W9-DGK-510

ACC Library
640 Bay Road
Queensbury, NY 12804

SHORT STORY WRITERS
REVISED EDITION

MAGILL'S CHOICE

SHORT STORY WRITERS

REVISED EDITION

Volume 2
William Faulkner — R. K. Narayan
379 – 758

edited by

CHARLES E. MAY
CALIFORNIA STATE UNIVERSITY, LONG BEACH

SALEM PRESS, INC.

Pasadena, California   Hackensack, New Jersey

Cover photo: Shawn Gearhart/©iStockphoto.com

Copyright © 1993, 1997, 2008, by Salem Press, Inc.
All rights in this book are reserved. No part of this work may be used
or reproduced in any manner whatsoever or transmitted in any form or
by any means, electronic or mechanical, including photocopy, record-
ing, or any information storage and retrieval system, without written
permission from the copyright owner except in the case of brief quota-
tions embodied in critical articles and reviews. For information address
the publisher, Salem Press, Inc., P.O. Box 50062, Pasadena, California
91115.

Some essays in these volumes originally appeared in *Critical Survey of
Short Fiction, Second Revised Edition*, 2001. New material has been added.

∞ The paper used in these volumes conforms to the American National Standard for Permanence of Paper for Printed Library Materials,
Z39.48-1992 (R1997).

Library of Congress Cataloging-in-Publication Data

Short story writers / edited by Charles E. May. — Rev. ed.
    v. cm. — (Magill's choice)
    Includes bibliographical references and index.
    ISBN 978-1-58765-389-6 (set : alk. paper) — ISBN 978-1-58765-390-2
(vol. 1 : alk. paper) — ISBN 978-1-58765-391-9 (vol. 2 : alk. paper) —
ISBN 978-1-58765-392-6 (vol. 3 : alk. paper) 1. Short story. 2. Short stories—Bio-bibliography—Dictionaries. 3. Novelists—Biography—Dictionaries. I. May, Charles E. (Charles Edward), 1941-

PN3373.S398 2008
809.3'1—dc22

                                                    2007032789

First printing

PRINTED IN CANADA

Contents – Volume 2

Complete List of Contents

Volume 1

Volume 2

Volume 3

SHORT STORY WRITERS

WRITERS

REVISED EDITION

William Faulkner

Born: New Albany, Mississippi; September 25, 1897
Died: Byhalia, Mississippi; July 6, 1962

Principal short fiction • *These Thirteen*, 1931; *Doctor Martino, and Other Stories*, 1934; *The Portable Faulkner*, 1946, 1967; *Knight's Gambit*, 1949; *Collected Short Stories of William Faulkner*, 1950; *Big Woods*, 1955; *Three Famous Short Novels*, 1958; *Uncollected Stories of William Faulkner*, 1979.

Other literary forms • William Faulkner published nearly twenty novels, two collections of poetry, and a novel-drama, as well as essays, newspaper articles, and illustrated stories. His early work has been collected and his University of Virginia lectures transcribed. As a screenwriter in Hollywood, he was listed in the credits of such films as *The Big Sleep* (1946), *To Have and Have Not* (1944), and *Land of the Pharaohs* (1955).

Achievements • William Faulkner is best known for his novels, particularly *The Sound and the Fury* (1929), *Absalom, Absalom!* (1936), and *As I Lay Dying* (1930), all of which have been translated widely. *A Fable* (1954) and *The Reivers* (1962) won Pulitzer Prizes, and *A Fable* and the *Collected Short Stories* won National Book Awards. Faulkner received the Nobel Prize in Literature for 1949.

Film versions have been made of several of his works: *Sanctuary* (1961), *Intruder in the Dust* (1949), *The Sound and the Fury* (1959), *The Reivers* (1969), and *Pylon* (1957; or *Tarnished Angels*). Others (*Requiem for a Nun*, 1951, and "Barn Burning") have been filmed for television.

Such attention attests to the fact that Faulkner has been one of the most influential writers in the twentieth century—both in the United States, where his work suggested to an enormous generation of southern writers the valuable literary materials that could be derived from their own region, and in Europe, particularly in France. He has had a later, but also profound, effect on Latin American fiction, most noticeably in the work of Colombian writer Gabriel García Márquez, who seeks, as Faulkner did, to create a fictive history of a region and a people. Faulkner's work has also been well received in Japan, which he visited as a cultural ambassador in 1955.

Biography • William Faulkner spent most of his life in Mississippi, although as a young man he went briefly to Paris and lived for a time in New Orleans, where he knew Sherwood Anderson. He trained for the Royal Air Force in Canada during World War I, but the war was over before he saw action. He attended the University of Mississippi in Oxford for a year, where he published poems and reviews in a campus periodical; and after dropping out, he worked for a time in the university post office. He married Estelle Oldham, and they had a daughter, Jill. Except for periodic and often unhappy stays in Hollywood to work on screenplays—in order to support a large number of dependents—Faulkner lived and wrote in Oxford, where he had available to him in the town and surrounding countryside the prototypes for the characters that inhabit his major works. During the late 1950's, he accepted a position as a writer-in-residence at the University of Virginia and traveled to Japan on behalf of the U.S.

Department of State. Although his literary reputation waned in the 1940's, when virtually all of his earlier works were out of print, Faulkner's stature as a writer grew after 1946, when *The Portable Faulkner* was published by Malcom Cowley, and especially after 1950, when he accepted the Nobel Prize, when his collected stories were published, and when his novels began to be reprinted. Faulkner drove himself harder physically as he grew older, and he was troubled throughout his life with alcohol binges, into which he would often fall after completing a book. These factors contributed to his death in 1962.

Analysis • William Faulkner has been credited with having the imagination to see, before other serious writers saw, the tremendous potential for drama, pathos, and sophisticated humor in the history and people of the South. In using this material and, in the process, suggesting to others how it might be used, he has also been credited with sparking the Southern Renaissance of literary achievement that produced much of the United States' best literature in the twentieth century.

In chronicling the tragedy of southern history, he delineated a vision tempered by his historical perspective that has freed the region from the popular conception of its character as possessing a universal gentility and a pervasive aristocracy, and he portrayed realistically a population often idealized and caricatured in songs, movies, and pulp fiction. In undercutting the false idealizations, Faulkner often distorted the stereotypes and rendered them somewhat grotesque in the interest of bringing them to three-dimensional life; and he attempted to show in the political and social presumptions of the South the portent of its almost inevitable destruction—first through war and then through an insidious new social order based on commercial pragmatism and shortsighted lust for progress. In this sense, the New South is shown to have much in common with mainstream America.

Faulkner's themes are often conveyed in an elaborate baroque style noted for its long, difficult sentences that challenge the reader to discern the speaker, the time, and even the subject of the narrative. Faulkner makes considerable use of stream-of-consciousness interior monologues, and his frequent meshings of time reinforce his conviction that the past and present are intricately interwoven in the human psyche.

"A Rose for Emily" • "A Rose for Emily," frequently anthologized and analyzed, is probably Faulkner's best-known story. Because of its elements of mystery, suspense, and the macabre, it has enjoyed a popular appeal. That Emily Grierson, an aging southern belle, murders the lover who spurned her and sleeps beside his decaying body for a number of years is only the most sensational aspect of the story. What is more interesting to the serious reader of Faulkner is the interplay between Emily Grierson and the two generations of townspeople who attempt to cope with her— one the old guard and the other a new generation with "modern ideas."

The opening paragraphs of the story inform the reader that when Miss Emily died, the whole town turned out for her funeral. She was a "fallen monument . . . a tradition, a duty and a care; a sort of hereditary obligation upon the town." The townspeople, who are by the time of Emily's death mostly of a generation younger than her own, have never been able to incorporate her into their community. For them, as well as for their fathers, she has stood as an embodiment of an older ideal of southern womanhood—even though in her later years she has grown obese, bloated, and pale as dough. The older generation, under the mayoralty of Colonel Sartoris ("who fathered the edict that no Negro woman should appear on the streets without an apron"), has relieved Miss Emily of her taxes and has sent its children to take her china-painting classes "in the same spirit that they were sent to church on Sunday with a twenty-five-cent piece for the collection plate." The new generation, however, is not pleased with the accommodations its fathers made with Miss Emily; it tries to impose taxes upon her and it no longer sends its children to take her lessons. Miss Emily has been encouraged in her ways by the old guard, however; she refuses to pay the town's taxes, telling the representatives of the new generation to "see Colonel Sartoris," who has been dead for ten years. The town is unable to handle Emily; it labels her "insane" and likewise comes to see her as the ghost of a feminine ideal out of the past. She becomes a recluse, living alone in her house with her black servant; and in her claim to privilege and impunity, she stands as a reminder to the town of the values—and sins—of its fathers, which are visited upon the third generation.

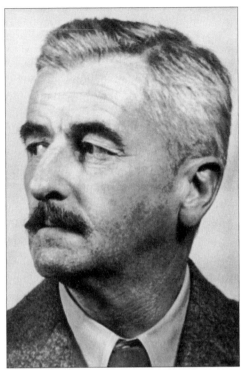

© The Nobel Foundation

It is tempting to think of Miss Emily as merely a decadent and perverse relic of the South's antebellum past; indeed, this is how the story has often been read. Such a neat interpretation, however, would seem to be defeated by the time element in the story. Emily lives in a house spiraled and cupolaed in the architectural style of the 1870's, on a once-elegant street that has been altered by industry and commercial development. Although the rickety town fathers of the Civil War era (1861-1865) come to her funeral dressed in their dusty uniforms and even believe that she was of their own generation and that they had danced with her when she was a young woman, clearly Emily is not of that generation; she is of the postwar South. She has not lingered as a relic from a warped racist culture; she has instead been created by defeated members of that culture who have continued to yearn after a world they have lost, a world that might well have existed largely in their imaginations, but a concept so persistent that the newer generation, for all its modern ideas, is powerless to control it. The reader is told that the town had long thought of Emily and her dead father "as a tableau, Miss Emily a slender figure in white in the background, her father a spraddled silhouette in the foreground, his back to her and clutching a horsewhip, the two of them framed by the backflung front door." It is clear that the newer generation of the twentieth century has adopted certain popular ideas about the Old South. This "tableau" could serve as the dust jacket for any number of romantic novels set in the plantation days.

Thus, the two generations are complicit in ignoring the real Emily and creating and maintaining the myth of Emily as an exemplum of southern womanhood from a lost age, just as the town aldermen—"three graybeards and one younger man, a member of the rising generation"—have conspired to cover up Emily's horrible crime. When the smell of the corpse of Emily's decaying lover, Homer Barron, had become so strong that it could no longer be ignored by the town, the aldermen had scattered lime around Emily's house secretly at night, although they knew she had recently purchased arsenic from the druggist and that Barron had disappeared; and when the smell went away, so did the town's concern about the matter. The old guard cannot bear, and does not wish, to accept the grim essence of the dream it has spun; the new generation, under the influence of the old, grudgingly accepts its burden of the past, but then wrenches it into a romantic shape that obscures the "fat woman in black" (overindulgent, moribund) that is Emily Grierson.

The story, then, is a comment on the postbellum South, which inherited the monstrous code of values, glossed over by fine words about honor and glory, that characterized the slave era; that postbellum South learns to ignore the unsavory elements of its past by ignoring Emily the recluse and murderess and by valorizing the romantic "tableau." This is, however, a complex matter. The new generation—a generation excluded from the nominal code of honor, valor, and decorum that the old Confederates believed to have sustained them and excluded from the benefits that were to be gained from the slave system of the "glorious" Old South—sees the Griersons as "high and mighty," as holding themselves "a little too high for what they really were." The new generation, pragmatic and small-minded, for the most part, has inherited a landscape sullied by cotton gins and garages. Miss Emily Grierson, as a privileged person and as a reminder of what the older generation forfeited in its defeat, is a goad in the minds of the uncharitable newer generation, which, when she does not marry, is "vindicated." When it hears the rumor that she has inherited nothing but the decaying house from her father, it is glad: "At last they could pity Miss Emily." Miss Emily out of sight, destitute, "insane," and deprived too of the lost legacy of the Old South can be re-created as a fictional heroine in white, part of the backdrop against which the popularized hero, her father, stands with his horsewhip—a faceless silhouette, cruel and powerful, an "ancestor" who can be claimed by the dispossessed generation as its own.

The incestuous image of the father and daughter suggests the corrupt nature of the New South, which, along with the corrupt nature of the Old South, is a favorite Faulknerian concern. Granted, the "tableau" on the face of it appears to be the cover of a romantic novel, and in that sense it seems to be merely a popular rendering of history; but it is the townspeople who arrange *father and daughter* in the lurid scene. It is the men of the new generation who black out the distinguishing features of Emily's dead father in their creation of the tableau, leaving a dark masculine space (more, one would guess, in the shape of foreman Homer Barron than of Mr. Grierson) into which they can dream themselves, as masters of a glorious age, as potent heroes for whom the wispy heroine wanes in the background. The newer generation has the "modern ideas" bred of the necessity of surviving in the defeated, industrialized South; but in its attitudes toward Emily Grierson, it reveals the extent to which the old decadent values of the fathers have been passed along.

The narrator of the story, one of the townspeople himself, has proved unreliable. Although it is true that Emily seems to be "a tradition, a duty, a care, . . . an hereditary obligation," a relic of the past miraculously sprung into being in spite of the disparity between her time and the historical time with which she is associated, the narrator only inadvertently reveals the truth of the matter: that both generations of the town are guilty of the desires and misplaced values that not only allow Miss Emily the murderess to come into being but also lead them to cover her crime and enshrine her in a tableau into which they, in their basest longings, can insert themselves. There is an incestuousness to all of this, an unhealthy interbreeding of values that allows each generation to perform despicable acts in the process of maintaining its ideas of what it would like to be. It is true that Emily is a "fallen monument"; but what the narrator fails to spell out explicitly is that the monument has been erected not only by the historical grandeur of her family, but also by the dispossessed generations that interpret her to their own ends. The monument is toppled by death, not by an ethical evolution in the town. The narrator is redeemed to some extent by "his" pity for Emily and by the recognition that the town, by driving her into mad isolation, has treated her badly.

As for Emily herself, she would seem to represent the worst elements of her neighbors, carried to their extreme conclusions. As the antebellum masters of the slaves presumed an all-powerfulness that allowed them to believe that they could own people, so does Miss Emily presume. Alive, Homer Barron—the outsider, the Yankee, a curious vitality in the pallid town—is outside Miss Emily's control. Dead, however, she can own him, can dress his corpse like a groom, can sleep beside him perhaps every night at least until her hair turns gray. As the new generation can blind itself to unpleasant truths about its history and itself, so can Emily become lost in delusion: Her father, dead for three days, is proclaimed not dead and she refuses to bury him; Homer's corpse is a "groom" (and, perhaps in some further depraved vision, connected with the dead father). Emily represents not only the decadence of Colonel Sartoris's racist era but also the decadence of the "modern" generation's use of that era. Thus "A Rose for Emily," often dismissed as Faulkner's ghost story, proves to be a clear expression of a recurring motif in Faulkner's works: the complexity of the connections between the present and the past.

"The Bear" • These connections are explored in a less sensational manner in "The Bear." This story, which Faulkner also made the centerpiece of his novel *Go Down, Moses*, is another of the most anthologized, most studied pieces of Faulkner's short fiction. Composed of five sections (although often only four are printed in anthology versions, the long and complex fourth section being omitted), "The Bear" covers the history of Isaac (Ike) McCaslin, heir to the land and to the shame of his slave-owner grandfather, L. P. C. McCaslin, who committed incest with his illegitimate daughter, thereby driving her mother to suicide. After discovering this horrifying ghost in old plantation ledgers, Ike feels bound to repudiate the inheritance that has descended to him from his grandfather—even though the repudiation costs him his wife and any hope of progeny—in an attempt to expiate his inherited guilt and to gain a measure of freedom from the vicious materialism that brought the slavery system into being. Thus he allows his patrimony to pass to his cousin McCaslin Edmonds, who plays devil's advocate in Ike's attempt to understand the South and his own place in it, the tragedy of the blacks and of his own class, and the significance of what he possesses without inheriting: an instinctual knowledge of nature and an infallible sense of what is just.

"The Bear" may be seen as a hunting story, part of the *Big Woods* collection that includes "The Bear Hunt" and "Race at Morning." As a hunting story it is concerned with Ike's maturing, with his pilgrimage year after year to the hunting grounds where he and a group of adult hunters stalk the ancient bear, Old Ben, an enduring symbol of nature. Ike's guide and teacher is Sam Fathers, an aging Native American who still holds a sure instinct for the truths to be found in nature, and under whose tutelage Ike comes to form a system of values that later will lead him to renounce his inheritance. From Sam, Ike acquires a sense of nature's terms and of humanity's need to meet her on her own terms—of the necessity of according dignity to the force of nature and to all creatures through whom it courses. To meet the embodiment of that force in Old Ben, Ike must leave behind the instruments of civilization: the gun, the compass, the watch. Eventually Ike is able to track down Old Ben with regularity, but even when he encounters the bear and is armed, he refuses to shoot it.

It would seem that the proof of nature's endurance, represented in the bear, is of paramount concern to Ike. When Old Ben is finally killed and Sam Fathers dies, the ritual of the hunt is over for Ike. Yet two years later, he returns to the woods and sees in its organic and deathless elements, which have incorporated the remains of Old Ben and Sam Fathers, a proof of nature's dualistic power to absorb death and bring forth new life from it. This force is at the same time awesome and terrifying, and it must be revered and confronted if humanity is to live meaningfully. Even as Ike makes this last pilgrimage, however, a lumber company hacks away at the forest and a train cuts through the wilderness, underscoring the idea of the damage a materialistic civilization can do to even the most powerful aspects of nature. Faulkner shows an era of United States history passing—an era of abundance and of human appreciation of what nature requires from humanity in their mutual interest.

When "The Bear" is examined from the point of view of the intricate fourth section, it goes beyond being merely a hunting story to comment profoundly on the passing age and that which is replacing it. The scene shifts from the vast wilderness of nature to the intense confines of Ike McCaslin's consciousness, which struggles to find a way to atone for the sins of his ancestors and of his class. The entanglement of past and present here is more complex than it is in "A Rose for Emily," for Ike must face the knowledge that bloods mingled in the past—black and white, slave and owner—have flowed in grossly inequitable courses to the present, as reflected in the sufferings of his mixed-blood relatives. Therefore, he renounces his patrimony, he sets out to redress old wrongs with his black relatives, and he seeks to give full recognition to the brotherhood he shares with these relatives by recognizing the strengths they contribute to his family and to southern society—the virtues of "pity and tolerance and forbearance and fidelity and love of children."

In contrast to the self-serving generation of postbellum townspeople in "A Rose for Emily," Ike—also of that era—is a man of conscience. This is not to suggest, however, that Ike is particularly "modern" in his ideas; rather he has modeled himself on older examples of integrity, not only Sam Fathers but also his father and his uncle, who had turned over their own inherited house to their slaves and built a humbler cabin for themselves. In Ike's own case, the personal sacrifices to integrity and conscience have been enormous—his wife's love; his hope of a son to carry on his mission; living alone and ultimately uncertain that his sacrifice will bear fruit beyond his limited scope to influence events. Nevertheless, Faulkner illustrates through his invention of Ike McCaslin the extent to which idealism can flourish, even when constantly challenged by the grimmest vestiges of past evils.

"Barn Burning" • "Barn Burning" is an inversion of "The Bear" in that its protagonist, ten-year-old Sarty Snopes, is seeking the world that Ike McCaslin wishes to repudiate. Not of the landed class, but the son of a tenant farmer who is always on the move because arson is his means of creating justice, Sarty associates the landed gentry with a "peace and dignity" and a civilized justice that is the direct opposite of the "fear and terror, grief and despair" that characterizes his life with his father, Ab Snopes. Ab uses fire as a weapon against the ruling class that he sees as the shaper of his economic fate, and he exhorts Sarty to be true to the blood ties which Ab sees as the only protection for his kind against the forces of an exploitative aristocracy. Sarty, however, rejects the "old blood" that he has not chosen for what seems to him a higher concept of fairness, and he longs to be free of his family and the turmoil it generates in his life.

For Sarty, Major DeSpain is the antithesis of Ab. DeSpain owns the farm on which Ab has most recently contracted to work. To Sarty, DeSpain and his columned house, as big as a courthouse, represent not what Ab sees, the sweat of black and white people to produce someone else's wealth, but the peace and dignity for which Sarty yearns and a system of justice that operates on principles of law rather than on personal revenge. Sarty's view is based on a naïve trust in civilization that blinds his inexperienced eyes to the inescapable connections between wealth and the mechanism of civilization.

Ab provokes a confrontation with DeSpain by deliberately tracking horse manure on an expensive rug. A series of moves and countermoves by Ab and DeSpain brings the pair to the point where, although DeSpain cannot begin to recover his loss from Ab, the local court nevertheless rules that Ab must take responsibility, within his means, for his act. This is enough to satisfy Ab yet again that the social system only works in behalf of the rich, and he sets out that night to redress this wrong by burning DeSpain's barn. Sarty cannot bear to allow this injustice, and so he is torn between real loyalty to his family and commitment to an ideal of justice. Specifically, he must decide whether to support his father's crime through silence or to betray the familial bond and warn DeSpain. Sarty chooses the ideal, warns DeSpain even as the barn begins to burn, and then flees the scene, unsure whether the shots he hears wound any of his family. Having made his choice, Sarty must set out alone to forge his own life.

"Barn Burning" offers a helpful picture of how Faulkner sees the economics of the postbellum South, where the poor whites remain the underclass rivals of black sharecroppers. Faulkner shows in other works how a new social order eventually evolved in which the descendants of Ab Snopes slip into the defeated, genteel society like silent bacteria and take over its commerce, coming finally to own the mansions that had previously belonged to the DeSpains and Compsons and Sartorises. Again and again Faulkner reiterates that it was the corrupt systems of slavery and of the plantation that ultimately ensured the fall of the Old South. Yet his view of Snopeses—violent, relentless, insidious men and inert, cowlike women, who by their numbers and crafty pragmatism will wrench the land and the wealth from the depleted gentility—is hardly positive.

In fact, "Barn Burning" is singular in that it is perhaps the only example of Faulkner's fiction in which the Snopeses are depicted sympathetically without first being made to appear ridiculous. As is often the case, Faulkner is extremely sensitive to the young boy caught in a painful rite of passage—as true for Sarty Snopes as it is for Ike McCaslin, Lucius Priest, Chick Mallison, and others not of the threatening Snopes clan. Moreover, "Barn Burning" makes an interesting case for Ab Snopes as the pitiable creation of the landed aristocracy, who seeks dignity and integrity for himself, although his only chance of achieving either would seem to lie in the democratic element of fire as the one defense available to all, regardless of social class. In this story,

Ab is placed in the company of Wash Jones, Joe Christmas, and other members of the underclass that Faulkner views with sympathy and whose portrayals are in themselves indictments of the civilization that has forced them to desperate means.

Although none of these examples quite suggests the very humorous ends to which Faulkner often turns his southern materials, it should be remembered that he was highly aware of the potential for comedy in all the situations described here and that even such delicate matters as the tensions between the races and the revolution in the social order are, in Faulkner's hands, as frequently the catalysts of tall tales and satire as they are of his most somber and lyrical prose. It is true that "A Rose for Emily" hints at a typically Faulknerian humor in that a whole town is turned on its end by the bizarre behavior of one of its citizens; but the grotesque nature of Miss Emily's secret smothers the promise of comedy in the story. Those seeking to experience Faulkner's comic voice are better served by reading such stories as "Shingles for the Lord," "Mule in the Yard," and "Spotted Horses."

In any case, whatever the mode Faulkner adopted in creating his Yoknapatawpha County and thereby re-creating the South, he produced a stunning body of work, and in both matter and style, his works have had an equally stunning impact on modern letters.

Constance Pierce
With updates by Terry Heller

Other major works

NOVELS: *Soldiers' Pay*, 1926; *Mosquitoes*, 1927; *Sartoris*, 1929; *The Sound and the Fury*, 1929; *As I Lay Dying*, 1930; *Sanctuary*, 1931; *Light in August*, 1932; *Pylon*, 1935; *Absalom, Absalom!*, 1936; *The Unvanquished*, 1938; *The Wild Palms*, 1939; *The Hamlet*, 1940; *Go Down, Moses*, 1942; *The Bear*, 1942 (novella); *Intruder in the Dust*, 1948; *Requiem for a Nun*, 1951; *A Fable*, 1954; *The Town*, 1957; *The Mansion*, 1959; *The Reivers*, 1962; *The Wishing Tree*, 1964 (fairy tale); *Flags in the Dust*, 1973 (original version of *Sartoris*); *Mayday*, 1976 (fable).

MISCELLANEOUS: *The Faulkner Reader*, 1954; *William Faulkner: Early Prose and Poetry*, 1962.

NONFICTION: *New Orleans Sketches*, 1958; *Faulkner in the University*, 1959; *Faulkner at West Point*, 1964; *Essays, Speeches and Public Letters*, 1965; *The Faulkner-Cowley File: Letters and Memories, 1944-1962*, 1966 (Malcolm Cowley, editor); *Lion in the Garden*, 1968; *Selected Letters*, 1977.

POETRY: *The Marble Faun*, 1924; *A Green Bough*, 1933.

SCREENPLAYS: *Today We Live*, 1933; *To Have and Have Not*, 1945; *The Big Sleep*, 1946; *Faulkner's MGM Screenplays*, 1982.

Bibliography
Fargnoli, A. Nicholas, and Michael Golay. *William Faulkner A to Z: The Essential Reference to His Life and Work*. New York: Facts on File, 2001. Encyclopedic reference work covering Faulkner's life and writings, with entries on individual short stories, characters, and much more.

Ferguson, James. *Faulkner's Short Fiction*. Knoxville: University of Tennessee Press, 1991. Attempt to redress the critical neglect of Faulkner's short fiction. Discusses Faulkner's poetic and narrative impulses, his themes of loss of innocence, failure to love, loneliness, and isolation; comments on his manipulation of time and point of view and how his stories relate to his novels.

Ford, Marilyn Claire. "Narrative Legerdemain: Evoking Sarty's Future in 'Barn Burning.'" *The Mississippi Quarterly* 51 (Summer, 1998): 527-540. In this special issue on Faulkner, Ford argues that Faulkner experiments with the doubling of perspective in "Barn Burning" in which the omniscient narrator fuses with the protagonist to create a story with multiple narrative layers.

Gray, Richard. *The Life of William Faulkner: A Critical Biography.* Oxford, England: Blackwell, 1994. A noted Faulkner scholar, Gray closely integrates the life and work. Part 1 suggests a method of approaching Faulkner's life, part 2 concentrates on his apprentice years, part 3 explains his discovery of Yoknapatawpha and the transformation of his region into his fiction, part 4 deals with his treatment of past and present, part 5 addresses his exploration of place, and part 6 analyzes his final novels, reflecting on his creation of Yoknapatawpha. Includes family trees, chronology, notes, and a bibliography.

Inge, M. Thomas, ed. *Conversations with William Faulkner.* Jackson: University Press of Mississippi, 1999. Part of the Literary Conversations series, this volume gives insight into Faulkner the person. Includes bibliographical references and index.

Jones, Diane Brown. *A Reader's Guide to the Short Stories of William Faulkner.* New York: G. K. Hall, 1994. Discusses more than thirty of Faulkner's stories in terms of publishing history, circumstances of composition, sources/influence, and relationship to other Faulkner works; includes interpretations of the stories and summarizes and critiques previous criticism.

May, Charles E., ed. *Masterplots II: Short Story Series, Revised Edition.* 8 vols. Pasadena, Calif.: Salem Press, 2004. Designed for student use, this reference set contains articles providing detailed plot summaries and analyses of these eight short stories by Faulkner: "Barn Burning" (vol. 1), "Delta Autumn" and "Dry September" (vol. 2), "Red Leaves" and "A Rose for Emily" (vol. 6), "Spotted Horses" and "That Evening Sun" (vol. 7), and "Wash" (vol. 8).

Minter, David. *William Faulkner: His Life and Work.* Baltimore: Johns Hopkins University Press, 1980. Shorter and less detailed than Joseph Blotner's biography, this volume gives more attention to exploring connections between Faulkner's life and his works.

The Mississippi Quarterly 50 (Summer, 1997). A special issue on Faulkner, including articles that discuss displaced meaning, dispossessed sons, the wilderness and consciousness, and subjectivity in *Go Down, Moses.*

Singal, Daniel J. *William Faulkner: The Making of a Modernist.* Chapel Hill: University of North Carolina Press, 1997. Study of the thought and art of Faulkner, charting the development of his ideas from their source in his reading to their embodiment in his writing. Depicts two Faulkners: the country gentleman and the intellectual man of letters.

Wagner-Martin, Linda. *New Essays on "Go Down, Moses."* New York: Cambridge University Press, 1996. After an introduction that summarizes contemporary reception and critical analysis of *Go Down, Moses,* Wagner-Martin collects essays that approach the work from the perspective of race, environment, gender, and ideology.

F. Scott Fitzgerald

Born: St. Paul, Minnesota; September 24, 1896
Died: Hollywood, California; December 21, 1940

Principal short fiction • *Flappers and Philosophers*, 1920; *Tales of the Jazz Age*, 1922; *All the Sad Young Men*, 1926; *Taps at Reveille*, 1935; *The Stories of F. Scott Fitzgerald*, 1951; *Babylon Revisited, and Other Stories*, 1960; *The Pat Hobby Stories*, 1962; *The Apprentice Fiction of F. Scott Fitzgerald, 1907-1917*, 1965; *The Basil and Josephine Stories*, 1973; *Bits of Paradise*, 1974; *The Price Was High: The Last Uncollected Stories of F. Scott Fitzgerald*, 1979; *Before Gatsby: The First Twenty-Six Stories*, 2001 (Matthew J. Bruccoli, editor).

Other literary forms • Four novels, four short-story collections, and a play make up the nine F. Scott Fitzgerald books published in his lifetime. They were issued in uniform editions by Scribner's with a British edition of each. His short stories were widely anthologized in the 1920's and 1930's in collections such as *The Best Short Stories of 1922, Cream of the Jug*, and *The Best Short Stories of 1931*. *The Vegetable: Or, From President to Postman* (1923) was produced at the Apollo Theatre in Atlantic City, and, while Fitzgerald was under contract to MGM, he collaborated on such screenplays as *Three Comrades, Infidelity, Madame Curie*, and *Gone with the Wind*. There have been numerous posthumous collections of his letters, essays, notebooks, stories, and novels; and since his death there have been various stage and screen adaptations of his work, including film versions of *The Great Gatsby* (1925) and *Tender Is the Night* (1934).

Achievements • F. Scott Fitzgerald, considered "the poet laureate of the Jazz Age," is best remembered for his portrayal of the "flapper" of the 1920's, a young woman who demonstrated scorn for conventional dress and behavior. Fitzgerald's fiction focuses on young, wealthy, dissolute men and women of the 1920's. His stories written for popular magazines such as the *Saturday Evening Post* and, later, *Esquire* were very much in demand. Fitzgerald's literary reputation, however, is chiefly based on the artistry of stories such as "Babylon Revisited" and "The Rich Boy," as well as the novel *The Great Gatsby*. In this important novel, Fitzgerald uses rich imagery and symbolism to portray lives of the careless, restless rich during the 1920's and to depict Jay Gatsby as the personification of the American Dream, the self-made man whose quest for riches is also a futile quest for the love of the shallow, spoiled Daisy.

Biography • F. Scott Fitzgerald was educated at St. Paul Academy and at the Newman School in Hackensack, New Jersey. While attending Princeton University he wrote for the *Princeton Tiger* and *Nassau Literary Magazine*. He left Princeton without a degree, joined the Army, and was stationed near Montgomery, Alabama, where he met Zelda Sayre. In 1920, they were married in New York City before moving to Westport, Connecticut. Their only child, Frances Scott Fitzgerald, was born in 1921. During the mid-1920's the Fitzgeralds traveled extensively between the United States and Europe, meeting Ernest Hemingway in Paris in 1925. The decade of the 1930's was a bleak one for the Fitzgeralds; Zelda had several emotional breakdowns and Scott sank into alcoholism. They lived variously in Montgomery and on the Turnbull estate outside

Baltimore. Fitzgerald went to Hollywood for the second time in 1931. After that they lived for a time in Asheville, North Carolina, where Zelda was hospitalized and where Fitzgerald wrote the Crack-up essays for *Esquire.* In 1937, Fitzgerald met Hollywood columnist Sheila Graham while he was living in Hollywood and writing under contract to MGM. Although he remained married to Zelda, he fell in love with Graham and lived with her through his remaining years. He began writing *The Last Tycoon* in 1939 and died, before it was completed, on December 21, 1940, at the age of forty-four.

Library of Congress

Analysis • F. Scott Fitzgerald was a professional writer who was also a literary artist. In practical terms this meant that he had to support himself by writing short stories for popular magazines in order to get sufficient income, according to him, to write decent books. Indeed, most of the money that Fitzgerald earned by writing before he went to Hollywood in 1937 was earned by selling stories to magazines. In his twenty-year career as a writer, he published 164 magazine stories; other stories were never published. All but eight of the stories that originally appeared in magazines became available in hardcover editions.

As one would expect of a body of 164 stories written in a twenty-year period mainly for popular consumption, the quality of the stories is uneven. At the bottom of this collection are at least a dozen stories, most of them written for *Esquire* during the last years of his life, which have few redeeming qualities; at the top of the list are at least a dozen stories which rank among the best of American short stories. One should not, however, be led to believe that these, as well as the hundred or more "potboilers" in the middle, do not serve a useful role in his development as an artist. Fitzgerald in the 1920's was considered the best writer of quality magazine fiction in America, and his stories brought the highest prices paid by slick magazines; the *Saturday Evening Post,* for example, paid him four thousand dollars per story even during the Depression. The noted wit Dorothy Parker commented that Fitzgerald could write a bad story, but that he could not write badly. Thus each story, no matter how weak, has the recognizable Fitzgerald touch—that sparkling prose which Fitzgerald called "the something extra" that most popular short stories lacked. Fitzgerald also learned at the beginning of his career that he could use the popular magazines as a workshop for his novels, experimenting in them with themes and techniques which he would later incorporate into his novels. An understanding of a Fitzgerald story should take into account this workshop function of the story as well as its artistic merits.

Fitzgerald's career as a writer of magazine fiction breaks logically into three periods: 1919-1924, years during which he shopped around for markets and published stories in most of the important periodicals of the times; 1925-1933, the central period characterized by a close association with the *Saturday Evening Post*—a relationship which almost precluded his publication of stories in other magazines; and 1934-1940, a period beginning with the publication of his first *Esquire* story and continuing through a subsequent relationship with that magazine which lasted until his death. During the first of these periods, Fitzgerald published thirty-two stories in ten different commercial magazines, two novels (*This Side of Paradise*, 1920, and *The Beautiful and Damned*, 1922), two short-story collections (*Flappers and Philosophers* and *Tales of the Jazz Age*), and one book-length play (*The Vegetable*). In the second period, during which *The Great Gatsby* and a third short-story collection (*All the Sad Young Men*) appeared, he enjoyed the popular reputation he had built with readers of the *Saturday Evening Post* and published forty-seven of the fifty-eight stories which appeared during this nine-year period in that magazine; the remaining eleven stories were scattered throughout five different magazines. In the final period, Fitzgerald lost the large *Saturday Evening Post* audience and gained the *Esquire* audience, which was smaller and quite different. Of the forty-four Fitzgerald stories to appear between 1934 and his death, twenty-eight appeared in *Esquire*. In addition to *Tender Is the Night*, which was completed and delivered before Fitzgerald's relationship with *Esquire* began, Fitzgerald published his final short-story collection (*Taps at Reveille*); he also drafted *The Last Tycoon* (1941) during the *Esquire* years. Twelve stories, nine of which have appeared in *Esquire*, have been published since his death.

An obvious conclusion may be drawn about Fitzgerald's professional career: He was at his best artistically in the years of his greatest popularity. During the composition of *The Great Gatsby*, Fitzgerald's commercial fiction was in such demand that large magazines such as the *Saturday Evening Post, Hearst's,* and *Metropolitan* competed for it. *Tender Is the Night* was written during the time when Fitzgerald's popularity with slick magazine readers was at its all-time high point; for example, in 1929 and 1930, important years in the composition of *Tender Is the Night*, he published fifteen stories in the *Saturday Evening Post*. In sharp contrast to the 1925-1933 stories, which are characteristically of an even, high quality, and many of which are closely related to two novels of this period, the stories of the *Esquire* years are, in general, undistinguished. In addition, with minor exceptions, the stories written in this final period have little relation to Fitzgerald's last "serious" work, *The Last Tycoon*. The *Esquire* years thus constitute a low point from both a popular and an artistic standpoint. They are years during which he lost the knack of pleasing the large American reading public and at the same time produced a comparatively small amount of good artwork.

In the first two years of Fitzgerald's storywriting, his sensitivity to audience tastes was naïve. "May Day" and "The Diamond as Big as the Ritz," not only the two best stories from these years but also two of the best stories in the Fitzgerald canon, were written for sale to mass-circulation magazines. Both, however, were too cynical about American values to be acceptable to a large, middle-American audience. By 1922 and the publication of "Winter Dreams" in *Metropolitan*, Fitzgerald had learned how to tailor his stories for slick magazine readers while at the same time using them to experiment with serious subjects and themes that he would later use in longer works.

"Winter Dreams" • Viewed in association with *The Great Gatsby*, "Winter Dreams" provides an excellent illustration of Fitzgerald's method of using his stories as a proving ground for his novels. In a letter to Maxwell Perkins, Fitzgerald describes "Winter Dreams" as a "sort of 1st draft of the Gatsby idea," and indeed, it contains sufficient similarities of theme and character to be called a miniature of *The Great Gatsby*. Parallels between Dexter Green and Jay Gatsby are striking: Both men have made a total commitment to a dream, and both of their dreams are hollow. Dexter falls in love with wealthy Judy Jones and devotes his life to making the money that will allow him to enter her social circle; his idealization of her is closely akin to Gatsby's feelings for Daisy Buchanan. Gatsby's idealized conception of Daisy is the motivating force that underlies his compulsion to become successful, just as Dexter's conception of Judy Jones drives him to amass a fortune by the time he is twenty-five. The theme of commitment to an idealized dream that is the core of "Winter Dreams" and *The Great Gatsby*, and the similarities between the two men point up the close relationship between the story and the novel. Because "Winter Dreams" appeared three years before *The Great Gatsby*, its importance in the gestation of the novel cannot be overemphasized.

Important differences in Fitzgerald's methods of constructing short stories and novels emerge from these closely related works. Much of the effectiveness of *The Great Gatsby* lies in the mystery of Gatsby's background, while no such mystery surrounds the early life of Dexter Green. In "Winter Dreams," Dexter's disillusionment with Judy occurs suddenly; when he learns that she is no longer pretty, the "dream was gone. Something had taken it from him . . . the moonlit veranda, and gingham on the golf links and the dry sun and the gold color of her neck's soft down. . . . Why these things were no longer in the world!" Because his enchantment could be shattered so quickly, Dexter's commitment to Judy is not of the magnitude of Gatsby's commitment to Daisy. Gatsby's disenchantment could only occur gradually. When he is finally able to see Daisy, "the colossal significance of the green light . . . vanished forever," but his "count of enchanted objects" had only diminished by one. Even toward the end of the novel, there is no way of knowing that Gatsby is completely disenchanted with Daisy. Nick says that "perhaps he no longer cared." The "perhaps" leaves open possibilities of interpretation that are closed at the end of "Winter Dreams." Although Dexter can cry at the loss of a dream, Gatsby dies, leaving the reader to guess whether or not he still held on to any fragment of his dreams about Daisy. The expansiveness of the novel obviously allowed Fitzgerald to make Gatsby and his dream believable while he could maintain the mystery of Gatsby's past and the origins of his dream. Fitzgerald could not do this as well with Dexter in "Winter Dreams." The point is that in writing "Winter Dreams" Fitzgerald was giving shape to his ideas about Jay Gatsby, and, after creating the story, he could better see the advantages of maintaining the sense of mystery that made Gatsby a more memorable character than his counterpart in "Winter Dreams."

"The Rich Boy" • Like "Winter Dreams," "The Rich Boy," published a year after *The Great Gatsby*, clearly illustrates the workshop function that the stories served. The story's rich boy, Anson Hunter, falls in love with the beautiful and rich Paula Legendre, but he always finds some reason for not marrying her, although he maintains that his love for her never stops. Anson, the bachelor, ironically becomes an unofficial counselor to couples with martial difficulties and, in his role as protector of the family name, puts an end to an affair that his aunt is having. Paula marries another man, divorces him, and, when Anson encounters her late in the story, he finds her happily remarried and pregnant. Paula, whose revered place has been jeopardized by her pregnancy, finally dies in childbirth, symbolically taking with her Anson's youth. He goes on a cruise, disillusioned that his only real love is gone. Yet he is still willing to flirt with any woman on the ship who will affirm the feeling of superiority about himself that he cherishes in his heart.

In "The Rich Boy," then, Fitzgerald uses many of the themes—among them, lost youth and disillusionment in marriage—that he had covered in previous stories; in addition, he uses devices such as the narrator-observer point of view that had been successful in *The Great Gatsby*, and he pulls from the novel subjects such as the idealization of a woman who finally loses her suitor's reverence. "The Rich Boy" also blends, along with the themes he had dealt with before, new topics that he would later distill and treat singly in another story, just as he first deals explicitly with the rich-are-different idea in "The Rich Boy" and later focuses his narrative specifically on that idea in "Six of One." Finally, particularly in the use of the theme of bad marriages in "The Rich Boy," there are foreshadowings of *Tender Is the Night* and the stories which cluster around it.

"Babylon Revisited" • The best of these *Tender Is the Night* cluster stories is "Babylon Revisited," which earned Fitzgerald his top *Saturday Evening Post* price of four thousand dollars and which is generally acclaimed as his finest story. "Babylon Revisited" represents a high point in Fitzgerald's career as a short-story writer: It is an artistically superior story which earned a high price from a commercial magazine. In the story's main character, Charlie Wales, Fitzgerald creates one whose future, in spite of his heroic struggle, is prescribed by his imprudent past, a past filled with heavy drinking and irresponsibility. He is destined to be haunted by reminders of his early life, embodied by Lorraine and Duncan, drinking friends from the past; to be judged for them by Marion, his dead wife's sister who, like Charlie's conscience personified, is disgusted by his past and demands punishment; and to be denied, for his penance, any right to fill the emptiness of his life with his daughter Honoria, who is in Marion's custody and who is the only really meaningful thing left. Fitzgerald fashions Charlie as a sensitive channel through which the reader can simultaneously view both Paris as it existed for expatriate wanderers before the Depression and the now-dimmed Paris to which Charlie returns.

The contrast is masterfully handled in that the course of Charlie's emotional life closely parallels the changing mood of the city—a movement from a kind of unreal euphoria to a mood of loss and melancholy. The contrast at once heightens the reader's sense of Charlie's loneliness in a ghost town of bad memories and foreshadows his empty-handed return to Prague, his present home. All of Charlie's present misery has resulted, in Fitzgerald's precise summary, from his "selling short" in the boom—an allusion to the loss of his dead wife Helen. Charlie, however, refuses to be driven back to alcohol, even in the face of being denied his daughter Honoria. Although he might easily have done so, Fitzgerald avoids drawing the reader into a sentimental trap of identification with Charlie's plight, the responsibility for and consequences of which must finally be borne only by Charlie. As he later did in Dick Diver's case in *Tender Is the Night*, Fitzgerald has shown in "Babylon Revisited" how one man works his way into an existence with nada at the core; how he manages to dissipate, "to make nothing out of something," and thus prescribe for himself a future without direction. It is also in the creation of this mood of Charlie's isolation that the artistic brilliance of the story, as well as its kinship to *Tender Is the Night*, lies.

The popular thrust of "Babylon Revisited" is a dual one in which Fitzgerald plays on what were likely to be ambivalent feelings of popular readers toward Charlie. On one hand, he is pictured first as an expatriate about whose resolution to remain abroad American audiences may have been skeptical. On the other, Charlie appears to have reformed and obviously loves his daughter. Marion, by contrast, is depicted as a shrew, and the reader is left to choose, therefore, between the punishment of a life sentence of loneliness for a penitent wrongdoer and the granting of his complete freedom and forgiveness rendered against the better judgment of the unsympathetic Marion. Fitzgerald guarantees that the reader will become emotionally involved by centering the story around the highly emotional relationship between a father and his daughter. Because Charlie is, in fact, guilty, to let him go free would be to let wrongdoing go unpunished—the strictest kind of violation of the Puritan ethic. To deprive Charlie of Honoria, however, would be to side with the unlikable Marion. Fitzgerald, then, resolves the conflict in the only satisfactory way—by proposing a compromise. Although Marion keeps Honoria for the moment, Charlie may be paroled, may come back and try again, at any time in the future.

The story, therefore, is successful on three major counts: It served as a workshop in which Fitzgerald shaped the mood of *Tender Is the Night*; it entertained with the struggle against unfair odds of a well-intentioned father for the affection of his daughter; and it succeeded on the mythic level, suggested in the title, as a story in which all ingredients conspire to lead to Charlie's exile—an isolation from the city that has fallen in the absence of a now-reformed sinner, carrying with it not only the bad but also the good which Charlie has come to salvage.

***Esquire* Stories** • About four years after the publication of "Babylon Revisited," Fitzgerald had lost the knack of writing *Saturday Evening Post* stories, and he began writing shorter pieces, many of which are sketches rather than stories, for *Esquire*. *Esquire*, however, was not a suitable medium to serve a workshop function as the *Saturday Evening Post* had been. On the one hand, it did not pay enough to sustain Fitzgerald through the composition of a novel; even if it had, it is difficult to imagine how Fitzgerald would have experimented in the framework of short *Esquire* pieces with the complex relationships that he was concurrently developing in *The Last Tycoon*. Moreover, there is the question of the suitability of Fitzgerald's *The Last Tycoon* material, regardless of how he treated it, for *Esquire:* The Monroe Stahr-Kathleen relationship in *The Last Tycoon*, for example, and certainly also the Cecelia-Stahr relationship, would have been as out of place in *Esquire* as the *Esquire* story of a ten-year binge, "The Lost Decade," would have been in the *Saturday Evening Post*. In short, *Esquire* was ill-suited to Fitzgerald's need for a profitable workshop for *The Last Tycoon*, and it is difficult to read the *Esquire* pieces, particularly the Pat Hobby stories about a pathetic movie scriptwriter, without realizing that every hour Fitzgerald spent on them could have been better spent completing *The Last Tycoon*. From a practical standpoint, it is fair to say that the small sums of income for which Fitzgerald worked in writing the *Esquire* stories may have interfered with the completion of his last novel, whereas the high prices Fitzgerald earned from the *Saturday Evening Post* between 1925 and 1933 provided the financial climate that made it possible for him to complete *Tender Is the Night*.

Indeed, if the *Esquire* stories in general and the Pat Hobby stories in particular, close as they were in terms of composition to *The Last Tycoon*, marked the distance

Fitzgerald had come in resolving the professional writer-literary artist dichotomy with which he had been confronted for twenty years, any study of the function of the stories in Fitzgerald's overall career would end on a bleak note. Two stories, "Discard" and "Last Kiss," neither of which was published in Fitzgerald's lifetime, indicate, however, that he was attempting to re-create the climate of free exchange between his stories and novels characteristic especially of the composition period of *Tender Is the Night.* "Last Kiss" provides a good commentary on this attempt. When the story appeared in 1949, the editors remarked in a headnote that the story contained "the seed" that grew into *The Last Tycoon.* The claim is too extravagant for the story in that it implies the sort of relationship between the story and the novel that exists between "Winter Dreams" and *The Great Gatsby,* a relationship that simply does not exist in the case of "Last Kiss" and *The Last Tycoon.* There are, however, interesting parallels.

"Last Kiss" • Fitzgerald created in "Last Kiss" counterparts both to Monroe Stahr and Kathleen in *The Last Tycoon.* Jim Leonard, a thirty-five-year-old film producer in "Last Kiss," is similar to Stahr in that he possesses the same kind of power: When the budding starlet, Pamela Knighton, meets Leonard, her agent's voice tells her: "This *is* somebody." In fact, on the Hollywood success ladder he is, in Fitzgerald's words, "on top," although, like Stahr, he does not flaunt this fact. Although Pamela is fundamentally different from Kathleen in her self-centered coldness, they also share a resemblance to "pink and silver frost" and an uncertainty about Americans. Kathleen is no aspiring actor, but her past life, like Pamela's, has an aura of mystery about it. Moreover, the present lives of both are complicated by binding entanglements: Pamela's to Chauncey Ward, and Kathleen's to the nameless man she finally marries. There are other parallels: The first important encounter between Leonard and Pamela, for example, closely resembles the ballroom scene during which Stahr becomes enchanted by Kathleen's beauty. In fact, the nature of Leonard's attraction to Pamela is similar to that of Stahr's to Kathleen; although there is no Minna Davis lurking in Leonard's past as there is in Stahr's, he is drawn to Pamela by the kind of romantic, mysterious force which had finally, apart from her resemblance to Minna, drawn Stahr to Kathleen. Moreover, both attachments end abruptly with the same sort of finality: Pamela dies leaving Jim with only film fragments to remember her by, and Kathleen leaves Stahr when she marries "the American."

The possibility that these parallels were the seeds of *The Last Tycoon* is small. The important point, however, is that "Last Kiss" is a popular treatment of the primary material that Fitzgerald would work with in the novel: Jim's sentimental return to the drugstore where he had once seen Pamela and his nostalgic remembrance of their last kiss earmark the story for a popular audience which, no doubt, Fitzgerald hoped would help pay his bills during the composition of the novel. Fitzgerald was unable to sell the story, probably because none of the characters generates strong emotion. It is sufficiently clear from "Last Kiss," however, that Fitzgerald was regaining his sense of audience. In the process of demonstrating how well he understood Hollywood, the story also captured much of the glitter that is associated with it in the popular mind. In order to rebuild the kind of popular magazine workshop that he had had for *Tender Is the Night,* it remained for him to subordinate his understanding of Hollywood to the task of re-creating its surface. If he had continued in the direction of "Last Kiss," he would perhaps have done this and thus returned to the kind of climate which had in the past proven to be most favorable for his serious novel work—one in which he wrote handfuls of stories for popular magazines while the novel was taking shape. It is also possible that he might have used such stories to make *The Last Tycoon* something more than a great fragment.

Regarding the role of the stories in Fitzgerald's career, one can finally state that they functioned as providers of financial incentive, as proving grounds for his ideas, as workshops for his craft, and as dictators of his popular reputation. The problem for the serious student of Fitzgerald's works is whether one should examine the popular professional writer who produced some 164 stories for mass consumption or limit one's examination of Fitzgerald to his acclaimed works of art, such as "Babylon Revisited," "The Rich Boy," *The Great Gatsby*, and *Tender Is the Night*. To do one to the exclusion of the other is to present not only a fragmented picture of Fitzgerald's literary output but also a distorted one. Just as the stories complement the novels, so do the novels make the stories more meaningful, and the financial and emotional climate from which they all came illuminates the nature of their interdependence.

Bryant Mangum
With updates by Mary Ellen Pitts

Other major works

PLAY: *The Vegetable: Or, From President to Postman*, pb. 1923.

NOVELS: *This Side of Paradise*, 1920; *The Beautiful and Damned*, 1922; *The Great Gatsby*, 1925; *Tender Is the Night*, 1934; *The Last Tycoon*, 1941.

MISCELLANEOUS: *Afternoon of an Author: A Selection of Uncollected Stories and Essays*, 1958; *F. Scott Fitzgerald: The Princeton Years, Selected Writings, 1914-1920*, 1996 (Chip Deffaa, editor).

NONFICTION: *The Crack-Up*, 1945; *The Letters of F. Scott Fitzgerald*, 1963; *Letters to His Daughter*, 1965; *Thoughtbook of Francis Scott Fitzgerald*, 1965; *Dear Scott/Dear Max: The Fitzgerald-Perkins Correspondence*, 1971; *As Ever, Scott Fitzgerald*, 1972; *F. Scott Fitzgerald's Ledger*, 1972; *The Notebooks of F. Scott Fitzgerald*, 1978; *A Life in Letters*, 1994 (Matthew J. Bruccoli, editor); *F. Scott Fitzgerald on Authorship*, 1996; *Dear Scott, Dearest Zelda: The Love Letters of F. Scott and Zelda Fitzgerald*, 2002 (Jackson R. Bryer and Cathy W. Barks, editors).

Bibliography

Bruccoli, Matthew J. *Some Sort of Epic Grandeur.* New York: Harcourt Brace Jovanovich, 1981. In this outstanding biography, a major Fitzgerald scholar argues that Fitzgerald's divided spirit, not his lifestyle, distracted him from writing. Bruccoli believes that Fitzgerald both loved and hated the privileged class that was the subject of his fiction.

Eble, Kenneth. *F. Scott Fitzgerald.* Rev. ed. Boston: Twayne, 1977. A clearly written critical biography, this book traces Fitzgerald's development from youth through a "Final Assessment," which surveys scholarship on Fitzgerald's texts.

Gale, Robert L. *An F. Scott Fitzgerald Encyclopedia.* Westport, Conn.: Greenwood Press, 1998. Provides everything students should know about Fitzgerald's life and works. Indispensable.

Hook, Andrew. *F. Scott Fitzgerald: A Literary Life.* New York: St. Martin's Press, 2002. Part of the Literary Lives series. Concise rather than thorough, but with some interesting details.

Jefferson, Margo. "Still Timely, Yet a Writer of His Time." *The New York Times*, December 17, 1996, p. C17. A brief biography of Fitzgerald on the occasion of his centennial year; calls him one of those rare artists with a cultural radar system that is constantly picking up sensations, responses, and fresh thoughts.

Kuehl, John. *F. Scott Fitzgerald: A Study of the Short Fiction*. Boston: Twayne, 1991. Part 1 discusses Fitzgerald's major stories and story collections, part 2 studies his critical opinions, and part 3 includes selections from Fitzgerald critics. Includes chronology and bibliography.

Mangum, Bryant. *A Fortune Yet: Money in the Art of F. Scott Fitzgerald's Short Stories*. New York: Garland, 1991. Discusses all of Fitzgerald's stories, both those in collections and those uncollected, focusing on their relationship to his novels and their role as a proving ground for his ideas.

May, Charles E., ed. *Masterplots II: Short Story Series, Revised Edition*. 8 vols. Pasadena, Calif.: Salem Press, 2004. Designed for student use, this reference set contains articles providing detailed plot summaries and analyses of these eight short stories by Fitzgerald: "Absolution" and "Babylon Revisited" (vol. 1), "Crazy Sunday" and "The Diamond as Big as the Ritz" (vol. 2), "The Freshest Boy" (vol. 3), "May Day" (vol. 5), "The Rich Boy" (vol. 6), and "Winter Dreams" (vol. 8).

Meyers, Jeffrey. *Scott Fitzgerald: A Biography*. New York: HarperCollins, 1994. In this biography, which makes use of previously unknown materials about Fitzgerald's life, Meyers discusses how such writers as Edgar Allan Poe, Ernest Hemingway, and Joseph Conrad influenced Fitzgerald's fiction.

Petry, Alice Hall. *Fitzgerald's Craft of Short Fiction*. Ann Arbor, Mich.: UMI Research Press, 1989. Study of Fitzgerald's short stories in relationship to his novels, American society, and his personal life. Summarizes and critiques critical reception to his short-story collections and discusses his relationship with his editor Max Perkins; analyzes all the major stories and a number of minor ones.

Tate, Mary Jo. *F. Scott Fitzgerald A to Z: The Essential Reference to His Life and Work*. New York: Facts on File, 1998. Comprehensive study of the man and his works. Provides bibliographical references and an index.

Gustave Flaubert

Born: Rouen, France; December 12, 1821
Died: Croisset, France; May 8, 1880

Principal short fiction • *Novembre*, wr. c. 1840, pb. 1885 (*November*, 1932); *Trois Contes*, 1877 (*Three Tales*, 1903).

Other literary forms • Gustave Flaubert is best known for his novels *Madame Bovary* (1857; English translation, 1886) and *L'Éducation sentimentale* (1869; *A Sentimental Education*, 1898), which offer a realistic view of life in his native Normandy and, in the latter somewhat autobiographical novel, in Paris. He also wrote narratives of his travels to the Pyrenees and Corsica in 1840 (1927), to Italy in 1845, and to Egypt and the Middle East in 1849-1851 (*Notes de voyage*, 1910). Much of the exotic material gleaned on these trips helped inspire *La Tentation de Saint Antoine* (1874; *The Temptation of Saint Anthony*, 1895) and *Salammbô* (1862; English translation, 1886), novels in which he fictionalized figures from history.

Achievements • Gustave Flaubert's *Madame Bovary* may be regarded as the great French novel, but upon its publication, in 1857, it was attacked for its immorality, and a famous lawsuit attempted to suppress it. In a sense, Emma Bovary differs little from many heroines of earlier novels, who engaged in enough amorous adventures to attract avid readers but whose eventual punishment served to uphold a moral perspective sufficient to keep the books socially respectable. What is new in *Madame Bovary*, as in Flaubert's other realist work, lies in the author's style. His detailed documentation of the society in which Emma lived emphasized the hypocrisy endemic in that society. Careful control of physical description delineates the personalities of the various characters and creates a style that has strongly influenced subsequent writers.

Flaubert's realistic compositions form only one aspect of his literary production. His other works, closer to the romantic tradition of the historical novel, testify to his depth and versatility.

Biography • Gustave Flaubert was the second of three surviving children of a provincial doctor. Although it was Gustave's older brother, Achille, who would succeed their father in his medical practice, young Gustave accompanied his father even into the dissecting room, where he gained a knowledge of anatomy and a habit of close observation that would contribute to his future literary style. Unlike Emma's husband, the inept country doctor Charles Bovary, Achille-Cléophas Flaubert was a respected professional. Even after his father's death, Flaubert wrote to his mother from Egypt of his pleasure at meeting during his travels a man who knew and respected his father's reputation.

Flaubert began the study of law but discontinued in part because of his poor health. Epileptic, he had infrequent seizures, but despite his robust appearance, his friends and family sought to protect him from excess strain. Flaubert's only sustained professional activity was as an author. Although he lacked other employment, he felt no particular pressure to rush his works into publication. During the years 1835

Library of Congress

to 1840, he composed a number of short pieces of prose, some fictitious and some personal memoirs, yet he published little. Most of these juvenilia were collected for publication only after his death.

During 1843-1845, Flaubert composed the first version of his autobiographical novel, *A Sentimental Education*, which would finally be published in a considerably revised version in 1869. The story that it tells of young Frédéric Moreau and his frustrated love for an older, married woman parallels Flaubert's own passion for the wife of Maurice Schlésinger, a financially successful bourgeois who provided a vehicle for the criticism of a materialistic society.

Flaubert's hesitation to publish increased in 1849 after reading the manuscript of *The Temptation of Saint Anthony* to his friends Maxima Du Camp and Louis Bouilhet, who harshly criticized it. In October, 1849, Flaubert and Du Camp set out together on a trip to Egypt and the Mediterranean coast as far as Constantinople. During the early part of this journey, Flaubert suffered from considerable depression, which he related to the poor reception of his book and doubts about his literary future. These doubts seem ironic in retrospect, given that in the fall of 1851 he was to begin writing *Madame Bovary*.

Despite a lengthy relationship with Louise Colet, Flaubert never married. His numerous affairs may have been somewhat compromised after his tour of the Orient, however, in that he returned home suffering from syphilis. The publication of *Madame Bovary* in 1857 brought Flaubert both fame and notoriety because of the accusation of its immorality. During the remaining years of his life, Flaubert divided his time between his residence in Paris and his country house in Normandy. He also occasionally traveled to North Africa, the setting of his novel *Salammbô* published in 1862, and to Germany and England. In 1877, three years before his death, he published what are now his best-known short stories, in *Three Tales*.

Analysis • Gustave Flaubert's *Three Tales*, published during the year 1877, when he was fifty-six years old, reflects the variety of styles of his literary production as a whole. "Un Cœur simple" ("A Simple Heart") employs the Norman realism of *Madame Bovary*. "La Légende de Saint Julien l'hospitalier" ("The Legend of St. Julian, Hospitaler") reflects the preoccupation with exotic locales and the history of the early Christians evident in *The Temptation of Saint Anthony* and Flaubert's travel narratives. "Hérodias" retains this exotic context while focusing on a singular heroine from the past, as Flaubert had done in *Salammbô*.

These three texts, Flaubert's only short fiction to be widely read, provide the usual choices for modern readers seeking an introduction to his work. Flaubert wrote them in a spontaneous burst of activity between September, 1875, and February, 1877, as if he were capping his career with a demonstration piece of his various styles.

"A Simple Heart" • "A Simple Heart," the life story of the good-hearted servant Félicité, draws its material from Flaubert's own life. In 1825, a servant, Julie, joined the Flaubert household and may have provided a model for the character of Félicité. Critics have further suggested comparisons between Félicité and the old woman Catherine Leroux, who, in the *Comices agricoles* scene of *Madame Bovary* (part 2, chapter 8), is awarded "for fifty-four years of service on the same farm, a silver medal—valued at twenty-five francs." Twenty-five francs may at that time have represented a fairly impressive sum but was nevertheless a mediocre value to place on fifty-four years of service. Flaubert, echoing his habit of undercutting both characters and social conventions with a final, damning detail, ends the official statement addressed to Catherine Leroux on this materialistic note.

In "A Simple Heart," as in *Madame Bovary*, the materialism of Norman society appears in the form of a continual preoccupation with money. Yet in both works, this harsh theme contrasts with a persistent romanticism linked to the vain hopes of the various characters. Cupidity in the form of jealousy appears in the very first sentence of "A Simple Heart": "For half a century, the bourgeois women of Pont-l'Évêque envied Madame Aubain because of her servant, Félicité." The motivations of characters throughout the story revolve around money, often to the disadvantage of trusting Félicité. Some figures appear prejudged, as society would have classified them economically, from their very first mention in the text. Thus, Madame Aubain's uncle, an impoverished aristocrat who visits early in the second section of the story, "always arrived at lunch time, with a horrid poodle whose paws spread dirt on all the furniture."

Even the characters dearest to Félicité do not hesitate to hurt her when money is involved. When Félicité befriends Nastasie Barette, who does exploit her by accepting numerous presents, Madame Aubain cuts off this opportunity for friendship by decreeing their prompt return from Trouville to Pont-l'Évêque. Even Félicité's beloved nephew, Victor, imposes on her generosity, although he does bring back to her gifts from his travels. His sudden departure on a voyage to the United States throws Félicité into despair, augmented by Madame Aubain's insensitive incomprehension of her suffering when she learns of Victor's death.

Throughout, characters are defined, usually in a negative manner, by the objects that surround them, objects that often appear in themselves hostile. The initial description of Madame Aubain's house in Pont-l'Évêque tells the reader that "it had interior differences of level that made people trip," and the family members appear through the presentation of their rooms, where the "two children's beds without mattresses" and the attic room of Félicité testify to the subordinate status of children and servants. Yet appearances can be deceiving, still with a bias toward the negative. Because of her harsh life and limited diet, Félicité "at the age of twenty-five appeared to be forty years old."

The considerable catalog of objects in these defining descriptions parallels Flaubert's technique in *Madame Bovary* and echoes much of the realistic style of Honoré de Balzac, whose death in 1850 had appeared to Flaubert as a great loss.

Thus, the detailed menu of the lunch at the Liébard farm recalls the even more expansive description in Emma Bovary's view of the dinner at the château, and Virginie, after her death, survives in memory in her clothes—reminiscent of the wedding bouquet of Charles's previous wife that greets Emma upon her arrival at the house at Tostes—clothes that Madame Aubain could bring herself to inspect only when "moths flew out of the wardrobe."

The central documentation, however, must be that of Félicité's own room. Flaubert makes a significant decision to withhold this description until the very end of the story. The mention of Félicité's room in the opening pages tells the reader only that it was in the attic and had a view over the fields. There is no description of the interior. By the time it is revealed, the room contains the debris of Félicité's life and "had the appearance both of a chapel and a bazaar, as it contained so many religious objects and varied things." The separation of the religious objects here from the others underlines their dual role. Religion, as will be seen, held great importance for Félicité, but the objects that represent her devotion share with the others in her room echoes of deterioration and loss. Further, the distinction blurs between religious and secular: "On the dresser, covered with a cloth like an altar, was a box made of seashells that Victor had given her." She retains with religious veneration objects linked to her memories.

Negative emphasis within the realistic catalog again parallels *Madame Bovary.* The determining events of Félicité's unhappy memories grow from the same avaricious society that surrounded Emma. The one man she loved, Théodore, abandoned her to marry "a very rich old woman," an action analogous both to Charles Bovary's first, arranged marriage to Héloïse and to Paul's later marriage in "A Simple Heart" to the daughter of a man who could help his career. Victor's death, attributed to poor medical treatment of his case of yellow fever, recalls Charles Bovary's unfortunate failure in the operation on Justin, and the heirs who pillage Madame Aubain's house parallel the actions of Emma's creditors.

The most obvious negative emphases, however, result from a series of exclusions. The bad can be defined most easily by contrast with the good. Often, this ranking comes from the arbitrary expectations of society, expectations that Flaubert documented in his *Dictionnaire des idées reçues* (1910, 1913; *Dictionary of Accepted Ideas,* 1954). Thus, Charles Bovary bought for Emma "a second-hand vehicle that, once equipped with new lanterns and pierced leather mud flaps, almost resembled a tilbury," and at the beach at Trouville, Virginie "went swimming in a shirt, for lack of a bathing costume; and her maid dressed her in a customs-inspection cabin that served for the bathers." Things, not allowed to be as they naturally exist, are described as "almost" something more prestigious.

Those moments of high prestige in which the characters participate, however, disappear from the text. At Virginie's funeral, for example, readers see the preparation of the body for the burial but not the more uplifting religious ceremony. Flaubert states simply, "after mass, it took three quarters of an hour to get to the cemetery." Similarly, though romance dominates Emma Bovary's life, Flaubert never shows her at the moment of central significance when she is a bride in church. Again, he emphasizes distance to be traversed: "The town hall being at half a league from the farm, they went there on foot, and came back in the same manner, once the ceremony was over at the church." The last phrase, added almost as an afterthought, effectively deemphasizes what could have been the most positive moment of Emma's life. One may certainly argue that liturgy, with its set patterns, need not be described in detail to be understood. Still, as Alphonse Daudet so aptly demonstrated in "Les Trois Messes basses," the personal circumstances woven into each liturgy make it a unique event. This must hold especially true for both weddings and funerals.

Although the drama of liturgical moments disappears from Flaubert's texts, a current of romanticism persists throughout "A Simple Heart." Linked in part to the religious element in the story, this romanticism includes references both to traditional romantic themes and to other passages in which Flaubert appears to parody such themes. This again echoes *Madame Bovary* and Flaubert's dual feelings concerning romantic passion. Emma Bovary's emotional confusion clearly derives from the false ideas of love, which she had taken from sentimental novels. Immediately after her marriage, she "sought to know exactly what people meant in real life by the words *felicity, passion* and *intoxication* that had appeared so beautiful to her in books." Flaubert's use of the word *félicité* in this description of Emma's disappointment anticipates the irony in the choice of the word as the name for his heroine in "A Simple Heart." Félicité does occasionally achieve joy but only despite the numerous forces working against her happiness.

Religion provides the central solace of Félicité's life. At the beginning of the story, she rises at dawn to attend Mass and falls asleep each night with her rosary in her hand. She derives a dual joy from attending catechism classes with Virginie. She admires the beauty of the stained-glass windows, much as Emma Bovary "rather than following the mass looked at the holy pictures framed in azure in her book," and thus Félicité gains a rudimentary religious education, such training "having been neglected in her youth." The repeated images in the church of the Holy Spirit in the form of a bird prepare for Félicité's vision at the end of the story.

Along with religion, a romantic joy in external nature touches Félicité. In a way that underlines her solitude, however, these fleeting moments of happiness come to Félicité only with the rare experience of love. Flaubert tells the reader very early that Félicité "had had, like anyone else, her tale of love," thus deemphasizing this formative experience. Still, during her interlude with Théodore, they were surrounded by the beauty of nature: "The wind was soft; the stars shone," but as Emma could not regain the luxury of the ball at the château, Félicité only rarely returns to the joys of nature. One other such interlude does occur when she accompanies the Aubain family to the countryside. This enjoyment coincides with the fulfillment that Félicité feels in taking care of Paul and Virginie when they are children, but even here there is a sense of deterioration from a better state of things past. The house they visit "was all that remained of a vacation house, now disappeared."

Consistent with the romantic pathetic fallacy identifying elements of nature with the emotional condition of the protagonist, nature remains pleasant in "A Simple Heart" while Félicité is relatively happy. Later, as she worries about Victor, who has gone to sea, she focuses on violent storms and finally learns that, "as in a memory of engravings in a geography book, he was eaten by savages, trapped in a forest by monkeys, or dying on a deserted beach." Like Emma, she takes her imaginings from an overly literal application of material from books.

As Flaubert cites these tales of savages and monkeys, modern elements of romantic travel literature, he draws on a rich source of contemporary allusion. Elsewhere, the names of Paul and Virginie he chooses for Madame Aubain's children recall the novel *Paul et Virginie* (1788), by Jacques-Henri Bernadin de Saint-Pierre, the exotic setting of which provided a model of preromantic nature description. Later, the appearance of the de Larsonnière family with their black servant and their parrot continued this current of exotic allusion.

Flaubert's critique of romanticism leads him to use a degree of exaggeration that approaches parody. When their uncle gives the children a geography book with engravings, "they represented different scenes of the world, cannibals with feathers on their heads, a monkey carrying off a young girl, bedouins in the desert, a whale being harpooned. . . ." These dramatic choices may have been typical of geography books of the time, but in Flaubert's description of Virginie after her death, the choices are entirely his own. He begins with a conventional tableau, where Virginie's pale face contrasted with a black crucifix echoes the contrast of light and darkness dear to the Romantics. As Félicité remains "for two nights" near the body, however, the description, drawn from Flaubert's realistic medical observations, inclines toward the grotesque.

Grotesque exaggeration linked to the theme of death culminates in the story of Félicité's parrot. She had become so attached to the bird, the last voice audible to her as she became progressively deaf, that she had it stuffed after its death. Its place among the religious objects in her room reinforced an association: "In church she always contemplated the Holy Spirit and observed that he somewhat resembled the parrot." The bird, however, badly preserved, deteriorated. At the end, when Félicité's friend brought the parrot to her to kiss, "worms were devouring it."

Félicité does not see the deterioration of the parrot. Her eyes as well as her ears are failing. The brief fifth and final section of the story brings the reader at last to the perspective of Félicité herself, who, thanks to the very narrowness of her perceptions, achieves the happiness promised in her name. Earlier references have slighted Félicité's intelligence and alluded to her lack of education, but what she does not know may protect her. The fifth section opens with the line "The grass sent the odor of summer," appealing to one sense that Félicité retains and bringing back to her the sense of joy in nature. A religious procession is about to pass by the house, and readers see it through Félicité's imagination. The holy sacrament is displayed on an altar containing many objects representative of life in the local area, including the stuffed parrot, Loulou. This accumulation of mismatched objects, however, no longer conveys the lack of aesthetic sense that it might have represented earlier. It has become a "mound of bright colors" amid which "Loulou, hidden under some roses, showed only a blue forehead, like a piece of lapis." Properly selected and arranged, even the realistic debris of village life can present a form of beauty. At the end, Félicité is vindicated in that her "simple heart" had led her to make instinctive choices that protect what beauty there was in her world.

The complex style of "A Simple Heart" derives from the tension between its realistic and romantic elements. A similar contrast in "La Légende de Saint Julien l'Hospitalier" ("The Legend of St. Julian, Hospitaler"), however, produces a much simpler narrative, where quantities of relatively generic images replace the nuances of the objects in Félicité's surroundings.

"The Legend of St. Julian, Hospitaler" • "The Legend of St. Julian, Hospitaler" conveys the life of its protagonist from birth to death, neatly divided into three parts: the growing violence of the young man, who fears that he will fulfill a prophecy that he will kill his parents, a period of flight that ends with Julien unwittingly killing his parents when they come to seek him, and his final repentance and salvation.

The story, set in a vaguely described medieval Europe, contains numerous exotic elements that link it to Flaubert's *The Temptation of Saint Anthony.* Although Antoine spends the greater part of his story doing penance and resisting temptations, however, Julien's violent years dominate a story with only a brief phase of penitence. The fairy-tale opening of "The Legend of St. Julian, Hospitaler"—"Julien's father and mother lived in a chateau, in the middle of a wood, on the slope of a hill"—contrasts with the more theatrical style with extensive dialogue that dominates *The Temptation of Saint Anthony.*

Exotic elements proliferate in "The Legend of St. Julian, Hospitaler" from the very first description, where the family's castle contains armaments of foreign origins, to the Asian merchants and pilgrims from the Holy Land who describe their journeys and to the diverse adversaries whom Julien faces during his extensive travels as a soldier. The analogy with the story of Oedipus, similarly destined to kill his father, adds a foreign element, but description in "The Legend of St. Julian, Hospitaler" lacks the details and contrasts of the Norman scene. When Julien kills animals while hunting and later finds himself surrounded by beasts intent on avenging his excessive savagery, the catalog of creatures retains the artistic sense of animals highlighted in a tapestry: "A marten slipped quickly between his legs, a panther bounded over his shoulder, a serpent wound around an ash tree." Except for the stag that speaks to Julien to warn him of his fate, the animals and other objects Julien encounters remain generic, devoid of descriptive detail.

Similarly, the pathetic fallacy linking landscape to emotion disappears in this text. When, in the second part, Julien marries and attempts to lead a settled life, the sky over his château "was always blue." Even in the emotional hunting scene that reawakens his savagery and leads to the death of his parents, readers see him surrounded by natural beauty: "The shadows of trees spread out across the moss. Sometimes the moon dappled the clearings."

Occasionally, description does serve, as elsewhere in Flaubert's work, to define the mood of characters. As Julien grows more ferocious in hunting, he returns home one night "covered with blood and dirt, with thorns in his hair and smelling like savage beasts." Flaubert, however, continues here, "He became like the beasts." The symbolism is more explicit and heavy-handed than in Flaubert's more realistic texts. A night lamp "in the form of a dove" symbolizes his parents' care for Julien but with a more simplistic suggestion than that in Félicité's vision of the Holy Spirit.

If the characters are not seen as motivated by the objects that surround them, a strong theme of fate provides an alternate controlling force. When Julien's thirst for blood is first aroused and he begins to kill birds with stones, "the wall being broken at that place, a piece of stone happened to be under his fingers. He turned his arm and the stone knocked down the bird." The stone, not Julien, is responsible, and later, when Julien attempts to repent, violent dreams come unbidden to renew his desire to kill.

Fate finds its voice in the prophecies governing Julien's life. At his birth, a beggar, "a Bohemian with plaited beard, silver rings on his arms, and blazing eyes," warns Julien's father of the violence to come, much as the beggar in *Madame Bovary* foreshadows Emma's death. At the end of the story, the leprous traveler whom Julien rescues flashes the same blazing eyes just before Julien is carried off to heaven. This salvation, ordained by Christ, responds to another kind of external—this time divine—manipulation.

"Hérodias" • Just as Julien's story follows what has been preordained, "Hérodias" must not depart from the set sequence of events from the biblical story. This time, Flaubert narrates not the entire life of his protagonist but the events of a single day. During the first two parts of the story, a delegation arrives from Rome and, while searching Herod's cellars for treasures, finds the imprisoned John the Baptist, called here Iaokanann, who rails against Herod's incestuous marriage. The third part narrates the banquet where Salomé's dance earns Iaokanann's death.

Again, Flaubert uses a considerable amount of description, much of it derived from his own visit to the shores of the Dead Sea, but the view remains that of the camera, avoiding detailed analysis of the characters' emotions. Readers first see Herod on a terrace with a panoramic view of the surrounding country. The descriptive catalog of the terrain and Herod's embattled position parallel the situation at the beginning of *Salammbô*. Later, an enumeration of armaments in Herod's cellars recalls the similar listing in "The Legend of St. Julian, Hospitaler," but very little of this relates to character exposition. Only the menacing "hot wind with the odor of sulfer" that blows as Hérodias, Herod's wife, arrives hints at the personal confrontations to come. Even when, at the end of the first part, Herod's view of a beautiful young girl on another terrace foreshadows Hérodias's manipulation of him, the portrait of the girl herself has the impersonality of an Asian painting.

A principal animation of "Hérodias" comes from recurrent animal imagery. Iaokanann appears in prison, covered with animal skins, "in the depths of his lair." He screams that he will cry out "like a bear, like a wild ass" and forces Hérodias finally to "roar" like a lion. Contrasting with this animal imagery, however, Salomé's dance appears mechanical. In a parallel scene in *Salammbô*, the heroine dances with a python "placing the middle of its body around the back of her neck," but Salomé, instructed by her mother, remains externally controlled "like a flower shaken by a storm."

Almost inevitably Iaokanann is beheaded. The story ends as two Christians carry the head away toward Galilee: "Since it was very heavy, they took turns carrying it." This final realistic touch parallels the closing of "The Legend of St. Julian, Hospitaler," where Flaubert adds, "There is the story of Saint Julien l'Hospitalier approximately as one finds it on the church window in my country." Each story, exoticism notwithstanding, ends grounded by a realistic touch.

Flaubert's instinctive return to realism reflects the importance of the documentary style, founded on his detailed observation of Norman life, through which he orchestrated objects to reflect the psychological composition of his characters. A comparison of "A Simple Heart" with Flaubert's more exotic short stories reveals a shift in the latter toward a formal objectivity. Animals like those of a tapestry and the image of a girl portrayed as if in a painting distance themselves from the emotional content of the story.

Flaubert's realistic manner bridges this distance. In "A Simple Heart," as in *Madame Bovary*, he develops a complexity that relies on the careful selection of objects to define both the feelings of his characters and the societal forces that often conflict with them. This conflict, closely tied to the clash of romantic and realistic elements, provides the basic tension that gives life to Flaubert's work.

Dorothy M. Betz

Other major works

PLAYS: *Le Château des cœurs,* wr. 1863, pr. 1874 (with Louis Bouilhet; *The Castle of Hearts,* 1904); *Le Candidat,* pr., pb. 1874 (*The Candidate,* 1904).

NOVELS: *La Première Éducation sentimentale,* wr. 1843-1845, pb. 1963 (*The First Sentimental Education,* 1972); *Madame Bovary,* 1857 (English translation, 1886); *Salammbô,* 1862 (English translation, 1886); *L'Éducation sentimentale,* 1869 (*A Sentimental Education,* 1898); *La Tentation de Saint Antoine,* 1874 (*The Temptation of Saint Anthony,* 1895); *Bouvard et Pécuchet,* 1881 (*Bouvard and Pécuchet,* 1896).

MISCELLANEOUS: *The Complete Works,* 1904 (10 volumes); *Œuvres complètes,* 1910-1933 (22 volumes).

NONFICTION: *Par les champs et par les grèves,* 1885 (with Maxime Du Camp; *Over Strand and Field,* 1904); *Correspondance, 1830-1880,* 1887-1893; *Dictionnaire des idées reçues,* 1910, 1913 (*Dictionary of Accepted Ideas,* 1954); *Notes de voyage,* 1910; *Correspondance,* 1981 (Alphonse Jacobs, editor; *Flaubert-Sand: The Correspondence of Gustave Flaubert and George Sand,* 1993); *Gustave Flaubert-Alfred Le Poittevin, Gustave-Flaubert-Maxine Du Camp: Correspondances,* 2000 (Yvan Leclerc, editor).

Bibliography

Addison, Claire. *Where Flaubert Lies.* New York: Cambridge University Press, 1996. Detailed study of Flaubert's life and art, focusing on the relationship between his personal life, historical context, and his fiction.

Bloom, Harold, ed. *Gustave Flaubert.* New York: Chelsea House, 1989. This collection of fourteen essays with an introduction by Bloom covers multiple aspects of Flaubert's life and work. Jane Robertson writes on the structure of "Hérodias," noting the relative difficulty of the work. Shoshana Felman's essay on "The Legend of St. Julian, Hospitaler" stresses legendary and symbolic elements in the story. Contains a chronology of Flaubert's life, a bibliography, and an index.

Brown, Frederick. *Flaubert: A Biography.* Boston: Little, Brown, 2006. This penetrating study of Flaubert in nineteenth century Paris paints a lively portrait of the man and his time.

Cronk, Nicholas. "Reading *Un Cœur Simple:* The Pleasure of the Intertext." *Nineteenth-Century French Studies* 24 (Fall/Winter, 1995/1996): 154-161. Discusses the story's allusion to eighteenth century works from the Rousseauesque tradition of sentiment and the Voltairean tradition of satire. Claims that Flaubert appropriates a character of Bernardin de Saint-Pierre's as a model for Félicité.

Greenbaum, Andrea. "Flaubert's *Un Cœur Simple.*" *The Explicator* (Summer, 1995): 208-211. Discusses the satire in Flaubert's story, particularly its mockery of religious devotion by means of the parrot, the story's satirical centerpiece.

May, Charles E., ed. *Masterplots II: Short Story Series, Revised Edition.* 8 vols. Pasadena, Calif.: Salem Press, 2004. Designed for student use, this reference set contains articles providing detailed plot summaries and analyses of these three short stories by Flaubert: "Hérodias" (vol. 3); "The Legend of St. Julian, Hospitaler" (vol. 4); and "A Simple Heart" (vol. 7).

Nadeau, Maurice. *The Greatness of Flaubert.* Translated by Barbara Bray. New York: Library Press, 1972. This biographical work devotes chapter 16 to the *Three Tales,* stressing how these works evolved from ideas that Flaubert had accumulated during his previous writing. Sources considered are largely biographical, and the chapter details the immediate context in which the three stories were written. Supplemented by a chronology and a bibliography.

Porter, Laurence M., ed. *Critical Essays on Gustave Flaubert.* Boston: G. K. Hall, 1986. This collection of sixteen essays includes work by a number of authorities in the field. Two studies treat the *Three Tales:* Raymonde Debray-Genette studies "Narrative Figures of Speech" in "A Simple Heart" in a structural analysis that still insists on the importance of illusion, and Benjamin F. Bart examines "Humanity and Animality" in "The Legend of St. Julian, Hospitaler." Bibliography, index.

Stipa, Ingrid. "Desire, Repetition, and the Imaginary in Flaubert's *Un Cœur Simple.*" *Studies in Short Fiction* 31 (Fall, 1994): 617-626. Argues that although Flaubert maintains an ironic perspective in the story, a pattern of repetitions of imagery makes the transformation of the parrot into a sacred symbol acceptable to the reader, a tactic that protects the protagonist from being the victim of the irony.

Unwin, Timothy, ed. *The Cambridge Companion to Flaubert.* New York: Cambridge University Press, 2004. Replete with tools for further research, this is an excellent aid to any study of Flaubert's life and work.

Wall, Geoffrey. *Flaubert: A Life.* New York: Farrar, Straus and Giroux, 2002. Critically acclaimed narrative biography that gives Lottman and Troyat a run for the standard. Offers plenty of fresh detail and a great read.

E. M. Forster

Born: London, England; January 1, 1879
Died: Coventry, England; June 7, 1970

Principal short fiction • *The Celestial Omnibus, and Other Stories,* 1911; *The Eternal Moment, and Other Stories,* 1928; *The Collected Tales of E. M. Forster,* 1947; *The Life to Come, and Other Stories,* 1972; *Arctic Summer, and Other Fiction,* 1980.

Other literary forms • E. M. Forster wrote six novels, one of which (*Maurice,* 1971) was published posthumously because of its homosexual theme. He also wrote travel books, essays, reviews, criticism, biography, and some poetry. Together with Eric Crozier he wrote the libretto for the four-act opera *Billy Budd* (1951), adapted from Herman Melville's famous work.

Achievements • As a novelist of rare distinction and one of the great literary figures of the twentieth century, E. M. Forster enjoyed international recognition and received many literary awards and honors. In 1921, as private secretary to the maharajah of Dewas State Senior, he was awarded the Sir Tukojirao Gold Medal. The publication of *A Passage to India* (1924) brought him much acclaim, including the Femina Vie Heureuse Prize and the James Tait Black Memorial Prize in 1925. In 1927, he was elected Fellow of King's College, Cambridge, and he delivered Clark Lectures at Trinity College. In 1937, the Royal Society of Literature honored him with the Benson Medal. In 1945, he was made Honorary Fellow, King's College, where he remained until his death in 1970. In 1953, he was received by Queen Elizabeth II as a Companion of Honor. Between 1947 and 1958, several universities, including Cambridge, conferred on him the honorary degree of doctor of laws. In 1961, the Royal Society of Literature named him a Companion of Literature. He attained the greatest recognition when, on his ninetieth birthday, on January 1, 1969, he was appointed to the Order of Merit by Queen Elizabeth.

Biography • Edward Morgan Forster was born in London on January 1, 1879. He was the great-grandson of Henry Thornton, a prominent member of the Evangelical Clapham Sect and a member of Parliament. His father, an architect, died early, and he was brought up by his mother and his great-aunt, Marianne Thornton (whose biography he published in 1956). He received his early education at Tonbridge School, but he did not like the public school atmosphere. His bitter criticism of the English public school system appears in his portrayal of Sawston School in his first two novels, *Where Angels Fear to Tread* (1905) and *The Longest Journey* (1907). From Tonbridge, Forster went on to the University of Cambridge—thanks to the rich inheritance left by Marianne Thornton, who died when he was eight—where he came under the influence of Goldworthy Lowes Dickinson (whose biography he wrote in 1934) and quickly began to blossom as a scholar, writer, and humanist.

After graduating from King's College, Forster traveled, with his mother, to Italy and Greece in 1901. His first short story, "Albergo Empedocle," was published in 1903. Between 1903 and 1910, he published four novels, nine short stories, and other, nonfictional items. His travels to Greece and Italy led to his representation of life in those countries as being less repressive than life in England. During World War I, he served as a volunteer with the Red Cross in Alexandria, Egypt. His stay there resulted in *Alexandria: A History and a Guide* (1922) and *Pharos and Pharillon* (1923). His two visits to India, the first in 1912 in company of Goldworthy Lowes Dickinson and the second in 1921 as private secretary to the maharajah of Dewas State Senior, provided him material for his masterpiece novel *A Passage to India* (1924) as well as *The Hill of Devi* (1953). With *A Passage to India*, Forster's reputation was established as a major English novelist of the twentieth century. He made a third visit to India in 1945 to attend a conference of Indian writers at Jaipur. He then wrote, "If Indians had not spoken English my own life would have been infinitely poorer." He visited the United States in 1947 to address the Symposium on Music Criticism at Harvard and again in 1949 to address the American Academy of Arts and Letters.

Though Forster stopped publishing fiction after 1924, he continued to produce significant nonfiction writing to the end. In a statement at the beginning of B. J. Kirkpatrick's *A Bibliography of E. M. Forster* (1965), Forster said: "The longer one lives the less one feels to have done, and I am both surprised and glad to discover from this bibliography that I have written so much." He died on June 7, 1970, at the age of ninety-one. Throughout his life he kept his faith in liberal humanism, in the sanctity of personal relationships, and, above all, in individualism. His charismatic personality and his personal warmth have led many people to believe that the man was greater than his books.

Analysis • All of Forster's best-known and most anthologized stories appeared first in two collections, *The Celestial Omnibus* and *The Eternal Moment*. The words "celestial" and "eternal" are especially significant because a typical E. M. Forster story features a protagonist who is allowed a vision of a better life, sometimes momentarily only. Qualifications for experiencing this epiphany include a questioning mind, an active imagination, and a dissatisfaction with conventional attitudes. The transformation resulting from the experience comes about through some kind of magic that transports him through time—backward or forward—or through space—to Mt. Olympus or to heaven. Whether or not his life is permanently changed, the transformed character can never be the same again after a glimpse of the Elysian Fields, and he is henceforth suspect to contemporary mortals.

Forster termed his short stories "fantasies," and when the discerning reader can determine the point at which the real and the fantastic intersect, he will locate the epiphany, at the same time flexing his own underused imaginative muscles. Perhaps "The Machine Stops," a science-fiction tale about a world managed by a computer-like Machine that warns men to "beware of first-hand ideas," was at the time of its writing (1909) the most fantastic of Forster's short fiction, but its portrayal of radio, television, and telephones with simultaneous vision seems to have been simply far-sighted.

Forster frequently uses a narrator who is so insensitive that he ironically enhances the perception of the reader. In "Other Kingdom," for example, when Mr. Inskip finds it "right" to repeat Miss Beaumont's conversation about a "great dream" to his employer, the reader correctly places the tutor on the side of unimaginative human, rather than in the lineup of Dryads to which the young lady will repair. When the narrator of "The Story of a Panic" boasts that he "can tell a story without exaggerating" and then unfolds a tale about a boy who obviously is visited by Pan and who finally bounds away to join the goat-god, the readers know that they must themselves inform the gaps of information. When the same narrator attributes the death of the waiter Gennaro to the fact that "the miserable Italians have no stamina. Something had gone wrong inside him," the reader observes the disparity between the two statements and rightly concludes that Gennaro's death has a supernatural cause—that he had been subjected to the same "panic" as had Eustace, and that only the latter had passed the test.

In *Aspects of the Novel* (1927), Forster suggests that fiction will play a part in the ultimate success of civilization through promotion of human sympathy, reconciliation, and understanding. In each of the short stories the protagonist gets a fingerhold on the universal secret, but he sometimes loses his grip, usually through the action of someone too blind, materialistic, or enslaved by time to comprehend the significance of the moment.

If, as Forster himself declares, the emphasis of plot lies in causality, he allows the reader an important participation, because the causes of transformation are never explicit, and the more mundane characters are so little changed by the miraculous events taking place around them that they are not puzzled or even aware that they occur.

"The Eternal Moment" • In "The Eternal Moment," the stiffly insensitive Colonel Leyland, Miss Raby's friend and traveling companion, is just such a character. Although Miss Raby is determined to accept the responsibility for the commercialization of the mountain resort Vorta engendered by her novel, Colonel Leyland can understand her feelings no more readily than can Feo, the uneducated waiter who is the immediate object of Miss Raby's search. Although Miss Raby ostensibly has returned to the village to see how it has been affected by tourism since she made it famous, she also is drawn to the spot because it was the scene of the one romantic, although brief, interlude of her life. For twenty years she has recalled a declaration of passionate love for her by a young Italian guide whose advances she had rejected. This memory has sustained her because of its reality and beauty. She finds the once rustic village overgrown with luxury hotels, in one of which Feo, her dream-lover, is the stout, greasy, middle-aged, hypocritical concierge.

Miss Raby, whose instincts have warned her that the progress of civilization is not necessarily good, sees that "the passage of a large number of people" has corrupted not only the village and its values, but also Feo. Observing that "pastoral virtues" and "family affection" have disappeared with the onslaught of touristry, she accosts the embarrassed peasant who had once offered her flowers. In a scene that is the quintessence of a human failure to communicate, Feo believes that she is attempting to ruin him, while she is actually appealing to him to help the old woman who owns the only hotel untouched by modernity. Colonel Leyland, who cannot bear the thought, much less the reality, of such intimate contact with a member of the lower class, gives up his idea of marrying Miss Raby. The rich novelist, whose entire life has been enriched by the "eternal moment" when she briefly and in imagination only had spanned class barriers, asks Feo if she can adopt one of his children. Rebuffed, she will live alone, able perhaps to blot out reality and relive the happiness that the memory of the "eternal moment" has brought her.

Another misunderstood protagonist is Eustace, the fourteen-year-old English boy considered a misfit by the group of tourists with whom he is seeing Italy. Listless and pampered, bad-tempered and repellent, Eustace dislikes walking, cannot swim, and appears most to enjoy lounging. Forced to go to a picnic, the boy carves from wood a whistle, which when blown evokes a "catspaw" of wind that frightens all of the other tourists into running. When they return to their picnic site in search of Eustace, they find him lying on his back, a green lizard darting from his cuff. For the first time on the trip the boy smiles and is polite. The footprints of goats are discerned nearby as Eustace races around "like a real boy." A dazed hare sits on his arm, and he kisses an old woman as he presents her with flowers. The adults, in trying to forget the encounter, are cruel to Eustace and to Gennaro, a young, natural, ignorant Italian fishing lad, who is a "stop-gap" waiter at the inn, and who clearly understands the boy's experience. As Eustace and Gennaro attempt to flee to freedom from human responsibility, the waiter is killed, the victim of a society which in its lack of understanding had attempted to imprison Eustace, oblivious to his miraculous change, or at least to its significance. He has turned into an elfin sprite of the woods, to which he escapes forever, leaving behind him Forster's customary complement of complacent, nonplussed tourists.

"Other Kingdom" • No Pan, but a Dryad, is Evelyn Beaumont of "Other Kingdom." Mr. Inskip, who narrates the tale, has been hired as a tutor of the classics by handsome, prosperous, and pompous Harcourt Worters. Inskip's charges are Worters's fiancé, Miss Evelyn Beaumont, and his ward, Jack Ford. When Worters announces that he has purchased a nearby copse called "Other Kingdom" as a wedding gift for Evelyn, she dances her gleeful acceptance in imitation of a beech tree. On a celebratory picnic Evelyn asks Jack to stand in a position that will hide the house from her view. She is dismayed to learn that Worters plans to build a high fence around her copse and to add an asphalt path and a bridge. Evelyn values the fact that boys and girls have been coming for years from the village to carve their initials on the trees, and she notes that Worters finds blood on his hands when he attempts to repeat the romantic ritual. Upon hearing that Worters has obtained Other Kingdom by taking advantage of a widow, she realizes that he is a selfish person who views her as one of his possessions to be enjoyed. Broken in spirit, she apparently agrees to his plan of fencing in the copse, but she dances away "from society and life" to be united with other wood nymphs and likely with Ford, who knows intuitively that she is a free spirit that can never be possessed.

"The Road from Colonus" • Although Eustace in "Story of a Panic" is a Pan-figure, Evelyn a Dryad, and Harcourt Worters a prototype of Midas, Mr. Lucas of "The Road from Colonus" is associated with Oedipus. The tale's title is reminiscent of Sophocles' play, and Ethel, Mr. Lucas's daughter, represents Antigone. As do Miss Raby, Eustace, and Evelyn Beaumont, Mr. Lucas enters into a special union with nature and humankind. Riding ahead of his daughter and her friends, he finds the "real Greece" when he spies a little inn surrounded by a grove of plane trees and a little stream that bubbles out of a great hollow tree. As he enters this natural shrine, he for the first time sees meaning to his existence, and he longs to stay in this peaceful spot. The other tourists, however, have schedules and appointments to adhere to, and they forcibly carry Mr. Lucas away from the scene of his revelation. That night the plane tree crashes to kill all occupants of the inn, and Mr. Lucas spends his remaining days fussing about his neighbors and the noises of civilization, especially those made by the running water in the drains and reminiscent of the pleasant, musical gurgles of the little stream in Greece.

"The Celestial Omnibus" • More fortunate than Mr. Lucas is the boy who rides "The Celestial Omnibus" from an alley where an old, faded sign points the way "To Heaven." After the driver, Sir Thomas Browne, delivers the boy across a great gulf on a magnificent rainbow to the accompaniment of music, and back home to his nursery, the boy's parents refuse to believe his tale. Mr. Bons, a family friend, attempts to prove the boy is lying by offering to make a repeat journey with him. On this trip the driver is Dante. Even though Mr. Bons is finally convinced that the boy has actually met Achilles and Tom Jones, he wants to go home. When Mr. Bons crawls out of the omnibus shrieking, "I see London," he falls and is seen no more. His body is discovered "in a shockingly mutilated condition," and the newspaper reports that "foul play is suspected." The boy is crowned with fresh leaves as the dolphins awaken to celebrate with him the world of imagination. Mr. Bons, when accosted with this world, rejected it so violently that he suffered physical pain.

In all of these "fantasies," a gulf separates reality from illusion, and the latter is clearly to be preferred. If one must inhabit the real world, one can bear its existence and even love its inhabitants if that person is one of the fortunate few receptive to a special kind of vision.

Sue L. Kimball
With updates by Chaman L. Sahni

Other major works

PLAY: *Billy Budd*, pb. 1951 (with Eric Crozier; libretto).

NOVELS: *Where Angels Fear to Tread*, 1905; *The Longest Journey*, 1907; *A Room with a View*, 1908; *Howards End*, 1910; *Maurice*, wr. 1913, pb. 1971; *A Passage to India*, 1924.

MISCELLANEOUS: *The Abinger Edition of E. M. Forster*, 1972-1998 (17 volumes; Oliver Stallybrass, editor).

NONFICTION: *Alexandria: A History and a Guide*, 1922; *Pharos and Pharillon*, 1923; *Aspects of the Novel*, 1927; *Goldsworthy Lowes Dickinson*, 1934; *Abinger Harvest—A Miscellany*, 1936; *Virginia Woolf*, 1942; *Development of English Prose Between 1918 and 1939*, 1945; *Two Cheers for Democracy*, 1951; *The Hill of Devi*, 1953; *Marianne Thornton: A Domestic Biography, 1797-1887*, 1956; *Commonplace Book*, 1978; *Selected Letters of E. M. Forster*, 1983-1985 (2 volumes; Mary Lago and P. N. Furbank, editors); *The Feminine Note in Literature*m 2001.

Bibliography

Beauman, Nicola. *E. M. Forster: A Biography*. New York: Alfred A. Knopf, 1994. In this biography devoted primarily to the first forty-five years of Forster's life, when he was developing as a fiction writer, Beauman discusses the origins of Forster's fictional themes in his family background and claims that his most successful years as a writer were also his unhappiest as a person due to his sexual repression and his conflicts over his homosexuality.

Caporaletti, Silvana. "Science as Nightmare: 'The Machine Stops' by E. M. Forster." *Utopian Studies* 8 (1997): 32-47. Discusses the dystopian theme in the story; claims the story denounces materialism and conformism imposed by rigid social conventions that repress diversity, spontaneity, and creativity.

_____. "The Thematization of Time in E. M. Forster's 'The Eternal Moment' and Joyce's 'The Dead.'" *Twentieth Century Literature* 43 (Winter, 1997): 406-419. Discusses how the two stories are influenced by Henri Bergson's dual concept of time as sequential and psychological. Argues that most of the characters in the stories reflect the contrast between these two modes of time.

Gardner, Philip, ed. *E. M. Forster: The Critical Heritage.* New York: Routledge, 1997. Critical essays on Forster's works. Includes bibliographical references and an index.

Iago, Mary. *E. M. Forster: A Literary Life.* New York: St. Martin's Press, 1995. Succinct study of Forster's novels and work for the British Broadcasting Corporation. Helpful notes.

McDowell, Frederick P. W. *E. M. Forster.* Rev. ed. Boston: Twayne, 1982. Brilliant, well-balanced, and compendious overview of Forster's life, times, career, work, and achievement. This book contains a useful chronology, a select bibliography, and an index. It also offers a concise and perceptive analysis of Forster's short stories.

May, Charles E., ed. *Masterplots II: Short Story Series, Revised Edition.* 8 vols. Pasadena, Calif.: Salem Press, 2004. Designed for student use, this reference set contains articles providing detailed plot summaries and analyses of these three short stories by Forster: "The Celestial Omnibus" (vol. 1), and "The Other Side of the Hedge" and "The Road from Colonus" (vol. 6).

Rapport, Nigel. *The Prose and the Passion: Anthropology, Literature, and the Writing of E. M. Forster.* New York: St. Martin's Press, 1994. Provides excellent interpretation and criticism of Forster's literary works.

Seabury, Marcia Bundy. "Images of a Networked Society: E. M. Forster's 'The Machine Stops.'" *Studies in Short Fiction* 34 (Winter, 1997): 61-71. Discusses the story as a vision of the computer revolution. Examines interrelations between technology and religious thinking in the story; explores what happens to people when they spend much of their time connected to computer networks.

Stone, Wilfred. *The Cave and the Mountain: A Study of E. M. Forster.* Stanford, Calif.: Stanford University Press, 1966. Well-researched and scholarly book. Contains a vast amount of useful information about Forster's background, career, esthetics, and work. Includes a detailed and illuminating chapter on the short stories. Using psychological and Jungian approaches, Stone offers insightful and masterly critiques of Forster's fiction. Supplemented by notes and a comprehensive index.

Mavis Gallant

Born: Montreal, Quebec, Canada; August 11, 1922

Principal short fiction • *The Other Paris*, 1956; *My Heart Is Broken: Eight Stories and a Short Novel*, 1964 (pb. in England as *An Unmarried Man's Summer*, 1965); *The Pegnitz Junction: A Novella and Five Short Stories*, 1973; *The End of the World, and Other Stories*, 1974; *From the Fifteenth District: A Novella and Eight Short Stories*, 1979; *Home Truths: Selected Canadian Stories*, 1981; *Overhead in a Balloon*, 1985; *In Transit*, 1988; *Across the Bridge*, 1993; *The Moslem Wife, and Other Stories*, 1994; *The Collected Stories of Mavis Gallant*, 1996; *Paris Stories*, 2002; *Varieties of Exile: Stories*, 2005.

Other literary forms • A journalist and essayist as well as a writer of fiction, Mavis Gallant has chronicled various social and historical events, such as the case of Gabrielle Russier, a young high school teacher in Marseille, who was driven to suicide by persecution for having become romantically involved with one of her students. *Paris Notebooks: Essays and Reviews* (1986) is a collection of essays in which Gallant offers observations relating to her many years spent in France, scrutinizing French culture and life in general. Her accounts of the student revolt of 1968 are particularly riveting.

In addition, Gallant wrote *The War Brides* (1978), a collection of biographical articles, and the play *What Is to Be Done?* (pr. 1982), a drama about two young women who idealize communism. Her essays, articles, and reviews have appeared regularly in *The New Yorker, The New York Times Book Review, The New Republic, The New York Review of Books,* and *The Times Literary Supplement.*

Achievements • Mavis Gallant's stature as a writer of short fiction is unassailable. The elegant simplicity of her pieces is an unchanging trait of her work and was in fact recognized in her first published piece, "Madeleine's Birthday," for which *The New Yorker* paid six hundred dollars in 1951. In 1981, Gallant was awarded Canada's Governor-General's Literary Award for fiction for *Home Truths.* Other awards include the Canadian Fiction Prize (1978), Officer of the Order of Canada (1981), and honorary doctorates from the University of Saint Anne, Nova Scotia (1984), York University (1984), the University of Western Canada (1990), Queen's University (1992), University of Montreal (1995), and Birnap's University (1995). She has also received the Canada-Australia Literary Prize (1985) and the Canadian Council Molson Prize for the Arts (1997).

Biography • Born in Montreal in 1922, Mavis Gallant (née Mavis de Trafford Young), an only child, was placed in a Roman Catholic convent school at the age of four. She attended seventeen schools: Catholic schools in Montreal, Protestant ones in Ontario, as well as various boarding schools in the United States. After the death of her father, Gallant lived with her legal guardians in New York, a psychiatrist and his wife. At the age of eighteen, Gallant returned to Montreal. After a short time working for the National Film Board of Canada in Ottawa during the winter of 1943-1944, Gallant accepted a position as reporter with the *Montreal Standard*, which she left in 1950. In 1951, Gallant be-

© Allison Harris

gan contributing short-fiction stories to *The New Yorker.* During the early 1950's, she moved to Europe, living in London, Rome, and Madrid, before settling in Paris in the early 1960's. It was through her travels and experiences in France, Italy, Austria, and Spain that she observed the fabric of diverse societies. During the initial years of her life in Europe, Gallant lived precariously from her writings, ultimately becoming an accomplished author, depicting loners, expatriates, and crumbling social structures. Gallant settled in Paris, working on a history of the renowned Dreyfus affair in addition to her work in fiction. Gallant settled in Paris, occasionally traveling to Canada, the United States, and England.

Analysis • The often somber tone of Mavis Gallant's work is strengthened by the combination of acute lucidness and understated stylistic richness. Gallant is a remarkable observer. She succeeds in creating worlds that are both familiar and foreign, appealing yet uninviting. Her mastery in the restrained use of language and in her incomparable narrative powers make her undeniably one of the world's greatest fiction writers.

"The Other Paris" • The title story of Mavis Gallant's first collection strikes the pitch to which the others that follow it are tuned. Most of these stories are about young Americans in Europe just entering into marriage, uncertain about what they should feel, unsure of their roles, and unable to find appropriate models around them for the behavior that they think is expected of them. The young protagonists in the stories grope through their ambivalences, looking for guidance in others who seem more sure of themselves, or clutching written words from some absent sibling—advice recorded in a letter, or written down by themselves about appropriate responses to their present situation. In the other stories in which a parent is present, the other parent, usually ill or divorced, is absent, and the rules of conduct become equally tenuous because of that absence. The European stories are set in the early 1950's, when the devastations of World War II are still being felt. Refugee figures haunt the fringes.

"The Other Paris" refers to the romantic illusions generated by films about that city which Carol feels she is missing. She is about to be married to Howard Mitchell, with whom she works in an American government agency, and with whom she is not yet in love. She keeps remembering her college lectures on the subject to reassure herself. Common interests and similar economic and religious backgrounds were what mattered. "The illusion of love was a blight imposed by the film industry, and almost entirely responsible for the high rate of divorce." Carol waits expectantly for the appropriate emotions to follow the mutuality of their backgrounds: Their fathers are both attorneys, Protestants, and from the same social class. In Carol's mind, the discovery of that mysterious "other Paris" is linked with the discovery of love. She believes the Parisians know a secret, "and if she spoke to the right person or opened the right door or turned down an unexpected street, the city would reveal itself and she would fall in love." She tries all the typical tourist things, such as listening to carols at the Place Vendôme, but everything has been commercialized. Newsreel cameras and broadcast equipment spoil the atmosphere she seeks. Plastic mistletoe with "cheap tinsel" is tied to the street lamps.

Odile, Howard's secretary, invites her to a private concert. Excitedly Carol thinks that she has finally gained entrance into the aristocratic secrets that are hidden from foreigners. Instead of the elegant drawing room she had anticipated, it is an "ordinary, shabby theatre" on an obscure street, nearly empty except for a few of the violinist's relatives. Odile is thin, dark, seldom smiles, and often sounds sarcastic because of her poor English. She is involved with Felix, pale, ill, hungry, and without papers, who sells things on the black market. He is twenty-one, she is more than thirty years old, and Carol finds the gap in their ages distasteful. They have no common interests, no mitigating mutual circumstances; yet, one night in Felix's dark, cluttered room, she discovers that they love each other. The thought makes her ill. In that dusty slum, with revulsion, she discovers that, at last, she has "opened the right door, turned down the right street, glimpsed the vision." On this paradox, that the sordid reality reveals the romantic illusion, the story closes with a time shift to the future in which Carol is telling how she met and married Howard in Paris and making it "sound romantic and interesting," believing it as it had never been at all.

"Autumn Day" • "Autumn Day" is another initiation story of a nineteen-year-old, Cissy, who follows her Army husband to Salzburg. She has a list of instructions: "Go for walks. Meet Army wives. Avoid people on farm." She attributes her unhappiness, her failure to feel like a wife, to the fact that they have no home. They are boarding in a farmhouse from which she takes dutiful long walks under the lowering Salzburg skies, gray with impending snow. An American singer practices a new setting of the poem "Herbsttag" ("Autumn Day"), whose most haunting line, which the narrator feels had something to do with her, is "who does not yet have a home, will never have one." She feels that the poet had understood her; it was exactly the life she was leading, going for lonely walks. She slides a note under the singer's door, asking if they might meet. After a complicated day she returns to the farmhouse to find the singer had invited her to lunch and had returned to America. Walt, her bewildered husband, finds her crying. He tries, timidly, to console her by insisting that they "will be all right" when they get their own apartment. She wonders if her present mood is indeed temporary or whether their entire marriage will be like this.

It is in depicting these border states of consciousness that Gallant excels. Her portraits of girls who are trying to become women without having internalized a strong role model to emulate are moving because the portrayal of their inner sense of being lost is augmented by the setting; it is externalized into the girls' awareness of being foreigners alone in a strange country. The psychic territory has been projected outward into an alien land. Both Cissy and her friend Carol have heard music which they feel contains some secret knowledge that can help them understand their feeling of having been somehow left out, excluded from a love they would like to feel. Both accommodate themselves to lives that are less than the songs promised they might be. "Autumn Day" closes with Cissy's ritually repeating the magic formula, like an incantation, like a figure in a fairy tale casting a spell over her own anxiety, "We'll be all right, we'll be all right, we'll be all right."

"Poor Franzi" • "Poor Franzi" is also set in Salzburg and in the same wavering space. The young American Elizabeth is engaged to the grandson Franzi of Baroness Ebendorf, an Austrian aristocrat, who dies in the course of the story. Because Franzi refuses to go to the funeral, Elizabeth feels obligated to attend. A party of American tourists serves as choric voices. They insinuate that the young Austrian has become engaged to the American girl simply to escape from the country. They gossip about his failure to visit the old woman in her last illness, his refusal to pay for the funeral, and his having burned her will. Her landlady, "out of helplessness and decency," had arranged for the last rites, which she could ill afford, a peasant paying homage to a noble line.

Elizabeth's nearsightedness is a physical correlative of her failure to see her fiancé's faults, which are obvious to everyone else. "Blind as a bat!" the other Americans mutter as she walks straight past them. She gazes at the edge of the horizon, but her myopia prevents her from distinguishing whether she is seeing clouds or mountains. She sees Franzi in this same suffused haze. Instead of the cynicism and selfishness his behavior so clearly outlines, there is a fuzzy aura blurred by her feeling of having to be protective of his great grief. Poor thing, he is all alone now; he must never suffer again. The soft shapes, "shifting and elusive," which better eyes than hers saw as the jutting rocks of the Salzburg mountains, become an emblem of her emotional condition. The story closes on this ambiguous haze: "What will happen to me if I marry him? she wondered; and what would become of Franzi if she were to leave him?"

The Collected Stories of Mavis Gallant • This anthology contains fifty-two stories that originally appeared in *The New Yorker* magazine. Gallant has divided her anthology into nine sections: thirty-five stories, with settings chronologically arranged between 1930 and 1990; five autobiographical stories with Linnet Muir, a young Canadian girl, as the main character; four about the Canadian Carette Sisters; four focused on Edouard, a Frenchman and his two "wives"; and four featuring Henri Grippes, a French "hack" writer and charlatan.

In the introduction, Gallant says she gets her ideas for stories through imaginary flashes. She compares the process to looking at a snapshot. Then she begins by developing a unique character with a name, age, nationality, profession, voice and accent, family history, destination, personality quirks, secrets, ambitions, and attitudes toward love, money, religion. Next, she writes scenes between her characters with dialogue and develops a plot that is "entire but unreadable." She says that revision takes her a long time; it is a "slow transformation from image to story."

The stories are written in a powerful and fluent style with precise details. Many have settings during and after World War II in Canada, France, and Germany, when people's lives are in a state of flux. Gallant's settings and characters are reproduced like filmed images, complete with background noise and dialogue. However, her extraordinary ability to get inside her characters' minds provides ironic contrast between external events and their fragmented thoughts and confused emotions. Typically, her main characters are rootless young women trapped by the past in an existential world, lonely, isolated, and uncertain of the direction their lives should take. Secondary characters often include neglected, love-starved children, surrounded by insensitive adults.

"The Moslem Wife" • The title of this story does not refer to a North African setting or to the Islamic religion. It refers to the role of Muslim women, who traditionally submit to the domination of fathers and husbands. These women have great responsibility for the management of their homes and the well-being of their families. Most have limited contact with the outside world.

Gallant compares the Muslim wife's lifestyle to that of Netta Asher, an inexperienced young English girl, whose family ties and cultural roots have been severed by death and circumstance. Netta's dying father provides for her future by signing a one-hundred-year lease on his resort hotel in southern France and marrying her to Jack, a philandering cousin. Thus, locked into her role as owner/manager of the hotel, Netta leads a confined life, while Jack enjoys much freedom. On the eve of Adolf Hitler's European conquest, Jack goes on holiday to England and does not return until World War II is over. Meanwhile, Netta takes care of Jack's temperamental mother and survives deprivation and the presence of Italian and German soldiers billeted at the hotel. Miserable and lonely, Netta longs to escape her "prison." However, when Jack, the perpetual adolescent, returns, Netta, still dependent on his masculine charm, remains locked into her role as "The Moslem Wife."

"Across the Bridge" • "Across the Bridge" is a lighthearted initiation story, set in Paris in the 1950's. It gives insight into postwar French families and their attempt to reestablish social classes and tradition. American teenagers, who enjoy considerable freedom to select their own love interests without parental involvement, will consider this story old-fashioned and foreign. However, ethnicity, religious background, and economic and social status are realistic factors that continue to influence a person's selection of a mate.

After much negotiation, teenage Sylvie Castelli's parents arrange her marriage to Arnaud Pons, a quiet, unromantic young man. The Italian/French Castellis have a modest fortune, but the Pons family has an old and respected name. On a bridge en route to having wedding invitations printed, Sylvie confesses to her mother that she is in love with Bruno, a boy she met at the park. Her doting parents allow her to break her engagement to Arnaud, and Mr. Castelli contacts Bruno's wealthy parents, who deny their son's interest in Sylvie and humiliate the Castellis. Eventually, Sylvie "crosses the bridge" from romantic, adolescent dreams to realistic maturity and on her own, without parental involvement, selects Arnaud as her fiancé. The question of whether pragmatic considerations offset romantic ideals and physical attraction remains unanswered as Sylvie and Arnaud begin their new relationship.

"The Doctor" • The Linnet Muir stories are fictionalized, coming-of-age memoirs based on Gallant's own experiences as a member of a dysfunctional family. Biographical data confirms much, but not all, of the content of the stories. During her childhood, Gallant, like Linnet, observed her parents' unhappy marriage. In "The Doctor" a precocious Linnet recalls the sterile and bewildering relationship between her parents, Charlotte and Angus Muir, and their eccentric friends, Mrs. Erskine and Dr.

Chauchard, Linnet's pediatrician, who is treating her for a lung disease from which she recovers.

After Gallant's father's untimely death, her mother placed her in a series of boarding schools and left her care and education to strangers. In her late teens, Gallant, like Linnet, attempted a reconciliation with her mother that failed. "In Youth Is Pleasure," an ironic title because of somber events in the story, eighteen-year-old Linnet asserts her independence, breaks off an unhappy relationship with her mother, and returns to Montreal from New York. There, she discovers family secrets: that her father suffered from tuberculosis of the bone and committed suicide and that her mother ran off with a lover.

Gallant became a successful journalist in Canada, an experience she considered boring, but one that sharpened her writing skills and techniques of observation. After selling her first short story, she left Canada and moved to France, where she hoped to establish new roots and become a successful writer. Similarly, in the story "Between Zero and One," Linnet works at a boring government job surrounded by men who are either too old or disabled to serve in the army during World War II. At first they resent Linnet, but later accept her. When Mrs. Ireland, an outspoken feminist, arrives, dynamics in the office change. After looking at a graph of statistics, Linnet becomes more assertive. She discovers that what occurs during a person's life-graph "Between Zero and One" determines the future.

Ruth Rosenberg
With updates by Kenneth W. Meadwell and Martha E. Rhynes

Other major works

PLAY: *What Is to Be Done*, pr. 1982.

NOVELS: *Green Water, Green Sky*, 1959; *Its Image on the Mirror*, 1964 (novella); *A Fairly Good Time*, 1970.

NONFICTION: *The Affair of Gabrielle Russier*, 1971; *The War Brides*, 1978; *Paris Notebooks: Essays and Reviews*, 1986.

Bibliography

Besner, Neil. *The Light of Imagination: Mavis Gallant's Fiction*. Vancouver: University of British Columbia Press, 1988. Extremely thorough analysis of Gallant's fiction from *The Other Paris* to *Overhead in a Balloon*. Includes a biographical review as well as a useful critical bibliography.

Clement, Lesley D. *Learning to Look: A Visual Response to Mavis Gallant's Fiction*. Montreal: McGill-Queen's University Press, 2000. This "visual" study of Gallant's work analyzes her descriptive powers, which generally take priority over plot per se.

Cote, Nicole, Peter Sabor, and Robert H. Jerry, eds. *Varieties of Exile: New Essays on Mavis Gallant*. New York: Peter Lang, 2003. Collection of essays on a range of topics, chiefly focusing on Gallant's view of Canada from her self-imposed Parisian "exile" as well as her depiction of other types of exile—literal, figurative, and psychological—in her work.

Dobozy, Tamas. "'Designed Anarchy' in Mavis Gallant's *The Moslem Wife, and Other Stories*." *Canadian Literature*, no. 158 (Autumn, 1998): 65-88. Discusses an anarchic aesthetic in the collection in which the stories challenge the impulse to create a master narrative and instead allow a variety of competing narratives that prevent a unified vision.

Hatch, Ronald. "Mavis Gallant." In *Canadian Writers Since 1960: First Series*. Vol. 53 in *Dictionary of Literary Biography*, edited by W. H. New. Detroit: Gale Research, 1986. Thorough general introduction to Gallant's fiction up to, and including, *Home Truths*. Supplemented by a bibliography of interviews and studies.

Jewison, Don. "Speaking of Mirrors: Imagery and Narration in Two Novellas by Mavis Gallant." *Studies in Canadian Literature* 10, nos. 1, 2 (1985): 94-109. A study of *Green Water, Green Sky* and *Its Image on the Mirror*. Focuses on the importance of mirrors from the perspective of imagery as well as of narration.

May, Charles E., ed. *Masterplots II: Short Story Series, Revised Edition*. 8 vols. Pasadena, Calif.: Salem Press, 2004. Designed for student use, this reference set contains articles providing detailed plot summaries and analyses of these nine short stories by Gallant: "Acceptance of Their Ways" and "Across the Bridge" (vol. 1); "Dédé" (vol. 2); "Going Ashore" (vol. 3); "The Ice Wagon Going Down the Street," "Jorinda and Jorindel," and "Lena" (vol. 4); "The Other Paris" (vol. 6); and "Speck's Idea" (vol. 7).

Schaub, Danielle. *Mavis Gallant*. New York: Twayne, 1998. Book-length discussion of Gallant's fiction focusing on the relationship between thematic tensions and narrative devices. Argues that Gallant's irony, stylistic devices, atmosphere, and structure create a tension that reflects the disconnectedness of her characters. Features chapters on Gallant's major short-story collections from *The Other Paris* to *Across the Bridge*.

Schenk, Leslie. "Celebrating Mavis Gallant." *World Literature Today* 72 (Winter, 1998): 18-26. In this interview, Gallant discusses the short story as a genre, the extent to which her stories are biographical or autobiographical, and her relationship to contemporary France. She also discusses some of her stories, including "Across the Bridge."

Simmons, Diane. "Remittance Men: Exile and Identity in the Short Stories of Mavis Gallant." In *Canadian Women: Writing Fiction*, edited by Mickey Pearlman. Jackson: University Press of Mississippi, 1993. Discusses characters in a number of Gallant's short stories who, suffering some early loss, are adrift and, by choosing to live abroad, are acting out their inner sense of exile.

Gabriel García Márquez

Born: Aracataca, Colombia; March 6, 1928

Principal short fiction • *Los funerales de la Mamá Grande,* 1962 (*Big Mama's Funeral,* stories included in *No One Writes to the Colonel, and Other Stories,* 1968); *Isabel viendo llover en Macondo,* 1967 (*Monologue of Isabel Watching It Rain in Macondo,* 1972); *No One Writes to the Colonel, and Other Stories,* 1968; *Relato de un náufrago,* 1970 (*The Story of a Shipwrecked Sailor: Who Drifted on a Liferaft for Ten Days Without Food or Water, Was Proclaimed a National Hero, Kissed by Beauty Queens, Made Rich Through Publicity, and Then Spurned by the Government and Forgotten for All Time,* 1986); *El negro que hizo esperar a los ángeles,* 1972; *La increíble y triste historia de la Cándida Eréndira y de su abuela desalmada,* 1972 (*Innocent Eréndira, and Other Stories,* 1978); *Leaf Storm, and Other Stories,* 1972; *Ojos de perro azul,* 1972; *Todos los cuentos de Gabriel García Márquez,* 1975 (*Collected Stories,* 1984); *Collected Novellas* (1990); *Crónica de una muerte anunciada,* 1981 (*Chronicle of a Death Foretold,* 1982); *Doce cuentos peregrinos,* 1992 (*Strange Pilgrims: Twelve Stories,* 1993).

Other literary forms • Besides his short fiction, including short stories and novellas, Gabriel García Márquez's fictional work includes full-length novels, such as his masterpiece and best-known novel, *Cien años de soledad* (1967; *One Hundred Years of Solitude,* 1970). Among his other novels are *El amor en los tiempos del cólera* (1985; *Love in the Time of Cholera,* 1988), *El general en su laberinto* (1989; *The General in His Labyrinth,* 1990), *Del amor y otros demonios* (1994; *Of Love and Other Demons,* 1995), and *Memoria de mis putas tristes* (2004; *Memories of My Melancholy Whores* (2005).

During García Márquez's long career as a journalist, he has written numerous articles, essays, and reports on a variety of topics, particularly relating to Latin American life and politics. He has published more than twenty volumes of nonfiction writings, most of which have not been translated into English. Among his translated nonfiction works are *Noticia de un secuestro* (1996; *News of a Kidnapping,* 1997), an account of the nefarious activities of drug lord Pablo Escobar in 1990, and *Vivir para contarla* (2002; *Living to Tell the Tale,* 2003), the first part of a projected three-volume autobiography.

Achievements • In 1967, Gabriel García Márquez's highly acclaimed novel *One Hundred Years of Solitude* appeared and was immediately recognized by critics as a masterpiece of fiction. As a work of high literary quality, this novel was unusual in that it also enjoyed tremendous popular success both in Latin America and in translation throughout the world. This work made García Márquez a major figure—perhaps *the* major figure—of contemporary Latin American literature.

García Márquez's work has been praised for bringing literary fiction back into contact with real life in all of its richness. His combination of realism and fantasy known as Magical Realism *(realismo mágico)* sets the stage for a full spectrum of Latin American characters. His stories focus on basic human concerns, and characters or incidents from one work are often integrated into others, if only with a passing reference.

García Márquez won the Colombian Association of Writers and Artists Award in 1954, for the story "Un dia despues del sabado." The novel *Cien años de soledad* (*One Hundred Years of Solitude*) garnered the French Prix de Meilleur Livre Étranger, the Italian Chianciano Award, and the Venezuelan Rómulo Gallego Prize. Awarding him the Nobel Prize in Literature in 1982, the Nobel committee compared the breadth and quality of his work to that of such great writers as William Faulkner and Honoré de Balzac. In 1988 García Márquez won the *Los Angeles Times* Book Award, for *El amor en los tiempos del cólera* (1985; *Love in the Time of Cholera*, 1988).

© The Nobel Foundation

Biography • Gabriel García Márquez was born in Aracataca, a town near the Atlantic coast of Colombia, on March 6, 1928. His parents, Luisa Santiaga and Gabriel Eligio Márquez, sent him to live with his maternal grandparents for the first eight years of his life. He attended school in Barranquilla and Zipaquirá and went on to law studies at the Universidad Nacional in Bogotá.

García Márquez's first short story was published in 1947 in the Bogotá newspaper *El Espectador.* The literary editor praised the work, and in the next five years several more short fictions were also published. When his studies were interrupted by political violence in 1948, García Márquez transferred to the Universidad de Cartagena, but he never received his degree. Instead, he began his career as a journalist, writing for *El Universal.* He soon had a daily column and became friends with the writers and artists of the "Barranquilla group." In 1950, he moved to Barranquilla and in 1954 to Bogotá, continuing his work as a journalist. During this time, he also published *Leaf Storm, and Other Stories* and received a prize from the Association of Artists and Writers of Bogotá.

In 1955, he was sent to Geneva, Switzerland, as a European correspondent. When *El Espectador* was closed down in January, 1956, García Márquez spent a period of poverty in Paris, working on *La mala hora* (1962; *In Evil Hour,* 1979) and writing some freelance articles. In the summer of 1957, he traveled through Eastern Europe before moving to Caracas, Venezuela, as a journalist. With the prospect of a steady job, he married Mercedes Barcha in March, 1958.

Interested since his university days in leftist causes, García Márquez worked for the Cuban news agency Prensa Latina in Bogotá after Fidel Castro came to power in 1959, then in Havana, Cuba, and later New York. After leaving the agency, he moved to Mexico City, where he worked as a journalist and screenwriter with Carlos Fuentes during the period 1961-1967. In 1962, *In Evil Hour* was published and won the Esso Literary Prize in Colombia. That same year, a collection of stories, *Los funerales de la*

Mamá Grande, also appeared. Then, in a spurt of creative energy, García Márquez spent eighteen months of continuous work to produce his best-selling novel *One Hundred Years of Solitude*, which won book prizes in Italy and France in 1969. In order to be able to write in peace after the tremendous success of this book, he moved to Barcelona, Spain, where he met Peruvian author Mario Vargas Llosa. In 1972, he won both the Rómulo Gallego Prize in Venezuela and the Neustadt International Prize for Literature. The money from both prizes was donated to political causes.

García Márquez left Barcelona in 1975 and returned to Mexico. That same year, *El otoño del patriarca* (1975; *The Autumn of the Patriarch*, 1975), about the life of a Latin American dictator, was published, and in 1981, his *Chronicle of a Death Foretold* appeared. His news magazine, *Alternativa*, founded in 1974 in Bogotá to present opposing political views, folded in 1980, but García Márquez continued his activism by writing a weekly column for Hispanic newspapers and magazines. His Nobel Prize speech in 1982 made a strong statement about conditions in Latin America yet sounded the note of hope in the face of oppression.

García Márquez continued his literary production after receiving the Nobel Prize, publishing, among other works, *El general en su laberinto* in 1989 (*The General in His Labyrinth*, 1990), based on the life of South American revolutionary leader Simón Bolívar. He also continued his political work, appearing at conferences with, variously, Colombian, Venezuelan, Mexican, and U.S. presidents discussing such issues as civil war and drug trafficking. In 1999 he fell ill in Bogotá, in one of his seven houses, and was diagnosed with cancer.

Analysis • Gabriel García Márquez's fiction is characterized by a thread of common themes, events, and characters that seem to link his work together into one multifaceted portrayal of the experiences of Latin American life. From the influences of his early childhood, when he learned from his grandmother how to tell the most fantastic stories in a matter-of-fact tone, to his later observations of the oppression and cruelties of politics, García Márquez captures the everyday life of the amazing people of coastal Colombia, with its Caribbean flavor, as well as the occasional resident of the highlands of Bogotá. He has an eye for the details of daily life mixed with humor and an attitude of acceptance and wonder. His characters experience the magic and joy of life and face the suffering of solitude and isolation but always with an innate dignity. García Márquez's vision touches real life with its local attitudes and values, and in the process it also reveals a criticism of politics, the Church, and U.S. imperialism, as they contribute to the Latin American experience.

García Márquez's body of work portrays a complete reality breaking out of conventional bounds. Characters from one story regularly show up or are mentioned in another, while his complex mix of fantasy and reality reveals a consummate storyteller capable of bringing to his work the magic of his non-European world. His impact as a writer lies in the fact that although his work describes the Latin American experience of life, it also goes beyond to reveal a universal human experience.

Ojos de perro azul • García Márquez's earliest stories have a bizarre, almost surreal, tone, reminiscent of Franz Kafka. Collected in *Ojos de perro azul*, these stories represent an experimental phase of García Márquez's development as a writer. They exemplify his new, or strange, realism, extending the reality of life into and beyond the experience of death. "La tercera resignación" ("The Third Resignation"), for example, deals with the thoughts and fears of a young man in his coffin. "Nabo, el negro que hizo esperar a los ángeles" ("Nabo, the Black Man Who Made the Angels Wait") tells of a man who is locked in a stable because he goes insane after being kicked in the head by a horse.

In "Isabel viendo llover en Macondo" ("Monologue of Isabel Watching It Rain in Macondo"), published the same year as his first novella, *Leaf Storm*, García Márquez captures the atmosphere of a tropical storm through the eyes of his protagonist. Here, the world of Macondo, used in *Leaf Storm* as well and made world-famous in *One Hundred Years of Solitude*, is presented amid the suffocating oppressiveness of tropical weather. Here as later, nature itself is often a palpable force in the fiction of García Márquez—often exaggerated and overwhelming in order to reflect the reality of Latin American geography and the natural forces within it. The repetition underscores the monotony of the continuing deluge, and the theme of solitude is reflected in the imagery as well as in the personal relationship of Isabel and Martin: "The sky was a gray, jellyish substance that flapped its wings a hand away from our heads."

No One Writes to the Colonel • After demonstrating his ability to capture the tropical atmosphere, García Márquez shows himself capable of capturing a portrait in words with his well-structured novella *No One Writes to the Colonel*. The central character is a dignified man with a deep sense of honor who has been promised a military pension. Every Friday, he goes to the post office to wait for mail that never comes, and then he claims that he really was not expecting anything anyway. He is a patient man, resigned to eternal waiting and hope when there is no reason to expect that hope to be fulfilled. "For nearly sixty years—since the end of the last civil war—the colonel had done nothing else but wait. October was one of the few things which arrived." His other hope is his rooster, which belonged to his son, who was executed for handing out subversive literature, but since he is too poor to feed the rooster, some townspeople work out an arrangement to provide food until after the big fight. The political background is introduced subtly as the story opens with the funeral of the first person to die of natural causes in this town for a long time. Violence, censorship, and political repression are a given, as is the pervasive poverty. The colonel continues passing out the literature in his son's place and waiting for his pension. His dignity sustains him in the face of starvation.

The dialogues between the colonel and his practical wife of many years are woven through the novella and reach a climax at the very end of the story. She presses him to sell the rooster, asking plaintively and persistently what they will eat:

> It had taken the colonel seventy-five years—the seventy-five years of his life, minute by minute—to reach this moment. He felt pure, explicit, invincible at the moment when he replied: "S—!"

Los funerales de la Mamá Grande • The image of dignity is developed again in the first story of *Los funerales de la Mamá Grande*, entitled "La siesta del martes" ("Tuesday Siesta") and also set in Macondo. Said to be García Márquez's favorite, it tells of a woman and her young daughter who arrive by train in the stifling heat at siesta time. The woman asks the priest to be allowed to visit her son in the cemetery. The young man was shot for being a thief, but she proudly claims him as her own with quiet self-control: "I told him never to steal anything that anyone needed to eat, and he minded me."

The title story, "Los funerales de la Mamá Grande" ("Big Mama's Funeral"), still set in Macondo, breaks the tone of the other stories into a technique of hyperbole, which García Márquez later used in *One Hundred Years of Solitude* to good effect. The opening sentence sets the tone:

> This is, for all the world's unbelievers, the true account of Big Mama, absolute sovereign of the Kingdom of Macondo, who lived for ninety-two years, and died in the odor of sanctity one Tuesday last September, and whose funeral was attended by the Pope.

The panorama and parody of the story mention Mama's power and property in high-sounding phrases, many from journalism. The pageantry is grandiose to the point of the absurd for this powerful individual, a prototype of the patriarch who appears in García Márquez's later work. She is a legend and local "saint," who seemed to the local people to be immortal; her death comes as a complete surprise. The story criticizes the manipulation of power but also skillfully satirizes the organized display or public show that eulogizes the holders of power with pomp and empty words. The story ends when the garbage men come and sweep up on the next day.

Innocent Eréndira, and Other Stories • Fantastic elements characterize the collection entitled *Innocent Eréndira, and Other Stories*. Two of the stories, "Un señor muy viejo con unas alas enormes" ("A Very Old Man with Enormous Wings") and "El ahogado más hermoso del mundo" ("The Handsomest Drowned Man in the World"), have adult figures who are like toys with which children, and other adults, can play. With the second story, García Márquez also tries a technique of shifting narrators and point of view to be used later in the novel *The Autumn of the Patriarch*.

A political satire is the basis for another story, "Muerte constante más allá del amor" ("Death Constant Beyond Love"). The situation that forms the basis for the satire is also incorporated into the longer "Innocent Eréndira." Geographically, in this collection García Márquez has moved inland to the barren landscape on the edge of the Guajiro desert. Here, he sets a type of folktale with an exploited granddaughter, a green-blooded monster of a grandmother, and a rescuing hero named Ulises. Combining myth, allegory, and references from other works, García Márquez weaves a story in which "the wind of her misfortune" determines the life of the extraordinarily passive Eréndira. Treated as a slave and a prostitute by her grandmother, Eréndira persuades Ulises to kill the evil woman—who turns out to be amazingly hard to kill. Throughout the story, García Márquez demonstrates the ability to report the most monstrous things in a matter-of-fact tone. Some critics have pointed out that the exaggeration that seems inherent in many of his tales may have its roots in the extraordinary events and stories that are commonplace in his Latin American world.

Chronicle of a Death Foretold • In the novella *Chronicle of a Death Foretold*, García Márquez blends his experience in journalism with his mastery of technique to tell a story based on an actual event that took place in 1955 in Sucre, where he lived at the time. Using records and witness testimony, he unfolds his story on the lines of a detective story. The incident is based on the revenge taken by Angela Vicario's brothers on their friend Santiago Nasar, who supposedly took Angela's virginity (although some doubt is cast on this allegation). The story is pieced together as the townspeople offer their memories of what happened, along with excuses for not having warned the victim. Tension builds as the reader knows the final outcome but not how or why it will occur. The use of dreams (ironically, Nasar's mother is an interpreter of dreams), the feeling of fatalism, and submission to the code of honor, all of which form a part of this society's attitudes, play a central role in the novella, as do García Márquez's use of vision and foreshadowing. Although the basis for the story is a journalistic report of a murder, the actual writing captures the themes of love and death as well as the complex interplay of human emotions and motives in a balanced and poetic account, which reveals García Márquez's skill as a writer.

Strange Pilgrims • Strange Pilgrims picks up the Magical Realism of the earlier short stories, orchestrating twelve works written between 1976 and 1982 so that seven stories, having to do with the death-force of life, are followed by five stories which evoke the vitality of death. The opening story portrays a septuagenarian ex-president whose imminent death proves to be illusory; the seventh story portrays a septuagenarian woman, to whom the approach of death proves to be illusory. In both stories, dying is detailed as a form of intensified living. The second and sixth stories deal with the supernatural, one through a corpse that does not putrefy and the other through a haunted bedroom, and both include Italian settings. The third and fifth stories carry fairy-tale variations: a sleeping beauty who, unkissed, awakes of her own volition, and a lady in distress who, imprisoned in a madhouse, transcends her incarceration. In the fourth story, the umbilicus of the seven, a woman, whose life consists of dreaming, awakens from her dreams only through death. The concluding five stories present, first, two stories of murder—between which is a story of suicide—and two stories dealing with strange fatalities. In one, the wave function of light drowns persons without diving gear; in the other, an apparently negligible rose-thorn prick on a young bride's ring fingertip inexorably causes her death.

Susan L. Piepke
With updates by Roy Arthur Swanson

Other major works

NOVELS: *La hojarasca*, 1955 (novella; translated as *Leaf Storm* in *Leaf Storm, and Other Stories*, 1972); *El coronel no tiene quien le escriba*, 1961 (novella; *No One Writes to the Colonel*, 1968); *La mala hora*, 1962 (revised 1966; *In Evil Hour*, 1979); *Cien años de soledad*, 1967 (*One Hundred Years of Solitude*, 1970); *El otoño del patriarca*, 1975 (*The Autumn of the Patriarch*, 1975); *El amor en los tiempos del cólera*, 1985 (*Love in the Time of Cholera*, 1988); *El general en su laberinto*, 1989 (*The General in His Labyrinth*, 1990); *Collected Novellas*, 1990; *Del amor y otros demonios*, 1994 (*Of Love and Other Demons*, 1995); *Memoria de mis putas tristes*, 2004 (*Memories of My Melancholy Whores*, 2005).

NONFICTION: *La novela en América Latina: Diálogo*, 1968 (with Mario Vargas Llosa); *Cuando era feliz e indocumentado*, 1973; *Chile, el golpe y los gringos*, 1974; *Crónicas y reportajes*, 1976; *Operación Carlota*, 1977; *De viaje por los países socialistas*, 1978; *Periodismo militante*, 1978; *Obra periodística*, 1981-1999 (5 volumes; includes *Textos costeños*, 1981; *Entre cachacos*, 1982; *De Europa y América, 1955-1960*, 1983; *Por la libre, 1974-1995*, 1999; *Notas de prensa, 1961-1984*, 1999); *El olor de la guayaba: Conversaciones con Plinio Apuleyo Mendoza*, 1982 (*The Fragrance of the Guava: Plinio Apuleyo Mendoza in Conversation with Gabriel García Márquez*, 1983; also known as *The Smell of Guava*, 1984); *La aventura de Miguel Littín, clandestino en Chile*, 1986 (*Clandestine in Chile: The Adventures of Miguel Littín*, 1987); *Noticia de un secuestro*, 1996 (*News of a Kidnapping*,

1997); *Por un país al alcance de los niños,* 1996 (*For the Sake of a Country Within Reach of the Children,* 1998); *Vivir para contarla,* 2002 (*Living to Tell the Tale,* 2003).

Bibliography

Bell, Michael. *Gabriel García Márquez: Solitude and Solidarity.* New York: St. Martin's Press, 1993. This book explores García Márquez's works from a number of different perspectives, ranging from comparative literary criticism to political and social critiques. Aso included are commentaries on García Márquez's styles, including journalism and Magical Realism.

Bell-Villada, Gene H. *García Márquez: The Man and His Work.* Chapel Hill: University of North Carolina Press, 1990. Includes biographical information on García Márquez, analyses of his major works, an index, and a bibliography.

Bloom, Harold, ed. *Gabriel García Márquez.* New York: Chelsea House, 1989. Essays by eighteen critics, with an introduction by Bloom, on the fiction of García Márquez. Includes two studies of *Chronicle of a Death Foretold,* estimates of the influences of Kafka and Faulkner, analyses of narrative stylistics, and inquiries into the author's types of realism.

Byk, John. "From Fact to Fiction: Gabriel García Márquez and the Short Story." *Mid-American Review* 6 (1986): 111-116. Discusses the development of García Márquez's short fiction from his early imitations of Kafka to his more successful experiments with Magical Realism.

Gerlach, John. "The Logic of Wings: García Márquez, Todorov, and the Endless Resources of Fantasy." In *Bridges to Fantasy,* edited by George E. Slusser, Eric S. Rabkin, and Robert Scholes. Carbondale: Southern Illinois University Press, 1982. Argues that the point of view of "A Very Old Man with Enormous Wings" makes readers sympathize with the old man by establishing his superiority over the villagers.

González, Nelly Sfeir de. *Bibliographic Guide to Gabriel García Márquez, 1986-1992.* Westport, Conn.: Greenwood Press, 1994. Annotated bibliography that includes works by García Márquez, criticism and sources for him, and an index of audio and visual materials related to the author and his works.

McMurray, George R., ed. *Critical Essays on Gabriel García Márquez.* Boston: G. K. Hall, 1987. Collection of book reviews, articles, and essays covering the full range of García Márquez's fictional work. Very useful for an introduction to specific novels and collections of short stories. Also includes an introductory overview by the editor and an index.

McNerney, Kathleen. *Understanding Gabriel García Márquez.* Columbia: University of South Carolina Press, 1989. Overview addressed to students and nonacademic readers. After an introduction on Colombia and a brief biography, the five core chapters explain his works in depth. Chapters 1 through 3 discuss three novels, chapter 4 focuses on his short novels and stories, and chapter 5 reviews the role of journalism in his work. Includes a select, annotated bibliography of critical works and an index.

McGuirk, Bernard, and Richard Cardwell, eds. *Gabriel García Márquez: New Readings.* New York: Cambridge University Press, 1987. Collection of twelve essays in English by different authors reflecting a variety of critical approaches and covering García Márquez's major novels as well as a selection of his early fiction: *No One Writes to the Colonel, Innocent Eréndira,* and *Chronicle of a Death Foretold.* Also includes a translation of García Márquez's Nobel address and a select bibliography.

Oberhelman, Harley D. *Gabriel Gárcia Márquez: A Study of the Short Fiction.* Boston: Twayne, 1991. Argues that García Márquez's short fiction is almost as important as his novels. Suggests that his stories have the same narrative pattern as his novels. Includes five interviews with García Márquez and essays by four critics.

Solanet, Mariana. *García Márquez for Beginners.* New York: Writers and Readers, 2001. Part of the "Beginners" series of brief introductions to major writers and their works. Very basic, but a good starting point.

Hamlin Garland

Born: West Salem, Wisconsin; September 14, 1860
Died: Hollywood, California; March 4, 1940

Principal short fiction • *Main-Travelled Roads: Six Mississippi Valley Stories*, 1891; *Prairie Folks*, 1893; *Wayside Courtships*, 1897; *Other Main-Travelled Roads*, 1910; *They of the High Trails*, 1916; *The Book of the American Indian*, 1923.

Other literary forms • Hamlin Garland's more than fifty published works include nearly every literary type—novels, biography, autobiography, essays, dramas, and poems. His best and most memorable novels are *Rose of Dutcher's Coolly* (1895), similar in plot to the later Theodore Dreiser novel *Sister Carrie* (1900), and *Boy Life on the Prairie* (1899), chronicling the social history of Garland's boyhood. One book of essays, *Crumbling Idols* (1894), presents his theory of realism ("veritism"). His autobiographical quartet, *A Son of the Middle Border* (1917), *A Daughter of the Middle Border* (1921), *Trail-Makers of the Middle Border* (1926), and *Back-Trailers from the Middle Border* (1928), recounts the story of his family. *A Daughter of the Middle Border* won the Pulitzer Prize for 1922. These books contain episodes that are treated in greater detail in some of his short stories.

Achievements • Hamlin Garland's work stands at an important transition point leading from Romanticism to realism, playing a role in ushering in the new literary trend. His best works are important for their depiction of a segment of society seldom delineated by other writers and for the relationship they show between literature and its socioeconomic environment. He used American themes—rather than Americanized European themes—and commonplace characters and incidents that turned the American writer away from his colonial complex, even away from the New England tradition of letters. His realism emancipated the American Midwest and West and the American farmer particularly from the romanticized conception that kept their story from being told before. Like Walt Whitman, Garland wanted writers to tell about life as they knew it and witnessed it. His realism foreshadowed the work of young writers such as Stephen Crane, E. W. Howe, and Harold Frederic. His naturalistic inclination, apparent in his belief that environment is crucial in shaping men's lives, preceded the naturalistic writing of Crane, Frank Norris, and Dreiser.

Aside from their value as literature, Garland's best stories are a comprehensive record of an otherwise relatively unreported era of American social history. Much read in his prime, he enjoyed considerable popularity even while antagonizing, with his merciless word pictures, the very people about whom he wrote. Garland was awarded honorary degrees from the University of Wisconsin, the University of Southern California, Northwestern University, and Beloit College. In 1918, he was elected to the board of directors of the American Academy of Arts and Letters. He won the Pulitzer Prize for Biography and Autobiography in 1922.

Biography • Of Scotch-Irish descent, Hannibal Hamlin Garland moved with his family from Wisconsin, where he was born in West Salem on September 14, 1860, to an

Iowa farm while still a child. Years spent on the farm made him seek escape through a career in oratory. To this end, he attended Cedar Valley Seminary, from which he graduated in 1881. He held a land claim in North Dakota for a year but mortgaged it for the chance to go East and enroll in Boston University. He succeeded in getting to Boston but was unable to attend the university; however, he embarked on a self-directed program of reading in the holdings of the Boston Public Library. While in Boston, he began writing, his first attempts being lectures, then stories and books. It was around this time also that he joined the Anti-Poverty Society and became an active reformer. He read Henry George and embraced the Single Tax theory as a solution to some of the many contemporary social problems.

Donald Pizer, along with many scholars, divides Garland's career into three general phases: a period of political and social reform activity that coincides with his most memorable fiction set in the Middle West (1884-1895); a period of popular romance-writing in which his settings shifted from the Midwest to the Rocky Mountains (1896-1916); and a period of increasing political and social conservatism, during which he wrote his major autobiographical works (1917-1940). In 1899, Garland married Zulime Taft, and they became parents of daughters born in 1904 and 1907. His list of acquaintances and friends grew to include such literary figures as William Dean Howells, Eugene Field, Joseph Kirkland, Edward Eggleston, Frank Norris, Stephen Crane, George Bernard Shaw, and Rudyard Kipling.

Garland lived the last years of his life in Hollywood, where he could be near his married daughter. In these later years, he turned more seriously to a lifelong fascination with the occult, producing two books on the subject. He died of cerebral hemorrhage in Hollywood on March 4, 1940.

Analysis • Hamlin Garland's most enduring short stories are those dealing with the Middle Border (the prairie lands of Iowa, Wisconsin, Minnesota, Nebraska, and the Dakotas). Collected for the most part in four books, they touch on nearly every subject of everyday life, from birth through youth, adulthood, courtship, and marriage, to death. They deal with the unromantic life of harassed generations on the farms and in the small towns of the prairie. Garland's belief that an author must write of "what is" with an eye toward "what is to be" causes him alternately to describe, prophesy, suggest, and demand. Although often subtle in his approach, he is sometimes, when championing the cause of the farmer, more the reformer than the artist. Social protest is the single most recurrent theme in his work. "A Stopover at Tyre" and "Before the Low Green Door" show with some skill the unrelenting drudgery of the farmer's life.

"Under the Lion's Paw" • "Under the Lion's Paw," Garland's most anthologized story, is his most powerful statement of protest. In it, one man, Tim Haskins, like thousands of struggling farmers, is exploited by another man, representative of scores of other land speculators. Haskins, through months of arduous labor, pushing his own and his wife's energies to their limits, has managed to make the dilapidated farm he is renting a productive place of which he can be proud. He has begun to feel confident that he can buy the farm and make a success of it. The owner, however, has taken note of the many physical improvements Haskins has made and recognizes its increased value. Thus, when Haskins talks to the owner about buying the place, he is astonished to learn that the purchase price has doubled and the rent has been increased. Haskins is "under the lion's paw," caught in untenable circumstances that will hurt him no matter what he does. If he gives up the farm, as his angry indignation dictates, he will lose all the money and time he has invested in the farm's improvements. If he buys, he will be under a heavy mortgage that could be foreclosed at any time. If he continues to rent at the higher fee, all his work will almost literally be for the owner's benefit, not for himself and his family. The personally satisfying alternative of simply striking the man dead is wildly considered by Haskins momentarily until the thought of the repercussions to his family brings him to his senses, and he agrees to buy on the owner's terms. The situation in itself is cruel. Garland clearly shows that it is even worse when one realizes that the exploitation of Haskins is only one of thousands of similar cases.

"Lucretia Burns" • "Lucretia Burns," another social protest story, is longer and has more action and a more complex major character than the similar "Before the Low Green Door." Although some of its impact is diminished by its tiresome discussions on reform and by its weak denouement, Garland has created in Lucretia an unforgettable character who makes the story praiseworthy. Lucretia is a strong personality who had "never been handsome, even in her days of early childhood, and now she was middle-aged, distorted with work and childbearing, and looking faded and worn." Her face is "a pitifully worn, almost tragic face—long, thin, sallow, hollow-eyed. The mouth had long since lost the power to shape itself into a kiss." She has reached a point of desperation that calls for some kind of action: confrontation (with her husband), capitulation, or a mental breakdown. She chooses to renounce her soul-killing existence and operate on a level of bare subsistence, with no more struggling to "get ahead" or do what is expected. When the spirit of rebellion overcomes her, she simply gives in to her chronic weariness and refuses to do more than feed her children and the husband for whom she no longer cares.

For a successful conclusion to this powerful indictment against the farm wife's hopeless life, Garland had several choices. Unfortunately, he chose the ineffectual ending in which a dainty, young, idealistic schoolteacher persuades Lucretia to give life another try. The reader, having seen Lucretia's determination to stop the drudgery in her life forever, is dissatisfied, knowing it would have taken a great deal more than a sympathetic stranger to convince Lucretia that her life was worth enduring.

This kind of lapse is not Garland's only flaw. Occasionally, he leads on his readers, telling them what they should think about a character. In "A Sociable at Dudleys," for example, he describes the county bully: "No lizard revelled in the mud more hideously

Library of Congress

than he. . . . His tongue dropped poison." Garland apparently abhorred the "vileness of the bully's whole life and thought." Moreover, in most of the stories, one can tell the heroes from the villains by the Aryan features and Scottish names of the former and the dark, alien looks of the latter. His heroes are further categorized into two prevailing physical types: Either they are tall, imposing, strong, even powerful and handsome (Tim Haskins is an older, more worn version of this type) or they are stocky, sturdy, ambitious, cheerful, and optimistic counterparts of the young Hamlin Garland as he described himself in *A Son of the Middle Border.* Will Hannan of "A Branch Road" falls into this category.

"A Branch Road" • "A Branch Road" develops another favorite theme of Garland— a romantic one in which boy meets girl; misunderstanding separates them; and then adversity reunites them. Although this plot is well-worn today, in the late nineteenth and early twentieth centuries. the reading public still liked it, and Garland occasionally catered to the larger reading public. "A Branch Road" is long enough for the author to develop character, setting, and plot in a more leisurely, less personal manner than in some of his other stories on the same theme, such as "A Day of Grace," "A Sociable at Dudleys," and "William Bacon's Man." In "A Branch Road," young Will Hannan and Agnes Dingman have fallen in love. Will is ecstatic when he goes to the Dingman farm to help with the threshing, secure in his belief that she cares as much for him as he for her.

Once at the farm, however, listening to the other men, both young and older, making casual, joking comments about Agnes's prettiness and her attraction to most of the young swains in the county, Will becomes apprehensive that they will notice her obvious preference for him and make light of his deep private feelings. To prevent this, he repays her smiling attentions to him with curt words and an aloof manner. Agnes is hurt and confused by this, not understanding his masculine pride and sensitivity to ridicule. She responds by keeping up a light-hearted demeanor by smiling and talking to the other men, who are delighted, a response that makes Will rage inwardly. The day is a disaster for Will, but because he is to take Agnes to the fair in a few days, he is confident that he will be able then to set things right.

On the morning of the day of the fair, however, the hopeful lover sets out early but promptly loses a wheel from his buggy, requiring several hours of delay for repair. By the time he gets to Agnes's house, she has gone to the fair with Will's rival, Ed Kinney. Will is so enraged by this turn of events that he cannot think. Dominated by his pride and jealous passion, blaming her and considering no alternatives, he leaves the county, heading West, without a word of farewell or explanation to Agnes.

Seven years later he returns to find Agnes married to Ed Kinney, mother of a baby, daughter-in-law to two pestering old people, and distressingly old before her time. Will manages to speak privately to her and learns how he and she had misunderstood each other's actions on that day long ago. He finds she had indeed loved him. He accepts that it is his fault her life is now so unhappy, that she is so abused and worn. In defiance of custom and morality, he persuades her to leave her husband and go away with him. They flee, taking her baby with them.

In outline, this is the familiar melodrama of the villain triumphing over the fair maiden while the hero is away; then, just in time, the hero returns to rescue the heroine from the villain's clutches. Actually, however, Garland avoids melodrama and even refrains from haranguing against farm drudgery. He avoids the weak denouement and chooses instead a rather radical solution to the problem: The abduction of a wife and baby by another man was a daring ending to an American 1890's plot. Yet Garland makes the justice of the action acceptable.

Will Hannan, a very sensitive young man living among people who seem coarse and crude, is propelled through the story by strong, understandable emotions: love, pride, anger, fear of humiliation, remorse, pity, and guilt. Love causes the anger that creates the confusion in his relationship with Agnes. Pride and fear of humiliation drive him away from her. Remorse pursues him all the time he is away and is largely responsible for his return. Pity and guilt make him steal Agnes away from the life to which he feels he has condemned her. Many of Garland's other stories do not have the emotional motivation of characters that "A Branch Road" has (in all fairness, most are not as long); nor are Garland's characters generally as complex. He seems less concerned with probing a personality's reaction to a situation than with describing the consequences of an act.

The theme of the return of the native to his Middle Border home is used in several stories, among them "Up the Coolly," "Mrs. Ripley's Trip," and "Among the Corn Rows."

"The Return of a Private" • Less pessimistic and tragic and more sentimental than these is "The Return of a Private," an elaboration of Garland's father's return from the Civil War (1861-1865) as told in the first chapter of *A Son of the Middle Border.* The story describes the sadness which old war comrades feel as they go their separate ways home. It describes the stirring emotions which the returning soldier feels as he nears his home and sees familiar landmarks; when he first catches sight of the homestead; when he sees his nearly disbelieving wife and the children who hardly remember him. They are tender scenes, but Garland the artist cannot contain Garland the reformer, who reminds the reader of the futility facing the soldier, disabled physically from war-connected fever and ague and handicapped financially by the heavy mortgage on his farm. The soldier's homecoming is shown as one tiny, bright moment in what has been and will continue to be an endless cycle of dullness and hardship. Garland obviously empathizes with the character and shows the homecoming as a sweet, loving time, but, as with so many of his stories, "The Return of a Private" is overcast with gloom.

Garland's stories show the ugly and the beautiful, the tragic with the humorous, the just with the unjust. He tries always to show the true, reporting the speech and dress of the people accurately, describing their homes and their work honestly. Truth, however, is not all that he seeks; he wants significance as well. To this end, his stories show the effects of farm drudgery on the men and women, of the ignorant practices of evangelists, of the thwarted ambitions of the youth because of circumstances beyond their control. Garland does not always suppress his reformer's instincts, and so in some stories he offers solutions. In his best stories, however, he simply shows the injustice and moves the reader, by his skillful handling of details, to wish to take action. Although his stories are often bitter and depressing, there is a hopefulness and optimism in Garland that compels him to bring them to a comparatively happy ending. In his best stories, he does for the Middle Border what Mary E. Wilkins Freeman does for New England, brings the common people into rich relation with the reader and shows movingly the plights of the less fortunate among them, especially women.

Jane L. Ball
With updates by Terry Heller

Other major works

PLAY: *Under the Wheel: A Modern Play in Six Scenes,* pb. 1890.

NOVELS: *A Little Norsk,* 1892; *A Member of the Third House,* 1892; *A Spoil of Office,* 1892; *Jason Edwards: An Average Man,* 1892; *Rose of Dutcher's Coolly,* 1895; *The Spirit of Sweetwater,* 1898 (reissued as *Witch's Gold,* 1906); *Boy Life on the Prairie,* 1899; *The Eagle's Heart,* 1900; *Her Mountain Lover,* 1901; *The Captain of the Gray-Horse Troop,* 1902; *Hesper,* 1903; *The Light of the Star,* 1904; *The Tyranny of the Dark,* 1905; *Money Magic,* 1907 (reissued as *Mart Haney's Mate,* 1922); *The Long Trail,* 1907; *The Moccasin Ranch,* 1909; *Cavanagh, Forest Ranger,* 1910; *Victor Ollnee's Discipline,* 1911; *The Forester's Daughter,* 1914.

NONFICTION: *Crumbling Idols: Twelve Essays on Art,* 1894; *Ulysses S. Grant: His Life and Character,* 1898; *Out-of-Door Americans,* 1901; *A Son of the Middle Border,* 1917; *A Daughter of the Middle Border,* 1921; *Trail-Makers of the Middle Border,* 1926; *The Westward March of American Settlement,* 1927; *Back-Trailers from the Middle Border,* 1928; *Roadside Meetings,* 1930; *Companions on the Trail: A Literary Chronicle,* 1931; *My Friendly Contemporaries: A Literary Log,* 1932; *Afternoon Neighbors,* 1934; *Joys of the Trail,* 1935; *Forty Years of Psychic Research: A Plain Narrative of Fact,* 1936.

POETRY: *Prairie Songs,* 1893.

Bibliography

Garland, Hamlin. *Selected Letters of Hamlin Garland.* Edited by Keith Newlin and Joseph B. McCullough. Lincoln: University of Nebraska Press, 1998. The volume's introduction serves as a good entry into Hamlin's biography.

Joseph, Philip. "Landed and Literary: Hamlin Garland, Sarah Orne Jewett, and the Production of Regional Literatures." *Studies in American Fiction* 26 (Autumn, 1998): 147-170. Compares some of Garland's early stories with the stories in Jewett's *Country of the Pointed Firs* to examine ideological conflict within literary regionalism. Argues that while Garland's support for social reform leads him to challenge some of the conventions of late nineteenth century realism, Jewett does not see class differences as a hindrance to U.S. destiny.

McCullough, Joseph. *Hamlin Garland.* Boston: Twayne, 1978. This study follows Garland through his literary career, dividing it into phases, with major attention to the first phase of his reform activities and the midwestern stories. A primary bibliography and a select, annotated secondary bibliography are included.

Martin, Quentin E. "Hamlin Garland's 'The Return of a Private' and 'Under the Lion's Paw' and the Monopoly of Money in Post-Civil War America." *American Literary Realism* 29 (Fall, 1996): 62-77. Discusses how Garland made money and power the central features in his two stories; discusses the connection between the stories and the financial system of Gilded Age America in the 1890's.

May, Charles E., ed. *Masterplots II: Short Story Series, Revised Edition.* 8 vols. Pasadena, Calif.: Salem Press, 2004. Designed for student use, this reference set contains articles providing detailed plot summaries and analyses of these three short stories by Garland: "Mrs. Ripley's Trip" (vol. 5), "The Return of a Private" (vol. 6), and "Under the Lion's Paw" (vol. 8).

Nagel, James, ed. *Critical Essays on Hamlin Garland.* Boston: G. K. Hall, 1982. Nagel's introduction surveys the critical responses to Garland's work. This volume is especially rich in reviews of Garland's books, and it also includes twenty-six biographical and critical essays.

Newlin, Keith. "Melodramatist of the Middle Border: Hamlin Garland's Early Work Reconsidered." *Studies in American Fiction* 21 (Autumn, 1993): 153-169. Discusses Garland's development of a dramatic method to express the privation of the Middle Border; argues that he was torn between his admiration for the universal truths of melodrama and his realization that melodrama was limited in its realistic presentation of life.

_____, ed. *Hamlin Garland: A Bibliography, with a Checklist of Unpublished Letters.* Troy, N.Y.: Whitston, 1998. Basically a primary bibliography, with one section listing articles that addressed Garland extensively. The introduction surveys the availability of primary and secondary sources. Newlin includes a chronology and title index.

Silet, Charles. *Henry Blake Fuller and Hamlin Garland: A Reference Guide.* Boston: G. K. Hall, 1977. This volume contains a comprehensive annotated guide to writing about Garland through 1975. For information about scholarly writing on Garland after 1975, see *American Literary Scholarship: An Annual.*

Silet, Charles, Robert Welch, and Richard Boudreau, eds. *The Critical Reception of Hamlin Garland, 1891-1978.* Troy, N.Y.: Whitston, 1985. This illustrated volume contains thirty-three essays that illustrate the development of Garland's literary reputation from 1891 to 1978. The introduction emphasizes the difficulty critics have had trying to determine the quality of Garland's art.

Nikolai Gogol

Born: Sorochintsy, Ukraine, Russian Empire (now in Ukraine); March 31, 1809
Died: Moscow, Russia; March 4, 1852

Principal short fiction • *Vechera na khutore bliz Dikanki*, vol. 1, 1831, vol. 2, 1832 (*Evenings on a Farm Near Dikanka*, 1926); *Arabeski*, 1835 (*Arabesques*, 1982); *Mirgorod*, 1835 (English translation, 1928).

Other literary forms • Nikolai Gogol established his reputation on his remarkable short stories, but he is often better known in the West for his play *Revizor* (pr., pb. 1836; *The Inspector General*, 1890) and for the first part of his novel *Myortvye dushi* (1842; *Dead Souls*, 1887). Still the subject of much debate and criticism, his *Vybrannye mesta iz perepiski s druzyami* (1847; *Selected Passages from Correspondence with Friends*, 1969) represents a range from literary criticism to tendentious and presumptuous evaluation of Russia as seen from abroad.

Achievements • In Russian literature of both the nineteenth and the twentieth centuries, it is impossible to overstate the importance of Nikolai Gogol as an innovator in style and subject matter. He created a great and enduring art form composed of the manners of petty officials, small landowners, and the fantastic and all-too-real people who inhabit the three worlds that he describes: the Ukraine, St. Petersburg, and the Russian heartland.

Outside Russia, his influence can be detected most noticeably in Franz Kafka's *Die Verwandlung* (1915; *The Metamorphosis*, 1936), which centers on a conceit not unlike Nikolai Gogol's hapless titular councillor in Gogol's "Nos" ("The Nose"). Inside Russia, Fyodor Dostoevski is reputed to have begun the saying that "we all came from under Gogol's 'Overcoat,'" meaning that Gogol's stories originated the themes, social and spiritual anguish, and other literary preoccupations of the rest of Russian literature.

Biography • Nikolai Vasilyevich Gogol was born in the Ukraine on March 31, 1809, to a Ukrainian landowner, Vasily Afanasievich Gogol-Yanovsky, and his young wife, Mariya Ivanovna. Vasily Afanasievich wrote plays in Ukrainian and sponsored artistic evenings at his home. Nikolai would write almost nothing in Ukrainian throughout his life. On his father's estate, Nikolai would absorb the manner and, significantly, the pace of provincial life, which would flavor his works from his early stories through *Dead Souls*.

At school and later in the *Gymnasium*, Nikolai remained something of a loner. He participated in activities, especially in drama performances, where he is said to have excelled. His classmates called him "the mysterious dwarf," though, for his predilection to aloofness and his unassuming stature.

Gogol's first work, *Hans Kuechelgarten* (1829), which he published at his own expense, was received so poorly that he bought all the unsold copies, burned them, and never wrote in verse again. He fled the country (in what was to become a characteristic retreat) and took refuge in Germany for several weeks. When he returned,

Library of Congress

he occupied a minor post in the civil service in St. Petersburg and began writing the stories that would begin to appear in 1831 and subsequently make him famous. His first collection of stories, *Evenings on a Farm Near Dikanka*, met with great critical and popular acclaim and set the stage for the series of successes that his later stories were to have.

In 1836, however, his play *The Inspector General* premiered, was produced most outlandishly in Gogol's mind, and created a minor scandal. Although this initial reaction was reversed and, through the intercession of the czar himself, the play was to continue its run, Gogol was nevertheless mortified at the antagonism that he had aroused in the spectators. He again left the country, only this time—with the exception of two rather short trips back to Russia—forever.

Gogol's last and most enduring works, "Shinel" ("The Overcoat") and *Dead Souls*, were thus written abroad. The irony of the profound resonance that his writing enjoyed at home was not lost on him. He began to doubt his ability to convey the "truth" to the Russians from such a distance and began to search for artistic inspiration. His self-doubt gave birth to his last literary production, *Selected Passages from Correspondence with Friends*. This product of his doubt was met with indignation and even anger in Russia. Vissarion Belinsky wrote his famous letter excoriating Gogol for his "fantastic book" and for writing from his "beautiful distance." Had Gogol forgotten the misery of Russia, its serfdom and servility, its "tartar" censorship, its totalitarian clout? Belinsky believed that the public was justified in its censure of this work; the public has the right to expect more from literature.

Gogol spent the last six years of his life fighting depression and artistic barrenness, trying to reach the "truth" in the second part of *Dead Souls*. However, he failed to finish this work and, shortly before his death, burned what he had written. Physically ill, spiritually empty, emotionally depleted, he died in pain in Moscow on March 4, 1852.

Analysis • Nikolai Gogol combines the consummate stylist with the innocent spectator, flourishes and flounces with pure human emotion, naturalism with delicate sensitivity. He bridges the period between Romanticism and realism in Russian literature. He captures the "real" against the background of the imagined and, in the estimation of at least one critic, the surreal. Frequently, the supernatural or some confounding coincidence plays a major role in his works. His heroes of the "little man" variety imprinted the most profound impression on his readers and critics alike. These petty clerks, all socially dysfunctional in some major respect, nevertheless explore the great depth of the human soul and exhibit certain personality traits characteristic of the greatest heroes in literature.

Gogol focuses his major creative occupation on the manners of his characters; his creative energy is nowhere more apparent than in the "mannerizing" in which he describes and characterizes. His genius does not dwell in philosophical dialogues, allegory, or involved interior monologue as do the realist novels of the latter half of the century. Nor does he engender his heroes with abandon and ennui, as do his near contemporaries Alexander Pushkin and Mikhail Lermontov. The depth of his psychological portraiture and the sweep of his romantic apostrophes, however, remain powerful and fascinating. In his plays, speech is swept aside from its characteristic place in the foreground; the dramatic foreground is given over to the manner or mannerisms of the characters. The actions literally speak louder than words. The social satire, deeply embedded in the manners of the characters, unfolds without special machinations and with few unnatural speech acts, such as asides. It is a tribute to Gogol's skill that his characters do not necessarily become superficial or unidimensional as a result but are imbued with certain attributes that display a wide range of human passion, particularly human dignity and the cognizance of the injustices created in social stratification.

One of Gogol's favored narrative devices can be called the chatty narrator. This narrator, seemingly prolix and sometimes random, will supply the reader with most of the information that will ever be revealed about a character. In a typical passage, the reader will encounter a character who might say something utterly commonplace such as: "I won't have coffee today, Praskovia Osipovna, instead I will take some hot bread with onions." The character says little that can be used to describe himself. The reader's attention, however, is then directed to the information supplied by the narrator: "Actually, Ivan Yakovlevich would have liked to take both, but he knew it was utterly impossible to ask for two things at the same time since Praskovia Osipovna greatly disliked such whims." Thus Ivan Yakovlevich is described by his manners—he speaks to his wife in a formal tone that relates very little information to the reader—but the narrator, in his chatty, nosy fashion reveals much about this individual and describes Ivan's wife, his subordinate position at home, and his struggle for dignity within this relationship at the same time. Thus, from a seeming excess of information, the reader becomes familiar with a character who might otherwise remain nondescript.

Gogol's narratives abound in descriptions, and these tend to be humorous. Many times, humor is created by the device of metonymy, whereby a part stands for the whole. Thus, women become "slender waists" and seem so light that one fears that they will float away, and men are mustaches of various colors, according to their rank. Another humorous effect might be created by the chatty narrator's remark about some individual in a very unfavorable light. This information that he, for some reason, knows in regard to the character informs the reader's opinion of that character and often lends either a humorous or a pathetic tone to his or her person. Also humorous is the effect created through realized metaphors, another favorite technique of Gogol. Thus, instead of "he ate like a pig," the person is actually transformed into a pig with all the attributes of a perfect pig, at least temporarily. In general, Gogol's works abound with descriptions packed with colors, similes, and wayward characterizations by his narrator or actors.

Gogol's works fall roughly into three categories, which in turn correspond approximately to three different periods in his creative life. The first period is represented solely by short stories that exhibit lush local color from the Ukraine and Gogol's own mixing of devils and simple folk. Seven of the eight stories from the collection *Evenings on a Farm Near Dikanka*, which appeared in 1831 (with the second part following in 1832), belong in this category, as well as the stories in *Mirgorod*, first published in 1835.

The second major period of Gogol's literary life features works either centered on a locus in the imperial center of Russia, St. Petersburg itself, or surrounding the bureaucrats and petty officials ubiquitous in the provinces of the empire. This period stretches roughly from 1835 to 1842 and includes the short stories "Nevsky Prospekti" ("Nevsky Prospect"), "Zapiski sumasshedshego" ("The Diary of a Madman"), "The Overcoat," "The Nose," the play *The Inspector General*, and the novel *Dead Souls*. The short story "Portret" ("The Portrait"), although definitely a product of this period, is singular for its strong echoes of the devil tales in the early period.

The last period can claim only one published work, *Selected Passages from Correspondence with Friends*, and is typically interpreted as a reversal in Gogol's creative development. If the analyst, however, can keep in mind Gogol's rather fanatic attachment to his artistic life as a devotional to God, then perhaps this otherwise unexplainable curve in his creative evolution might seem more understandable.

The two volumes of *Evenings on a Farm Near Dikanka* contain eight stories. However atypical they were to become in terms of setting and subject matter, these tales of the Ukraine, with various elements of the supernatural adding terror, exhibit many of the qualities found in the mature writer of the second period. They are magical and engaging, heroic and base, simply enjoyable to read and quite poignant.

"A May Night" • An excellent example of these tales is "Mayskaya Noch: Ili, utoplennitsa" ("A May Night: Or, The Drowned Maiden"). The plot is a simple love story in which the lovers are not allowed to wed because of the objection of the man's father. The seeming simplicity, however, is overwhelmed by acts of Satan, witches, and *rusalki*. (In folk belief, *rusalki* are female suicides who endlessly inhabit the watery depths of ponds, tempting men and often causing their deaths.) When the antics of Ukrainian Cossack youths do not by themselves bring the matter to resolution, the *rusalka* puts a letter into the young man's hand, which secures for him his marriage.

The characters are depicted in ways highly reminiscent of the oral folktales. Levko, the hero, sings to his beloved to come out of her house. He speaks of his "brighteyed beauty," her "little white hands," and her "fair little face." All these figures of speech are fixed epithets common in folklore. He promises to protect her from detection—"I will cover you with my jacket, wrap my sash around you, or hide you in my arms—and no one will see us,"—forfending the possible intrusion three ways. Likewise, he promises to protect her from any cold—"I'll press you warmer to my heart, I'll warm you with my kisses, I'll put my cap over your little white feet"— that is, a threefold protection. The reinforcement of images in threes is also quite common in folklore. Thus, clearly, Gogol is invoking folklore in his artistic works. Nevertheless, there are hints of the mature Gogol in the landscape descriptions. Even the intervention of the supernatural to produce, in this case, the successful outcome of the story belongs to the second period as well as to the first.

"Ivan Fyodorovich Shponka and His Aunt" • One story, in retrospect, however, stands out clearly from the others. "Ivan Fyodorovich Shpon'ka i ego tetushka"

("Ivan Fyodorovich Shponka and His Aunt") certainly presages the later works that will come to be regarded as Gogol's most characteristic. Set in the Ukraine, the story begins with an elaborate frame involving the following: The original storyteller of the tale wrote the story entirely and gave it to the narrator (for reasons that are not explained), but the narrator's wife later used the paper to wrap her pies, so the end of the story was unfortunately lost. Readers are assured, however, that should they desire, they may contact the original storyteller, who still lives in that village and who will certainly oblige in sharing the ending.

There are many details in this frame alone that are very typical of the mature Gogol. First, the narrator does not take responsibility for the story—that is, that it is left unfinished; the abrupt end is presented as something over which he has no control. Second, the woman is the undoing of the man, although, in this case, the undoing is caused by her stupidity (she is illiterate) and not by an inherent evil. Moreover, the narrator could have rectified the situation himself, but, seemingly, he was fated to forget to ask the storyteller for another copy of the ending. Most of all, the story in the frame abounds with chatty, seemingly irrelevant details that serve to characterize the narrator, his wife, and the storyteller but that, ultimately, motivate the plot and occasion the sometimes precipitous changes in the course of the narrative.

The motifs described above reappear in forms both changed and unchanged throughout Gogol's work. A woman will appear in many guises in three of the four stories in *Mirgorod*. In "Taras Bulba," a long story with the color and force of an epic, a Polish beauty causes the son, Andrei, to defect to the enemy. Later, the traitor will be murdered by his father's own hands, described in the father's own words as a "vile dog."

"Viy" • In another story from this collection, "Viy," a young student, Khoma Brut, meets an old woman on his way home on vacation. When he stays for the night in her barn, she comes after him with outstretched arms. Khoma tries to avoid her three different ways, but she persists and, to his amazement, he loses the use of his arms and legs. The old woman turns out to be a witch who wickedly torments and then rides on the back of the young philosopher. Remembering some exorcisms, however, he renders her harmless and, in fact, exchanges places with her, now riding on her back. Khoma makes an incredible trek in this fashion until she falls in a faint. Now, watching her prone form, he is amazed to find not a witch or an old woman but a fair young maiden. Khoma races off, making it all the way to Kiev, but is called back to watch over her corpse for three nights, which was the last request of the dying maiden. During the third night, he is overcome by the supernatural devil, Viy, who emanates from the dead woman and thus brings his own doom.

"The Tale of How Ivan Ivanovich Quarreled with Ivan Nikiforovich" • This tale revolves around the motif of the evil woman, although almost imperceptibly. Here, it is a "stupid" woman who sets out the gun while cleaning the house, which causes Ivan Ivanovich to envy this possession of his neighbor Ivan Nikiforovich. This seemingly insignificant act is the very act that causes an ensuing argument and that in turn builds into a lasting enmity between the former friends and then lasts in the courts for a decade. In Russia, this story is often invoked when people quarrel over imagined improprieties or insignificant trifles.

"Nevsky Prospect" • In *Arabesques*, the two most famous stories, "Nevsky Prospect" and "The Diary of a Madman," similarly feature the demonic power of women over men. "Nevsky Prospect" indeed centers on this "demonic" nature of women. Two tales are told, one of the "sensitive young man," the artist Piskarev, and the other of a rather older, down-to-earth lieutenant named Pirogov. The artist, perhaps fooled by the falling darkness, is stunned by the dazzling beauty of a woman walking by on Nevsky Prospect, a main avenue in St. Petersburg. At the same moment, Pirogov notices and blindly takes off after a blond woman, "convinced that no beauty could resist him." Piskarev, almost overwhelmed at his own audacity, meekly follows his beauty to her "home," only to find out that she is, indeed, a prostitute. This development soon becomes the undoing of the poor artist as he falls into daytime and nighttime dreaming in a vain attempt to rescue his former exalted vision and save her image from the reality of her vile lifestyle. He takes to opium and, finally emboldened, decides on the desperate act of proposing marriage to her. When she rebuffs him, he goes mad and takes his own life. Pirogov, on the other hand, for all of his self-confidence and experience, fares only slightly better after following his blond beauty home—to her husband. He blindly but cunningly continues his pursuit of her, only to end up being humiliated and physically abused. Indignant, he sets out to put his case before the court, but, somehow, after eating a little and spending some time rather pleasantly, he becomes diverted and seemingly forgets the whole thing. The narrator then closes the story with the admonition not to trust Nevsky Prospect, since nothing is as it seems, especially not the ladies.

"The Diary of a Madman" • "The Diary of a Madman" appears to be the personal journal of Popryshchin, whose name sounds very much like "pimple." The story is written as a series of entries with the chronology becoming entirely skewed at the end in accordance with the degree of dementia within the protagonist. The appearance of Popryshchin, the poor government clerk, marks the introduction of a new incarnation of the meek Shponkin type who will populate many of Gogol's works thereafter and enter the world of Russian literature as a prototype for many writers, notably Dostoevski. Popryshchin, a rather older, undistinguished man, adores the director's daughter but recognizes that pursuing her is useless. Moreover, he sees that his infatuation for her will be his doom: "Dear God, I'm a goner, completely lost!" Virtually at the same moment that he admits his futile position, his attention is drawn to the thin voice of Madgie, the young lady's dog, who is speaking to Fido. This rather fantastic conversation is centered on the letter that poor Fido seemingly never received from Madgie. Popryshchin's delusions continue to build up, with him even reading the canine correspondence. It is actually through Madgie's letters that Popryshchin learns of the young lady's love for, and engagement to, a handsome young chamberlain. Moreover, Popryshchin finds the young man's description unflattering. The sentence, "Sophie always laughs at him," becomes the crowning blow to his sanity. Shortly thereafter he goes mad, imagining himself to be the king of Spain. He is committed to Spain, more accurately, to a mental hospital, where he is constantly tormented. The pathos of the "little man" is palpable, conveyed through the evocation of a beautiful image—a troika coming to fly to him and rescue him—juxtaposed to the hateful attendants dousing him repeatedly with cold water.

"The Overcoat" • Another "little man" follows closely in Popryshchin's footsteps. In "The Overcoat," Akaky Akakievich, whose humorous name is a reminder of fecal matter (kaka), represents such a meek and orderly person that he can perform only one duty: copying papers. This duty he discharges perfectly and with great pleasure, sometimes so much so that he occasionally brings the document home and, in his spare time, copies it again. Akaky Akakievich lives in St. Petersburg, victim of almost unimaginable poverty with barely enough means to keep himself alive. It was, indeed, a terrible day when he could no longer persuade his tailor to have his overcoat remade; he would have to buy a new one. The physical privations that were necessitated by this desperate position are reminiscent of saintly asceticism. However, Akaky begins to sublimate his anguish and dreams of the great overcoat as though of a wife. With the mention of the word "wife," the reader who is accustomed to Gogol might immediately suspect the potential danger of this coat, since women in Gogol's fiction are almost always the undoing of a man. True to form, after withstanding all the hardships, enduring all the misgivings and new sensations, Akaky wears the new coat only once before he is mugged and the coat stolen from him. Dazed and exposed in the cold of St. Petersburg, he musters the courage to petition a "Person of Consequence" who dismisses him pompously. Akaky then falls into a fever from which he will not emerge alive. The tale, however, takes on a fantastic ending. Akaky comes back from the dead, intimidates and robs the Person of Consequence of his overcoat, and then, apparently satisfied, leaves the scene forever.

"The Nose" • The supernatural revenge makes "The Overcoat" quite singular in Gogol's work. The fantastic element, however, appears again in another story of the same period, "The Nose." A barber, Ivan Yakovlevich, takes a roll for breakfast and finds, much to his alarm, a human nose in it, and he recognizes the nose as that of the Collegiate Assessor Kovalyov. Ivan Yakovlevich tries to rid himself of the nose. Meanwhile, its erstwhile owner wakes up to find a completely smooth area where his nose and incipient pimple had been the previous evening. He sets out on foot with the empty spot concealed by a handkerchief, only to witness his own former nose walking about freely, moreover in the uniform of a civil councillor—that is, a higher-ranking individual than Kovalyov himself. He accosts the nose very deferentially, but the nose claims to be an independent individual and not part of Kovalyov at all. In desperation, he sets out for the police department but, thinking better of it, decides to place an advertisement in the local newspaper. There, the clerk, thinking about it, decides against publishing such an advertisement to avoid potential scandals for the paper. Luckily for Kovalyov, the nose is returned to him by a police officer, but to his horror, it will not stick to his face. Then, as absurdly as the story began, it ends. Kovalyov wakes up with the nose back in its former place, goes to Ivan Yakovlevich and has a shave (the barber now not touching the olfactory organ), and it is as though nothing happened.

Many of Gogol's characters have penetrated into everyday Russian speech. If someone works hard at a brainless job, he is called an "Akaky Akakievich," for example, an attestation how well the writer created a type of Russian "little man" who, however uncreative, still captures the hearts and alliances of readers. There is something real about these absurd, impossible characters, something in their unidimensionality that transcends their locus and becomes universal. Gogol, while embroidering in highly ornate circumlocution, directly touches the wellspring of humanity in even the lowliest, most unattractive character. In his descriptions, there are simultaneously resonances of slapstick humor and the depths of human misery and social injustice.

Gogol left quite an imprint on the course of Russian literature. Very few subsequent writers will produce anything that does not at all reverberate the Gogolian legacy. Even in the twentieth century, writers incorporate his artistic ideas or emulate his style to a degree.

Christine Tomei

Other major works

PLAYS: *Vladimir tretey stepeni*, wr. 1832, pb. 1842; *Zhenit'ba*, wr. 1835, pr., pb. 1842 (*Marriage: A Quite Incredible Incident*, 1926); *Revizor*, pr., pb. 1836 (*The Inspector General*, 1890); *Utro delovogo cheloveka*, pb. 1836, pr. 1871 (revision of *Vladimir tretey stepeni*; *An Official's Morning*, 1926); *Igroki*, pb. 1842, pr. 1843 (*The Gamblers*, 1926); *Lakeyskaya*, pb. 1842, pr. 1863 (revision of *Vladimir tretey stepeni*; *The Servants' Hall*, 1926); *Otryvok*, pb. 1842, pr. 1860 (revision of *Vladimir tretey stepeni*; *A Fragment*, 1926); *Tyazhba*, pb. 1842, pr. 1844 (revision of *Vladimir tretey stepeni*; *The Lawsuit*, 1926); *The Government Inspector, and Other Plays*, pb. 1926.

NOVELS: *Myortvye dushi*, part 1, 1842, part 2, 1855 (*Dead Souls*, 1887); *Taras Bulba*, 1842 (revision of his 1835 short story; English translation, 1886).

MISCELLANEOUS: *The Collected Works*, 1922-1927 (6 volumes); *Polnoe sobranie sochinenii*, 1940-1952 (14 volumes); *The Collected Tales and Plays of Nikolai Gogol*, 1964.

NONFICTION: *Vybrannye mesta iz perepiski s druzyami*, 1847 (*Selected Passages from Correspondence with Friends*, 1969); *Letters of Nikolai Gogol*, 1967.

POETRY: *Hanz Kuechelgarten*, 1829.

Bibliography
Fanger, Donald L. *The Creation of Nikolai Gogol*. Cambridge, Mass.: Belknap Press of Harvard University Press, 1979. Fanger presses deeply into the background material and includes in his purview works both published and unpublished, in his effort to reveal the genius of Gogol's creative power. This book is worthwhile in many respects, particularly for the wealth of details about Gogol's life and milieu. Includes twenty-eight pages of notes and an index.

Fusso, Susanne, and Priscilla Meyer, eds. *Essays on Gogol: Logos and the Russian Word*. Evanston, Ill.: Northwestern University Press, 1992. Collection of essays on Gogol from a conference at Wesleyan University. Bibliography and index.

Hart, Pierre R. "Narrative Oscillation in Gogol's 'Nevsky Prospect.'" *Studies in Short Fiction* 31 (Fall, 1994): 639-645. Argues that the story is a commentary on the author's development of strategies to deal with reality; discusses the urban scene in the story, suggesting that the city forces the protagonist into a final defensive position.

Karlinsky, Simon. *The Sexual Labyrinth of Nikolai Gogol*. 1976. Reprint. Chicago: University of Chicago Press, 1992. Look at Gogol's literature and his relations with men. Contains annotated bibliography of Gogol's works in English. Index.

Luckyj, George Stephen Nestor. *The Anguish of Mykola Hohol a.k.a. Nikolai Gogol*. Toronto: Canadian Scholars' Press, 1998. Explores Gogol's life and how it affected his work. Includes bibliographical references and an index.

Maguire, Robert A. *Exploring Gogol*. Stanford, Calif.: Stanford University Press, 1994. The most comprehensive study in English of Gogol's entire writing career. Incorporates a chronology, detailed notes, and an extensive bibliography.

_____, ed. *Gogol from the Twentieth Century: Eleven Essays.* Princeton, N.J.: Princeton University Press, 1974. This collection of essays, with a lengthy introduction by the editor and translator, represents some of the most famous and influential opinions on Gogol in the twentieth century. Some of the most problematic aspects of Gogol's stylistics, thematics, and other compositional elements are addressed and well elucidated. Bibliography, index.

May, Charles E., ed. *Masterplots II: Short Story Series, Revised Edition.* 8 vols. Pasadena, Calif.: Salem Press, 2004. Designed for student use, this reference set contains articles providing detailed plot summaries and analyses of these five short stories by Gogol: "The Diary of a Madman" (vol. 2), "The Nose" and "Old-World Landowners" (vol. 5), "The Overcoat" (vol. 6), and "Viy" (vol. 8).

Rancour-Laferriere, David. *Out from Under Gogol's "Overcoat": A Psychoanalytic Study.* Ann Arbor, Mich.: Ardis, 1982. This specialized study proves very exciting to the reader of Gogol. Much of the discussion focuses on the particular usage of words by Gogol. Even students with no command of Russian will find the explication understandable since the examples are clear and self-defining. Much of the discussion consists of very modern literary-analytical technique and may prove of good use to the reader. Contains a bibliography that includes many background works.

Tosi, Alessandra. "Andrei Kropotov's 'Istoriia o Smurom Kaftane': A Thematic Source for Gogol's 'Shinel'?" *The Slavonic and East European Review* 76 (October, 1998): 601-613. Compares Gogol's "The Overcoat" with Kropotov's earlier story; in both stories a trivial garment takes on significance for the main characters and ultimately causes their ruin. Discusses the similarity in the twists in the plots; suggests that Kropotov's story may have been source for Gogol's.

Nadine Gordimer

Born: Springs, Transvaal, South Africa; November 20, 1923

Principal short fiction • *Face to Face: Short Stories*, 1949; *The Soft Voice of the Serpent, and Other Stories*, 1952; *Six Feet of the Country*, 1956; *Friday's Footprint, and Other Stories*, 1960; *Not for Publication, and Other Stories*, 1965; *Livingstone's Companions: Stories*, 1971; *Selected Stories*, 1975; *A Soldier's Embrace*, 1980; *Something out There*, 1984; *Reflections of South Africa*, 1986; *Crimes of Conscience*, 1991; *Jump, and Other Stories*, 1991; *Why Haven't You Written? Selected Stories, 1950-1972*, 1992; *Loot, and Other Stories*, 2003; *Beethoven Was One-Sixteenth Black, and Other Stories*, 2007.

Other literary forms • Nadine Gordimer is well known for several of her novels, including *A World of Strangers* (1958), *The Conservationist* (1974), *Burger's Daughter* (1979), and *The House Gun* (1998), as well as the acclaimed *My Son's Story* (1990). She has also published extensively in nonfiction and has made notable contributions to South African scholarship with such books as *Lifetimes Under Apartheid* (1986; with David Goldblatt) and *Living in Hope and History: Notes from Our Century* (1999). Her other publications have included volumes essays; two edited works on the literature of her homeland, *South African Writing Today* (1967) and *Telling Tales* (2004); and several teleplays.

Achievements • As a courageous chronicler of life in South Africa, particularly through her short fiction, Nadine Gordimer is known throughout the world. She published her first collection of short stories in 1949 and has continued to publish books into the twenty-first century. One of her latest collections, *Beethoven Was One-Sixteenth Black, and Other Stories* (2007), contains a diverse mix of stories, ranging from a tale about a former anti-apartheid activist trying to understand his own racial identity to a fantasy about a parrot with an embarrassing habit of reproducing the voices and intimate conversations of people whom it overhears.

Gordimer received the W. H. Smith and Son Prize in 1971 for *Friday's Footprint, and Other Stories*. Two years later she won the James Tait Black Memorial Prize for *A Guest of Honour* (1970). The next year, *The Conservationist* shared with Stanley Middleton's *Holiday* (1974) the prestigious Booker Prize. Gordimer was also a recipient of France's Grand Aigle d'Or, and in 1991 she won what many consider the ultimate literary honor—the Nobel Prize in Literature.

An opponent of all forms of discrimination, Gordimer rejected candidacy for the Orange Prize in 1998 because the award was restricted to female writers. She has been the vice president of PEN International and an executive member of the Congress of South African Writers. Her other honors have included the Modern Literature Association Award and the Bennett Award in the United States and the Chevalier de l'Ordre des Arts et des Lettres in France. Her short fiction has been published in such magazines as *The New Yorker.*

One American reviewer summed up Gordimer's importance in literature, writing: "Gordimer is in the great mainstream of the short story—Maupassant, Chekhov, Turgenev, James, Hemingway, Porter." Most of Gordimer's fiction has been published in paperback form, enabling a greater number of readers and critics to recognize and enjoy her work.

Biography • Nadine Gordimer grew up a rebel. Both her parents were immigrants to South Africa; her mother was English, her father an eastern European Jew. In Springs, the gold-mining town near Johannesburg in which she spent her early years, Gordimer frequently played hooky from her convent school. When she did attend, she would sometimes walk out. She found it difficult to tolerate all the pressures for conformity.

In the white, middle-class South African environment in which Gordimer grew up, a girl could aspire only to marry and rear a family. After leaving school and then working at clerical jobs for a few years, girls would eventually be singled out as prospec- tive wives by young men from fami-

© The Nobel Foundation

lies much like their own. From there, within months the girls would actualize the greatest dreams of young womanhood: They would have their engagement parties, linen showers, and wedding ceremonies, and they would bear their first children. None of these dreams would be served by the girls' education; books, in perhaps leading their minds astray, would interfere with the years of the girls' preparation for the mold.

At an early age, however, Gordimer did not fit the mold—she was an avid reader. By nine, she was already writing, and at the age of fourteen she won a writing prize. Her favorite authors were Anton Chekhov, W. Somerset Maugham, Guy de Maupassant, D. H. Lawrence, and the Americans Katherine Anne Porter, O. Henry, and Eudora Welty. As Gordimer became a young woman, she became increasingly interested in politics and the plight of black South Africans. She did not, however, launch her writing career as a way to bring change.

A male friend was an important influence on Gordimer. He told her that she was too ignorant and too accepting of society's values. Gordimer has written, "It was through him, too, that I roused myself sufficiently to insist on going to the university." Since she was twenty-two at the time and still being supported by her father, her family did not appreciate her desire to attend the university.

Gordimer commuted to Johannesburg to attend the University of Witwatersrand. While at the university, she met Uys Krige, an Afrikaans poet who had shunned his privileged Afrikaner heritage, lived in France and Spain, and served with the International Brigade in the Spanish Civil War (1936-1939). He, too, was a profound influence on her. She had been "a bolter," as she put it, at school; she was in the process of bolting from her family and class and the culture of white South Africa, and Krige gave her a final push. She would be committed to honesty alone. She began to send stories to publications in England and the United States. They were well received, and she began to build her reputation as a short-story writer and novelist. She published her first collection of stories, *Face to Face*, in 1949.

During the 1950's, Gordimer married her first husband, Reinhold Cassirer, a German Jew who had fled Berlin. They had a son, Hugo, with whom Gordimer would collaborate during the mid-1990's on a documentary about Berlin and Johannesburg. A second marriage later produced another child.

During the mid-1980's Gordimer turned to a new medium. She wrote teleplays of four of her stories–*Praise, Oral History, Country Lovers*, and *A Chip of Glass Ruby* (all 1985); she also participated in the production of other teleplays. Taken together, the films present a compelling vision of Gordimer's South Africa. A filmed interview of Gordimer by Joachim Braun often accompanies the showing of her films. In this interview, Gordimer had many interesting things to say about both her work and the tragic state of her country. Always passionate about politics, Gordimer was a member of the African National Congress during the 1990's and an enthusiastic supporter of South Africa's peaceful transition to full democracy. She continued writing and publishing prolifically into the twenty-first century and published her fifteenth collection of short stories, *Beethoven Was One-Sixteenth Black, and Other Stories*, in 2007, at the age of eighty-four.

Analysis • Nadine Gordimer is a distinguished novelist and short-story writer. About *Selected Stories*, drawn from her earlier volumes of stories, a reviewer said that the stories "are marked by the courage of moral vision and the beauty of artistic complexity. Gordimer examines, with passionate precision, the intricacies both of individual lives and of the wide-ranging political and historical forces that contain them." About the stories in *A Soldier's Embrace*, a reviewer wrote, "Their themes are universal: love and change, political transition, family, memory, madness and infidelity, to name a few. . . . What makes Nadine Gordimer such a valuable—and increasingly valued—novelist and short-story writer is her ability to meet the demands of her political conscience without becoming a propagandist and the challenges of her literary commitment without becoming a disengaged esthete." Over the course of her career, three of her books were banned in South Africa.

It would be easy for Gordimer to declare self-exile. Unlike James Joyce, however, she chose not to abandon the inhospitable country of her birth, accepting the obligation of citizenship to help make her country better. She did this by practicing her art, for it is an art that enables her diverse compatriots to understand better themselves and one another.

The settings and characters in Gordimer's stories cut across the whole spectrum of South African life. She writes about black village life and black urban experiences. She writes about the Afrikaans-speaking whites, English-speaking whites, Indians, and others. Her protagonists are as likely to be male as female, and reviewers have commented on her uncanny ability to make her male characters fully realized. In *The House Gun*, Gordimer ponders the deeply personal question of whether parents can even trust their own child not to commit murder. With amazing range and knowledge, she reveals the intricacies of individual lives and of the historical and political forces that shape them.

Reading one of Gordimer's stories is always exciting, because one does not know what will have caught her interest—urban or rural blacks, urban or rural Afrikaners, leisured or working or revolutionary whites, an African or a European setting. It is a great surprise, for example, to discover a story in the form of a letter from a dead Prague father to the son who predeceased him. It is a made-up letter in which Hermann Kafka tells off ungrateful, congenitally unhappy Franz.

As she has demonstrated again and again during more than thirty years of writing, Gordimer does not restrict her focus to people and scenes that are the most familiar. One marvels in reading "A City of the Dead, a City of the Living," for example, at what the author, a well-off white woman, knows of black-township life, at the total credibility of characters Samson Moreke and his wife, Nanike. Gordimer's knowledge and credibility are characteristic of all of her short fiction. "A City of the Dead, a City of the Living," "Sins of the Third Age," and "Blinder" could easily be included among the twenty best short stories of the twentieth century.

"Is There Nowhere Else Where We Can Meet?" • Among Gordimer's most gripping stories are those in which blacks and whites are at cross-purposes. "Is There Nowhere Else Where We Can Meet?" from *The Soft Voice of the Serpent, and Other Stories* is one of the simplest and best of this group. On a country road, a young white woman's handbag is torn from her by a passing local, whose bedraggled condition had evoked the woman's pity. The day is very cold, yet he is shoeless and dressed in rags. When she attains safety and has brought her fear under control, she decides not to seek aid or inform the police. "What did I fight for" she thinks. "Why didn't I give him the money and let him go? His red eyes, and the smell and those cracks in his feet, fissures, erosion."

"Six Feet of the Country" • The title piece of Gordimer's 1956 collection, *Six Feet of the Country*, is another exceptional story. A young black laborer walks from Rhodesia to find work in South Africa, where he has family who are employed on a weekend farm of a white Johannesburg couple. When he arrives at the farm, the illegal immigrant becomes ill and dies. There ensues a prolonged entanglement with the authorities, who insist on having the body so that it can be examined and the bureaucratic requirement for a statement of the cause of death can be fulfilled. With great reluctance, the family surrenders the body. When at last the casket is returned to the farm for burial, they discover that the body in it is that of a stranger. In the course of spinning out a plot about the fate of a corpse, Gordimer provides great insight into the lives of the farm laborers, the proprietors, and the police official, and she also reveals the relative inability of the laborers to deal with illness and the bureaucracy.

"A Chip of Glass Ruby" • "A Chip of Glass Ruby," in *Not for Publication, and Other Stories*, is about an Indian family in the Transvaal. The wife and mother is loving and unassuming and a very competent manager of a household that includes nine children. To the chagrin of her husband, Bamjee, she is also a political activist. It makes no sense to him that she takes grave risks for blacks, who are regarded as lower even than Indians. During the course of the story, she is arrested and imprisoned and participates in a prison hunger strike. Bamjee, a poor, small-time fruit and vegetable dealer, cannot understand any of this: He asks, "'What for?' Again and again: 'What for?'" His birthday comes, and he himself does not even remember. The eldest daughter brings word from her mother, in the prison, however, that his birthday must not be forgotten. Bamjee is moved and begins to have a glimmer of understanding of the wonderful woman who is his wife. As the daughter explains: "It's because she always remembers; remembers everything—people without somewhere to live, hungry kids, boys who can't get educated—remembers all the time. That's how Ma is."

"The Intruder" • "The Intruder," which appears in *Livingstone's Companions*, focuses on the decadence of an upper-class man of English descent. After shedding his last wife, hard-drinking, stay-out-late James Seago takes up with the beautiful teenage daughter of Mrs. Clegg, a woman of his age who affects a bohemian morality. Seago refers to the daughter, Marie, whom he uses sexually and enjoys having in his lap as he drinks, as his teenage doll, his marmoset, his rabbit. Because he has financial problems, Seago is plausibly able to postpone committing himself to her in marriage. Once they are married, Seago's irresponsible life of nightly partying does not change. Having married his pet, however, he must live with her, and so they set up housekeeping in an unpleasant flat. Marie becomes pregnant. The arrival of a child will force changes in Seago's way of life: For one thing, they will have to find living quarters more suitable for a child; for another, his wife-pet will have to give her primary attention to the child, not him. Arriving home early one morning after a night of partying, they fall into bed exhausted. A few hours later, Marie awakens hungry. She wanders out of the bedroom and finds the rest of the flat a wreck. All the kitchen staples have been spilled or thrown about; toothpaste is smeared about the bathroom. In the living room, on one of the sofa cushions, is "a slime of contraceptive jelly with haircombings—hers." Gordimer only hints at the perpetrator. It seems more than likely, though, that it is James Seago, who again is rebelling at the prospect of being forced into a responsible mode of life.

"Abroad" • In "Abroad," the main character is an Afrikaner. Manie Swemmer is a likable, middle-aged widower who has worked hard his entire life at construction and with cars. His grown sons have moved to neighboring black-run Zambia, known as Northern Rhodesia while still a British colony. Manie decides to take the train up to Zambia and visit his sons. Arriving in Lusaka, the capital, Manie is met by his younger son, Willie. Having expected to stay with Willie, Manie is surprised to learn that Willie does not have quarters of his own but is staying at a friend's, where there is no room for his father. To his dismay, Manie learns that all the local hotels are booked. The irrepressible Manie, though, manages to talk the manager of the Regent into placing him in a room that already has been rented as a single. The problem is that it is rented to an Indian, although an educated Indian. Although Manie has been given a key to the room and has placed his belongings inside, when he returns later, the Indian, from the inside, has bolted the door and locked out the Afrikaner. Manie then is offered a bed in a room intended for black guests. The blacks have not yet arrived, and Manie uses the door bolt to lock them out. "Abroad" is a beautiful story about a well-meaning Afrikaner who is excited by the racial mixing of the new nation and who wants to stretch himself to his liberal limit. His feelings toward blacks, though, are still conditioned by his South African base, where all blacks are automatically regarded as inferior. "I've only just got here, give me a bit of time," Manie tells the desk clerk. "You can't expect to put me in with a native, right away, first thing."

"A Soldier's Embrace" • Upon gaining its independence from Portugal in 1975, Mozambique became another black-ruled neighbor of South Africa. "A Soldier's Embrace," the title story of Gordimer's 1980 collection, is about the changeover, the exultation, and the disillusionment of a liberal white couple. The story begins with a brilliant scene of the celebration of the victory of the guerrillas who have been fighting the colonial power. Swept up by the street crowd, the woman finds herself embraced by two soldiers, one a white peasant youth, the other a black guerrilla. She puts an arm around each and kisses each on the cheek. Under the new regime, one is certain, a human being will be a human being; all groups will be treated equally. Although many whites take flight to Europe, the woman and her husband, a lawyer, are eager to participate in building the new nation. Weeks and months pass, however, and, despite the friends the lawyer has among highly placed blacks, the government does not ask the lawyer for his services. There is an atmosphere of hostility toward whites. There is looting and violence. When a friend in nearby Rhodesia, soon to be Zimbabwe, offers the lawyer a position in that country, with reluctance and relief he and his wife pack and go. The couple have wanted the country in which they have spent their adult years to be black-run; when that comes about, they find that there is no role for them.

Something Out There • In the novella that provides the title for Gordimer's volume of short fiction *Something Out There*, a race war looms but has not yet erupted. Acts of violence are taking place; any one of them might well precipitate such a war. In the novella, the "something out there" is a baboon. Gordimer's intention is to suggest that the response of white South Africans to the baboon corresponds to the irrational way they have been responding to the carefully planned symbolic acts of violence by guerrillas. Those acts of violence are handwriting on the wall announcing the coming of race war, which still could be prevented if the writing were read intelligently.

All that the whites want, however, is to be left alone. They want the animal "to be confined in its appropriate place, that's all, zoo or even circus." They want South African blacks to be confined to their appropriate places—locations and townships, black homelands, villages in the bush. As the baboon is "canny about where it was possible somehow to exist off the pickings of plenty," so, too, is the South African black majority, before the cataclysm, somehow able to exist off pickings of white wealth. That wealth will not be shared, only protected, "while charity does not move those who have everything to spare, fear will"—the fear of the baboon, the fear of the guerrilla.

What is the fate of the baboon? It is finally shot and slowly bleeds to death from its wounds. The implication is clear: A similar fate awaits the guerrillas. Gordimer's prime minister speaks: "This government will not stand by and see the peace of mind of its peoples destroyed. . . . We shall not hesitate to strike with all our might at those who harbour terrorists. . . ." The four guerrillas who are the novella's human protagonists, in counterpoint to the movements of the baboon, succeed in blowing up a power station; three escape and it is made clear that they will carry out further attacks. The meaning in this plot—though not in all Gordimer plots on this subject—is that a ruthless government will be a match for those attempting to destroy it.

The fact that the white population is greatly outnumbered makes no difference. They have the education, the technology, the will to defend to the death what they have. Racial justice is an idea with which only a few whites—the man and woman on the power-station mission—are concerned. Protecting privilege and property is what most whites care most about. They cannot understand the few who act from disinterested motives. A minor character in "Something Out There" is a decent white police sergeant. He is totally mystified by the white guerrillas whom he interrogates:

"There's something wrong with all these people who become enemies of their own country. . . . They're enemies because they can't enjoy their lives the way a normal white person in South Africa does."

One of the black guerrillas is dispassionate, determined, fearless Vusi, whose life is dedicated to bringing about black majority rule. Vusi says. "They can't stop us because we can't stop. Never. Every time, when I'm waiting, I know I'm coming nearer." A Vusi, however, is rare. "At the Rendezvous of Victory," another story in this volume, looks ahead to the ultimate black victory. It is about the man who served as commander in chief of the liberation army, known as General Giant. As a warrior, he was invaluable; as a cabinet minister after victory, he is a great burden to his prime minister. He led his people to victory and freedom; in freedom, his chief interest is women.

"A City of the Dead, a City of the Living" • In "A City of the Dead, a City of the Living," a young black man who has committed illegal acts for his people's liberation and who is on the run from the police is given shelter by a township family. With their small house already overcrowded, the family is inconvenienced, but the husband knows his duty. His wife, nursing her fifth child, does not like the idea of taking in a stranger, but the man is pleasant and helpful, and she softens. She softens and begins to feel attracted to him. Frightened, she goes to the police to inform on him, thus betraying the cause of her people's liberation.

"Sins of the Third Age" • "Sins of the Third Age," surprisingly, is not a political story. It is about a couple who survived World War II as displaced persons. Nothing remained of their pasts. They met and in a strange country began to build their lives together. Gordimer is wonderfully evocative as she suggests the passing of years and the deepening of their love. The wife's job as an interpreter takes her on frequent trips, many times to Rome and Milan. On one of her trips, she gets the idea that they should buy a home in Italy for their retirement, near a Piedmontese village. He retires first and goes to Italy to prepare the house. After several months, he appears suddenly and announces, "I've met somebody." His affair eventually ends, but the betrayal destroys the vitality of the marriage. To have done otherwise than to take her husband for granted would have been betrayal on her part. She trusted, and she loses.

"Blinder" • "Blinder" is still another fine story in the 1984 volume. It is about an aging servant woman's loss of her lover, a man who was the main consolation of her life. Ephraim's first loyalty, however, was to his wife and children in his home village; the wife got his earnings, and after his death, her children get his bicycle. When Ephraim suddenly dies, Rose's white family expected her to increase her drinking, to go on a "blinder." Instead, she plays hostess to Ephraim's wife, who has come to the city to see about a pension.

"The Defeated" • "The Defeated" was originally published in the collection *Why Haven't You Written? Selected Stories, 1950-1972* and was reprinted in 1993. It is a first-person narrative concerning a European Jewish family that runs a concession store for black South Africans in a forbidden, filthy part of town. The narrator, a young girl, befriends Miriam Saiyetovitz, whose immigrant parents work long hours selling goods to indecisive customers. The shop they live above is across from an eating establishment teeming with the smells of slaughtered animals. Mrs. Saiyetovitz, "ugly, with the blunt ugliness of a toad; the ugliness not entirely at home in any element— as if the earth were the wrong place, too heavy and magnetic for a creature already blunt," and her dull husband devote their lives to giving their daughter everything they possibly can. When Miriam describes all the birthday gifts her friend received, her mother assures her they will throw her a huge party. As the two girls grow up together and it comes time for university, Miriam's parents labor to send her to a good college. Miriam grows further apart from them, moving into the upper classes as she attends pool parties and eventually marries a doctor. Ultimately, she abandons the two people who made her comfortable life possible. When the narrator, now a grown woman, goes to visit Mr. and Mrs. Saiyetovitz, she learns that they hardly see their daughter or her baby son at all.

In "The Defeated," Gordimer conjures up an evocative variety of discordant but powerful moments: the sweaty smell of the black Africans mingling with the odor of bloodied meat, the toadlike mother juxtaposed with her blossoming daughter, the quietly rage-filled father who takes terrible advantage of his status as a white man to humiliate his black customers. Also noticeable is the contrast between the narrator's relatively benign home life and the concession area where black South Africans are forced to shop among the refuse. "The Defeated" deftly envelops in its fold class differences, the burgeoning of female sexuality, and the tragedy of wasted lives, both of immigrants and of dispossessed indigenous peoples. Gordimer does not openly judge Miriam, but it is clear through the telling of her growing alienation that Miriam is only one of the upwardly mobile Afrikaners whose sights are set on material gain and not on remaining true to those who sacrificed happiness for them.

Paul Marx
With updates by Carol Bishop

Other major works

NOVELS: *The Lying Days*, 1953; *A World of Strangers*, 1958; *Occasion for Loving*, 1963; *The Late Bourgeois World*, 1966; *A Guest of Honour*, 1970; *The Conservationist*, 1974; *Burger's Daughter*, 1979; *July's People*, 1981; *A Sport of Nature*, 1987; *My Son's Story*, 1990; *None to Accompany Me*, 1994; *The House Gun*, 1998; *The Pickup*, 2001; *Get a Life*, 2005.

TELEPLAYS: *A Chip of Glass Ruby*, 1985; *Country Lovers*, 1985; *Oral History*, 1985; *Praise*, 1985.

NONFICTION: *On the Mines*, 1973 (with David Goldblatt); *The Black Interpreters: Notes on African Writing*, 1973; *Lifetimes Under Apartheid*, 1986 (with Goldblatt); *The Essential Gesture: Writing, Politics, and Places*, 1988 (Stephen Clingman, editor); *Conversations with Nadine Gordimer*, 1990 (Nancy Topping Bazin and Marilyn Dallman Seymour, editors); *Three in a Bed: Fiction, Morals, and Politics*, 1991; *Writing and Being*, 1995; *A Writing Life: Celebrating Nadine Gordimer*, 1999 (Andries Walter Oliphant, editor); *Living in Hope and History: Note from Our Century*, 1999.

ANTHOLOGIES: *South African Writing Today*, 1967 (with Lionel Abrahams); *Telling Tales*, 2004.

Bibliography

Bazin, Nancy Topping, and Marilyn Dallman Seymour, eds. *Conversations with Nadine Gordimer.* Jackson: University Press of Mississippi, 1990. The scope of this volume renders it invaluable. It reveals some of Gordimer's insights and attitudes toward her works and their origins, in conversations spanning thirty years. Supplemented by an index and a bibliography.

Driver, Dorothy, Ann Dry, Craig MacKenzie, and John Read, comps. *Nadine Gordimer: A Bibliography of Primary and Secondary Sources, 1937-1992.* London: Hans Zell,

1994. More than three thousand entries listed chronologically. Each critical book or article entry indicates which Gordimer works are covered. Includes a chronology of Gordimer's career to 1993. Several helpful indexes.

Ettin, Andre Vogel. *Betrayals of the Body Politic: The Literary Commitments of Nadine Gordimer.* Charlottesville: University Press of Virginia, 1995. Ettin examines all Gordimer's genres of writing and discovers the recurring themes: betrayal, politics of family, concept of homeland, ethnicity, and feminism.

Head, Dominic. *Nadine Gordimer.* Cambridge, England: Cambridge University Press, 1994. Head interprets Gordimer's first ten novels. Indexed. Select bibliography of works by and about Gordimer. Chronology of Gordimer's career and major South African political events to 1991.

King, Bruce, ed. *The Later Fiction of Nadine Gordimer.* New York: St. Martin's Press, 1993. The introduction, surveying the variety in Gordimer's novels from *The Late Bourgeois World* to *My Son's Story,* is followed by five general essays dealing thematically or stylistically with multiple novels, seven essays dealing with one or two novels in depth, and three essays dealing with short stories. Indexed. Notes on contributors.

Lazar, Karen. "Feminism as 'Piffling'? Ambiguities in Nadine Gordimer's Short Stories." In *The Later Fiction of Nadine Gordimer,* edited by Bruce King. New York: St. Martin's Press, 1993. Examines a number of Gordimer's short stories in terms of her changing attitudes toward women's oppression and feminism, ranging from her early view that many women's issues are "piffling" to views that reveal Gordimer's politicization on the question of gender.

Lomberg, Alan R. "Once More into the Burrows: Nadine Gordimer's Later Short Fiction." In *The Later Fiction of Nadine Gordimer,* edited by Bruce King. New York: St. Martin's Press, 1993. Analysis of how Gordimer continues to examine concerns raised in early stories in her later ones. After discussing how two early stories are developed into a later novella, Lomberg analyzes other stories that Gordimer has written again and again, particularly those that treat love affairs.

May, Charles E., ed. *Masterplots II: Short Story Series, Revised Edition.* 8 vols. Pasadena, Calif.: Salem Press, 2004. Designed for student use, this reference set contains articles providing detailed plot summaries and analyses of nine short stories by Gordimer: "Another Part of the Sky" (vol. 1); "The Defeated" (vol. 2); "Livingstone's Companions" (vol. 4); "Open House" (vol. 5); and "Something Out There," "The Smell of Death and Flowers," "A Soldier's Embrace," "Town and Country Lovers," and "The Train from Rhodesia" (vol. 7).

Smith, Rowland, ed. *Critical Essays on Nadine Gordimer.* Boston: G. K. Hall, 1990. Excellent selection of essays on Gordimer's works. Includes bibliographical references and an index.

Temple-Thurston, Barbara. *Nadine Gordimer Revisited.* New York: Twayne, 1999. Part of Twayne's World Authors series, this is a good updated study of the author and her works. Bibliographical references and an index are provided.

Trump, Martin. "The Short Fiction of Nadine Gordimer." *Research in African Literatures* 17 (Spring, 1986): 341-369. Argues that in her best stories Gordimer describes the hardships of South Africans, particularly women, who suffer social inequality; summarizes a number of stories that illustrate this focus.

Graham Greene

Born: Berkhamsted, Hertfordshire, England; October 2, 1904
Died: Vevey, Switzerland; April 3, 1991

Principal short fiction • *The Basement Room, and Other Stories*, 1935; *The Bear Fell Free*, 1935; *Twenty-four Stories*, 1939 (with James Laver and Sylvia Townsend Warner); *Nineteen Stories*, 1947 (revised 1954; as *Twenty-one Stories*); *A Visit to Morin*, 1959; *A Sense of Reality*, 1963; *May We Borrow Your Husband?, and Other Comedies of the Sexual Life*, 1967; *Collected Stories*, 1972; *How Father Quixote Became a Monsignor*, 1980.

Other literary forms • Graham Greene published twenty-six novels including the posthumously issued *No Man's Land* (2004). His other novels include *The Power and the Glory* (1940; reissued as *The Labyrinthine Ways*), *The Heart of the Matter* (1948), *Brighton Rock* (1938), *The End of the Affair* (1951), and *The Human Factor* (1978). In addition to his many novels and short-story collections, Greene published five plays; three collections of poetry of which the last two, *After Two Years* (1949) and *For Christmas* (1950), were privately printed; travel books, including two centering on Africa; several books of literary essays and film criticism; a biography, *Lord Rochester's Monkey: Being the Life of John Wilmot, Second Earl of Rochester* (1974); and two autobiographical works, *A Sort of Life* (1971) and *Ways of Escape* (1980). In addition, Greene published journals, book reviews, and four children's books.

Achievements • Although the Nobel Prize eluded Graham Greene, he remains one of the most important novelists of the twentieth century. With more screen adaptations than any other modern author, translations into twenty-seven different languages, and book sales exceeding twenty million dollars, Greene enjoyed a combination of critical success and popular acclaim not seen by a British author since the time of Charles Dickens.

In 1984, Great Britain made Greene a Companion of Literature, and in 1986, a member of the elite Order of Merit. France bestowed on Greene one of its highest honors, naming him a Commander of Arts and Letters. In addition, Greene's most famous novels–*The Power and the Glory, The End of the Affair,* and *The Heart of the Matter*—have been acknowledged as literary masterpieces. Combining the outer world of political intrigue and the inner world of the human psyche, Greene's world is one of faith and doubt, honor and betrayal, love and hate. Both the depth and breadth of Greene's work make him one of Britain's most prolific and enduring writers.

Biography • Educated at Berkhamsted School and Balliol College, Oxford, Graham Greene served in the Foreign Office, London, from 1941 to 1944. He married Vivien Dayrell-Browning in 1927 and had two children. He was a staff member of the *London Times* from 1926 to 1930, and he served as movie critic (1937-1940) and literary editor (1940-1941) of *The Spectator*. He also served as director for Eyre and Spottiswoode, publishers (1944-1948), and for The Bodley Head, publishers (1958-1968). The recipient of numerous awards, Greene received the Hawthornden Prize for *The Labyrinthine Ways* in 1941; the Black Memorial Prize for *The Heart of the Matter* in 1949; the

© Amanda Saunders

Shakespeare Prize, Hamburg, 1968; and the Thomas More Medal, 1973. Other awards of distinction include a D.Litt. from the University of Cambridge in 1962, a D.Litt. from Edinburgh University, 1967, Honorary Fellow at Balliol College (Oxford) in 1963, Companion of Honor in 1966, and Chevalier of the French Legion of Honor in 1969. With fifty-four books to his credit, Greene remained a productive writer throughout his life. His last publication was in 1988, but he was said to be working on a new book at the time of his death on April 3, 1991. Greene spent his last years in Antibes, France, and died in Vevey, Switzerland.

Analysis • "Goodness has only once found a perfect incarnation in a human body and never will again, but evil can always find a home there. Human nature is not black and white but black and grey." So said Graham Greene in his essay "The Lost Childhood," and the statement as well as any defines the worldview manifested in his fiction. The "perfect incarnation" is Jesus Christ, and it is against this backdrop of the divine-made-human that Greene draws and measures all the actions of his stories. Whether the stories are explicitly religious in theme, such as "The Hint of an Explanation," or not, or whether Greene chooses to view humanity in a tragic or comic light, the basic vision is the same: human nature steeped in evil and struggling with the fundamental problems of egotism, love and hate, responsibility, innocence and guilt.

As a result of this vision, the central action in Greene's fictional world is invariably betrayal—the Judas complex—betrayal of one's fellow human beings, of one's self, or of one's God. For Greene's heroes and heroines there is no escape; they fall by virtue of their very humanity. Yet their flawed humanity is not presented and then judged from the standpoint of any simplistic orthodoxy. As a thinker and as a fiction writer Greene was a master of paradox, creating a world of moral and theological mystery in which ignobility and failure may often be the road to salvation. Indeed, in Greene's world the worst sin is a presumed innocence which masks a corrosive egotism that effectively cuts human beings off from their fellow creatures and from God.

"The Hint of an Explanation" • Greene's paradoxical treatment of his major themes within a theological perspective is best evident in "The Hint of an Explanation." The story develops in the form of a conversation between the narrator, an agnostic, and another passenger, a Roman Catholic, while the two are riding on a train in England. Although he confesses to have occasionally had intuitions of the existence of God, the agnostic is intellectually revolted by the whole notion of "such a God who can so abandon his creatures to the enormities of Free Will . . . 'When you think of what God—if there is a God—allows. It's not merely the physical agonies, but think of the corruption, even of children.'" The question posed by the agnostic is the mystery of evil—why an omniscient God permits it. In response, the Catholic reminds him that the limitations of human understanding make a full answer impossible for human beings. Nevertheless, he insists, there are "hints" of an explanation, hints caught by men when they are involved in events that do not turn out as they were intended— "by human actors I mean, or by the thing behind the human actors." The suggested "thing" behind the human actors is Satan, and it is the Catholic traveler's conviction of Satan's ultimate impotence and defeat, derived paradoxically from an experience of evil in his own childhood, that provides the underpinning for his own belief in divine providence.

As a child, the Catholic son of a Midland bank manager was tempted by the town freethinker to steal a consecrated Host while serving Mass and deliver it to him. The tempter, a baker named Blacker, is corruption incarnate; he both entices the boy by letting him play with an electric train and promising to give it to him, and at the same time threatens to bleed him with a razor if the boy will not do his bidding. The boy is conscious of the *eternal* consequences his actions will have: "Murder is sufficiently trivial to have its appropriate punishment, but for this act the mind boggled at the thought of any retribution at all." Still, driven by fear of Blacker, he steals the communion wafer—the Body of Christ—and prepares to deliver it to the baker. Nevertheless, when Blacker appears that evening under the boy's bedroom window to collect the Host, his diabolical purposes are defeated when the boy abruptly swallows the communion wafer rather than deliver it into the hands of the Enemy.

As he now recalls this episode from his childhood for the agnostic stranger, the Catholic sees in it a "hint" of the manner in which the mystery of the divine will operates, for that episode was the "odd beginning" of a life that eventually led him to become a priest. Looking back on it now, he sees in his struggle with Blacker nothing less than the struggle between God and Satan for the human soul, and the inevitable defeat of "that Thing," doomed to hopelessness and unhappiness.

Although the story is clear in its religious theme, any danger of its being merely a tract disguised as fiction is skillfully circumvented both by the paradoxical quality of Greene's thought and by his technical skill as a writer. For one thing, Greene undercuts the threat of dogmatic rigidity by creating enormous compassion for the malevolent figure of Blacker, imprisoned in his own misery, at the same time leaving the door open for his eventual redemption through defeat. Moreover, much of this compassion derives from the reader's awareness that, as a human being, Blacker is as much the victim of satanic forces working through him as he is agent of his own fate. Greene sustains a delicate dramatic balance between man's free will and responsibility on the one hand, and on the other, the suggestion or "hint" of supernatural forces at work in human affairs. Greene leaves the reader with a sense of the ineffable mystery of reality, and even the rather hackneyed and mechanical surprise ending of the story—the discovery in the last paragraph that the Catholic is indeed a priest—is consistent with the dramatic logic of the story.

"The Hint of an Explanation" bears many of the trademarks that made Greene one of the most important and widely read artists of the twentieth century, earning him both popularity and high critical esteem. His technical skill and sheer virtuosity as a storyteller stemmed equally from his mastery of the high formalist tradition of Henry James and Joseph Conrad and from the conventions of the melodramatic thriller, with its roots in classical, Renaissance, and Jacobean drama. Mastery of the themes and devices of the thriller—love and betrayal, intrigue, unexpected plot turns, the use of the hunt or chase, danger and violence—gave him a firm foundation upon which to base his subtle explorations of the spiritual condition of human beings in the twentieth century. In short, one of his most important contributions to the short story lies in the way in which he took the conventional form of popular fiction and infused it with a dimension of mystery that often penetrates to the deepest theological levels of experience. Although occasionally the action in Greene's stories may seem contrived, it is contrivance brought off with great dynamism—the energy and unpredictability of life's happenstances—and not the sealed, airless contrivance wrought by the aesthetic purists (whom Greene denounced), those modern fiction writers who have elevated artistic form to an absolute.

Although the social milieu of Greene's fiction is most often the commonplace world of modern England and Europe, it is his ability to infuse this landscape with the sense of mystery that gives the stories their imaginative power and depth. Often the most fertile ground for imagination is childhood, and this may well account for the fact that, as in "The Hint of an Explanation," Greene frequently makes childhood the locus of action for his themes of innocence, egotism, and betrayal. Yet his depiction of childhood is not a sentimentalized, romantic portraiture of innocence betrayed by a hostile world. Greene focuses on childhood because he finds in children a sense of reality which is keener and more alive, a sharper moral imagination, and a more vivid awareness of the personal consequences of their choices as they struggle with the demands of love and hate, loyalty and betrayal. In an essay on James, Greene remarked that "to render the highest justice to corruption you must retain your innocence: you have to be conscious all the time within yourself of treachery to something valuable." Greene's fictional children, still unjaded by maturity, *feel* the potential for treachery both within themselves and surrounding them. Greene was able to make this complex childhood world palpable and render it with great psychological fidelity, perhaps seen best in one of his finest stories, "The Basement Room."

"The Basement Room" • Betrayal and the spiritually fatal consequences of choosing a specious innocence over the unalterable fact of the fallen state are the driving forces in "The Basement Room." Phillip Lane, a seven-year-old upper-class boy, develops a strong bond of friendship with Baines, the family butler, while his parents are gone on a fortnight's holiday. With Baines, whom he sees as a "buccaneer" and man-of-the-world, Philip feels that he has begun "to live," and indeed he *is* initiated into a complex world of love and hate, deceit, the demands of friendship, and eventually betrayal. For Baines and Phillip have a common enemy: Mrs. Baines, a bitter shrew who bullies both her husband and young Phillip. During a day's outing with Baines, Phillip also meets the butler's mistress, Emmy, whom Baines introduces as his "niece." When Mrs. Baines is called away suddenly because of family illness, Baines, in a holiday mood, brings Emmy home for the night, convinced that Phillip will loyally keep his secret.

"Life," however, so complex and confusing in its demands, is too much for young Phillip. The suspicious Mrs. Baines returns unexpectedly during the night and terrifies him, demanding to know where "they" are. Too frightened to answer, Phillip manages to reach the bedroom door in time to see the enraged Mrs. Baines attacking her husband in the upstairs hallway, and in the ensuing struggle she topples over the bannister and is killed. Phillip runs frightened from the house, while the butler quickly removes her body to the foot of the stairs of their basement apartment to make it appear that she has accidentally fallen there. Phillip wanders aimlessly in the streets, waiting for someone to lift the burden of responsibility from him, for "life" has now become intolerable. "He loved Baines, but Baines had involved him in secrets, in fears he didn't understand. That was what happened when you loved—you got involved; and Phillip extricated himself from life, from love, from Baines." So when he is returned home by the police, Phillip betrays Baines, blurting out the facts that condemn the butler.

The effect of Phillip's betrayal—choosing an egotistic "innocence" over the ambiguous responsibilities of love in a fallen world—is disastrous to his own spiritual growth. At the end of the story, Greene skillfully shifts the scene forward to Phillip's own deathbed where, having "never faced it [life] again in sixty years . . . ," he agonizingly relives the moment of his betrayal, murmuring the policeman's question to Baines ("Who is she? Who is she?") as he sinks into death. Greene's point is clear: Phillip's spiritual development stopped at the age of seven when he refused the consequences of his love for Baines. Instead of the reality of being a fallen, yet free and mature, creature, he chose egotism and the illusion of innocence. The innocence Phillip elects, however, is not a true childlike quality. On the contrary, the childhood Phillip loses is exactly that keen awareness of the potentialities for love and treachery, of the power of evil and the vital sense of mystery inspiring terror and awe which constitutes for Greene the real human condition. We are reminded of Greene's quoting from Æ's poem "Germinal": "In the lost childhood of Judas, Christ was betrayed."

"The Destructors" • Greene's depiction of the lost childhood theme in "The Basement Room" is devastating and terrible, but he can also present the same theme in a manner which is devastatingly funny. Such is the case in "The Destructors," in which the callous youngster Trevor leads a gang of neighborhood boys in the systematic dismantling of the house of Mr. Thomas—"Old Misery" as the children call him—a retired builder and decorator. Because his own father was once an architect, Trevor fully understands the value of Old Misery's house; indeed, it is an elegant, two-hundred-year-old structure built by Sir Christopher Wren, which embodies the refinements of tradition. In fact, Old Misery's house is an emblem of civilization itself, the whole legacy of humane values and order and design passed from generation to generation, still imposing even though it stands amid the ruins of bombed-out postwar London. Fully conscious of its historical and cultural significance, Trevor diabolically mobilizes the gang of youths to bring the house down, working from the inside "like worms, don't you see, in an apple."

Trevor ingratiates himself with Old Misery by asking to tour the inside of the house and then, learning that the owner will be away for a weekend holiday, sets his plan of destruction in motion. Working floor by floor, the gang wrecks everything—furniture, china and ornamental bric-a-brac, doors, personal mementos, porcelain fixtures, the winding staircase, and parquet floors; even Old Misery's hidden cache of pound notes is burned up. The evil inspired by Trevor goes beyond simple thievery; it is destruction for its own sake, a satanic love of chaos. When Trevor's minion Blackie asks him if he hates Old Misery, the leader replies coldly that "There'd be no fun if I hated him. . . . 'All this love and hate,' he said, 'it's soft, it's hooey. There's only things, Blackie. . . .'" In Trevor's remark Greene has touched the nerve of a fundamental side of the modern consciousness, its brutal amorality and contempt for the past.

Greene's inventive genius manages to make "The Destructors" humorous, although terrifyingly so. Trevor's plan to destroy the house is endangered when Old Misery returns prematurely from his holiday, but Trevor is up to the challenge and instantly contrives a plot to trap the aged owner in his own outdoor privy. Locked in by the gang for the night, Old Misery can only sit helplessly and wonder what the faint sounds of hammering and scraping mean. The next morning a driver arrives to remove his lorry from the parking lot next door, and as he pulls away, unaware of the rope tying his truck to the foundation beams, Old Misery's house comes down in a heap of rubble. The driver manages to free Old Misery from the privy, but he cannot restrain himself from laughing at the scene of devastation. "'How dare you laugh,' Mr. Thomas said, 'It was my house. My house.'" The driver can only reply, chuckling, "I'm sorry. I can't help it, Mr. Thomas. There's nothing personal, but you got to admit it's funny."

"The Destructors" represents Greene at his best in presenting his vision of human perversity and folly in a comic vein. The depiction of Trevor's unmitigated evil is frightening, but it is finely balanced by the humor of the final scene; and in the lorry driver's laughter and the absurdly pathetic character of Old Misery the reader finds a basic affirmation of the common values of human existence which, paradoxically, triumph over the cold diabolism of young Trevor. It is he who is the ultimate loser. Knowing the world only as "things," he himself has become a thing—T. the destructor—and he cannot respond either with love or hate to the life around him.

Greene's stories, with their remarkable craftsmanship, exercise a powerful fascination on the reader. Even at their most melodramatic, his stories unfailingly create a plausible sense of reality because they touch the full range of human experience: petty foibles, corruption, deceit, love, responsibility, hope, and despair. Whether Greene's emphasis is tragic or comic, or a wry mingling of both, the reader is again and again confronted in the stories with the fundamental mystery of existence on earth, making them at once rich, entertaining, and profound.

John F. Desmond
With updates by Karen Priest

Other major works

CHILDREN'S LITERATURE: *The Little Train*, 1946; *The Little Fire Engine*, 1950 (also known as *The Little Red Fire Engine*, 1952); *The Little Horse Bus*, 1952; *The Little Steam Roller: A Story of Mystery and Detection*, 1953.

PLAYS: *The Heart of the Matter*, pr. 1950 (with Basil Dean; adaptation of his novel); *The Living Room*, pr., pb. 1953; *The Potting Shed*, pr., pb. 1957; *The Complaisant Lover*, pr., pb. 1959; *Carving a Statue*, pr., pb. 1964; *The Return of A. J. Raffles: An Edwardian Comedy in Three Acts Based Somewhat Loosely on E. W. Hornung's Characters in "The Amateur Cracksman,"* pr., pb. 1975; *For Whom the Bell Chimes*, pr. 1980, pb. 1983; *Yes and No*, pr. 1980, pb. 1983; *The Collected Plays of Graham Greene*, pb. 1985.

ANTHOLOGIES: *The Old School: Essays by Divers Hands*, 1934; *The Best of Saki*, 1950; *The Spy's Bedside Book: An Anthology*, 1957 (with Hugh Greene); *The Bodley Head Ford Madox Ford*, 1962, 1963 (4 volumes); *An Impossible Woman: The Memories of Dottoressa Moor of Capri*, 1975.

NOVELS: *The Man Within*, 1929; *The Name of Action*, 1930; *Rumour at Nightfall*, 1931; *Stamboul Train: An Entertainment*, 1932 (pb. in U.S. as *Orient Express: An Entertainment*, 1933); *It's a Battlefield*, 1934; *England Made Me*, 1935; *A Gun for Sale: An Entertainment*, 1936 (pb. in U.S. as *This Gun for Hire: An Entertainment*); *Brighton Rock*, 1938; *The Confidential Agent*, 1939; *The Power and the Glory*, 1940 (reissued as *The Labyrinthine Ways*); *The Ministry of Fear: An Entertainment*, 1943; *The Heart of the Matter*, 1948; *The Third*

Man: An Entertainment, 1950; *The Third Man and The Fallen Idol*, 1950; *The End of the Affair*, 1951; *Loser Takes All: An Entertainment*, 1955; *The Quiet American*, 1955; *Our Man in Havana: An Entertainment*, 1958; *A Burnt-Out Case*, 1961; *The Comedians*, 1966; *Travels with My Aunt*, 1969; *The Honorary Consul*, 1973; *The Human Factor*, 1978; *Dr. Fischer of Geneva: Or, The Bomb Party*, 1980; *Monsignor Quixote*, 1982; *The Tenth Man*, 1985; *The Captain and the Enemy*, 1988; *No Man's Land*, 2004.

MISCELLANEOUS: *The Portable Graham Greene*, 1973 (Philip Stout Ford, editor).

NONFICTION: *Journey Without Maps: A Travel Book*, 1936; *The Lawless Roads: A Mexican Journal*, 1939 (reissued as *Another Mexico*); *British Dramatists*, 1942; *Why Do I Write? An Exchange of Views Between Elizabeth Bowen, Graham Greene, and V. S. Pritchett*, 1948; *The Lost Childhood, and Other Essays*, 1951; *Essais Catholiques*, 1953 (Marcelle Sibon, translator); *In Search of a Character: Two African Journals*, 1961; *The Revenge: An Autobiographical Fragment*, 1963; *Victorian Detective Fiction*, 1966; *Collected Essays*, 1969; *A Sort of Life*, 1971; *The Pleasure Dome: The Collected Film Criticism, 1935-40, of Graham Greene*, 1972 (John Russell-Taylor, editor; pb. in U.S. as *The Pleasure-Dome: Graham Greene on Film, Collected Film Criticism, 1935-1940*); *Lord Rochester's Monkey: Being the Life of John Wilmot, Second Earl of Rochester*, 1974; *Ways of Escape*, 1980; *J'accuse: The Dark Side of Nice*, 1982; *Getting to Know the General: The Story of an Involvement*, 1984.

POETRY: *Babbling April: Poems*, 1925; *After Two Years*, 1949; *For Christmas*, 1950.

RADIO PLAY: *The Great Jowett*, 1939.

SCREENPLAYS: *Twenty-one Days*, 1937; *The New Britain*, 1940; *Brighton Rock*, 1947 (adaptation of his novel; with Terence Rattigan); *The Fallen Idol*, 1948 (adaptation of his novel; with Lesley Storm and William Templeton); *The Third Man*, 1949 (adaptation of his novel; with Carol Reed); *The Stranger's Hand*, 1954 (with Guy Elmes and Giorgino Bassani); *Loser Takes All*, 1956 (adaptation of his novel); *Saint Joan*, 1957 (adaptation of George Bernard Shaw's play); *Our Man in Havana*, 1959 (adaptation of his novel); *The Comedians*, 1967 (adaptation of his novel).

TELEPLAY: *Alas, Poor Maling*, 1975.

Bibliography

Bayley, John. "Graham Greene: The Short Stories." In *Graham Greene: A Reevaluation*. New York: St. Martin's Press, 1990. Basing his comments on his analysis of "The Hint of an Explanation," Bayley argues that many Greene stories have a hidden subject in a sense that none of his novels does. Claims that by means of almost invisible contrasts and incongruities, the story leads the reader both away from and toward its central revelation.

De Vitis, A. A. *Graham Greene*. Rev. ed. Boston: Twayne, 1986. Most interesting in this volume are an overview of critical opinion about Greene, a chronology, and a chapter on the short stories. Supplemented by a thorough primary bibliography and an annotated bibliography of secondary sources.

Kelly, Richard. *Graham Greene*. New York: Frederick Ungar, 1984. General introduction to Greene and his work. The chapter on the short stories discusses "The Destructors," "The Hint of an Explanation," and "The Basement Room" as the best of Greene's stories.

_____. *Graham Greene: A Study of the Short Fiction*. New York: Twayne, 1992. Discusses the influence of Henry James, Guy de Maupassant, and W. Somerset Maugham on Greene's stories, but also discusses how the stories reflect Greene's own personal demons. Includes an interview with Greene, his introduction to his *Collected Stories*, and three previously published essays by other critics.

May, Charles E., ed. *Masterplots II: Short Story Series, Revised Edition.* 8 vols. Pasadena, Calif.: Salem Press, 2004. Designed for student use, this reference set contains articles providing detailed plot summaries and analyses of six short stories by Greene: "Across the Bridge," "The Basement Room," and "Cheap in August" (vol. 1); "The Destructors" and "A Drive in the Country" (vol. 2); and "The Hint of an Explanation" (vol. 3).

Meyers, Jeffrey, ed. *Graham Greene: A Revaluation.* New York: St. Martin's Press, 1990. These essays by eight scholars offer critical analyses of Greene's accomplishments, in the shadow of his death.

Miller, R. H. *Understanding Graham Greene.* Columbia: University of South Carolina Press, 1990. Guide to all of Greene's writing. The style is concise yet informative and evaluative, but the author runs too quickly through the canon. Bibliography and index.

O'Prey, Paul. *A Reader's Guide to Graham Greene.* New York: Thames and Hudson, 1988. Critical overview of Greene's fiction. The excellent introduction familiarizes the reader with Greene's major themes. Supplemented by a complete primary bibliography and a brief list of critical works.

Sherry, Norman. *The Life of Graham Greene.* 2 vols. New York: Viking Press, 1989-1995. The first two parts of what is certainly the most comprehensive, most authoritative account of Greene's life yet published, written with complete access to his papers and the full cooperation of family, friends, and the novelist himself. Includes a generous collection of photographs, a bibliography, and an index.

Smith, Grahame. *The Achievement of Graham Greene.* Sussex, England: Harvester Press, 1986. Includes an excellent introduction, with an overview of themes and biographical data. Contains chapters on "Fiction and Belief" and "Fiction and Politics," as well as sections titled "The Man of Letters" and "Greene and Cinema." Augmented by a select bibliography.

Brothers Grimm

Jacob Grimm

Born: Hanau, near Kassel, Hesse-Kassel (now in Germany); January 4, 1785
Died: Berlin, Prussia (now in Germany); September 20, 1863

Wilhelm Grimm

Born: Hanau, near Kassel, Hesse-Kassel (now in Germany); February 24, 1786
Died: Berlin, Prussia (now in Germany); December 16, 1859

Principal short fiction • *Kinder-und Hausmärchen*, 1812, 1815 (revised 1819-1822; *German Popular Stories*, 1823-1826; 2 volumes; better known as *Grimm's Fairy Tales*).

Other literary forms • The Brothers Grimm published important studies of German tales and mythology, as well as philological works recognized for their importance to the study of the German language.

Achievements • The tales collected and edited by the Brothers Grimm are the defining instances of *Märchen*, a term only approximately translated by "fairy tale." At a time when the changes wrought by the Industrial Revolution threatened to make the traditions of oral storytelling disappear, Jacob and Wilhelm Grimm were able to preserve these tales in written form. Now, in the Anglo-Saxon world at least, the tales recounted by the Brothers Grimm are more familiar than any stories except those of the Bible. The literary influence of the collection has been considerable: It has shaped much of subsequent children's literature and has inspired a great many sophisticated fictions, particularly among the German Romantics, the English Victorians, and the so-called Fabulators of the mid-twentieth century. Most important, however, has been the direct human influence of the tales. The collection epitomizes the psychological wisdom of generations of storytellers, and the tales themselves provide for nearly every child in the West a first map of the territory of the imagination.

Biography • Both of the Brothers Grimm devoted their lives to literary and philological scholarship. Following in their father's footsteps, they studied law at Marburg, but, under the influence of Johann Gottfried Herder and Clemens Brentano, they turned from the law, and between 1806 and 1826, first at Marburg and later at the library of the Elector in Kassel, they collaborated in the study of folklore, producing not only the *Märchen* but also *Deutsche Sagen* (1816-1818; *German Legends*, 1981), on local historical legends and other works. In 1830, they left Kassel to become librarians and later professors at Göttingen. After a decade of largely independent work, the two collaborated again on a monumental lexicon of the German language, the *Deutsches Wörterbuch* (1854). The project was begun in 1838, was carried to Berlin when the brothers were appointed professors at the university in 1841, and was completed only in 1961—Wilhelm had died working on the letter *D*, Jacob at *F*.

Wilhelm Carl Grimm was in his own right an editor of medieval texts who did important work on runes and Germanic legend. Jacob Ludwig Carl Grimm was one of the greatest scholars in the history of a nation of scholars. His *Deutsche Mythologie* (1835; *Teutonic Mythology*, 1880-1888), attempted to establish a theoretical base for the *Märchen* collected earlier, viewing them as the detritus of a German mythology suppressed by Christianity. In thus laying the groundwork for all further speculation on the origins of folklore and myth, he has come to be acknowledged as the founder of the scientific study of folklore. At the same time, he is the uncontested founder of the systematic study of the German language and indeed of historical linguistics itself; this assessment is based on the strength of his work that begins with the formulation of Grimm's law in *Deutsche Grammatik* (1819-1837) and culminates in the *Deutsches Wörtebuch.*

Analysis • *Grimm's Fairy Tales* came into being in the context of German Romanticism, particularly with its renewed interest in the medieval past. Just as European society was becoming urban, industrial, and literate, a growing nationalism turned attention to folk culture. The Brothers Grimm first began collecting songs and stories for the poet Clemens Brentano and his brother-in-law Achim von Arnim, who had themselves collaborated on an influential collection of folksongs, *Des Knaben Wunderhorn* (1805, 1808; the boy's wonderhorn), still familiar from Gustav Mahler's many settings of its songs. The Grimms drew on oral as well as printed sources, interviewing both peasant storytellers and middle-class urban informants. The resulting collection of some two hundred stories preserved a substantial body of folklore, fortuitously, at the very moment when its milieu was being irreparably destroyed by the modernization of nineteenth century Europe. Translated into at least seventy languages, *Grimm's Fairy Tales* stands as the model for every subsequent collection of folklore, however much more sophisticated in theory or method. The brothers' own notes and commentaries on the tales, included in the second edition, form the basis of the science of folklore.

One source of the appeal of these tales is their complex chemistry of both art and artlessness. The Grimms did not think of themselves as authors of short fiction but as what would now be considered anthropologists. They set for themselves the task of contriving, from many different versions of any tale, an account that achieved artistic integrity without sacrificing folkloric quality. This meant sometimes restoring details that seemed to have been dropped or distorted in the course of oral tradition, or deleting what seemed purely literary invention. Many decisions were arbitrary since this was, after all, the beginning of a discipline, and the Grimms sometimes changed their minds, as differences between the first and second editions make clear. They were guided on the whole, however, by an aim of reconstructing prototypes which they assumed to be oral. Thus, in each tale they were responding to two different challenges. First, they attempted to preserve and even enhance the atmosphere of performance through traditional rhetorical devices such as repetition of songs and narrative formulas in which the audience would share and through the general circumstantial quality characteristic of every spellbinding teller. At the same time, their versions were meant to be definitive and fixed in print, a medium with aesthetic demands of its own that had to be met.

"Six Soldiers of Fortune" • As a result, within the Grimm style, which is instantly recognizable as a matter of motif, several substyles of narrative are apparent. There are some tales that strike the reader as archetypal for their transparency of structure. "Six Soldiers of Fortune," for example, assembles a group of soldiers, each with a unique preternatural power, makes use of, and so in a sense exhausts, each power in a deadly contest for the hand of a princess, and then dismisses the group with a treasure to divide. Perhaps most lucid of all is the haunting "The Fisherman and His Wife"; this tale combines heightening ambitions and lowering weather against the measured rhythm of wishes demanded and granted, all strung on the thread of a summoning spell sung six times to the generous fish, an enchanted prince who disturbingly *remains* enchanted throughout the tale, until in the end everything is as it was. In this tale, no wish is of-

Library of Congress

fered at first, until the wife, knowing with the logic of fairy tale that enchanted fish grant wishes, sends her husband back. After wishing herself from hovel to cottage to castle, however, her third wish is for a change not of station but of identity. She wishes to be king, and this moves beyond the rule of three to the inordinate and outlandish: emperor, pope, ruler of the sun and moon, things she cannot be.

"The Lady and the Lion" • Other tales seem authentic not for their clarity but for a sense of free-ranging invention in loose, barely articulated forms. "The Lady and the Lion" is a prime example of a tale that seems ready to go anywhere a teller is inclined to take it. It relies heavily on familiar but heterogeneous motifs, and so while it fascinates readers from moment to moment (especially if heard rather than read) with an almost Asian opulence of invention, it seems in the end unmotivated.

"Godfather Death" • The tension between the commitment to transcribe tales as told and the need to devise viable written artifacts can best be exemplified by contrasting two stories. In "Godfather Death," a man seeking a godfather for his thirteenth child rejects God himself and the Devil but accepts Death because he "makes all equal." When the boy is grown, Death gives him an herb that restores life, with these instructions: "If I stand by the head of the sick-bed, administer this herb and the man will recover; but if I stand at the foot, the man is mine, and you must say that nothing can save him." The boy becomes a famous healer. Once when the King is sick, with Death at his feet, the boy risks using the herb to save him, but Death pardons him with a warning. Later, however, the King's daughter is in the same situation, and for love of her the doctor again overrules Death. Death seizes him with an icy hand and leads him to a cave where thousands of candles are burning, some very large, some mere stubs. "Show me the light of my life," says the doctor, and he finds it guttering. He begs his godfather to replace it, and the story ends like this:

Death behaved as if he were going to fulfill his wish, and took hold of a tall new candle, but as he desired to revenge himself, he purposely made a mistake in fixing it, and the little piece fell down and was extinguished. The physician too fell on the ground; now he himself was in the hands of Death.

"The Wonderful Glass" • *Grimm's Fairy Tales* preserves another version of this story, "The Wonderful Glass," which is, from the point of view of a written tale, almost incoherent. It is less carefully composed than "Godfather Death": Only one stranger appears, the child is merely "another child," and the gift of healing is given oddly not to the child but to his father; in fact the child plays no role at all. The father never misuses the gift but one day decides to visit the godfather. Five steps lead to the house. On the first a mop and a broom are quarreling, on the next he finds a "number of dead fingers," on the next a heap of human heads give him directions, on the next a fish is frying itself in a pan. At the top the doctor peeks through the keyhole and sees the godfather with a set of horns on his head. When he enters the house, the godfather hides under the bedclothes. When he says, "I saw you through the keyhole with a pair of horns on your head," the godfather shouts, "That is not true," in such a terrible voice that the doctor runs away and is never heard of again. "The Wonderful Glass" is hardly worth preserving except as a transcript of a clumsy horror story. The immense superiority of "Godfather Death" may suggest how the Grimms' decision to proceed by artful selection among versions rather than by wholesale recasting in another mode produced masterpieces. Again and again their editorial tact added formal power to the visual interest and psychological depth of the inherited stories.

"Rapunzel" • "Rapunzel," for example, begins like many of the *Märchen* ("Snow White," "Sleeping Beauty," "The Almond Tree"), with a couple who wish for a child. A small window in their house overlooks a witch's garden, and one night the husband climbs over the high wall to steal some "rapunze," a salad green. He is soon caught by the witch, however, and to save his life he promises to amend the theft by giving her his child when it is born. It was pregnancy that made his wife crave rapunze; the unborn child thus causes the theft and by a rough justice replaces the thing stolen. The witch takes her at birth, names her Rapunzel, and walls her up, even more securely than the plant she replaces, in a tower accessible only by a high window. This generates the central image of the tale: the long-haired nubile girl imprisoned in the tower. Like the husband, the Prince (potential husband of the next generation) climbs over the wall to steal the witch's Rapunze(l), and he, too, is eventually caught by the possessive witch. Learning of the Prince's visits, she banishes Rapunzel to a wasteland, first cutting off her hair, which will be used to lure the Prince to a confrontation. He escapes, but in his terror falls on thorns that blind him. After years of wandering, he hears Rapunzel's voice again, they embrace, and her tears restore his sight.

"Rapunzel" is usually read as a story of maturation, with Rapunzel as the central figure, but she is a passive character throughout, an instrument in the relations of others. It is at least equally a tale of possessiveness and longing. The parents desire a child; in the wife's craving for greens the reader sees the child at once gained and lost. Like the parents (although more like Rumpelstiltskin) the witch desires a child, and the Prince's longing is obvious—it is the chief character trait of princes throughout the *Märchen*. The remarkable dearth of magic is related to these themes. In spite of the presence of the witch, the only magic is the healing tears of love. In other versions the witch's magic harms the prince; here it is mysteriously not her doing, but ronic coincidence. The pathos of that reticence is owed to the Brothers Grimm; their instinct for invoking folk style is apparent in the repeated motifs but above all in their inspired invention of the phrase, "Rapunzel, Rapunzel, let down your hair," which sounds, even when the reader knows better, like the archaic root of the whole story.

Thus, the Grimms reconciled the values of folklore with what were recognized as the requirements of short fiction, but they were scrupulously aware that the versions they contrived were only moments seized out of the continuing tradition of telling and retelling. The proper habitation of the *Märchen* is in the mouths of storytellers. Form, the proportion of parts, and even readers' sympathies are always being accommodated to new audiences in new circumstances. As early as 1893, Marian Cox could study 345 variants of "Cinderella" alone. *Grimm's Fairy Tales*, then, were folktales accommodated to print: more symmetrical, more compressed, as a rule spatially rather than linearly conceived, and with formal rhythms replacing the lost rhythm of speech. The brothers' devotion to their originals or to the sources behind their originals, however, is apparent. As the example of "Rapunzel" suggests, their versions are much less stylized than other literary versions; the reader never feels the presence of an author as in those printed versions that antedate the Grimms, such as Charles Perrault and Giambattista Basile. They would never say, as Perrault does, that Sleeping Beauty was beautiful even though she dressed like someone's grandmother in clothes out of fashion for a century.

Thanks to the Grimms, the *Märchen* have survived in a new kind of world, but the process of accommodation continues. One of the measures of how thoroughly these tales have been internalized in the West is the shock every reader feels on first reading the Grimms' own account of tales so profoundly familiar. This is not how they are remembered, and the difference frankly reveals how tastes have changed in the intervening years. Through several generations of editors, and especially of parents, the *Märchen* have become more magical, much more romantic, and decidedly less violent than the Grimms' own versions.

Magic is a most important variable. Although there is plenty of it in the tales, modern readers will find the Grimms often unexpectedly discreet in the use of magic.

"The Little Farmer" • There is even at least one plainly antimagical story, "The Little Farmer," in which the protagonist defeats a whole town because the people are gullible about magic (eventually they are all drowned when, after the farmer tells them he collected a fine flock of sheep under water, they see fleecy clouds reflected on the surface as confirmation of his story and jump in). There is much use of gratuitous magic, not only for ornament but also, in particular, to establish a tone of fantasy at the start of a story. The beginning of "Sleeping Beauty" offers an extreme example: A frog jumps out of the water, prophesies that the queen will soon bear a daughter, and disappears never to be mentioned again. Indeed, supernatural helpers put in abrupt appearances throughout the tales.

"Snow White" • Often in reading *Grimm's Fairy Tales*, however, the reader finds coincidence or rationalization where memory led him to expect magic. Thus, in "Snow White," although the wicked queen has her magic mirror, much that could be magic is more nearly pharmacology. Even the revival of Snow White is not, as Walt Disney and memory would have it, by the magic of a kiss from Prince Charming, but like this: The dwarfs gave the coffin to the Prince, who had his servants carry it away.

Now it happened that as they were going along they stumbled over a bush, and with the shaking a bit of the poisoned apple flew out of her throat. It was not long before she opened her eyes, threw open the cover of the coffin, and sat up, alive and well. "Oh dear, where am I?," cried she. The King's son answered, full of joy, "you are near me. . . . Come with me to my father's castle and you shall be my bride." And Snow White was kind, and went with him.

An earlier generation of commentators would have woven from bush and fruit a myth of fall and redemption, but at least as interesting is the calculated avoidance of overt magic even in resurrection. The blinding of the Prince in "Rapunzel" is treated with similar ambiguity.

Violence • Apart from the treatment of magic, the most unexpected feature of the Grimms' tales is their violence. The stories are full of treachery, mutilation, cannibalism, and over and over again the visual and visceral impact of the sight of red blood against pale skin, white snow, black wood, or stone. This is most shocking in the well-known stories. When Snow White's stepmother cannot resist coming to the wedding to see if the girl really is "a thousand times more fair," she finds that "they had ready red-hot iron shoes, in which she had to dance until she fell down dead."

The ending of "Cinderella" is similar, although it is better integrated with the shape of the story. The two stepsisters cut off parts of their feet to fit into the tiny slipper, but as each in turn passes the grave of Cinderella's true mother, which is marked by a hazel tree grown from a twig she asked as a gift from her father and watered with her tears, two birds perched in the tree, her helpers earlier, make known the mutilations so that at last Cinderella can put on the shoe that was made for her. As a result, she marries the Prince, and the tale ends with the same birds pecking out the eyes of the stepsisters.

Violence in *Grimm's Fairy Tales* nearly always has a human origin. The reader grows accustomed to witches, stepmothers, and evil elder siblings, but the overwhelming sense of the world here is optimistic. The stories regularly assert a harmony between humans and nature, often seen as more reliable than human harmony: The birds will help when other people will not. By their plotting, the stories also project a harmony in time. In the end, the good live happily ever after, while for the evil there are dire and, to most modern readers, disproportionate punishments. The harmonious close of a Grimm tale is grounded on a faith in justice. Indeed, several of the tales have this as their theme: No crime can remain hidden; truth will come to light. Behind this is a sense of divine Providence, for beneath all the magic the milieu of these tales is thoroughly Christian. There is hardly a trace of the tragic weight of Germanic myth in even the most harrowing of the *Märchen*.

"The Singing Bone" • Consider "The Singing Bone": Through the clear water of a river, a herdsman sees on the sandy bottom a bone as white as snow. He retrieves it to make a mouthpiece for his horn, and at once it begins to sing its own story, "I killed the wild boar, and my brother slew me,/ Then gained the Princess by pretending it was he." The marvel is brought to the King, the victim's skeleton is found, the wicked brother is ordered drowned, and the bones are "laid to rest in a beautiful grave." This is quite brutal, even in summary, but the formal symmetries of the violence here reinforce the demonstration of justice. If a modern reader tends to worry about the bereft Princess and is less than satisfied with a beautiful grave, it may be that he has lost faith in any ultimate distribution of justice. That may be the chief reason that so much of the violence of the Grimms' tales is now suppressed in the telling.

The Grimms' theory of folklore as the doctrine of a mythology is now discredited, but they were right to sense the tremendous resonance of these tales in the imagination. More recently, psychological approaches from Sigmund Freud and Carl Jung down to Bruno Bettelheim have pointed to the archetypal force of these stories. This force is not the Grimms' creation; it is a wisdom concentrated through a long process of transmission. What the Grimm brothers contributed was an array of formal devices learned in the context of literate fiction—devices that increased the strength and resilience of the tales in the period when their survival was most threatened.

Along with the form of the stories, what the Grimms' retelling often particularly enhanced were the visual images. The traditional tales were full of images of seminal power from which much of the psychological impact emanated. In stories meant to be heard, however, the visual imagination is free, and images can be invoked by a word or two. Consciously or not, the Brothers Grimm realized that in the act of reading, the visual imagination is engaged, so images must be sharpened and developed in order to act on a preoccupied eye. As a result, *Grimm's Fairy Tales* is crowded with images of emblematic power such as the gingerbread house, the palace of sleepers, Snow White in her glass coffin, and Little Red Riding Hood and the bedded wolf. These images have attracted the finest illustrators (and animators) of every intervening generation to join with storytellers in transmitting a body of tales that speaks to readers, it seems, in the native language of the imagination.

Laurence A. Breiner

Other major works

NONFICTION: *Deutsche Sagen*, 1816-1818 (*German Legends*, 1981; 2 volumes); *Deutsche Grammatik*, 1819-1837 (by Jacob Grimm alone); *Über deutsche Runen*, 1821 (by Wilhelm Grimm alone); *Die deutsche Heldensage*, 1829 (by Wilhelm Grimm alone); *Deutsche Mythologie*, 1835-1837 (4 volumes; by Jacob Grimm alone; *Teutonic Mythology*, 1880-1888); *Geschichte der deutschen Sprache*, 1848 (by Jacob Grimm alone); *Deutsches Wörterbuch*, 1852-1862 (3 volumes).

Bibliography

Bettelheim, Bruno. *The Uses of Enchantment: The Meaning and Importance of Fairy Tales.* New York: Random House, 1976. Bettelheim's book discusses the major motifs and themes of fairy tales from a Freudian psychological perspective, focusing on their meanings for the growing child. He discusses many of the tales collected by the Brothers Grimm and in part 2 examines in detail eight of the stories still popular today. He includes a useful bibliography, though many of the books listed are in German, and an index.

Grimm, Jacob, and Wilhelm Grimm. *The Complete Fairy Tales of the Brothers Grimm.* Edited and translated by Jack Zipes. New York: Bantam Press, 1992. This is perhaps the best of the many translations in English. The introduction is informative, and data are also given on the informants the Grimm brothers used in their research. Also included are thirty-two tales that the Grimms dropped from earlier editions, as well as eight variants showing how the Grimms edited and re-created tales as they were compiling their collection.

Haase, Donald, ed. *The Reception of Grimms' Fairy Tales: Responses, Reactions, Revisions.* Detroit: Wayne State University Press, 1993. Valuable essays on public and critical opinions of the Grimms' tales.

Kamenetsky, Christa. *The Brothers Grimm and Their Critics: Folktales and the Quest for Meaning.* Athens: Ohio University Press, 1992. Surveys the Grimms' lives, theories and practices, critical appraisals of their folktales, and extensive bibliographical resources.

Michaelis-Jena, Ruth. *The Brothers Grimm.* London: Routledge and Kegan Paul, 1970. Michaelis-Jena has written a thorough biography of Jacob and Wilhelm Grimm, and she includes a chapter called "The 'Nursery and Household Tales' and Their Influence," which provides information on early reactions to the collection and its translations, noting that the tales spurred an interest in collection of other national folktales. Contains an index and bibliography.

Murphy, G. Ronald. *The Owl, the Raven, and the Dove: The Religious Meaning of the Grimms' Magic Fairy Tales.* New York: Oxford University Press, 2000. Examines the religious aspects of the tales. Includes bibliographical references and an index.

Paradiz, Valerie. *Clever Maids: The Secret History of the Grimm Fairy Tales.* New York: Basic Books 2005. Examination of the source of the Grimm brothers' collection of fairy tales, specifically; Paradiz argues that many of the tales were contributed not by peasants from the German countryside but rather by educated and aristocratic German women.

Tatar, Maria. *The Hard Facts of the Grimms' Fairy Tales.* Princeton, N.J.: Princeton University Press, 1987. Tatar provides close readings of many of the tales, mostly from a psychological perspective, though the book is aimed at a more scholarly audience than Bettelheim's. She examines typical motifs and situations and attempts to bring in the perspectives of folklorists, cultural anthropologists, and literary critics, as well as that of the psychologists. Notes, index.

Zipes, Jack. *The Brothers Grimm: From Enchanted Forests to the Modern World.* New York: Routledge, 1988. Zipes's book arose out of talks he gave at various conferences. The work is quite scholarly, and many of the chapters examine the effects of the tales on modern society and place them in a sociohistorical context. Supplemented by notes, a good bibliography, and an index.

Bret Harte

Born: Albany, New York; August 25, 1836
Died: Camberley, Surrey, England; May 5, 1902

Principal short fiction • *Condensed Novels,* 1867; *The Lost Galleon, and Other Tales,* 1867; *The Luck of Roaring Camp, and Other Sketches,* 1870; *Stories of the Sierras,* 1872; *Mrs. Skaggs's Husbands,* 1873; *Tales of the Argonauts,* 1875; *Thankful Blossom,* 1877; *Drift from Two Shores,* 1878; *The Story of a Mine,* 1878; *The Twins of Table Mountain,* 1879; *Flip and Found at Blazing Star,* 1882; *In the Carquinez Woods,* 1883; *Maruja,* 1885; *A Millionaire of Rough-and-Ready,* 1887; *The Crusade of the Excelsior,* 1887; *A Phyllis of the Sierras,* 1888; *Cressy,* 1889; *The Heritage of Dedlow Marsh,* 1889; *A Waif of the Plains,* 1890; *A First Family of Tasajara,* 1891; *Sally Dows,* 1893; *A Protégée of Jack Hamlin's,* 1894; *The Bell-Ringer of Angel's,* 1894; *In a Hollow of the Hills,* 1895; *Barker's Luck, and Other Stories,* 1896; *Three Partners,* 1897; *Stories in Light and Shadow,* 1898; *Tales of Trail and Town,* 1898; *Mr. Jack Hamlin's Meditation,* 1899; *Condensed Novels: Second Series,* 1902; *Trent's Trust,* 1903; *The Story of Enriquez,* 1924.

Other literary forms • Bret Harte attempted practically every form of *belles lettres* common in the nineteenth century. He wrote several collections of poems, almost entirely forgotten in the years since his death. Indeed, his poetic reputation to modern readers depends completely on the success of one poem, his comic verse masterpiece "Plain Language from Truthful James," more commonly known as "The Heathen Chinee," published in 1870. He wrote and edited newspaper material, essays, the novel *Gabriel Conroy* (1876), and some excellent satirical work, notably his *Condensed Novels*; and he collaborated with Mark Twain on a play, *Ah Sin* (1877), based on his poem "The Heathen Chinee."

Achievements • Bret Harte's influence on "local color" fiction, especially the literature of the American West, was profound but not totally fortunate. He was one of the earliest writers, and certainly the most influential one, to set stories on the mining frontier that evolved from the California gold rush of 1849. His interest in the Western story and his success in transforming his raw material into popular fiction led many subsequent writers to explore American Western themes that they might otherwise have dismissed as unworthy of serious notice. Harte's stories, however, focusing on colorful characters that he deemed worthy of treatment for their own sake, tend to undervalue plot and setting, and his contrived plots and sentimental treatment of character gave subsequent Western fiction an escapist, juvenile bent, which it took a long time to outgrow.

Biography • Born in Albany, New York, as Francis Brett Harte (he would later drop the "Francis" and change the spelling of his middle name to Bret), Harte went to California in 1854, where for a while he lived many of the lives he was later to re-create imaginatively in the biographies of his fictional characters. Among other occupations, he worked an unsuccessful mining claim on the Stanislaus River; he may have been a guard for the Wells Fargo stagecoach lines; and he was employed in various capacities at the San Francisco mint before drifting into journalism. He was associ ated with the founding (1864) of C. H. Webb's journal the *Californian*, in which some of his own early work was published. Subsequently he became editor of the *Overlane Monthly* (1868-1870), in which many of his most famous works first saw print. Notable among these are the short story "The Luck of Roaring Camp" and the comic poem "Plain Language from Truthful James," which led to an offer from *The Atlantic Monthly* of a ten-thousand-dollar yearly contract, annually renewable, for exclusive rights to his material. On the strength of this contract Harte moved to Boston, but the contract was never renewed after the first year. Indeed, Harte's later work never came up to the standard of his earlier, and although he was a tireless writer his production rapidly de generated into hack work. He moved to Europe, serving for a brief time as American consul in Krefeld, Germany, and in Glasgow, Scotland, before finally settling in Lon don, where he lived the rest of his life. He was happy in London, where people viewed his work more charitably than in the United States and where he was respected as an authentic voice of "the '49."

Analysis • In any discussion of Bret Harte, one must begin by making a clear distinc tion between *importance* and *quality*, that is, between the influence of an author's work and its intrinsic value. That Harte was an extremely important writer, no one will deny. Almost entire credit should be given to him for the refinement of the gold fields of California into rich literary ore. More than a mere poet of "the '49," he firmly estab lished many of the stock character types of later Western fiction: the gentleman gam bler, the tarnished lady, the simple though often lovably cantankerous prospector, all invariably possessed of hearts of gold. These prototypes, so beloved of later Western writers both of fiction and film, seemed to spring, like rustic Athenas, full-grown from his fertile brain. Yet with all his admitted importance there have been doubts from the very beginning about the intrinsic quality of his work. After publication of *The Luck of Roaring Camp, and Other Sketches* and the overwhelming success of his famous comic poem "Plain Language from Truthful James" in the same year, the set of brilliant to morrows confidently predicted for him developed instead into rediscovery only of a series of remembered yesterdays. What, the critic should initially ask, is the reason be hind Harte's meteoric rise and his equally precipitous fall?

Perhaps a partial answer may be found by examination of a term often applied to Harte's work: It is, critics are fond of saying, "Dickensian." There is much truth to this critical commonplace, for the influence of Charles Dickens is everywhere to be found in Harte's writing, from the often brilliantly visualized characters, through the sentimental description, to the too-commonly contrived plot. Perhaps the first of these influences is the most important, for, like Dickens, when Harte is mentioned one immediately thinks of memorable characters rather than memorable stories. What would Dickens be without his Bob Cratchit, Mister Micawber, and Little Nell? Similarly, what would Harte be without his gambler John Oakhurst or his lovable but eccentric lawyer, Colonel Starbottle? The answer to these rhetorical questions, how ever, conceals a major limitation in Harte's literary artistry which the often too-facile comparison to Dickens easily overlooks. For in Dickens's case, in addition to the characters mentioned above, equally powerful negative or evil ones may be added who are completely lacking in Harte's own work. Where are the Gradgrinds and Fagins and Uriah Heeps in Harte's writing? The answer, to the detriment of Harte's stories, is that they are nowhere to be found. The result, equally unfortunate, is that Harte's stories lack almost completely any tragic vision of the world or of human beings' place in it. Misfortune in Harte's stories is uniformly pathetic rather than tragic, and the unfortunate result is that too often these stories settle for a "good cry" on the part of the reader rather than attempting any analysis of humanity's destiny or its place in an unknown and often hostile universe.

"The Outcasts of Poker Flat" • A brief glance at one of Harte's best-known stories, "The Outcasts of Poker Flat," may serve at once to indicate both the strengths and the limitations of his work. This story tells of the fortunes of four "outcasts" from the California gold camp of Poker Flat, who have been escorted to the city limits by a vigilance committee, operating in the flush of civic pride, and told never to return on peril of their lives. The four outcasts are Mr. John Oakhurst,

Library of Congress

a professional gambler; "the Duchess" and "Mother Shipton," two prostitutes; and "Uncle Billy," a "confirmed drunkard," suspected as well of the more serious crime of robbing sluices. The four outcasts hope to find shelter in the neighboring settlement of Sandy Bar, a long day's journey away over a steep mountain range; but at noon the saddle-weary Duchess calls a halt to the expedition, saying she will "go no further." Accordingly, the party goes into camp, despite Oakhurst's pointing out that they are only half way to Sandy Bar and that they have neither equipment nor provisions. They do, however, have liquor, and the present joys of alcohol soon replace the will to proceed toward Sandy Bar where, in all fairness to the outcasts, their reception may not be overwhelmingly enthusiastic. Oakhurst does not drink, but out of a feeling of loyalty stays with his companions.

Some time later during the afternoon, the party is joined by two refugees from Sandy Bar, Tom Simson and his betrothed, Piney Woods. They have eloped from Sandy Bar because of the objections of Piney's father to their forthcoming marriage and are planning to be wed in Poker Flat. It transpires that Simson, referred to throughout the story as "the Innocent," had once lost to Oakhurst his "entire fortune—amounting to some forty dollars"—and that after the game was over Oakhurst had taken the young man aside and given him his money back, saying simply "you're a good little man, but you can't gamble worth a cent. Don't try it over again." This had made a friend-for-life of the Innocent and also serves to show that Poker Flat's view of Oakhurst as a monster of iniquity is not to be taken totally at face value. Since it is now too late to travel on, both the outcasts and the young lovers decide to encamp in a ruined house near the trail.

During the night Uncle Billy abandons the group, taking all the animals with him. It also begins to snow. The party, predictably, is snowed in, although the situation does not appear too grave since the extra provisions which the Innocent has brought with him and which Uncle Billy did not take in his departure are enough, with careful husbandry, to last the party for ten days. All begin to make the cabin habitable, and they spend the first few days listening to the accordion the Innocent has brought and to a paraphrase of the *Iliad* which the Innocent has recently read and with which, much to Oakhurst's delight, he regales the company.

The situation, however, deteriorates. Another snowstorm totally isolates the camp, although the castaways are able to see, far below them, the smoke of Poker Flat. On the tenth day, Mother Shipton, "once the strongest of the party," who had mysteriously been growing weaker, dies. Her serious decline, it turns out, is a result of the fact that she had not eaten any of her carefully husbanded rations, which she had selflessly saved for her companions. Oakhurst then makes a pair of snowshoes out of a pack saddle and gives them to the Innocent, whom he sends off to Poker Flat in a last attempt to bring aid. If the Innocent reaches Poker Flat within two days, Oakhurst says, all will be well. He follows the Innocent part way on his journey toward Poker Flat, but does not return.

Meanwhile, back at the camp, the situation goes from bad to worse. Only the Duchess and Piney are left, and—although they discover and are properly grateful for the pile of wood which Oakhurst has secretly gathered and left for them—the rigors of a cruel world prove too strong. They die of starvation in the snow, and a rescue party arriving too late is properly edified by their moral courage—and, the reader trusts, properly chastened by recognition of Poker Flat's own despicable conduct. Oakhurst, we discover at the end of the story, in the best tradition of *noblesse oblige*, has committed suicide. The story concludes with a rehearsal of his epitaph, written by himself on a deuce of clubs and pinned to a pine tree with a bowie knife: "Beneath this tree lies the body of John Oakhurst, who struck a streak of bad luck on the 23d of November 1850, and handed in his checks on the 7th of December, 1850."

It is pointless to pretend that "The Outcasts of Poker Flat" does not have a certain power; indeed, the evidence of its continuing popularity, as shown through inclusion in countless anthologies of every persuasion, clearly indicates that the story is not a totally negligible effort. Yet after thoughtful readers have finished the story, they are conscious of a certain dissatisfaction. The question to be asked is, "Why?"

The obvious answer seems to be that the story has little new to say. In European literature, prostitutes with hearts of gold were scarcely novel figures by the 1860's; furthermore, the fact that holier-than-thou individuals, who are likely not only to cast the first stone but also to be sorry when it hits, can scarcely have been new to any reasonably perceptive reader. What Harte no doubt intended was to evoke an emotion on the part of the reader, an emotion of sorrow and pity for the poor victims of the social ingratitude (one hates to say *injustice*) of Poker Flat. The argument, from one perspective, is the oldest in the world—the tiresome *tu quoque* statement that the holier-than-thou are little better than the lowlier-than-them. Yet this easy answer will not entirely work. As has been pointed out many times, considered purely from the perspective of "ideas," most literature *is* commonplace.

Perhaps a better question is to ask how Harte approached his parable and whether his fictional method works. To this the answer must be "No," for if readers consider the story carefully, they must agree that it simply is not successful, even in its own terms. They have, as Harte's friend and sometime collaborator Mark Twain would have said, been "sold."

Let us examine the story closely. A group of outcasts is sent up a long day's journey to another place. They stop only halfway—that is, half a day's journey—there. The place they left, in fact, is clearly visible behind them. Four in number, they are joined by two others; when Uncle Billy deserts, their number is five. Harte tells us that with careful management they have ten days' food, even though they have no animals. (What Uncle Billy could possibly have wanted with the seven animals he stole, particularly since he had no provisions to put on them, is never clarified, nor is the bothersome detail of how he could have managed the theft in the first place, considering he had to remove them single-handedly from under the noses of his companions, one of whom, John Oakhurst, is, Harte specifically tells us, "a light sleeper." The animals do not simply wander off; Harte calls our attention to the fact that they had been "tethered." Uncle Billy must therefore have released them on purpose.) In any event, the unfortunate castaways survive on meager rations for a week until Oakhurst suddenly remembers how to make snowshoes. Why he could not remember this skill on the second day or perhaps the third, is never clarified, but no matter. The reason is obvious, at least from Harte's point of view of the logic of the story. It is necessary for Harte to place his characters in a situation of romantic peril in order that their sterling qualities be thrown into high relief; to place his characters *in extremis*, however, Harte totally sacrifices whatever logic the story may have in its own terms.

When Uncle Billy leaves, then, the group discovers that it has sufficient supplies for ten days—that is, fifty man days' worth of food. Mother Shipton eats none of hers, dying of starvation at the end of a week. This means that the party now has some twenty-two man days of food left, with at the most only three people to eat it, since Mother Shipton is already dead and Oakhurst is about to commit suicide. This is, according to the data Harte has previously given, easily a week's rations. Why, then, do the two surviving ladies die of starvation before the rescue party arrives some four days later?

The answer has nothing to do with the story, which is designed, rather, for the moral Harte wishes to impale upon it. For in his single-minded pursuit of the commonplace notion that appearances may be deceiving and that there is a spark of goodness in all of us, Harte has totally sacrificed all fictional probabilities. Any potential tragic effect the story might presumably possess evaporates in the pale warmth of sentimental nostalgia.

This inability to allow his stories to speak for themselves is Harte's besetting fictional weakness. Rather than allowing his tales to develop their own meaning, he obsessively applies a meaning to them, a meaning which, in far too many cases, cheapens the fictional material at his disposal. Perhaps the fault is that Harte, in his relentless search for this new California literary ore, did not really know where to find it. The mother lode consistently escaped him, and whatever flakes his search discovered were too often small and heavily alloyed.

James K. Folsom
With updates by John W. Fiero

Other major works

PLAYS: *Two Men of Sandy Bar*, pr. 1876; *Ah Sin*, pr. 1877 (with Mark Twain); *Sue*, pr. 1896 (with T. Edgar Pemberton).

NOVELS: *Gabriel Conroy*, 1876.

MISCELLANEOUS: *The Luck of Roaring Camp, and Other Writings*, 2001.

NONFICTION: *Selected Letters of Bret Harte*, 1997 (Gary Scharnhorst, editor).

POETRY: "Plain Language from Truthful James," 1870 (also known as "The Heathen Chinee"); *East and West Poems,* 1871; *Poems,* 1871; *Poetical Works,* 1880; *Poetical Works of Bret Harte,* 1896; *Some Later Verses,* 1898.

Bibliography

Barnett, Linda D. *Bret Harte: A Reference Guide.* Boston: G. K. Hall, 1980. With a brief introduction outlining the historical directions of Harte scholarship and criticism, this work provides a good annotated bibliography and checklist through 1977.

May, Charles E., ed. *Masterplots II: Short Story Series, Revised Edition.* 8 vols. Pasadena, Calif.: Salem Press, 2004. Designed for student use, this reference set contains articles providing detailed plot summaries and analyses of three short stories by Harte: "The Luck of Roaring Camp" (vol. 5), "The Outcasts of Poker Flat" (vol. 6), and "Tennessee's Partner" (vol. 7).

Morrow, Patrick. *Bret Harte.* Boise, Ida.: Boise State College Press, 1972. This brief but excellent study analyzes Harte's major work in both literature and criticism. Although concise, it is a very helpful introduction. Supplemented by a select bibliography.

Nissen, Axel. *Bret Harte: Prince and Pauper.* Jackson: University Press of Mississippi, 2000. This scholarly biography provides a new assessment of the life and achievements of the writer.

O'Connor, Richard. *Bret Harte: A Biography.* Boston: Little, Brown, 1966. Lively, anecdotal, and gossipy account limited to Harte's life, this work is not critical in focus. It does list Harte's best-known literary characters.

Scharnhorst, Gary. *Bret Harte.* New York: Twayne, 1992. Critical biography of Harte, providing analyses of stories from four different periods of his life, fully informed by critical reception of Harte's work. An afterword summarizes Harte's critical reputation.

_____. *Bret Harte: A Bibliography.* Lanham, Md.: Scarecrow Press, 1995. Excellent tool for the student of Harte.

_____. *Bret Harte: Opening the American Literary West.* Norman: University of Oklahoma Press, 2000. Study of the writer/editor and his struggle to make the West part of the wider American culture.

_____. "Mark Twain, Bret Harte, and the Literary Construction of San Francisco." In *San Francisco in Fiction: Essays in a Regional Literature,* edited by David Fine and Paul Skenazy. Albuquerque: University of New Mexico Press, 1995. Discusses Harte's acceptance of the eastern canon's taste in such stories as "The Idyl of Red Gulch" and his romanticized depiction of San Francisco as a rough-and-tumble boomtown in several late stories.

Stevens, J. David. "'She War a Woman': Family Roles, Gender, and Sexuality in Bret Harte's Western Fiction." *American Literature* 69 (September, 1997): 571-593. A discussion of gender in Harte's Western fiction; argues that what critics have labeled sentimental excess in Harte's fiction is in fact his method of exploring certain hegemonic cultural paradigms taken for granted in other Western narratives; discusses stories that deal with the structure of the family and how they critique gender roles.

Nathaniel Hawthorne

Born: Salem, Massachusetts; July 4, 1804
Died: Plymouth, New Hampshire; May 19, 1864

Principal short fiction • *Twice-Told Tales*, 1837 (expanded 1842); *Mosses from an Old Manse*, 1846; *The Snow-Image, and Other Twice-Told Tales*, 1851.

Other literary forms • Nathaniel Hawthorne is a major American novelist whose early *Fanshawe: A Tale* (1828) did not lead immediately to further long fiction. After a period largely given to tales and sketches, he published his classic study of moral prejudice in colonial New England, *The Scarlet Letter* (1850). In the next decade, three more novels—he preferred to call them romances—followed: *The House of the Seven Gables* (1851), *The Blithedale Romance* (1852), and *The Marble Faun* (1860). He wrote books for children, including *A Wonder-Book for Boys and Girls* (1852), and travel sketches of England, *Our Old Home* (1863). His posthumously published notebooks and letters are also important.

Achievements • This seminal figure in American fiction combined narrative skill and artistic integrity as no previous American writer had done. A dozen of Nathaniel Hawthorne's short stories remain anthology favorites, and few modern American students fail to become familiar with *The Scarlet Letter*.

Hawthorne's influence on subsequent American writers, especially on his younger American friend Herman Melville, and on Henry James, William Faulkner, and Robert Lowell, has been enormous. Although he wrote comparatively little literary theory, his prefaces to his novels, preeminently the one to *The House of the Seven Gables*, and scattered observations within his fiction reflect a pioneering concern with his craft.

Biography • It is fitting that Nathaniel Hawthorne's birth in 1804 came on the Fourth of July, for, if American writers of his youth were attempting a literary declaration of independence to complement the successful political one of 1776, Hawthorne's fiction of the 1830's, along with Edgar Allan Poe's poetry and fiction and Ralph Waldo Emerson's essays and lectures of the same decade, rank as the fruition of that ambition.

Undoubtedly his hometown of Salem, Massachusetts, exerted a powerful shaping influence on his work, even though his sea-captain father died when Nathaniel, the second of three children, was only four and even though Nathaniel did not evince much interest in the sea. No one could grow up in Salem without a strong sense of the past, especially a boy one of whose ancestors, John Hathorne (as the family name was then spelled), had served as a judge in the infamous witchcraft trials of 1695.

In 1813, confined to home by a foot injury for two years, young Nathaniel formed the habit of reading for hours at a stretch. On graduating from Bowdoin College in 1825, where he was a classmate of Franklin Pierce, the future president, and Henry Wadsworth Longfellow, the future poet, the bookish Hawthorne returned to Salem and began a decade of intensive reading and writing. He published a novel,

Fanshawe: A Tale (later repudiated), in 1828 and began to compose the short stories that eventually brought him into prominence. The first collection of these, *Twice Told Tales*, appeared in 1837.

In 1838, he became engaged to Sophia Peabody, of Salem, and the following year was appointed to a position in the Boston Custom House, but he left in 1841 to join the infant Brook Farm community in West Roxbury, Massachusetts. As a rather solitary man with no prior practical experience of farming, he did not thrive there and left before the end of the year. Marrying in 1842, the couple settled at the Old Manse in Concord. Although he befriended Henry David Thoreau, Hawthorne found the Concord Transcendentalists generally pretentious and boring. During the administration of James K. Polk, he left Concord for another customhouse appointment, this time back in Salem. From this period comes his second short-story collection, *Mosses from an Old Manse*.

Moving thereafter to Lenox in the Berkshires, Hawthorne met the younger writer Herman Melville and produced, in a few weeks in 1850, *The Scarlet Letter*, which was the first of his successful novels; *The House of the Seven Gables* and another collection of short fiction, *The Snow-Image, and Other Twice-Told Tales*, followed the next year. Back in Concord at "The Wayside" in 1852, he wrote a campaign biography for his friend Pierce, which resulted in Hawthorne's appointment as U.S. consul in Liverpool, England. That same year he also wrote the novel *The Blithedale Romance*, based loosely on his Brook Farm experience.

In England, Hawthorne kept an extensive journal from which he later fashioned *Our Old Home*. Resigning his office in 1857, Hawthorne traveled with his family on the Continent; in Florence, he began his last novel, published in 1860 as *The Marble Faun*. By the time he returned to Concord, his health was failing, and although he worked at several more novels, he did not get far into any of them. In 1864, he set forth on a trip with Pierce but died in Plymouth, New Hampshire, on May 19.

Analysis • Nathaniel Hawthorne's reading in American colonial history confirmed his basically ambivalent attitude toward the American past, particularly the form that Puritanism took in the New England colonies. Especially interested in the intensity of the Puritan-Cavalier rivalry, the Puritan inclination to credit manifestations of the supernatural such as witchcraft, and the psychology of the struggle for liberation from English rule, Hawthorne explored these themes in some of his earliest stories. As they did for his Puritan ancestors, sin and guilt preoccupied Hawthorne, who, in his move from Salem to Concord, encountered what he considered the facile dismissal of the problem of evil by the Concord intellectuals. He developed a deeply ambivalent moral attitude that colored the situations and characters of his fiction.

In the early masterpiece "My Kinsman, Major Molineux," Hawthorne's concern with the coming of age of the United States blends with the maturation of a lad on the verge of manhood. Introduced to the complexities of evil, characters such as Robin of this story and the title character of "Young Goodman Brown" have great difficulty summoning the spiritual strength to resist dark temptations.

Often, Hawthorne's characters cannot throw off the burden of a vague and irrational but weighty burden of guilt. Frequently, his young protagonists exhibit a cold, unresponsive attitude toward a loving fiancé or wife and can find no spiritual sustenance to redeem the situation. Brown, Parson Hooper of "The Minister's Black Veil," and Reuben Bourne of "Roger Malvin's Burial" are examples of such guilt-ridden and essentially faithless men.

Another prevalent type of protagonist rejects love to become a detached observer, such as the husband of "Wakefield," who for no apparent reason deserts his wife and spends years living nearby in disguise. In the stories of his middle and later periods, these detached characters are usually scientists or artists. The former include misguided idealists such as Aylmer of "The Birthmark" and the scientist Rappaccini in "Rappaccini's Daughter," who experiments remorselessly on female family members in search of some elusive abstract perfection. Hawthorne's artists, while less dangerous, tend also to exclude themselves from warm and loving relationships.

At their most deplorable, Hawthorne's isolated, detached characters become, like Ethan Brand in the story of the same name and Roger Chillingworth of *The Scarlet Letter*, violators of the human heart,

Library of Congress

unreclaimable souls whose estrangement from normal human relationships yields them little in compensation, either material or spiritual.

Characteristically, Hawthorne builds his stories on a quest or journey, often into the woods or wilderness but always into an unknown region, the protagonist emerging enlightened or merely chastened but invariably sadder, with any success a bitterly ironical one, such as Aylmer's removal of his wife's birthmark, which kills his patient. The stories are pervasively and often brilliantly symbolic, and Hawthorne's symbolic imagination encompasses varieties ranging from more or less clear-cut allegory to elusive multiple symbolic patterns whose significance critics debate endlessly.

A century and a half after their composition, Hawthorne's artistry and moral imagination, even in some of his seriously flawed stories, continue to engage readers and critics. Two of Hawthorne's most enduringly popular stories—"Roger Malvin's Burial" and "My Kinsman, Major Molineux"—appeared initially in the 1831 edition of a literary annual called *The Token* but remained uncollected until long afterward. Both seem to have been intended for a book, *Provincial Tales*, that never materialized, and both begin with paragraphs explicitly linking the narratives to historical events.

"Roger Malvin's Burial" • "Roger Malvin's Burial" is set in the aftermath of a 1725 confrontation with Native Americans called Lovell's Fight. Roger is a mortally wounded soldier; Reuben Bourne, his less seriously injured companion, must decide whether to stay with his older friend on the desolate frontier or make his way back to his company before he becomes too weak to travel. Urged to the latter course by

Roger, his prospective father-in-law, Reuben makes the older man as comfortable as he can at the base of a huge rock near an oak sapling, promises to return as soon as he can, and staggers away. Eventually, he is discovered by a search party and taken home to be ministered to by Dorcas, his fiancé. After several days of semiconsciousness, Reuben recovers sufficiently to answer questions. Although he believes he has done the right thing, he cannot bring himself to contradict Dorcas's assumption that he had buried her father, and he is undeservedly lionized for his heroic fidelity.

Eighteen years later, this unhappy and uncommunicative husband takes Dorcas and their fifteen-year-old son Cyrus to the frontier, presumably to resettle but really to "bury" Roger and expiate his own guilt. On the anniversary of the day Reuben had left Roger, Dorcas and Cyrus are led to the rock and the now blasted oak tree, a fatal gunshot is fired, and in a chillingly ambiguous way Reuben relieves himself of his "curse." This pattern of irrational guilt and ambivalent quest would be repeated in other stories, using New England historical incidents and pervasive symbols such as the rock and oak of "Roger Malvin's Burial."

"My Kinsman, Major Molineux" • "My Kinsman, Major Molineux" is justly considered one of Hawthorne's greatest stories. The historical introduction here serves to establish the setting as a time of bitter resentment toward Massachusetts colonial governors. The location is left deliberately vague, except that Robin, the young protagonist, must arrive by ferry in a town where he hopes to meet his kinsman, a colonial official. Robin has come from the country with an idea of getting a boost toward a career from Major Molineux. The town is tense and lurid when he enters at nightfall, and the people act strangely. In particular, whenever Robin mentions the name of his kinsman, he is rebuffed. Although frequently described as "shrewd," Robin seems naive and baffled by the events of this disquieting evening.

Eventually, he is treated to the nightmarish spectacle of the public humiliation of his kinsman, though it appears that Major Molineux is the more or less innocent victim of colonial vindictiveness toward the authority of the Crown. At the climax, Robin finds himself unaccountably laughing with the townspeople at Molineux's disgrace. By the end of the evening, Robin, convinced that nothing remains for him to do but to return home, is counseled by the only civil person he meets to wait a few days before leaving, "as you are a shrewd youth, you may rise in the world without the help of your kinsman, Major Molineux."

At one level, this is clearly a rites-of-passage story. Robin has reached the point of initiation into an adult world whose deviousness and obliquity he has hardly begun to suspect, but one in which he can hope to prosper only through his own efforts. The conclusion strongly implies that he cannot go home again, or that if he does, life will never be the same. As the stranger suggests, he may well be obliged to stay and adjust to the new world that he has discovered. The historical setting proclaims "My Kinsman, Major Molineux" an imaginative account of the colonial struggle toward the challenges and perils of an independence for which the people are largely unprepared. The ferry ride, reminiscent of the underworld adventures of epic heroes such as Odysseus and Aeneas—and perhaps more pointedly yet, the Dante of the *Inferno*—leads to a hellish region from which newcomers cannot normally expect to return. The multiplicity of interpretations that this story has provoked attests to its richness and complexity.

Several of Hawthorne's best stories first appeared in 1835. One of these, "Wakefield," has been criticized as slight and undeveloped, but it remains intriguing. It poses in its final paragraph an exacting problem: "Amid the seeming confusion of our mysterious world, individuals are so nicely adjusted to a system, and systems to one another and to a whole, that, by stepping aside for a moment, a man exposes himself to a fearful risk of losing his place forever." Wakefield "steps aside" by leaving his wife for no apparent reason and secretly taking up residence in the next street. The setting of this story, unusual for Hawthorne, is London, and the couple have been married for ten years. Wakefield seems to be an embryonic version of the ruthless experimenter of several later stories, but here his action is more of a joke than an experiment. He is "intellectual, but not actively so"; he lacks imagination; and he has "a cold but not depraved nor wandering heart." When he leaves, he promises to be back in three or four days, but he stays away for twenty years. He adopts a disguise, regularly walks by his old home and peers in, and even passes his wife in the street. Wakefield has a purpose that he cannot define, but the author describes his motive merely as "morbid vanity." He will frighten his wife and will find out how much he really matters. He does not matter that much, however, for his wife settles into the routine of her "widowhood." Finally, passing his old home in a rain shower, he suddenly decides to enter, and at this point the story ends, leaving unanswered the question of whether he has lost his place forever.

"The Minister's Black Veil" • Of the many Hawthorne stories that point toward his masterpiece in the novel *The Scarlet Letter,* "The Minister's Black Veil" boasts the character most akin to Arthur Dimmesdale of the novel. Like Dimmesdale, Parson Hooper has a secret. He appears one morning at a Milford meeting house (a reference to "Governor Belcher" appears to place the story in Massachusetts in the 1730's or early 1740's) with his face shrouded by a black veil, which he never thereafter removes. Unlike Dimmesdale, he thus flaunts his secret while concealing it. The whole story revolves around the veil and its meaning. His sermon, unusually energetic for this mild minister, is "secret sin." That afternoon, Hooper conducts a funeral service for a young woman, and Hawthorne hints darkly that Hooper's sin may have involved her. In the evening, at a third service, Hooper's veil casts gloom over a wedding ceremony. The congregation speculates endlessly but inclines to avoid the minister.

One person who does not avoid him is a young woman named Elizabeth, who is engaged to Hooper. Elizabeth unavailingly begs him to explain or remove the veil and then breaks their engagement. In the years that follow, the lonely minister exerts a strange power over his flock. Dying sinners always insist on his visiting them and never expire before he reaches them, although his presence makes them shudder. Finally, Hooper himself sickens, and Elizabeth reappears to nurse him. On his death bed, he questions the aversion of his onlookers and insists that he sees a similar veil over each of their faces. He then expires and is buried with the veil still over his face. A question more important than the nature of Hooper's transgression concerns his increase in ministerial efficacy. Is Hooper's veiled state a kind of extended stage trick? (In death a smile lingers on his face.) Is it advantageous to be ministered to by a "mind diseased?" Is Hooper's effectiveness an implicit condemnation of his and his congregation's religion? Such questions Hawthorne's story almost inevitably raises and almost equally inevitably does not presume to answer directly.

"The May-Pole of Merrymount" • "The May-Pole of Merrymount" is simple in plot but complex in theme. One midsummer's eve, very early in the colonial life of the

Massachusetts settlement at Mount Wollaston, or Merry Mount, a reenactment of ancient Maypole rites accompanies the wedding of an attractive young couple, Edith and Edgar. Into the scene storms a belligerent group of Puritans under John Endicott, who hacks down the Maypole, arrests the principals, including the flower-decked priest and the bridal couple, and threatens punishment to all, though Edith's and Edgar's will be light if they can accommodate themselves to the severe Puritan life hereafter.

Hawthorne uses history but does not follow it strictly. The historical Endicott's main motive in attacking Merry Mount was to stop its denizens from furnishing firepower and firewater—that is, guns and liquor—to Native Americans. The real Merry Mounters were not so frivolous, nor the Puritans necessarily so austere as Hawthorne depicts them. His artistic purpose required the sharp contrast of two ways of life among early Massachusetts settlers, neither of which he is willing to endorse. The young couple are caught between the self-indulgence of their own community and the "dismal wretches" who invade their ceremony. Like many of Hawthorne's characters, Edith and Edgar emerge into adulthood in an environment replete with bewildering moral conflicts. It is possible to see the conflict here as one between "English" and "American" values, the Americans being the sober seekers of a new, more disciplined, presumably more godly order than the one they chose to leave behind; the conflict can also be seen as one between a form of religion receptive to "pagan" excesses and a strict, fiercely intolerant one; yet another way of seeing it is as one between hedonists and sadists—for the pleasure principle completely dominates Hawthorne's Merry Mount, while the Puritans promise branding, chopping of ears, and, instead of a Maypole, a whipping post for the miscreants.

The resolution of the story echoes John Milton's description of Adam and Eve leaving Eden at the end of *Paradise Lost* (1667), but Hawthorne has Endicott throw a wreath of roses from the Maypole over the heads of the departing newlyweds, "a deed of prophecy," which signifies the end of the "systematic gayety" of Merry Mount, which also symbolizes the "purest and best of their early joys" that must sustain them in the strict Puritan regimen that lies ahead.

"Young Goodman Brown" • "Young Goodman Brown," first appearing in print in 1835, is set in Salem at the end of the seventeenth century—the era of the witchcraft trials. Again, the names of some minor characters are historical, but Brown and his wife, Faith, whom the young protagonist leaves one night to go into the woods, are among his most allegorical. In its outline the allegory is transparent: When a "good man" abandons his faith, he can expect to go to the devil. Hawthorne complicates his story by weaving into it all sorts of subtleties and ambiguities. Brown's guide in the woods is simultaneously fatherlike and devilish. He encounters a series of presumably upright townspeople, including eventually Faith herself, gathering for a ceremony of devil-worship. At the climactic moment, Brown urges Faith to "look up to heaven, and resist the wicked one." The next thing he knows, he is alone in the forest, all his companions having fled—or all having been part of a dream. Brown returns home in the morning, his life radically altered. He can no longer trust his neighbors, he shrinks from his wife, and he lives out his years a scowling, muttering misanthrope.

As in "The May-Pole of Merrymount," Hawthorne's motive in evoking an episode of New England history is not primarily historical: No one proceeds against witches; there is no allusion to Judge John Hathorne. Rather, the setting creates an atmophere of guilt, suspicion, and unstable moral imagination. Breathing this atmosphere, Brown falls victim not to injustice or religious intolerance but to himself. In a sense it does not matter whether Brown fell asleep in the woods and dreamed the Black Sabbath. Regardless of whether he has lost faith, he has manifestly lost hope. His apparent capacity to resist evil in the midst of a particularly unholy temptation dispels his own guilt no more than the guilt he, and seemingly only he, detects in others. "Young Goodman Brown" is a masterful fictive presentation of the despairing soul.

All the preceding stories had been published by the time Hawthorne turned thirty-one. For about three more years, stories continued to flow, although most of those from the late 1830's are not among his best. He broke a subsequent dry spell with a series of stories first published in 1843 and 1844, many of which were later collected in *Mosses from an Old Manse* in 1846. Most notable of these later stories are "The Birthmark," "The Artist of the Beautiful," and "Rappaccini's Daughter."

"The Birthmark" • In these later efforts, the artist-scientist appears frequently. Aylmer of "The Birthmark" becomes obsessed by the one flaw in his beautiful wife, Georgiana, a birthmark on her left cheek that had not previously bothered her or her prior lovers. To Aylmer, however, it is a "symbol of imperfection," and he undertakes its removal. Hawthorne foreshadows the result in many ways, not the least by Georgiana's observation that her brilliant husband's "most splendid successes were almost invariably failures." She submits to the operation nevertheless, and he succeeds at removing the mark but fails to preserve her life, intertwined somehow with it.

Aylmer equates science with religion; words such as "miracle," "votaries," "mysteries," and "holy" abound. He is also an artist who, far from subjecting Georgiana to a smoky laboratory, fashions an apartment with beautiful curtains and perfumed lamps of his creation for her to inhabit during the experiment. Neither hero nor villain, Aylmer is a gifted man incapable of accepting moral limitations and therefore unable to accept his wife as the best that life could offer him.

The artist appears in various guises in Hawthorne's later stories and novels. He may be a wood-carver as in "Drowne's Wooden Image," a poet like Coverdale of *The Blithedale Romance*, a painter like Kenyon of *The Marble Faun*, or, as in "The Artist of the Beautiful," a watchmaker with the ambition "to put the very spirit of beauty into form." Owen Warland is also a peripheral figure, not yet alienated from society like many twentieth century artists real and fictional but regarded as quaint and ineffectual by his companions. Like Aylmer, he attempts to improve on nature, his creation being a mechanical butterfly of rare and fragile beauty. Owen appears fragile himself, but it is part of Hawthorne's strategy to reveal his inner toughness. He can contemplate the destruction of his butterfly by a child with equanimity, for the artifact itself is only the "symbol" of the reality of art. Owen suffers in living among less sensitive and spiritual beings and in patiently enduring their unenlightened patronization, but he finds security in his capacity for beauty.

"Rappaccini's Daughter" • "Rappaccini's Daughter" has three familiar Hawthorne characters. His young initiate this time is an Italian university student named Giovanni Guasconti, whose lodgings in Padua overlook a spectacular garden, the pride and joy of a scientific experimenter, Dr. Rappaccini, whose human subject is his daughter Beatrice. A scientific rival, professor Baglioni, warns Giovanni that Rappaccini much prefers science to humankind, but the young man falls in love with Beatrice and thus comes within Rappaccini's orbit. This scientist is more sinister than Aylmer and exerts his power over Beatrice more pervasively than does Aylmer over Georgiana. Beatrice's very life is bound up with the powerful poison with which he grows the exotic flowers in his garden. Giovanni, who has himself imbibed the poison, tries to counter its effect on Beatrice by offering her a medicine obtained from Baglioni, but its effect on her, whose whole life has depended on the poison, is fatal.

This story and its four main characters have generated a bewildering variety of interpretations. One reason for the critical quarrels is a subtle shift in point of view late in the story. For most of the way, the reader is with Giovanni and knows what Giovanni knows, but about four-fifths of the way, an omniscient narrator begins to comment on the limitations of his perceptions, the truth being deeper than he can plumb. This double perspective creates difficulties in gauging his character and that of the other three principals.

Hawthorne's allegorical propensities also complicate one's understanding of the story. For example, Beatrice can be seen as an Eve, an already corrupted temptress in the garden; as a Dantean, who guides her lover through what is for him, initially at least, Paradise; and as the Pomona of Ovid's tale of Vertumnus, the vegetarian god who wins her love and takes her away. (There is a statue of Vertumnus in Rappaccini's garden.) Obviously, Beatrice is not consistently any of these figures, but each of them leads to further allegorizing.

Perhaps the ultimate explanation of the interpretive difficulties arising from "Rappaccini's Daughter" is the author's profound ambivalence. In this fictional world, good and evil, beauty and deformity, are inextricably intermingled. Is Baglioni, for example, wise counselor or jealous rival, the protector of Giovanni or the vindictive agent of Beatrice's destruction? He fulfills these roles and others. In this story he conjoins with three other familiar Hawthorne types, the young initiate into life's malignities, the trusting victim of a detached manipulator, and the insensitive violator of his victim's integrity. Nearly every conceivable critical method has been applied to "Rappaccini's Daughter"; ultimately each reader must make up his or her own mind about its primary significance.

After these three stories of the mid-1840's, all viewed incidentally as landmarks of science fiction by historians of that genre, Hawthorne, back in Salem and busy with his customhouse duties, wrote little for several years. Before turning his attention to long fiction in 1850, however, he completed a few more short stories in the late 1840's, the most important of which is "Ethan Brand."

"Ethan Brand" • Like several of his best stories, this one occupies the time from nightfall to the following dawn, but unlike "Young Goodman Brown" and "My Kinsman, Major Molineux" it has a contemporary setting. Bartram is a lime burner attending his fire on Mount Greylock in northwestern Massachusetts with his son Joe, when a man appears, a former lime burner who long ago decided to devote his life to searching for the Unpardonable Sin, which, by cultivating his intellect at the expense of his moral sense, he found in his own heart. All this he explains to the unimaginative and uncomprehending Bartram. The sensitive son fears the glint in the stranger's eye, and even Bartram cringes at Ethan Brand's sinister laugh. Since Brand has passed into local folklore, Bartram dispatches Joe to inform the villagers that he is back, and soon a contingent of neighbors comes on the scene. When Brand demonstrates his abrogation of human brotherhood, they retire, and Brand offers to watch Bartram's fire so that the latter and his son can retire for the night to their nearby hut. When Bartram and Joe awake in the morning, they find Brand gone, but a look into the fire reveals his skeleton burned to lime, his hardened heart also burnt but distinctly outlined.

What was the sin? Hawthorne subtitled this story "A Chapter from an Abortive Romance." No fragments of such a romance have ever turned up, although the story alludes briefly to past relationships between Brand and some of the villagers, including an "Esther" on whom Brand had performed a "psychological experiment, and wasted, absorbed, and perhaps annihilated her soul, in the process." Hawthorne seems to have intended no specifying of this or any other of Brand's activities but succeeded in delineating a character who represents the ultimate development—at least in his short fiction—of the coldly intellectual seeker who has denied his heart, exploited others in relentless quasi-scientific experimentation, and isolated himself from humanity. Hawthorne would depict such characters in more detail in his novels but never one who acknowledged his sin so completely and regarded suicide as the only act remaining to him.

At one time, Hawthorne's short stories were viewed mainly as preliminaries to the novels to which he turned shortly after publishing "Ethan Brand" in January of 1850, but he is now recognized as a master of the short story. Unlike all other major American writers of his time, he devoted his creative energies almost exclusively to fiction. Only Edgar Allan Poe, who began to publish his fiction shortly after Hawthorne's early stories appeared, approaches his position as the United States' first artist of short fiction. If Poe excelled at the psychology of terror, Hawthorne prevailed at the psychology of guilt. Both brilliantly characterized the isolated or alienated individual, but only Hawthorne regularly enriched the cultural significance of his stories by locating these characters within the context of an American past and thus contributing imaginatively to his readers' sense of that past.

Robert P. Ellis

Other major works

CHILDREN'S LITERATURE: *Grandfather's Chair,* 1841; *Biographical Stories for Children,* 1842; *True Stories from History and Biography,* 1851; *A Wonder-Book for Boys and Girls,* 1852; *Tanglewood Tales for Boys and Girls,* 1853.

EDITED TEXT: *Peter Parley's Universal History,* 1837.

NOVELS: *Fanshawe: A Tale,* 1828; *The Scarlet Letter,* 1850; *The House of the Seven Gables,* 1851; *The Blithedale Romance,* 1852; *The Marble Faun,* 1860; *Septimius Felton,* 1872 (fragment); *The Dolliver Romance,* 1876 (fragment); *Doctor Grimshawe's Secret,* 1883 (fragment); *The Ancestral Footstep,* 1883 (fragment).

MISCELLANEOUS: *Complete Works,* 1850-1882 (13 volumes); *The Complete Writings of Nathaniel Hawthorne,* 1900 (22 volumes); *The Centenary Edition of the Works of Nathaniel Hawthorne,* 1962-1997 (23 volumes).

NONFICTION: *Life of Franklin Pierce,* 1852; *Our Old Home,* 1863; *The American Notebooks,* 1941; *The French and Italian Notebooks,* 1980; *Letters of Nathaniel Hawthorne,* 1984-1987 (4 volumes); *Selected Letters of Nathaniel Hawthorne,* 2002 (Joel Myerson, editor).

Bibliography

Bunge, Nancy. *Nathaniel Hawthorne: A Study of the Short Fiction.* New York: Twayne, 1993. Discusses Hawthorne's major short stories in three categories: isolation and community, artists and scientists, and perspective, humility, and joy. Includes excerpts from Hawthorne's journals, letters, and prefaces; also includes excerpts on Hawthorne from Herman Melville, Edgar Allan Poe, Henry James, and several contemporary critics.

Keil, James C. "Hawthorne's 'Young Goodman Brown': Early Nineteenth-Century and Puritan Constructions of Gender." *The New England Quarterly* 69 (March, 1996): 33-55. Argues that Hawthorne places his story in the seventeenth century to explore the nexus of past and present in the attitudes of New Englanders toward theology, morality, and sexuality. Points out that clear boundaries between male and female, public and private, and work and home were thresholds across which nineteenth century Americans often passed.

Kelsey, Angela M. "Mrs. Wakefield's Gaze: Femininity and Dominance in Nathaniel Hawthorne's 'Wakefield.'" *ATQ*, n.s. 8 (March, 1994): 17-31. In this feminist reading of Hawthorne's story, Kelsey argues that Mrs. Wakefield finds ways to escape and exceed the economy of the male gaze, first by appropriating the look for herself, then by refusing to die, and finally by denying her husband her gaze.

Mackenzie, Manfred. "Hawthorne's 'Roger Malvin's Burial': A Postcolonial Reading." *New Literary History* 27 (Summer, 1996): 459-472. Argues that the story is postcolonial fiction in which Hawthorne writes the emerging American nation and recalls European colonial culture; claims that Hawthorne rehearses the colonialist past in order to concentrate and effectively "expel" its inherent violence.

McKee, Kathryn B. "'A Small Heap of Glittering Fragments': Hawthorne's Discontent with the Short Story Form." *ATQ*, n.s. 8 (June, 1994): 137-147. Claims that Hawthorne's "Artist of the Beautiful" and "Downe's Wooden Image" are examples of his dissatisfaction with the short story as a form; argues that the fragile articles at the center of the tales mirror the limitations Hawthorne saw in the short-story genre.

May, Charles E., ed. *Masterplots II: Short Story Series, Revised Edition.* 8 vols. Pasadena, Calif.: Salem Press, 2004. Designed for student use, this reference set contains articles providing detailed plot summaries and analyses of eleven short stories by Hawthorne: "The Ambitious Guest," "The Artist of the Beautiful," and "The Birthmark" (vol. 1); "Dr. Heidegger's Experiment" (vol. 2); "Ethan Brand: A Chapter from an Abortive Romance" (vol. 3); "The Minister's Black Veil" and "My Kinsman, Major Molineux" (vol. 5); "Rappaccini's Daughter" and "Roger Malvin's Burial" (vol. 6); and "Wakefield" and "Young Goodman Brown" (vol. 8).

Newman, Lea Bertani Vozar. *A Reader's Guide to the Short Stories of Nathaniel Hawthorne.* Boston: G. K. Hall, 1979. For each of fifty-four stories, this valuable guide furnishes a chapter with four sections: publication history; circumstances of composition, sources, and influences; relationship with other Hawthorne works; and interpretations and criticism. The discussions are arranged alphabetically by title and keyed to a bibliography of more than five hundred secondary sources.

Scharnhorst, Gary. *The Critical Response to Hawthorne's "The Scarlet Letter."* New York: Greenwood Press, 1992. Includes chapters on the novel's background and composition history, on the contemporary American reception, on the early British reception, on the growth of Hawthorne's reputation after his death, on modern criticism, and on *The Scarlet Letter* on stage and screen.

Swope, Richard. "Approaching the Threshold(s) in Postmodern Detective Fiction: Hawthorne's 'Wakefield' and Other Missing Persons." *Critique* 39 (Spring, 1998): 207-227. Discusses "Wakefield" as a literary ancestor of "metaphysical" detective fiction, a postmodern genre that combines fiction with literary theory. "Wakefield" raises many of the questions about language, subjectivity, and urban spaces that surround postmodernism.

Von Frank, Albert J., ed. *Critical Essays on Hawthorne's Short Stories*. Boston: G. K. Hall, 1991. Divided into nineteenth and twentieth century commentary, with a section of new essays, an introduction, and a chronology of the tales.

Wineapple, Brenda. *Hawthorne: A Life*. New York: Alfred A. Knopf, 2003. Analysis of Hawthorne's often contradictory life that proposes that many of Hawthorne's stories are autobiographical.

Ernest Hemingway

Born: Oak Park, Illinois; July 21, 1899
Died: Ketchum, Idaho; July 2, 1961

Principal short fiction • *Three Stories and Ten Poems*, 1923; *In Our Time*, 1924, 1925; *Men Without Women*, 1927; *Winner Take Nothing*, 1933; *The Fifth Column and the First Forty-nine Stories*, 1938; *The Snows of Kilimanjaro, and Other Stories*, 1961; *The Nick Adams Stories*, 1972; *The Complete Stories of Ernest Hemingway*, 1987.

Other literary forms • During the four decades in which Ernest Hemingway worked at his craft, he published seven novels, a collection of fictional sketches, and two non-fiction accounts of his experiences in Spain and in Africa; he also edited a collection of war stories and produced a considerable number of magazine and newspaper articles. The latter have been collected in posthumous editions. Manuscripts of two unfinished novels, a series of personal reminiscences, and a longer version of a bullfighting chronicle have been edited and published posthumously as well. In 1981, Hemingway's first biographer, Carlos Baker, brought out an edition of the writer's correspondence.

Achievements • After spending a decade in relative obscurity, Ernest Hemingway finally became a best-selling author with the appearance of *A Farewell to Arms* in 1929. His long association with the publishing firm Charles Scribner's Sons, where the legendary Max Perkins was his editor for more than two decades, assured him wide publicity and a large audience. His passion for high adventure and his escapades as a womanizer made him as famous for his lifestyle as for his literary accomplishments.

For *Whom the Bell Tolls* (1940) was selected to receive the Pulitzer Prize in 1940, but the award was vetoed. In 1952, the Pulitzer committee did give its annual prize to *The Old Man and the Sea* (1952). Two years later, Hemingway was awarded the Nobel Prize in Literature.

Even more significant than these personal awards has been the influence that Hemingway has exerted on American letters. His spare style has become a model for authors, especially short-story writers. Further, Hemingway has received significant critical attention, though not all of it laudatory. His tough, macho attitude toward life and his treatment of women have been the subjects of hostile reviews by feminist critics during the 1970's and 1980's.

Biography • Ernest Hemingway was born in Oak Park, Illinois, a Chicago suburb, in 1899, the second child of Clarence (Ed) and Grace Hemingway's six children. Growing up in a doctor's house, under the domination of a forceful mother, would provide Ernest grist for his literary mill in years to come. The family's frequent trips to northern Michigan would also figure in his development as a writer, providing him a locale for numerous stories and an appreciation for wild terrain.

After graduating from high school, Hemingway left Chicago to take a job on the Kansas City *Star.* Shortly after the United States entered World War I, he quit his job and went to Italy as a Red Cross volunteer. There, he was wounded while assisting Italian soldiers. He spent several weeks in a Milan hospital, where he met Agnes von Kurowsky, who would serve as a model for Catherine Barkeley in *A Farewell to Arms*.

Hemingway returned to the U.S. in 1919 and began writing stories—none of which sold. In 1920, he met Hadley Richardson, whom he married the following year. They returned to Europe late in 1921, and for the next decade, Hemingway spent his time in Paris or in other locales on the Continent, sharpening his skills as a short-story writer. Two collections of his work were published by literary presses. The many expatriates who he met in Paris served as models for his first full-length novel, *The Sun Also Rises*, which appeared to favorable reviews in 1926. In the same year, he and Hadley separated, and Hemingway pursued his relationship with Pauline Pfeiffer, whom he married in 1927.

© The Nobel Foundation

In 1928, Hemingway began the novel that would establish his reputation, *A Farewell to Arms*. Published in 1929, it sold quite well and freed the novelist to pursue other interests for several years. Though he had his residence in Key West, Florida, during the 1930's, he spent considerable time in Spain studying the art of bullfighting and took Pauline on a big-game safari in Africa. Out of these experiences came *Death in the Afternoon* (1932) and *The Green Hills of Africa* (1935); neither received the acclaim that the earlier novels had enjoyed.

In 1937, Hemingway managed to secure a position as a reporter to cover the Spanish Civil War (1936-1939). While in Spain, he spent most of his time with Martha Gellhorn, a young writer whom he had met the previous year in Florida. They were married in 1939 after Hemingway divorced Pauline. The Spanish Civil War furnished him materials for a major novel, *For Whom the Bell Tolls*, and a play, *The Fifth Column* (1938), which had a brief run on Broadway.

After the outbreak of World War II, Hemingway found a way to be with the American troops, joining his third wife as a war correspondent in Europe. His relationship with Gellhorn deteriorated as the war progressed, and by 1945, they had agreed to divorce. Hemingway made Mary Welsh his fourth wife in 1946, after courting her for two years. The two spent Hemingway's remaining years together in Cuba or in various retreats in the United States and in Europe. During the years following World War II, Hemingway started several major projects, but few came to fruition. A notable exception was *The Old Man and the Sea*, which ran in *Life* magazine, sold millions in hardback, and became a motion picture. Growing bouts of depression became harder and harder to fight off, however, and in 1961, Hemingway finally committed suicide while staying at his second home, in Ketchum, Idaho.

Analysis • Any study of Ernest Hemingway's short stories must begin with a discussion of style. Reacting against the overblown, rhetorical, and often bombastic narrative techniques of his predecessors, Hemingway spent considerable time as a young man working to perfect the spare form of narration, dialogue, and description that became the hallmark of his fiction. Nowhere does he achieve greater mastery of his medium than in his short stories. He expressed his belief and described his own method in a passage in *Death in the Afternoon:* "If a writer of prose knows enough about what he is writing about he may omit things that he knows and the reader, if the writer is writing truly enough, will have a feeling of those things as strongly as though the writer has stated them." Following this dictum, Hemingway constructed stories that sometimes make readers feel as if they are unseen auditors at some closet drama, or silent observers at intimate moments in the lives of characters struggling with important, although often private, issues.

"Hills Like White Elephants" • The technique is readily apparent in "Hills Like White Elephants." Set in Spain during the hot summer, the story contains little overt action. Hemingway sketches the background deftly in a single opening paragraph of half a dozen sentences, each of which provides vital information that establishes a physical setting and a symbolic backdrop for the tale. On one side of the little junction station, there are fertile fields; on the other, a barren landscape. Only three characters appear: a man identified as an American, a girl, and a woman who serves them in the little café at which they have stopped to wait for the train that passes through the unnamed town on the route from Barcelona to Madrid. The entire story consists of a single scene in which the man and the girl sit in the café, drink various alcoholic beverages, and converse.

Much of the dialogue seems little more than small talk, but there is an underlying sense of tension from the very first exchange between the man and the girl after they order their beer. The girl mentions that the hills in the distance "look like white elephants," to which her companion replies, "I've never seen one." She immediately responds, "No, you wouldn't have," and he fires back, "I might have. . . . Just because you say I wouldn't have doesn't prove anything." The harshness of their responses contrasts with the inconsequential nature of the subject of their discussion, suggesting that the relationship between them is somehow strained but that neither wishes to discuss openly the real issue over which they are at odds.

For nearly half the story, the two try to make conversation that will ease the tension, but their remarks serve only to heighten it. The man finally mentions, in an almost offhand way, the subject that is really on his mind: He wants the woman to have an abortion. "It's really an awfully simple operation," he tells her. "It's just to let the air in. . . . it's all perfectly natural." The woman, who sits silent through his pleading, finally replies, "Then what will we do afterward?" The man repeatedly assures her that things will be fine if she agrees only to terminate her pregnancy, since in his view the baby will destroy the lifestyle to which they have become accustomed. The woman is wiser; she knows that their relationship has already been poisoned forever and that her pregnancy is not the sole cause. Theirs has been a peripatetic, rootless life, as barren in some ways as the countryside in which they now find themselves.

This summary of the story, like summaries of so many of Hemingway's stories, is inevitably an artificial construct that does not convey the sense of significance that readers get from discovering the larger issues lurking beneath the surface of the dialogue and description. This story is about choice, a vital choice for the woman, who must face the dilemma of either acquiescing to the man's wishes and undergoing what is for her more than a routine operation or risking the loss of a man for whom she has had some genuine feelings of love. Ultimately, either through his insistence or through her own realization that she must try to salvage their relationship even though she senses it will be futile to do so, she agrees to his demands. Her closing remark, on which the story ends, carries with it the strong note of cynicism that pervades the entire story: "I feel fine," she tells the man as they wait for the train's imminent arrival.

In addition to his distinctive style, Hemingway has made his mark in the literary world through the creation of a special kind of hero. The "Hemingway hero," as this figure has come to be known, is usually a man scarred by some traumatic experience—war, violence, a love affair gone bad. Often a physical maiming serves as a symbolic reminder of the psychological dysfunction that characterizes these figures. Despite having received a bad deal from the world, the Hemingway hero perseveres in his search for a good life, creating his own meaning out of the chaos of existence— the hallmark of existential heroes in both American and continental literature. These heroes do what is right without expecting reward, either in this life or in the next.

"In Another Country" • Two fine examples of Hemingway heroes appear in the story "In Another Country." The tale is set in Italy during World War I. A young American officer is recuperating at an Italian hospital, where he mingles with Italian soldiers who have seen considerably more action than he has seen. The extent of their physical injuries mirrors the psychological scars that the war has inflicted on them. One of them, a major who had been a champion fencer before the war, diligently undergoes therapy on a machine designed to restore his withered hand. He is hard on the young American for entertaining thoughts that full recovery for any of them is possible, yet he insists that they all go through the motions—not only with their therapy but also with other activities as well. He demands that the young man learn Italian correctly, for example, arguing that one must follow the rules in life, even when they seem meaningless. Clearly bitter over his fate, he nevertheless keeps up his treatment, until an even more ironic blow strikes him: His young wife contracts pneumonia, and while he is going through the motions to recover the use of a hand damaged beyond restoration, she lies dying. His anger at the cruelty of her impending senseless death drives him to lash out at the institution of marriage; when she dies, however, he breaks down in tears and abandons his therapy. The young American, witness to the Italian's great love, comes to understand how nothing of value can last in this world. The lesson is bitter, but it is one that Hemingway heroes must learn if they are to go on living in a world where the only certainties are chance and chaos.

The young American in "In Another Country" is similar to the main figure in Hemingway's stories, Nick Adams. Seen often as an alter ego for the writer himself, Nick appears in almost twenty stories, and from them readers can piece together his history. A youth who spends time in Michigan and who has many of his ideals shattered by his participation in World War I, Nick develops the characteristics of the Hemingway hero: He becomes convinced of the world's essential callousness, yet he steels himself against its cruelties by observing the rituals that give his own life meaning. Hence, in "Big Two-Hearted River," Nick uses the activities associated with fishing as a kind of therapy to recover from the trauma of war.

"The Killers" • One of the most anthologized of the Nick Adams stories is "The Killers." In this tale, Nick is a young man, still quite naïve and still given to romanticizing events in his life. Two Chicago gunmen arrive at the small diner where Nick is eating. They bully the waiter, bind and gag Nick and the cook, and wait impatiently for a boxer named Ole Andresen, a frequent patron of the diner, so that they can kill him. When Andresen fails to come to dinner, the gangsters finally leave. Knowing that they will seek out Andresen, Nick runs to the boxer's boarding house to warn him. Surprisingly, Andresen refuses to run away; he is content to wait for whatever fate brings him. Nick cannot understand how anyone can accept his lot with such resignation. The lesson for him—and for Hemingway's readers—is that there comes a point when it is impossible to keep moving on, to keep effecting changes by running away. All people must stand and meet the destiny allotted to them, no matter how bitter and unfair that may seem.

"Soldier's Home" • Like Nick Adams and the young American in "In Another Country," the hero of "Soldier's Home" has been scarred by his experience in World War I and has discovered upon his return to his hometown that he cannot find a sympathetic audience for his complaints. The people who did not go to war have already formed their opinions of what happened "over there" and have spent their patriotic energies feting the first groups of returning servicemen. Krebs, the protagonist of the tale, had remained in Germany with the occupation forces for a year beyond the declaration of the armistice. He is greeted with suspicion by his fellow townspeople; they cannot understand why he has waited so long to come home. When he tries to tell people what the war was actually like for him, he is rebuffed. He finds that only when he invents tales of heroism do people pay attention to him. Krebs has slipped into a continual state of ennui; no suggestion for action, either from family or friends, strikes him as worthwhile. In this sense, he fails to fulfill the role of typical Hemingway heroes, most of whom go on doggedly with their lives, all the while knowing that their efforts are doomed to failure. The overriding atmosphere of this story is one of pessimism, almost defeatism without hint of defiance—a rather unusual stance for Hemingway.

Two of Hemingway's greatest short stories are set in Africa, a land to which the author traveled on safari in 1933-1934. Often anthologized and frequently the subject of critical discussion, both "The Snows of Kilimanjaro" and "The Short Happy Life of Francis Macomber" detail relationships between weak men and strong women, displaying Hemingway's hostility toward women who seem to prey upon men, sapping their creativity and in some cases emasculating them.

"The Snows of Kilimanjaro" • "The Snows of Kilimanjaro" tells the story of a writer who is no longer able to practice his craft. Harry, the protagonist, has lost his ability to write well, having chosen to live a life of adventure and luxury. When the story opens, Harry is lying on a cot in the African plains, dying of the gangrene that he contracted by failing to take routine care of a scratch. Much of the story is given over to dialogue between Harry and his wife (presumably his second or third wife), a rich woman on whom he depends now for his livelihood; the tension in their marriage is seen by Harry at times as the cause of his inability to produce the kind of work that had once made him the darling of critics and the public. As Harry sees it, "He had destroyed his talent by not using it, by betrayals of himself and what he believed in." In his imagination, he writes fragments of the wonderful tales that he wishes to tell; these are presented in italic passages interspersed throughout the story.

Though the wife holds out hope that she will be able to get Harry back to a hospital, the writer knows that he is condemned to die of his wound—itself a trivial cut, but in this case fatal because of the circumstances in which Harry finds himself. The physical landscape mirrors Harry's failed aspirations. He is dying on the plains in sight of Africa's highest mountain; he can see the summit, but he knows he will never reach it. Similarly, the gangrenous wound and the resultant decay parallels the decay of the writer who fails to use his talents. Both the striving for some imaginary heights and the senseless destruction of the hero are highlighted in the short epigraph that begins the story. In it, Hemingway notes the presence of a leopard carcass, frozen near the summit of Kilimanjaro. "No one has explained," Hemingway writes, "what the leopard was seeking at that altitude." No one can really explain, either, why men such as Harry strive to be good writers, nor can anyone explain why some succeed while others are blocked from achieving their goals.

Hemingway portrays the wife in this story with only a modicum of sympathy. She seems concerned about her husband, but only because she entertains some romantic notion that believing strongly in something will make it so; she is convinced that she can save her husband despite clear evidence that he is beyond hope. Harry calls her names and blames her for his failure, and though he realizes in the moments before he dies that she is not actually the cause of his failure—"when he went to her [to marry her] he was already over"—she never achieves a level of dignity that merits the reader's sympathy.

"The Short Happy Life of Francis Macomber" • The story that critics often cite as Hemingway's finest is also set in Africa. "The Short Happy Life of Francis Macomber" details the relationship of Francis and Margot Macomber, wealthy Americans on an extended hunt with their professional guide, Robert Wilson. Told nonchronologically, the story reveals Francis's initial cowardice in the face of danger, his eventual triumph over his fear, and his untimely death at the moment when he is able to display his courage.

It would be hard to characterize Francis Macomber as a Hemingway hero. In fact, he is quite the opposite. He has money, but he possesses none of the qualities that Hemingway considers admirable in a man. Francis is dominated psychologically by his wife, and much of what he does is aimed at proving his manhood to her. Their African safari is but another effort on his part to display his worthiness for her continued affection. Unfortunately, Francis is a coward. The story opens with a scene that displays the strain that he is under, having just displayed his inability to stand up to danger. Through conversation among the three principal characters, the reader is able to infer that Francis had failed to complete a kill on a lion he had wounded. When he had gone into the bush to finish off the animal, the lion had charged, and Francis had run away; Wilson had been forced to kill the animal. Margot had observed his behavior, and she is now openly disdainful of her husband. She even plays up to Wilson right in front of Francis. As a final insult, after the Macombers retire to their tent for the evening, Margot slips out and goes to Wilson's tent to spend the night with him.

The following day, Francis has a chance to redeem himself. He and Wilson go out to hunt again; this time the quarry is buffalo. Margot remains in the vehicle once more, and the incident with the lion is repeated: Macomber wounds a bull, which slumps off deep into the brush, and he must go in after the beast to finish the job that he started. This time, when the bull charges, Francis holds his ground and fires at the animal, but the beast keeps on coming at him. Almost immediately, Margot fires from the car, but she hits her husband rather than the buffalo. Francis is killed instantly.

Margot Macomber is a classic Hemingway woman—the kind for which Hemingway has been criticized severely in the years since feminist critics have gained influence in American literary studies. She is physically attractive, though she is reaching the age at which her beauty is starting to fade. She is portrayed as being almost desperate to find some kind of security and is willing to use her sexual wiles to obtain it. She is cruel toward Francis when he shows himself a coward: She rejects physical contact with him and openly fawns over Wilson, though she taunts him, too, about his rather callous attitude toward killing. When Wilson mentions that hunting from a car (which he had done with the Macombers earlier) is a violation of the sport hunting laws and doing so could cost him his license, Margot leaps on the opportunity to suggest that she will use this information to blackmail him at some later time.

Unlike the Macombers, Wilson, Hemingway's white hunter, possesses several of the qualities that the author admires. He is good at his job. He understands people like Francis and Margot, and he has little respect for either of them because they are essentially fakes. He makes his living by taking advantage of the desires of people like them to dabble in life's more dangerous experiences. Having confronted danger almost every day, Wilson has become accustomed to living with his fears. He has even developed a certain callousness toward hunting and especially toward people who go on safaris. The behavior of the Macombers does not shock him. On the contrary, he is prepared for Margot's gesture of infidelity; he carries a double cot with him so he can accommodate wives like her who find their husbands despicable and the white hunter irresistible. Though Wilson is not admirable, in his self-awareness he achieves a certain esteem that is clearly missing in either of the Macombers.

The major critical question that dominates discussion of this story is: Did Margot kill her husband intentionally, or is Francis's death an accident? This is not idle speculation, for the answer at which one arrives determines the interpretation of the story's central theme. If Francis's death is indeed accidental, one can argue that Hemingway is making an ironic statement about the nature of self-fulfillment. At the moment that Francis achieves his greatest personal triumph, his life is ended. The fates simply destroy the possibility of his taking control of his life now that he has displayed himself capable of facing danger. Few details in the story, however, suggest that Francis should be considered a real hero. He may appear heroic at the instant of his death, but nothing he does before he faces the buffalo makes him worthy of emulation, and little that follows his death indicates that he has won new respect or lasting remembrance. Wilson does remind Margot that, had he lived, Francis would have had the courage to leave his wife. One must remember, though, that Wilson is the person who accuses Margot of murdering her husband, and he is searching to attach a motive to Margot's actions.

If one assumes that Margot shoots her husband intentionally, the ending of the story prompts a different interpretation. Francis is a type of the man struggling to break free of the bond that strong women have placed on weak men—and, by extension perhaps, on all men. This harsh antifeminist viewpoint is supported by Hemingway's portrayal of Margot as a classic femme fatale, valued for her beauty and grasping for security in a world where men ostensibly are dominant but where in reality women use their sexuality to gain and maintain control. Francis's killing of the buffalo is symbolic of his ability to destroy the barriers that are keeping him from breaking free of his wife; when she realizes what the event means, Margot takes immediate action to prevent her husband from carrying through on his triumph. However, Hemingway never lets the reader see into the mind of Margot Macomber (though he does share the inner thoughts of Francis, Wilson, and even the lion), so it is impossible to settle on a definitive reading of the wife's motivation and hence of the story itself. As so often happens in real life, readers are left to draw conclusions for themselves from the events which they witness.

A key scene in "The Short Happy Life of Francis Macomber" may serve as a key to understanding Hemingway's philosophy of life. After Macomber has wounded the lion, he and Wilson have a lengthy discussion about the necessity of going after the animal to kill it. "Why not leave him there?" Macomber asks. "It isn't done," Wilson replies; "But," the professional hunter continues, "you don't have to have anything to do with it [the final kill]." Wilson seems to be speaking for Hemingway here. Once something is started, it must be completed. Society depends on that dictum. This is more profound than it may seem at first. As anyone who has read Hemingway's *The Green Hills of Africa* knows, the author sees the safari as a metaphor for life itself. The activities on the safari are self-generated: No one is forced to undertake anything on the hunt, but once one agrees to participate, one has an obligation to carry through according to the rules of the game. Wilson, who sees himself in terms of his profession, must finish the kill even if his dilettante employer refuses to do so. One's duty, Hemingway says in *Death in the Afternoon*, is what one decides to do. Men and women are free to choose their destiny, knowing their struggle will always end in death; doing well that which they choose to do is what makes people heroic.

Laurence W. Mazzeno

Other major works
NOVELS: *The Sun Also Rises*, 1926; *The Torrents of Spring*, 1926; *A Farewell to Arms*, 1929; *To Have and Have Not*, 1937; *For Whom the Bell Tolls*, 1940; *Across the River and into the Trees*, 1950; *The Old Man and the Sea*, 1952; *Islands in the Stream*, 1970; *The Garden of Eden*, 1986; *True at First Light*, 1999.

DRAMA: *Today Is Friday*, pb. 1926; *The Fifth Column*, pb. 1938.

NONFICTION: *Death in the Afternoon*, 1932; *Green Hills of Africa*, 1935; *A Moveable Feast*, 1964; *By-Line: Ernest Hemingway, Selected Articles and Dispatches of Four Decades*, 1967; *Ernest Hemingway: Selected Letters, 1917-1961*, 1981; *Dateline, Toronto: The Complete "Toronto Star" Dispatches, 1920-1924*, 1985; *The Dangerous Summer*, 1985; *Ernest Hemingway on Writing*, 1999 (Larry W. Phillips, editor); *Hemingway on Fishing*, 2000 (Nick Lyons, editor); *Hemingway on Hunting*, 2001 (Sean Hemingway, editor); *Hemingway on War*, 2003 (Sean Hemingway, editor); *Dear Papa, Dear Hotch: The Correspondence of Ernest Hemingway and A. E. Hotchner*, 2005 (Albert J. DeFazio, III, editor); *Hemingway and the Mechanisms of Change: Statements, Public Letters, Introductions, Forewords, Prefaces, Blurbs, Reviews, and Endorsements*, 2006 (Matthew J. Bruccoli, editor).

Bibliography
Benson, Jackson J., ed. *New Critical Approaches to the Short Stories of Ernest Hemingway.* Durham, N.C.: Duke University Press, 1990. Section 1 covers critical approaches to Hemingway's most important long fiction; section 2 concentrates on story techniques and themes; section 3 focuses on critical interpretations of the most impor-

tant stories; section 4 provides an overview of Hemingway criticism; section 5 contains a comprehensive checklist of Hemingway short fiction criticism from 1975 to 1989.

Bloom, Harold, ed. *Ernest Hemingway.* Broomall, Pa.: Chelsea House, 2000. Includes articles by a variety of critics who treat topics such as Hemingway's style, unifying devices, and visual techniques.

Burgess, Anthony. *Ernest Hemingway.* New York: Thames and Hudson, 1999. Originally published in 1978 as *Ernest Hemingway and His World*, an insightful appreciation of Hemingway by one of Great Britain's leading writers. Includes bibliographical references and an index.

Dubus, Andre. "A Hemingway Story." *The Kenyon Review*, n.s. 19 (Spring, 1997): 141-147. Dubus, a respected short-story writer himself, discusses Hemingway's "In Another Country." States that, whereas he once thought the story was about the futility of cures, since becoming disabled he has come to understand that it is about healing.

Lamb, Robert Paul. "The Love Song of Harold Krebs: Form, Argument, and Meaning in Hemingway's 'Soldier's Home.'" *The Hemingway Review* 14 (Spring, 1995): 18-36. Claims that the story concerns both war trauma and a conflict between mother and son. Discusses the structure of the story; argues that by ignoring the story's form, one misses the manner of Hemingway's narrative argument and the considerable art that underlies it.

May, Charles E., ed. *Masterplots II: Short Story Series, Revised Edition.* 8 vols. Pasadena, Calif.: Salem Press, 2004. Designed for student use, this reference set contains articles providing detailed plot summaries and analyses of fifteen short stories by Hemingway: "After the Storm," "An Alpine Idyll," "The Battler," "Big Two-Hearted River," and "A Canary for One" (vol. 1); "A Clean, Well-Lighted Place" (vol. 2); "Hills Like White Elephants" (vol. 3); "In Another Country," "Indian Camp," and "The Killers" (vol. 4); "My Old Man" (vol. 5); "The Short Happy Life of Francis Macomber" (vol. 6); and "The Snows of Kilimanjaro," "Soldier's Home," and "The Three-Day Blow" (vol. 7).

Nolan, Charles J., Jr. "Hemingway's Complicated Enquiry in *Men Without Women.*" *Studies in Short Fiction* 32 (Spring, 1995): 217-222. Examines the theme of homosexuality in "A Simple Enquiry" from Hemingway's *Men Without Women.* Argues that the characters in the story are enigmatic, revealing their complexity only after one has looked carefully at what they do and say.

Reynolds, Michael. *The Young Hemingway.* New York: Blackwell, 1986.

_____. *Hemingway: The Paris Years.* New York: Blackwell, 1989.

_____. *Hemingway: The American Homecoming.* New York: W. W. Norton, 1992.

_____. *Hemingway: The 1930's.* New York: W. W. Norton, 1997.

_____. *Hemingway: The Final Years.* New York: W. W. Norton, 1999. These five volumes by Michael Reynolds come as close to being a definitive study of the life and work of Hemingway as anything yet published. Monumental in scope and exhaustive in detail.

Wagner-Martin, Linda, ed. *Hemingway: Seven Decades of Criticism.* East Lansing: Michigan State University Press, 1998. Collection of essays ranging from Gertrude Stein's 1923 review of Hemingway's stories to recent responses to *The Garden of Eden.* Includes essays on "Indian Camp," "Hills Like White Elephants," and *In Our Time* as self-begetting fiction.

Amy Hempel

Born: Chicago, Illinois; December 14, 1951

Principal short fiction • *Reasons to Live*, 1985; *At the Gates of the Animal Kingdom*, 1990; *Tumble Home: A Novella and Short Stories*, 1997; *The Dog of the Marriage*, 2005; *The Collected Stories of Amy Hempel*, 2006.

Other literary forms • Primarily a short-story writer, Amy Hempel has published comparatively little in othe genres. During the mid-1980's, she was a contributing editor to *Vanity Fair*. She also edited *Unleashed: Poems by Writers' Dogs* in 1995.

Achievements • Amy Hempel's stories have appeared in leading American journals and have been widely anthologized in publications such as *The Best American Short Stories* and *The Best of the Missouri Review, 1978-1990* ("Today Will Be a Quiet Day" appeared in both), *The Pushcart Prize, The Norton Anthology of Short Fiction* (1978), and *New American Short Stories: The Writers Select Their Own Favorites* (1987).

Biography • Amy Hempel was born in Chicago, the eldest of three children (she has two younger brothers). Her family moved to Denver when she was in the third grade, and when she was in high school they moved to San Francisco. Her mother committed suicide when Hempel was eighteen, and at about the same time, Hempel was involved in two serious auto accidents. She spent a number of years in California and studied at both Whittier College and San Francisco State University, and she held a variety of jobs in her twenties. She attended the Bread Loaf Writers' Conference in Vermont for a while but started writing in earnest when she studied with author Gordon Lish in a fiction workshop at Columbia University in 1982. (Lish arranged for her first collection of stories to be published in 1985.) After settling in New York City with her husband, Hempel worked as an editor and contributor to several periodicals and taught and lectured at a number of writing programs and workshops.

Analysis • Amy Hempel is one of the original short-story writers upon whom the term "minimalist" was conferred but, as several critics have noted, "miniaturist" may be a more accurate term. Some of her stories are very short (including the one-sentence "Housewife," which appears in *Tumble Home*). Even in her longer stories the style is compressed and economical in the extreme, the action limited, and the characters constantly making cryptic, ironic comments to one another. In an interview, Hempel said:

> A lot of times what's not reported in your work is more important than what actually appears on the page. Frequently the emotional focus of the story is some underlying event that may not be described or even referred to in the story.

Her stories demonstrate this minimalist philosophy again and again. Hempel's stories often revolve around sadness, loss, and survival: Characters are in hospitals or in recovery or in trouble. However, even in these stories of crisis, Hempel is distinguished by her humor; characters, even children, always have clever things to say to one another, and their conversations are full of metaphors, parables, and symbolic lessons. Hempel's stories often feature dogs, other animals, and best girlfriends, thus often bordering on sentimentality. What saves the stories from falling into that easier literary condition, if anything, is their sardonic wit.

"In the Cemetery Where Al Jolson Is Buried" • "In the Cemetery Where Al Jolson Is Buried" is probably Hempel's best-known work. Originally published in *Tri-Quarterly*, it has been reprinted in *The Editors' Choice: New American Stories* (1985) as well as in the popular *Norton Anthology of Short Fiction*, and it is quintessentially Hempel. The situation is dire: The narrator is visiting a friend in the hospital whom she has avoided visiting for two months; the friend is dying, and both women are in denial. Their conversation is filled with popular trivia, jokes, and funny stories—but many of these hint at the situation (like the narrator's fear of flying). After an earthquake, the narrator relates, a teacher got her sixth-grade students to shout, "*Bad* earth!" at the broken playground. She asks her friend, "Did you know when they taught the first chimp to talk, it lied?" In the end, the friend dies, although the narrator cannot express the thought and says euphemistically, "On the morning she was moved to the cemetery, the one where Al Jolson is buried." In the last image of the story, the narrator describes what happened when the signing chimp had a baby and it died: "her wrinkled hands moving with animal grace, forming again and again the words: Baby, come hug, Baby, come hug, fluent now in the language of grief." Only the narrator is inarticulate in that language, but the sublimation of her feelings makes the story a powerful emotional experience for readers. As is often the case in reading Amy Hempel, less is surely more.

"Today Will Be a Quiet Day" • This short story was also published in Hempel's first collection, *Reasons to Live*, and was later included in *The Best American Short Stories*, *The Pushcart Prize XI*, and *The Best of the Missouri Review: Fiction, 1978-1990*, the journal where it first appeared.

The story describes a father in San Francisco taking his son and daughter out for the day. The father drives north across the Golden Gate Bridge; the three eat lunch in Petaluma, and then the daughter drives them home by a different route. Little happens, in other words, and the story is filled with their conversation, joke-telling, and jousting—like the title, an inscription the son once imagined on his tombstone. The father has taken them out for the day because

> He wanted to know how they were, is all. Just—how were they. . . . You think you're safe, the father thought, but it's thinking you're invisible because you closed your eyes.

A friend of the boy has recently killed himself, readers learn, and the father wants to make sure his own kids are okay. The imagery of the story underlines the question of the difference between appearance and reality: The restaurant where they have lunch still looks like the gas station it originally was; the daughter discovers that the dog she thought was taken to live on a ranch has been put to sleep. At the end of the story, all three are in sleeping bags in the master bedroom of their house. Has the mother died recently? Are the parents divorced? Something hidden has given a tension to the simple events of the story. As they fall asleep, the father asks if they want the good news or bad news first and then says he lied, that there is no bad news. For a little while longer, perhaps, he is going to be able to protect his two teenagers from the dangers of the world, but this protective posture, as Hempel intimates to readers, is precarious.

"The Harvest" • "The Harvest" was originally published in *The Quarterly* and collected in *At the Gates of the Animal Kingdom,* Hempel's second collection of stories, and it is the best example of her metafictional style, a style which has occasionally appeared in her fiction. The story is narrated by a young woman who has been in an auto accident: She and her date were headed for dinner in his car when they were hit, and in the accident the narrator almost lost her leg—or did she? In the second half of the story, she starts to unravel her narrative, and to describe the things she left out of the story, made up, or exaggerated—the marital status of the man, the seriousness of her injuries—and by the end, readers question what, if anything, took place. A psychiatrist tells the girl that victims of trauma often have difficulties distinguishing fiction from reality, and the insight underlines what Hempel is doing in "The Harvest": telling a story that becomes a narrative about making up a story—or about storytelling itself.

"The Most Girl Part of You" • This story was first published in *Vanity Fair* and was subsequently reprinted in *New American Short Stories* and in *At the Gates of the Animal Kingdom,* and it displays the basic Hempel style. A teenage narrator tells of her relationship with her friend, "Big Guy," whose mother hung herself eight days earlier. Although the surface conversation is, as usual, full of jokes, clearly there is something deeper going on. Big Guy sews the girl's name into the skin of his hand, sucks ice to try to crack his teeth, and cuts the insect bites on her body with a razor. When Big Guy starts to make love to her after a dance, the girl claims she is "ready to start to truly be alive," but readers sense something else—his instability, her insecurity, and her obvious pity for his tragedy. The title of the story comes from a film she was forced to watch at school years earlier, *The Most Girl Part of You,* and her own mother has apparently encouraged her sexual initiation. To readers, that introduction to adult sexuality seems wrong. Like the iceberg Ernest Hemingway used to describe a story's hidden content, a large part of this story's cryptic meaning may lie beneath the tense fictional surface.

Tumble Home: A Novella and Short Stories • This collection contains seven stories and the title novella, an eighty-page letter the narrator is writing to an artist she may or may not have met, describing her life inside a mental hospital. Little happens, and readers learn more about the narrator's friends in the institution—Karen, Warren, and Chatty—than about the narrator's own life. There is hardly anything remarkable in their conversations except the wit and sardonic humor of Hempel's elliptical, first-person style. The other stories in the collection—several of them just a few pages long—reflect typical Hempel concerns. "Sportsman," probably the strongest story here, for example, describes the breakup of Jack and Alex. Jack drives east from California to stay with his friends Vicki and her husband, "the doctor," who live on Long Island. Vicki arranges for Jack to see Trina, a psychic, but then Alex calls from California to say that her mother has suffered a stroke. The story ends with Jack and Trina headed into New York City on a date, but the resolution of the relationships here is far from certain. As usual, appearances can be deceiving. The city looks pretty good, Jack comments; "Give it a minute," the psychic responds. Like Raymond Carver, Hempel often tells deceptively simple stories about contemporary characters in deeper trouble than they realize.

David Peck

Other major works
ANTHOLOGY: *Unleashed: Poems by Writers' Dogs*, 1995 (with Jim Shepard).

Bibliography
Aldridge, John W. *Talents and Technicians: Literary Chic and the New Assembly-Line Fiction.* New York: Charles Scribner's Sons, 1992. In a chapter that considers Carver, Ann Beattie, and Frederick Barthelme, Aldridge accuses Hempel of "chronic minimalist constipation" and claims that behind her stories, several of which he analyzes, "there seems to be nothing but a chilly emotional void generated by either an incapacity to feel or a determination to express no feeling if one is there."

Ballantyne, Sheila. "Rancho Libido, and Other Hot Spots." Review of *Reasons to Live*, by Amy Hempel. *The New York Times Book Review*, April 28, 1985, p. 9. Laudatory review that offers useful insights on minimalism and Hempel's treatment of California's culture.

Blythe, Will, ed. *Why I Write: Thoughts on the Craft of Fiction.* Boston: Little, Brown, 1998. As one of twenty-six contributors to this collection, Hempel suggests some of the reasons that she creates her short fiction.

Hallett, Cynthia J. "Minimalism and the Short Story." *Studies in Short Fiction* 33 (1996): 487-495. In an essay that uses Hempel, Raymond Carver, and Ernest Hemingway as primary examples, Hallett attempts to lay down a theoretical foundation for minimalist fiction.

Hemple, Amy. Interview by Suzan Sherman. *BOMB*, Spring, 1997, 67-70. In this wide-ranging interview, Hempel talks about her background as a writer, the origins of many of her stories, and her theories about reading and writing short fiction.

May, Charles E., ed. *Masterplots II: Short Story Series, Revised Edition.* 8 vols. Pasadena, Calif.: Salem Press, 2004. Designed for student use, this reference set contains articles providing detailed plot summaries and analyses of three short stories by Hempel: "Going" (vol. 3), "In the Cemetery Where Al Jolson Is Buried" (vol. 4), and "Today Will Be a Quiet Day" (vol. 7).

Towers, Robert. "Don't Expect Too Much of Men." Review of *At the Gates of the Animal Kingdom*, by Amy Hempel. *The New York Times*, March 11, 1990, sec. 7, p. 11. Contains helpful remarks on Hempel as a miniaturist.

O. Henry

Born: Greensboro, North Carolina; September 11, 1862
Died: New York, New York; June 5, 1910

Principal short fiction • *Cabbages and Kings*, 1904; *The Four Million*, 1906; *Heart of the West*, 1907; *The Trimmed Lamp*, 1907; *The Gentle Grafter*, 1908; *The Voice of the City*, 1908; *Options*, 1909; *Roads of Destiny*, 1909; *Let Me Feel Your Pulse*, 1910; *Strictly Business*, 1910; *The Two Women*, 1910; *Whirligigs*, 1910; *Sixes and Sevens*, 1911; *Rolling Stones*, 1912; *Waifs and Strays*, 1917; *Postscripts*, 1923; *O. Henry Encore*, 1936; *Tales of O. Henry*, 1969; *The Voice of the City, and Other Stories: A Selection*, 1991; *The Best of O. Henry*, 1992; *Collected Stories: Revised and Expanded*, 1993; *Selected Stories*, 1993; *The Best Short Stories of O. Henry*, 1994; *One Hundred Selected Stories*, 1995.

Other literary forms • Although almost all of O. Henry's literary output is in the short-story form, he contributed verse and anecdotes to *Rolling Stone*, the humorous weekly magazine which he founded and edited in 1894. He also experimented with playwriting, collaborating on a musical comedy based on "He Also Serves," with two other gentlemen; the play was staged once, in mid-1909. He also prepared a play based on "The World and the Door."

Achievements • A widely read and published writer, O. Henry wrote short stories that influenced not only the development of magazine fiction as a popular form but also the evolution of modern narrative. Indeed, even very diverse European and South American writers adopt the devices O. Henry perfected. This phenomenon is no accident: His short stories have been widely reprinted and translated, especially in Russia and France, and have been adapted for radio, stage, and television performances.

O. Henry was, however, especially popular in the United States. Extremely humorous, clever, and entertaining, he also managed to capture all that was recognizably and uniquely American—the variegated language, attitudes, spirit, geographical locations, social environments, and, most important, the inclination to identify with the downtrodden, the underdog. O. Henry's contribution to American letters was so obvious that a long-lived literary prize—the annual O. Henry Memorial Award for Prize Stories—was established in 1918 by the New York Society of Arts and Sciences.

Biography • Receiving little formal education, O. Henry, pseudonym of William Sydney Porter, found themes and plots for his short stories in his early jobs as pharmacist, ranch hand, draftsman, and bank teller. After being arrested for embezzlement in 1894, he fled to Honduras, where much of the material for *Cabbages and Kings* was acquired. He returned to Texas in 1897 to be with his dying wife and was convicted and sent to prison one year later. During his imprisonment he began to achieve national prominence for his stories and subsequently continued his writing career in New York. He signed contracts with the *Sunday World* and *Munsey's* for weekly stories drawn from his own experiences in the city. In 1907, he married his childhood sweetheart; three years later he died, finally succumbing to alcohol-induced cirrhosis of the liver and diabetes.

Library of Congress

Analysis • O. Henry's widely varied background provided not only plots for his tales but also characters drawn from all walks of life. Ham in "The Hiding of Black Chief," Caesar in "A Municipal Report," and Lizzie in "The Guilty Party" are only isolated examples of O. Henry's proficiency in creating a vivid sense of the texture of language for the reader by reproducing native dialect, be it Western, southern, or even "New Yorkese." This linguistic sensitivity contributes to O. Henry's versatility as a local colorist, as does his literary self-education. Echoes of Charles Dickens appear in "Elsie in New York," allusions to Greek and Roman mythology in "Hygeia at the Solito" and "The Reformation of Calliope," and parodic references to Arthur Conan Doyle in "The Adventure of Shamrock Jolnes."

O. Henry's popularity stems not only from his depiction of commonplace events and human responses but also from the surprise endings of his "well-made" plots. Talented as an ironist, he both comments upon and sympathizes with the ranch hands, bank clerks, and shop girls whose sorrows and foibles he re-creates. Although much of his humor redounds from his likely use of puns and literary allusions, much might be called the humor of recognition—the rueful grin that occurs when a reader sees his or her own petty flaws mirrored in a character and predicts the almost inevitable downfall. The downfall, however, is often given the comic turn which made O. Henry famous. Kid Brady in "Vanity and Some Sables," for example, would rather go to jail for the theft of furs than tell his girlfriend that her "Russian sables" cost $21.50 in a bargain basement; Maida, the shop girl in "The Purple Dress" who "starves eight months to bring a purple dress and a holiday together," gives up her carefully garnered money to save a spendthrift friend from eviction. Molly sacrifices her furs—and her vanity—to prove Kid's honesty, and Maida is outdone by her tailor in generosity so that she gets both her dress and the marriageable head clerk: These are the twist endings that turn minor personal tragedies into comic triumphs.

"The Gift of the Magi" • Possibly one of the most anthologized of O. Henry's stories is "The Gift of the Magi," a tale about the redeeming power of love. The protagonists, a couple named James and Della Young, struggle to live on a small salary. By Christmas Eve, Della's thrift has gained her only $1.87 for her husband's gift, which she had hoped would be "something fine and rare and sterling." She decides to sell one of the family "treasures"—her long, beautiful chestnut hair—to buy a platinum chain for her husband's prized possession, his watch. The first reversal is that he has bought her a set of pure tortoiseshell combs with which to adorn her long hair; the second, that he has sold his watch to do so.

In this story about the true spirit of gift-giving, both the family treasures and the protagonists take on Old Testamentary significance. Della's hair, the reader is told, puts the queen of Sheba's wealth to shame; Jim's watch rivals all of Solomon's gold. Both unselfishly sacrifice their most precious possession for the other, thereby ushering in a new dispensation on Christmas Eve. Even more, these "two foolish children" acquire allegorical value in their act of giving insofar as they replicate the giving of the three wise men: "Of all who give and receive gifts, such as they are the wisest," O. Henry tells us: "They are the magi." In O. Henry's version, then, the "Gift of the Magi" turns out not to be gold, frankincense, or myrrh, not even hair-combs or a watch chain, but rather, selfless love.

"Past One at Rooney's" • This love is what O. Henry posits as a cure for such social ills as the almost inevitable gang fights and prostitution he portrays in his New York stories. In "Past One at Rooney's," a tale introduced as a modern retelling of William Shakespeare's *Romeo and Juliet* (c. 1595-1596), a gangster, hiding from the police, falls in love with a prostitute. They lie about their occupations for the sake of the other: Eddie MacManus pretends to be the son of a Wall Street broker, while Fanny claims to be a factory girl. When a policeman recognizes MacManus, however, she gives up her new identity to prevent the arrest. Pulling her night's money out of her garter, she throws it at the policeman and announces that MacManus is her procurer. Once they are allowed to leave, MacManus confesses that he really is wanted by the police but intends to reform; and seeing that she still loves him, saves her (as she had "saved" him by sacrificing her hoped-for respectability) through marriage. Such stories of the "golden-hearted prostitute" are plentiful in the O. Henry canon and in themselves provide another clue to O. Henry's popularity—his emphasis on the remnant of human compassion in the most cynical of characters.

Roads of Destiny • O. Henry is interested as well in what might be called the moment of choice: the decision to act, speak, or dress in a way which seems to determine the whole course of a life. The title story of the volume *Roads of Destiny*, a story allegorical in nature, suggests that the choice is not so much among different fates as among different versions of the same fate. Environment, in short, determines character, unless some modicum of self-sacrificing love as in "The Gift of the Magi" intervenes. More concretely, O. Henry saw poverty and exploitation as the twin evils of urban life. Often cited for his sympathetic portrayal of the underpaid store clerk who struggles to survive, he is, as well, a biting critic of those who perpetuate an inhumane system to satisfy personal greed or lust. "An Unfinished Story," for example, castigates an aging lady-killer who is "a connoisseur in starvation. He could look at a shop-girl and tell you to an hour how long it had been since she had eaten anything more nourishing than marshmallows and tea." Piggy, with whom O. Henry himself ruefully identified, preyed on shop girls by offering them invitations to dinner. The working girl might thus keep her conscience and starve, or sell herself and eat: This was her condition as well as her choice.

"The Trimmed Lamp" • Where a choice need not be made through hunger alone is the middle moral ground on which many of O. Henry's stories take place. "The Trimmed Lamp," the titular story of another volume, suggests two opposing ways to deal with an exploitative economic system. Nancy, a country girl content to work for small wages in a department store, mimics not only the quietly elegant dress but also the manners of her wealthy customers, while her friend Lou, a highly paid laundry presser, spends most of her money on expensive, conspicuous clothing. Nancy exploits the system by educating herself in the best it has to offer; Lou works for the system and profits monetarily. In the long run Nancy's education teaches her the difference between purchased quality, such as the clothes Lou wears, and intrinsic quality, which cannot be bought. She refuses an offer of marriage from a millionaire because he is a liar: As O. Henry writes, "the dollar-mark grew blurred in her mind's eye, and shaped itself into . . . such words as 'truth' and 'honor' and now and then just 'kindness.'" Lou, in contrast, becomes the mistress of a wealthy man, leaving her quiet, serious fiancé to Nancy. The final vignette, a plainly clothed but vibrantly happy Nancy trying to comfort her sobbing, fashionably dressed friend, illustrates the divergence between their two philosophies. Although neither can escape completely from the economic system, Nancy refuses to measure human worth in monetary terms; instead, she adopts the same set of values posited in "The Gift of the Magi."

"The Ransom of Red Chief" • Many of the stories O. Henry writes are quite outside the moral framework that is suggested in "The Trimmed Lamp." Like others written about the "gentle grafters" who populated the nether side of his world, the story of "The Ransom of Red Chief" is of the "biter bit" variety. O. Henry's humorous focus on the problems that two kidnappers have with their charge—a redhaired version of Tom Sawyer with the same unflagging energy for mischief—deflects the moral question about the criminal action. Johnny enjoys his adventure; he styles himself Red Chief and tries to scalp one of his captors at daybreak, then rides him to the stockade to "rescue" settlers, feeds him oats, and worries him with questions about why holes are empty. His father's reply to a demand for ransom shows that he understands *who* is in captivity; he offers to take his son back for a sum of $250.

The Gentle Grafter • Similarly, the exploits recounted in *The Gentle Grafter* are modern tall tales, the heroes at times acquiring a mythological aura, at times appearing to be no different from the average man on the street. Grafting, in short, is an occupation which carries the same code of responsibilities as any legitimate business, as is made clear in "Shearing the Wolf." When two con men, Jeff Peters and Andy Tucker, discover that the leading hardware merchant in town intends to frustrate someone else's scheme to sell forged money, they agree that they cannot "stand still and see a man who has built up a business by his own efforts and brains and risk be robbed by an unscrupulous trickster." The twist is that the "trickster" is the merchant and the "businessman" is the forger.

In a number of respects, then, O. Henry contributed immeasurably to the development of the American short story. To be sure, many of his works are considered ephemeral today, primarily because they first appeared as magazine fiction; but a careful perusal reveals that behind the humor lies the mirror of the social reformer. In the characters and situations one notices common human problems of the beginning of the twentieth century; in the humor one notices the attempt to deal with apparently insurmountable social problems. With his clever plot reversals, O. Henry does more than create a new story form; he keeps the reader alive to the connotations of language and aware that in a world dominated by an unfair economic system, human kindness may be the answer.

Patricia Marks
With updates by Terri Frongia

Other major works
PLAY: *Lo*, pr. 1909 (with Franklin P. Adams).
MISCELLANEOUS: *Rolling Stones*, 1912; *O. Henryana*, 1920.
NONFICTION: *Letters to Lithopolis*, 1922; *The Second Edition of Letters to Lithopolis from O. Henry to Mabel Wagnalls*, 1999 (with Mabel Wagnalls).

Bibliography
Arnett, Ethel Stephens. *O. Henry from Polecat Creek*. Greensboro, N.C.: Piedmont Press, 1963. Described by Porter's cousin as a delightful and authentic story of O. Henry's boyhood and youth, this entertaining biography of the early years goes far in illuminating the character-shaping environment and experiences of both Porter and his fiction. Supplemented by illustrations, notes, a bibliography, and an index.

Current-Garcia, Eugene. *O. Henry: A Study of the Short Fiction*. New York: Twayne, 1993. Introduction to O. Henry's stories, largely drawn from Current-Garcia's earlier Twayne volume. Focuses on O. Henry's frequent themes, his romanticism, and his narrative techniques, such as his use of the tall-tale convention. Includes critical excerpts from discussions of O. Henry by other critics.

Eichenbaum, Boris. *O. Henry and the Theory of the Short Story*. Translated by I. R. Titunik. Ann Arbor: University of Michigan Press, 1968. Originally published in Russia in 1925, this study reflects both the Russian interest in O. Henry as a serious writer and the brand of criticism known as Russian Formalism. Because Formalism was more concerned with technical achievement than thematic profundity, O. Henry, who was a technical master, is a perfect candidate for the exercise of this kind of analysis.

Evans, Walter. "'A Municipal Report': O. Henry and Postmodernism." *Tennessee Studies in Literature* 26 (1981): 101-116. Recognizing modern criticism's either trite interpretation or complete indifference to O. Henry's work, through the fiction of postmodernists like Vladimir Nabokov, John Barth, Robert Coover, and William Gass, Evans embarks on a radical revisioning of Porter's literary contributions.

Gallegly, Joseph. *From Alamo Plaza to Jack Harris's Saloon: O. Henry and the Southwest He Knew*. The Hague: Mouton, 1970. By investigating contemporary photographs, literature, popular pursuits, news items, and personalities—both real and fictional—from the contemporary scene of the author, Gallegly provides significant insight into the southwestern stories.

Langford, Gerald. *Alias O. Henry: A Biography of William Sidney Porter*. New York: Macmillan, 1957. Well-documented biography that considers in detail Porter's marriages and the evidence used in his embezzlement trial. The foreword provides a brief but penetrating overview of O. Henry's critical reputation (including overseas) and his place within the context of American literature. Supplemented by illustrations, an appendix about *Rolling Stones*, notes, and an index.

May, Charles E., ed. *Masterplots II: Short Story Series, Revised Edition*. 8 vols. Pasadena,

Calif.: Salem Press, 2004. Designed for student use, this reference set contains articles providing detailed plot summaries and analyses of five short stories by O. Henry: "The Furnished Room" and "The Gift of the Magi" (vol. 3), "Mammon and the Archer" and "A Municipal Report" (vol. 5), and "The Ransom of Red Chief" (vol. 6).

Monteiro, George. "Hemingway, O. Henry, and the Surprise Ending." *Prairie Schooner* 47, no. 4 (1973-1974): 296-302. In rehabilitating O. Henry and his most famous technique, Monteiro makes comparisons with Hemingway's own—but very different—use of the same device. This significant difference Monteiro ascribes to Hemingway's essentially uneasy reception of Porter's work and to the two authors' divergent outlooks on life.

Stuart, David. *O. Henry: A Biography of William Sydney Porter.* Chelsea, Mich.: Scarborough House, 1990. Good, updated volume on O. Henry. Includes bibliographical references.

Watson, Bruce. "If His Life Were a Short Story, Who'd Ever Believe It?" *Smithsonian* 27 (January, 1997): 92-102. Biography strewn with anecdotes and some literary criticism. Includes photographs.

Langston Hughes

Born: Joplin, Missouri; February 1, 1902
Died: New York, New York; May 22, 1967

Principal short fiction • *The Ways of White Folks,* 1934; *Simple Speaks His Mind,* 1950; *Laughing to Keep from Crying,* 1952; *Simple Takes a Wife,* 1953; *Simple Stakes a Claim,* 1957; *The Best of Simple,* 1961; *Something in Common, and Other Stories,* 1963; *Simple's Uncle Sam,* 1965; *The Return of Simple,* 1994; *Short Stories,* 1996.

Other literary forms • Although perhaps best known for his poetry, Langston Hughes explored almost every literary genre. His prose fiction includes novels, humorous books, historical, biographical, autobiographical, and cultural works, translations, lyrics, librettos, plays, and scripts. His total output includes more than seventy volumes, as well as numerous articles, poems, and stories, most which which were published in book form for the first time in the sixteen-volume *Collected Works of Langston Hughes* (2001-2004).

Achievements • Langston Hughes has been acknowledged both before and after his death as the most influential African American writer in the English-speaking world. As a leader of the Harlem Renaissance, he not only wrote in a variety of genres but also edited and encouraged the literary, dramatic, and musical productions of other people of color. Recognition came during his lifetime as early as 1925, when he won the Poetry Prize given by *Opportunity* magazine and the Spingarn prizes of *Crisis* magazine for both poetry and essay writing. His novel *Not Without Laughter* (1930) won the Harmon Gold Medal in 1931. That year he received his first Rosenwald Fellowship, an award repeated in 1941. The John Simon Guggenheim Memorial Foundation Fellowship in 1935, the National Academy of Arts and Letters Award for Literature in 1946, and the Ainsfield-Wolf Award in 1953 continued to keep him in the forefront of the literary community, particularly in New York, throughout his life. His alma mater, Lincoln University, awarded him an honorary doctorate in 1943, and he received others from Howard University and Case Western Reserve University in 1963 and 1964, respectively.

Biography • James Mercer Langston Hughes came from an educated family whose energies were spent primarily in entrepreneurial efforts to combat poverty and institutionalized racism in order to survive. His life repeats a well-known pattern of early twentieth century African American families: a resourceful mother who rented out their home to boarders, a father who had to leave home to find work, a grandmother who cared for him during his early years, and a stepfather. He grew up in the Midwest—Kansas, Illinois, and Ohio—and participated in athletics as well as in literary activities in high school.

Graduating from Central High School in Lincoln, Illinois, in 1920, Hughes attended Columbia University before shipping out on liners bound for Africa and Holland. He also traveled extensively in Europe before returning to the United States in 1925. Then, in 1929, he received a bachelor's degree from Lincoln University, Pennsylvania. Hughes at first subsisted with the help of patrons, but gradually began to earn a living on the proceeds from his writings and his poetry readings. Although mainly basing himself in Harlem, New York City, Hughes continued to travel extensively. He won numerous prizes, grants, and fellowships for his literary achievements before his death in 1967.

Analysis • Langston Hughes records in *The Big Sea: An Autobiography* (1940) his feelings upon first seeing Africa: "when I saw the dust-green hills in the sunlight, something took hold of me inside. My Africa, Motherland of the Negro peoples! And me a Negro! The real thing!" The trip to Africa confirmed what he already knew—that the subject matter of his writings would reflect his desire "to write seriously and as well as I knew how about the Negro people." Most of Hughes's short stories concern themselves with black people presented from many different perspectives and in both tragic and comic dimensions. Even when a white is the protagonist of a story, as in "Little Dog," the gentle black man to whom Miss Briggs is attracted is given special focus. Hughes, however, is not racist in his presentation. People, regardless of their racial background, are people first participating in a common humanity before they are individuals distorted by prejudice based on ignorance, by fear, or by social conditions which create a spiritual and psychological malaise, sometimes crippling in its effect.

"Little Dog" • "Little Dog" tells the story of a white and gaunt middle-aged woman, head bookkeeper of a coal and coke firm for twenty-one years, who, because of her own sense of prudence, responsibility, and concern, sublimates her own desires to care for her mother, and then, after her mother's death, is left alone and lonely. Although she keeps busy, is comfortably situated, and does not think too much of what she may be missing, she occasionally wonders why she knows no one whom she can appreciate as a friend. One day she inexplicably stops the taxicab in which she is riding in front of a pet shop featuring in its window "fuzzy little white dogs," and she purchases for herself a puppy at a very steep price. She arranges with the janitor of her apartment building, "a tow-headed young Swede," to provide food for her dog, which she names Flips, and soon her life revolves around activities centering on Flips.

One day the janitor does not show up to feed the dog; several days pass until Miss Briggs decides she needs to go down to the basement to search out the janitor. With her dog by her side, she knocks at a door behind which she hears sounds of "happy laughter, and kids squalling, and people moving." The door is opened by a small black boy and soon Miss Briggs discovers that the "tall broad-shouldered Negro" standing amid the children is the new janitor.

The image patterns and juxtapositions in the story now begin to form meaningful patterns. The white woman, living "upstairs" with the "fuzzy white dog," is contrasted with the black man and his "pretty little brown-black" children who live "downstairs." The gentle and kind black man begins to service Miss Briggs's needs, bringing more food than is good for the dog because he believes the woman desires it and because he is being paid for it; Miss Briggs, however, never tells him that meat every few days is sufficient. Soon Miss Briggs finds herself hurrying home, never realizing that it is no longer the dog but rather the nightly visits of the janitor that compel her to hurry. One evening her words inadvertently reveal her subconscious needs. The black janitor has just left after delivering Flips's food and she can hear him humming as he returns to his family. Suddenly Miss Briggs says to Flips: "Oh, Flips . . . I'm so hungry."

Now, although she never consciously knows why, Miss Briggs decides she needs to move; "she could not bear to have this janitor come upstairs with a package of bones for Flips again. . . . Let him stay in the basement, where he belonged." The accumulation of references to bones, meat, and services provides for the reader, if not for Miss Briggs, a moment of epiphany: "He almost keeps me broke buying bones," Miss Briggs says to the tall and broad-shouldered black janitor. "True," the janitor answers her. The sustenance the black man provides for the dog is no sustenance for the gaunt and bony woman, nor is the dog, like children, sufficient to keep memory of the departed alive. Miss Briggs moves and shortly is completely forgotten by the people in the neighborhood in which she had lived.

Library of Congress

"Thank You M'am" • If Miss Briggs seems a portrait of a woman dead before she is buried, Mrs. Luella Bates Washington Jones of "Thank You M'am" is a picture of middle-aged woman still vital and vigorous, although she, too, lives alone; and although it appears she has no children of her own, she is still potent, giving new life to a young black boy who attempts to mug her. The child is no match for the woman, who is identified with her purse so large "that it had everything in it but a hammer and nails." She drags him home with her, sees that he washes, and shares with him her frugal meal. Her presence is so overpowering that the boy is more fearful of trying to get away than of staying, but she breaks down his resistance when she speaks to him of common problems. "I was young once and I wanted things I could not get." The boy waits expecting the "but" to follow. The woman anticipates: "You thought I was going to say, *but I didn't snatch people's pocketbooks.* Well, I wasn't going to say that. . . . I have done things, too, which I would not tell you, son. . . . Everybody's got something in common." The woman's actions, however, tell the boy more than her words do, and at the end of the story the boy is unable to use words, although his lips try to phrase more than "Thank you M'am."

"Professor" • One of Hughes's most frequently praised stories is "Professor." Focused through the point of view of its protagonist, Dr. T. Walton Brown (*T* for Tom, Uncle Tom?), the story examines how a black professor of sociology "bows" and "bobs" like a puppet on a string to members of the wealthy white establishment, doing only those things of which they approve, saying what they want to hear, although at times he knows the lies diminish him.

Bitterly ironic in tone, the story begins with the juxtaposition of Brown in dinner dress against the lobby of a run-down segregated hotel and Brown cared for by a white chauffeur who tucks the professor carefully into the luxury of a limousine to carry him through the black ghetto to a private house as large as a hotel. Brown's posture and attire are carefully contrasted with the "two or three ash-colored children" who run across the street in front of the limousine, "their skinny legs and poor clothes plain in the glare of the headlights." So also are the streets and buildings contrasted—"the Negro streets": "pig's knuckle joints, pawnshops, beer parlors—and houses of vice, no doubt—save that these latter, at least, did not hang out their signs" with the "wide lawns and fine homes that lined the beautiful well-lighted boulevard where white people lived."

Brown has bought entry into the white establishment by prostituting himself, by accepting the degradation of the constant diminishing of his selfhood and his negritude. He listens to his white counterpart say: "Why, at our city college here we've been conducting some fine interracial experiments. I have had some colored ministers and high school teachers visit my classes. We found them most intelligent." Although at times Brown is moved to make slight and subtle protest, in the end he agrees with the biased white people, saying "You are right."

Brown's behavior is dictated by his desire for the money the white people offer him as long as he conforms to their expectation. Money will buy Brown prestige, will enable his college to survive, and will further his career. Money will also "take his family to South America in the summer where for three months they wouldn't feel like Negroes." Thus, he dances to the "tune of Jim Crow education," diminishing both himself and his race. Although carefully constructed, the story offers no subtleties beyond the ironies present; image patterns are at a minimum, complex symbolism nonexistent. Characterization, too, is sparse. The reader learns only enough about the professor to make his behavior immediately credible, but a traditional plot line moves with careful pacing to climax and pointed resolution, and the theme overshadows technique.

"Fine Accommodations" • Similar in theme and technique to "Professor" is "Fine Accommodations." In this story, a young black porter learns that the Dr. Jenkins, booked into sleeping car accommodations, is not the leader of his race and "fine man" the naïve porter expects but rather another Uncle Tom who keeps on "being a big man" by "bowing to Southern white customs," by helping to keep poor black people just where they have always been "all the time—poor and black." At the end of the story, the porter makes the point of the story: "The last Negro passenger I had in that drawing room was a pimp from Birmingham. Now I got a professor. I guess both of them have to have ways of paying for such fine accommodations."

"Big Meeting" • From the perspective of complexity, subtlety, and power, "Big Meeting" is a considerably better story. Told in the first person by a young black boy who with a companion is observing a church revival meeting held in the woods, the story recounts the boy's moment of epiphany when he realizes, if only subconsciously, that as a cynical observer rather than a participant in the ritual he is more akin to the white folks gathered to watch than to his own people. Making use of dialect and gospel songs, Hughes builds the story to a powerful sermon where the preacher recounts the betrayal of Christ to the accompaniment of echoing refrains and then moves the sermon to the cadences of poetry:

They brought four long nails
And put one in the palm of His left hand.
The hammer said . . . Bam!
They put one in the palm of His right hand.
The hammer said . . . Bam!
They put one through His left foot . . . Bam!
And one through His right foot . . . Bam!
. . . "Don't drive it!" a woman screamed. "Don't drive them nails!
For Christ's sake! Oh! Don't drive 'em!"

In the woods observing the action, the narrator and his companion are near enough to a car full of white people to overhear what they are saying as they comment in ways showing their biases, limitations, and prejudices. As the narrator hears these comments, he begins to respond, but not enough to cause him to identify with the participants in the service. Rather, both he and his companion seem more concerned with the behavior of their mothers who are taking part in the church rituals.

At the climax of the story, the narrator hears his mother's voice: "Were you there when they crucified my Lord?/ Were you there when they nailed Him to the tree?" At the same time as the mother cries out the questions, the preacher opens his arms wide against the white canvas tent, and his body reflects a crosslike shadow. As the mother asks the question again, the white people in the car suddenly drive away creating a swirl of dust, and the narrator cries after them, "Don't go. . . . They're about to call for sinners. . . . Don't go!"

The boy's cry to the white people reflects his understanding of the parallel setup between the white people and the betrayers of Christ. Hughes goes further than this, however, and provides in the last sentence of the story an epiphanic moment: "I didn't realize I was crying until I tasted my tears in my mouth." The epiphany projects a revelation dimly understood by the narrator but clearly present—that as bad as the white people's behavior seemed, his own rejection of his people and heritage was worse.

Mary Rohrberger
With updates by Emma Coburn Norris

Other major works

CHILDREN'S LITERATURE: *Popo and Fijina: Children of Haiti*, 1932 (story; with Arna Bontemps); *The First Book of Negroes*, 1952; *The First Book of Rhythms*, 1954; *The First Book of Jazz*, 1955; *The First Book of the West Indies*, 1955; *The First Book of Africa*, 1960.

PLAYS: *Little Ham*, pr. 1935; *Mulatto*, pb. 1935; *Troubled Island*, pr. 1935 (opera libretto); *Don't You Want to Be Free?*, pb. 1938; *Freedom's Plow*, pb. 1943; *Street Scene*, pr., pb. 1947 (lyrics; music by Kurt Weill and Elmer Rice); *Simply Heavenly*, pr. 1957 (opera libretto); *Black Nativity*, pr. 1961; *Five Plays*, pb. 1963 (Walter Smalley, editor); *Tambourines to Glory*, pr., pb. 1963; *Jerico-Jim Crow*, pr. 1964; *The Prodigal Son*, pr. 1965.

ANTHOLOGIES: *The Poetry of the Negro, 1746-1949*, 1949 (with Arna Bontemps); *The Book of Negro Folklore*, 1959 (with Bontemps); *New Negro Poets: U.S.A.*, 1964; *The Book of Negro Humor*, 1966; *The Best Short Stories by Negro Writers: An Anthology from 1899 to the Present*, 1967.

NOVELS: *Not Without Laughter*, 1930; *Tambourines to Glory*, 1958.

MISCELLANEOUS: *The Langston Hughes Reader,* 1958; *The Collected Works of Langston Hughes,* 2001-2004 (16 volumes).

NONFICTION: *The Big Sea: An Autobiography,* 1940; *Famous American Negroes,* 1954; *Famous Negro Music Makers,* 1955; *The Sweet Flypaper of Life,* 1955 (photographs by Roy De Carava); *A Pictorial History of the Negro in America,* 1956 (with Milton Meltzer); *I Wonder as I Wander: An Autobiographical Journey,* 1956; *Famous Negro Heroes of America,* 1958; *Fight for Freedom: The Story of the NAACP,* 1962; *Black Magic: A Pictorial History of the Negro in American Entertainment,* 1967 (with Meltzer); *Black Misery,* 1969 (illustrations by Arouni); *Arna Bontemps—Langston Hughes Letters,* 1980; *Remember Me to Harlem: The Letters of Langston Hughes and Carl Van Vechten, 1925-1964,* 2001 (Emily Bernard, editor).

POETRY: *The Weary Blues,* 1926; *Fine Clothes to the Jew,* 1927; *Dear Lovely Death,* 1931; *The Negro Mother,* 1931; *Scottsboro Limited: Four Poems and a Play in Verse,* 1932; *The Dream Keeper, and Other Poems,* 1932; *A New Song,* 1938; *Shakespeare in Harlem,* 1942; *Jim Crow's Last Stand,* 1943; *Lament for Dark Peoples,* 1944; *Fields of Wonder,* 1947; *One Way Ticket,* 1949; *Montage of a Dream Deferred,* 1951; *Selected Poems of Langston Hughes,* 1959; *Ask Your Mama: Or, Twelve Moods for Jazz,* 1961; *The Panther and the Lash: Or, Poems of Our Times,* 1967; *The Poems, 1921-1940,* 2001 (volume 1 of *The Collected Works of Langston Hughes;* Dolan Hubbard, editor); *The Poems, 1941-1950,* 2001 (volume 2 of *The Collected Works of Langston Hughes;* Hubbard, editor); *The Poems, 1951-1967,* 2001 (volume 3 of *The Collected Works of Langston Hughes;* Hubbard, editor).

SCREENPLAY: *Way Down South,* 1939 (with Clarence Muse).

TRANSLATIONS: *Masters of the Dew,* 1947 (of Jacques Roumain; with Mercer Cook); *Cuba Libre,* 1948 (of Nicolás Guillén; with Ben Carruthers); *Gypsy Ballads,* 1951 (of Federico García Lorca); *Selected Poems of Gabriela Mistral,* 1957.

Bibliography

Bloom, Harold, ed. *Langston Hughes.* New York: Chelsea House, 1989. Useful collection of some of the best literary criticism of Hughes's works, with several articles on his poetry, but these reprinted essays do not have notes and Bloom's introduction is perfunctory. Supplemented by a useful bibliography and an index.

Borden, Anne. "Heroic 'Hussies' and 'Brilliant Queers' Genderracial Resistance in the Works of Langston Hughes." *African American Review* 28 (Fall, 1994): 333-345. Discusses Hughes's focus on the interrelationship between gender and racial issues, as well as his treatment of gender issues within the black community—particularly the ways in which gender affects the struggle to maintain community in racist society.

Dickinson, Donald C. *A Bio-Bibliography of Langston Hughes, 1902-1967.* 2d ed. Hamden, Conn.: Archon Books, 1972. With its preface by Arna Bontemps, a major scholar and critic of the Harlem Renaissance and a contemporary of Hughes, the reader has both older and updated assessments of Hughes's achievement. Part 1 is the biography, which incorporates information throughout Hughes's life; part 2 includes all of his work through 1965, except short newspaper articles, song lyrics, and phonographic records. Even a glance at the bibliography gives an indication of the range of Hughes's imaginative achievement.

Harper, Donna Sullivan. *Not So Simple: The "Simple" Stories by Langston Hughes.* Columbia: University of Missouri Press, 1995. Good analysis of Hughes's tales that includes useful bibliographical references and an index.

Hokanson, Robert O'Brien. "Jazzing It Up: The Be-bop Modernism of Langston

Hughes." *Mosaic* 31 (December, 1998): 61-82. Examines how Hughes uses be-bop jazz to challenge both the boundaries between music and poetry and the distinctions between popular and high culture; argues that Hughes's work constitutes a distinctively "popular" modernism that uses jazz to ground its poetic experimentation in the vernacular tradition of African American culture.

May, Charles E., ed. *Masterplots II: Short Story Series, Revised Edition.* 8 vols. Pasadena, Calif.: Salem Press, 2004. Designed for student use, this reference set contains articles providing detailed plot summaries and analyses of three short stories by Hughes: "Gospel Singers" (vol. 3); "On the Road" (vol. 5); and "Thank You, M'am" (vol. 7).

Leach, Laurie F. *Langston Hughes: A Biography.* Westport, Conn.: Greenwood Press, 2004. Overview of Hughes's life and development as a playwright, poet, and journalist.

Ostrom, Hans. *Langston Hughes: A Study of the Short Fiction.* New York: Twayne, 1993. Includes critical analyses of Hughes's short fiction; excerpts from his essays and speeches on his life, racial issues, and writings; and remarks from critics on his works. Contains a life chronology and selected bibliography.

Rampersad, Arnold. *The Life of Langston Hughes.* 2 vols. New York: Oxford University Press, 1986-1988. This major critical biography illustrates not only the triumphs but also the struggles of the man and the writer. The importance of Hughes in the Harlem Renaissance and his symbolic significance in the developing artistic and imaginative consciousness of African American writers come alive in concrete examples.

Schwarz, A. B. Christa. *Gay Voices of the Harlem Renaissance.* Bloomington: Indiana University Press, 2003. Schwarz examines the work of four leading writers from the Harlem Renaissance—Countée Cullen, Langston Hughes, Claude McKay, and Richard Bruce Nugent—and their sexually nonconformist or gay literary voices.

Trotman, C. James, ed. *Langston Hughes: The Man, His Art, and His Continuing Influence.* New York: Garland, 1995. Fine collection of essays dealing with such topics as the Harlem Renaissance, "Race, Culture, and Gender," and Hughes's continuing influence on poetry, fiction, and drama.

Zora Neale Hurston

Born: Eatonville, Florida; January 7, 1891
Died: Fort Pierce, Florida; January 28, 1960

Principal short fiction • *Spunk: The Selected Short Stories of Zora Neale Hurston*, 1985; *The Complete Stories*, 1995.

Other literary forms • Though best known for her novels, especially *Their Eyes Were Watching God* (1937), Zora Neale Hurston wrote in most major genres during her forty-year career. In addition to two posthumously published collections of her short stories, she wrote a few early poems, several short plays, folklore collections, essays, reportage, and an autobiography. Three of her plays were published during the 1920's and 1930's, and a fourth, *Polk County*, that she published in 1944, was produced in 2002. Her four novels include *Jonah's Gourd Vine* (1934), *Their Eyes Were Watching God* (1937), *Moses, Man of the Mountain* (1939), and *Seraph on the Suwanee* (1948). Posthumously published collections of her nonfiction writings include *Go Gator and Muddy the Water: Writings* (1999), *Every Tongue Got to Confess: Negro Foktales from the Gulf States* (2001), and *Zora Neale Hurston: A Life in Letters* (2002).

Achievements • Zora Neale Hurston is best known as a major contributor to the Harlem Renaissance literature of the 1920's. Not only was she a major contributor, but also she did much to characterize the style and temperament of the period; indeed, she is often referred to as the most colorful figure of the Harlem Renaissance. Though the short stories and short plays that she generated during the 1920's are fine works in their own right, they are nevertheless apprentice works when compared to her most productive period, the 1930's. During the 1930's, Hurston produced three novels, all telling examples of her creative genius, as well as two collections of folklore, the fruits of her training in anthropology and her many years of fieldwork. It is Hurston's interest in preserving the culture of the black South that remains among her most valuable contributions. Not only did she collect and preserve folklore outright, but also she used folklore, native drama, and the black idiom and dialect in most of her fiction.

Although Hurston's popularity declined during the 1940's and 1950's, and although she died in relative obscurity in 1960, scholars and critics sparked a Hurston revival during the mid-1970's. Hurston's popularity has never been greater, as her works are considered mainstays in any number of canons, among them African American literature, folklore, southern literature, feminist studies, and anthropology.

Biography • Zora Neale Hurston was born in 1891 in the all-black town of Eatonville, Florida, near Orlando. She was the youngest daughter and the seventh of eight children born to John and Lucy Hurston. Her father was a minister and local government official who wrote many of Eatonville's laws upon its incorporation and served several terms as mayor. Her mother was a homemaker who cared not only for her children but also for an extended family that included, at various times, her own mother and her brother Jim. By all accounts, Hurston's childhood was happy, almost idyllic, free from the poverty and racism that characterized much of the black experience in the South. Indeed, this wholesome upbringing informed much of Hurston's later work and earned for her the designation as an early black cultural nationalist.

Whatever idyllic aspects Hurston's childhood possessed were shattered when Hurston was about nine. The death of Hurston's beloved mother, who encouraged the young Zora to "jump at the sun," precipitated a change. This was followed by her father's remarriage to a woman who had no interest in the children and the subsequent dismantling of the relative happiness of the Hurston household. The next several years of Hurston's life found her much displaced, living variously with older siblings and receiving only sporadic schooling.

Although exact dates are difficult to place in Hurston's early chronology because she frequently lied about her age, various sources reveal that Hurston joined a Gilbert and Sullivan traveling show when she was about fourteen as a wardrobe maid to one of the show's stars. Hurston worked for this show for several years, traveling throughout the South, sometimes without pay. It was with this show, however, that Hurston's talents as raconteur were first noticed, as she often entertained the company with stories, anecdotes, and tales from the black South, told with their own humor, mimicry, and dialect.

Hurston left her job with the Gilbert and Sullivan show in Baltimore, and, out of an intense desire to complete her education, she enrolled in the high school department of the Morgan Academy (now Morgan State University) in that city, completing the high school program in 1919. From Morgan, Hurston entered Howard University, at that time known as "the Negro Harvard," in Washington, D.C. At Howard, Hurston soon came to the attention of Alain Locke, adviser to the Howard Literary Society and later a principal critic of the New Negro movement. Locke invited Hurston to join the literary society, and she soon began publishing in *Stylus*, the Howard University literary magazine. Her first published short story, "John Redding Goes to Sea," appeared in *Stylus* in 1921.

Hurston's talent soon came to the attention of Charles S. Johnson, founder and editor of the National Urban League's magazine *Opportunity*, which held annual contests for young writers. Johnson encouraged Hurston to submit her works to *Opportunity*, which she did; "Drenched in Light" appeared in December, 1924, and "Spunk" in June, 1925. Both "Spunk" and a short play, "Color Struck," were second-place prizewinners in their respective divisions in *Opportunity*'s 1925 contest, and another short story, "Black Death," won honorable mention.

Hurston traveled to New York to attend the 1925 contest awards banquet and found herself in the midst of the Harlem Renaissance, the great outpouring of artistic expression revolving around Harlem. She became an active member of the Harlem literati and soon became the Harlem Renaissance's most colorful figure. In the fall of 1925, Hurston entered Barnard, the women's college of Columbia University, on a scholarship arranged by Annie Nathan Meyer. There, she studied anthropology under Franz Boas and received her degree in 1928.

Beginning in 1927, Hurston traveled throughout the South, collecting folklore, first under the sponsorship of the Association for the Study of Negro Life and History, and later through various fellowships, including a Guggenheim, and the private sponsorship of Charlotte Osgood Mason, a wealthy white patron of Harlem Renaissance writers including Langston Hughes and Alain Locke.

In 1930, Hurston and Hughes collaborated on a black folk play, *Mule Bone*, an undertaking that severed the personal and professional relationship between Hurston

Library of Congress

and Hughes; the break was never mended and kept the play from being published in its entiret until 1991, long after the death of both authors. The dispute precipitated by the question o principal authorship, while cer tainly unfortunate, nevertheles illustrates the fiercely indepen dent temperament that Hurston maintained throughout her life time.

Though the 1930's got off to a rough start with the controvers with Hughes, the decade proved to be Hurston's most productive She published her first novel, *Jo nah's Gourd Vine,* in 1934, fol lowed in rapid succession by the folklore collection *Mules and Men* in 1935; another novel, the now classic *Their Eyes Were Watching God* in 1937; another folklore col lection, *Tell My Horse,* in 1938 and another novel, *Moses, Man o the Mountain,* in 1939. In addi

tion, Hurston wrote several short stories and several essays, notably those on black cul ture, published in Nancy Cunard's massive collection, *Negro,* in 1934.

In 1942, Hurston published her autobiography, *Dust Tracks on a Road.* Althougl the book won the *Saturday Review*'s Ainsfield-Wolf Award for race relations, it proved to be the last significant work of Hurston's career, although she did publish another novel, *Seraph on the Suwanee,* in 1948. There are several reasons for the decline in Hurston's popularity, the most important among them being that her folk-based lit erature did not fit into protest literature, the dominant literary trend of the 1940's, coupled with Hurston's growing conservatism. Further, in September, 1948, shortly before the publication of *Seraph on the Suwanee,* Hurston was falsely charged with se ducing a minor, but before the charges could be dismissed as unfounded, the black press, in particular the *Baltimore Afro-American,* had spread the story to its readers and had severely, almost irreparably, damaged Hurston's reputation. Disillusioned and outraged at her treatment by the court and the black press, Hurston moved back to the South, where she lived for the remainder of her life.

The 1950's was a tragic decade for Hurston. Her career was stagnant, and al though she kept writing, she received rejection after rejection. She did, however, do some reporting for the *Pittsburgh Courier,* a black paper with a national circulation; published several essays; and accepted several speaking engagements. She supported herself with occasional work, including substitute teaching and writing freelance ar ticles for various papers.

Toward the end of the 1950's, Hurston's health became increasingly fragile. She suffered from overweight, hypertension, poor diet, gallbladder trouble, ulcers, and various stomach ailments. In 1959, she suffered a stroke, and in October of that year was placed in the Saint Lucie County welfare home, where, alone and penniless, she died on January 28, 1960. She was buried by subscription a week later in Fort Pierce's segregated cemetery, the Garden of the Heavenly Rest.

Analysis • The bulk of Zora Neale Hurston's short fiction is set in her native Florida, as are most of her novels. Even when the setting is not Florida, however, the stories are informed by the life, habits, beliefs, and idioms of the people whom Hurston knew so well, the inhabitants of Eatonville primarily. One criticism often leveled at Hurston was that she frequently masqueraded folklore as fiction, or, in other cases, imposed folklore on the fictive narrative. Whatever the merits of such criticism may be, Hurston's short stories abound with an energy and zest for life that Hurston considered instructive for her readers.

"John Redding Goes to Sea" • Hurston's first published short story is entitled "John Redding Goes to Sea." It was published in the May, 1921, issue of the *Stylus*, the literary magazine of Howard University, and was reprinted in the January, 1926, issue of *Opportunity*. Although the story is obviously the work of a novice writer, with its highly contrived plot, excessive sentimentality, and shallow characterizations, its strengths are many, strengths upon which Hurston would continue to draw and develop throughout her career.

The plot is a simple one: Young John Redding, the titular character, wants to leave his hometown to see and explore parts and things unknown. Several circumstances conspire, however, to keep him from realizing his dream. First, John's mother, the pitifully possessive, obsessive, and superstitious Matty Redding, is determined not to let John pursue his ambitions; in fact, she pleads illness and threatens to disown him if he leaves. Second, John's marriage to Stella Kanty seems to tie him permanently to his surroundings, as his new wife joins forces with his mother to discourage John's desire to travel. Further, his mother's tantrums keep John from even joining the Navy when that opportunity comes his way. Later, when John is killed in a tempest while working with a crew to build a bridge on the St. John's River, his father forbids his body to be retrieved from the river as it floats toward the ocean. At last, John will get his wish to travel and see the world, although in death.

If the plot seems overdone and the sentimentality overwhelming, "John Redding Goes to Sea" does provide the reader with the first of many glimpses of life among black Floridians—their habits, superstitions, strengths, and shortcomings. For example, one of the more telling aspects of the story is that Matty believes that her son was cursed with "travel dust" at his birth; thus, John's desire to travel is Matty's punishment for having married his father away from a rival suitor. Hurston suspends judgment on Matty's beliefs; rather, she shows that these and other beliefs are integral parts of the life of the folk.

Another strength that is easily discernible in Hurston's first short story is her detailed rendering of setting. Hurston has a keen eye for detail, and nowhere is this more evident than in her descriptions of the lushness of Florida. This adeptness is especially present in "John Redding Goes to Sea" and in most of Hurston's other work as well.

By far the most important aspect of "John Redding Goes to Sea" is its theme that people must be free to develop and pursue their own dreams, which is a recurring theme in the Hurston canon. John Redding is deprived of self-expression and self-determination because the wishes and interpretations of others are imposed upon him. Hurston clearly has no sympathy with those who would deprive another of freedom and independence; indeed, she would adamantly oppose all such restrictive efforts throughout her career as a writer and folklorist.

"Spunk" • Another early short story that treats a variation of this theme is "Spunk," published in the June, 1925, issue of *Opportunity*. The central character, Spunk Banks, has the spunk to live his life as he chooses, which includes taking another man's wife and parading openly around town with her. Although Hurston passes no moral judgment on Banks, she makes it clear that she appreciates and admires his brassiness and his will to live his life according to his own terms.

When the story opens, Spunk Banks and Lena Kanty are openly flaunting their affair in front of the Eatonville townspeople, including Lena's husband, Joe Kanty. The other town residents make fun of Joe's weakness, his refusal to confront Spunk Banks. Later, when Joe desperately attacks Spunk with a razor, Spunk shoots and kills him. Spunk is tried and acquitted but is killed in a work-related accident, cut to death by a circle saw.

Again, superstition plays an important role here, for Spunk claims that he has been haunted by Joe Kanty's ghost. In fact, Spunk is convinced that Joe's ghost pushed him into the circle saw, and at least one other townsman agrees. As is customary in Hurston's stories, however, she makes no judgment of the rightness or wrongness of such beliefs but points out that these beliefs are very much a part of the cultural milieu of Eatonville.

"Sweat" • Another early Eatonville story is "Sweat," published in 1926 in the only issue of the ill-fated literary magazine *Fire!*, founded by Hurston, Hughes, and Wallace Thurman. "Sweat" shows Hurston's power as a fiction writer and as a master of the short-story form. Again, the story line is a simple one. Delia Jones is a hardworking, temperate Christian woman being tormented by her arrogant, mean-spirited, and cruel husband of fifteen years, Sykes Jones, who has become tired of her and desires a new wife. Rather than simply leaving her, though, he wants to drive her away by making her life miserable. At stake is the house for which Delia's "sweat" has paid: Sykes wants it for his new mistress, but Delia refuses to leave the fruit of her labor.

Sykes uses both physical and mental cruelty to antagonize Delia, the most far-reaching of which is Delia's intense fear of snakes. When Delia's fear of the caged rattlesnake that Sykes places outside her back door subsides, Sykes places the rattlesnake in the dirty clothes hamper, hoping that it will bite and kill Delia. In an ironic twist, however, Delia escapes, and the rattlesnake bites Sykes as he fumbles for a match in the dark house. Delia listens and watches as Sykes dies a painful, agonizing death.

Although "Sweat" makes use of the same superstitious beliefs as Hurston's other stories, a more complex characterization and an elaborate system of symbols are central to the story's development. In Delia, for example, readers are presented with an essentially good Christian woman who is capable of great compassion and long suffering and who discovers the capacity to hate as intensely as she loves; in Sykes, readers are shown unadulterated evil reduced to one at once pitiful and horrible in his suffering. In addition, the Christian symbolism, including the snake and the beast of burden, adds considerable interest and texture to the story. It is this texture that makes "Sweat" Hurston's most rewarding work of short fiction, for it shows her at her best as literary artist and cultural articulator.

"The Gilded Six-Bits" • Although Hurston turned to the longer narrative as the preferred genre during the 1930's, she continued writing short stories throughout the remainder of her career. One such story is "The Gilded Six-Bits," published in 1933, which also examines relationships between men and women. In this story, the marriage bed of a happy couple, Joe and Missie May Banks, is defiled by a city slicker, Otis D. Slemmons. Missie May has been attracted by Slemmons's gold money, which she desires to get for her husband. The gold pieces, however, turn out to be gold-plated. Hurston's message is nearly cliché—"all that glitters is not gold"—but she goes a step further to establish the idea that true love transcends all things. Joe and Missie May are reconciled at the end of the story.

Last Stories • Hurston's last stories are fables that seem to have only comic value but do, however, advance serious thoughts, such as the ridiculousness of the idea of race purity in "Cock Robin, Beale Street" or the equal ridiculousness of the idea that the North was better for blacks, in "Story in Harlem Slang." Although these stories are not artistic achievements, they do provide interesting aspects of the Hurston canon.

In many ways, Hurston's short stories are apprentice works to her novels. In these stories, she introduced most of the themes, character types, settings, techniques, and concerns upon which she later elaborated during her most productive and artistic period, the 1930's. This observation, however, does not suggest that her short stories are inferior works. On the contrary, much of the best of Hurston can be found in these early stories.

Warren J. Carson
With updates by the Editors

Other major works

PLAYS: *Color Struck*, pb. 1926; *The First One*, pb. 1927; *Mule Bone*, pb. 1931 (with Langston Hughes); *Polk County*, pb. 1944, pr. 2002.

NOVELS: *Jonah's Gourd Vine*, 1934; *Their Eyes Were Watching God*, 1937; *Moses, Man of the Mountain*, 1939; *Seraph on the Suwanee*, 1948.

MISCELLANEOUS: *I Love Myself When I Am Laughing . . . and Then Again When I Am Looking Mean and Impressive: A Zora Neale Hurston Reader*, 1979.

NONFICTION: *Mules and Men*, 1935; *Tell My Horse*, 1938; *Dust Tracks on a Road*, 1942; *The Sanctified Church*, 1981; *Folklore, Memoirs, and Other Writings*, 1995; *Go Gator and Muddy the Water: Writings*, 1999 (Pamela Bordelon, editor); *Every Tongue Got to Confess: Negro Foktales from the Gulf States*, 2001; *Zora Neale Hurston: A Life in Letters*, 2002 (Carla Kaplan, editor).

Bibliography

Bloom, Harold, ed. *Zora Neale Hurston*. New York: Chelsea House, 1986. From the series Modern Critical Views. An excellent collection of criticism of Hurston's work and life. Includes early commentary by Franz Boas and Langston Hughes, as well as later studies.

Chinn, Nancy, and Elizabeth E. Dunn. "'The Ring of Singing Metal on Wood': Zora Neale Hurston's Artistry in 'The Gilded Six-Bits.'" *The Mississippi Quarterly* 49

(Fall, 1996): 775-790. Discusses how Hurston uses setting, ritual, dialect, and the nature of human relationships in the story; argues that the story provides a solution to the problem of reconciling her rural Florida childhood with her liberal arts education and training.

Cooper, Jan. "Zora Neale Hurston Was Always a Southerner Too." In *The Female Tradition in Southern Literature*, edited by Carol S. Manning. Urbana: University of Illinois Press, 1993. Examines the hitherto neglected role that Hurston played in the Southern Renaissance between 1920 and 1950. Argues that Hurston's fiction is informed by a modern southern agrarian sense of community. Suggests that the Southern Renaissance was a transracial, cross-cultural product of the South.

Cronin, Gloria L., ed. *Critical Essays on Zora Neale Hurston*. New York: G. K. Hall, 1998. Useful collection of essays by various scholars that includes bibliographical references and an index.

Donlon, Jocelyn Hazelwood. "Porches: Stories: Power: Spatial and Racial Intersections in Faulkner and Hurston." *Journal of American Culture* 19 (Winter, 1996): 95-110. Comments on the role of the porch in Faulkner and Hurston's fiction as transitional space between the public and the private where the individual can negotiate an identity through telling stories.

Hill, Lynda Marion. *Social Rituals and the Verbal Art of Zora Neale Hurston*. Washington, D.C.: Howard University Press, 1996. Chapters on Hurston's treatment of everyday life, science and humanism, folklore, and color, race, and class. Hill also considers dramatic reenactments of Hurston's writing. Includes notes, bibliography, and an appendix on "characteristics of Negro expression."

Hurston, Lucy Anne. *Speak, So You Can Speak Again: The Life of Zora Neale Hurston*. New York: Doubleday, 2004. Brief biography written by Hurston's niece. Most notable for the inclusion of rare photographs, writings and other multimedia personal artifacts. Also contains an audio CD of Hurston reading and singing.

Lyons, Mary E. *Sorrow's Kitchen: The Life and Folklore of Zora Neale Hurston*. New York: Charles Scribner's Sons, 1990. Perhaps the only straightforward biography of Hurston, written with the younger reader in mind. Especially useful for those who need a primer on Hurston's background in all-black Eatonville.

May, Charles E., ed. *Masterplots II: Short Story Series, Revised Edition*. 8 vols. Pasadena, Calif.: Salem Press, 2004. Designed for student use, this reference set contains articles providing detailed plot summaries and analyses of four short stories by Hurston: "Drenched in Light" (vol. 2), "The Gilded Six-Bits" (vol. 3), and "Spunk" and "Sweat" (vol. 7).

Newsom, Adele S. *Zora Neale Hurston: A Reference Guide*. Boston: G. K. Hall, 1987. Catalog of Hurston criticism spanning the years 1931-1986, arranged chronologically with annotations. This source is an invaluable aid to serious scholars of Hurston. Also contains an introduction to the criticism on Hurston. An especially useful resource for all inquiries.

West, Margaret Genevieve. *Zora Neale Hurston and American Literary Culture*. Gainesville: University Press of Florida, 2005. Chronicle of Hurston's literary career and a look at why her writing did not gain popularity until long after her death.

Washington Irving

Born: New York, New York; April 3, 1783
Died: Tarrytown, New York; November 28, 1859

Principal short fiction • *The Sketch Book of Geoffrey Crayon, Gent.*, 1819-1820; *Bracebridge Hall*, 1822; *Tales of a Traveller*, 1824; *The Alhambra*, 1832; *Legends of the Conquest of Spain*, 1835; *The Complete Tales of Washington Irving*, 1975, 1998 (Charles Neider, editor).

Other literary forms • Washington Irving distinguished himself in a variety of genres. His finest and most typical book, *The Sketch Book of Geoffrey Crayon, Gent.*, blends essay, sketch, history, travel, humor, and short story; his first best-seller was a satire, *A History of New York* (1809); he coauthored a successful play, *Charles the Second: Or, The Merry Monarch* (1824); but he devoted the latter and most prolific part of his career to books of travel and especially of history.

Achievements • Washington Irving was America's first internationally recognized author. Although he achieved national attention with his satiric *A History of New York*, his fame abroad was made with *The Sketch Book of Geoffrey Crayon, Gent.* Irving was a prolific writer throughout his life, from his first collaborations with his brother William and friend James Kirke Paulding, to his many biographies of well-known historical figures, including George Washington. Among his most successful works were his collections of sketches and tales, a distinction then made between realistic and imaginative types of fiction. His sketches often make use of historical sources, while the tales usually derive from traditional folktales. His best-known stories, "Rip Van Winkle" and "The Legend of Sleepy Hollow," although largely copied from German folktales, still maintain an originality through their American settings and Irving's own gently humorous style.

Biography • The eleventh and last child of a successful merchant, Washington Irving, somewhat frail and indulged as he was growing up, was the favorite child of his Anglican mother and Presbyterian minister father. As a young man, Irving studied law in the office of Josiah Ogden Hoffman, to whose daughter he was attracted, and enjoyed the social and cultural advantages of New York City as something of a gentleman-playboy. At this time, he dabbled in satirical writing in serial publications. He gained a certain amount of cosmopolitan sophistication with a tour of Europe in 1804-1806, during which time he kept a journal.

Irving was admitted to the New York bar at the age of twenty-three and nominally began to work as a lawyer on Wall Street, although he practiced little. Instead, he wrote serial essays with his brother and James Kirke Paulding for a periodical they called *Salmagundi*, modeled on Joseph Addison's *Spectator*, "to instruct the young, reform the old, correct the town, and castigate the age." This amounted to making light fun of fashion and social mores in high society, although occasionally they made jabs at Thomas Jefferson's "logocratic" democracy.

"Diedrich Knickerbocker's" *A History of New York* followed in 1809; originally in-

Library of Congress

tended as a parody of a pretentious New York guidebook, it had
become instead a comic history of
the Dutch in New York. When Matilda Hoffman died in the same
year, Irving, distraught, stopped
writing for a time. He moved in
1811 to Washington, D.C., to
lobby for the Irving brothers' im-
porting firm. Still affected by Matilda's death, he drifted into several different occupations, lost the
brothers' firm to bankruptcy, yet
benefited from his literary contacts to the point where he began
to pursue writing with renewed effort. By the time he published *The
Sketch Book of Geoffrey Crayon, Gent.*
in 1819, he was on his way to supporting himself through his writing. In order to find original materials for his sketches, he made
various trips through Europe and
America, including a ministry to
Spain; he returned to New York fi-
nally in 1832. His long absence, reminiscent of Rip Van Winkle's, provided him with a
new perspective on the United States, whose western frontier was beginning to open;
he packed again, this time for the West, and wrote many of his books out of the experience. He finally returned home to the Hudson, ensconced in family and friends,
where he died in 1859.

Analysis • Washington Irving's masterpiece, *The Sketch Book of Geoffrey Crayon, Gent.*,
has a historical importance few American books can match. No previous American
book achieved a really significant popular and critical success in England, the only
arena of opinion which then mattered; but Irving demonstrated that an American
could write not only well but also brilliantly even by British standards. In fact,
throughout the century English as well as American schoolboys studied Irving's book
as a model of graceful prose.

Irving had achieved some popularity in his own country well before the British triumphs. In 1807-1808, Irving, his brother William, and James Kirke Paulding collaborated on the independently published periodical series, *Salmagundi*. Since the project was a true collaboration, scholars are in doubt as to precisely who deserves credit
for precisely what, but two pieces deserve particular notice. "Sketches from Nature"
sentimentally sketches two old bachelors, one of whom restores the spirits of the
other by leading him through scenes reminiscent of their youth. "The Little Man in
Black" is supposedly a traditional story passed through generations of a single family.
Irving here introduces another old bachelor, who wanders into the village a stranger
to all and sets up housekeeping in a decrepit house rumored to be haunted. First ostracized by the adults, then tormented by the local children, ultimately he dies by

starvation, in his last moments forgiving all, a true but misunderstood Christian. Both pieces display Irving's graceful style, his prevalent sentimentality, and his wholehearted commitment to charming, pleasing, and entertaining his audience. Both feature an old bachelor stereotype which he inherited from the Addisonian tradition and continued to exploit in later works. The pieces differ in their formal focus, however, and aptly illustrate the two poles of Irving's fictional nature. The second shows his fondness for the tale tradition: He cites a source in family folklore; the narrative hangs on striking incident; and he flavors the atmosphere with a suggestion of the supernatural. The first features virtues of the periodical essay: evocation of character divorced from dramatic incident; a style dominated by smoothness (Edgar Allan Poe's term was "repose") and by descriptions strong on concrete detail; and an essentially realistic atmosphere. Irving's unique genius led him to combine the best of both traditions in his finest fiction and thereby to create the modern short story in America.

Irving's early career coincided with the rise of Romanticism, and the movement strongly influenced his greatest book, *The Sketch Book of Geoffrey Crayon, Gent.* Here he capitalized on the element which strongly marks his most successful stories: imagination. Consistently, Irving's most successful characters, and stories, are those which most successfully exploit the imagination.

"The Spectre Bridegroom" • In "The Spectre Bridegroom," the title character triumphs not through strength, physical skills, or intelligence, but rather through manipulating the imaginations of those who would oppose his aims. The story's first section humorously describes a bellicose old widower, the Baron Von Landshort, who has gathered a vast audience, consisting mostly of poor relatives properly cognizant of his high status, to celebrate his only daughter's marriage to a young count whom none of them has ever seen. In the story's second part, the reader learns that as the count and his friend Herman Von Starkenfaust journey to the castle, they are beset by bandits; the outlaws mortally wound the count who, with his last breath, begs Von Starkenfaust to relay his excuses to the wedding party. The story's third part returns to the castle where the long-delayed wedding party finally welcomes a pale, melancholy young man. The silent stranger hears the garrulous Baron speak on, among other matters, his family's longstanding feud with the Von Starkenfaust family; meanwhile the young man wins the daughter's heart. He shortly leaves, declaring he must be buried at the cathedral. The next night the daughter's two guardian aunts tell ghost stories until they are terrified by spying the Spectre Bridegroom outside the window; the daughter sleeps apart from her aunts for three nights, encouraging their fears the while, and finally absconds. When she returns with her husband, Von Starkenfaust, who had pretended to be the Spectre, they both are reconciled with the Baron and live happily ever after.

By becoming in one sense artists themselves, Herman and his bride both manipulate the imaginations of the Baron, the aunts, and the entire wedding party to make their courtship and elopement possible; here, happily, the dupes lose nothing and share the ultimate happiness of the dupers. There are at least three dimensions to "The Spectre Bridegroom": As it is read, one can imaginatively identify with the duped family and believe the Spectre genuine, or alternately identify with the young couple innocently manipulating their elders. A third dimension enters when the reader recalls the personality of the frame's Swiss tale-teller, occasionally interrupting himself with "a roguish leer and a sly joke for the buxom kitchen maid" and himself responsible (it is surely not the modest and proper Geoffrey Crayon or Washington Irving) for the suggestive antlers above the prospective bridegroom's head at the feast.

"Rip Van Winkle" • The narrative perspectives informing Irving's single greatest achievement, "Rip Van Winkle," radiate even greater complexities. At the simplest level the core experience is that of Rip himself, a good-natured idler married to a termagant who drives him from the house with her temper. While hunting in the woods, Rip pauses to assist a curious little man hefting a keg; in a natural amphitheater he discovers dwarfish sailors in archaic dress playing at ninepins. Rip drinks, falls asleep, and awakens the next morning alone on the mountainside. In a subtle, profound, and eerily effective sequence, Irving details Rip's progressive disorientation and complete loss of identity. The disintegration begins mildly enough—Rip notices the decayed gun (a thief's substitute he thinks), his dog's absence, some stiffness in his own body—each clue is emotionally more significant than the last, but each may be easily explained. Rip next notices changes in nature—a dry gully has become a raging stream, a ravine has been closed by a rockslide; these are more dramatic alterations, but still explainable after a long night's sleep.

Upon entering the village, he discovers no one but strangers and all in strange dress; he finds his house has decayed, his wife and children have disappeared; buildings have changed as well as the political situation and even the very manner and behavior of the people. In a terrible climax, when Irving for once declines to mute the genuine horror, Rip profoundly questions his own identity. When he desperately asks if anyone knows poor Rip Van Winkle, fingers point to another ragged idler at the fringe, the very image of Rip himself as he had ascended the mountain. Even Poe or Franz Kafka never painted a loss of identity more absolute, more profound, more credible, more terrible. After a moment of horror, Irving's sentimental good humor immediately reasserts itself. Rip's now-adult daughter appears and recognizes him; the ragged idler turns out to be his son, Rip, Jr. Rip himself hesitates for a moment, but, upon learning that his wife has died "but a short time since," declares his identity and commences reintegrating himself in the community, eventually to become an honored patriarch, renowned for recounting his marvelous experience.

Thus is the nature of the core narrative, which is almost all most people ever read. The reader values the story for its profound mythic reverberations; after all, throughout Western civilization Irving's Rip has become an archetype of time lost. The reader may also appreciate Irving's amoral toying with lifestyles, and although the Yankee/Benjamin Franklin lifestyle Rip's wife advocates and which leads to her death (she bursts a blood vessel while haggling) fails to trap Rip, he triumphs by championing the relatively unambitious, self-indulgent lifestyle Irving identifies with the Dutch. Still, many people feel tempted to reject the piece as a simplistic fairy tale dependent on supernatural machinery for its appeal and effect. This is a mistake.

Those who read the full story as Irving wrote it will discover, in the headnote, that Irving chose to relate the story not from the point of view of an omniscient narrator but from that of Diedrich Knickerbocker, the dunderheaded comic persona to whom years earlier he had ascribed the burlesque *A History of New York*. The presence of such a narrator—and Irving went to some trouble to introduce him—authorizes the reader to reject the supernatural elements and believe, as Irving tells us many of

Rip's auditors believed, that in actuality Rip simply tired of his wife, ran away for twenty years, and concocted a cock-and-bull story to justify his absence. Looking closer, the reader discovers copious hints that this is precisely what happened: Rip's reluctance to become Rip again until he is sure his wife is dead; the fact that when his neighbors hear the story they "wink at each other and put their tongues in their cheeks"; the fact that, until he finally established a satisfactory version of the events, he was observed "to vary on some points every time he told it." In the concluding footnote, even dim Diedrich Knickerbocker acknowledges the story's doubtfulness but provides as evidence of its truth the fact that he has heard even stranger supernatural stories of the Catskills, and that to authenticate his story Rip signed a certificate in the presence of a justice of the peace. "The story, therefore, is beyond the possibility of doubt." Irving clearly intends to convince his closest readers that Rip, like the couple in "The Spectre Bridegroom," triumphed over circumstances by a creative manipulation of imagination.

"The Legend of Sleepy Hollow" • In "The Legend of Sleepy Hollow" our source is again Diedrich Knickerbocker, and again, creatively manipulating the imaginations of others proves the key to success. The pleasant little Dutch community of Sleepy Hollow has imported a tall, grotesquely lanky Yankee as schoolmaster, Ichabod Crane. Although he is prey to the schoolboys' endless pranks, he himself ravenously and endlessly preys on the foodstuffs of the boys' parents. Ichabod finally determines to set his cap for the pretty daughter of a wealthy farmer, but Brom Bones, the handsome, Herculean local hero, has likewise determined to court the girl. The climax comes when the principals gather with the entire community at a dance, feast, and "quilting frolic" held at Katrina Van Tassel's home. Brom fills the timorous and credulous Ichabod full of tales of a horrible specter, ghost of a Hessian soldier beheaded by a cannonball, who inhabits the region through which Ichabod must ride that night to return home. As he makes his lonely journey back, Ichabod encounters the dark figure who carries his head under his arm rather than on his neck and who runs him a frightful race to a bridge. At the climax the figure hurls his head and strikes Ichabod, who disappears, never to be seen in the village again. Brom marries Katrina, and years later the locals discover that Ichabod turned lawyer, politician, newspaperman, and finally became a "justice of the Ten Pound Court."

Again it is the character who creatively manipulates the imagination who carries the day; the manipulatee wins only the consolation prize. Again the Dutch spirit triumphs over the Yankee. In this story there is something quite new, however; for the first time in American literature there is, in the characterization of Brom Bones, the figure of the frontiersman so important to American literature and American popular culture: physically imposing, self-confident, rough and ready, untutored but endowed with great natural virtues, gifted with a rude sense of chivalry, at home on the fringes of civilization, and incorporating in his own being the finer virtues of both the wilderness and the settlements. Irving here brilliantly anticipated both the essence of southwestern humor and of James Fenimore Cooper's seminal Westerns.

Irving wrote a great many other stories, including several romantic tales set in Spain, most of them flawed by superficiality and sentimentality; he also produced a number of gothic stories, some of which are still read with pleasure, among them "The Adventure of the German Student" and "The Devil and Tom Walker." Irving,

however, reached his highest point in his first published short story, "Rip Van Win
kle." He never equaled it in any subsequent story—but then, only a tiny handful o
writers ever have.

Walter Evan
With updates by Ann A. Merrit

Other major works

MISCELLANEOUS: *The Complete Works of Washington Irving*, 1969-1989 (30 volumes).

PLAY: *Charles the Second: Or, The Merry Monarch*, pb. 1824 (with John Howard
Payne).

NONFICTION: *A History of New York*, 1809; *Biography of James Lawrence*, 1813; *A His
tory of the Life and Voyages of Christopher Columbus*, 1828; *A Chronicle of the Conquest o
Granada*, 1829; *Voyages and Discoveries of the Companions of Columbus*, 1831; *A Tour of the
Prairies*, 1835; *Astoria*, 1836; *The Adventures of Captain Bonneville*, 1837; *The Life of Olive
Goldsmith*, 1849; *The Life of George Washington*, 1855-1859 (5 volumes).

Bibliography

Aderman, Ralph M., ed. *Critical Essays on Washington Irving*. Boston: G. K. Hall, 1990
Collection of essays on Irving, from both the nineteenth and twentieth centuries
Includes discussions of Irving's art and literary debts, the relationship of his sto
ries to his culture, and his generic heritage.

Hiller, Alice. "'An Avenue to Some Degree of Profit and Reputation': *The Sketch Boo*
as Washington Irving's Entree and Undoing." *Journal of American Studies* 31 (Au
gust, 1997): 275-293. Claims that some of Irving's personal correspondence re
veals that *The Sketch Book* may have been pitched deliberately at the British market,
resulting in a paralysis of Irving's powers of writing.

McFarland, Philip. *Sojourners*. New York: Atheneum, 1979. Although not a conven
tional biography, this study of Washington Irving's life situates the writer in his var
ious geographic, historic, and literary contexts. McFarland explores in detail the
life of Irving, interweaving his biography with those of other important Americans
of the time, among them Aaron Burr, the abolitionist John Brown, and John J.
Astor.

May, Charles E., ed. *Masterplots II: Short Story Series, Revised Edition*. 8 vols. Pasadena,
Calif.: Salem Press, 2004. Designed for student use, this reference set contains arti
cles providing detailed plot summaries and analyses of four short stories by Irving:
"Adventure of the German Student" (vol. 1), "The Devil and Tom Walker" (vol. 2),
"The Legend of Sleepy Hollow" (vol. 4), and "Rip Van Winkle" (vol. 6).

Murray, Laura J. "The Aesthetic of Dispossession: Washington Irving and Ideologies
of (De)colonization in the Early Republic." *American Literary History* 8 (Summer,
1996): 205-231. Argues that Euro-Americans cultivated their sense of vulnerability
with respect to Great Britain and in so doing rhetorically excused themselves from
their colonizing role with regard to Native Americans.

Myers, Andrew B., ed. *A Century of Commentary on the Works of Washington Irving*.
Tarrytown, N.Y.: Sleepy Hollow Restorations, 1976. This collection, divided into
four chronologically ordered sections, offers writings on Washington Irving. Part
1 includes essays by contemporaries of Irving, such as William Cullen Bryant and
Henry Wadsworth Longfellow; part 2 covers evaluations from the beginning of
the nineteenth century. Early twentieth century scholars of American literature,

such as Fred Lewis Pattee, Vernon Louis Parrington, and Van Wyck Brooks, are represented in part 3, and part 4 covers the period 1945 to 1975. The collection gives an excellent overview of the development of Irving criticism and provides a point of departure for further investigations.

Piacentino, Ed. "'Sleepy Hollow' Comes South: Washington Irving's Influence on Old Southwestern Humor." *The Southern Literary Journal* 30 (Fall, 1997): 27-42. Examines how nineteenth century southern backwoods humorists adapted Washington Irving's "The Legend of Sleepy Hollow" to a southern setting; discusses a number of works with clear parallels to Irving's story.

Plummer, Laura, and Michael Nelson. "'Girls Can Take Care of Themselves': Gender and Storytelling in Washington Irving's 'The Legend of Sleepy Hollow.'" *Studies in Short Fiction* 30 (Spring, 1993): 175-184. Argues that Sleepy Hollow is female-centered; the tales that circulate in the region focus on emasculated, headless spirits and serve to drive out masculine interlopers like Ichabod and thus preserve the old Dutch domesticity based on wives' tales.

Rubin-Dorsky, Jeffrey. *Adrift in the Old World: The Psychological Pilgrimage of Washington Irving.* Chicago: University of Chicago Press, 1988. In this study of Irving's short fiction, Rubin-Dorsky sets out to establish Irving's Americanness, thus reversing a critical tradition that marked him as primarily imitative of British prose style. By placing Irving within his historical context, Rubin-Dorsky underscores Irving's central position in early American letters.

Tuttleton, James W., ed. *Washington Irving: The Critical Reaction.* New York: AMS Press, 1993. Essays of critical interpretation of Irving's works.

Williams, Stanley T. *The Life of Washington Irving.* 2 vols. New York: Oxford University Press, 1935. This thorough biography provides a wealth of biographical and literary detail about Irving. Volume 1 is most useful for those interested in Irving's short fiction, as it covers his life and his work up to *The Alhambra.*

Shirley Jackson

Born: San Francisco, California; December 14, 1916
Died: North Bennington, Vermont; August 8, 1965

Principal short fiction • *The Lottery: Or, The Adventures of James Harris*, 1949 (also pb. as *The Lottery, and Other Stories*); *Just an Ordinary Day*, 1996 (Laurence Jackson Hyman and Sarah Hyman Stewart, editors); *Shirley Jackson Collected Stories*, 2001.

Other literary forms • Shirley Jackson's dozen published books include novels, humorous fictionalized autobiographies, and children's books. Many of her stories, essays, and public speeches remain uncollected. Several works have been adapted to other media: "The Lottery" for television, *We Have Always Lived in the Castle* (1962) for stage, and *The Bird's Nest* (1954) and *The Haunting of Hill House* (1959) for the cinema.

Achievements • Shirley Jackson is probably best known for her short story "The Lottery," which was first published in the June 26, 1948, edition of *The New Yorker*. As with the majority of her works, both short stories and novels, "The Lottery" explores the darker side of the human psyche, often in a manner disturbing to the reader. In addition to using ordinary settings for extraordinary occurrences, Jackson often injects an element of the supernatural. This is seen, for example, in the story "The Visit" and in the novel *The Haunting of Hill House*. In addition, Jackson has published *Life Among the Savages* (1953), a highly humorous account of her home life. In 1961, Jackson received the Edgar Allan Poe Award for her story "Louisa, Please." She was awarded the Syracuse University Arents Pioneer Medal for Outstanding Achievement in 1965. In 2001, Peterson Publishing brought out a new edition of her best short fiction in its Great Author series.

Biography • Shirley Jackson was born in California on December 14, 1919, and moved with her family to New York when she was sixteen. After an unsuccessful year at the University of Rochester, Jackson enrolled, at the age of twenty, in the University of Syracuse. This was to be the beginning of an independent life for the author, as she would finally be away from the dominating presence of her mother. At Syracuse, Jackson met Stanley Edgar Hyman, the man she would marry in 1940. Hyman achieved fame in his own right as a teacher, writer, and critic. The marriage between Jackson and Hyman was tumultuous in many ways but provided a stabilizing factor for Jackson. Her literary production increased markedly after the marriage and the birth of their four children. Jackson's own phobias, however, kept creeping into this successful, if odd, relationship. She was an agoraphobic and a depressive. Part of the latter affliction was contributed to by her asthma and arthritis, as well as Hyman's extramarital affair in the early 1960's. In addition, Jackson had never really been a social person—she was much too individualistic to fit into any of the polite social molds. In 1963, Jackson began to turn around psychologically. Her husband made a new commitment to the marriage, and an enlightened psychiatrist began to help her work with the agoraphobia. Her writing continued to be an outlet for her. Although Jackson recovered emotionally, she never recovered physically. She was obese and a chain smoker. She died on August 8, 1965, at the age of forty-eight.

Analysis • Shirley Jackson's stories seem to center on a single concern: Almost every story is about a protagonist's discovering or failing to discover or successfully ignoring an alternate way of perceiving a set of circumstances or the world. Jackson seems especially interested in how characters order their worlds and how they perceive themselves in the world. Often, a change in a character's perspective leads to anxiety, terror, neurosis, or even a loss of identity. Although it is tempting to say that her main theme is the difference between appearance and reality, such a statement is misleading, for she seems to see reality as Herman Melville's Ishmael comes to see it, as a mirror of the perceiving soul. It is rarely clear that her characters discover or lose their grasp of reality; rather, they form ideas of reality that are more or less moral and more or less functional. For Jackson, reality is so complex and mysterious that one inevitably only orders part of it. A character may then discover parts that contradict a chosen order or that attract one away from the apparent order, but one can never affirm the absolute superiority of one ordering to another. In this respect, Jackson's fictional world resembles those of Stephen Crane and Ernest Hemingway. Perhaps the major differences between her fiction and theirs is that her protagonists are predominantly women; she explores some peculiarly feminine aspects of the problem of ideas of order.

Jackson's middle-class American women seem especially vulnerable to losing the security of a settled worldview. Their culture provides them with idealistic dream visions of what their lives should be, and they have a peculiar leisure for contemplation and conversation imposed upon them by their dependent roles. Men in her stories seem so busy providing that they rarely look at and think about the order of things. Her career women are more like these men. In "Elizabeth" and "The Villager," the protagonists succeed, albeit precariously, in preserving ideas of themselves and their worlds despite the contradictory facts that seem increasingly to intrude. In these two stories, one sees a sort of emotional cannibalism in the protagonists as they attempt to preserve belief in an order that reality seems no longer disposed to sustain. Several stories show a woman's loss of an ordering dream. These divide into stories about women who experience the terror of loss of identity and those who may find a liberating and superior order in what would ordinarily be called infantile fantasy.

Among those who lose a dream are the protagonists of "The Little House" and "The Renegade." In "The Little House," a woman's first possession of her own small country house is ruined by the terrifying insinuations of her new neighbors; they leave her alone on her first night after relating to her their fears that the previous owner was murdered and that the murderer will return. In "The Renegade," a mother discovers an unsuspected cruelty in her neighbors and even in her children when her dog is accused of killing chickens. Although Jackson's humorous autobiographical stories are of a different order, the often anthologized "Charles" tells of a mother's discovery that the nemesis of the kindergarten whose antics her son reports each day is not the mythical Charles, but her own son, Laurie.

Perhaps the most successful escape into fantasy is Mrs. Montague's in "The Island." All her physical needs are provided by a wealthy but absent son and the constant attendance of Miss Oakes. Mrs. Montague lives in her dream of a tropical paradise, virtually untouched by her actual world. This escape is judged by the ironic frame of Miss Oakes's relative poverty and her inevitable envy, suffering, spite, and ugliness; she has no chance of such an escape herself. Some movements into fantasy are terrifying or at least ambiguous. In "The Beautiful Stranger," Margaret resolves a tension in her marriage by perceiving the man who returns from a business trip as a stranger, not her husband. By the end of the story, this fantasy has led to her losing herself, unable to find her home when she returns from a shopping trip. A similar but more ambiguous situation develops in "The Tooth," in which a woman escapes into a vision of an island to evade the pain of an aching tooth. Many of Jackson's protagonists conceive of an island paradise as an ideal order when their control of the immediate is threatened.

Some ideas of order remain impenetrable. In "Louisa, Please," a variation on Nathaniel Hawthorne's "Wakefield," a runaway daughter returns home after a long absence to discover that her family has built a life around her loss and will not be convinced of her return. In "Flower Garden" and "After You, My Dear Alphonse," protagonists find themselves unable to change or to abandon racist ideas because the ideas are too strong or because of community pressure.

"The Visit" • A closer look at three especially interesting stories reveals more about Jackson's themes and gives some indication of her technical proficiency. In "The Visit," Margaret comes to visit a school friend, Carla Rhodes, for the summer. The beautiful Rhodes estate includes a dream house with numerous fantastic rooms. The house seems not quite real; nearly every room is covered with tapestries depicting the house in different hours and seasons, and there is a mysterious tower of which no one speaks. For Margaret, the house and the family are ideal, especially when Carla's brother, Paul, arrives with his friend, the Captain. This idyll lasts until the evening of Paul's departure, when Margaret discovers that Paul has been a hallucination or a ghost, for the Captain is Carla's brother and no one else has seen Paul. This revelation clarifies several mysteries that have developed, especially that of Margaret's strange visit to the tower. Paul has told Margaret that an old aunt often secludes herself in the tower. When Margaret pays her a visit, she undergoes a not really frightening but certainly haunting experience with old Aunt Margaret. At the end of the story, the reader must conclude Aunt Margaret to be an apparition, that she is probably the Margaret who died for love and whose picture in mosaic appears on the floor of one room. Young Margaret has lost a phantom lover as old Margaret lost her Paul. Young Margaret realizes this at the same time that she is made aware of time's effect on the house: the age and weakness of the Rhodeses, the bitter darkness of their true son, and the physical decay of the buildings. Furthermore, she begins to doubt her own place and identity as she wonders if her visit to the house will ever end. The home of her dreaming now threatens to become an imprisoning nightmare.

In retrospect, the device by which Jackson encourages the reader to share Margaret's hallucination or haunting may seem contrived. This choice, however, seems effective because the more fully the reader shares Margaret's perceptions and the more subdued (without being absent) are the disturbing elements, the more fully will the reader share the shock of her awakening into nightmare. Also technically effective are the apparent connections with Poe's "The Fall of the House of Usher." Most important among these is the succession of mirror images: multiple pictures of the house, between the house and Mrs. Rhodes, among members of the family, between the two Margarets, and between the decline of the family and of the house. These connections seem deliberately chosen in part to emphasize the contrasts between Margaret and Poe's narrator. Because Margaret's response to the house is so positive, the shock of her discovery is greater by contrast. Furthermore, when she dis-overs this house to be like what one knows the House of Usher to be, one sees the analogy between her terror at imprisonment and that of Poe's narrator when he sees a universe unnaturally lit by a blood red moon, yet another image of the coffin lit from within. Margaret actually enters one of the dream worlds promised American girls. Under its spell, she overlooks its flaws and forgets about time, but when the Captain breaks the spell, pointing out signs of decay, Paul departs and Margaret becomes acutely aware of time as her nightmare begins.

"Pillar of Salt" • Time is often the destroyer of feminine ideals in Jackson's stories because they seem to depend on a suspension of time. In "Pillar of Salt," another Margaret loses her secure world. A trip to New York City with her husband forces a new perspective on her which produces her anxiety and, finally, paranoia. It remains unclear, however, whether her paranoia is illness or a healthy reaction to an inimical environment.

The couple's first week in the city is idyllic, and the fast pace is a pleasant change from New Hampshire. At a party at the end of the first week, however, Margaret begins to feel isolated, unnoticed among strangers who behave in strange ways. She learns there is a fire in the building but is unable to persuade anyone else to leave. The fire turns out to be two buildings away, but she is the only one to heed the warning and flee the building. She comes to see this nightmarish experience as symbolic of her experience in New York and perhaps of her life as a whole. She begins to notice new details about the city: dirt, decay, speed, stifling crowds. She feels increasingly isolated and insignificant. Of this life she thinks, "She knew she was afraid to say it truly, afraid to face the knowledge that it was a voluntary neck-breaking speed, a deliberate whirling faster and faster to end in destruction." Even her friends' Long Island beach cottage shows the spreading blight; there they find a severed human leg on the sand. Margaret comes to believe that her former order was illusory. Upon returning to the city, she begins to hallucinate, to see the destruction of the city in fast motion. Windows crumble. Her bed shakes. Driven from her apartment, she finds herself unable to return, paralyzed in a fast-moving, anonymous crowd on the wrong side of a mechanical and murderous river of traffic.

Margaret comes to see herself in a modern Sodom, paralyzed not because she has disobeyed God, but because she has seen in prophetic vision the truth about the city: It is no home for human beings but rather is impersonally intent upon destruction. The allusion of the title and her critique of city life verify her perception; however, those who do not share her vision remain capable of functioning. As in "The Visit," the internal view of Margaret encourages a close identification between reader and character which makes judgment difficult until the reader can step back; but stepping back from "Pillar of Salt" plunges the reader deeper into mystery. In both stories, the protagonist moves from dream to nightmare, but in "Pillar of Salt," the reader is much less certain that the move is to a better or more accurate view of reality.

"The Lottery" • Shirley Jackson's reputation rests primarily upon her most anthologized story, "The Lottery." Her lecture on this story (printed in *Come Along with Me*) suggests that her creation of a normal setting convinced many readers that the story was largely factual. In fact, the central problem of the story seems to be to reconcile the portrait of typical small-town life in which the characters seem just like the reader with the horrifying ritualistic killing these people carry out. Here, apparently incompatible ideas of order are thrust upon the reader for resolution, perhaps in order to complicate the reader's conceptions.

"The Lottery" develops by slowly raising the level of tension in the semipastoral setting until a series of carefully arranged revelations brings about a dramatic and shocking reversal. The villagers gather at mid-morning on a late June day for an annual event, the lottery, around which a great deal of excitement centers. Jackson supplies details which arouse reader curiosity: Nearly all towns have a similar lottery; it is as old as the town; it has an elaborate ritual form which has decayed over time; every adult male *must* participate; some believe the orders of nature and of civilization depend on carrying it out correctly. The family of the man who draws the marked lot must draw again to determine the final winner. The tension built out of reader curiosity and the town's moods reverses toward the sinister when the "winner's" wife reveals that she does not want to win. Once this reversal is complete, the story moves rapidly to reveal the true nature of the lottery, to choose a victim for annual sacrifice by stoning. Jackson heightens the horror of this apparently unaccountable act with carefully chosen and placed details.

Several commentators have attempted to explain the story through reconstructing the meaning of the ritual and through carefully examining the symbols. Helen Nebeker sees the story as an allegory of "man trapped in a web spun from his own need to explain and control the incomprehensible universe around him, a need no longer answered by the web of old traditions." These attempts to move beyond the simple thriller seem justified by the details Jackson provides about the lottery. This ritual seems clearly to be a tradition of prehistoric origin, once believed essential for the welfare of the community. Even though its purpose has become obscure and its practice muddled, it continues to unify and sustain the community. Critics tend to underemphasize the apparent health and vitality of the community, perhaps feeling that this ritual essentially undercuts that impression. It is important to notice that one function of the lottery is to change the relationship between community and victim. The victim is chosen at random, killed without malice or significant protest, and lost without apparent grief. This story may be what Richard Eastman has called an open parable, a fable which applies at several levels or in several contexts.

"The Lottery" creates an emotional effect of horror at the idea that perhaps in human civilization, the welfare of the many depends often on the suffering of the few: the victim race, the exploited nation, the scapegoat, the poor, the stereotyped sex, the drafted soldier. In these cases, instead of a ritual, other aspects of the social order separate oppressor and victim, yet the genuine order and happiness of the majority seems to depend on the destruction of others. In this respect, "The Lottery" resembles many stories of oppression, such as Franz Kafka's "The Bucket Rider" and some stories by Richard Wright; its purpose may be to jar readers into thinking about ways in which their lives victimize others.

Jackson places the reader of "The Lottery," which lacks a protagonist, in a position similar to that of the protagonists of "The Visit" and "Pillar of Salt." The story moves from a relatively secure agrarian worldview to an event which fantastically complicates that view. Here, as in most of her stories, Jackson emphasizes the complexity of reality. Nature and human nature seem unaccountable mixtures of the creative and destructive. Her best people are in search of ways to live in this reality without fear and cruelty.

Terry Heller
With updates by Victoria E. McLure

Other major works

CHILDREN'S LITERATURE: *Nine Magic Wishes,* 1963; *Famous Sally,* 1966.

PLAY: *The Bad Children,* pb. 1958.

NOVELS: *The Road Through the Wall,* 1948 (also pb. as *The Other Side of the Street*); *Hangsaman,* 1951; *The Bird's Nest,* 1954 (also pb. as *Lizzie*); *The Sundial,* 1958; *The Haunting of Hill House,* 1959; *We Have Always Lived in the Castle,* 1962.

MISCELLANEOUS: *Come Along with Me: Part of a Novel, Sixteen Stories, and Three Lectures,* 1968 (Stanley Edgar Hyman, editor).

NONFICTION: *Life Among the Savages,* 1953; *The Witchcraft of Salem Village,* 1956; *Raising Demons,* 1957.

Bibliography

Hall, Wylie. *Shirley Jackson: A Study of the Short Fiction.* New York: Twayne, 1993. Introduction to Jackson's stories, with comments by Jackson herself, and a few short, previously published, critical articles by others. Discusses Jackson's interest in the occult, her fascination with dream situations, her focus on children, and her most famous story, "The Lottery."

Hattenhauer, Darryl. *Shirley Jackson's American Gothic.* New York: State University of New York Press, 2003. Strong argument for Jackson's modernity. Analyzes her use of the supernatural as metaphor and illuminates the influences of Jackson's substance abuse, marital strife, and political leanings on her work.

Kittredge, Mary. "The Other Side of Magic: A Few Remarks About Shirley Jackson." In *Discovering Modern Horror Fiction,* edited by Darrell Schweitzer. Mercer Island, Wash.: Starmont House, 1985. Useful study of the use of magic and the supernatural in Jackson's works. The author draws interesting comparisons between Jackson's fiction and nonfiction works.

May, Charles E., ed. *Masterplots II: Short Story Series, Revised Edition.* 8 vols. Pasadena, Calif.: Salem Press, 2004. Designed for student use, this reference set contains articles providing detailed plot summaries and analyses of three short stories by Jackson: "Charles" (vol. 1); and "The Lottery" and "One Ordinary Day, with Peanuts" (vol. 5).

Murphy, Bernice M., ed. *Shirley Jackson: Essays on the Literary Legacy.* Jefferson, N.C.: McFarland, 2005. Collection of essays that reveals Jackson's better and lesser known works.

Oppenheimer, Judy. *Private Demons: The Life of Shirley Jackson.* New York: G. P. Putnam's Sons, 1988. This volume is the first extensive biography of Jackson. It is finely detailed and provides the reader an excellent view of this author. Oppenheimer interviewed close to seventy persons for this book, including Jackson's family members, friends, and neighbors. Contains numerous photographs.

Parks, John G. "'The Possibility of Evil': A Key to Shirley Jackson's Fiction." *Studies in Short Fiction* 15, no. 3 (Summer, 1978): 320-323. This useful article concentrates on Jackson's short stories. Parks draws useful comparisons with authors such as Flannery O'Connor and Nathaniel Hawthorne.

Rubinstein, Roberta. "House Mothers and Haunted Daughters: Shirley Jackson and Female Gothic." *Tulsa Studies in Women's Literature* 15 (Fall, 1996): 309-331. Explains how Jackson's fiction demonstrates her increasingly gothic representation of the bonds between mothers and daughters; discusses this theme in a number of Jackson's stories.

Schaub, Danielle. "Shirley Jackson's Use of Symbols in 'The Lottery.'" *Journal of the Short Story in English* 14 (Spring, 1990): 79-86. Discusses how Jackson distracts the reader's attention into thinking the story is a fable or fairy tale; discusses the symbolic use of setting, atmosphere, numbers, names, and objects in the story.

Stark, Jack. "Shirley Jackson's 'The Lottery.'" In *Censored Books*, edited by Nicholas Karolider, Lee Burgess, and John M. Kean. Lanham, Md.: Scarecrow Press, 1993. Discusses some of the reasons for the story's being censored in schools and some of the values of teaching the story to teenagers; argues that it encourages reflection on some of the issues teens need to understand to become good citizens.

Yarmove, Jay A. "Shirley Jackson's 'The Lottery.'" *The Explicator* 52 (Summer, 1994): 242-245. Discusses the importance of setting, historical time, and irony of character names in the allegorical meaning of the story. Compares the ending of the story to the ending of Hardy's *Tess of the D'Urbervilles*.

Henry James

Born: New York, New York; April 15, 1843
Died: London, England; February 28, 1916

Principal short fiction • *A Passionate Pilgrim*, 1875; *The Madonna of the Future*, 1879; *The Siege of London*, 1883; *Tales of Three Cities*, 1884; *The Author of Beltraffio*, 1885; *The Aspern Papers*, 1888; *The Lesson of the Master*, 1892; *The Private Life, Lord Beaupre, The Visits*, 1893; *The Real Thing*, 1893; *Terminations*, 1895; *Embarrassments*, 1896; *The Two Magics: The Turn of the Screw and Covering End*, 1898; *The Soft Side*, 1900; *The Better Sort*, 1903; *The Novels and Tales of Henry James*, 1907-1909 (24 volumes); *The Finer Grain*, 1910; *A Landscape Painter*, 1919; *Travelling Companions*, 1919; *Master Eustace*, 1920; *Stories of Writers and Other Artists*, 1944; *Henry James: Selected Short Stories*, 1950; *Henry James: Eight Tales from the Major Phase*, 1958; *The Complete Tales of Henry James*, 1962-1965 (12 volumes; Leon Edel, editor); *The Figure in the Carpet, and Other Stories*, 1986; *The Jolly Corner, and Other Tales*, 1990; *The Uncollected Henry James: Newly Discovered Stories*, 2004.

Other literary forms • Henry James was a prolific writer who, from 1875 until his death, published at least one book every year. In addition to his considerable output of short fiction, he wrote novels, dramas, biographies, autobiographies, reviews, travelogues, art and literary criticism, literary theory, and letters. His most notable novels include *Daisy Miller* (1878), *The Europeans* (1878), *The Portrait of a Lady* (1880-1881), *Washington Square* (1880), *The Bostonians* (1885-1886), *The Tragic Muse* (1889-1890), *The Turn of the Screw* (1898), *The Wings of the Dove* (1902), and *The Ambassadors* (1903). James was a pioneer in the criticism and theory of fiction. Much of his criticism appears in Leon Edel and Mark Wilson's edition of *Henry James: Literary Criticism* (1984). James's creative method and the sources of many of his works are documented in *The Complete Notebooks of Henry James* (1987).

Achievements • Henry James contributed to the development of the modernist novel, invented cryptic tales that border on the postmodern, and laid the groundwork for the contemporary theory of narrative. He completed twenty novels (two uncompleted novels were published posthumously). He also wrote 112 short stories, 7 travel books, 3 autobiographies, numerous plays, 2 critical biographies, and voluminous works of criticism. James brought the American novel to its fruition and gave it an international flavor. He transformed the novel of physical adventure to one of psychological intrigue. His character studies are probing and intense. His precise use of limited point of view invites the reader to become actively engaged in interpreting events and ferreting out meaning. His works also achieve a masterful blend of summarized action and dramatic scenes. In his short fiction, he created the forerunners of the modern antiheroes and invented metafictional stories about the nature of art and writing. Also, his critical works and many prefaces have given modern critics a vocabulary for discussing character and point of view. James edited a deluxe edition of his complete works, received honorary degrees from Harvard University and the University of Oxford, and was awarded the Order of Merit from King George V. His works have influenced Joseph Conrad, James Joyce, Virginia Woolf, and Graham Greene.

Biography • Henry James's career is usually divided into four periods: his formative years, his apprenticeship, his middle years, and his major phase. James was descended from Irish Protestants. His grandfather, a poor immigrant, lived out the American Dream and died one of the wealthiest men in the United States. James's father, Henry James, Sr., renounced the Calvinistic work ethic and indulged in the mysticism of Emanuel Swedenborg and the socialism of Charles Fourier.

Through most of his youth, James was shuttled back and forth between Europe and the United States, thus gaining an international perspective on art and life. He learned French and received a European education through a variety of tutors and schools. As a young man, he was exposed to the greatest museums and art galleries in the world. His eye for painting aided him in creating a painterly quality in his work. In 1858, his family moved to Newport, Rhode Island, which was to become the scene of some of his early works of fiction. In 1862, he went to Harvard University to study law but attended James Russell Lowell's lectures and decided to pursue a literary career. In 1864, he published his first short story and continued to write stories and criticism for the rest of his life. In 1869, he spent a year abroad. With the death of his favorite cousin, Minnie, in 1870, he believed that his youth had come to an end.

James entered his apprentice years between 1865 and 1882. During these years, he published his first collection of short fiction, *A Passionate Pilgrim*, and his first significant novel, *Roderick Hudson* (1876). He achieved popular success with *Daisy Miller* and went on to write *The American* (1876-1877), *Washington Square* (1880), and *The Portrait of a Lady* (1880-1881). These works dealt with the international theme and explored the problems of American innocence exposed to the corrupting influence of European society.

During the 1880's, James began to take up some of the themes of the naturalists. With *The Bostonians* (1885-1886) and *The Princess Casamassima* (1885-1886), James began to treat the issues of social reformers. These novels, along with *The Tragic Muse* (1889-1890), were not successful. Between 1890 and 1895, James attempted to establish his reputation as a dramatist, but he was unable to please theater audiences, and his play *Guy Domville* (1894) was booed.

In 1897, James settled down in Lamb House in Sussex, and by 1900 he had entered his major phase and had written three richly textured novels: *The Wings of the Dove* (1902), *The Ambassadors* (1903), and *The Golden Bowl* (1904). He died in 1916 in London and was buried in the United States.

Analysis • Henry James believed that an author must be granted his *donnée*, or central idea, and then be judged on the execution of his material. James's stories are about members of high society. The characters do not engage in dramatic actions but spend much of their time in cryptic conversations, which slowly reveal the intense psychological strain under which they are laboring. James's narrators are often confused individuals trying to puzzle out and evaluate themselves and the people around them. Romance is frequently at the center of James's tales, but his lovers have difficulty coming to terms with their own feelings, and often love goes unrecognized and unfulfilled. Marriage is often rejected by his characters, and when it does appear, it is often the scene of heartaches and hidden resentments. Death and dying are also a part of James's stories. Even though he focuses on the death of women and children, he avoids both the macabre and the sentimental. His stories can be divided into three categories: international romances, tales about writers and artists, and introspective narratives about wasted lives.

James has not been given the same recognition for his short fiction that Nathaniel Hawthorne and Edgar Allan Poe have received; yet James devoted much of his literary life to the creation of short fiction and made many attempts to master the form. Several times in his life he expressed the desire to give up writing novels and to devote himself solely to creating short fiction. For half a century, James employed himself in the writing of 112 pieces of short fiction, beginning with "A Tragedy of Error" in 1864 and ending with "The Round of Visits" in 1910. He began writing stories ten years before he published his first novel, and over his lifetime, his stories appeared in thirty-five different periodicals on both sides of the Atlantic.

Library of Congress

James called his short fiction "tales," and he divided his tales into types. The anecdote, which focuses on one character and one incident, is a brief, compact, and highly distilled story comparable to a sonnet. The longer *nouvelle*, which often ran between twenty thousand and forty-five thousand words, allowed James greater development in his short fiction, not for multiplying incidents but for probing the depths of a character's experience. James expanded his stories because he wanted to explore the richness of human experience that lies hidden behind the surface of everyday life.

James's major tales can be divided into three periods: His early stories focus on the international theme; during his middle years, his stories center on writers and artists; and his final stories focus on older characters who have gone through life but never really lived. James's international stories focus on taking characters with set expectations and placing them in foreign environments. *Daisy Miller* is one of James's early novelettes and deals with a young American girl who finds herself out of place in a European environment.

Daisy Miller • In *Daisy Miller*, young Frederick Winterbourne, an American living in Europe, becomes fascinated with the garrulous Daisy Miller, who is vacationing on the Continent. The free-spirited Daisy amiably flirts with Winterbourne. Although he is attracted to her, he is aware that she and her negligent mother are the source of gossip among European Americans, who are scandalized by the forward ways of the unchaperoned young American. After seeing Daisy in Vevey, he again meets her in Rome, where she is frequently seen with Giovanelli, who is thought to be an Italian adventurer. Ostracized by her American compatriots, she continues to be seen with Giovanelli and risks her life by spending a moonlit night with him at the Colosseum, where she contracts malaria and dies. The puzzled Winterbourne attends her funeral and realizes that she is innocent.

In *Daisy Miller,* James explores the dilemma of an innocent American woman who flouts the social codes of European society. More than that, however, he explores the mind of Winterbourne, a Europeanized American who tries to figure out whether Daisy is naïve or reckless. Like other Jamesean heroes, Winterbourne cannot commit himself to a woman with whom he is falling in love. Finding her attractive but shallow, he is compelled to lecture her on mores, and when he sees her at the Colosseum, he "cuts her dead." Unable to break Winterbourne's stiffness, she sends him a message from her deathbed, noting that she was fond of him. Convinced that he has been unjust to her, Winterbourne escapes into his studies and becomes entangled with a foreign woman.

James's heroine, like Herman Melville's Billy Budd, represents American innocence. Both have found themselves in a world order that puts them at risk, and both are sacrificed by those who should have helped them. In addition to introducing the international theme, *Daisy Miller* introduces two Jamesean types: the sacrificed woman and the egotist who rejects her love. Though James later rejected his subtitle *A Study,* the novelette *Daisy Miller* is a study of the complexity of human relationships. The enigmatic but vivacious Daisy is sacrificed at the Colosseum like the early Christians, while the reticent and regretful lover experiences a sense of loss as he retreats from the world of spontaneity and life.

"The Aspern Papers" • In "The Aspern Papers," James takes the international theme beyond the romance and weaves a darker and more complex tale. In order to obtain the letters of the American poet Jeffrey Aspern, an unnamed American editor takes up residence with Aspern's former mistress Juliana Bordereau and is willing to make love to her middle-aged niece, Miss Tita. He pays exorbitant rent for a room in their Venetian hideaway and spends lavishly to create a garden in their courtyard. Feeling that he is inspired by the mystic presence of Aspern and willing to take any measure to obtain the letters, he breaks into Juliana's drawer and is caught. He retreats, and the dying Juliana hides the papers in her mattress. After Juliana dies, Miss Tita offers to give him the papers if he will marry her. He rejects her proposal only to reconsider it too late, after Miss Tita has burned the papers.

The unnamed narrator goes by an alias. Later, he reveals his name to Miss Tita but not to the reader. He is one version of the unidentifiable American hero who either shuffles names like James Fenimore Cooper's Leatherstocking or assumes various identities like Melville's heroes. He is a man without an identity, a parasite living on the reputation of a famous writer. He is also a typical American monomaniacal quester, fixed on an obsessive quest and willing to sacrifice all in pursuit of it. The narrator sees himself as part of a grandiose scheme; the garden that he plants becomes the symbol of a lost Eden. In Miss Tita, James again sets up woman as a sacrificial victim. Like other Jamesean heroes (and heroes from American literature in general), the narrator rejects marriage. Also, in his quest for knowledge, he is willing to sacrifice the private lives of Juliana and Aspern.

"The Real Thing" • In his next set of stories, which focus on artists and writers, James explores the relationship between life and art, and the conflict between the artist's public and private life. In "The Real Thing," James tells the story of an unnamed artist who hires two highly polished aristocrats forced to earn their living as models. Major Monarch and his wife contrast with the artist's other models, Miss Churm, a feisty cockney, and Oronte, a low-life Italian. The artist discovers that his lower-class models can transform themselves into aristocrats, whereas the real aristocrats present either a static or a distorted picture of reality. An old friend tells him to get rid of the aristocrats because they are ruining his work and jeopardizing his career. The artist, however, respects and sympathizes with their plight but eventually has to dismiss them.

In "The Real Thing," James explores not only the relationship between art and life but also the human dilemma of an artist faced with the conflict of saving his career or upholding his responsibility to two people with whom he sympathizes. The story is built on a series of finely balanced contrasts. The Monarchs are pure aristocrats. The artist thinks that they have come to sit for a portrait, but they have come to be hired as models. The Monarchs are aristocrats, yet they cannot model aristocrats, whereas Miss Churm and Oronte are commoners who can easily transform themselves into gentry. Ironically, the Englishwoman models for Italian types, while the Italian model does Englishmen. The servant-class models start out waiting on the Monarchs, but later the Monarchs wait on the servants. Thus, class distinctions are reversed. The artist wants to paint artistic portraits for which the aristocratic Monarchs are suitable, yet he devotes himself to commercial illustrations, using a working woman who can impersonate an empress. The aristocrats display themselves like slaves at an auction, whereas the servants do their job without auditioning. The lower-class models are professionals; the aristocrats are amateurs. The artist friend is supposedly a good judge of models, but he is a second-rate painter.

The greatest irony of all is that people who have no sense of self can become transformed into commercial art, while people holding on to their identity, their own clothes, and their own manners become too photographic, too typical, and too much the real thing. Although the artist must rid himself of the two aristocrats, his experience with them has moved him more deeply than his work with the professional models. The story is a gem of balance and contrast that transforms an aesthetic dilemma into an ethical one and explores the relationship of art to life, servant to master, self to role, portraiture to illustration, and commercial art to lived experience. "The Real Thing" is an often-anthologized story and a perfect illustration of James's craft in the anecdote or traditional short story.

"The Figure in the Carpet" • The theme of the relationship between art and life is broadened in James's stories about writers. During his middle period, James created a series of stories in which a young would-be writer or critic surveys the life and work of a master writer. In "The Figure in the Carpet," a story about an eccentric writer who has gained significant critical attention, James probes the nature of criticism itself. An unidentified critic trying to gain a name for himself is called upon to review *The Middle*, the latest novel of the famous author Hugh Vereker, because the lead critic, George Corvick, has to meet his fiancé, Gwendolen Erme. The narrator writes a glowing review of Vereker's work, then attends a party in hope of seeing the great author. When a socialite presents Vereker with the narrator's review, he calls it "the usual twaddle." Vereker later apologizes to the critic but says that critics often misunderstand the obvious meaning, which stands out in his novels like a figure in a carpet. The critic probes Vereker for clues, but the author says that the clues run throughout his entire work. After searching for the secret meaning in Vereker's work, the critic gives up the quest as a hoax. His fellow critic Corvick, however, uses the quest for the narrative secret as an excuse to work more closely with his fiancé, Gwendolen. Frustrated in their efforts, Corvick leaves the country. While away, he writes Gwendolen that he has figured out the secret, and he and Gwendolen get married. When Corvick dies, Gwendolen will not reveal the secret to the narrator, who is even willing to marry her to obtain it. Gwendolen does marry a mediocre critic, Drayton Deane. After the deaths of Gwendolen, Vereker, and Vereker's wife, the narrator tries to obtain the secret from Deane, who knows nothing about it.

In "The Figure in the Carpet," James again turns to the monomanical unnamed narrator on a quest for secret knowledge hidden in a text. Like the narrator of "The Aspern Papers," the critic is willing to marry a woman to gain greater knowledge about an author's work. James said that the story was about misunderstood authors and the need for more analytical criticism. Yet the story sets up typical Jamesean paradoxes. Is Vereker being honest or is "the figure" merely a hoax on critics? Does Corvick really know the secret or is he using his knowledge to win Gwendolen? What is the puzzling connection between interpreting a work and exploring the intimate relationships between men and women? Why do the many so-called possessors of the secret die? This story has been cited as a model for the critical act by many modern critics. Its metafictional qualities and its strange mixture of love and death with the act of interpretation give it a distinctly postmodern quality.

The stories written in James's later years take on a mystical tone. The artist is replaced by a sensitive individual who has alienated himself from the world. The characters are few and often focus on only two people. The characters remain obsessive, but now they are in pursuit of that part of themselves that haunts them. The Jamesean love story is played out into old age, with the woman as a patient bystander, a reflector of the man's battle with himself. The image of the hunt found in Cooper, Melville, and Ernest Hemingway is now symbolic of an internal quest for the terrors hidden within the self. The artists, who in earlier stories sought to gain a second chance or find a next time, now become egocentric gentlemen facing the life that they could have had. The venture into the wilderness becomes a metaphor for the descent into the unconscious.

"The Altar of the Dead" • In "The Altar of the Dead," George Stransom constantly memorializes the death of his bride, Mary Antrim, who died of a fever after their wedding day. Like a character from a Poe short story, he maintains an obsessive devotion to his dead love and is chained to the observance of the anniversary of his wife's death. While remembering his wife, he meets his friend Paul Creston and Paul's second wife. In a strange way, James returns to the international theme by making Creston's new wife an American who has married for money. Stransom meditates on Creston's first wife and idealizes her in her death. Later the same day, Stransom learns of the death of his boyhood friend, Acton Hague, a man who betrayed Stransom in some undisclosed manner. Hague becomes the only dead friend that Stransom rejects, as Stransom becomes more and more absorbed with the dead and creates an altar of candles to them. A mysterious woman becomes a fellow mourner at Stransom's shrine. It takes him months to learn her name and years to find out her address. He finally comes to her apartment after the death of her aunt, only to find that her room is a personal shrine to Acton Hague, who rejected the woman. Since Stransom cannot light a candle for Hague, the relationship ends. The loss of the woman casts a shadow over his daily devotions at his altar. Dismayed, he has a vision of his dead wife, Mary, smiling at him from heaven. Just then, the mysterious woman

returns to him as he dies in her arms. The last candle on the altar is lit not only for
Acton Hague but also for Stransom.

Stransom has left the world of the living and has become obsessed with the dead.
He forms a distant relationship with a fellow mourner, but she is only a part of his isolated world. Her feelings are never considered. Instead of forming a meaningful relationship, he continues to withdraw from human love. Stransom, like other heroes in
James's later tales, becomes an example of James's reticent lover, a man who has rejected life and embraced death. The death of Stransom in the woman's arms unites
the love and death theme predominant in the later tales.

"The Beast in the Jungle" • "The Beast in the Jungle" is a powerful story about one
man's quest for his illusive identity. John Marcher meets May Bartram when they are
both in their thirties. Ten years earlier, Marcher revealed to her that he was singled
out for a terrible fate. When Marcher recalls that he told her about his premonition,
they form a relationship, and May begins to wait with him. Blindly, he rules out love
as the strange fate that awaits him and forms a friendship with May, taking her to op-
eras, giving her gifts, and spending hours talking about his fate. As the years pass, he
becomes skeptical that the "beast" will ever come. He feels reluctant to take May
along with him on a "tiger hunt." Finally, May becomes ill. She knows his fate but will
not tell him because she wants to make him a man like any other. He realizes that he
might save her, but he is too preoccupied with his own destiny to become involved
with her. She eventually tells him that his fate has already passed him by and that he
never recognized it. When she dies, he contemplates that her death might be the terrible fate, but he rules out this premise. Marcher, an outsider at May's funeral, eventually goes abroad only to return to the grave of his friend to see another mourner
stricken with grief. Suddenly, the beast leaps out at Marcher, as he realizes that he has
failed to love and has been unable to feel deeply about anything. He has been an
empty man who has watched his life from the outside but has failed to live it.

Marcher, like Stransom, is held prisoner to an obsession that removes him from
the world of human relationships. He cannot give himself to another, so he must
await his fate. James called the story a negative adventure. Indeed, Marcher's trek
into the wilderness is his own confrontation with his unconscious fears. In his
monomaniacal obsession, he sacrifices May, who becomes dedicated to waiting for
him to discover his fate, while he prides himself on his disinterestedness. In "The
Beast in the Jungle," as in other James stories, the woman becomes useful to the man
as a siphon for his own obsessions. Marcher fails to recognize and accept love and
wastes his life by projecting all his endeavors onto a nebulous future. He is so
wrapped up in his own ego that he fails to believe that the death of a lifelong friend
is a terrible fate. In the end, he is brought into the world of the dead. Like Stransom,
he has lived outside the present and now has only a lost past on which to look
back. Like Winterbourne at the funeral of Daisy Miller, he begins to realize what
the woman has meant to him. The cemetery where he stands is compared to a
garden, which can be seen as an Eden, where Marcher realizes his own ignorance
and comes to a painful awareness of his loss of paradise. The cemetery is also called a
wilderness, a wilderness that will take him beyond the settled life and into the terrible recesses of his own heart. Marcher is a version of the American future-oriented pioneer unattached to family and loved ones, an Emersonian hero caught in the void
of his own solipsistic world. He also becomes one of the first modern antiheroes,
inauthentic men who live outside themselves, men to whom nothing really happens.

"The Jolly Corner" • Stransom becomes absorbed in the past, in the world of the dead, and he neglects to establish a relationship with the woman who mourns with him. Marcher becomes involved in a vacuous destiny, unable to see the love that surrounds him. In "The Jolly Corner," Spencer Brydon, another alienated man who rejects the present, pursues his obsession with a past that might have been. Having lived abroad, Brydon returns to New York after a thirty-three-year absence only to find that the world has changed around him. James again explores what happens to an individual who finds himself in an alien culture. When Brydon comes to settle some property that he owns in the United States, he begins to wonder about his talents as a businessman and contemplates the kind of man he might have been had he stayed in the United States. He eventually develops a morbid obsession with his alter ego, the other self that he might have been. One night, Brydon enters the empty house called the Jolly Corner in search of his doppelgänger. When he finally comes face to face with it, he faints at the monstrous sight. Upon recovery, he finds himself in the lap of Alice Staverton, who reassures him that she does not find his shadow self so horrible. In the end, he rejoices that he has gained knowledge about himself.

Spencer Brydon's return to the United States plays an ironic twist on James's international theme, as a Europeanized American returns to a United States that he feels alienated from and then conjures up an American self that horrifies him. Like Marcher, Brydon finds himself on a hunt stalking his secret self, his fate that might have been. Again, James uses the image of the hunt to symbolize an internal journey into the subconscious mind. As the doors of life's options open and close around Brydon in the haunted house of his lost youth, the monster leaps out at him as it did at Marcher. Both men, like Stransom, collapse upon the women they have neglected. Alice Staverton is the woman who waited and shared his destiny, the way that May Bartram did Marcher's. She not only knew his double but also accepted it. The use of the double figure was popular in romantic and gothic literature, but in "The Jolly Corner," James gave a deeper psychological and philosophical undertone to the motif. In his last group of stories, James used the mystery adventure format to probe the inner psyche of his characters and to examine characters obsessed with living life outside the present.

James brought a greater psychological realism to the genre of short fiction, expanded its length in order to encompass an in-depth range of inner experiences, transformed the mystery story into metafictional narratives that have a distinctly postmodern quality, and reshaped the quest motif of American literature into existential probings about authenticating one's identity.

Paul Rosefeldt

Other major works

PLAYS: *Daisy Miller,* pb. 1883 (adaptation of his novel); *The American,* pr. 1891, pb. 1949 (adaptation of his novel); *Guy Domville,* pb. 1894, privately; pr. 1895, pb. 1949; *The Reprobate,* pb. 1894, pr. 1919; *Theatricals: Tenants and Disengaged,* pb. 1894; *Theatricals, Second Series: The Album and The Reprobate,* pb. 1895; *The High Bid,* pr. 1908, pb. 1949; *The Other House,* wr. 1909, pb. 1949; *The Outcry,* wr. 1909, pr. 1917, pb. 1949; *The Saloon,* pr. 1911, pb. 1949 (one act); *The Complete Plays of Henry James,* pb. 1949 (Leon Edel, editor).

NOVELS: *Roderick Hudson,* 1876; *The American,* 1876-1877; *An International Episode,* 1878-1879 (novella); *Daisy Miller,* 1878; *The Europeans,* 1878; *Confidence,* 1879-1880;

The Portrait of a Lady, 1880-1881; *Washington Square*, 1880; *The Bostonians*, 1885-1886; *The Princess Casamassima*, 1885-1886; *The Reverberator*, 1888; *The Tragic Muse*, 1889-1890; *The Awkward Age*, 1897-1899; *The Spoils of Poynton*, 1897; *What Maisie Knew*, 1897; *In the Cage*, 1898; *The Turn of the Screw*, 1898; *The Sacred Fount*, 1901; *The Wings of the Dove*, 1902; *The Ambassadors*, 1903; *The Golden Bowl*, 1904; *The Outcry*, 1911; *The Ivory Tower*, 1917; *The Sense of the Past*, 1917.

NONFICTION: *Transatlantic Sketches*, 1875; *French Poets and Novelists*, 1878; *Hawthorne*, 1879; *Portraits of Places*, 1883; *A Little Tour in France*, 1884; *The Art of Fiction*, 1884; *Partial Portraits*, 1888; *Essays in London*, 1893; *William Wetmore Story and His Friends*, 1903; *English Hours*, 1905; *The American Scene*, 1907; *Views and Reviews*, 1908; *Italian Hours*, 1909; *A Small Boy and Others*, 1913 (memoirs); *Notes of a Son and Brother*, 1914 (memoirs); *Notes on Novelists*, 1914; *The Middle Years*, 1917; *The Art of the Novel: Critical Prefaces*, 1934 (R. P. Blackmur, editor); *The Notebooks of Henry James*, 1947 (F. O. Matthiessen and Kenneth B. Murdock, editors); *The Scenic Art*, 1948 (Allan Wade, editor); *Henry James Letters*, 1974-1984 (5 volumes; Leon Edel, editor); *Henry James: Literary Criticism*, 1984; *The Art of Criticism: Henry James on the Theory and Practice of Fiction*, 1986; *The Complete Notebooks of Henry James*, 1987; *Dear Munificent Friends: Henry James's Letters to Four Women*, 1999 (Susan E. Gunter, editor); *Henry James on Culture: Collected Essays on Politics and the American Social Scene*, 1999 (Pierre A. Walker, editor); *Dearly Beloved Friends: Henry James's Letters to Younger Men*, 2001 (Susan E. Gunter and Steven H. Jobe, editors).

Bibliography

Bell, Millicent. "'The Pupil' and the Unmentionable Subject." *Raritan* 16 (Winter, 1997): 50-63. Claims the story is about that which was once considered almost unmentionable by the genteel: money. James focuses on the extinct code of manners and taste by which refined persons were not supposed to talk much about money.

Dewey, Joseph, and Brooke Horvath, eds. *"The Finer Thread, the Tighter Weave": Essays on the Short Fiction of Henry James*. West Lafayette, Ind.: Purdue University Press, 2001. Critical study. Includes bibliographical references and an index.

Flannery, Denis. *Henry James: A Certain Illusion*. Burlington, Vt.: Ashgate, 2000. Analysis of illusion in the works of James. Bibliography and index.

Gage, Richard P. *Order and Design: Henry James Titled Story Sequences*. New York: Peter Lang, 1988. Gage examines James's published short-story collections, such as *Terminations*, *Embarrassments*, and *The Soft Side*, in order to show how James collected his stories around a central theme. Focusing on the interrelatedness of James's works, Gage shows how James's stories can be divided into organized units based upon a holistic design.

Hocks, Richard A. *Henry James: A Study of the Short Fiction*. Boston: Twayne, 1990. Hocks's book is a good introduction to James's short fiction. The book divides James's stories into three periods: the early social realism, the middle tales dealing with psychological and moral issues, and the later works of poetic expressionism. Detailed analyses of the major works are provided, along with selections of James's writings on short fiction and a collection of critical articles on selected works.

Horne, Philip. "Henry James and the Economy of the Short Story." In *Modernist Writers and the Marketplace*, edited by Ian Willison, Warwick Gould, and Warren Chernaik. London: Macmillan, 1996. Discusses some of the commercial and social constraints and opportunities that affected James's writing of short fiction in the last half of his career.

Lustig, T. J. *Henry James and the Ghostly*. Cambridge, England: Cambridge University Press, 1994. Discusses James's ghost stories and the significance of the "ghostly" for James's work generally. Among the best-known James stories discussed are "The Jolly Corner" and "The Turn of the Screw." Lustig devotes a third of this study to "The Turn of the Screw," which he argues is a story about reading.

Martin, W. R., and Warren U. Ober. *Henry James's Apprenticeship: The Tales, 1864-1882*. Toronto: P. D. Meany Publishers, 1994. Analysis of the stories James wrote in the first fifteen years of his career, suggesting how the vision he was creating in those stories prepared for the writing of his first masterpiece, *The Portrait of a Lady*. Discusses the sources of his basic theme of the victimized innocent.

May, Charles E., ed. *Masterplots II: Short Story Series, Revised Edition*. 8 vols. Pasadena, Calif.: Salem Press, 2004. Designed for student use, this reference set contains articles providing detailed plot summaries and analyses of twelve short stories by James: "The Altar of the Dead" and "The Beast in the Jungle" (vol. 1); "Europe," "The Figure in the Carpet," and "The Great Good Place" (vol. 3); "In the Cage," "The Lesson of the Master," and "The Jolly Corner" (vol. 4); "The Middle Years" (vol. 5); "The Pupil" and "The Real Thing" (vol. 6); and "The Tree of Knowledge" (vol. 7).

Rawlings, Peter. "A Kodak Refraction of Henry James's 'The Real Thing.'" *Journal of American Studies* 32 (December, 1998): 447-462. Discusses "The Real Thing" and its treatment of issues of representation and reproduction as an allegory in which the tyrannical forces of the real and the vulgar, unless subjected to the processes of selection and idealization, can be all-vanquishing.

Wagenknecht, Edward. *The Tales of Henry James*. New York: Frederick Ungar, 1984. The book contains brief analyses of fifty-five of James's major tales as well as thumbnail sketches of other stories. It provides a good reference work for someone looking for short summaries and critical bibliographies (found in the footnotes) but lacks detailed criticism of individual works as well as historical perspective.

Sarah Orne Jewett

Born: South Berwick, Maine; September 3, 1849
Died: South Berwick, Maine; June 24, 1909

Principal short fiction • *Old Friends and New,* 1879; *Country By-Ways,* 1881; *The Mate of the Daylight, and Friends Ashore,* 1884; *A White Heron, and Other Stories,* 1886; *The King of Folly Island and Other People,* 1888; *Strangers and Wayfarers,* 1890; *Tales of New England,* 1890; *A Native of Wimby,* 1893; *The Life of Nancy,* 1895; *The Queen's Twin,* 1899; *Stories and Tales,* 1910; *The Uncollected Short Stories of Sarah Orne Jewett,* 1971.

Other literary forms • Sarah Orne Jewett wrote four novels, and she published popular books for children, including *Play Days* (1878) and *Betty Leicester* (1890). Her main work of nonfiction was a history, *The Story of the Normans* (1887).

Achievements • Sarah Orne Jewett is best known as a local colorist who captured with fidelity the life of coastal Maine in the late nineteenth century in sensitive and moving portraits, mainly of women's lives. Except for *The Country of the Pointed Firs,* widely considered her masterpiece, Jewett's long fiction is thought less successful than her short stories. During her lifetime, she was considered one of the best short-story writers in America. Most of her stories appeared first in popular magazines such as *The Atlantic,* under the editorship of William Dean Howells, and *Harper's.* American literary historian F. O. Matthiessen said in his 1929 study of Jewett that she and Emily Dickinson were the two best women writers America had produced. Willa Cather offered Jewett similar praise and credited her with positively changing the direction of her literary career in a brief but rich acquaintance near the end of Jewett's life.

Biography • Sarah Orne Jewett spent most of her life in South Berwick on the Maine coast, where she was born on September 3, 1849. Daughter of a country doctor, she aspired to medicine herself, but moved toward writing because of early ill health (which led her father to take her on his calls, for fresh air), the special literary education encouraged by her family, and her discovery as a teenager of her "little postage stamp of soil" in reading Harriet Beecher Stowe's *The Pearl of Orr's Island* (1862). Her father, especially, encouraged her to develop her keen powers of observation, and her grandfathers stimulated her interest in storytelling. After the death of her father in 1878, she began a lifelong friendship with Annie Fields that brought her into contact with leading writers in America and Europe, such as Henry James and George Eliot. Jewett and Fields traveled together in Europe, the Caribbean, and the United States, and after the death of Mr. Fields, they lived together for extended periods.

Jewett began writing and publishing at the age of nineteen. During her career she developed and maintained the purpose of helping her readers to understand and love the ordinary people of her native Maine, and later she told stories about other misunderstood people such as the Irish and southern whites. In her career, she produced more than twenty volumes of fiction for children and adults, history, prose sketches, and poetry. Her short stories show rapidly increasing subtlety and power. Her early books were well received, but beginning with *The Mate of the Daylight,*

James Notman

and Friends Ashore, reviewers routinely praised her collections highly. It was not unusual for reviewers to be puzzled by how much they liked Jewett's stories. A frequent response was that the stories seemed to lack plot and action and yet at the same time they were absorbing and charming. Late twentieth century critics, notably feminist critics, have suggested that Jewett was developing a kind of storytelling in opposition to the popular melodramas with their fast-paced romance or adventure plots. Jewett's stories came more and more to focus on intimate relations of friendship, especially between older women, but eventually in one way or another between all kinds of people.

By the time Jewett wrote her masterpiece, the novella *The Country of the Pointed Firs,* she had fully developed a form of narration that pointed toward the James Joyce of *Dubliners* (1914). This novella, and a number of her best stories such as "Miss Tempy's Watchers" and "The Queen's Twin," would set up a problem of tact, of how to overcome barriers to communion between two or more people, and then through a subtle process of preparation would make overcoming these barriers possible. The story would end with an epiphany that involved communion between at least two people. Though she wrote a variety of other kinds of stories in her career, this type of development was probably her major accomplishment, and it achieved its fullest realization in *The Country of the Pointed Firs.*

A tragic carriage accident on her birthday in 1902 left her in such pain that she gave up fiction writing and devoted herself to her friends. In the fall of 1908, she met Willa Cather, to whom she wrote several letters that inspired Cather to write about Nebraska. Cather recognized Jewett's help by dedicating to Jewett her first Nebraska novel, *O Pioneers!* (1913). Jewett died at her South Berwick home on June 24, 1909.

Analysis • When a young reader wrote to Sarah Orne Jewett in 1899 to express admiration of her stories for girls, Jewett encouraged her to continue reading:

> You will always have the happiness of finding friendships in books, and it grows pleasanter and pleasanter as one grows older. And then the people in books are apt to make us understand 'real' people better, and to know why they do things, and so we learn sympathy and patience and enthusiasm for those we live with, and can try to help them in what they are doing, instead of being half suspicious and finding fault.

Here Jewett states one of the central aims of her fiction, to help people learn the arts of friendship. Chief among these arts is tact, which Jewett defines in *The Country of the*

Pointed Firs as a perfect self-forgetfulness that allows one to enter reverently and sympathetically the sacred realms of the inner lives of others. In her stories, learning tact is often a major element, and those who are successful are often rewarded with epiphanies—moments of visionary union with individuals or with nature—or with communion—the feeling of oneness with another person that for Jewett is the ultimate joy of friendship.

"A White Heron" • "A White Heron," which first appeared in *A White Heron*, is often considered Jewett's best story, perhaps because it goes so well with such American classics as Nathaniel Hawthorne's *The Scarlet Letter* (1850), Herman Melville's *Moby Dick* (1851), and William Faulkner's "The Bear" (1942). With these works, the story shares a central, complex symbol in the white heron and the major American theme of a character's complex relationship with the landscape and society. As a story about a young person choosing between society and nature as the proper spiritual guide for a particular time in her life, however, "A White Heron" is atypical for Jewett. One main feature that marks the story as Jewett's, however, is that the main character, Sylvia, learns a kind of tact during her adventure in the woods, a tact that grows out of an epiphany and that leads to the promise of continuing communion with nature that the story implies will help this somewhat weak and solitary child grow into a strong adult.

Sylvia, a young girl rescued by her grandmother, Mrs. Tilley, from the overstimulation and overcrowding of her city family, meets a young ornithologist, who fascinates her and promises her ten dollars if she will tell him where he can find the white heron he has long sought for his collection. Childishly tempted by this magnificent sum and her desire to please the hunter, who knows so much of nature yet kills the birds, she determines to climb at dawn a landmark pine from which she might see the heron leave its nest. She succeeds in this quest, but finds she cannot tell her secret to the hunter. The story ends with the assertion that she could have loved the hunter as "a dog loves" and with a prayer to the woodlands and summer to compensate her loss with "gifts and graces."

Interesting problems in technique and tone occur when Sylvia climbs the pine. The narrative tone shifts in highly noticeable ways. As she begins her walk to the tree before dawn, the narrator expresses personal anxiety that "the great wave of human interest which flooded for the first time this dull little life should sweep away the satisfactions of an existence heart to heart with nature and the dumb life of the forest." This statement seems to accentuate an intimacy between reader and narrator; it states the position the narrative rhetoric has implied from the beginning and, in effect, asks if the reader shares this anxiety. From this point until Sylvia reaches the top of the tree, the narrator gradually merges with Sylvia's internal consciousness. During the climb, Jewett builds on this intimacy with Sylvia. Both narrator and reader are aware of sharing in detail Sylvia's subjective impressions of her climb and of her view, and this merging of the subjectivities of the story (character, narrator, and reader) extends beyond the persons to objects as the narrator unites with the tree and imagines its sympathy for the climber. The merging extends further yet when Sylvia, the reader, and the narrator see with lyric clarity the sea, the sun, and two hawks that, taken together, make all three observers feel as if they could fly out over the world. Being atop the tallest landmark pine, "a great mainmast to the voyaging earth," one is, in a way, soaring in the cosmos as the hawks soar in the air.

At this point of clarity and union, the narrative tone shifts again. The narrator speaks directly to Sylvia, commanding her to look at the point where the heron will rise. The vision of the heron rising from a dead hemlock, flying by the pine, and settling on a nearby bough is a kind of colloquy of narrator and character and, if the technique works as it seems to intend, of the reader, too. This shift in "place" involves a shift in time to the present tense that continues through Sylvia's absorption of the secret and her descent from the tree. It seems clear that the intent of these shifts is to transcend time and space, to unite narrator, reader, character, and the visible scene which is "all the world." This is virtually the same technical device which is the central organizing device of Walt Whitman's "Crossing Brooklyn Ferry," and the intent of that device seems similar as well. The reader is to feel a mystical, "transcendental" union with the cosmos that assures one of its life and one's participation in that life.

A purpose of this union is to make justifiable and understandable Sylvia's choice not to give the heron's life away because they have "watched the sea and the morning together." The narrator's final prayer makes sense when it is addressed to transcendental nature on behalf of the girl who has rejected superfluous commodity in favor of Spirit, the final gift of Ralph Waldo Emerson's nature in his essay, "Nature." Though this story is atypical of Jewett insofar as it offers a fairly clear transcendental view of nature and so presents a moment of communion with the nonhuman, it is characteristic of Jewett in that by subtly drawing reader and narrator into the epiphany, the story creates a moment of human communion.

"The Only Rose" • More typical of Jewett's best work is "The Only Rose," which was first published in *The Atlantic* in January, 1894, and was then collected in *The Life of Nancy*. This story is organized by three related epiphanies, each centering on the rose, and each involving a blooming.

In the first "miracle of the rose," Mrs. Bickford and Miss Pendexter are hypnotized into communion by contemplating the new bloom on Mrs. Bickford's poor bush. In this epiphany, Miss Pendexter enters into spiritual sympathy with Mrs. Bickford, realizing that her silence this time is unusual, resulting not from having nothing to say, but from "an overburdening sense of the inexpressible." They go on to share the most intimate conversation of their relationship. The blooming flower leads to a blooming in their friendship. It also leads, however, to Mrs. Bickford's dilemma: On which of her three dead husbands' graves should she place this single rose? Her need to answer this question points to a deeper need to escape from her comparatively isolated and ineffectual life by shifting from an ethic of obligation to an ethic of love. Her heart has been frozen since her first husband's death, and it is long past time now for it to thaw and bloom again. Miss Pendexter understands something of this and tactfully leaves Mrs. Bickford to work it out for herself.

The second miracle of the rose occurs almost at the end of the story, when John confesses his love for Lizzie to his Aunt Bickford as he drives her to the graveyard. The symbolic rose of young and passionate love moves him to speak, even though he is unsure of the propriety of speaking up to the wealthy aunt from whom he hopes to receive an inheritance. His story of young love and hope, however, takes Mrs. Bickford out of herself, and she forgets her troubles in sharing his joy. As a result, he blooms, blushing a "fine scarlet."

The final miracle is that while she is taking the flowers to the graves, she realizes which of her husbands should have the rose. At the same time that John is taking the rose for his Lizzie, Mrs. Bickford is giving it in her heart to Albert, the first husband, whom she loved so passionately in her youth. Her realization of this event makes her blush "like a girl" and laugh in self-forgetfulness before the graveyard as she remembers that the first flower Albert gave her was just such a rose.

In the overall movement of the story, Mrs. Bickford is lifted out of herself and prepared for a richer and deeper communion with her friends and relatives. The single rose blossom seems mysteriously to impose an obligation upon her, but probably it really awakens the ancient spring of love within her that was perhaps covered over by grief at losing Albert so young and by the difficult life that followed his loss. When she finally struggles free of the weight of the intervening years, she recovers her hidden capacity for friendship and joy, for forgetting herself and joining in the happiness of others. She has epiphanies, rediscovers tact, and begins again to experience communion.

"Martha's Lady" • "Martha's Lady" first appeared in *The Atlantic* in October, 1897, and was then collected in *The Queen's Twin*. This story illustrates Jewett's mature control over her technique and material. She represents a kind of sainthood without falling into the syrupy sentimentality of popular melodrama.

Into a community beginning to show the effects of a Puritan formalism comes Helena Vernon, a young city woman who is unselfconsciously affectionate and beautiful and, therefore, a pleasure to please. She delights her maiden cousin, Harriet Pyne, charms the local minister, who gives her a copy of his *Sermons on the Seriousness of Life*, and transforms Martha, Harriet's new and awkward servant girl. In fact, Helena transforms to some extent everyone she meets in the village of Ashford, taking some of the starch out of their stiff and narrow way of life. After Helena leaves to marry, prosper, and suffer in Europe, Martha carries her memory constantly in her heart: "To lose out of sight the friend whom one has loved and lived to please is to lose joy out of life. But if love is true, there comes presently a higher joy of pleasing the ideal, that is to say, the perfect friend." This is the ideal of sainthood that the narrative voice asks the reader to admire. Thanks largely to Martha's living this ideal of always behaving so as to please Helena, she and Harriet live a happy life together for forty years. Helena returns to visit, worn, but with the same youthful spirit, and to reward with a kiss what she recognizes as Martha's perfect memory of the services Helena enjoyed as a girl. This recognition acknowledges Martha's faithfulness to her ideal and creates that moment of communion that is the ultimate reward for such faithfulness.

What prevents this story from dissolving into mush? Nearly all the special features of Jewett's technical facility are necessary. She avoids overelaboration. It is not difficult for an alert reader to notice the parallel to the Christ story type; a liberating figure enters a legalistic society to inspire love in a group of followers, which results in an apotheosis after her departure. The disciple remains true to the ideal until the liberator comes again to claim the disciple. Jewett could have forced this analogy on the reader, but she does not. Only a few details subtly suggest the analogy—character names, calling Martha a saint, and her relics—but these need not compel the reader in this direction, which, in fact, adds only a little to the story's power.

Although avoiding overelaboration, Jewett also avoids internal views. On the whole, the story is made of narrative summary and brief dramatic scenes. Emotion is revealed through action and speech; this technical choice produces less intensity of feeling than, for example, the intimate internal view of Sylvia in "The White Heron." The result is a matter-of-factness of tone that keeps Martha's sainthood of a piece with the ordinary world of Ashford. This choice is supported by nearly every other technical choice of the story—the attention to detail of setting, the gentle but pointed humor directed against religious formalism, and the emergence of Martha from the background of the story. Jewett's intention seems to be on the one hand to prevent the reader from emoting in excess of the worth of the object, but on the other to feel strongly and warmly the true goodness of Martha's faithfulness to love. Another purpose of this narrative approach is to demonstrate tact. In "A White Heron," both Sylvia and the reader enter the quest for the heron with mixed motives, but the nature of the journey—its difficulties, its joys, the absorption it requires— tends to purify motives and to prepare the spirit for epiphany. Sylvia's vision from atop the pine culminates in communion with the wild bird, a vision she has earned and that she may repeat if she realizes its value.

Jewett's light touch, her own tact in dealing with such delicate subjects, is one of her leading characteristics, and it flowers magnificently in the fiction of the last ten years of her writing career. Although the stories discussed above illustrate Jewett's most powerful and moving storytelling, they do not illustrate so fully another of the main characteristics of her stories—humor. Humor is often present in her stories and can be found in more abundance than might be expected in "The Only Rose" and "Martha's Lady." She also wrote a number of funny stories that discriminating readers such as Cather would not hesitate to compare with the work of Mark Twain. "The Guests of Mrs. Timms," though more similar to the stories of Jane Austen than Twain, is a popular story of the humorous ironies that result when a socially ambitious widow calls on another widow of higher status without announcing her visit in advance. Among her best humorous stories are "Law Lane," "All My Sad Captains," "A Winter Courtship," and "The Quest of Mr. Teaby," but there are many others that are a delight to read.

Terry Heller

Other major works

CHILDREN'S LITERATURE: *Play Days: A Book of Stories for Children*, 1878; *The Story of the Normans*, 1887; *Betty Leicester: A Story for Girls*, 1890.

NOVELS: *Deephaven*, 1877 (linked sketches); *A Country Doctor*, 1884; *A Marsh Island*, 1885; *The Country of the Pointed Firs*, 1896; *The Tory Lover*, 1901.

NONFICTION: *Letters of Sarah Orne Jewett*, 1911 (Annie Fields, editor); *Sarah Orne Jewett Letters*, 1956 (Richard Cary, editor).

POETRY: *Verses: Printed for Her Friends*, 1916.

Bibliography
Auten, Janet Gebhart. "'Nothing Much Happens in This Story': Teaching Sarah Orne Jewett's 'A White Heron.'" In *Short Stories in the Classroom*, edited by Carole L. Hamilton and Peter Kratzke. Urbana, Ill.: National Council of Teachers of English, 1999. Recounts several experiences in teaching the story to high school students, making suggestions about the value of the story to exploring conflicts of interest and expanding the canon.

Cary, Richard, ed. *Appreciation of Sarah Orne Jewett: Twenty-nine Interpretive Essays.* Waterville, Maine: Colby College Press, 1973. This book collects a good cross section of the major writing on Jewett from 1885 until 1972. Contains biographical sketches, extended reviews, examinations of her technique, interpretations of some individual works, and evaluations of her career.

Donovan, Josephine. *Sarah Orne Jewett*. New York: Frederick Ungar, 1980. This critical study includes a chronology and an examination of Jewett's literary career, following the development of her major themes through her works. Donovan is especially interested in Jewett's feminist themes. She provides primary and secondary bibliographies.

Graham, Margaret Baker. "Visions of Time in *The Country of the Pointed Firs*." *Studies in Short Fiction* 32 (Winter, 1995): 29-37. Discusses the concept of time in Jewett's book from Julia Kristeva's feminist perspective; argues that Jewett presents masculine, linear time and feminine, cyclical time, yet transcends both to achieve monumental time. Contends the narrator of the stories transcends the notion of superficial change and sees that the mythical and the historical are the same.

Matthiessen, F. O. *Sarah Orne Jewett*. Boston: Houghton Mifflin, 1929. This short biographical study may be the most readily available in libraries. Matthiessen surveys Jewett's life without going into great detail.

May, Charles E., ed. *Masterplots II: Short Story Series, Revised Edition*. 8 vols. Pasadena, Calif.: Salem Press, 2004. Designed for student use, this reference set contains articles providing detailed plot summaries and analyses of five short stories by Jewett: "The Courting of Sister Wisby" (vol. 2), "Miss Tempy's Watchers" and "A Native of Winby" (vol. 5), "The Town Poor" (vol. 7), and "A White Heron" (vol. 8).

Mobley, Marilyn Sanders. *Folk Roots and Mythic Wings in Sarah Orne Jewett and Toni Morrison*. Baton Rouge: Louisiana State University Press, 1991. Critical study that asserts the importance of myth and folklore in the work of two women of different races and generations who draw on the cultural roots of their people.

Nagel, Gwen L., ed. *Critical Essays on Sarah Orne Jewett*. Boston: G. K. Hall, 1984. This collection includes sixteen contemporary reviews of Jewett's books, reprints of eight critical essays from 1955 to 1983, and eight original essays. These deal with biography as well as interpretation. The introduction surveys the history of critical writing on Jewett.

Nagel, Gwen L., and James Nagel. *Sarah Orne Jewett: A Reference Guide*. Boston: G. K. Hall, 1978. Introduced with a survey of criticism on Jewett, this reference guide lists and annotates writing about Jewett from 1873 to 1976. It is invaluable as a source for secondary writing and for forming impressions of how Jewett's reputation has developed. For discussions of criticism since 1976, see *American Literary Scholarship: An Annual*.

Silverthorne, Elizabeth. *Sarah Orne Jewett: A Writer's Life*. Woodstock, N.Y.: Overlook Press, 1993. Silverthorne describes the increasing interest in Jewett's treatment of women, ecology, and regional life. Silverthorne had access to letters and manuscripts unavailable to previous biographers, and she takes full advantage of Jewett scholarship.

Ruth Prawer Jhabvala

Born: Cologne, Germany; May 7, 1927

Principal short fiction • *Like Birds, Like Fishes, and Other Stories*, 1963; *A Stronger Climate: Nine Stories*, 1968; *An Experience of India*, 1971; *How I Became a Holy Mother, and Other Stories*, 1976; *Out of India: Selected Stories*, 1986; *East into Upper East: Plain Tales from New York and New Delhi*, 1998.

Other literary forms • Ruth Prawer Jhabvala is the author of several novels, ranging from *To Whom She Will* in 1955 (pb. in U.S. as *Amrita*) to *My Nine Lives: Chapters of a Possible Past* in 2004. Her 1975 novel *Heat and Dust* won a Booker McConnell Prize and a National Book League award. In screenplay form, that work won an award from the British Academy of Film and Television Arts. Her screenplay adaptation of E. M. Forster's *A Room with a View* (1908) won a Writers Guild of America Award in 1986 and an Academy Award in 1987. Jhabvala's screenplay *Mr. and Mrs. Bridge* (1990) received a New York Film Critics Circle Award. In 1993, her screenplay adaptation of Forster's *Howards End* (1910) was nominated for an Academy Award. She also adapted Henry James's novel *The Golden Bowl* (1904) to the screen in 2000 and Diane Johnson's novel *Le Divorce* (1997) in 2003.

Achievements • In addition to the many awards she has won for her fiction, Ruth Prawer Jhabvala received a John Simon Guggenheim Memorial Foundation Fellowship in 1976 and a Neil Gunn International Fellowship in 1979. She was a MacArthur Foundation fellow from 1986 to 1989.

Biography • Ruth Prawer was born in Cologne, Germany, on May 7, 1927, the second child of Marcus Prawer, a Polish-Jewish lawyer, and Eleanora Cohn. The family left Germany in 1939. Most of their relatives perished in World War II.

In England, Prawer was educated at a grammar school and at Queen Mary College, London University. In 1951, she received her master's degree in English literature; her thesis was on the eighteenth century short story. Soon afterward, she married Cyrus S. H. Jhabvala, an Indian Parsi, who had studied architecture at the university. They settled in New Delhi, India, where, with her husband's encouragement, she began producing fiction. Shortly after the birth of their first daughter, Jhabvala completed a novel, *To Whom She Will* (1955). In 1957, her stories began appearing in *The New Yorker*.

In 1961, film producers James Ivory and Ismail Merchant asked Jhabvala to write a screenplay of her novel *The Householder* (1960). Thus began a collaboration that produced some of the most admired films of the twentieth century. In 1975, Jhabvala moved to New York City but continued to maintain a close relationship with her husband.

Analysis • Ruth Prawer Jhabvala's lack of ties to any one place may account for her objectivity as a writer. However, her detachment does not prevent her from empathizing with her characters, nor does her rootlessness make her less conscious of the importance of place. Jhabvala's experiences may have made her more capable of understanding how feelings of isolation affect individuals, whether they are Indian women, restricted by too many traditions, or Manhattanites, burdened by too many options.

Jhabvala's early stories reflect the delight that, in her story "Myself in India," she describes as a Westerner's initial reaction to India. Like Jane Austen, to whom she has been compared by critics, Jhabvala here emphasizes the comic elements in family life, though she does satirize self-deception, snobbery, or pretentiousness. In these lighthearted stories, Jhabvala's characters emerge from their adventures relatively unscathed. For example, the narrator of "My First Marriage," from *Like Birds, Like Fishes and Other Stories,* regards her seduction and abandonment as incidents that merely make her more interesting.

During the 1970's, Jhabvala's short fiction became more pessimistic. Some of her characters seek to escape from the world by following spiritual leaders, as does the protagonist in the title story of *An Experience of India*; others, like the minister in "Rose Petals," from the same collection, have hopes of improving society; still others, such as the minister's wife, dedicate their lives to amusing themselves. Whether they reside in New Delhi or New York, the characters in *East into Upper East* live with the same uncertainties. Although these later stories often end unresolved, one can find satisfaction in their artistic perfection.

"The Old Lady" • "The Old Lady," from *Like Birds, Like Fishes, and Other Stories,* is typical of Jhabvala's early works. Its plot is minimal: The author simply records a few hours of ordinary life in a prosperous Indian family. Besides the servants, the household includes the old lady, her daughter Leila, her son Bobo, and Leila's daughter Munni. Leila's estranged husband Krishna and her older brother Satish, a lawyer, appear for lunch. The household is filled with tension. Leila finds her husband irritating and is annoyed with her mother, her brother, and her daughter for being so fond of him. During their lunch together, Leila embarrasses the inoffensive Krishna and quarrels with Bobo and Satish. Afterward, she criticizes her mother for being too old-fashioned to understand divorce. However, to Satish's annoyance, nothing is decided. The protagonist recognizes this atmosphere as the one that prevailed when her husband was still living. Then she, too, was unhappy; now, however, she has learned from a guru how to distance herself from the emotional turmoil around her. There is a wonderful comic irony in the fact that though her offspring think themselves so much cleverer than their mother, she alone has found the secret of happiness.

"A Course of English Studies" • One of the recurring subjects of Jhabvala's short fiction is the conflict between East and West. In the early story "A Course of English Studies" from *An Experience of India*, an encounter between East and West is shown as essentially comic. Both of the major characters are worthy targets of satire, the silly Indian girl Nalini, who comes to a British university in order to have a literary love affair, and Dr. Norman Greaves, the weak-willed English teacher whom Nalini chooses as her lover. The story is told from Nalini's perspective, and though it is told in a third-person narrative, the style reflects her breathless enthusiasm. Although Nalini has no common sense, she is a brilliant tactician, and as she is unhampered by principles and incapable of feeling shame or embarrassment, Greaves does not stand a chance against her. Nalini thoroughly enjoys the affair; it is Greaves who lives in apprehension. After Nalini pays a visit to his wife and begins planning to take him back to India with her, Greaves terminates the relationship. Nalini recovers rapidly. Convinced that the English poets were wrong about their countrymen's capacity for passion, she decides that she should return to India alone. In other stories, Jhabvala shows cross-cultural adventures as dangerous and potentially tragic, but the lovers in "A Course of English Studies" end up no worse for their affair, though probably no wiser.

"How I Became a Holy Mother" • The title story from the collection *How I Became a Holy Mother, and Other Stories* focuses on a phenomenon which the author finds puzzling, the migrations of Westerners to India in search of spiritual enlightenment. The story is told in the first person by Katie, who at the age of twenty-three tires of her life in London and heads for India. Katie settles down in an ashram, which is relatively clean, has a picturesque setting, and is headed by an energetic but undemanding master. Katie enjoys conversing with the master and with the best looking of his Indian disciples, Vishwa, who eventually becomes her lover. However, she sees right through the master's chief sponsor, the rich, tyrannical "Countess," who plans to take Vishwa to the West with her. Determined not to lose him, Katie lets the Countess discover them making love. The master solves the problem by suggesting that they go on tour together, with Vishwa cast as the Guru and Katie as a Holy Mother. The story is particularly interesting because, unlike so many of Jhabvala's spiritual pilgrims, this protagonist does not allow herself to be overwhelmed by India. Though Jhabvala has said that one can resist India only by escaping from it, here she suggests that common sense may be one's best defense.

"Fidelity" • Although it is set in Manhattan, "Fidelity," from *East into Upper East*, is much like such stories of one-sided devotion as "Bombay" and "On Bail," from *Out of India*, and the poignant "Expiation," one of the New Delhi stories in *East into Upper East*. In "Fidelity," Sophie loves her self-centered, habitually unfaithful husband, Dave, so much that she will not tell him she has a terminal illness for fear of causing him pain. Sophie knows how easily Dave is driven to tears. She also knows that he is having trouble with the young girl for whom he left her. However, as Dave admits to his sister, he has more than his mistress to worry about. If he does not come up with a significant amount of money, he will be sent to prison for fraud, as happened once before. After his nephew Michael has paved the way for him, Dave appears at Sophie's bedside. Although he pretends concern about her health, Dave is much too focused on himself to notice that she is dying. However, Sophie has decided that the easiest way to give Dave the money he needs is to die as soon as possible. While he holds her, she prepares to take the pills that will end her life, and though Dave has no idea what is really happening, as usual, he prepares to shed his convenient tears. "Fidelity" demonstrates Jhabvala's power to reveal the very souls of her characters without intruding into the narrative.

Rosemary M. Canfield Reisman

Other major works

NOVELS: *To Whom She Will*, 1955 (pb. in U.S. as *Amrita*, 1956); *The Nature of Passion*, 1956; *Esmond in India*, 1958; *The Householder*, 1960; *Get Ready for Battle*, 1962; *A Backward Place*, 1965; *A New Dominion*, 1972 (pb. in U.S. as *Travelers*, 1973); *Heat and Dust*,

1975; *In Search of Love and Beauty*, 1983; *Three Continents*, 1987; *Poet and Dancer*, 1993; *Shards of Memory*, 1995; *My Nine Lives: Chapters of a Possible Past*, 2004.

SCREENPLAYS: *The Householder*, 1963; *Shakespeare Wallah*, 1965 (with James Ivory); *The Guru*, 1968; *Bombay Talkie*, 1970; *Autobiography of a Princess*, 1975 (with Ivory and John Swope); *Roseland*, 1977; *Hullabaloo over Georgie and Bonnie's Pictures*, 1978; *The Europeans*, 1979 (with Ivory); *Quartet*, 1981 (with Ivory); *The Courtesans of Bombay*, 1982; *Heat and Dust*, 1983 (based on her novel); *The Bostonians*, 1984 (with Ivory; based on Henry James's novel); *A Room with a View*, 1986 (based on E. M. Forster's novel); *Maurice*, 1987 (based on Forster's novel); *Madame Sousatzka*, 1988 (with John Schlesinger); *Mr. and Mrs. Bridge*, 1990 (based on Evan S. Connell, Jr.'s novels); *Howards End*, 1992 (based on Forster's novel); *The Remains of the Day*, 1993 (based on Kazuo Ishiguro's novel); *Jefferson in Paris*, 1995; *Surviving Picasso*, 1996; *A Soldier's Daughter Never Cries*, 1998 (based on Kaylie Jones's novel); *The Golden Bowl*, 2000 (based on James's novel); *Le Divorce*, 2003 (with James Ivory; based on Diane Johnson's novel).

TELEPLAYS: *The Place of Peace*, 1975; *Jane Austen in Manhattan*, 1980; *The Wandering Company*, 1985.

Bibliography

Chakravarti, Aruna. *Ruth Prawer Jhabvala: A Study in Empathy and Exile*. Delhi, India: B. R. Publishing, 1998. Discusses other European authors who have written about India, and Jhabvala's role as expatriate. Useful for scholars and students approaching Jhabvala for the first time. Includes bibliographical references and an index.

Crane, Ralph J. *Ruth Prawer Jhabvala*. New York: Twayne, 1992. In a chapter entitled "Sufferers, Seekers, and the Beast That Moves: The Short Stories," Jhabvala's first five volumes of short fiction are discussed. Crane maintains that the differences among Jhabvala's stories reflect her own ambivalence toward India. Includes biographical chapter, chronology, notes, and bibliography.

_____, ed. *Passages to Ruth Prawer Jhabvala*. New Delhi, India: Sterling, 1991. Only one of the essays in this volume deals specifically with short stories. However, much of what is said about theme in the analyses of the novels is applicable to the short fiction as well.

Godden, Rumer. "A Cool Eye in a Parched Landscape." *The New York Times Book Review*, May 25, 1986, 1, 20. Points out stories in *Out of India* that exemplify the internal struggle that Jhabvala discusses in "Myself in India."

Gray, Paul. "Tributes of Empathy and Grace." *Time* 127 (May 12, 1986): 90. In *Out of India*, women repeatedly sacrifice themselves for undeserving men. However, Jhabvala's Western women choose to immerse themselves in India, while her Indian women have fewer options.

Jhabvala, Ruth Prawer. "The Artistry of Ruth Prawer Jhabvala." Interview by Bernard Weinraub. *New York Times Magazine*, September 11, 1983, 64. An important interview/profile, in which Jhabvala explains why she left India for New York City.

_____. "Introduction: Myself in India." In *Out of India: Selected Stories*. New York: William Morrow, 1986. Jhabvala defines the "cycle" of reactions to India which all Westerners seem to experience. Essential reading.

Mason, Deborah. "Passage to America." *The New York Times Book Review*, November 29, 1998, 20, 22-23. The stories in *East into Upper East* prove once again that Jhabvala is a "spellbinding urban fabulist," whose rootless characters escape from reality in various ways. "The Temptress" is the only story of true redemption.

May, Charles E., ed. *Masterplots II: Short Story Series, Revised Edition.* 8 vols. Pasadena, Calif.: Salem Press, 2004. Designed for student use, this reference set contains articles providing detailed plot summaries and analyses of three short stories by Jhabvala: "The Englishwoman" (vol. 2), "In a Great Man's House" (vol. 4), and "The Man with the Dog" (vol. 5).

Sucher, Laurie. *The Fiction of Ruth Prawer Jhabvala: The Politics of Passion.* New York: St. Martin's Press, 1989. Utilizes four novels and nine short stories to prove that Jhabvala's detachment masks her real romanticism, as seen in her interest in feminine sexual politics. Includes bibliography.

Urstad, Tone Sundt. "Protecting One's Inner Self: Ruth Prawer Jhabvala's 'Rose Petals.'" *Studies in Short Fiction* 33 (Winter, 1996): 43-49. "Rose Petals" exemplifies what Jhabvala has stated about how different people react to India's overwhelming social problems. An excellent starting point for the study of Jhabvala's short fiction.

James Joyce

Born: Dublin, Ireland; February 2, 1882
Died: Zurich, Switzerland; January 13, 1941

Principal short fiction • *Dubliners*, 1914.

Other literary forms • James Joyce's name is synonymous with twentieth century fiction, a revolution to which he devoted himself with remarkable single-mindedness. The results are to be found in three extremely influential works of fiction–*A Portrait of the Artist as a Young Man* (1914-1915, serial; 1916, book), *Ulysses* (1922), and *Finnegans Wake* (1939). Though his work in other genres is of much less significance, Joyce also wrote two books of poetry, as well as one play. His youthful critical essays, crucial to an understanding of his artistic origins, were collected posthumously and edited by Richard Ellmann and Ellsworth Mason as *The Critical Writings of James Joyce* (1959). The raw material for *A Portrait of the Artist as a Young Man*, edited by Theodore Spencer, was also published posthumously as *Stephen Hero* (1944).

Achievements • James Joyce is acknowledged by many as the twentieth century's greatest prose artist and is also, arguably, that century's most famous author. Despite his small output and the increasing difficulty of his works, Joyce's name stands as a monument to commitment and artistic integrity. Since the end of World War II, there has hardly been a novelist in the West who has not felt Joyce's influence. Continuing interest in his complex mind and work is sustained by a vast array of academic commentators.

The reasons for Joyce's eminence are not hard to find. Each of his works, beginning with the short stories of *Dubliners*, is notable for its startling originality of language and conception. His fiction, moreover, placed his native city, Dublin, indelibly on the map of the world's culture. His life, a continual struggle against ill health, exile, and the almost total neglect of publishers, has come to be perceived as an eloquent expression of self-determination in an age of totalitarian conformity.

Biography • James Augustine Joyce was born on February 2, 1882, the eldest child of John Stanislaus and Mary Jane (May) Murray Joyce. The family was typical of the growing ranks of the Irish Catholic middle class of the day, socially confident, politically optimistic, though less than well established economically. During Joyce's early years, however, the family remained in comfortable circumstances, and at the age of six, Joyce was enrolled in Clongowes Wood College, an elite Jesuit boarding school outside Dublin. After two years at Clongowes, Joyce's education was interrupted because of a decline in family fortunes, the result in large part of John Joyce's improvidence. In 1893, Joyce began to attend Belvedere College, another Jesuit school, in Dublin, where, in addition to undergoing a thorough exposure to the narrow Roman Catholicism of the day, he won a number of academic prizes. In 1898, Joyce entered University College, Dublin, from which he graduated in 1902.

Throughout the 1890's, the Joyce family continued to experience hard times.

Library of Congress

Their setbacks had a parallel in the reversal of Ireland's political fortunes during the same period. In 1891, Charles Stewart Parnell, the disgraced leader of the Irish cause, died. This event was the occasion of Joyce's first-known literary work, an accusatory poem directed against the foremost of Parnell's lieutenants, who had turned against him, entitled "Et tu, Healy." The 1890's also saw the rise of a literary and intellectual movement in Ireland. By the time Joyce had begun his undergraduate career, this movement was sufficiently evolved to be criticized, a task that Joyce took upon himself, most notably in a pamphlet entitled "The Day of the Rabblement." While at college, Joyce also distinguished himself by other literary essays, mostnotably with an article on Henrik Ibsen—an important early influence—which appeared in the prestigious *Fortnightly Review.*

In 1902, Joyce left Ireland for Paris, intending to study medicine in order to secure an income to support his writing. This unsuccessful trip was abruptly curtailed by news of his mother's terminal illness. After her death in 1903, Joyce spent an unproductive year in Dublin, relieved only by writing poems and the initial versions of some of the *Dubliners* stories and by meeting Nora Barnacle, his wife-to-be. With her, he left Ireland in 1904, remaining abroad, with a few brief exceptions, for the rest of his life.

Joyce and his wife began life in Pula, then a backwater in the Austro-Hungarian Empire, later known as the town of Pulj in Yugoslavia. Most of their lives before World War I, however, were spent in Trieste. There, their two children were born, Giorgio in 1905 and Lucia two years later. Joyce earned an uncertain and reluctant living teaching English as a foreign language and worked on the stories of *Dubliners* and *A Portrait of the Artist as a Young Man.* A number of prospective publishers deemed the stories to be too scandalous to issue, and *Dubliners* languished in limbo until 1914.

That year was to prove decisive to Joyce's development as a writer. Through the good offices of the Irish poet William Butler Yeats, the American poet Ezra Pound contacted Joyce and arranged for *A Portrait of the Artist as a Young Man* to be serialized. In that year, also, Joyce started his most celebrated work, *Ulysses,* and moved with his family to Zurich, where they lived for the duration of the war. Briefly returning to Trieste in 1919, the family moved to Paris, where *Ulysses* was published in 1922. Beset by ill health and by the mental illness of his daughter, though immune from financial difficulties through the generosity of a patron, Harriet Shaw Weaver, Joyce remained in Paris working on his opaque masterpiece, *Finnegans Wake,* until World

War II obliged him to resettle in Zurich. There, Joyce died of complications arising from perforated ulcers on January 13, 1941.

Analysis • In August, 1904, James Joyce wrote to his friend C. P. Curran: "I am writing a series of epicleti. . . . I call the series *Dubliners* to betray the soul of that hemiplegia or paralysis which many consider a city." This note announces, in effect, a transformation of the short story as a form. The note's pretentious jargon reveals the attitude of the young Joyce's artistic demeanor. In addition, it calls attention to some of the main technical and thematic characteristics of a volume that had to wait a further ten years for a publisher to consider it acceptable.

There is still some scholarly debate over the term "epicleti," whose etymology remains obscure. It is clear, however, that Joyce's use of the term shows him to be in pursuit of an aesthetic method. This self-conscious search for a method reveals Joyce as a preeminently twentieth century modernist author. As with his eminent contemporaries and advocates T. S. Eliot and Ezra Pound, to write was to articulate a theory of writing. Moreover, the search was successfully concluded, as the closing chapter of *A Portrait of the Artist as a Young Man* records. It culminated in the "epiphany," which means "showing forth" and which describes not only Joyce's method but also his objectives in using one.

Joyce used the term "epiphany" to describe some of his own early artistic efforts in prose. These sketches sometimes resemble prose poems, calibrating moments of intense perception and emotional heightening. At other times, they take the form of life studies of banal moments in everyday life. The overall intention is one of unmasking hidden states, whether of the exalted or humdrum variety. In both instances, the pieces are marked by a fastidious language, which clearly anticipates the "style of scrupulous meanness" in which Joyce said *Dubliners* is written.

Dubliners • Artistic theory is not the only novelty of *Dubliners*. Joyce's note to Curran also draws attention to his subject matter. From a strictly historical point of view, Joyce's characterization of his birthplace is to some extent misleading. The stories of *Dubliners* tend to overlook those factors that distinguished the city in Joyce's time. The impact and significance of the establishment in Dublin of Ireland's national theater, the Abbey, for example, which opened in 1904, may be lost on non-Irish readers of Joyce's stories. In general, Joyce is at pains to belittle the various attempts at cultural self-renewal, which were a marked feature of Dublin life in the early years of the twentieth century, as the satire of the story "A Mother" shows—although in "The Dead" this satirical attitude is significantly modified. Joyce also fails to provide a cross section of the city's social composition, there being no stories featuring the upper echelon. The city was not quite the paraplegic of Joyce's diagnostic imagination.

The stories' emphasis is on what Joyce asserts to be typical of his city. This democratic vision of his brings to the reader's notice a range of marginalized citizens. These include children, the alienated, the helpless and hopeless, and particularly women—*Dubliners* has a feminist undercurrent, all the more noteworthy because of its time. These citizens, often known merely by a single name, represent the social, cultural, and moral cost of living in a city that was less a capital than one of the British Empire's provincial administrative centers. The fact that their humdrum and unpromising lives should be subjected to the artistic and intellectual powers that Joyce possessed is significant on a number of counts. From the standpoint of literary history, *Dubliners* combines the two prevailing literary modes of Joyce's day. In a refinement of an approach pioneered by the great French novelist Gustave Flaubert, Joyce subjects material that had hitherto been the artistic property of the naturalists to the aesthetic commitments of the Symbolists. One way of describing the function of the epiphany is to note its author's organization of commonplaces in such a manner that they ultimately yield possibilities of meaning greater than their culturally preconditioned, or factual, appearances admit.

From the point of view of Irish literary history, the stories of *Dubliners* eloquently, though untypically, participate in the overall effort of the Irish Literary Revival to address national realities. The careful delineation of lost lives, which characterizes most of *Dubliners*, is a unique contribution to the spirit of the critique, which informs much of the stories' Irish cultural context. It is not surprising to learn that they were considered too controversial to publish with impunity, or that, by virtue of being so, they confirmed their author's belief that they constituted "a chapter in the moral history of my country."

A further notable feature of the book is that, unlike many collections of short stories, particularly those of that period, *Dubliners* is a collection of stories that, however limited in range, is disparate while at the same time functioning as a coherent whole. Its coherence is not merely a matter of Joycean cunning, whereby the collection's opening story is entitled "The Sisters" and centers on a death, while the final story is called "The Dead" and takes place at a party hosted by sisters. The history of the book's composition, to which must be added a recognition of the complications brought about by publishers' lack of commitment, precludes any such facile observation, since "The Dead" was conceived and written after Joyce's initial version of *Dubliners* had been completed and submitted for publication. Two other stories were added to the original dozen, "Two Gallants" and "A Little Cloud." Rather more subtly, the collection achieves coherence by numerous overlapping means. These include the integrity of its style, its thematic consistency, the largely uniform character of its *dramatis personae*, and its use of a major device in the overall scheme of Joyce's aesthetic, repetition and variation.

In addition, Joyce himself had an integrated vision of the work's coherence, one whereby the whole would be seen to be greater than the sum of the parts. This view holds good particularly when applied to the twelve stories of the initial *Dubliners*, where it describes a mode of symmetrical organization as well as a principle of thematic development, so that a case can readily be made for the work as a whole comprising a "moral history." According to Joyce, *Dubliners* may be divided into four consecutive sections. The first of these consists of the three opening stories, "The Sisters," "An Encounter," and "Araby." These are followed by a sequence of stories dealing with adolescence, "The Boarding House," "After the Race," and "Eveline." Three stories of mature life come next, "Clay," "Counterparts," and "A Painful Case." Finally the volume closes with a trio of stories devoted to public life, "Ivy Day in the Committee Room," "A Mother," and "Grace."

Although the symmetry of this quartet of trios is disrupted by the introduction of further stories, two of the new additions, both written in 1906, enlarge rather than negate their respective categories. The range of the stories of adolescence is considerably broadened by the addition of "Two Gallants." Similarly, the motifs of entrapment and disillusion, typical of the stories of mature life, are further adumbrated in the history of Chandler, the protagonist of "A Little Cloud." In "The Dead," written in 1907, Joyce's artistry as a writer of short fiction is seen to best advantage. In addition, this story crystallizes and elevates to a higher plane of intellection and feeling many of the themes of *Dubliners*, the result being what is generally acknowledged to be one of the finest short stories in the English language.

The titles of the stories of *Dubliners* offer a clue to the nature of their contents. Such titles as "An Encounter," "A Painful Case," "Counterparts," "A Mother," and "The Dead"—to take some of the most obvious cases in point—seem deliberately to offer little or nothing to the reader, neither a sense of expectation nor a sense of anything particularly distinctive within the material, even though Joyce insisted to his publishers that presenting his fellow citizens to the world at large had undoubted novelty value. Yet the very anonymity of many of the titles points with precision to both their character and their method. The stories' protagonists are for the most part colorless, unpromising, defeated, and lacking in interiority. For the most part, they are unaware of these facts about their personalities and conditions, and the stories evolve somewhat remorselessly to a point where these hapless characters are on the threshold of recognizing, or deliberately overlooking, their morally abject lives. The fact, therefore, that the stories' titles frequently evoke generic types or states is a pointer to one of their prominent attributes. The stories that do not conform to this general rule have titles that are extremely localized and opaque in a different sense. Few readers will know automatically that the ivy day referred to in "Ivy Day in the Committee Room" refers to the custom of commemorating the Irish political leader Charles Stewart Parnell, or that "Araby," in addition to its generic connotations, refers to an actual bazaar that was held in Dublin in mid-May, 1894. This obscure fact makes the story's protagonist the same age as Joyce was when the bazaar was held.

The sense of comparative anonymity and insignificance suggested by the titles is replicated in the case of the protagonists, a large number of whom are either anonymous or known by a single name, as though they had not yet succeeded in attaining the measure of identity required to merit being fully named. The very title *Dubliners* is clearly generic, and Joyce, approaching his material from such a standpoint, reveals his interest in the typical, the representative, and the norm. In this sense, Joyce shows his deep sense of the short-story form, with its traditional emphasis on the delineation of representative characters in representative contexts. Such an interest is amplified with great deftness and versatility in the language of the stories, which frequently draws on official, generic codes of utterance. Gabriel's speech on hospitality in "The Dead" is an important example of one such code, particularly when contrasted with the highly wrought meditation that closes the story. The sermon that concludes "Grace" is another, despite being rendered in the narrative mode known as free indirect style for satirical purposes. A third example is the mimicry of the newspaper report of police evidence in "A Painful Case." The collection as a whole is saturated by formal and informal exploitation of the characters' various modes of utterance from which a sense of their cultural orientation and impoverishment may be extrapolated.

As with all Joyce's works, the latently satirical manipulation of cliché is a crucial feature of *Dubliners*. In addition, by virtue of the author's uncanny ear not merely for the demotic but for the quality of consciousness that such utterances reveal, the stories possess a convincing patina of objectivity, as though it is the restless but unobtrusive activity of their language that produces their effects, rather than anything as unrefined as the author's direction and intentions. Thus, the doctrine of the artist's impersonality, which has numerous important implications for modernist aesthetics and which Joyce, possibly following the example of Gustave Flaubert, invokes in *A Portrait of the Artist as a Young Man*, is utilized in *Dubliners* to telling effect.

It is in the matter of the stories' presumed objectivity that *Dubliners* fell afoul of the publishing industry of the day. Joyce freely availed himself of the civic furniture of his native city, including by name actual business premises—pubs and hotels, notably—as well as churches and other well-known amenities and distinctive features of the social life of his birthplace. By so doing, he not only went further in his pursuit of documentary verisimilitude than the vast majority of even naturalistic writers of Joyce's generation but also revealed a conception of language—or of what happens to language once it is written—which, in its mature development in *Ulysses* and *Finnegans Wake*, provided a complex, integrated code of cultural semiotics. Joyce's use of placenames, the names of businesses, and most notoriously the names of English royalty, shows his understanding that a name is a word, not a supposedly photographic facsimile of the entity it denotes. *Dubliners* is replete with names chosen with a sensitivity to their artistic and cultural resonance as well as to their geographical precision. For example, the North Wall, Eveline's terminus in the story that bears her name, is both correct in a documentary sense and thematically appropriate. A subtler instance is Mr. Duffy's residence at Chapelizod, a short distance outside Dublin. Not only does the choice of residence underline Duffy's standoffish nature, but also the name of where he lives is a corruption of Chapel Iseult. This name invokes the legend of the lovers Tristan and Iseult, of whose tragic love Duffy's affair is a banal but nevertheless heartfelt shadow. Use of the legend is an anticipation of the method in *Ulysses*, where the heroic stuff of epic forms an ironic but by no means belittling counterpoint to the trial of twentieth century human beings.

Neither of Joyce's English and Irish publishers was very interested in the long-term consequences or subtle immediacies of Joyce's art. Both feared that his use of actual names would lead them into serious legal difficulties, which would be compounded by what was considered a use of blasphemous language and an impersonation of the thoughts of Edward, Prince of Wales, in "Ivy Day in the Committee Room," Joyce's favorite story in the collection. Joyce, against his better judgment, toned down the impersonation and made a number of other minor adjustments, while basically upholding his right of documentary representation in the service of artistic integrity and objectivity.

The most conclusive evidence for the stories' objectivity, however, is provided by their use of the epiphany. Much critical ink has been consumed in attempting to explicate this device. Undoubtedly it is a key concept not only in the appreciation of the art of Joyce's short stories but also in the comprehension of the form's development under the influence of *Dubliners*. At the same time, the reader who does not possess a firm grasp of the concept may still read *Dubliners* with satisfaction, insight, and sympathy. The epiphany makes its presence felt, typically, at the conclusion of a *Dubliners* story. It is here that the reader is likely to experience a certain amount of distancing from the action, which cannot be accounted for merely by the foreignness of the characters and their locale. These, in themselves, do not inhibit either the forward movement of the narrative or that movement's potential for significance. At the point when that potential might well be expected to be realized, however, it may strike the reader as being deferred or repressed.

This discovery is intended to alert the reader that the narrative technique of a Dubliners story only superficially conforms to the introduction-development-denouement model of story organization. Early critics of the work, indeed, complained that for the most part, through their lack of dramatic issue or intriguing theme, the stories were no more than sketches, not seeing that what Joyce was interested in was as much manner as matter, and that only a minimalist approach of the kind he used would grace with art the marginal conditions of his characters and articulate, in a mode that did not violate the impoverished spirit of his paralyzed raw material, its worthiness and the value of bringing it to the reader's attention. Concern for the reader's attention is therefore critical, since so much of what Joyce was writing about had already been effectively written off socially, culturally, politically, and spiritually. The comprehensive nature of this silencing is spelled out in the collection's opening story, "The Sisters."

The strain placed on the reader's attention by the typical conclusion of the stories is Joyce's method of expressing his concern that the material's impact not be diminished by meeting the preconditioned expectations of how its conflicts might be resolved. Rather than have the story reach a conclusion, with its connotations of finality and mastery, Joyce ends the story, breaks off the action before all its implications and ramifications have been extrapolated. He thereby extends to the reader an invitation, which may also be a duty, to draw out the inferences of this act of narrative termination. The development of inferences is the means whereby the story achieves the statement of itself, an achievement that describes the epiphany in action.

In order to participate in the activity of revelation that the term "epiphany" connotes, the reader will note that not only does a *Dubliners* story conventionally, if loosely, observe the Aristotelian unities of time, place, and action, but also that unity is achieved by the tissue of correspondences, insinuations, nuances, echoes, and general interplay that exists among the various phases of a given story's action and the language. The introduction of the train at the end of "A Painful Case" is an obvious example of Joyce's cunning and tacit strategies. One of the outcomes of these effects is to offset any purely deterministic sense of plot. The compulsiveness and irreversibility of action, on a sense of which plot tends to be based, is offset, modified, or at the very least has its crudely dramatic character diminished by Joyce's effects. As a result, the reader is placed in a position of assembling what the story's fabric of data signifies. It is the reader, typically, rather than the protagonist, who recognizes the epiphanic moment, the moment at which the tendencies of the action become undeniably clear. At this moment, the reader attains the point of maximum perspective. It is a moment of closure but of reinvestment, of withdrawal and of sympathy, of estrangement and acceptance. Its result is to make the reader morally complicit with the material, since were it not for the epiphany's appeal to the reader the material's significance, or rather its ability to signify, would be moot. The empowered reader becomes the type of citizen whom the representative protagonist of a *Dubliners* story cannot be. The stories represent a mastery over material and circumstances with which the reader is called upon to identify, but which the characters cannot embody.

Although it is possible to consider the stories of *Dubliners* from many different artistic, cultural, and moral perspectives, the theme of independence or the lack of it is the one that seems most central to Joyce's concerns. His preoccupation with the paralyzed condition of his native city may be described as an awareness of how little the spirit of independence moved there. The numerous implications of this lack are addressed in story after story. The typical trajectory of the story is the optimistic going out, the counterpart of which is the disillusioned return. In even such a simple story as "An Encounter," the youngster's naïve dream of adventure and access to the adult world is both realized and made unrecognizable and unacceptable by the form it takes. Encounters with worldly others, such as the flirtatious couples at the bazaar at

the end of "Araby," or Frank in "Eveline," the sophisticated foreigners in "After the
Race," or Ignatius Gallaher in "A Little Cloud," all leave the protagonists reduced
and defeated. The world is a more complex and demanding environment than their
dreams of fulfillment might have led them to believe. The self withdraws, pained that
the world is not a reflection of its needs. As in "Two Gallants," when the world can
be manipulated to serve the ego, the process is crude, exploitative, and morally despicable.

"Ivy Day in the Committee Room" • Some of the most far-reaching implications of
the independence theme may be seen in "Ivy Day in the Committee Room." There
the heirs of a dramatically successful political movement for a constitutional form of
Irish independence are depicted as bemused, opportunistic, devoted to rhetoric
rather than action, stagnant in thought and deed. Their conspicuous lack of will is
matched by their inconsistency of thought. Yet, while satire is a pronounced feature
of the story, Joyce also makes clear that the characters cannot be merely scorned.
The poem that affects them is certainly not a fine piece of writing, as the story's closing comment would have readers believe. On the contrary, it is a heartfelt performance, genuine in its feeling and authentic in its response. The negative elements of
these characters' lives and the bleak outlook for the productive commissioning of
their human potential become, in Joyce's view, as compelling a set of realities as the
triumph of the will or worldly fulfillment.

"The Dead" • This view receives its most comprehensive expression in "The Dead,"
making the story, for that reason alone, the crowning achievement of *Dubliners*. From
the playful malapropism of its opening sentence to its resonant closing periods, this
story provides, in scale, thematic variety, psychological interest, and narrative tempo
a complete and enriched survey of Joyce's artistic and moral commitments at the
close of the first phase of his writing career. Whereas previously, the collection's stories were representations of a quality, or poverty, of consciousness to which the characters were unable to relate, in "The Dead" Gabriel achieves an awareness of his particular consciousness. The moment of recognition, the epiphany, in which Gabriel
realizes what his wife's story of lost love says about his own emotional adequacy, is not
an experience whose meaning the reader infers. It is a meaning whose articulation by
Gabriel the reader overhears. Unlike many of the other stories, however, "The Dead"
does not end on this note of recognition. Gabriel, for all that "The Dead" has shown
him having difficulty in being self-possessed and autonomous, acknowledges the
force and significance of Gretta's revelation. He relates to those limitations in himself, which the story of Michael Furey underlines. In doing so, he attains a degree of
sympathy, honesty, and freely chosen solidarity with the finite, mortal nature of human reality, his mind enlarging as its sense of defeat becomes a central and constraining fact of life. The balance achieved in "The Dead" between subjective need and objective fact, between romance and reality, between self-deception and self-awareness
gives the story its poise and potency and makes it a persuasive recapitulation of the
other *Dubliners* stories' concerns.

    It is by the conclusive means of "The Dead" that Joyce's *Dubliners* identifies itself
with the critique of humanism, which was a fundamental component of the revolution in the arts at the beginning of the twentieth century. The invisibility of the author's personality, the tonal and stylistic restraint with which the stories are told, and
the aesthetic subtlety of the epiphany add up to rather more than simply a revolution

in short fiction. They also, by their nature, draw attention to the force of the negative as a reality in the lives of the characters, a reality that Joyce, by refusing to overlook it, helped place on the agenda of twentieth century consciousness.

George O'Brien

Other major works

PLAY: *Exiles*, pb. 1918.

NOVELS: *A Portrait of the Artist as a Young Man*, 1914-1915, serial (1916, book); *Ulysses*, 1922; *Finnegans Wake*, 1939; *Stephen Hero*, 1944 (edited by Theodore Spencer).

NONFICTION: *Letters of James Joyce*, 1957-1966 (3 volumes); *The Critical Writings of James Joyce*, 1959; *Selected Letters of James Joyce*, 1975 (Richard Ellmann, editor); *The James Joyce Archives*, 1977-1979 (64 volumes); *On Ibsen*, 1999; *Occasional, Critical, and Political Writing*, 2000.

POETRY: *Chamber Music*, 1907; *Pomes Penyeach*, 1927; "Ecce Puer," 1932; *Collected Poems*, 1936.

Bibliography

Alter, Robert. *Canon and Creativity: Modern Writing and the Authority of Scripture*. New Haven, Conn.: Yale University Press, 2000. Lucid argument for the complex influence that the Bible has exerted on three important and diverse authors: Franz Kafka, Hayyim Hahman Bialik, and James Joyce.

Benstock, Bernard. *Narrative Con/Texts in "Dubliners."* Urbana: University of Illinois Press, 1994. Includes analyses of narrative principles, symbolic systems, theological contexts, and a variety of themes and techniques in *Dubliners*.

Blades, John. *How to Study James Joyce*. Houndmills, England: Macmillan, 1996. Excellent study guide for students of Joyce. Includes bibliographical references, outlines, and syllabi.

Bosinelli, Rosa M. Bollettieri, and Harold F. Mosher, Jr., eds. *ReJoycing: New Readings of "Dubliners."* Lexington: University Press of Kentucky, 1998. Fourteen new essays on *Dubliners* that argue Joyce questioned literary, cultural, and political developments of his time. The essays examine themes, style, intertexuality, politics, linguistics, and gender conflicts in Joyce's stories.

Brunsdale, Mitzi M. *James Joyce: A Study of the Short Fiction*. New York: Twayne, 1993. General introduction to Joyce's stories, focusing on the five most familiar stories from *Dubliners*. Also includes excerpts from Joyce's own nonfiction criticism and from other critics.

Fargnoli, Nicholas, and Michael P. Gillespie. *James Joyce A to Z: The Essential Reference to the Life and Work*. New York: Oxford University Press, 1995. Dictionary-type reference book with approximately eight hundred entries on characters, concepts, locales, terminology, and critics of Joyce.

Jones, Ellen Carol, and Morris Beja, eds. *Twenty-first Joyce*. Gainesville: University Press of Florida, 2004. This useful reference work collects 13 scholarly essays written by Joyce experts. Part of the Florida James Joyce Series.

Leonard, Garry M. *Reading "Dubliners" Again: A Lacanian Perspective*. Syracuse, N.Y.: Syracuse University Press, 1993. Using Lacan's Freudian approach to language's role in creating our experience of reality, Leonard examines the stories in *Dubliners*, urging readers to explore their kinship with the moral paralysis of the characters.

May, Charles E., ed. *Masterplots II: Short Story Series, Revised Edition*. 8 vols. Pasadena, Calif.: Salem Press, 2004. Designed for student use, this reference set contains articles providing detailed plot summaries and analyses of twelve short stories by Joyce: "Araby" and "The Boarding House" (vol. 1); "Clay," "Counterparts," and "The Dead" (vol. 2); "Eveline" and "Grace" (vol. 3); "Ivy Day in the Committee Room" and "A Little Cloud" (vol. 4); "A Painful Case" (vol. 6); "The Sisters" (vol. 7); and "Two Gallants" (vol. 8).

Schwarz, Daniel R., ed. *"The Dead" by James Joyce*. New York: St. Martin's Press, 1994. Casebook of essays on "The Dead," from such critical perspectives as reader-response theory, new historicism, feminism, deconstruction, and psychoanalysis.

Studies in Short Fiction 32 (Summer, 1995). A collection of sixteen new essays on *Dubliners*, along with eleven reviews of new books on Joyce. Includes general essays on techniques and themes of *Dubliners* as well as analyses of "Araby," "The Sisters," "Grace," "The Dead," and discussions comparing Joyce's stories with those of William Trevor and Edna O'Brien.

Theall, Donald F. *James Joyce's Techno-Poetics*. Toronto: University of Toronto Press, 1997. Representative of a new wing of Joyce studies, Theall's work examines Joyce as a progenitor of today's cyberculture. Includes bibliography and index.

Franz Kafka

Born: Prague, Bohemia, Austro-Hungarian Empire (now in Czech Republic);
July 3, 1883
Died: Kierling, Klosterneuburg, near Vienna, Austria; June 3, 1924

Principal short fiction • *Betrachtung,* 1913 (*Meditation,* 1948); *Das Urteil,* 1913, 1916 (*The Sentence,* 1928; also as *The Judgment,* 1945); *Die Verwandlung,* 1915 (novella; *The Metamorphosis,* 1936); *Ein Landarzt: Kleine Erzählungen,* 1919 (*The Country Doctor: A Collection of Fourteen Short Stories,* 1945); "In der Strafkolonie," 1919 ("In the Penal Colony," 1941); *Ein Hungerkünstler: Vier Geschichten,* 1924 (*A Hunger Artist,* 1948); *Beim Bau der Chinesischen Mauer: Ungedruckte Erzählungen und Prosa aus dem Nachlass,* 1931 (*The Great Wall of China, and Other Pieces,* 1933); *Erzählungen,* 1946 (*The Complete Stories,* 1971); *The Penal Colony: Stories and Short Pieces,* 1948; *Selected Short Stories,* 1952.

Other literary forms • Franz Kafka did not attempt to write drama or poetry. His métier was prose. He was a perfectionist who apparently intended only a portion of what he had written for publication. Much of his reputation rests on his three posthumously published novels: *Der Prozess* (1925; *The Trial,* 1937), *Das Schloss* (1926; *The Castle,* 1930), and *Amerika* (1927; *America,* 1938). Those three novels and several volumes of Kafka's short stories were prepared for publication by the executor of his literary estate, Max Brod, who took great liberties in rearranging Kafka's often chaotic manuscripts. During the 1990's, better trained scholars reedited Kafka's original manuscripts and made new translations that superseded the editions that had been in print for more than sixty years.

Kafka also wrote voluminously in other categories of prose that bear the same distinctive style as his creative work. His diaries and letters contain many comments that aid in the understanding of his stories, and his meticulous legal reports are exemplary professional documents.

Achievements • Every year, more secondary literature is published about Franz Kafka than about almost any other author except William Shakespeare. This attests the extraordinary power and alluringly enigmatic content of his works. Although his inimitable prose style describes everything as if it were self-evident, he invariably introduces elements of the fantastic and surreal and portrays the demise of his characters as almost inevitable. His works are imbued with a sense of horror as isolated characters struggle futilely against malign forces that they do not understand.

Kafka unintentionally became the voice of the age. Coming after the philosophers Martin Heidegger and Edmund Husserl, and being contemporary with the founder of psychoanalysis, Sigmund Freud, he captured the existential angst of the generation. As a result of the Industrial Revolution, the father no longer worked from the home but dominated the family from a distance. The figure of authority was a stranger.

Biography • Franz Kafka's literary achievements are all the more remarkable when one considers that he lived to be only forty, was increasingly ill with tuberculosis dur-

ing the last seven years of his life and up until two years before his death held a full-time position as lawyer.

Although his lifestyle was in keeping with that of his mother's bachelor brothers, one of whom was a country doctor, Kafka and his father were very different in personality. The efforts of the robust, self-confident, and sometime abusive businessman to rear a frail insecure, and sensitive son led to a constant state of friction between the two. Unlike his younger sisters, who married and established families of their own, Kafka lived mainly with his parents, attempting always to relate to the father who could not understand him.

Kafka's parents had a strong marriage but did not have much time for their children, who were cared for by household help. During the day, the parents worked together in their store. In the evening, the two of them played cards. Kafka did well in school, contrary to his fears, and received a good education, especially in Latin, from dedicated teachers.

In 1901, Kafka entered the German University in Prague and obtained his doctorate in law in 1906. He resigned from his first position, stating as his reason that he was upset by the cursing and swearing, even though it had not been directed at him. Through the intercession of a friend, he then obtained a position with the Workers Accident Insurance Institute and remained with the firm from 1908 to 1922, when his declining health necessitated an early retirement. His work was appreciated, and he received many benefits from the firm.

Kafka was never without friends, and he had a good sense of humor—something that could be emphasized more in the interpretation of his works. He liked to read his stories aloud and sometimes broke down in uncontrollable laughter over the plots that he had invented. Marriage was something that Kafka both desired and feared. He was engaged twice to Felice Bauer, a woman who lived in another city. He had met her briefly through a friend and soon afterward initiated an epistolary relationship. This became a pattern that he repeated with two other women, always being reluctant to be with them in person. Only in the last year of his life did he overcome his inhibitions enough to live for a few months with a woman half his age, Dora Dymant.

Dymant did not realize the value of Kafka's literary works and at his request burned many manuscripts. Kafka also stipulated in his will that his friend and exec tor, the author Max Brod, was to burn everything not published during Kafka's lifetime. It was an ambivalent request, because Brod had said he would never do so.

Although Jewish, Kafka was relatively unaffected by anti-Semitism. The gravestone for him and his parents is in the Strasnice Cemetery in Prague. His three sisters were later killed in concentration camps.

Analysis • Franz Kafka's stories are not about love or success. They do not leave the reader feeling comfortable. Writing was, for him, a necessity. On August 6, 1914, Kafka wrote in his diary: "My talent for portraying my dreamlike inner life has thrust all other matters into the background; my life has dwindled dreadfully, nor will it cease to dwindle. Nothing else will ever satisfy me." The meaning of the images from his dreamlike inner life was not always clear to him at the time of writing. Sometimes he realized only several years later what he may have subconsciously meant. Toward the end of his life, he decided that psychoanalysis was a waste of time and abandoned that approach in retrospective reading. Critics may not be of the same opinion.

"The Metamorphosis" • The opening sentence of "The Metamorphosis" is one of the most famous in modern fiction: "As Gregor Samsa awoke one morning from uneasy dreams he found himself transformed in his bed into a gigantic insect." In the story's first section, Gregor accepts his fantastic transformation matter-of-factly, perhaps wishing to bury its causes in his subconscious mind. Instead of worrying about the mystery of his metamorphosis, he worries about the nature and security of his position as traveling salesperson for a firm whose severity he detests.

In the second section, Gregor's isolation and alienation intensify. Readers learn about his relations, past and present, with his family; they have been characterized by concealment, mistrust, and exploitation on the father's part. Gregor's mother is gentle, selfless, weak, and shallow; in the story's development she becomes increasingly her husband's appendage. His sister Grete is his favorite; however, although she ministers to his new animal needs, she fails him emotionally. In the third section, Gregor, defeated, yields up all hope of returning to the human community. His parents and sister shut him out, as his miserable existence slopes resignedly toward death.

Gregor's metamorphosis accomplishes several of his aims: First, it frees him from his hated job with an odious employer by disabling him from working; second, it relieves him of the requirement to make an agonizing choice between his filial duty to his parents—particularly his father—and his desperate yearning to emancipate himself from such obligations and dependence. It thus enables him to "bug out" of his loathsome constraints yet do so on a level of conscious innocence, with Gregor merely a victim of an uncontrollable calamity. Moreover, Gregor's fantasies include aggressive and retaliatory action against the oppressive firm. He accomplishes this by terrorizing the pitiless, arrogant office manager, who tells him, "I am speaking here in the name of your parents and of your chief." On the conscious level, Gregor pursues the clerk to appease him and secure his advocacy for Gregor's cause at the office; subconsciously, his threatening appearance and apparently hostile gestures humiliate his hated superiors.

Gregor's change also expresses his sense of guilt at having betrayed his work and his parents, at having broken the familial circle. It is a treacherous appeasement of this guilt complex, inviting his isolation, punishment, and death. His loss of human speech prevents him from communicating his humanity. His enormous size, though an insect (he is at least two feet wide), his ugly features, and his malodorous stench invite fear and revulsion. Yet his pacific temperament and lack of claws, teeth, or wings make him far more vulnerable than when his body was human. His metamorphosis therefore gives him the worst of both worlds: He is offensive in appearance but defenseless in fact, exposed to the merciless attack of anyone—such as his furious father—ready to exploit his vulnerability.

"The Metamorphosis," then, can be seen as a punishment fantasy with Gregor Samsa feeling triply guilty of having displaced his father as leading breadwinner for the family, for his hatred of his job, and resentment of his family's expectations of him. He turns himself into a detestable insect, thereby both rebelling against the authority of his firm and father and punishing himself for this rebellion by seeking estrangement, rejection, and death. Insofar as Gregor's physical manifestation constitutes a translation of the interior self to the external world, "The Metamorphosis" is a stellar achievement of expressionism.

"The Judgment" • Kafka wrote "Das Urteil" ("The Judgment") in one sitting through the night of September 22-23, 1912. It was an eminently satisfying experience, the only one of his works that he said came out of him like a birth. When he sat down to write, he had intended to depict a war scene. Then, the story took its own direction, and when he finished, early in the morning, he was not sure what it meant. He knew only that it was good.

In the course of "The Judgment," the main character, Georg Bendemann, experiences a complete reversal in his plans. At the outset, he announces his engagement to Frieda Brandenfeld. At the end, he commits suicide. The transition from good news to bad and the descent from normalcy into apparent madness are subtly accomplished. With hindsight, one can see that warning signs are held up all the way. Yet none of these signs is in itself shocking enough to alienate the reader. Only their cumulative effect is overwhelming. Kafka's stories wield their powerful influence over the reader's mood by always remaining plausible. While never losing the semblance of logical reportage, Kafka creates scenes of horror, which both spring from and give rise to psychological suffering. Anything resembling such scenes has come to be called "Kafkaesque."

Kafka writes metaphorically, letting characters, actions, and objects represent emotional and psychological states. Thus, the works are understood best not as narrative advancing a plot but in terms of the protagonist's attempts to transcend absurdity, depersonalization, and alienation. There is a strong autobiographical element in all the stories.

Most critics equate Georg Bendemann with Kafka, and Georg's father with Kafka's father. The issue to be dealt with, then, is why the father would violently oppose the son's engagement to a woman from a well-to-do family. To accept that, one has to subscribe to an inverse standard. Kate Flores interprets this aspect of "The Judgment" in an anthropological way, explaining that for precivilized man it was an act of insubordination to supplant the dominant male. Certainly, "The Judgment" does contain elements of a primal struggle. Also consistent with this reading is the father's tenacious hold on Georg's watch chain, as if to halt the inexorable advance of time and the aging process. There is also the fact that Kafka's father did indeed deride one of his engagements, although at a much later date than when "The Judgment" was written.

Kafka's stories support many interpretations. It is important, when reading "The

Judgment," that one not concentrate on the apparent polarity of father and son to the exclusion of the curious figure of the friend in Russia, to whom the first third of the story is devoted. In fact, preposterous though it may seem, the most comprehensive reading results from considering all three male figures—the friend in Russia, Georg Bendemann, and his father—to be different aspects of the same person, namely Kafka. It is significant that only one name is provided.

The friend in Russia immediately becomes associated with writing, because Georg has been writing to him for years. This association is reinforced when the father, surprisingly, also claims to have been writing to the friend. After Georg has brought up the matter of an engagement on three separate occasions, the friend in Russia responds by showing some interest, but as with his emotionless reaction to the death of Georg's mother, the friend's interest in human affairs seems perfunctory. He has few social contacts, has let his business slide, and seems to be in a general state of ill health and decline. His life has dwindled dreadfully. This identifies him with Kafka the writer.

Georg Bendemann's business seems to have been operating in inverse proportion to that of his friend in Russia. It is thriving, and he has recently become engaged. The thriving business and the engagement go hand in hand in "The Judgment." Both are traditionally recognized outward signs of success. Kafka, at the time of writing "The Judgment," was already a successful lawyer, well established in his firm and becoming interested in Felice Bauer, who seems to be represented in the story by her close namesake, Frieda Brandenfeld. Frieda makes a remark to Georg that, on the surface, is very puzzling. She tells him that since he has friends such as the one in Russia, he should never have gotten engaged. This is the warning sign that either Frieda or the friend in Russia will have to go. The application to Kafka's life seems clear: Either Felice or the writing will have to go.

The most interesting and complex of the three male figures is the father. While appearing to oppose Georg, the older man can, in this case, actually be relied on to say what Georg wants to hear. Faced with the irreconcilable conflict between loyalty to his longtime friend in Russia and loyalty to his new fiancé, Georg finds himself inexplicably going to his father's room, where he has not been for some time. The sunlight is blocked by a wall, the father is surrounded by ancient newspapers, and the window is shut. It is a trip into the dark and the past, which is sealed off from the outside world. The father represents the subconscious. He is also the progenitor, and he is still, despite some deceptive signs of senility, the figure of authority.

The father's first remark, which points beyond the frame of the surface story, is his question of whether Georg really has a friend in St. Petersburg. What the father really seems to be asking is whether the friend can continue to be called a friend when he has been so neglected. Georg at this point is still inclined to decide in favor of Frieda and an outwardly successful life, so he endeavors to quell the troubling reference to his friend by carrying his father from the dark out into the light and then covering him up, thereby forcibly suppressing the question of the friend.

Contrary to Georg's intent, this results in the father's exploding into action. In an extraordinarily dramatic scene, he hurls off the blankets, leaps to his feet, and, standing upright on the bed and kicking, denounces Georg's plans for marriage and accuses him of playing the false friend all these years. Georg realizes that he should be on his guard against attack but then forgets again and stands defenseless before his father.

The father's second remark that seems rather incredible in terms of the surface story is that the friend in Russia has not been betrayed after all, because he, the father, has also been writing to him all along and representing him. Suppressed talents are only strengthened in the subconscious. The father now unquestionably has the upper hand and pronounces his judgment over Georg: He was an innocent child, but he has been a devilish human being. Presumably, it was during childhood that Georg cultivated the friend now in Russia. As an adult, getting ever more into business and thoughts of marriage, Georg has been devilish by denying his true self, the writer. The father finishes by sentencing Georg to death by drowning. To drown is to be plunged into the creative element.

Georg confirms the validity of his father's verdict by carrying out the sentence. It is important for the reader to remember that as the father crashes on the bed exhausted, the subconscious having asserted itself, and as Georg lets himself fall from the bridge, effectively ending the business career and the engagement, it is the formerly faded and foreign true self, the writer, who remains. Thus, what seems on first reading to be a horror story of insanity and suicide is actually not a disaster at all but an exercise in self-preservation. No sooner had Kafka become romantically involved with Felice than he had worked out subconsciously how detrimental such a relationship would be to his career as a writer. With such personal material, it is no wonder the writer in Kafka felt inspired to finish "The Judgment" in one sitting. Ironically, his conscious mind was at that point still so far behind the insights of the subconscious that he dedicated the story to none other than Felice Bauer.

The subtitle of Heinz Politzer's book on Kafka, *Parable and Paradox*, evokes the elusive nature of Kafka's story lines, which are charged with opposing forces seeking synthesis. Although most of the stories are grim, the reader cannot help but be amused at the outrageous, at times burlesque turns of events. Only the bleak and disquieting desperation of the characters contradicts the humor inherent in their situations. Also, many of the stories end with the main character dead or reduced to a state of utter hopelessness. Many of the longer stories, such as "The Judgment," are so complex that they can be confusing. Kafka's shorter stories, consisting of only a paragraph or a page or two, sometimes leave a more lasting impression, because they each center on one main event.

"Give It Up!" • Politzer begins his study with a lengthy discussion of a 124-word commentary that Kafka wrote late in 1922. In the commentary, which has become known as "Give It Up!," a traveler heading for the train station early one morning becomes disconcerted when he checks his watch against a clock tower and thinks that he must be late. In his haste, he becomes uncertain of the way and has to ask a police officer. The officer repeats the question, then tells the man to give up and turns away from him. The police officer's reply is both hilarious and profoundly unsettling. It is hilarious because it is completely out of line with what a police officer would say. It is unsettling because it lifts the story out of the mundane into a world where not only time but also, apparently, place have lost their relevance and it is impossible to determine one's way. The issue has become existential.

"Before the Law" • Kafka innately distrusted figures of authority and frequently portrayed them maliciously misleading and abusing those who came under their power. The 1922 commentary is simply a lighter variation on the theme that Kafka stated unforgettably in 1914 in his parable "Vor dem Gesetz" ("Before the Law").

This moving and perfect piece of writing was later incorporated into chapter 19 of Kafka's novel *Der Prozess* (1925; *The Trial,* 1937).

In the two-page parable, a man from the country seeks access to the law. He is told by the doorkeeper that he may not enter at the moment but possibly later. The man is deterred from entering without permission by the doorkeeper's telling him that this is only the first of many doors that are guarded by increasingly powerful doorkeepers. The man spends the rest of his life there waiting for admittance and gives away everything he owns in unsuccessful attempts to bribe the doorkeeper. Finally, in his dying hour, he asks why no one else has come to that door, only to hear the doorkeeper say: "This door was intended only for you. I am now going to shut it."

The parable is not enlightening. By the time the man finds out that he should go through the door after all, it is shut in his face. The story seems, rather, to be a comment on the human condition as Kafka experienced it in early twentieth century Europe. The rise of science and industry had displaced but could not replace religion, with the result that human beings could no longer find their way. The human institutions, the apparent absolutes represented by the law, prove to be fallible, imperfect, and unreliable. Nothing now can fill the human need for direction in life. Reality has become fragmented and disjunctive. "Before the Law" is particularly poignant because the reader cannot help but believe that, before the law, human beings are all people from the country, simple, helpless creatures who have lost their way.

"The Bucket Rider" • The way out of this impossible situation is brilliantly described with humor and sadness in Kafka's three-page story "Der Kübelreiter" ("The Bucket Rider"), written during a coal shortage in the winter of 1916. The main character has no coal, and it is bitterly cold. He also has no money but goes to the coal dealer anyway, to ask for only a shovelful. To show how desperate he is, he rides there on his empty coal bucket, sailing through the air and calling down from high above the dealer's house. The dealer is deeply moved by the voice of an old customer, but it is his wife who goes to the street to investigate. Once she finds that the bucket rider cannot pay immediately, she claims to see no one and waves him away with her apron. The bucket is too light to offer any resistance. The rider ascends "into the regions of the ice mountains" and is "lost for ever."

This story contains the delightful, dreamlike element of the fantastic that is a source of great beauty in Kafka's works. The moment the main character decides to ride on his bucket, which occurs at the beginning of the second paragraph, he is lifted out of everyday reality, in which he would surely have frozen to death. Kafka shows, once again, that it is useless to plead with others, especially those who have some authority. Rather than send his main character on an empty bucket back to his freezing room, Kafka has the bucket whisk him away into the ice mountains, never to return. Coal and indeed all mundane concerns cease to be a problem as the bucket rider leaves behind the human habitat. Thwarted by everyday pettiness, he has moved instead into a timeless mental space that seems infinitely more interesting. In "The Bucket Rider," Kafka represents that space with the image of distant ice mountains. In his fifty-second aphorism, he writes a literal description of that saving space: "There is only a spiritual world; what we call the physical world is the evil in the spiritual one, and what we call evil is only a necessary moment in our endless development." The bucket rider has transcended the evil phase.

"A Country Doctor" • The winter of 1916 was one of Kafka's most prolific periods and one in which he seemed especially visually oriented and inclined toward the fantastic. His seven-page masterpiece "Ein Landarzt" ("A Country Doctor") is one of his most involved works. It contains all Kafka's main themes and the salient features of his style.

As in "The Bucket Rider," the setting of "A Country Doctor" is an icy winter, and the mood is one of confused, melancholy desperation. The situation is hopeless, and the doctor sees no way out of it. Unlike "The Bucket Rider," which has only one main event, "A Country Doctor" is a richly textured work. The most rewarding interpretive approach is that employed here in examining "The Judgment." There are three main male characters: the country doctor, the groom, and the sick boy. They seem to represent different aspects of the same person, and the story, once again, seems to be autobiographical.

The country doctor is an older man who has been working for a long time in his profession, and he is disillusioned. The local people, while placing many demands on him, do nothing to help him. Not one of the neighbors would lend him a horse in an emergency. In keeping with the spirit of the age, the people have lost their faith in religion and look instead to science and medicine to perform the miracles, backing up the doctor's efforts with choral chanting as if he were a medicine man. He is the only one sadly aware of the limitations of his profession but plays out the charade in a resigned fashion, eventually lying outright to the boy by minimizing the severity of his fatal wound.

Kafka was a professional as well, a lawyer who in 1916 had already worked nine years after articling. Although he was a dedicated and valued member of his firm, he regarded his work as a necessary evil, as his means of earning a living so that he could write in his spare time. He was not disillusioned with law, but neither did he harbor any cherished illusions about his distinguished profession. He believed that, as it did to the man from the country in "Before the Law," law was wearing him out. Readers will equate the country doctor with Kafka the lawyer.

In order of appearance, the second male character in "A Country Doctor" is the groom. That he belongs to the country doctor or is part of him is evidenced by the servant girl's remark, "You never know what you're going to find in your own house." Certainly, the groom represents a source not tapped in a long time—so long, in fact, that the country doctor is surprised when the man emerges from the abandoned pigsty. By association with the steaming horses, by the birthlike nature of their emergence, and by his rape of Rose, the groom stands for vitality, sensuality, and sex. He is also associated with savagery and filth.

At the time of writing "A Country Doctor," Kafka had broken off his first engagement to Felice Bauer and had had several short-lived affairs. He was attracted to women but still believed that marriage and his work as a writer were mutually exclusive. His belief that marriage was not for him was based also on his perception of the sexual act as something terrible. Just as the groom represents a repressed aspect of the country doctor, who had all but ignored Rose, so, too, he represents the sexual fulfillment that Kafka decided again and again to sacrifice in order to continue his writing. Readers will equate the groom with Kafka the lover.

The groom and the two horses emerge from the pigsty together, then go off in different directions. While the groom was pursuing Rose, the unearthly horses transported the country doctor to the sick boy. Perhaps the boy was only to be reached by supernatural means. There is a fairy-tale quality to the ten-mile journey. It took only a moment, and the blinding snow was gone, replaced by clear moonlight. The nature of the journey is significant for the reader's interpretation of the boy. Kafka has placed him in the spiritual world.

Whereas the country doctor is only one of many, as stressed by the indefinite article in the title, the boy is unique. His father, family, and the villagers have no understanding of the boy's condition. Clearly, the boy is having a hard time of it in these surroundings. Even the doctor feels ill "in the narrow confines of the old man's thoughts." Disheartened, the boy at first wants to die. So does the doctor. Once the doctor becomes aware of the unique nature of the boy's great wound, however, which is both attractive and repulsive, rose-colored and worm-eaten, the boy decides that he wants to live. By then, though, it is too late. The blossom in his side is destroying him.

Like the friend in Russia in "The Judgment," the boy in "A Country Doctor" appears sickly but turns out to be of supreme importance. Kafka was not physically strong. In 1916, his tuberculosis had not yet been diagnosed, but he suffered from stomach problems. He lived with his parents, who were concerned that the long hours he spent writing were ruining his health. It is therefore fitting that those characters in his stories who represent Kafka the writer appear to be sickly. Readers will equate the boy with Kafka the writer.

Like the surface level of "The Judgment," the surface level of "A Country Doctor" reads like a tragedy of unequaled proportions. Unable to help the boy, the country doctor finds himself also unable to get home, for the trip away from the boy is as slow as the trip to him was fast. "Exposed to the frost of this most unhappy of ages," the doctor realizes that, as a result of this trip, he has not only sacrificed his servant girl but also lost his flourishing practice to his successor. What this translates into, though, is a triumph. Kafka the writer has subjugated Kafka the lawyer and Kafka the lover. The famous, peremptorily fatalistic last line of the story reveals its double meaning. "A false alarm on the night bell once answered—it cannot be made good, not ever." Once Kafka accepted his gift as a writer, he could never abandon that link with the spiritual world.

Kafka's works show, simultaneously and paradoxically, not only the existential angst inherent in the human condition but also a way out of that hopeless state. If the various characters are considered as elements of a personality seeking integration, the stories end not bleakly but on a transcendent note. Kafka's refuge was in his writing, in the spiritual world, and in laughter.

Jean M. Snook
With updates by Gerhard Brand and the Editors

Other major works

NOVELS: *Der Prozess*, 1925 (*The Trial*, 1937); *Das Schloss*, 1926 (*The Castle*, 1930); *Amerika*, 1927 (*America*, 1938; better known as *Amerika*, 1946).

MISCELLANEOUS: *Hochzeitsvorbereitungen auf dem Lande und andere Prosa aus dem Nachlass*, 1953 (*Dearest Father: Stories and Other Writings*, 1954; also known as *Wedding Preparations in the Country, and Other Posthumous Prose Writings*, 1954).

NONFICTION: *Brief an den Vater*, wr. 1919, pb. 1952 (*Letter to His Father*, 1954); *The Diaries of Franz Kafka*, 1948-1949; *Tagebücher, 1910-1923*, 1951; *Briefe an Milena*, 1952 (*Letters to Milena*, 1953); *Briefe, 1902-1924*, 1958; *Briefe an Felice*, 1967 (*Letters to Felice*, 1974); *Briefe an Ottla und die Familie*, 1974 (*Letters to Ottla and the Family*, 1982).

Bibliography

Ben-Ephraim, Gavriel. "Making and Breaking Meaning: Deconstruction, Four-Level Allegory, and *The Metamorphosis*." *The Midwest Quarterly* 35 (Summer, 1994): 450-467. Argues that Kafka's ability to combine oppositions without resolving them enables him to simultaneously build and dismantle an allegorical ladder ascending the four levels of traditional interpretation.

Bloom, Harold, ed. *Franz Kafka*. New York: Chelsea House, 1986. Collection of essays, on Kafka himself and on themes that pervade his works, by distinguished scholars. Includes essays on the short stories "Up in the Gallery," "A Country Doctor," "Der Bau" ("The Burrow"), and "Die Verwandlung" ("The Metamorphosis"). Contains an excellent index that itemizes specific aspects of the works.

Corngold, Stanley. *Franz Kafka: The Necessity of Form*. Ithaca, N.Y.: Cornell University Press, 1988. Chapter 3 (43 pages) contains what is very likely the definitive analysis of "The Metamorphosis." Also includes excellent analysis of "The Judgment," in chapters 2 and 7, discussions of form and critical method, and comparisons with other authors. Corngold also wrote a critical bibliography of "The Metamorphosis" in *The Commentator's Despair* (1973).

Flores, Angel, ed. *The Problem of "The Judgement": Eleven Approaches to Kafka's Story*. New York: Gordian Press, 1976. English translation, followed by a valuable collection of essays on the short story that Kafka considered his best. Harmut Binder reveals a surprising number of background sources in literature and legend. Kate Flores writes a convincing analysis based on the nature of human fatherhood. Walter Sokel provides an extensive interpretation. Very worthwhile.

Hayman, Ronald. *K: A Biography of Kafka*. London: Weidenfeld & Nicolson, 1981. More than a biography, this study contains many helpful discussions of the literary works, showing how they arose in response to specific situations and linking them with contemporary passages from Kafka's diary and letters. A moving portrayal particularly of Kafka's last days, when his steps toward liberation coincided tragically with the final stages of tuberculosis.

Heinemann, Richard. "Kafka's Oath of Service: 'Der Bau' and the Dialectic of Bureaucratic Mind." *PMLA* 111 (March, 1996): 256-270. Analyzes "Der Bau," as a literary representation of what Kafka called the bureaucratic mind, which reflects both the acceptance of authority as a foundation for attachment to a community and the paralysis of a restlessly critical consciousness that makes impossible any reconciliation between self and other.

Jofen, Jean. *The Jewish Mysticism of Kafka*. New York: Peter Lang, 1987. Detailed, learned examination of Kafka's connections to Jewish writers, including Y. L. Peretz, Martin Buber, Morris Rosenfeld, and other Yiddish authors. Contains notes but no bibliography.

May, Charles E., ed. *Masterplots II: Short Story Series, Revised Edition*. 8 vols. Pasadena, Calif.: Salem Press, 2004. Designed for student use, this reference set contains articles providing detailed plot summaries and analyses of ten short stories by Kafka: "The Burrow" (vol. 1); "A Country Doctor" (vol. 2); "The Great Wall of China" (vol. 3); "A Hunger Artist," "The Hunter Gracchus," "In the Penal Colony," "Jackals and Arabs," and "Josephine the Singer; Or, The Mouse Folk" (vol. 4); "The Metamorphosis" (vol. 5); and "A Report to an Academy" (vol. 6).

Oz, Amos. "A Log in a Freshet: On the Beginning of Kafka's 'A Country Doctor.'" *Partisan Review* 66 (Spring, 1999): 211-217. Argues that the story is not a story of crime and punishment, nor is it a fable about making the wrong decision. The feelings of guilt the doctor experiences are not the result of any action. Under the terms of Kafka's contract, the doctor is guilty a priori, convicted from the start, despite his innocence.

Reiner, Stach. *Kafka: The Decisive Years*. Orlando, Fla.: Harcourt, 2005. First published in Germany in 2002, this stellar work serves as the first of a projected three-volume Kafka biography. Inclues photos, thorough notes, bibliography, and several indexes.

Speirs, Ronald, and Beatrice Sandberg. *Franz Kafka*. New York: St. Martin's Press, 1997. Chapters on "a writer's life" and on the novels and short stories. Provides detailed notes and extensive bibliography.

Jamaica Kincaid

Born: Saint Johns, Antigua; May 25, 1949

Principal short fiction • *At the Bottom of the River*, 1983.

Other literary forms • In addition to her short stories, Jamaica Kincaid has written the novels *Annie John* (1985), *Lucy* (1990), *The Autobiography of My Mother* (1996), and *Mr. Potter* (2002). Her nonfiction writings include a book-length essay concerning her native island Antigua, *A Small Place* (1988) and *Among Flowers: A Walk in the Himalaya* (2005). She has also written a children's book, *Annie, Gwen, Lilly, Pam, and Tulip* (1986) and has edited several anthologies, including *The Best American Essays 1995* (1995), *My Favorite Plant: Writers and Gardeners on the Plants They Love* (1998), and *The Best American Travel Writing 2005* (2005).

Achievements • Jamaica Kincaid's short-story collection *At the Bottom of the River* received the Morton Dauwen Zabel Award from the American Academy of Arts and Letters in 1983. Her novel *Annie John* was one of three finalists for the international Ritz Paris Hemingway Award in 1985. Her short story "Xuela" was included in *The Best American Short Stories 1995*; "In Roseau" was included in *The Best American Short Stories 1996*.

Biography • Born in 1949, Jamaica Kincaid, then Elaine Potter Richardson, lived with her homemaker mother and carpenter father on Antigua, a small West Indian island measuring nine by twelve miles. The family was impoverished: Their house had no running water or electricity. The young girl's chores included drawing water from a community faucet and registering with the public works so that the "night soil men" would dispose of the family's waste. Even so, her childhood was idyllic. She was surrounded by the extraordinary beauty of the island, was accepted by her community, and was loved and protected by her mother. When Kincaid was nine, however, her mother gave birth to the first of three more children—all boys. At that point, the closeness that Kincaid had enjoyed was at first disturbed and then destroyed. She credits the lies that she began to tell her mother as the catalyst for her fiction writing: "I wasn't really lying. I was protecting my privacy or protecting a feeling I had about something. But lying is the beginning of fiction. It was the beginning of my writing life." Also at this time, she began to comprehend the insidious impact of colonialism. (Antigua was a British colony until 1967, and only in 1981 did it receive full independence.) The Antiguans' docile acceptance of their inferior status enraged her. Thus the serenity she had known as a child was displaced by loneliness and anger.

In 1966, Kincaid, seeking to disassociate herself from her mother, left Antigua not to return for nineteen years and then only after she was a naturalized citizen of the United States and an established writer. Arriving in Scarsdale, New York, the seventeen-year-old Kincaid worked as a live-in baby-sitter. She did not open her mother's letters, and when, after a few months, she took an au pair position in New York City, she did not send her mother her new address. For the next three years, she cared for the four young girls of Michael Arlen, a writer for *The New Yorker* and a future coleague when she herself would become a staff writer for the magazine. Her childhood and early New York experiences are fictionalized in *At the Bottom of the River,* *Annie John,* and *Lucy.*

During her first few years in New York, she wanted to continue her education at a university but found her Antiguan schooling to be inferior; instead, she first studied for a high school diploma, took a few photography courses at a community college, and then attended Franconia College in New Hampshire on scholarship, leaving after a year because, although only in her twenties, she felt too old. After jobs as a secretary and receptionist, she wrote for a teen magazine. In 1973, she changed her name to Jamaica Kincaid, perhaps suggesting that she had

Sigrid Estrada

achieved her own identity. Associating with New York writers and artists, she met George Trow (*Lucy* is dedicated to him), who wrote "Talk of the Town" for *The New Yorker.* She collaborated on a few columns, and eventually one of her pieces was accepted by editor William Shawn, who was known for encouraging fledgling writers. In 1978, the magazine published her first short story, "Girl." Soon after, she married Allen Shawn, the editor's son. In 1983, her first collection, *At the Bottom of the River,* was published to generally favorable reviews, as was her subsequent work, which has earned for her a devoted following. She continued to write short stories, usually published in *The New Yorker,* and give lectures and readings. She and Allen Shawn, a composer and professor at Bennington College, along with their two children—Annie, named after her mother, and Harold—settled in Bennington, Vermont. In addition to being a writer, Kincaid developed a passion for gardening, a subject on which she wrote for *The New Yorker.* She also published a collection of her gardening writings, *My Favorite Plant,* in 1998.

Analysis • Jamaica Kincaid is noted for her lyrical use of language. Her short stories and novels have a hypnotic, poetic quality that results from her utilization of rhythm and repetition. Her images, drawn from her West Indian childhood, recall Antigua, with its tropical climate, Caribbean food, local customs, and folklore laced with superstitions. Many of her stories move easily from realism to surrealistic fantasy, as would a Caribbean folktale. She is also praised for her exploration of the strong but ambiguous bond between mother and daughter and her portrayal of the transformation of a girl into a woman. Thus her work touches upon the loss of innocence that comes when one moves out of the Eden that is childhood. These are the features that are found not only in her short fiction but also in her novels, the chapters of which *The New Yorker* originally published as short stories, and in *Annie, Gwen, Lilly, Pam, and Tu-*

lip, a children's book that was part of a project designed by the Whitney Museum of American Art, the original publisher, who sought to bring together contemporary authors and artists for a series of limited editions aimed primarily at collectors.

Kincaid's concern with racism, colonialism, class divisions, and sexism is rooted in her history: "I never give up thinking about the way I came into the world, how my ancestors came from Africa to the West Indies as slaves. I just could never forget it. Or forgive it." She does not hesitate to tackle these issues in her writing. In her nonfictional *A Small Place*, she directs the force of her language toward an examination of her native island of Antigua, presenting the beauty as well as the racism and corruption rooted in its colonial past. In her fiction, these same issues are not slighted; for example, *Annie John* and *Lucy* address various forms of oppression and exploitation.

Jamaica Kincaid's short stories, strongly autobiographical, are often set in the West Indies or incorporate images from the islands and include many events from her youth and young adulthood. In general, her stories chronicle the coming of age of a young girl. Because the mother-daughter relationship is central to the process, Kincaid often examines the powerful bond between them, a bond that the child must eventually weaken, if not break, in order to create her own identity. Kincaid has been accurately called "the poet of girlhood and place."

"Girl" • The first of the ten stories in *At the Bottom of the River* is the often-praised and quoted "Girl." Barely two pages in length, the story outlines the future life of a young girl growing up on a small Caribbean island. The voice heard belongs to the girl's mother as she instructs her daughter in the duties that a woman is expected to fulfill in a culture with limited opportunities for girls. Twice the girl interrupts to offer a feeble protest, but her mother persists.

The girl is told how to wash, iron, and mend clothes; how to cook fritters and pepper pot; how to grow okra; and how to set the table—in short, everything that will enable her to care for a future husband. She is told how to smile, how to love a man, and how to get rid of an unborn baby should it be necessary. Most important, however, her mother warns her about losing her reputation because then the girl (and this is unsaid) loses her value as a potential wife. Almost as a refrain, the mother cautions "On Sundays try to walk like a lady and not like the slut you are so bent on becoming" or "This is how to behave in the presence of men who don't know you very well, and this way they won't recognize immediately the slut I have warned you against becoming." On the island, the girl's most important asset is her virginity.

The language is a prime example of Kincaid's ability to work a hypnotic spell. The story consists of a series of variations on particular instruction: "This is how to sew on a button; this is how to make a buttonhole for the button you have just sewed on; this is how to hem a dress when you see the hem coming down and so to prevent yourself from looking like the slut I know you are so bent on becoming." The rhythm and repetition create a lyric poetic quality that is present to some degree in all Kincaid's fiction. Her prose demands to be read out loud.

"Girl" suggests the child's future life on the island, but several stories in the collection re-create the atmosphere of her present existence. The story "In the Night" recounts her daily experiences. Thus, details such as crickets or flowers that would be important to her are recorded, often in the form of lists or catalogs: "The hibiscus flowers, the flamboyant flowers, the bachelor's buttons, the irises, the marigolds, the whiteheadbush flowers, lilies, the flowers on the daggerbush," continuing for a full paragraph. Here cataloging, a familiar feature of Kincaid's prose, represents a child's attempt to impose an order on her surroundings. The young narrator does not question her world but only reports what she observes. Thus witchcraft exists side by side with more mundane activities: "Someone is making a basket, someone is making a girl a dress or a boy a shirt . . . someone is sprinkling a colorless powder outside a closed door so that someone else's child will be stillborn." This melding of the commonplace with the supernatural occurs frequently in Kincaid's fiction. The narrator's troubles, such as wetting the bed, are those of a child and are easily resolved by her mother. Her plans for the future, marrying a woman who will tell her stories, also are typical of a child. This is an idyllic world before the fall from innocence, a world in which everything is ordered, listed, and cataloged. Nothing is threatening, since the all-powerful mother protects and shields.

"Holidays" • In several other stories, including "Wingless" and "Holidays," the girl is again shown to be occupied by the usually pleasant sensations of living: walking barefoot, scratching her scalp, or stretching, but sometimes, as illustrated in "Holidays," experiencing pain: "spraining a finger while trying to catch a cricket ball; straining a finger while trying to catch a softball; stepping on dry brambles while walking on the newly cut hayfields." The trauma, however, is clearly limited to physical sensations. When the child thinks of the future, the images are those of wishful thinking, similar to daydreams. This tranquil state of youth, however, is only temporary, as "Wingless" implies. The narrator, wingless, is still in the "pupa stage."

"The Letter from Home" • In "The Letter from Home," the narrator's growing awareness makes it impossible for her to maintain the comforting simplicity of her child's world. Questions about life and death intrude: "Is the Heaven to be above? Is the Hell below?" These inquiries, however, are set aside in favor of the present physical reality—a cat scratching a chair or a car breaking down. Even love and conception are reduced to the simplest terms: "There was a bed, it held sleep; there was movement, it was quick, there was a being." She is not ready to confront the idea of death, so when death beckons, she "turned and rowed away."

"What I Have Been Doing Lately" • Just as the philosophical questions about life and death disrupt the bliss of childhood, so does the journey toward selfhood, which Kincaid symbolically represents as a journey over rough or impassable terrain or water. In "What I Have Been Doing Lately," the obstacle is water: "I walked for I don't know how long before I came to a big body of water. I wanted to get across it but I couldn't swim. I wanted to get across it but it would take me years to build a boat. . . . I didn't know how long to build a bridge." Because the journey is difficult, as any passage to adulthood would be, the narrator is hesitant, afraid of finding the world not beautiful, afraid of missing her parents, so she goes back to bed: She is not ready yet. Soon, however, she will not have the option of retreating and waiting.

"My Mother" • The journey toward selfhood necessitates a separation from the mother, as is suggested in the story "My Mother." The protection that was vital during childhood becomes stifling in adolescence: "Placing her arms around me, she drew my head closer and closer to her bosom, until finally I suffocated." Furthermore, the girl's feelings are ambiguous. Realizing that she has hurt her mother, she cries, but then she utilizes those tears to create a pond, "thick and black and poisonous," to form a barrier over which they "watched each other carefully." The all-protecting mother of the earlier stories transforms herself into a mythic monster and thus threatens the emerging selfhood of the daughter. The daughter, however, also grows "invincible" like her mother, and she, too, metamorphoses into a similar beast. Strong as the daughter has become, however, she can never vanquish her mother: "I had grown big, but my mother was bigger, and that would always be so." Only after the daughter completes her own journey toward selfhood is her mother no longer a threat: "As we walked along, our steps became one, and as we talked, our voices became one voice, and we were in complete union in every way. What peace came over me then, for I could not see where she left off and I began, or where I left off and she began."

"At the Bottom of the River" • The concluding and title story is also the longest in the collection, at about twenty pages. "At the Bottom of the River" suggests answers to the questions raised in the other stories. Again, Kincaid employs the symbol of a journey through forbidding terrain to suggest traveling through life. What is the purpose of the journey, for what does one ultimately face but death? One man, overwhelmed, does nothing. Another discovers meaning in his family, his work, and the beauty of a sunrise, but still he struggles and "feels the futility." How can one live with the paralyzing knowledge that "dead lay everything that had lived and dead also lay everything that would live. All had had or would have its season. And what should it matter that its season lasted five billion years or five minutes?" One possible response is suggested in the life of "a small creature" that lives in the moment, aware only of the sensation of grass underfoot or of the sting of a honeybee.

The narrator, who at first knew only the love of her mother, suffers from its necessary withdrawal. Adrift, she embarks on a symbolic journey in which she submerges herself in a river-fed sea. Discovering a solution at the bottom of the river, she emerges with a commitment to the present. Death, because it is natural, cannot be destroyed, but the joys derived from the commonplace—books, chairs, fruit—can provide meaning, and she "grow[s] solid and complete."

"Xuela" • Kincaid's story "Xuela" became the first chapter of her novel *The Autobiography of My Mother* (1996). Like many of her other stories, it is set against a rich description of the botany and geography of tropical Dominica, and it continues Kincaid's meditation on the theme of mothers and daughters. Xuela, the daughter who shares her mother's name, also shares with many Kincaid women an anger at the mother who has rejected her and a fury at the world which little understands—and little cares—about her needs.

In the story's first sentence, the reader learns that Xuela's mother died in giving her birth, and the rest of the story is the record of the first seven years of Xuela's life. Her father places the infant in the care of Eunice, his laundrywoman and visits her every two weeks when he delivers the dirty clothes he cares for as little as he cares for his baby daughter either physically or emotionally, oblivious as he is to his laundrywoman's lack of affection for her foster child.

The child, however, knows very well that her foster mother has no use for her, and she grows ever more bitter and withdrawn. When she breaks Eunice's treasured china plate, she cannot bring herself to utter the words "I'm sorry." Like the turtles she captures and carelessly kills, Xuela has withdrawn into a shell which threatens to destroy her with enforced isolation.

At that point her father sends Xuela to school. The few other students are all boys;

like their teacher they are "of the African people" and unable to respond to the powerful element of Carib Indian in Xuela's ancestry. The teacher wears her own African heritage like a penance and is quick to label Xuela's intelligence as a sign of her innate evil. When the child is found writing letters to her father, he removes her from the school and takes her to live with him and his new wife, another woman who has no love for the child. Like her insensitive teacher, her father's power as a jailer seems to suggest the destructive powers of colonialism, another Kincaid theme.

Through all these trials, the child is sustained by a vision of her mother, who appears to her in sleep. In the dream, she sees her true mother descending a ladder to her, but always the dream fades before she can see more than her mother's heels and the hem of her robe. Frustrating as it is, the dream also comes to represent the presence of the only person outside herself that Xuela can identify with unreserved love.

The story's themes of the mother who, from the child's point of view, has willfully withdrawn her love joins with the theme of the child's wakening to the use of sexuality to replace her lost mother's love, linking this story to the rest of Kincaid's work.

Kincaid's stories are praised for their strong images, poetic language, and challenging themes, and they are criticized for their lack of plot and sometimes obscure symbolism. Any reader, however, who, without reservations, enters Kincaid's fictive world will be well rewarded.

Barbara Wiedemann
With updates by Ann D. Garbett and the Editors

Other major works

CHILDREN'S LITERATURE: *Annie, Gwen, Lilly, Pam, and Tulip*, 1986 (with illustrations by Eric Fischl).

ANTHOLOGIES: *The Best American Essays 1995*, 1995; *My Favorite Plant: Writers and Gardeners on the Plants They Love*, 1998; *The Best American Travel Writing 2005*, 2005.

NOVELS: *Annie John*, 1985; *Lucy*, 1990; *The Autobiography of My Mother*, 1996; *Mr. Potter*, 2002.

NONFICTION: *A Small Place*, 1988; *My Brother*, 1997; *My Garden (Book)*, 1999; *Talk Stories*, 2001; *Among Flowers: A Walk in the Himalaya*, 2005.

Bibliography

Bloom, Harold, ed. *Jamaica Kincaid*. Philadelphia: Chelsea House, 1998. Collection of individually authored chapters on Kincaid, this critical study includes bibliographical references and an index.

Bouson, J. Brooks. *Jamaica Kincaid: Writing Memory, Writing Back to the Mother*. Albany: State University of New York Press, 2005. Examination of Kincaid's life, including her relationship with her mother, her homeland of Antigua, and her conflicting relations with her father and brother.

De Abruna, Laura Nielsen. "Jamaica Kincaid's Writing and the Maternal-Colonial Matrix." In *Caribbean Women Writers*, edited by Mary Condé and Thorunn Lonsdale. New York: St. Martin's Press, 1999. Discusses Kincaid's presentation of women's experience, her use of postmodern narrative strategies, and her focus on the absence of the once-affirming mother or mother country that causes dislocation and alienation.

Ellsberg, Peggy. "Rage Laced with Lyricism." Review of *A Small Place*. *Commonweal* 115

(November 4, 1988): 602-604. In her review of *A Small Place,* with references to *At the Bottom of the River* and *Annie John,* Ellsberg justifies the anger that is present in *A Small Place,* anger that is occasioned by exploitation.

Emery, Mary Lou. "Refiguring the Postcolonial Imagination: Tropes of Visuality in Writing by Rhys, Kincaid, and Cliff." *Tulsa Studies in Women's Literature* 16 (Fall, 1997): 259-280. Emery uses one of Jean Rhys's novels to illustrate a dialectical relationship between the European means of visualization and image-making in postcolonial literatures as something not just of the eye. Argues that the use of the rhetorical trope of ekphrasis (an artistic hybrid) reflects the cultural hybrid nature of postcolonial literature.

Ferguson, Moira. *Jamaica Kincaid: Where the Land Meets the Body.* Charlottesville: University Press of Virginia, 1994. Includes bibliographical references and an index.

_____. "A Lot of Memory: An Interview with Jamaica Kincaid." *The Kenyon Review,* n.s. 16 (Winter, 1994): 163-188. Kincaid discusses the inspiration for her writing and the reasons she wrote her first book in an experimental style; describes the influence of the English tradition on fiction in the Caribbean; comments on the nature of colonial conquest as a theme she explores through the metaphor of gardening.

MacDonald-Smythe, Antonia. *Making Homes in the West Indies: Constructions of Subjectivity in the Writings of Michelle Cliff and Jamaica Kincaid.* New York: Garland, 2001. Focuses on these two Caribbean women writers.

May, Charles E., ed. *Masterplots II: Short Story Series, Revised Edition.* 8 vols. Pasadena, Calif.: Salem Press, 2004. Designed for student use, this reference set contains articles providing detailed plot summaries and analyses of three short stories by Kincaid: "At the Bottom of the River" (vol. 1), "Girl" (vol. 3), and "My Mother" (vol. 5).

Paravisini-Gebert, Lizabeth. *Jamaica Kincaid: A Critical Companion.* Westport, Conn.: Greenwood Press, 1999. Two biographical chapters are followed by penetrating analyses of *At the Bottom of the River, Annie John, Lucy,* and *The Autobiography of My Mother.*

Simmons, Diane. *Jamaica Kincaid.* New York: Twayne, 1994. Lucid critical overview of Kincaid's life and work. A good introduction to her work for nonspecialist readers.

Barbara Kingsolver

Born: Annapolis, Maryland; April 8, 1955

Principal short fiction • *Homeland, and Other Stories*, 1989.

Other literary forms • Barbara Kingsolver is known primarily for her long fiction, which includes *The Bean Trees* (1988), *Animal Dreams* (1990), *Pigs in Heaven* (1993), *The Poisonwood Bible* (1998), and *Prodigal Summer* (2000). She has also written travel articles, book reviews, essays, and poetry. Her nonfiction work *Holding the Line: Women in the Great Arizona Mine Strike of 1983* (1989) compellingly presents the plight of miners in southern Arizona's copper mining company towns. Her other nonfiction books include *High Tide in Tucson: Essays from Now or Never* (1995), *Last Stand: America's Virgin Lands* (2002), and *Small Wonder* (2002).

Kingsolver's only published volume of poetry is *Another America* (1992, 1998). The form in which verses are presented in that collection invites awareness of diverse perspectives, with Kingsolver's poetry and its Spanish translations printed on facing pages. A selection of her essays in *High Tide in Tucson: Essays from Now or Never* (1995) offers thoughts on parenting, home ownership, cultural habits, travel, and writing. Her observations on the natural order of things, from child rearing to exploring a volcanic crater in Hawaii, range from self-deprecatingly humorous to awe-inspired. All celebrate one's connection to and citizenship of the world.

Achievements • Kingsolver has received many awards for her writing. In 1986 the Arizona Press Club gave her its feature-writing award. She received American Library Association awards in 1989 for *The Bean Trees* and in 1990 for *Homeland*. The Edward Abbey Ecofiction Award (1990) for *Animal Dreams* and the prestigious PEN Western Fiction Award (1991) added to her reputation. In 1993 and 1994 she received the Los Angeles Book Award and Mountain and Plains Booksellers Association Award for *Pigs in Heaven*. She also received an Enoch Pratt Library Youth Book Award for *The Bean Trees*. Her other awards include the Enoch Pratt Library Lifetime Achievement Medal in 2005; the 2002 International IMPAC Dublin Literary Award for *Prodigal Summer*, an award for the Best American Science and Nature Writing in 2001; a National Humanities Medal in 2000; the 1999 Patterson Fiction Prize; a *New York Times* Ten Best Books selection for *The Poisonwood Bible* in 1998; a citation of accomplishment from the United Nations National Council of Women in 1989. In 1995, De Pauw University conferred an honorary doctorate on her. She spent two semesters as a visiting writer at Emory and Henry College. True to her activist principles, she is the founder of the Bellwether Prize, given in support of literature of social change.

Biography • Born in Annapolis, Maryland, on April 8, 1955, Barbara Kingsolver spent most of her childhood in eastern Kentucky's rural Nicholas County and began writing before beginning high school. She studied biology at DePauw University in Indiana and graduated magna cum laude in 1977. While working for a master's degree in science at the University of Arizona, she took a creative writing class. Between her stints as a student, she lived for a time in Greece and France. After completing her master's degree, she did science writing for the University of Arizona and began to write feature articles, which appeared in such national publications as *Smithsonian Harper's*, and *The New York Times*. After marrying Joseph Hoffman in 1985, she wrote *The Bean Trees* during insomniac interludes she experienced while pregnant with her daughter Camille. She later divorced Hoffman and married Steven Hopp, with whom she settled in Tucson, Arizona. Kingsolver has been a political activist all of her adult life.

Analysis • Barbara Kingsolver's short stories are notable for their clear-eyed, sometimes ironic, and always empathic look at the daily lives of ordinary people. Her narrators are mostly female or compassionate omniscient voices telling stories of homecomings, intergenerational misunderstandings, and mundane events such as scheduling errands or getting to know one's neighbors. She pays close attention to the tensions that control events like Thanksgiving dinners and accurately captures the dynamics of husband and wife and of mother and daughter. In her stories, characters struggle to understand who they are in the context of family history and their present circumstances. The epiphanies of Kingsolver's women are small but searingly personal. They range from deciding not to have a child to a sudden understanding of a mother's point of view. In a News Hour online interview with David Gergen, editor-at-large for *U.S. News and World Report*, Kingsolver explained her fascination with the quotidian episodes in families' and couples' lives:

> We need new stories. We need stories that can help us construct, reconstruct the value of . . . solidarity, of not . . . the lone solo flier, but the family, the community, the value of working together.

Kingsolver's short fiction is not minimalist. She belongs to generations of storytellers who create settings rich in sensual and situational detail. Her characters are clearly situated and her stories have a satisfying beginning, middle, and end as do the stories of nineteenth century writers such as Sarah Orne Jewett and Mary E. Wilkins Freeman. She is also distinctly contemporary because her characters reach an episode's end when they achieve some insight or understanding of their condition. They do not, however, find sentimental or easy answers. Each story concludes with characters more able to cope with the literal and emotional landscapes of their lives.

Like poet and essayist Adrienne Rich, Kingsolver embraces the political. She believes art should reflect the world she sees daily, so she writes, for example, about the plight of mine workers in the American Southwest and the displacement of American Indians. College professors, aging hippies, and small-town eccentrics all wrestle with bigotry and stereotyping as they move through their lives. Kingsolver's characters avoid the cynicism of many contemporary fictional voices, seeking instead a synthesis that will see them through or the moral vision that will allow them to rise above prejudices they cannot control. She combines the narrative structure of nineteenth century realists with the frank look at life espoused by John Steinbeck, one of her inspirations. Kingsolver's characters offer an alternative to ironic, angry characters. They struggle with the inequities of American life without losing their ability to maintain human connection. Kingsolver creates characters who confront life without relinquishing hope. Her vision is distinctive and welcome.

Homeland, and Other Stories • Barbara Kingsolver's collection is divided between stories in which the difficulties of small-town life are controlled by the fears and sensibilities of people wedded to the status quo and those in which the clash between alternative lifestyles and the ordinary routines of existence is prominent. With one exception, the narrators are women or feature omniscient narrators, whose voices elucidate women's lives and points of view. The stories frequently have a postmodern view of time, jumping nonchronologically from one episode or memory to the next, the changes marked by spaces in the text as well as by narrated events. Kingsolver interestingly blurs the line between character and narrator by interspersing narrative passages with snippets of dialogue. Often the narrator's contributions could just as easily be spoken by the main character; this shared quality underlines the universal relevance of private stories. Kingsolver's sto-

ries, built around family routines, usually emphasize a thoughtful female character grappling with a problem. These range from spending quality time with a child ("Quality Time"), facing the need to break off a love affair ("Stone Dreams"), coping with suffering the failure of a long-standing relationship ("Blueprints"), and fighting economic and social injustice ("Why I Am a Danger to the Public") to deciding whether or not to have a child ("Covered Bridges").

Another theme is how one comes to terms with one's past. "Survival Zone" and "Extinctions" have dual tensions: The eternal city/country dilemma surfaces differently in each story, and each considers the opportunities for a life in the larger world as opposed to a well-known existence. "Rose-Johnny" tackles the divisive and mean-spirited effects of racial prejudice in a small southern town. A young girl, curious and kindhearted, tells the story, which highlights the socially sanctioned cruelty of adults. Kingsolver's characters realize the beginnings of personal solutions or they relate histories that reveal insights won after the scrutiny of their pasts. Either way, readers know life always goes on in its complicated and demanding way. Survival is mandatory; understanding possible.

"Homeland" • The title story of Kingsolver's collection *Homeland, and Other Stories* retrospectively tells the tale of an aging Cherokee grandmother's last days. Gloria St. Clair, Great Mam's granddaughter, a grown woman with her own grown children, narrates a family history that begins with the Cherokee Trail of Tears. Great Mam's band had eluded relocation by hiding and was finally allowed to settle where they chose. Still, they called the refugee years "The Time When We Were Not." Gloria's reference initiates the reader into history as a personal experience. A reminiscence of the family's trip back to Great Mam's birthplace, the Hiwassee Valley in Tennessee, follows. Gloria's father, a coal miner just back to work after a season of wildcat strikes, decides this trip is necessary for his mother, who is in her waning days; he plans it despite his wife's skepticism.

Great Mam and Gloria's special relationship evolves along with the story. During lazy afternoons or quiet evenings in the dark, Great Mam tells Gloria stories of the animals "as if they were relatives [her] parents had neglected to tell [her] about." The trip, with the three children bumping along in the back of a pickup truck, as well as the fact that they slept three to a bed, reveals the family's economic situation. Gloria's mother represents a third dynamic, the social status quo; she is thankful God spared her children a "Cherokee nose." Mrs. Murray rises above the common-law, racially mixed marriage of her husband's parents. Gloria balances between her mother and her love for the soft-spoken woman, who tells her how the world began and calls her Waterbug. She fatalistically laments her lack of attention to stories she now knows were rare treasures. The trip fails, the home of a once-proud people houses a troop of sideshow Indians in Cherokee Park. Great Mam does not get out of the truck but remarks to Gloria, "I've never been here before." Great Mam's death is unremarkable, personal, and poignant for Gloria and a troublesome irritation for her mother—the three of them a perfect metaphor for the pain of America's position on "the Indian question."

"Islands on the Moon" • Annemarie and her mother Magda are intimate antagonists because Annemarie thinks her mother "doesn't seem mid-forties, she seems like Grandma Moses in moonstone earrings." Annemarie has been alienated from her mother, an aging hippie with wild hair, since her father's death, and her aggravation only increases when Magda turns up pregnant at the same time that she does. As it turns out, Annemarie is not presently married and is contemplating remarrying her first husband. Her own son, Kevin, is moving steadily beyond her reach. Magda breaks her practice of keeping her distance because she wants Annemarie to accompany her when she has amniocentesis, a test to which she would not have agreed had her doctor not threatened to drop her as a patient if she refused. On the way to the clinic, the two have an automobile accident and are rushed to the hospital. The shock of the accident and their time side by side in the hospital free a torrent of resentments from Annemarie. Her persistence prompts Magda to say, "I never knew what you expected from me, Annemarie. I never could be the mother you wanted." When Annemarie makes the ultimate accusation, that Magda does not miss her husband, Magda recounts her husband's obsessive attempts to try to think of all the things she would need to remember to do after he was gone. Stunned, Annemarie understands her error. "How could I not ever have known that, that it wrecked your life, too?" she asks her mother. At the story's end, Annemarie reaches over to touch her unborn sister, establishing a tenuous bond which now has a chance to flourish.

Karen L. Arnold
With updates by the Editors

Other major works

ANTHOLOGY: *The Best American Short Stories, 2001,* 2001.

NOVELS: *The Bean Trees,* 1988; *Animal Dreams,* 1990; *Pigs in Heaven,* 1993; *The Poisonwood Bible,* 1998; *Prodigal Summer,* 2000.

NONFICTION: *Holding the Line: Women in the Great Arizona Mine Strike of 1983,* 1989;

High Tide in Tucson: Essays from Now or Never, 1995; *Last Stand: America's Virgin Lands,* 2002 (photographs by Annie Griffiths Belt); *Small Wonder,* 2002.
POETRY: *Another America/Otra America,* 1992.

Bibliography

DeMarr, Mary Jean. *Barbara Kingsolver: A Critical Companion.* Westport, Conn.: Greenwood Press, 1999. Good overview of Kingsolver's work, emphasizing her ecofeminism.

Draper, James P. "Barbara Kingsolver." In *Contemporary Literary Criticism: Yearbook 1993.* Vol. 81. Detroit: Gale Research, 1994. Collection of critical views of Kingsolver's work.

Epstein, Robin. "Barbara Kingsolver." *Progressive* 60 (February, 1996): 33-38. An informative interview with Kingsolver; Kingsolver believes that most readers do not think that her writing is overly political; she feels that she has a responsibility to discuss her beliefs with the public.

Fleischner, Jennifer, ed. *A Reader's Guide to the Fiction of Barbara Kingsolver: "The Bean Trees," "Homeland, and Other Stories," "Animal Dreams," "Pigs in Heaven."* New York: Harper Perennial, 1994. Good resource for the student new to Kingsolver's work.

Gaard, Greta. "Living Connections with Animals and Nature." In *Eco-Feminism: Women, Animals, Nature,* edited by Greta Gaard. Philadelphia: Temple University Press, 1993. Discusses the implications of a personal/political commitment to the natural world.

Kingsolver, Barbara. Interview by Lisa See. *Publishers Weekly* 237 (August 31, 1990): 46. Kingsolver discusses her early literary influences and her research and writing methods.

May, Charles E., ed. *Masterplots II: Short Story Series, Revised Edition.* 8 vols. Pasadena, Calif.: Salem Press, 2004. Designed for student use, this reference set contains articles providing detailed plot summaries and analyses of three short stories by Kingsolver: "Homeland" (vol. 3), "Islands on the Moon" (vol. 4), and "Rose-Johnny" (vol. 6).

Pence, Amy. "Barbara Kingsolver." *Poets and Writers* 21, no. 4 (July/August, 1993): 14-21. Pence looks at Kingsolver's writing and her commitments to political activism and family.

Ross, Jean W. "CA Interview." In *Contemporary Authors.* Vol. 134, edited by Susan M. Trotsky. Detroit: Gale Research, 1992. Brief biographical and professional information sections are followed by an interview covering Kingsolver's writing methods, the sources of some of her characters, the importance of her background, and some of her nonfiction writing.

Ryan, Maureen. "Barbara Kingsolver's Lowfat Fiction." *Journal of American Culture* 18, no. 4 (Winter, 1995): 77-123. Ryan compares Kingsolver's first three novels with her first short-story collection.

Rudyard Kipling

Born: Bombay, India; December 30, 1865
Died: Hampstead, London, England; January 18, 1936

Principal short fiction • *Quartette*, 1885 (with John Lockwood Kipling, Alice Macdonald Kipling, and Alice Kipling); *In Black and White*, 1888; *Plain Tales from the Hills*, 1888; *Soldiers Three: A Collection of Stories*, 1888; *The Phantom 'Rickshaw, and Other Tales*, 1888; *The Story of the Gadsbys*, 1888; *Under the Deodars*, 1888; *Wee Willie Winkie, and Other Child Stories*, 1888; *The City of Dreadful Night, and Other Places*, 1890; *The Courting of Dinah Shadd, and Other Stories*, 1890; *Life's Handicap*, 1891; *Mine Own People*, 1891; *Many Inventions*, 1893; *The Jungle Book*, 1894; *The Second Jungle Book*, 1895; *Soldier Tales*, 1896; *The Day's Work*, 1898; *Stalky and Co.*, 1899; *Just So Stories*, 1902; *Traffics and Discoveries*, 1904; *Puck of Pook's Hill*, 1906; *Actions and Reactions*, 1909; *Rewards and Fairies*, 1910; *A Diversity of Creatures*, 1917; *Land and Sea Tales for Scouts and Guides*, 1923; *Debits and Credits*, 1926; *Thy Servant a Dog*, 1930; *Limits and Renewals*, 1932; *Collected Dog Stories*, 1934.

Other literary forms • Rudyard Kipling's literary career began in journalism, but his prose sketches and verse brought him early fame. He wrote several novels, most lastingly *Kim* (1901), and he also wrote works of history, including a study of his son's military regiment from World War I. In his lifetime as well as posthumously, however, his fame depended upon his poetry and short stories, both of which he wrote for adult audiences and for children. Kipling's autobiography, *Something of Myself: For My Friends Known and Unknown* (1937), was published after his death.

Achievements • By his early twenties, Rudyard Kipling had become one of the best-known writers in the English language. His first poems and stories were written and published in India, but his popularity quickly spread throughout the English-speaking world and beyond. Although he published several novels, the short-story form proved to be his most successful métier. Drawing upon his experiences in India, many of his early stories featured the adventures of ordinary soldiers, junior officers, and civil officials, and his use of dialect was a recognized feature of his literary technique. Awarded the Nobel Prize in Literature in 1907, he also received honorary degrees from many universities.

Kipling wrote extensively about the benefits of the United Kingdom's paramount position in the world, and over time his public persona was perceived to be that of a political reactionary. Although some of his finest short stories were written in the last two decades of his life, by that time, to many of his contemporaries, he had become yesterday's man, irrevocably associated with political imperialism, a dying creed even before his death in 1936. After his death, however, his stories received much critical study and acclaim, and Kipling is considered to be one of the major practitioners of the short-story art ever to write in English.

Biography • Joseph Rudyard Kipling was born in Bombay, India, in 1865. His father, John Lockwood Kipling, was an artist and teacher. His mother, Alice Macdonald

Kipling, was from a family of exceptional sisters. One married the Pre-Raphaelite painter, Sir Edward Coley Burne-Jones, and another was the mother of Stanley Baldwin, the British prime minister in the years between the two world wars.

As was customary at the time, Rudyard and his younger sister remained in England when their parents returned to India, and Kipling dramatized his misery at being left behind in his later writings. He attended a second-rank private school that prepared middle-class boys for careers in the military; small, not athletic, and forced to wear glasses, Kipling was not an outstanding or popular student, but his literary interests proved a defense and a consolation. The university was not an option for him, primarily for financial reasons, and he returned to India, where his parents had found a position for him on an English-language newspaper.

Kipling was fascinated by India. Often unable to sleep, he spent his nights wandering the streets. He had written some poetry as a schoolboy and continued to do so, while also composing newspaper sketches featuring his Anglo-Indian environment. By the end of the 1880's, he had already published several volumes of short stories and poems. No British writer since Charles Dickens had become so well known, and Kipling was only in his mid-twenties. His works were often satiric, and some readers believed that he cast aspersions upon the British army and imperial authorities in India, but the opposite was closer to Kipling's own feelings. He doubted that the English at home understood the sacrifices that the average soldier, the young officer, and the district commissioners were making to preserve Great Britain's prosperity and security.

Kipling left India in 1889 and established himself in London, where he became acquainted with the major literary figures of the day, including Thomas Hardy and Henry James. In 1890, he published his first novel, *The Light That Failed*. With the American Wolcott Balestier, Kipling, in spite of his previous unwillingness to attach himself to any literary partnership, wrote a second novel, *The Naulahka: A Story of East and West* (1892). Kipling's relationship with Balestier was very close, and, after the latter's death, he married Balestier's sister, Caroline (Carrie), in 1892. Kipling subsequently settled in Vermont, near his wife's family. Although residing there for four years before returning to England, Kipling never admired the United States and had difficulty with Carrie's family.

Kipling's fame reached its pinnacle in the years before the South African (Boer) War broke out in 1899. His portrayal of the Empire struck a chord in the British psyche during the 1890's; a changing political climate, however, began to make Kipling's public posture as an imperialist less acceptable. Still, he continued to write, both for children and for adults. In 1902, he purchased Bateman's, a country house in Sussex, which remained his home for the rest of his life.

Long a frustrated man of action and a Francophile from his schoolboy years, he vehemently opposed Germany during World War I. His only son was killed in action in 1915. Kipling's health had begun to decline, his marriage was less than fulfilling, and although he received much formal praise, his later stories were not widely read. He died in 1936 and was buried in Westminster Abbey, more a recognition for his earlier than his later career. Only after his death was it possible to separate the public man—imperialist and antiliberal—from the literary artist whose best stories have continued to survive.

Analysis • Many of Rudyard Kipling's earliest short stories are set in the India of his early childhood years in Bombay and his newspaper days in Lahore. The intervening years at school in England had perhaps increased his sensitivity to the exotic Indian locale and British imperial presence. Kipling was a voracious reader of English, French, and American writers, trained by his newspaper experience in the virtues of conciseness and detail. His art arrived almost fully revealed in his earliest works. Kipling focused, however, not on the glories and conquests of empire but on the lives—work and activities, passions and emotions—of ordinary people responding to what were often extraordinary or inexplicable events. Love, especially doomed love, terror and the macabre, revenge and its consequences—these were the elements upon which his stories turned, even later when the settings were often English. His fame or notoriety was almost instantaneous, in part because of the locations and subject matter of the stories, because of his use of dialect in re-creating the voices of his nonestablishment characters, and because Kipling's early writings appeared at a time when England and Western civilization as a whole were caught up in imperial dreams and rivalries.

A number of his stories pivot around the relations between men and women. Kipling has been called a misogynist, and often his characters, particularly those in the military, blame women for their own and others' misfortunes. Most of his stories employ a male voice, and many critics agree that Kipling's women are not often fully realized, particularly in his early years. The isolation of British soldiers and officials in India could itself explain these portrayals. There were boundaries in that esoteric environment—sexual, social, racial—that were violated only at a cost, but in Kipling's stories they are crossed because his characters choose to do so or cannot help themselves.

"Beyond the Pale" • In "Beyond the Pale," Christopher Trejago seduces and is seduced by a fifteen-year-old Hindu widow, Bisea, before misunderstanding and jealousy cause the lovers to terminate the relationship. Later, Trejago returns to their place of rendezvous only to discover that Bisea's hands have been cut off at the wrists; at the instant of his discovery, he is attacked by a sharp object that injures his groin. One of Kipling's shortest stories, it exhibits several of his continuing concerns. Love, passion, even understanding are often doomed, whether between man and woman or between British and Indians, while horror and unexpected shock can occur at any time and have lasting effects; revenge is a human quality. Stylistically, the story is rich in the descriptive detail of the dead-end alley where Bisea and Trejago first met but is enigmatic in explaining how the affair became known, leading to Bisea's maiming. The story does not end with the assault on Trejago. As often with Kipling, there is a coda. Trejago is forced to carry on, with a slight limp and the remembrance of horror leading to sleepless nights.

"Love-o'-Women" • Dangerous boundaries and illicit relationships also feature in his "Love-o'-Women," the story of Larry Tighe, a gentleman who had enlisted as a common soldier, a gentleman-ranker who stepped down out of his proper world. Kipling often used the technique of a story-within-a-story, told by a narrator who may or may not be telling the total truth but whose own personality and perception are as important as the plot itself, accomplished most notably in "Mrs. Bathurst." Here, in "Love-o'-Women," the tale opens with Sergeant Raines shooting one of his own men, Corporal Mackie, who had seduced Mrs. Raines. After Raines's trial, several soldiers ruminate on the dead Mackie's fate. One of them, Terrence Mulvaney, comments that Mackie is the lucky one: He died quickly. He then tells the story of Tighe, whoc laimed the nickname of Love-o'-Women and made a career in the military of seducing daughters and wives, governesses and maids. When Tighe attempts to commit suicide by exposing his body to enemy fire during a battle, Mulvaney saves him and learns that Tighe deeply regrets what he has done, including his treatment and loss of his only real love, a woman named Egypt who turned to prostitution. Dying of syphilis, Tighe collapses in Egypt's arms; she then shoots herself. Kipling did not necessarily believe in justice in the world, and, although reared a Christian, he was not orthodox in his religious beliefs but believed that there was a mortality for which one must answer. In "Love-o'-Women," sin required confession, contrition, and penance.

Library of Congress

"The Phantom 'Rickshaw" • Ghosts or phantoms also often played a role in Kipling's stories. In "The Phantom 'Rickshaw," Jack Pansay, an English official in India, begins a shipboard flirtation with a married woman, Mrs. Keith-Wessington, while returning from England. The affair continues in India, but Pansay grows tired of her, becoming engaged to someone else. Mrs. Wessington refuses to accept the termination of the romance and subsequently dies after losing control of her rickshaw while attempting to renew the affair. Soon, as a ghostly presence, she and her rickshaw begin to appear to Pansay, and feeling that his rejection had killed her, he himself sinks into decline. Although his doctor believes that his illness is merely the result of overwork, Pansay believes otherwise: His death is the payment required for his treatment of Mrs. Wessington.

"The Wish House" • From the beginning of his literary career, Kipling was considered to be a master in the use of dialect. Mulvaney's telling of Tighe's tale was rendered in an Irish dialect. In Kipling's Indian stories, Mulvaney's Irish was joined by characters speaking London Cockney, Yorkshire in northern England, and others. In many of his later stories, Kipling incorporated various English dialects, such as the Sussex dialect spoken by Grace Ashcroft and Liz Fettley in "The Wish House." He generally used dialect when portraying the speech of persons from the undereducated classes or foreigners—persons different from his middle-class readers—and his treatment is often successful, even though some critics have claimed that his dialect re-creations were not entirely accurate. It has also been argued that, at times, the use of dialect gets in the way of the reading and understanding of the story itself, although this is more true of his early stories than his later ones.

In "The Wish House," Grace Ashcroft goes to an abandoned house, inhabited by wraiths, where it was possible to take on the pain of some loved one; for her, it was her former lover. Like the blind woman in "They," however, she is driven by a love that is ultimately a selfish one: She is willing to accept his pain as hers not only because she loved him but also because she hopes that he will never marry and find happiness with anyone else.

"The Brushwood Boy" • On occasion, Kipling attempted to create the speaking style of the middle or upper classes. Here the use of words and phrases can be disconcerting to the reader, particularly after the diction and slang of an era has become dated. In "The Brushwood Boy," George Cottar, the perfect public-school graduate and heroic young officer, resorts to "By Jove" on a regular basis. Possibly accurate then, it is artificial and stereotyped to a later generation. The same might be said about Kipling's attempts to re-create the voices of children: Sometimes they are successful, sometimes not. If dialogue and dialect can deepen and extend the meaning and quality of a story, they can also date a story and detract from it.

During the 1890's, after his marriage to Carrie and the birth of his three children, Kipling, although continuing to write short stories and novels for an adult audience, also turned his hand to works for children. Kipling had an empathetic feeling for children; some critics suggest that he never entirely outgrew his own childhood, with its traumas and rewards. *The Jungle Book* was published in 1894 and *The Second Jungle Book* the following year. The series of stories of the baby Mowgli reared by wolves in the jungle is perhaps the most enduring of Kipling's many short-story collections. Several generations of children read about Father and Mother Wolf, the tiger Shere Khan, the sleepy bear Baloo, the panther Bagheera, and Kaa, the python. In later decades, other children came to know them through the Walt Disney cartoon feature, but there is a quality in the Kipling stories that did not translate fully to the screen. Like authors of other animal stories, Kipling anthropomorphized his creatures, and they exhibit recognizable human characteristics, but his jungle contains a quality of danger, of menace, which was not replicated in the Disney production.

"The King's Ankus" • Kipling's City of the Cold Lair in "The King's Ankus," inhabited only by the evil White Cobra, places the reader in a dark, dangerous, and claustrophobic building, a house of fear and death. A continuing motif in the stories involves references to the Law of the Jungle—Charles Darwin's survival of the fittest—an ideology very prominent in the imperialist years of the late nineteenth century. The villainous Shere Khan, Mowgli's rival who is always eager to put Mowgli to death, belonged to that jungle world, while the Monkey-People as portrayed in "Kaa's Hunting" and human beings, driven from their village in "Letting in the Jungle," did not. Both species did not properly follow the law; both were cowardly, vindictive, thoughtless, greedy, and irrational.

Just So Stories • The *Just So Stories* were published in 1902. These were composed for an audience younger and more innocent than the readers of *The Jungle Book* stories. The teller of the tales, or fables, addresses his hearer as "O My Best Beloved," who was Kipling's eldest child, Josephine, who died at the age of six, in 1899. The *Just So Stories* appeal on two levels. First, they purport to answer some of the eternal questions of childhood such as "How the Camel Got His Hump" and "How the Leopard Got His Spots." In so doing, Kipling's genius for specific details captivates the reader. From "How the Whale Got His Throat" comes the following:

If you swim to latitude Fifty North, longitude Forty West (that is magic), you will find sitting *on* a raft, *in* the middle of the sea, with nothing on but a pair of blue canvas breeches, a pair of suspenders (you *must* not forget the suspenders, Best Beloved), and a jack-knife, one shipwrecked Mariner.

Second, the settings of the tales enchant with their exotic locale, such as the Howling Desert of the camel, the High Veldt of the leopard, and "the banks of the turbid Amazon" in those High and Far-Off Times.

Puck of Pook's Hill • The fourth collection of Kipling's children's stories was *Puck of Pook's Hill*, published in 1906. Now ensconced in the English countryside at Bateman's, Kipling turned to the history of England. Puck, "the oldest Old Thing in England," appears to two young children, Dan and Una, and through the use of magic conjures up for them various past eras from pre-Roman times onward. The nationalistic bias of the tales is not heavy-handed, and generally the narrative and the conversations of the characters are appropriate for children, while Puck's world, if not Puck himself, is more familiar and less exotic than Kipling's earlier children's books. Among re-created practical Romans, patriotic Saxons, and archetypal peasants, the most evocative tale is "Dymchurch Flit," recited by the narrator in a Sussex dialect. In the aftermath of Henry VIII's Protestant Reformation, England's fairies ("pharisees") wished to flee from the land, and a peasant woman gives her two disabled sons through a "pure love-loan" to ferry them to the Continent. At the end of each conjuring of the past, however, Puck causes the children to forget him and his creations; he and his magic belong in the stories, not in so-called real life. Although Puck uses magic, the stories themselves are more realistic, being grounded in history, than either the fables of *The Jungle Book, The Second Jungle Book,* or *Just So Stories.*

"Mrs. Bathurst" • One of Kipling's most successful short stories was "Mrs. Bathurst," published in 1904 and set in South Africa. On one level, the story is told through an unidentified first-person narrator. He and his friend Inspector Hooper, a railway investigator who had just returned from surveying railway equipment in the interior, are passing time drinking beer on a hot day. Hooper has something in his pocket for which he occasionally reaches but never quite removes. They are shortly joined by Pycroft, a sailor, and Sergeant Pritchard, whom the narrator knows but Hooper does not. Pycroft and Pritchard begin to reminisce about sailors whom they have known: Boy Niven who led them astray in the forests of British Columbia supposedly searching for his uncle's farm, Spit-Kit Jones who married "the cocoanut-woman," and Moon, who had "showed signs o'bein' a Mormonastic beggar" and who deserted after sixteen years of service. The talk then turns to "V," who had disappeared just recently while up-country, only eighteen months before his pension. "V" was also known as Click because of his false teeth, which did not quite fit. Hooper is interested in what Pycroft and Pritchard have to say about "V" and asks them if "V" has any tattoos. Pritchard takes umbrage, believing that Inspector Hooper is seeking information in order to arrest his friend "V." Apologies are made, and then Hooper asks to hear more about "Vickery," though until that moment only "V" had been used in the discussion.

The narrator asks why Vickery ran away, and Pycroft, through a smile, lets it be known that there was a woman involved. Mrs. Bathurst, a widow, owned a hotel in New Zealand frequented by sailors and others. Asked to describe her, Pycroft answered that "'Tisn't beauty, so to speak, nor good talk necessarily. It's just It." Pycroft has now become the primary narrator, and Vickery and Mrs. Bathurst are filtered through his memories and perceptions. According to Pycroft, Mrs. Bathurst had "It," and Vickery was captivated although he did not let that be known to Pycroft at the time. Last December, as Pycroft tells the story, while on liberty in Cape Town, he ran into Vickery who, visibly disturbed, demanded that Pycroft accompany him to a biograph or cinematograph. This early motion picture—a recent novelty—featured scenes from England. Sitting in the front row, Vickery and Pycroft watched various London views appear on the "magic-lantern sheet." The scene shifted to London's Paddington Station, and among the passengers who came down the platform in the direction of the camera was Mrs. Bathurst, who "looked out straight at us with that blindish look. . . . She walked on and on till she melted out of the picture—like a shadow jumpin' over a candle."

At Vickery's urging, Pycroft accompanies him for five consecutive evenings to the cinematograph. On one occasion, Vickery agitatedly claims that Mrs. Bathurst is looking for him. Then, under obscure circumstances, Vickery is assigned upcountry, and before he leaves he tells Pycroft that the motion picture of Mrs. Bathurst would appear again in a town where he would be able to see her once more. Vickery also abruptly informs Pycroft that he is not a murderer, for his wife had died during childbirth after Vickery had shipped out. Confused, Pycroft asked for the rest of the story but was not enlightened: "'The rest,' 'e says, 'is silence,'" borrowing from *Hamlet* (c. 1600-1601). Pycroft heard no more from Vickery.

At this point Hooper again reaches into his pocket and makes a reference to false teeth being acceptable evidence in a court of law. He then tells of his recent experience in the interior. Told to watch for a couple of tramps, Hooper recites how he could see them from a long way off, one standing and one sitting. They were dead.

> There'd been a bit of a thunderstorm in the teak, you see, and they were both stone dead and black as charcoal. That's what they really were, you see—charcoal. They fell to bits when we tried to shift 'em. The man who was standin' up had the false teeth. I saw 'em shinin' against the black. . . . Both burned to charcoal.

Again, Hooper reaches to his pocket, and again he does not bring forth anything. Although no other evidence appears, Pritchard for one seems to assume that the other body, unidentified by Hooper, is Mrs. Bathurst. Pycroft concludes that he for one is glad that Vickery is dead, wishing only to drink the last of the beer.

Throughout the story, Mrs. Bathurst is perceived through a series of images, as seen and related by Pycroft and Pritchard, who had known her in New Zealand, as told by Vickery to Pycroft, as she appears flickering on the motion-picture screen and as the unidentified narrator recites these varying images to the reader. If one theme in "Mrs. Bathurst" is the difficulty of perceiving the reality behind the images, another is the compulsive and destructive power of love. This was not a new aspect in Kipling's work, but perhaps never before had the woman, and even the man, Vickery, been quite so filtered from the reader through the various narrators and now including her image on the screen. Vickery's death apparently resulted because of his experience with Mrs. Bathurst. What was that experience? Was he escaping from her or seeking her out? Was he guilty of something? Apparently he was not guilty of murdering his wife. Had love or its consequences driven him mad? One critic has pointed out the element of "synchronicity," or the significant coincidence as an element in "Mrs. Bathurst." Many twentieth century writers, from James Joyce to Anthony

Powell, have employed this device. In "Mrs. Bathurst," the most notable example was the coincidence of Vickery and then Pycroft discovering Mrs. Bathurst on the motion-picture screen. The story is of seemingly disjointed events, like individual scenes in a motion picture. Combined, they may have a coherence, but what that coherence is, or means, remains obscure, merely flickering images. Readers have puzzled over "Mrs. Bathurst" ever since the story first appeared.

"They" • Several of Kipling's later stories continue to develop his earlier themes. In 1904, Kipling wrote "They." A ghost story, or perhaps a fantasy, its setting is a beautiful, isolated country house in England inhabited by a young blind woman who, through her sheer need, has been able to bring back the spirits of dead children and thus to transcend the grave, the ultimate barrier. Like Mrs. Bathurst and other of Kipling's female characters, the blind woman has a power that profoundly affects the world around her.

"Mary Postgate" • "Mary Postgate," a powerful story of repression and revenge, portrays a middle-aged spinster and companion who passively accepts the abuse of the young boy of the house, Wyndham Fowler. He treated her shabbily for years, throwing things at her, calling her names such as "Posty" and "Packhead," and belittling her abilities. Then, while in training as a pilot in World War I, Wynn is accidentally killed. Postgate has long repressed and denied any feelings and does so again when his death is announced; her only regret is that he died before he had the chance to "kill somebody." While she is in town getting paraffin to burn Wynn's effects, a building collapses, killing a young girl; although the local doctor tells her that the crash occurred from natural causes, she refuses to accept it, convinced that the Germans have bombed the house. Returning home to light the fire, she comes across an injured pilot in the garden and, assuming that he is German, refuses to summon a doctor, electing instead to watch him die. In choosing the pilot's death, Postgate not only is having her revenge for the death of Wynn and the girl killed supposedly at the hands of the hated German enemy but also is gaining her personal revenge for the hollowness of her own life. The pilot in the garden might well be German, but for Mary it makes no difference: It could be anyone. As he dies and as the fire consumes Wynn's effects, Mary experiences a rush of ecstasy comparable to a sexual release. "Mary Postgate" is a deeply felt exploration of a damaged human psyche.

"Dayspring Mishandled" • "Dayspring Mishandled" is one of Kipling's last and finest stories. It, too, is a story of revenge, but revenge ultimately not taken. It tells of two writers, Manallace and Castorley, cynically writing for pulp publication: "If you save people thinking you can do anything with 'em." After they quarrel, Castorley decides to write real literature and becomes a pseudoexpert on Geoffrey Chaucer; Manallace, who does have literary abilities, chooses not to pursue his talent and continues the easy path. Over an unspecified insult by Castorley to a woman for whom Manallace has been caring—typically in Kipling, much is left unsaid—Manallace vows revenge, creating a fake Chaucerian manuscript that Castorley publicly proclaims as legitimate, thus earning a knighthood. Manallace plans to reveal the fake, perhaps to the press, perhaps to Castorley himself to drive him insane, but he delays his plan as Castorley's health begins to fail and as he is put under the care of a doctor, Gleeag, who Manallace later suspects is poisoning Castorley. Lady Castorley urges Manallace to help Castorley assemble his collected works for publication and implies that she knows about the forgery; Manallace believes that she is having an affair with Gleeag, the doctor, and that she wants knowledge of the fake Chaucer manuscript to come out in hopes that the shock will kill her husband. On his deathbed, Castorley confesses his fears to Manallace: The manuscript was "*too* good," and his wife has reminded him that "a man could do anything with anyone if he saved him the trouble of thinking," which is exactly what Manallace has done with Castorley by allowing him to validate the fake without really thinking. Castorley dies of what Gleeag, Lady Castorley's paramour, said was "Malignant kidney-disease—generalized at the end."

Like most of Kipling's best stories, "Dayspring Mishandled" explores the recurring themes of passion and revenge, the failure of human nature, the confusion in relationships, frustrated ambition, and the inability to see clearly, even in the understanding of oneself. It is rich in allusions and references that remain unexplained and are left for the reader to explore. Kipling's most popular stories were the product of his early life, but some of his greatest stories—too often ignored for a time—were written toward the end.

Eugene S. Larson

Other major works

NOVELS: *The Light That Failed,* 1890; *The Naulahka: A Story of East and West,* 1892 (with Wolcott Balestier); *Captains Courageous: A Story of the Grand Banks,* 1897; *Kim,* 1901.

MISCELLANEOUS: *The Sussex Edition of the Complete Works in Prose and Verse of Rudyard Kipling,* 1937-1939 (35 volumes).

NONFICTION: *American Notes,* 1891; *Beast and Man in India,* 1891; *Letters of Marque,* 1891; *The Smith Administration,* 1891; *A Fleet in Being: Notes of Two Trips with the Channel Squadron,* 1898; *From Sea to Sea,* 1899; *Letters to the Family,* 1908; *The New Army in Training,* 1914; *France at War,* 1915; *The Fringes of the Fleet,* 1915; *Sea Warfare,* 1916; *Letters of Travel, 1892-1913,* 1920; *The Irish Guards in the Great War,* 1923; *A Book of Words,* 1928; *Something of Myself: For My Friends Known and Unknown,* 1937; *Uncollected Prose,* 1938 (2 volumes); *Rudyard Kipling to Rider Haggard: The Record of a Friendship,* 1965 (Morton N. Cohen, editor); *The Letters of Rudyard Kipling,* 1990-2004 (6 volumes; Thomas Penney, editor); *Writings on Writing,* 1996 (Sandra Kemp, editor); *Kipling's America: Travel Letters, 1889-1895,* 2003 (D. H. Stewart, editor).

POETRY: *Schoolboy Lyrics,* 1881; *Echoes,* 1884 (with Alice Kipling); *Departmental Ditties,* 1886; *Barrack-Room Ballads, and Other Verses,* 1892; *The Seven Seas,* 1896; *An Almanac of Twelve Sports,* 1898; *Recessional, and Other Poems,* 1899; *The Five Nations,* 1903; *Collected Verse,* 1907; *A History of England,* 1911 (with C. R. L. Fletcher); *Songs from Books,* 1912; *Sea Warfare,* 1916; *Twenty Poems,* 1918; *Rudyard Kipling's Verse, 1885-1918,* 1919; *The Years Between,* 1919; *Q. Horatii Flacci Carminum Librer Quintus,* 1920 (with Charles L. Graves, A. D. Godley, A. B. Ramsay, and R. A. Knox); *Songs for Youth,* 1924; *Sea and Sussex from Rudyard Kipling's Verse,* 1926; *Rudyard Kipling's Verse, 1886-1926,* 1927; *Songs of the Sea,* 1927; *Poems, 1886-1929,* 1929; *Selected Poems,* 1931; *Rudyard Kipling's Verse, 1885-1932,* 1933; *Rudyard Kipling's Verse,* 1940 (definitive edition).

Bibliography

Adams, Jad. *Kipling.* London: Haus Books, 2005. This biography reveals Kipling's inspiration for his poetry and portrays sides of his character that are rarely seen.

Battles, Pau. "'The Mark of the Beast': Rudyard Kipling's Apocalyptic Vision of Empire." *Studies in Short Fiction* 33 (Summer, 1996): 333-344. A reading of Kipling's story as his most powerful critique of the Empire; argues that "The Mark of the Beast" is an allegory of the relationship between the colonizer and the colonized.

Bauer, Helen Pike. *Rudyard Kipling: A Study of the Short Fiction.* New York: Twayne, 1994. Discusses the themes of isolation, work, the Empire, childhood, the supernatural, and art in Kipling's short stories. Includes Kipling's comments on writing and excerpts from a formalist and a postcolonial analysis of Kipling.

Coates, John. *The Days's Work: Kipling and the Idea of Sacrifice.* Madison, N.J.: Fairleigh Dickinson University Press, 1997. Explores one of Kipling's favorite themes.

Daniel, Anne Margaret. "Kipling's Use of Verse and Prose in 'Baa Baa, Black Sheep.'" *Studies in English Literature 1500-1900* 37 (Autumn, 1997): 857-875. Argues that the story relies on a literary self-consciousness to bring under artistic control the possible untruths and chaos of memory; claims that Kipling's use of both prose and poetry creates a comfortable connection with his audience.

Dillingham, William B. *Rudyard Kipling: Hell and Heroism.* New York: Palgrave Macmillan, 2005. This biography offers a close look at some of Kipling's most noted works while exploring the complexities of his personality.

Gilmour, David. *The Long Recessional: The Imperial Life of Rudyard Kipling.* New York: Farrar, Straus and Giroux, 2002. Interesting account of Kipling's life and his complex and changing views of the British Empire, written with an awareness of the rise of terrorism emanating from the postcolonial developing world.

Mallett, Phillip, ed. *Kipling Considered.* New York: St. Martin's Press, 1989. This collection contains essays on *Plain Tales from the Hills, Stalky and Co.*, Kipling and Conrad, and "Mrs. Bathurst." The most helpful for readers interested in Kipling's short stories is Clare Hanson's discussion of the meaning of form in Kipling's short stories; Hanson establishes a theoretical framework for the short story as a genre and discusses Kipling's "Mary Postgate" to illustrate her concepts.

May, Charles E., ed. *Masterplots II: Short Story Series, Revised Edition.* 8 vols. Pasadena, Calif.: Salem Press, 2004. Designed for student use, this reference set contains articles providing detailed plot summaries and analyses of eight short stories by Kipling: "The Gardener" (vol. 3); "Lispeth" (vol. 4); "The Man Who Would Be King" (vol. 5); "The Strange Ride of Morrowbie Jukes," "They," and "Thrown Away" (vol. 7); and "Wireless" and "The Wish House" (vol. 8).

Orel, Harold, ed. *Critical Essays on Rudyard Kipling.* Boston: G. K. Hall, 1990. Sections on Kipling's poetry, his writing on India, his work as a mature artist, his unfinished memoir, and his controversial reputation. Introduced by a distinguished critic. No bibliography.

Ricketts, Harry. *Rudyard Kipling: A Life.* New York: Carroll & Graf, 2000. In a detailed and lively account of Kipling's life, Ricketts also analyzes the literary works that emerged from that popular but controversial career.

Ring Lardner

Born: Niles, Michigan; March 6, 1885
Died: East Hampton, New York; September 25, 1933

Principal short fiction • *Bib Ballads*, 1915; *Gullible's Travels*, 1917; *Treat 'em Rough*, 1918; *Own Your Own Home*, 1919; *The Real Dope*, 1919; *How to Write Short Stories*, 1924; *The Love Nest, and Other Stories*, 1926; *Round Up: The Stories of Ring Lardner*, 1929; *Lose with a Smile*, 1933; *Ring Around the Bases: The Complete Baseball Stories of Ring Lardner*, 1992 (Matthew J. Bruccoli, editor).

Other literary forms • Ring Lardner is known chiefly as a short-story writer, but in his own time was better known as a sportswriter, columnist, and humorist. He also wrote two novel-length works, *You Know Me Al* (1915) and *The Big Town* (1921), and he tried his hand at writing musical comedies, *June Moon* (1929; in collaboration with George S. Kaufman) being his only successful one. Most of Lardner's nonfictional prose remains uncollected, although a few works have appeared in book form, including an early piece about the return of the Chicago White Sox from a worldwide tour, a book of verse about successful business and professional men (*Regular Fellows I Have Met*, 1919), three humorous essays, "The Young Immigrunts," "Symptoms of Being Thirty-five," and "Say It with Oil," and a burlesque autobiography, *The Story of a Wonder Man* (1927).

Achievements • Ring Lardner added significantly to a tradition dating back at least as far as Mark Twain's *Adventures of Huckleberry Finn* (1884). Using first-person monologue (usually humorous, always steeped in colloquialisms, occasionally in the form of correspondence), Lardner allowed his characters to reveal themselves, warts and all. As such, the superficiality and insincerity of his narrators is starkly contrasted with the often harsh truths they unintentionally reveal. This allowed Lardner to illustrate some of the less edifying aspects of American society and human nature in general. He also captured the spoken language (and slang) of ordinary people, rendering it as an art form unto itself. Thus, in addition to their entertainment value, Lardner's stories provide a telling picture of American manners and morals during the first third or so of the twentieth century. Finally, Lardner was a pioneer in the fruitful marriage between the game of baseball and American letters, laying the foundation for later works by prominent authors such as Mark Harris (*Bang the Drum Slowly*, 1956), W. P. Kinsella (*Shoeless Joe*, 1982, filmed as *Field of Dreams*, 1989), Bernard Malamud (*The Natural*, 1952), and Philip Roth (*The Great American Novel*, 1973).

Biography • Ring Lardner was born into a wealthy, genteel family and educated at home by his mother and a tutor before he attended the public high school. After a brief stay at the Armour Institute in Chicago, where his father sent him to study mechanical engineering, he held a series of jobs with newspapers, chiefly as a sportswriter, which led him into writing fiction about ball players and athletes. He married Ellis Abbott in 1911; they had four sons. He died in 1933 of a heart attack.

Analysis • The question that almost inevitably arises in any discussion of Ring Lardner's stories is: What is Lardner's attitude toward his characters and by extension toward the culture out of which they come? Is Lardner, in other words, a misanthrope who hated not only his own characters but also himself, or is he, rather, a disappointed idealist who found in the world of his immediate experience constant instances of cruelty, vulgarity, and insensitivity? Those who point to Lardner's sheltered upbringing and the apparently happy family life both of his early years and of his later married life favor the latter view, while those who wish to find in his fiction some affirmation of the goodness of human beings prefer the former. Obviously, no final answer to the question is possible.

"Champion" • If one reads an early story such as "Champion," one sees a heavy-handed author stacking the cards against his brutal hero, Midge Kelly. Midge beats his disabled brother to steal his half dollar and, when their mother objects, beats her, too. Thereafter Midge's life is a succession of victories and brutalities: He becomes a prizefighter who wins fight after fight and, at the same time, does in those who have befriended him. Although his disabled brother is sick and unable to get out of bed and longs to have a letter from his famous brother, Midge refuses to write. When his wife and son are ill and destitute, he tears up a letter from his wife begging for help. He fires the manager who has helped make him a champion fighter and heaps money on a woman who is obviously using him, although he later casts her off, too, and then takes for himself the wife of his new manager. Through the obvious card-stacking one sees Lardner's intention. He hates brutality and he hates the way brutality is not only ignored but also rewarded in our society. Midge Kelly is not a believable character; he is a symbol on which Lardner heaps all of the abuse he can muster. If it were not for the brutality, "Champion" would be a maudlin tearjerker.

The truth seems to be that, underneath the pose of the realist, observer, and reporter of American crudities, Ring Lardner was a sensitive, even a sentimental man. The monologue form exactly suited his need to keep the sentimentality out of sight while letting his crude, vulgar, insensitive types condemn themselves out of their own mouths, but it was also a way of allowing the victims of the bullies to engage the reader's sympathies without having to make them stereotyped victims: people with disabilities who are beaten, mothers knocked down by their sons, abandoned wives and babies. Lardner's best stories present the reader with a story in which the real author has all but disappeared while his narrator tells his ironically revealing, self-condemning tale.

"Haircut" • One of the best of Lardner's stories, "Haircut," is told by a barber who is giving a haircut to an unnamed stranger in a small Midwestern town. The hero of the barber's tale is Jim Kendall, a practical joker, whom the barber describes as "all right at heart" but whom the reader quickly sees as a man who enjoys inflicting pain on other human beings under the guise of being funny. To pay his wife back for getting his paycheck (he gives her no money to run the household), Kendall tells her to meet him with their children outside the tent of a visiting circus. Instead of joining her there with the tickets as he promised, he hides out in a saloon to savor the joke he is playing on his family. Meanwhile, a new doctor in the town, "Doc" Stair, appears on the scene, and feeling sorry for the mother with the crying children, buys the tickets for them. When Kendall hears how Doc Stair spoiled his fun, he gets furious and vows revenge. He tricks a young woman, Julie Gregg, who is "sweet on" Doc Stair, into com-

Library of Congress

ing into the doctor's office late at night. No one is there but Kendall and his friends hiding in the dark. When Julie calls out the doctor's first name, "Oh, Ralph," Kendall and his crowd leap out and mimic her. When she retreats, they chase her home. Another frequent victim of Kendall's jokes, a "cuckoo" named Paul who is fond of Julie and the doctor and who hears the doctor say that a man like Kendall ought not to be allowed to live, invites himself to go duck hunting with Kendall. Kendall gives Paul his gun to hold, the gun goes off, and Kendall is killed. Doc Stair, the coroner, rules the shooting accidental. Although in this story the chief villain is given his comeuppance, a subtler cruelty is revealed by the barber who says of Kendall that in letting a man like Paul hold his gun, he probably got what he deserved.

"Golden Honeymoon" • Another of Lardner's best stories, "Golden Honeymoon," is a gentler satire; indeed, critics have disagreed about whether this is the portrait of a happy marriage or a vicious attack on marriage in general. Doubtless the truth lies somewhere in between, for the old man who tells the story of his and his wife's trip to Florida on their golden honeymoon is a boring windbag. He is impressed with himself and his son, who is "high up in rotary"; with the commonplace, vulgar details of their trips to cafeterias, church socials, card games, and movies; and with their encounter with his wife's old beau. The main action of the story concerns the conflict that arises between the couple over the reappearance fifty years later of the suitor, who is married to a woman the narrator describes as a rotten cardplayer. Although he is not as brutal or despicable as other Lardner narrators, he has many of the same faults: insensitivity, vanity, pettiness, and even a little cruelty. When he wins a game of checkers, he gloats; when he loses at horseshoes, he pouts. When his wife hurts her back on the croquet court, he laughs at her, and when he is beaten at horseshoes, he quarrels with his wife and she quits speaking to him. The story ends "happily"—that is, the two make up and get "kind of spoony"—but the essential portrait remains that of a boring, vain, pompous old man.

"Some Like Them Cold" • "Some Like Them Cold" is a story told through the exchange of letters between a young woman named Mabelle Gillespie who allows herself to be picked up by a young man in the La Salle Street Station in Chicago. Chas. F. Lewis (as he signs his letters) is on his way to New York to break into the songwriting business. He is a typical Lardner monologuist—vain, crude, and cruel—and Mabelle is the familiar Lardner victim—sensitive, trusting, and foolish. Her letters to Lewis play up her virtues as a "home body"; his become increasingly short, emphasizing how well he is getting on in the Big Town and offering accounts of women who chase him. After he announces his marriage to a woman whom he had earlier described as cold and indifferent to home life, he advises Mabelle not to speak to "strange men who you don't know nothing about as they may get you wrong and think you are trying to make them." "Some Like Them Cold" was later converted by Lardner into the successful musical comedy *June Moon.*

"Ex Parte" • A story technically subtler is "Ex Parte," told in the first person by a man attempting to justify his part in the breakup of his marriage. As he tells it, he and his wife were happy on their honeymoon but as soon as they moved into the house he had bought as a surprise for her (he had promised they would choose a house together), their marriage began to go bad. The trouble is that the house and furniture (picked out by a decorator) are too shiny and new-looking to suit his wife; she hates the house and admires the converted barn and early American furniture of her school friend. Even the nicks and burns on her friend's dining room table seem beautiful to her. So the narrator, after consuming a large quantity of "early American Rye," goes home and mutilates their table with a blow torch. His wife leaves him, and he is now trying to get his friends to take his side in the quarrel.

What is unusual about this story is that, instead of the typical opposition of bully and victim, there is rather a battle between two people equally insensitive and shallow: the husband who likes bright, shiny new things and the wife who likes antiques. For both, marriage is simply a matter of having the right things.

To call Ring Lardner either a misanthrope or a humorist, or even a realist who observed American manners, is to miss the point. Lardner was a moralist, like his friend F. Scott Fitzgerald, and, although at times he could be merely funny or sentimental or tiresome, his best stories are homilies, camouflaged by humor, on meanness, cruelty, and vanity. Lardner had a remarkable ear for a certain kind of native American speech, and he used that talent for giving his stories the ring of truth and passing on to succeeding generations a small but enduring collection of excellent short stories.

W. J. Stuckey
With updates by Ira Smolensky

Other major works

PLAY: *June Moon,* pr. 1929 (with George S. Kaufman).

NOVELS: *You Know Me Al,* 1915; *The Big Town,* 1921.

NONFICTION: *My Four Weeks in France,* 1918; *Regular Fellows I Have Met,* 1919; "The Young Immigrunts," 1920; "Symptoms of Being Thirty-Five," 1921; "Say It with Oil," 1923; *What of It?,* 1925; *The Story of a Wonder Man,* 1927; *Letters from Ring,* 1979 (Clifford M. Caruthers, editor; revised as *Letters of Ring Lardner,* 1995).

Bibliography

Blythe, Hal, and Charlie Sweet. "Lardner's 'Haircut.'" *The Explicator* 55 (Summer, 1997): 219-221. Poses the question of why Whitey would tell his tale of homicide to a stranger; argues that Whitey feels guilty because he has been involved and thus, like the Ancient Mariner, stops strangers to tell his tale.

Bruccoli, Matthew J., and Richard Layman. *Ring Lardner: A Descriptive Bibliography.* Pittsburgh: University of Pittsburgh Press, 1976. This highly accessible and useful summary of Lardner's work provides a good starting point for getting a sense of Lardner's overall achievements, range, and productivity.

Cowlishaw, Brian T. "The Reader's Role in Ring Lardner's Rhetoric." *Studies in Short Fiction* 31 (Spring, 1994): 207-216. Argues that readers of Lardner's stories perceive a set of corrective lessons conveyed satirically by an implied author. Readers who accept the role of implied reader and thus align themselves with the implied author as perceptive and intelligent people accept these lessons and thus fulfill the basic purpose of satire, which is social correction.

Friedrich, Otto. *Ring Lardner*. Minneapolis: University of Minnesota Press, 1965. Admirably concise work that discusses Lardner's command of different dialects. Puts the darker side of Lardner's psyche into the context of myths and misconceptions popular at the time he wrote. An expert on the historical period both in the United States and Europe, Friedrich provides a lucid and insightful introduction to Lardner's main themes and techniques.

Geismar, Maxwell. *Ring Lardner and the Portrait of Folly*. New York: Thomas Y. Crowell, 1972. Probably the most ambitious work of literary criticism devoted entirely to Lardner. Geismar draws a full-blown critique of American materialism out of Lardner's work, arguing that Lardner's sarcasm and satire masked a deeply felt idealism.

Lardner, James. "Ring Lardner at 100—Facing a Legacy." *The New York Times Book Review* 90 (March 31, 1985): 3. James Lardner reflects on the life and work of his grandfather, Ring Lardner, and describes the Ring Lardner Centennial Conference held at Albion College in Michigan; discusses Lardner's satire, although he contends he gives his characters more depth than one usually associates with satire.

Lardner, Ring. *Letters of Ring Lardner*. Edited by Clifford M. Caruthers. Washington, D.C.: Orchises, 1995. Lardner's correspondence reveals biographical elements of his life.

Lardner, Ring, Jr. *The Lardners: My Family Remembered*. New York: Harper and Row, 1976. Lardner's third son, a successful screenwriter, provides a charming portrait of the Lardner family. As portrayed here, Ring Lardner, Sr., was humble and completely unpretentious about his work. He was also a good family man and had an interesting circle of friends, including F. Scott Fitzgerald.

May, Charles E., ed. *Masterplots II: Short Story Series, Revised Edition*. 8 vols. Pasadena, Calif.: Salem Press, 2004. Designed for student use, this reference set contains articles providing detailed plot summaries and analyses of four short stories by Lardner: "The Golden Honeymoon," "Haircut," and "Harmony" (vol. 3); and "Some Like Them Cold" (vol. 7).

Robinson, Douglas. *Ring Lardner and the Other*. New York: Oxford University Press, 1992. Examines Lardner's themes in his fiction. Includes bibliographical references and an index.

Yardley, Jonathan. *Ring*. New York: Random House, 1977. This well-written, thorough biography is especially good at drawing the very strong connection between Lardner as journalist and Lardner as short-story writer. According to Yardley, the journalistic desire of unadorned facts that Lardner had to present leads logically to an unflinching examination of human nature and American society through the medium of fiction.

Mary Lavin

Born: East Walpole, Massachusetts; June 11, 1912
Died: Dublin, Ireland; March 25, 1996

Principal short fiction • *Tales from Bective Bridge*, 1942; *The Long Ago, and Other Stories*, 1944; *The Becker Wives, and Other Stories*, 1946; *At Sallygap, and Other Stories*, 1947; *A Single Lady, and Other Stories*, 1951; *The Patriot Son, and Other Stories*, 1956; *Selected Stories*, 1959; *The Great Wave, and Other Stories*, 1961; *The Stories of Mary Lavin*, 1964-1985 (3 volumes); *In the Middle of the Fields, and Other Stories*, 1967; *Happiness, and Other Stories*, 1969; *Collected Stories*, 1971; *A Memory, and Other Stories*, 1972; *The Shrine, and Other Stories*, 1977; *A Family Likeness, and Other Stories*, 1985; *In a Café*, 1995.

Other literary forms • Mary Lavin's novel *Gabriel Galloway* was serialized in *The Atlantic Monthly* in 1944 and was later published as a book under another title, *The House in Clewe Street* (1945). *The House in Clewe Street* and the novel *Mary O'Grady* (1950, 1986) are a loosely connected series of episodes in family life, structured to dramatize the lives of family members over several generations. Without an overall unity, the novels lack direction and force; there are, however, numerous examples within the novels of the social mores and restrictive attitudes more artfully handled in the short stories. Lavin's fine children's stories, *A Likely Story* (1957) and *The Second-Best Children in the World* (1972), capture the imaginative life of children.

Achievements • As a major Irish writer, Mary Lavin is a realist in the tradition of Frank O'Connor and Seán O'Faoláin. The resemblance to those important Irish writers, however, stops there. Her characters are usually solidly middle class, and they tend to be shopkeepers and clerks, a population that is, perhaps, less "submerged" than that of O'Connor's fiction. For Lavin, social class is a determining factor in a character's behavior and fate. She stresses the limitations imposed by a character's social role. In addition, she does not use humor as a major fictional device. Instead of humor, there is often an ironic twist to the plot. Lavin's plots also tend to avoid the simple solution provided by techniques such as reversal and recognition. Instead, she closely examines the problems that her characters encounter. If there is a resolution, it is by no means a simple one.

Lavin is the recipient of numerous awards and honors, including the James Tait Black Memorial Prize in 1944, the Katherine Mansfield-Menton Prize in 1962, the Ella Lynam Cabot Fellowship in 1971, the Gregory Medal in 1974, and the American Irish Foundation Award in 1979. Lavin was president of the Irish Academy of Letters from 1971 to 1973, and she received the American Irish Foundation award in 1979.

Lavin was honored at the Kells Heritage Festival in County Meath in 1993, when an Irish television documentary about her life and work, *An Arrow in Flight*, was screened. Also in 1993, Aosdana, the Irish body that honors writers, musicians, and visual artists, granted her its highest distinction by electing her to the rank of Saoi, "in recognition of creative work which has made an outstanding contribution to the arts in Ireland." The Irish President at the time, Mary Robison, praised Lavin's ability to "catch the tones of the Irish family and the tensions therein."

Biography • Born in East Walpole, Massachusetts, on June 11, 1912, and the only child of Irish-born Nora Mahon and Tom Lavin, Mary Lavin emigrated to Ireland in her ninth year. Educated at Loreto Convent in Dublin and University College, Dublin, she wrote her master's thesis on Jane Austen; she then taught French at Loreto Convent for two years while preparing her unfinished doctoral thesis on Virginia Woolf. In 1942, she married William Walsh, and they had three daughters: Valentine, Elizabeth, and Caroline. After the death of her husband in 1954, Lavin had little time to write fiction since she had to bring up her children and run the farm at Bective. A John Simon Guggenheim Memorial Foundation Fellowship in 1959, however, and another in 1962, gave her the time and confidence to create fiction once more. She published a number of stories that were then collected in *The Great Wave, and Other Stories*. Thereafter, the years became serene and productive. Lavin received a number of awards and prizes, including a third Guggenheim Fellowship, in 1972, and a D.Litt. from the National University of Ireland in 1968. In 1969, she married an old friend from her university days, Michael MacDonald Scott, a laicized Jesuit.

Lavin, who had been living in a nursing home in Blackrock, a southern suburb of Dublin, died on March 25, 1996, at the age of eighty-three. She was praised by both the president of Ireland, Mary Robison, and the Taoiseach, John Bruton, who said her life was characterized by the ability to "make the ordinary extraordinary." She was eulogized in Irish and English newspapers by many of the most famous Irish critics and authors, such as William Trevor, Clare Boylan, W. J. McCormack, and Maurice Harmon. Publication of the first full-length biography of Lavin was stalled in May, 1998, because one of her daughters was unhappy with her portrayal in the book.

Analysis • Neither national nor international events find their way into Mary Lavin's fiction, which is crammed with incidents from the lives of Dublin shopkeepers, country people, island fishermen and their families, nuns, priests, her parents, her children, and her husbands. Lavin's characters, much more important than the plots, which are rather mundane, are usually autobiographical. They represent the author and her acquaintances at various stages in her lifetime: childhood, student life, marriage, motherhood, and widowhood.

Whereas James Joyce was haunted by a father-son conflict, Lavin was plagued by a mother-daughter conflict, resulting in what might be called an Electra complex. It partially accounts for the frequent revelations of unhappy marriages between mismatched couples, although the differences were a source of attraction before the birth of children or the assumption of responsibilities. More often than not, the wife characters are domineering, unhappy, practical slaves to social mores. Some other women characters—nuns, spinsters, sisters, and widows—are vain, flighty, insecure, and emotionally labile. Husband characters, in contrast, no matter how beaten they are by their wives and circumstances, have a certain poetic vision, while the priests, bachelors, brothers, and widowers appear robust, in command of life and their emotions.

"Miss Holland" • "Miss Holland," Lavin's first short story, published in *Dublin Magazine* and reprinted in *Tales from Bective Bridge*, is the story of a typical spinster. Agnes Holland, lonely and ill prepared to face life, traveled for years with her father, who made all the decisions. At his death, Agnes must adjust to the world without anyone to help her. The story, set in England, begins with Agnes searching for a place to live; she finally decides to live at the guest house of Mrs. Lewis because of a playful cat.

Also living there are two men and three women with whom Agnes has nothing in common. She is not a conversationalist and cannot join in the spirited exchanges held during dining hours. Since the other boarders are younger, age is a further obstacle. Agnes feels trapped by her surroundings; there is nothing from the past that she can recollect which will bridge the gap between her and the boorish boarders. Agnes thinks she must try to enter this strange world and wants to discover something to share with the group, needing to be part of her environment.

The black cat affords the opportunity. Agnes sees him jumping in the sun after running through the flower bed where he plucked one red carnation; the image is like that of a Spanish dancer, and she can hardly wait to tell the group. At dinner she and a male guest begin to speak simultaneously, so Agnes waits to let him tell his story. To her horror, she learns that he has shot the cat. Amused, the other guests begin to laugh. Agnes is silent, withdrawing from the boisterous group; no longer can she associate with such people. Having no place else to go because she must live on the small amount of money left to her by her father, she determines to live on past memories of more genteel days. All the ugly characteristics of the uncultured men and women rush to her mind, separating her from them. Loneliness will become a fixed part of life, borne with dignity. Agnes's emotional drama is the conflict of the story. Forever opposed to vulgarity, Agnes realizes she can no longer use her imagination to disguise poor taste and must protest "because my people before me went that way."

"At Sallygap" • Annie Ryan in "At Sallygap" and Ella in "A Happy Death" are typical examples of the wife characters who pressure their husbands. Childless, Annie is a real terror. Artistic Manny Ryan, a fiddler who years earlier was heading to Paris with a band, jumped ship for Annie. He thought she was loving, fragile, and in need of him. Their marriage, however, symbolizes the paralysis and stagnation of Irish urban life. After years of labor, they have nothing more tangible than a tiny Dublin shop where they work and live. Manny knows that "All the Dublin people were good for was talking." Annie was no exception. Her tongue lashes out at Manny usually because he is not aggressive enough in commercial dealings. Annie dominates him while wishing he would be the dominant spouse. Manny's gentility, unfortunately, serves as a red flag for Annie's temper.

By ordering him to go to Sallygap to set up a trade in fresh eggs, Annie gives him a brief escape from his hateful marriage. A lover of nature, Manny draws strength from the rural scenes. On missing the last bus, he walks home, free "at last from the sordidness of the life he led." While Manny feels elated, however, Annie, accustomed to her husband's regularity, goes through a variety of emotions awaiting his return. First, she plans to taunt him. Then, thinking he is out drinking to get the courage to fight back, she relishes that prospect and prepares herself for a grand battle. Next, fear overcomes her: Perhaps Manny is dead. No, he would be brought home alive with a "latent mutinous instinct" activated, which she hopes will enliven their relationship. On hearing his footsteps, however, Annie realizes nothing has changed. Manny is sober and servile, "imprisoned forever in her hatred."

"A Happy Death" • In "A Happy Death," Ella, with three daughters to rear, has to control her emotions in dealing with her dying husband Robert. To supplement their income, Ella rents rooms in their home, using some of the money to buy clothes for Robert so he can get a better job at the library. Outraged when he is demoted from clerk to porter because of his coughing, she demands that he quit, but he refuses and works as a porter. Ella cannot comprehend Robert's need to work and bring her his wages, so she convinces herself that he works to spite her and lower the family's social class. The emotional charges between Ella and Robert build up until his death and explode in Ella afterward.

Through a series of flashbacks, a device Lavin uses in most of her stories, the reader learns of Ella's happy courtship with Robert, her admiration of his white skin and his interest in poetry, and their elopement against her parents' wishes. Their happiness is fleeting. After they are married, she burns his poetry books, sees his white skin as a sign of weakness, and understands why her shopkeeping parents opposed her marriage to unemployed Robert. When Robert is hospitalized, with a flush of excitement Ella insists on keeping up appearances. He must have the best ambulance, a private ward, a new nightshirt, and oranges which he cannot eat.

The daughters are embarrassed by their mother's vain fussing over Robert; it is unnatural to send out for grapes, apples, and newspapers when they know he can neither eat not read. Ella, however, wants everyone to know Robert is a person of importance, with people who care for him. More fruit, biscuits, and sweets are brought to him, making it difficult for the nurses to find space for the thermometer.

Eventually, Ella realizes that the unconscious Robert is dying and prays for his happy death; meanwhile, her prayers and behavior at the bedside are a continued source of distress to her daughters. Thrusting a crucifix in Robert's face, Ella tries to get him to say an act of contrition; he does not. Then he regains his senses long enough to call out for Ella with the lovely golden hair. Misunderstanding her request for him to repeat "I am heartily sorry," Robert thinks she is sorry for having offended him and says, "There's nothing to be sorry about. You always made me happy, just by being near me." Robert's delirious mind recollects their youth and plans for "just the two of them," ignoring the daughters, and a look of "rapturous happiness" returns to his face before he dies. Bewildered, Ella refuses comfort from the priest, nurse, and her daughters. Screaming and sobbing, she is led from the ward, disbelieving God's refusal to answer her prayers for Robert's happy death. Ironically, she does not know that her prayers have been answered.

"Say Could That Lad Be I" • The young boy in "Say Could That Lad Be I," an early story in the first collection, *Tales from Bective Bridge*, and Tom in "Tom" from the collection *The Shrine, and Other Stories*, are portraits of Lavin's father. The farm boy, mischievous and carefree, has a dog, White Prince, the greatest fighter in the countryside. On a visit to his grandmother, the boy takes along White Prince. It is a great mistake to lock him in the cottage when he goes on an errand for his grandmother, since the dog jumps through a closed window and follows his master to the village. After a disturbance in a shop, White Prince flies through its window, causing even greater destruction. Pretending that it is not his dog, the boy walks back to his grandmother. On the road, White Prince, dragging a leg of mutton in his mouth, joins his master. There is not much the lad can do but wash the mutton, present it to his grandmother, and head home before the townspeople pounce on him.

"Tom" • In "Tom," Lavin opens the story by saying, "My father's hair was black as the Devil's, and he flew into black, black rages." Everything about him was black except for "the gold spikes of love with which he pierced me to the heart when I was a child." The author leaves little doubt about the affection she held for her father. In this story she recounts with pride his exploits at school, his walks under a sky filled with birds, his travels to Dublin, Liverpool, Scotland, and America, plus his return to Ireland.

Lavin's portrait of her mother is quite different. She states with disinterest that her mother had numerous memories filling her head, but they could all be reduced to her mother at the piano with her singing sisters and their beaux about her. Her courtship with Tom was more ardent on his part than hers. Yet she, at thirty years old, realized she had snared a desirable fifty-year-old bachelor even though she disliked him at first because of his coarseness, ignorance, and arrogance. Lavin surmises her mother would have preferred her Protestant suitor, Mr. Barrett, a land agent on a large estate. Because of the age difference, Nora lived twenty-four years after Tom's death; Lavin agrees it was an unfair relationship. Her father had her "mother's beauty when he could proudly display it but she did not have his support when she needed it most."

Mary, in contrast, had Tom's support when she needed it. While at the university, he took her to Roscommon, revisiting his boyhood haunts and sharing his memories. Ignoring the material changes, he points out the unchanging mounds, stone walls, and streams running over mossy stones. Although he recognizes old friends, very aged and worn, they do not recognize him. A childhood friend, Rose Magarry, on seeing him says he is Tom's son, "Sure, you're the dead spit of him!" Silently, they leave without correcting the woman.

"Senility" • Tom does not follow the same rules that Nora does, and Mary accepts his lifestyle without complaint. If he was ever a burden to her, it does not appear in Lavin's fiction. Incidentally, the old mother in "Senility" from the same collection is an exquisite portrait of a widowed woman who lives with her daughter. The emotional tension between them is acute, and neither mother nor daughter will release it. The son-in-law acts as a referee in a continuing war of nerves.

When not writing about her family, Lavin presents other people's problems. Always busy with her own difficulties as the correspondence with Lord and Lady Dunsany reveals, she records some fresh insights about psychotic behavior in a tightly structured society. In writing about insanity, she is more comprehensive in *Mary O'Grady*, her second novel, with a description of Patrick's withdrawal from his family and its effect on the members, but the short stories also document the exploits of schizophrenic people, giving the impression that such people are an integral part of Irish society.

"Eterna" • Eterna, the nun in "Eterna," is an excellent example of a woman who cannot face life. A young doctor called to treat the novice Eterna finds her arrogant, despite an outward appearance of humility. He discovers that her infected arm was caused by turpentine soaking through the bandage over a cut which she received by falling off a ladder. Eterna, he learns, is an artist. As the eldest of ten from a poor family, she was educated by the nuns because of her talent and joined the order to continue her work; she could not remain with her impoverished family, and the doctor learns that in time she would not remain with the order.

Years after his calls at the convent in a provincial town, he sees Eterna again at the national Gallery in Dublin. She has a crazed look, wears outlandish clothes, and fixes her daft gaze on him. It brings back his memories of her former life and his brief, questioning visits with her. He flees from the gallery and rushes to his car to await his wife. She, who also knew Eterna, is nonchalant about his encounter with the artist, saying, "If she'd gone a bit cracked, what about it . . . she was probably headed that way from the start." She then tells her husband that people have to clip their wings in order to keep their feet on the ground.

The many widows in Lavin's fiction have their feet on the ground, representing their author after the death of her first husband. Mary and Maudie from "In a Café," Brede from "Bridal Sheets," the unnamed widow from "In the Middle of the Fields," and Vera Traska from "The Cuckoo-Spit," "Happiness," "Trastevere," and "Villa Violella" trace Lavin's battle against loneliness and her eventual adjustment to another self and remarriage.

"Happiness" • Vera in "Happiness" is a central widow character. Her story is told in the first person by her eldest daughter, an unusual technique for Lavin, who generally uses the omniscient third-person point of view. Kate, the eldest daughter in "The Will," the novice in "My Vocation," the neighbor-narrator in "The Small Bequest," the niece-narrator in "A Wet Day," the daughter in "The Mouse," and the husband in "My Molly" are other exceptions to the omniscient viewpoint.

The daughter in "Happiness" describes Vera's thoughts about happiness and how it must not be confused with pleasure or perceived as the opposite of sorrow. The narrator then introduces her younger sisters, Bea and Linda (the latter was only a year old at the time of their father's death), Father Hugh (Michael Scott), a family friend filling the place of the lost father, and Grandmother, whom "God Almighty couldn't make happy." This is a portrait of Lavin's family. Episodes from Lavin's life with husband Robert (William Walsh) and grandfather Tom reveal happy moments. The black period immediately after Robert's death is an unhappy period when the narrator and Bea guard against their mother's suicide. Their trips to Europe are in vain because Vera cannot forget her husband, but since the children learn geography and history, the trips are not completely a waste. In rearing her daughter after returning home, Vera rejects advice from relatives, friends, and strangers, who want her to accept life as a vale of tears.

By accepting life's chaos, symbolized by her disordered study, Vera painfully pursues life. Father Hugh is there to help, but at times she has him "as distracted as herself." Writing, working for her family, and gardening consume much energy, and it is not surprising that Vera eventually collapses while working in her garden. Father Hugh carries her into the house, where she dies four hours later, recalling the day Robert died. It is necessary for Vera to die and natural that she would remember Robert's last day. A finality to that relationship opens new doors for Mary Lavin, through which she and Father Michael Scott can pass. "Happiness," more autobiographical than fictive, is the story of an insecure, emotionally fragile woman dealt some cruel blows.

In a Café • The final book Mary Lavin saw through publication was *In a Café*, which included reprints of such stories as "In the Middle of the Fields" and "In a Café"; revised versions of such stories as "The Convert" and "The Will"; and one story, "The Girders," which had never been published before. According to Elizabeth Lavin, one of her three daughters, who was responsible for selecting the stories, Lavin had been revising a number of stories for a collected edition of her short fiction; this shorter selection was published when she broke her hip and had to halt the revision process.

The new story in the collection was found by Lavin's daughter quite by accident.

According to those who knew her, Lavin was quite sensitive about the stories she sent under contract to *The New Yorker* which were rejected. She reportedly had a big heap of such stories under a bed. Her daughter has said that she is sure she will discover many more unpublished Lavin stories, which will probably see print in the near future.

It is not known whether "The Girders" is a *New Yorker* reject or a story Lavin had not gotten around to submitting for publication. However, it is a typical Lavin story, straightforward and unadorned—an example of what William Trevor has referred to as her ability to be subtle "without making a palaver about it." The story reflects a typical Irish conflict between nostalgia for the country and pride in progress and work in the city. The central character is a man who works on large construction sites in Dublin as part of the economic boom in Ireland in the last decade of the twentieth century. Life in the city for the man seems crazed and giddy, but he knows that outside was a world "still as sane and sweet as ever." Thus, he longs to make enough money to return to the country.

When the man has an accident that cripples his feet and necessitates his return to his mother's house in the country, he is not so sure that this is what he wants. The story ends with him looking out the hospital window at the construction girders and thinking he will never see them again. Instead, he would be looking at the trees and fields for the rest of his life. As he thinks of them, the fields seem a monotonous green and the trees clumsy and stupidly twisted. Now the girders of the great buildings do not look so cruel at all, and "the cranes looked as frail as the silk wings of a dragonfly that wouldn't harm a thing."

Eileen A. Sullivan
With updates by James Sullivan and Charles E. May

Other major works

CHILDREN'S LITERATURE: *A Likely Story*, 1957; *The Second-Best Children in the World*, 1972.

NOVELS: *The House in Clewe Street*, 1945; *Mary O'Grady*, 1950, 1986.

Bibliography

Caswell, Robert W. "Political Reality and Mary Lavin's *Tales from Bective Bridge.*" *Eire-Ireland* 3 (Spring, 1968): 48-60. Caswell argues that Lavin's stories lack the "political reality" found in the works of Frank O'Connor and Seán O'Faoláin. He also states that she does not show nationalism as a driving force of her characters. Yet Caswell still feels that Lavin captures a distinctly Irish identity.

Hawthorne, Mark D. "Words That Do Not Speak Themselves: Mary Lavin's 'Happiness.'" *Studies in Short Fiction* 31 (Fall, 1994): 683-688. Claims that in this well-known Lavin story the narrator's attempt to understand and account for her mother's enigmatic use of the word "happiness" illustrates the futility of trying to understand verbal constructs; the inability to communicate is a major theme in the story.

Kelly, A. A. *Mary Lavin: A Study.* New York: Barnes & Noble Books, 1980. Perhaps the best critical book available on Lavin. Kelly discusses Lavin's use of the social hierarchy in her fiction. There are also excellent chapters on the themes of the family and religion found in Lavin's work.

Lynch, Rachel Sealy. "'The Fabulous Female Form': The Deadly Erotics of the Male

Gaze in Mary Lavin's *The House on Crewe Street.*" *Twentieth Century Literature* 43 (Fall 1997): 326-338. An analysis of Lavin's novel, concentrating on gender relation and Lavin's use of satire.

May, Charles E., ed. *Masterplots II: Short Story Series, Revised Edition.* 8 vols. Pasadena Calif.: Salem Press, 2004. Designed for student use, this reference set contain articles providing detailed plot summaries and analyses of six short stories by Lavin: "The Great Wave" and "Happiness" (vol. 3); "The Nun's Mother" (vol. 5) "A Wet Day," "The Widow's Son," and "The Will" (vol. 8).

Murray, Thomas J. "Mary Lavin's World: Lovers and Strangers." *Eire-Ireland* 7 (Summer, 1973): 122-131. Murray finds much "sterility" in the characters and situations in Lavin's fiction. The role of women in many of the stories, Murray argues, is to destroy the life-affirming fantasies of men.

Neary, Michael. "Flora's Answer to the Irish Question: A Study of Mary Lavin's 'The Becker Wives.'" *Twentieth Century Literature* 42 (Winter, 1996): 516-525. Discusses the protagonist of the story as a passive projection of a national Irish ideal; shows how the story deals with the Irish struggle to establish an identity from within.

Peterson, Richard F. *Mary Lavin.* Boston: Twayne, 1980. This book offers a brief biography of Lavin and then examines specific examples of the stories and novels. A useful introduction to the writer.

Shumaker, Jeanette Roberts. "Sacrificial Women in Short Stories by Mary Lavin and Edna O'Brien." *Studies in Short Fiction* 32 (Spring, 1995): 185-197. Examines sacrificial women in two stories by Lavin and two by O'Brien; claims that in the stories female martyrdom (en)gendered by the Madonna myth has different forms, from becoming a nun to becoming a wife, mother, or "fallen woman."

Vertreace, Martha. "The Goddess Resurrected in Mary Lavin's Short Fiction." In *The Anna Book: Searching for Anna in Literary History,* edited by Mickey Perlman. Westport, Conn.: Greenwood Press, 1992. Argues that Lavin creates a number of mother figures in her stories based on pre-Christian goddesses worshiped in ancient Ireland. Suggests that characters who interact with this figure are redeemed through her by relinquishing other forms of creativity, such as artistic expression.

D. H. Lawrence

Born: Eastwood, Nottinghamshire, England; September 11, 1885
Died: Vence, France; March 2, 1930

Principal short fiction • *The Prussian Officer, and Other Stories*, 1914; *England, My England*, 1922; *St. Mawr: Together with "The Princess,"* 1925; *Rawdon's Roof*, 1928; *The Woman Who Rode Away, and Other Stories*, 1928; *Love Among the Haystacks, and Other Stories*, 1930; *The Lovely Lady, and Other Stories*, 1933; *A Modern Lover*, 1934; *The Complete Short Stories of D. H. Lawrence*, 1961.

Other literary forms • D. H. Lawrence is one of the most prolific writers in English literary history. His major works include ten volumes of poetry, a collection of critical essays, four books of travel writings, several translations, and plays, in addition to the four novels (among others) for which he is popularly known. His most famous novel, *Lady Chatterley's Lover* (1928), brought him fame and further assured that he would be remembered as a novelist rather than a poet and short-story writer. After his novels, his most widely read and anthologized works are short stories and poems. In many of his works, Lawrence uses identical situations, plots, images, and themes.

Achievements • The subject and style of Lawrence's works, of whatever kind, are so distinct and consistent that his name has given birth to an adjective, "Lawrentian," to describe a way of looking at the world and a method for presenting it. The bold originality and powerful style of his early novels attracted the attention of upper-class British writers and intellectuals such as the philosopher Bertrand Russell and even the prime minister Herbert Asquith. Lawrence's values, however, were not the same as theirs, and he spent most of his life as a nomad, searching for amenable landscapes and cultures. All of his works record that search and reveal its remarkable unity of purpose.

After Lawrence's death, his critical reputation eventually declined, though his works continued to sell. Then, in 1955, the influential modern English critic F. R. Leavis published a study of the novels and declared Lawrence to be the most important writer of his generation and as good as Charles Dickens. He praised *Sons and Lovers* (1913) as the first honest treatment of the British working class. Also in 1955 the American critic Harry T. Moore published the first authoritative biography, *The Intelligent Heart*, introducing Lawrence to a public as fascinated by his life as by his work. His reputation is worldwide; in 1982, there were nearly three hundred titles pertaining to Lawrence translated into thirty languages.

Biography • David Herbert Lawrence's life went through four distinct stages. The first may be indicated as the Nottingham or Eastwood years, the formative years before March, 1912. Lawrence's father, Arthur, was a miner and his mother, a teacher. Married beneath her status, Lydia Beardsall Lawrence detested the commonness of her husband and vowed that her sons would never work the pits. She therefore doggedly saw Lawrence through a teacher-training program at Nottingham University College. The class struggle at home mirrored the larger class struggle, of which Lawrence was acutely aware.

Within the grim industrial village life there remained a lyrical beauty in intimate relations. In Eastwood, Lawrence was romantically involved with two women who represented the contradictory nature of love. Jessie Chambers (Muriel in *Sons and Lovers*), his mother's choice, was too spiritual and possessive for Lawrence. He was physically attracted to another, Louie Burrows, but the oedipal bonds were too strong to break. When Lydia Lawrence died in December, 1910, Lawrence drifted aimlessly and over the next few months severed all romantic attachments. Then, in March, 1912, he met Frieda Weekley, the wife of his modern languages professor. They were married in May.

The next period lasted until the end of World War I and his subsequent departure from England. Lawrence published poems that treat his marriage to Frieda as at once physical and spiritual. He was at work on a long novel, *The Sisters*, which he split into two and published the first part, *The Rainbow*, in 1915. The work was suppressed by British censors because of its frank portrayal of sexual relations, and Lawrence was unable to find an American publisher. In 1917, he and Frieda applied for passports, which they were denied, ostensibly because Frieda's family was German and some of her relatives (notably, the infamous Red Baron) served prominently in the German army. For the next two years, the Lawrences lived in dire poverty, in cottages and on funds lent by friends.

Years of wandering characterize the third period. After relatively short residencies in various Italian towns, Lawrence visited Ceylon (now Sri Lanka) and Australia, and then from September, 1922, until September, 1925, lived in Taos, New Mexico, and Chapala and Oaxaca in Mexico, interspersed with a short return to England in late 1924. He traveled to the United States at the invitation of Mabel Dodge Luhan, who had read *Sea and Sardinia* (1921) and was convinced that only Lawrence could describe the "soul" of the Southwest landscape and Native Americans. His American works lyrically reveal the landscape but show little empathy for the people and their history.

In November, 1925, the Lawrences moved to Spotorno, Italy. In June, 1926, Lawrence declared that he no longer wanted to write fiction and began a series of watercolors and large oil paintings. From a villa near Florence in 1927, Lawrence wrote his last novel and *succès de scandale*, *Lady Chatterley's Lover*, and collected his lyrical accounts of travels in Mexico and the American Southwest. His last works, just before he moved to Bandol and then Vence in the French Provence, included his studies of the Etruscan tombs at Tarquinia; a short novel, *The Escaped Cock*, which is an idiosyncratic account of Christ's death and resurrection; *Apocalypse* (1931), a study of the Book of Revelation; and *Last Poems* (1932), which deals with the experience of dying. All of them reflect Lawrence's preparation for his own death, from tuberculosis, in March, 1930.

Analysis • D. H. Lawrence's early stories are set, except for "The Prussian Officer," in the English Midlands; their plot and characters are a thinly veiled autobiography and are built on incidents that Lawrence would develop at length in other forms, notably the novels and plays that he was writing concurrently. Some readers prefer the stories to Lawrence's longer forms, which they regard as too insistent and repetitious; his stories, like his poems, are more structured, their images more intense. Like the longer works, however, the stories reveal Lawrence's central belief in a "fatal change" in the early twentieth century: "the collapse from the psychology of the free human individual into the psychology of the social being." Lawrence tried always to see unity in the behavior of human beings and the historical changes through which ages lived. In the longer works and in many essays, he developed a didactic style appropriate to his sweeping interpretation of human history and types of personality. In the stories, he lyrically and more intimately explores how the quality of individuals' lives is affected by their human relationships.

Odour of Chrysanthemums" • A majority of the stories more frequently treat the failure of human relationships. "Odour of Chrysanthemums" is one of five accounts of such a discovery of lost human possibilities; other versions appear in three novels and a play, *The Widowing of Mrs. Holroyd* (1914), from this period. A proud miner's wife, Elizabeth Bates, waits with her two children for her husband, who is late coming from the pits. At first, she angrily surmises that he has gone to a pub; as time passes, the anger changes to fear. The husband has been killed in a mining accident, and his fellow colliers bring his body home. The climax of the story is one of Lawrence's best scenes, as the miner's mother and wife wash the corpse. In early versions of the story, from 1911, Lawrence treated the mother's and wife's whimperings and reveries equally; in the collected version in 1914, however, he added the powerful dramatic epiphany of Mrs. Bates's feeling of shame for having denied her husband's body. "She had denied him what he was . . . refused him as himself." The discovery is also liberating: "She was grateful to death, which restored the truth. And she knew she was not dead." The symbol of flowers is a derivative, almost gratuitous device. Their fragrance equates to memory, as the wife recalls the events of her married life: birth, defeat and reconciliation, and death.

Before Lawrence's own fulfillment with Frieda Weekley, it is problematic whether he could have known, or treated so honestly, the complex nature of human sexuality or the separateness of lovers. Without the revisions, the story is successful only as an account of lost love and patent realizations, much like others in *The Prussian Officer, and Other Stories*. "The Shadow in the Rose Garden" and "The Shades of Spring" are stories about return and realization, but they lack dramatic climaxes. In "The Shadow in the Rose Garden," an unnamed woman returns on her honeymoon to the town where she first fell in love. There, she discovers that her first lover, whom she believed a South African (Boer) War casualty, is alive but confined to an insane asylum. In an unresolved ending, her husband learns that she is still attached to the soldier and concludes that it "would be violation to each of them to be brought into contact with the other." In "The Shades of Spring," Hilda Millership—rejected by a cultured suitor, John Syson—gives herself to her gamekeeper, Arthur Pilbury, on Syson's wedding night. Later, still foppishly attached to Hilda, Syson returns to her farm, learns about Hilda's affair, and is taunted by the gamekeeper for not having seduced her.

Both stories lack the dramatic structure of "Odour of Chrysanthemums." They exemplify a style that Lawrence told his literary agent in 1914 he wanted to outgrow: a method of "accumulating objects in the light of a powerful emotion, and making a scene of them." Nevertheless, these early stories use situations, characters, and symbols that one finds in all Lawrence's work. At the end of "The Shades of Spring," for example, a bee stings Pilbury, and Hilda sucks the wound and smears his mouth with bloody kisses. This gesture is one of the first symbolic statements of a Lawrentian paradigm: Blood symbolizes natural, unconscious life, in contrast to the mechanically intellectual and socially correct existence of Syson.

"The Blind Man" • These two ways of living are also represented in a contrast between *feeling* and *seeing*, between intuitive knowledge and acquired, social knowledge. "The Blind Man" is Lawrence's most powerful treatment of both the necessity and the consequence of intimate physical contact. Isabel Pervin is married to Maurice, who was blinded and scarred in World War I and is completely dependent on her. The focus of the story is not their love but Maurice's sudden passion for his wife's cousin and her former admirer, Bertie Reid. Maurice asks Isabel to invite Bertie for a visit, hoping that he can become his closest friend. Isabel's ambivalent feelings about Bertie, fond yet contemptuous, derive from her knowledge of his lifestyle. "He had his friends among the fair sex—not lovers, friends." She knew that he was "unable to enter into close contact of any sort." This failure at relationships, Lawrence bitingly asserts, made him a "brilliant and successful barrister, also a litterateur of high repute, a rich man, and a great social success"—in short, the epitome of the aristocratic Englishman. The story, however, is more serious than it is satirical. At the electrifying climax, Maurice first runs his hand over Bertie's face and body, and then to Bertie's horror, puts Bertie's hand over his scars and into his eye sockets. Maurice tells Isabel of the experience, which he regards as a ritual of undying friendship, but she sees Bertie's revulsion and his urge to flee such intimacy.

In his own life, Lawrence was attracted to the ritual of *Blutbruderschaft*, in which two male friends mix their blood from self-imposed cuts, and he used that ritual along with a nude wrestling scene, in *Women in Love* (1920). The equivalent contact in "The Blind Man," heightened by Maurice's disfigurement, shows the failure of male relationships as a corollary of failed sexual love. Lawrence had been reading Carl Jung's "Psychology of the Unconscious" and "found much truth" in the oedipal "mother-incest idea." At times, Frieda could become for Lawrence the devouring mother: A man "casts himself as it were into her womb, and . . . the Magna Mater receives him with gratification. . . . It is awfully hard, once the sex relation has gone this way, to recover. If we don't recover we die." Lawrence professed to "believe tremendously in friendship between man and man, a pledging of men to each other inviolably."

"The Prussian Officer" • Although male friendship remained for all Lawrence's life an ideal, he was never able to produce an account of successful male relations whether the bonds were sexual or not. "The Blind Man" symbolically rejects male friendship as a way out of an unavoidable sexual regression, despite what Lawrence professed to believe. In an earlier story, "The Prussian Officer," Lawrence had not yet acquired the skill of using symbolic gestures. He thus treats more directly the destructive nature of suppressed desires—in this case, for an overtly sexual male relationship. Originally entitled "Honour and Arms," the story's title was changed by an editor, much to Lawrence's dismay. Although the revised title focuses on the dominant character and necessarily minimizes another, it removes the pun and limits Lawrence's intent to show how repressed or unconscious desires can erupt in sadistic violence in any relationship.

The Prussian captain, attracted to his young orderly, Anton Schoner, vents his forbidden attraction, first in sadistic assaults and then by refusing to let the orderly see his sweetheart. The orderly's "normal" heterosexuality eventually yields to unconscious responses toward the captain, which drive Schoner to murder him. Lawrence treats the murder like a rape: "It pleased him . . . to feel the hard twitchings of the prostrate body jerking his own whole frame. . . ." The theme common to both "The

Prussian Officer" and "The Blind Man" lies in the similarity between otherwise dissimilar characters. Anyone who has avoided his feelings, or acknowledged but repressed them, on being forced to recognize them, destroys himself—or, more usually, as in Bertie's case, flees to avoid entrapment in any permanent sexual relationship.

"The Horse Dealer's Daughter" • In contemporaneous stories of heterosexual love, physical contact has the opposite effect. A woman is, like Sleeping Beauty, awakened by physical touch to know and accept, usually gradually, her unconscious desires. In "The Horse Dealer's Daughter," a doctor rescues a drowning girl, takes her to his home, and strips off her wet clothes. When she awakens, she embraces him and stirs him into love for her. (Lawrence develops the same plot in a longer version in *The Virgin and the Gipsy*, 1930.)

"You Touched Me" • "You Touched Me" also explores the theme of touch, complicated by an additional motive of inherited wealth. The lower-class male, ironically named Hadrian, has been adopted from a charity house. After wartime service, he returns to his adoptive father, Ted Rockley, a dying invalid cared for by his two natural spinster daughters, Emmie and Matilda. One night, Matilda goes into Hadrian's room, genuinely mistaking it as her father's, and caresses his face before discovering who he is. The touch stirs Hadrian's desire and determines him to conquer the proud Matilda. Ted Rockley approves Hadrian's offer to marry and threatens to leave his estate to Hadrian if Matilda refuses. Matilda's reason for agreeing to marriage is not the point, though it adds a realistic, common touch. The point is that her touching Hadrian validates his desire and gives him rights.

"You Touched Me" shares its plot with a longer work of this period, *The Fox*. In both narratives, a young man returns to England from Canada and falls in love with an older woman. In *The Fox*, the plot complication is not inheritance but a romantic and economic liaison of the loved one, Nellie March, with another woman, Jill Banford. As he does with other homosexual characters, Lawrence simply kills Jill: The young man, Henry Grenfel, cuts down a tree so that it falls where Jill is standing. Henry's repeated warnings to Jill to move and her refusal to do so leave vague whether the act was suicide or murder.

Homoeroticism in stories such as *The Fox* and the subject of sexual awakenings in all his works elicited the popular view of Lawrence's works as being pornographic. It was a charge against which Lawrence vigorously defended himself. His narratives were erotic, designed to awaken readers to their sexuality when they identified with his characters, but they were not pornographic, designed for genital arousal. Pornography offered a life-denying and self-consuming masturbatory release; the erotic stimulated the need for fulfillment with another. According to Lawrence, the British public was not accustomed to the open treatment of sexual relations as healthy. Instead, earlier writers had denied normal sexuality and reduced virile male characters to enervated victims of accidents or war. Nineteenth century readers could accept such vital characters as Rochester in Charlotte Brontë's *Jane Eyre* (1847) only when they were physically ruined or subjugated to a feminine domesticity. The impotent characters, Lawrence believed, that recur so often are both cause and effect of the decline of modern British civilization. In 1917, hoping to flee to the United States, Lawrence wrote to Bertrand Russell, "I cannot do any more work for this country . . . there is no future for England: only a decline and fall. That is the dreadful and unbearable part of it: to have been born into a decadent era, a decline of life, a collapsing civilization."

"The Crown" • Even a dying civilization has its beauty, Lawrence decided, but it was a demonic and apocalyptic one. In the most important essay for understanding his credo, "The Crown," Lawrence characterized modern society as the end of a civilization. It was self-indulgent, self-destructive, sensuous, power-seeking, monotheistic, and light-denying. A new and balanced society would eventually follow. Meanwhile, for generations caught at the end of such epochs, the only way out of a narcissistic egoism was to indulge demonically in sex or bloodlust. Destruction, like creation, required vitality. Lawrence hoped that demonic vitality, spent at last, would lead to a new civilization. Even if it made things worse, it was preferable to apathy.

Lawrence always saw correspondences between individuals, the kinds of societies that they fostered, and the religious myths that they created. The most cogent interpretation that Lawrence gives of the Christian myth is an oedipal one recorded in an unpublished foreword to *Sons and Lovers:*

> The Father was flesh—and the Son, who in himself was finite and had form, became Word. For form is the uttered Word, and the Son is the Flesh as it utters the word, but the unutterable Flesh is the Father.
>
> And God the Father, the Inscrutable, the Unknowable, we know in the Flesh, in woman. She is the door for our ingoing and our out-coming. In her we go back to the Father.

Much of this echoes Jung's "Psychological Approach to the Trinity." For both Lawrence and Jung, father and son constitute polarities in the male psyche. At the personal level, Lawrence has been separated from his father by the mother's interventions. The only way back to the father was to reject the mother and replace her with another female object of desire. The wife replaces mother and restores the son to the father.

Like civilization, Christianity had hardened into meaningless dogma. Lawrence's travels were undertaken not only to avoid a dying British culture but also to discover the nature of other, pre-Christian religions. In the Native American culture, Lawrence found, for a while, what he was seeking: the "oldest religion," when "everything was alive, not supernaturally but naturally alive." The Native Americans' "whole life effort" was to "come into immediate *felt* contact and, so derive energy, power, and a dark sort of joy." Their efforts to become one with the cosmos, without intermediation, was the "root meaning" of religion. Such rapturous description suggests an equivalence to Lawrence's "blood-consciousness" as an attempt to revive a vital religion. The stories and short novels set in the American Southwest and Mexico blend religious vitality and demonic indulgence. Many readers, unaware of Lawrence's metaphysical framework, disparage the stories for what they see as his approval of brute, male force against women. At the naturalistic level, the stories are gratuitously violent, but in the context of Lawrence's credo, they become fabulistic, not realistic. Character and action should be interpreted as symbolic. The presentation of a scene does not necessarily indicate the author's approval.

The juxtaposition of characters in three stories of the Southwest—"The Princess," "The Woman Who Rode Away," and the short novel *St. Mawr*—recalls the structure of earlier stories. Egotistical, haughty, coddled but unfulfilled American and European women come under the sway of dark-skinned heroes who embody Lawrence's ideal.

Lawrence's male Native Americans are distinguished from even the most intuitive British men, like Maurice in "The Blind Man" or Henry in *The Fox:* They have rejected a white culture, including religion, which threatens to demean and confine them. Having escaped the coming Christian apocalypse, they are neither self-indulgent nor spiritual but living embodiments of a phallic mystery, the "only mystery" that the female characters have not unraveled. Their attempts to "know" that mystery leads to their alienation or destruction.

"The Princess" • In "The Princess," Dollie Urquhart travels, after her aristocratic father's death, to a dude ranch in New Mexico. There, she is drawn ineluctably to Domingo Romero, a guide at the ranch and the last of a line of great Native American landholders. Romero is himself unfulfilled and waits for one of two Lawrentian fates: to die or to be "aroused in passion and hope." One day, Dollie arranges a trip, with a female companion and Romero as guide, over the Rockies to a spot where animals can be observed in their "wild unconsciousness." Even though the companion's horse is injured, Dollie and Romero continue the trip. The cold mountains both terrify and seduce Dollie, as Lawrence makes the mountains represent what she is seeking, in perhaps his most successful use of settings as symbols. The guide and his charge spend the night in a miner's shack. Frightened by dreams of snow, a symbol of spiritual death, Dollie goes to Romero for "warmth, protection" and to be "taken away from herself," and Romero obliges. The next day, when Dollie tells him that she does not like "that sort of thing," Romero is broken and angry. Like Hadrian in "You Touched Me," he argues that Dollie's coming to him has given him the right to marry her. When she refuses, he strips her and violates her repeatedly, but she refuses to relent. Romero had successfully reached some "unrealised part" of her that she had never wanted to feel. Soon, rangers rescue Dollie and kill Romero. Unable to find her old self, "a virgin intact," she goes "slightly crazy."

"The Woman Who Rode Away" • In "The Woman Who Rode Away," the knowledge sought by the unnamed woman is much more profound. She wants to visit a remote tribe of Chilchuis and "to know their gods." She does not know that for years the Chilchui have waited for a female sacrificial victim to appease their gods. The woman uses the ploys that society has taught her to engage the Chilchuis, but they remain indifferent. They "were not human to her, and they did not see her as a beautiful white woman . . . no woman at all." Instead, she sees in the dark eyes of her guard a "fine spark" of derision. In a masterful confusion of object and metaphor, Lawrence has the Chilchui ask if the woman will "bring her heart to the Chilchui." Her affirmative response convinces the Chilchuis that she was sent in fulfillment of the prophecy. An aged Chilchui appears, drugs her, cuts away her clothes, and touches her body with his fingertips, which he has moistened at his mouth. At the dawn of the winter solstice, four Chilchuis lay her on a stone and hold her legs and arms. At her head, with knife poised and one eye on the sky, the old priest figure waits for the moment to strike.

St. Mawr • In *St. Mawr,* Lawrence uses not a Native American or even a human figure but a red stallion to symbolize ideal maleness. Lou Witt's husband, typically for Lawrence, has lost his sense of what it means to be a man. The other two male characters, the grooms Phoenix and Lewis, a Navajo and a Welshman, respectively, retain some of their fierce male separateness. None of them, however, measures up to the horse, who "stands where one can't get at him" and "burns with life." When St. Mawr throws Rico, an event full of symbolic suggestion, Lou plans to sell the horse. Then she discovers that the new female owner plans to geld him. To avoid that fate Lou moves with the horse to New Mexico. St. Mawr thrives in the new, stark, mountain landscape, but Lou feels thwarted and diminished. As in "The Woman Who Rode Away," Lawrence ritualizes Lou's quest and transforms her into another mythic sacrificial figure. "She understood now the meaning of the Vestal Virgins. . . . They were symbolic of herself, of woman weary of the embrace of incompetent men." So she turns to "the unseen gods, the unseen spirits, the hidden fire" and devotes herself "to that, and that alone."

The Man Who Died • In Lawrence's last major story, Lou's character and function as the waiting Vestal Virgin are transformed into the mythological figure of Isis, although with a peculiarly Lawrentian twist. *The Man Who Died* is Lawrence's ultimate revision of Christianity's emphasis on the Crucifixion. The work is divided in two parts. The first, published with the title that Lawrence wanted for all editions, "The Escaped Cock," follows the traditional story of Christ's rising and healing. He perceives intellectually the life around him but laments, "The body of my desire has died and I am not in touch anywhere." In 1927, when Lawrence wrote "The Escaped Cock," he may have seen the ending as incomplete, but he did not return to create a second part for two years.

In part 2, Lawrence recasts Christ as the dismembered Osiris whose parts are reassembled by Isis. Reborn in part 1, Christ can function only as a pagan male seasonal deity, dying in winter, while the eternal feminine, symbolized in Isis, waits for his rebirth in spring to reanimate her. Lawrence thus effectively unites two themes that obsess all his works: the renewal of the sexes and the concomitant discovery of a revitalized religion. At one level, Christ and Isis are merely man and woman, but as both deity and human, this new Christ integrates the physical and the spiritual. Lawrence is not advocating a return to paganism, as a facile reading might conclude, but a return of Christianity to its archetypal origins. The new Christ says, "On this rock I built my life," the rock of the living woman. It is not the rock of Saint Peter, of masculine control, but of phallic marriage.

Alvin Sullivan

Other major works

PLAYS: *The Widowing of Mrs. Holroyd*, pb. 1914; *Touch and Go*, pb. 1920; *David*, pb. 1926; *The Plays*, pb. 1933; *A Collier's Friday Night*, pb. 1934; *The Complete Plays of D. H. Lawrence*, pb. 1965

NOVELS: *The White Peacock*, 1911; *The Trespasser*, 1912; *Sons and Lovers*, 1913; *The Rainbow*, 1915; *Mr. Noon*, wr. 1920-1922, pb. 1984; *The Lost Girl*, 1920; *Women in Love*, 1920; *Aaron's Rod*, 1922; *Kangaroo*, 1923; *The Ladybird, The Fox, The Captain's Doll*, 1923; *The Boy in the Bush*, 1924 (with M. L. Skinner); *The Plumed Serpent*, 1926; *Lady Chatterley's Lover*, 1928; *The Escaped Cock*, 1929 (best known as *The Man Who Died*); *The Virgin and the Gipsy*, 1930.

NONFICTION: *Study of Thomas Hardy*, 1914; *Twilight in Italy*, 1916; *Movements in European History*, 1921; *Psychoanalysis and the Unconscious*, 1921; *Sea and Sardinia*, 1921; *Fantasia of the Unconscious*, 1922; *Studies in Classic American Literature*, 1923; *Reflections on the Death of a Porcupine, and Other Essays*, 1925; *Mornings in Mexico*, 1927; *Pornog-*

raphy and Obscenity, 1929; À Propos of Lady Chatterley's Lover, 1930; Assorted Articles, 1930; Apocalypse, 1931; Etruscan Places, 1932; The Letters of D. H. Lawrence, 1932 (Aldous Huxley, editor); Phoenix: The Posthumous Papers of D. H. Lawrence, 1936 (Edward McDonald, editor); The Collected Letters of D. H. Lawrence, 1962 (2 volumes; Harry T. Moore, editor); Phoenix II: Uncollected, Unpublished, and Other Prose Works, 1968 (Moore and Warren Roberts, editors); The Letters of D. H. Lawrence, 1979-2000 (8 volumes; James T. Boulton and others, editors); Selected Critical Writings, 1998; Cafe Letters and Articles, 2004; Introductions and Reviews, 2005.

POETRY: Love Poems, and Others, 1913; Amores, 1916; Look! We Have Come Through!, 1917; New Poems, 1918; Bay, 1919; Tortoises, 1921; Birds, Beasts, and Flowers, 1923; The Collected Poems of D. H. Lawrence, 1928; Pansies, 1929; Nettles, 1930; The Triumph of the Machine, 1931; Last Poems, 1932; Fire, and Other Poems, 1940; Phoenix Edition of Complete Poems, 1957; The Complete Poems of D. H. Lawrence, 1964 (Vivian de Sola Pinto and Warren Roberts, editors).

Bibliography

Balbert, Peter. *D. H. Lawrence and the Phallic Imagination.* New York: St. Martin's Press, 1989. Well-reasoned response to feminist critics who accused Lawrence of misogyny. For "The Woman Who Rode Away," Balbert gives a revisionist study that shows the causes for misreadings in other works.

Bell, Michael. *D. H. Lawrence: Language and Being.* Cambridge, England: Cambridge University Press, 1992. Discusses the development of Lawrence's metaphysics not only in terms of his emotional life but also in terms of Martin Heidegger's metaphysics. Although this study focuses primarily on Lawrence's novels, its comments on his thought are relevant to his short fiction as well.

Black, Michael. *D. H. Lawrence: The Early Fiction.* New York: Cambridge University Press, 1986. In this sensitive study, Black discovers new layers of meaning in five of the eight stories that he examines. He rejects earlier psychoanalytic readings as too reductionist. As soon as critics characterized Lawrence's works as oedipal, they went no further.

Ellis, David. *D. H. Lawrence: Dying Game, 1922-1930.* New York: Cambridge University Press, 1997. The third volume of the Cambridge biography of Lawrence links his writings with the incidents of his life; argues that more than most authors, Lawrence's fiction was associated with his daily living. Discusses his fiction and revisions during the 1920's, including his work on *Lady Chatterley's Lover* and "The Rocking-Horse Winner."

Harris, Janice Hubbard. *The Short Fiction of D. H. Lawrence.* New Brunswick, N.J.: Rutgers University Press, 1984. Harris's book is the first to treat chronologically all Lawrence's short fiction. Weak discussions of some works (for example "England, My England") are more than compensated for by enlightening readings of others (such as *The Man Who Died*).

Jackson, Dennis, and Fleda Brown Jackson, eds. *Critical Essays on D. H. Lawrence.* Boston: G. K. Hall, 1988. Various critical insights may be found in this collection of twenty essays, which includes articles by scholars and by well-known writers such as Anaïs Nin and Sean O'Casey. All literary genres in which Lawrence was involved are represented by one or more contributions here. Also of note is the editors' introduction, which deals with trends in critical and biographical literature about Lawrence.

May, Charles E., ed. *Masterplots II: Short Story Series, Revised Edition.* 8 vols. Pasadena,

Calif.: Salem Press, 2004. Designed for student use, this reference set contains arti
cles providing detailed plot summaries and analyses of these eleven short storie
by Lawrence: "The Blind Man" (vol. 1); "The Horse Dealer's Daughter" (vol. 4)
"The Man Who Loved Islands" and "Odour of Chrysanthemums" (vol. 5); "The
Prussian Officer" and "The Rocking-Horse Winner" (vol. 6); "Sun," "Tickets
Please," and "Two Blue Birds" (vol. 7); and "The White Stocking" and "The
Woman Who Rode Away" (vol. 8).

Schneider, Daniel J. *The Consciousness of D. H. Lawrence: An Intellectual Biography.* Law
rence: University Press of Kansas, 1986. Tracing all the major works chronologi
cally, Schneider treats Lawrence's religious nature at all stages of his life. Nineteen
stories, both early and late, are briefly analyzed to show how Lawrence shaped
over the years, his credo about kinds of consciousness and knowledge.

Squires, Michael, and Keith Cushman, eds. *The Challenge of D. H. Lawrence.* Madison
University of Wisconsin Press, 1990. This group of essays, which deal both with in
dividual works and with broader literary contexts, supplies some interesting and
provocative insights. Of particular note is the first article, by Wayne C. Booth, a
self-confessed "lukewarm Lawrentian" who maintains that Lawrence's works are
better appreciated upon rereading and reconsideration.

Thornton, Weldon. *D. H. Lawrence: A Study of the Short Fiction.* New York: Twayne
1993. Makes a case for the technical skill, psychological depth, and thematic sub
tlety of Lawrence's short fiction by focusing on his most important short stories.
Argues that Lawrence's work is always exploratory, a means of working through
his own tentative ideas.

Ursula K. Le Guin

Born: Berkeley, California; October 21, 1929

Principal short fiction • *The Word for World Is Forest*, 1972; *The Wind's Twelve Quarters*, 1975; *Orsinian Tales*, 1976; *The Water is Wide*, 1976; *Gwilan's Harp*, 1981; *The Compass Rose*, 1982; *The Visionary: The Life Story of Flicker of the Serpentine, with Wonders Hidden*, 1984; *Buffalo Gals and Other Animal Presences*, 1987; *Fish Soup*, 1992; *A Fisherman of the Inland Sea: Science Fiction Stories*, 1994; *Solitude*, 1994 (novella); *Unlocking the Air, and Other Stories*, 1996; *Tales from Earthsea*, 2001; *The Birthday of the World, and Other Stories*, 2002; *Changing Planes*, 2003.

Other literary forms • Although Ursula K. Le Guin has published fifteen volumes of short fiction, she is best known for her novels, especially the Earthsea books, which include *A Wizard of Earthsea* (1968), *The Tombs of Atuan* (1971), *The Farthest Shore* (1972), and *Tehanu: The Last Book of Earthsea* (1990). Other well-known novels include *The Left Hand of Darkness* (1969), *The Lathe of Heaven* (1971), *The Dispossessed: An Ambiguous Utopia* (1974), *Always Coming Home* (1985), and the four linked novellas *Four Ways to Forgiveness* (1995). Her unlinked novels include *The Telling* (2000) and *The Other Wind* (2001).

Le Guin has also published eight volumes of poetry, including *Wild Angels* (1975), *Hard Words, and Other Poems* (1981), *Going Out with Peacocks, and Other Poems* (1994), *Sixty Odd: New Poems* (1999), and *Incredible Good Fortune: New Poems* (2006). Her nonfiction writings include *The Language of the Night: Essays on Fantasy and Science Fiction* (1979), *Dancing at the Edge of the World: Thoughts on Words, Women, and Places* (1988), *Steering the Craft: Exercises and Discussions on Story Writing for the Lone Navigator or the Mutinous Crew* (1998), and *The Wave in the Mind: Talks and Essays on the Writer, the Reader, and the Imagination* (2004). Le Guin's edited works include *The Norton Book of Science Fiction: North American Science Fiction, 1960-1990* (1993) and *Selected Stories of H. G. Wells* (2005). Her translations include *Tao Te Ching: A Book About the Way and the Power of the Way* (1997) and *Selected Poems of Gabriela Mistral* (2003).

Achievements • Ursula K. Le Guin is recognized as a leading American writer of science fiction and fantasy. Her short stories, especially "The Ones Who Walk Away from Omelas," winner of a 1974 Hugo Award, often appear in college literature anthologies. Le Guin has received many awards and honors for her work. *The Left Hand of Darkness* and *The Dispossessed* received both the Nebula and Hugo Awards. Volumes of the Earthsea books earned awards for adolescent literature, including the *Boston Globe*/Horn Book Award for *A Wizard of Earthsea*, a Newbery Honor Book Citation for *The Tombs of Atuan*, and the National Book Award for Children's Literature for *The Farthest Shore*. Her other awards include a Hugo for *The Word for World Is Forest*, a Nebula and Jupiter Award in 1975 for "The Day Before the Revolution," and Jupiters for *The Dispossessed* and "The Diary of the Rose." She was given a Gandalf Award in 1979, an American Book Award nomination and the Janet Heidinger Kafka Prize for Fiction for *Always Home* in 1986, and Nebula Awards for *Tehanu* in 1991 and for *Solitude* in 1995.

Biography • Ursula Kroeber was born on October 21, 1929, in Berkeley, California, the daughter of anthropologist Alfred L. Kroeber and author Theodora Kroeber. She received her bachelor's degree from Radcliffe College in 1951 and her master's from Columbia University in 1952. While on a Fulbright Fellowship in Paris in 1953, she married Charles A. Le Guin. They had three children: daughters Elisabeth and Caroline and a son, Theodore. She taught French at Mercer University and the University of Idaho before settling in Portland, Oregon, in 1959. In 1962, she began publishing fantasy and science fiction. In addition to writing, she was active in the Democratic Party, in writing workshops, and in Tai Chi Chuan, a Chinese form of exercise. Throughout her life, Le Guin has been reticent about discussing her personal life.

Analysis • As literary scholars and critics give more attention to fantasy and science fiction, Ursula K. Le Guin attracts a large share of their interest because she creates possible worlds that cast an informative light on perennial human problems, she explores gender issues that make her fiction popular among feminist readers, and she is precise and powerful in her use of language.

When Le Guin writes about her craft and her works, she often refers to Jungian psychology and Daoist philosophy as major components of her worldview. In her 1975 essay "The Child and the Shadow," Le Guin uses Jungian psychology to support her contention that fantasy is "the language of the night," an important means by which the collective unconscious speaks to the growing individual. In Le Guin's understanding of Jungian thought, consciousness, the part of the self that can be expressed in everyday language, emerges from the unconscious as a child matures. The individual's unconscious is shared in its essentials with all other humans and so is called the collective unconscious.

To become an adult, an individual must find ways of realizing the greatest potential of the unconscious. For Le Guin, these are summed up in the recognition by the individual that on unconscious levels, an individual is identical with all other humans. This recognition releases the irrational forces of social binding, such as compassion, love, creativity, and the sense of belonging to the human community. A major problem in achieving this recognition is learning to deal with "the shadow." Choosing to be one person involves choosing not to be other persons that one could be. Both the positive and the negative choices must be maintained to sustain an identity; the negative choices become one's shadow. The process of achieving adulthood is blocked by the shadow, an unconscious antiself with which one must deal in order to take possession of the rest of the unconscious.

For Le Guin, children become adults when they can cease projecting evil impulses onto others and to recognize that these impulses are part of their selves. This process, she believes, is symbolically represented in the many fairy tales and fantasies in which an animal helps the protagonist to discover and attain his true identity. Such stories speak to the unconscious, telling the child by means of myth and symbol how to achieve wholeness of self.

Le Guin's writings tend to equate Daoism, a Chinese philosophy expressed about two thousand years ago in the *Dao De Jing*, with Jungian psychology. This goal of wholeness, as expressed in the Circle of Life, or yin and yang symbol of Daoist philosophy, is a recurrent theme in her fiction. The Circle of Life is a diagram of the dynamic relationship between being and nonbeing in the universe. Le Guin celebrates the balancing of such oppositions.

This metaphysic leads to an ethic of passive activity. All acts in the world of being imply their opposites, the assertion of being activating the potential for nonbeing of the end one seeks. Acts of coercion aimed at controlling human behavior are especially prone to produce equal and opposite reactions. Therefore, Le Guin's more successful characters do not try to influence people's actions by direct persuasion or by force but rather by being models of the desired activity.

Courtesy, Allen and Unwin

Le Guin's science fiction differs from her fantasy and psychomyths in that the distinguishing feature of the story's world is technology rather than magic. Her best science-fiction stories accept the unique technology as a given and center on fully realized characters coming to terms with the problems or implications of that technology. "The Eye Altering" recounts the struggle of colonists trying to adjust to a new planet that does not quite mesh with their metabolism, especially the difficulties they encounter when they discover that they are bearing children who, in fact, are better suited to this new planet than to Earth. In "The Diary of the Rose," the psychoscope, a therapeutic tool, allows a form of mind reading. An apprentice analyst confronts the problem of how to treat a patient who seems perfectly sane but who is accused of political deviation. Several of Le Guin's best science-fiction stories became the seeds of later novels or developed in relation to her novels. "Winter's King" led to *The Left Hand of Darkness*. Written after *The Dispossessed*, "The Day Before the Revolution" is about the death of Odo, the woman who founded Odonianism, the anarchist philosophy of Anarres society in *The Dispossessed*. In "The New Atlantis," Le Guin combines psychomyth and science fiction. While a future America sinks into the sea under the weight of political tyranny and ecological sin, a mythical new world awakens and rises from the sea. In each of these stories, the fates of fully realized characters are more central than the science-fiction settings and technology.

Though Le Guin's stories nearly always contain multiple layers of meaning that repay rereading, they are usually also engaging and entertaining on first reading. She interests the reader in her characters or she sets up her problems in images and symbols that stimulate the imagination and lead to speculation. Many of her stories are also witty. Sometimes the wit is broad, as in "The Author of the Acacia Seeds," which tells of efforts to translate the writings of ants. Sometimes, her wit is more subtle, as in "Sur," an account of the "real" first expedition to the South Pole, made by a group of women who kept their feat a secret to avoid embarrassing Roald Amundsen.

This brief account cannot deal with many of Le Guin's themes. She has shown significant interest in feminism and other political and social themes. Her family background in anthropology contributed to her interest in imagining cultures and contact between alien cultures. Over the span of her career, she has tended to move from more traditional forms of fantasy and science fiction toward imagining alternative cultures and their interactions.

"Darkness Box" • Several of these aspects of Le Guin's worldview appear in "Darkness Box," one of her earliest publications. "Darkness Box" is a fairy tale allegory that takes place in a world of cycles. In this world, time does not pass. There is no source of light, though it is always midmorning. Certain events repeat themselves exactly and perpetually. A young prince rides with his army to the seashore to repel an invasion by his rebel brother. The brother always comes from the sea; he is always defeated and killed. At the same time that he leaves, the prince returns to the palace of his father, who exiled the brother. The prince always rides out again with his army to meet the restored and returning invaders. Into this cycle intrudes what appears to be a unique set of events that are sequential rather than cyclical. The son of a witch finds a box on the shore and gives it to the prince. The king recognizes it as a box he cast into the sea and warns the prince not to open it. The prince's longing for music that ends, for wholeness, leads him to knock the box open and restrains him from closing it. Darkness spills out, the darkness of shadows and their opposite, the sun. He begins to experience conflict, death, and the passing of time. Having achieved a shadow, he has entered into time and being.

Read as a Jungian myth of maturation, the tale represents the collective unconscious as a place of unrealized potentials for identity. The prince is a potential ego, his exiled brother a potential shadow, their endless battle a portent of the struggle consciousness must undergo to create a mature personality. Opening the box that lets out darkness becomes a symbolic representation of the birth of the ego, the entrance into time, and self-creation with real consequences for the self, such as the creation of a shadow and the acceptance of mortality.

Read as a Daoist allegory, the tale represents nonbeing, the dark half of the Circle of Life, as a place of unrealized potential for being. Nonbeing is timeless and changeless yet full of possibilities. In this reading, opening the box realizes some of the potentials for being. A real world begins, a world of cause and effect in time, a world bounded by nonbeing as reflected in the introduction of true death. Though not all of Le Guin's stories so directly communicate the Jungian and Daoist aspects of her worldview, many become richer and deeper when viewed in this context.

Le Guin defines fantasy as the manipulation of myths and symbols to communicate with the unconscious. Some of her fantasies she called psychomyths: "more or less surrealistic tales, which share with fantasy the quality of taking place outside any history, outside of time, in that region of the living mind which . . . seems to be without spatial or temporal limits at all."

"The Ones Who Walk Away from Omelas" • "The Ones Who Walk Away from Omelas" is probably Le Guin's best-known psychomyth. This story combines fiction and essay in an unusual way. The narrator describes the beautiful and happy city of Omelas beginning its summer festival. Gradually, she reveals that this is an imagined city. The narrator cautions the reader against doubting that a utopian city filled with joy might also be a place of dynamic and meaningful life. The reader is encouraged to follow his own fancy in imagining a truly happy city. She suggests attitudes toward technology, sexual pleasure, and drug use that would foster happiness, then returns to a description of the festival.

Guessing that the reader will be skeptical even after helping to imagine this wonderful city, she then reveals two more facts. First, the happiness of Omelas depends upon one small child being locked forever in a dark room, deprived of all comfort and affection. Any effort to provide care and justice for that child would destroy the happiness of Omelas. Second, there are people who cannot bear to accept their happiness under this condition. These are the ones who walk away.

Structured as a mutually imagined myth, this story seems designed to provoke examination of the tendencies of human imagination. Why must people find a dark side of beauty in order to believe in it? Why is happiness unimaginable without suffering? How do people manage to find ways of accepting life under these terms? Why are some people unable to accept that living almost inevitably entails gaining from the suffering of others? Although this story is somewhat different in form from her more typical fantasies, it seems to share with them the central aim of fantasy Le Guin described in "The Child and the Shadow": to reduce the reader's inclination "to give up in despair or to deny what he sees, when he must face the evil that is done in the world, and the injustices and grief and suffering that we must all bear, and the final shadow at the end of all."

A Fisherman of the Inland Sea • The importance of imagination in achieving balance continues in *A Fisherman of the Inland Sea*. The volume begins with an eleven-page introduction in which Le Guin dichotomizes readers into "us"—science-fiction readers—and people who cannot or will not program their VCRs, which is how she characterizes those who spurn the genre. She also explains thematic aspects of the eight stories in the collection, the last three of which are space-exploration fantasies that involve imagined cultures and technologies she has previously developed, namely the Hanish world and the ansible. She adds to these a time-space device called a "churten" drive, which allows instantaneous transmission of matter across any points in space.

"The First Contact with the Gorgonids" is a straightforward "justice served" narrative that explains how the much-abused housewife, Annie Laurie Debree, became the hero of Grong Crossing, at the expense of her difficult husband, Jerry. The second story, "Newton's Sleep," explores the psychological impact of an earthwide holocaust on the surviving escapees. "Ascent of the North Face" is predicated on the language pun of the title and rolls out in journal-entry style. "The Rock That Changed Things" depicts the evolutionary dynamic of an oppressed race as it attains autonomy, reminiscent of *The Word for World Is Forest*. The fifth story, "The Kerastion," describes a coherent set of cultural behaviors that involve the production of a musical instrument from human flesh. Taken together, these five stories show Le Guin to be varied in approach and treatment and interested in different subjects.

The trilogy of space stories begins with "The Shobies' Story." The Hanish-Gethenian-Human crew of ten take a test flight using a new "churten" drive. Their noninterval "transilence" to a distant location becomes problematic as they seek to interpret their separate realities. They are able to reintegrate into a unified story of their travel only out of a willingness to achieve group harmony. The next test, described in "Dancing to Ganam," involves a smaller crew of Cetians and Hanish that included Dalzul, a charismatic leader. Their arrival in another world, where they are treated as gods, ends in Dalzul's sacrifice, apparently as a willed conclusion from the collective group. The collection's title story, "Another Story: Or, A Fisherman of the Inland Sea," continues the "churten" theme. The narrator, Hideo, begins with the fable of a fisherman who catches the attention of the sea king's daughter, agrees to stay with her for a night, then finds that more than one hundred years have passed in the short time of his absence. Hideo leaves home and a nascent love interest, Isidri, in order to study temporal physics. Eventually, he becomes disjunct in time, when experimenting with the churten drive, and arrives back at home fifteen years earlier, just after he had decided to leave. Instead, he chooses to stay and follow a different path Hideo then accepts the love of Isidri but wonders what has happened in the temporal paradox of his future.

Terry Heller
With updates by Eunice Pedersen Johnston, Scott Vander Ploeg, and the Editors

Other major works

CHILDREN'S LITERATURE: *The Adventure of Cobbler's Rune*, 1982; *The Visionary*, 1984; *A Visit from Dr. Katz*, 1988; *Catwings*, 1988; *Solomon Leviathan's 931st Trip Around the World*, 1988; *Catwings Return*, 1989; *Fire and Stone*, 1989; *A Ride on the Red Mare's Back*, 1992; *More Tales of the Catwings*, 1994; *Wonderful Alexander and the Catwings*, 1994; *Tales of the Catwings*, 1996; *Tom Mouse and Ms. Howe*, 1998; *Tom Mouse*, 1998; *Jane on Her Own: A Catwings Tale*, 1999; *Gifts*, 2004; *Voices*, 2006.

ANTHOLOGIES: *Norton Book of Science Fiction: North American Science Fiction, 1960-1990*, 1993; *Selected Stories of H. G. Wells*, 2005.

NOVELS: *Planet of Exile*, 1966; *Rocannon's World*, 1966; *City of Illusions*, 1967; *A Wizard of Earthsea*, 1968; *The Left Hand of Darkness*, 1969; *The Lathe of Heaven*, 1971; *The Tombs of Atuan*, 1971; *The Farthest Shore*, 1972; *The Dispossessed: An Ambiguous Utopia*, 1974; *Very Far Away from Anywhere Else*, 1976; *The Eye of the Heron*, 1978; *Leese Webster*, 1979; *Malafrena*, 1979; *The Beginning Place*, 1980; *Always Coming Home*, 1985; *Tehanu: The Last Book of Earthsea*, 1990; *Searoad: Chronicles of Klatsand*, 1991; *Four Ways to Forgiveness*, 1995 (four linked novellas); *The Telling*, 2000; *The Other Wind*, 2001.

NONFICTION: *From Elfland to Poughkeepsie*, 1973; *The Language of the Night: Essays on Fantasy and Science Fiction*, 1979 (Susan Wood, editor); *Dancing at the Edge of the World: Thoughts on Words, Women, and Places*, 1988; *Napa: The Roots and Springs of the Valley*, 1989; *Steering the Craft: Exercises and Discussions on Story Writing for the Lone Navigator or the Mutinous Crew*, 1998; *The Wave in the Mind: Talks and Essays on the Writer, the Reader, and the Imagination*, 2004.

POETRY: *Wild Angels*, 1975; *Hard Words, and Other Poems*, 1981; *In the Red Zone*, 1983; *Wild Oats and Fireweed: New Poems*, 1988; *Blue Moon over Thurman Street*, 1993; *Going Out with Peacocks, and Other Poems*, 1994; *Sixty Odd: New Poems*, 1999; *Incredible Good Fortune: New Poems*, 2006.

TRANSLATIONS: *Tao Te Ching: A Book About the Way and the Power of the Way*, 1997 (of Laozi); *Selected Poems of Gabriela Mistral*, 2003.

Bibliography

Bittner, James W. *Approaches to the Fiction of Ursula K. Le Guin*. Ann Arbor: UMI Research Press, 1984. This author discusses both Le Guin's short stories and her novels, making connections among her works to show how certain themes are apparent in all of them.

Collins, Jerre. "Leaving Omelas: Questions of Faith and Understanding." *Studies in Short Fiction* 27 (Fall, 1990): 525-535. Argues that "The Ones Who Walk Away from Omelas" can be read either as a religious allegory of the "suffering servant" or as an allegory of Western capitalism; however, rejection of the capitalist exploitation story undermines the redemption story. Thus, Le Guin indirectly supports the scapegoat theodicy she tries to undermine.

Cummins, Elizabeth. *Understanding Ursula K. Le Guin.* Columbia: University of South Carolina Press, 1990. Analysis of Le Guin's work emphasizing the different worlds she has created (Earthsea, the Hannish World, Orsinia, and the West Coast) and how they provide the structure for all of her fiction.

De Bolt, Joe, ed. *Ursula K. Le Guin: Voyager to Inner Lands and to Outer Space.* Port Washington, N.Y.: Kennikat Press, 1979. This volume is a collection of critical essays that discusses Le Guin's work from a variety of perspectives, including anthropology, sociology, science, and Daoist philosophy.

Kaler, Anne K. "'Carving in Water': Journey/Journals and the Images of Women's Writings in Ursula Le Guin's 'Sur.'" *Literature, Interpretation, Theory* 7 (1997): 51-62. Claims that Le Guin's story "Sur" provides a cleverly coded map for women striving to be professional writers; to illustrate the paths that women writers must take into the tundras ruled by male writers, she uses the devices of disorder, dislocation, and reversal in the journey/journal.

May, Charles E., ed. *Masterplots II: Short Story Series, Revised Edition.* 8 vols. Pasadena, Calif.: Salem Press, 2004. Designed for student use, this reference set contains articles providing detailed plot summaries and analyses of three short stories by Le Guin: "The Ones Who Walk Away from Omelas" (vol. 5), "Schrödinger's Cat" (vol. 6), and "Sur" (vol. 7).

Reid, Suzanne Elizabeth. *Presenting Ursula K. Le Guin.* New York: Twayne, 1997. This critical biography helps young readers to understand how her childhood, family, and life have helped to shape Le Guin's work.

Rochelle, Warren. *Communities of the Heart: The Rhetoric of Myth in the Fiction of Ursula K. Le Guin.* Liverpool, England: University of Liverpool Press, 2001. Analyzes Le Guin's construction of myth and use of mythological themes in her work.

Walsh, William. "I Am a Woman Writer; I Am a Western Writer: An Interview with Ursula Le Guin." *The Kenyon Review,* n.s. 17 (Summer/Fall, 1995): 192-205. Le Guin discusses such topics as the genre of science fiction, her readership, the feminist movement, women writers, and the Nobel Prize.

White, Donna R. *Dancing with Dragons: Ursula K. Le Guin and the Critics.* Columbia, S.C.: Camden House, 1999. Part of the Studies in English and American Literature, Linguistics, and Culture series, this volume examines Le Guin's works and critical reaction to them.

Doris Lessing

Born: Kermānshāh, Persia (now Bākhtarān, Iran); October 22, 1919

Principal short fiction • *This Was the Old Chief's Country,* 1951; *Five: Short Novels,* 1953; *No Witchcraft for Sale: Stories and Short Novels,* 1956; *The Habit of Loving,* 1957; *A Man and Two Women,* 1963; *African Stories,* 1964; *The Black Madonna,* 1966; *Winter in July,* 1966; *Nine African Stories,* 1968; *The Temptation of Jack Orkney, and Other Stories,* 1972 (also known as *The Story of a Non-Marrying Man, and Other Stories*); *The Sun Between Their Feet: Volume 2 of Doris Lessing's Collected African Stories,* 1973; *This Was the Old Chief's Country: Volume 1 of Doris Lessing's Collected African Stories,* 1973; *Sunrise on the Veld,* 1975; *A Mild Attack of Locusts,* 1977; *Collected Stories,* 1978 (2 volumes; also known as *Stories,* 1978); *London Observed: Stories and Sketches,* 1991 (also known as *The Real Thing: Stories and Sketches,* 1992); *Spies I Have Known, and Other Stories,* 1995; *The Old Age of El Magnifico,* 2000; *The Grandmothers,* 2003.

Other literary forms • In addition to her twenty volumes of short fiction, Doris Lessing's many books include poetry, memoirs, reportage, plays, essays, and reviews. She is best known, however, for her novels, particularly *The Golden Notebook* (1962), and the five-volume Children of Violence series, which includes *Martha Quest* (1952), *A Proper Marriage* (1954), *A Ripple from the Storm* (1958), *Landlocked* (1965), and *The Four-Gated City* (1969). She explored the genre she terms "space fiction" in the volumes *Shikasta* (1979), *The Marriages Between Zones Three, Four, and Five* (1980), *The Sirian Experiments* (1981), *The Making of the Representative for Planet 8* (1982), and *Documents Relating to the Sentimental Agents in the Volyen Empire* (1983), as well as "inner space fiction" in novels such as *Briefing for a Descent into Hell* (1971) and *The Memoirs of a Survivor* (1974). During the mid-1980's, she returned to more realistic fiction, publishing, among others, two novels under the pseudonym Jane Somers. Lessing's latest novels include *Playing the Game* (1995), *Love, Again* (1996), *Mara and Dann* (1999), *Ben, in the World* (2000), *The Sweetest Dream* (2001), *The Story of General Dan and Mara's Daughter, Griot and the Snow Dog* (2005), and *The Cleft* (2007).

Lessing has also written several plays that have been produced; these are collected in *Play with a Tiger, and Other Plays* (1996). Her many nonfiction books include the autobiographical works *Going Home* (1957), *African Laughter: Four Visits to Zimbabwe* (1992), *Under My Skin* (1994), and *Walking in the Shade* (1997). Many of her critical writings have been collected in *Time Bites: Views and Reviews* (2005).

Achievements • Doris Lessing was a finalist for the Booker McConnell Prize for *Briefing for a Descent into Hell, The Sirian Experiments,* and *The Good Terrorist* (1985). She was nominated for the Australian Science-Fiction Achievement Award in 1982 for *The Sirian Experiments. The Good Terrorist* won her the W. H. Smith and Son Literary Award, the Palermo Prize, and the Premio Internazionale Mondello. In 1995 the nonfiction *Under My Skin* (1994) earned the James Tait Black Memorial Prize and the *Los Angeles Times* Book Prize. *Walking in the Shade* received a nomination for the 1997 National Book Critics Award in the biography/autobiography category. Lessing has been a nominee for the Nobel Prize in Literature.

Biography • Born to British parents in Persia, where her father, Alfred Cook Tayler, worked in a bank, Doris May Lessing moved to Southern Rhodesia (now Zimbabwe) in 1925, when she was five. There she lived on a remote farm, south of the Zambezi River. "Our neighbors were four, five, seven miles off. In front of the house . . . no neighbors, nothing; no farms, just wild bush with two rivers but no fences to the mountains seven miles away." In her teens, she moved to a "very small town that had about ten thousand white persons in it. The black population did not count, though it was fairly large." This was the Africa of rigid racial separation; Lessing would later chronicle its horrors.

Ingrid Von Kruse

While still in her teens, Lessing married and had two children. She later married again and, in 1949, left her second husband to go to England, bringing her son with her. The emptiness of the African veld and the life of small African towns are the themes of much of her earlier work, including the early volumes of the Children of Violence series. The scene then shifts in her fiction, as it did in her life, to England, and particularly London.

Lessing was a member of communist groups in both Africa and England. In Africa, she describes the group as "having no contact with any kind of reality. . . . I found this when I came to England and had a short association with the British Communist party." Lessing's disillusionment with the difference between the official Communist Party and the "beautiful purity" of the ideas which lie behind communism is an extremely important theme in her fiction. For many of her characters, disillusionment with the possibility of a political solution to the inequities and horror of modern life, leads them first to madness, suicide, or acquiescence. Later, beginning with *The Four-Gated City*, it leads them to visionary solutions. Once her characters give up politics as a solution, they come more and more to accept the mystic resolutions of the Eastern traditions, especially those of Sufism, an ancient form of Islamic human-centered mysticism. In *Prisons We Choose to Live Inside* (1987), a series of lectures she gave for the Canadian Broadcasting Corporation, she reaffirms her view that the survival of the human race depends on its recognizing its connection to all nature rather than stressing a sense of separation.

In 1995 Lessing returned to Southern Africa to visit her daughter and grandchildren. It was her first return to the region in which she grew up since being forcibly removed in 1956 for her political views. The same year she also received an honorary degree from Harvard University and collaborated with illustrator Charlie Adlard to publish the novel *Playing the Game*. In 1996 she published *Love, Again*, her first novel in seven years. In 1997 *Walking in the Shade*, the second volume of her autobiography, was issued.

Analysis • Doris Lessing engaged in a lifelong process of self-education, becoming involved with all the important intellectual and political movements of the twentieth century: Freudian and Jungian psychology, Marxism, feminism, existentialism, mysticism, sociobiology, and speculative scientific theory. All these interests appear in her fiction, which consequently serves as a record of the changing climate of the times. She has also displayed in her writing an increasing anxiety about humanity's ability to survive.

In Doris Lessing's short fiction, the reader meets characters remarkable for their intelligence, their unceasing analysis of their emotions, and their essential blindness to their true motivations. The people who move through her stories, while very vividly placid in the details of their lives, are in essence types. As Lessing says in her preface to *The Golden Notebook*, they are "so general and representative of the time that they are anonymous, you could put names to them like those in the old Morality Plays." Those whom the reader meets most frequently in the short fiction are Mr. I-am-free-because-I-belong-nowhere, Miss I-must-have-love-and-happiness, Mrs. I-have-to-be-good-at-everything-I-do, Mr. Where-is-a-real-woman, and Ms. Where-is-a-real-man; and there is one final type Lessing names, Mrs. If-we-deal-very-well-with-this-small-problem-then-perhaps-we-can-forget-we-daren't-look-at-the-big-ones. This last type is the character so often met at the beginning of Lessing's stories, the character who has become uneasily aware of a discrepancy between intention and action, between the word and the deed, but who would prefer not to take the analysis too far. Lessing is inexorable, however, and in story after story characters are driven to new, usually unpleasant knowledge about themselves and their motivations. Typically, the stories end with the situation unresolved. The reader sees the awakening but not the translation of new knowledge into action. For Lessing, the jump from dealing very well with small problems to looking at the big ones is the jump from History to Vision and lies beyond the scope of short fiction.

The great obstacle facing Lessing's characters in their movement toward self-knowledge, toward vision, is emotion—particularly romantic love. Lessing sees romantic love as essentially egocentric; people love what they wish to see in the beloved, not what is really there. They love so that they will feel loved in return. They love, in the terms of the title story of one of her collections, from "the habit of loving." This, Lessing insists, is nothing but masochistic self-indulgence. Love robs people of their ability to reason clearly, diverts their energy into useless and potentially harmful channels, causes them to agonize over choices which make, in the end, very little real difference.

Worse, in terms of her visionary philosophy, romantic love, by keeping people focused on the particular, prohibits their making the necessary connections between the individual and the collective consciousness. In story after story, readers watch people live out the same patterns, search for love at all costs, focus on the small problems, the matter at hand: Does he love me? Readers watch them try to believe that this is fundamentally what matters, that there is meaning in the small patterns of their lives. Lessing would deny that this is so. There is meaning, she seems to say, but it lies beyond these insignificant details. One must break through them, destroy them, in order to find it.

Some of her characters, although by no means all, do so. Anna Wulf, the writer-heroine of *The Golden Notebook*, succeeds in first dismantling the old patterns and then in synthesizing new ones, as does the anonymous narrator of "How I Finally Lost My Heart."

"How I Finally Lost My Heart" • An uncharacteristic story in its resemblance to fable, "How I Finally Lost My Heart" is fascinating in its diagrammatic exposition of Lessing's views on romantic love. The story opens as the unnamed "I," a woman, is awaiting the arrival of her escort for the evening, a man designated only as C. The narrator explains that C is the third "serious" love of her life, the first two being A and B. Earlier in the day, the speaker has had lunch with A and tea with B and is pleased that she has been able to enjoy their company with equanimity; she is, finally, "out of love" with them. Recognizing her sensation at this discovery as one of relief, the speaker begins to question her exhilaration at the thought of spending the evening with C, "because there was no doubt that both A and B had caused me unbelievable pain. Why, therefore, was I looking forward to C? I should rather be running away as fast as I could."

The narrator's questioning leads her to a new recognition of what lies behind the human desire to be "in love." It is not, she concludes, that "one needs a person who, like a saucer of water, allows one to float off on him/her, like a transfer." It is not, then, that one needs to "lose one's heart" by blending with another. Rather, "one carries with one a sort of burning spear stuck in one's side, that one waits for someone else to pull out; it is something painful, like a sore or a wound, that one cannot wait to share with someone else." One needs to "lose one's heart" literally, to get rid of it by giving it to someone else. The catch is that we are expected to take their heart in return. Lessing envisages a grotesque sort of barter, two people demanding of each other, "take my wound."

Moving to the telephone to call C and suggest that they agree to keep their hearts to themselves, the speaker is forced to hang up the phone:

> For I felt the fingers of my left hand push outwards around something rather large, light and slippery—hard to describe this sensation, really. My hand is not large, and my heart was in a state of inflation after having had lunch with A, tea with B, and then looking forward to C. . . . Anyway, my fingers were stretching out rather desperately to encompass an unknown, largish, lightish object, and I said: Excuse me a minute to C, looked down, and there was my heart, in my hand.

There her heart stays, attached to her hand, for four days, growing to the flesh of her palm. She cannot remove it by any "act of will or intention of desire," but when, distracted by events outside her window, she temporarily forgets herself, she feels it begin to loosen. One can "lose one's heart" only by forgetting about it, but it is still attached, and who is one to give it to?

She has previously covered the heart with aluminum foil, in part because it is messy and in part because, unaccustomed to the air, "it smarts." Now wrapping a scarf around her hand, heart and all, she walks about London, finally taking a train on the underground. In the train, she sits across from a woman maddened by love, who ceaselessly, jerkily, accuses her lover or husband of giving his mistress a gold cigarette case. The woman is on the verge of total breakdown, of lapsing into total immobility and, watching her, the narrator forgets herself. She feels the heart loosen from her hand, plucks it off and gives it to the mad woman:

> For a moment she did not react, then with a groan or a mutter of relieved and entirely theatrical grief, she leaned forward, picked up the glittering heart, and clutched it in her arms.

The woman has "taken heart"; she now has the energy of the heart and the "theatrical" grief it brings with it. She can once again play love as a game, insisting that her husband or lover "take her wound." The narrator, finally, is free. "No heart. No heart at all. What bliss. What freedom."

"How I Finally Lost My Heart," although uncharacteristic in its style, can serve as a paradigm for most of Lessing's stories on the relations between men and women. It is valuable because it points out so clearly her vision that the important choice is not among A and B and C, but it is rather the choice of freedom or bondage. If people choose freedom and break out of the patterns of romantic love, they are then able to see clearly and can move on to new ways of loving. This will necessitate new forms of the family, which Lessing sees, in its traditional structure, as the institutionalized destruction of its individual members. If, however, they remain convinced that the important choice is that of who to love, not how to love, they remain in delusion.

"A Man and Two Women" • This same lesson is exemplified in the more traditional story "A Man and Two Women," one of Lessing's many explorations of the strains and restrictions of marriage. The plot is simple: Two couples, good friends, arrange to spend some time together in a country cottage. The couple who own the cottage, Dorothy and Jack, have recently had a baby. Of the visiting couple, Stella and Paul, only Stella is actually able to come. The story is impressive in its precise delineation of the relationships among the members of the quartet and in its explorations of Dorothy's languor and withdrawal after childbirth. The real excitement, however, lies in Stella's slow examination of her own marriage in light of the situation she finds between Jack and Dorothy. Both marriages are perceived by the couples to be extraordinary in their strength and exuberance, yet both are strained. The connection between Jack and Dorothy is threatened by the strength of Dorothy's attachment to her new son. Also, Stella realizes that her connection with Paul has been more strained by their occasional infidelities than she has realized.

In the final scene, Jack begins to make love to Stella, something Dorothy has goaded him into, declaring that she does not care what he does; he has become insignificant to her. At first, Stella responds:

> She thought: What is going to happen now will blow Dorothy and Jack and that baby sky-high; it's the end of my marriage. I'm going to blow everything to bits. There was almost uncontrollable pleasure in it.

Remembering the baby, however, she pulls back and waits for Jack to drive her to the station, making the final comment "It really was a lovely night"—a mundane comment for a return to the usual.

Using the paradigm of "How I Finally Lost My Heart," readers see that the story ends with Stella's struggle over choosing A or B, Jack or Paul, and with her desire to abandon herself to love. "There was almost uncontrollable pleasure in it." She agonizes only over whom she will ask to "take my wound." Although she perceives that both her marriage and Jack's marriage are failures, she leaves with her heart in her hand, carrying it back to Paul. She sees more clearly than she did at the opening of the story, but she is not yet able to act on her perceptions. She has not yet lost her heart.

"A Man and Two Women" ends, then, in ambiguity but not in pessimism. Stella may not yet be able to act on her perceptions, but she is admirable in her willingness to reexamine her life. Readers should consider emulating her. They are left not with a blueprint for action but with feelings and emotions that must be examined. It is typical of Lessing's short fiction that they, like Stella, are awakened to reality and then are left to take their own directions.

"The New Café" • In her collection *The Real Thing: Stories and Sketches,* Lessing offers glimpses of life in her hometown of London in the 1980's, played out in a series of everyday human experiences. As usual, Lessing's stories on a surface level are simple enough, common to even the most detached observer of urban life. However, her aim is much deeper, as demonstrated in "The New Café," the story of a woman entranced by the conduct of a fellow customer who appears at once distant and interested in his flirtatious banter with female acquaintances, but whose charms suddenly disappear during a mysterious encounter with a young mother and her child on a London street. In recalling the story, Lessing's narrator notes:

> here, as in all good cafés, may be observed real-life soap operas, to be defined as series of emotional events that are certainly not unfamiliar, since you are bound to have seen something like them before, but to which you lack the key that will make them not trite, but shockingly individual.

"Sparrows" • With "Sparrows," set again in a café, the trite once more becomes the profound, as a series of diners react to a family of sparrows who persist in feeding off scraps of food thrown by guests or left at tables. The seemingly innocuous behavior of the birds elicits reactions ranging from outright indifference to the intrigue expressed by members of one family who see in the sparrows' actions a lesson that applies to their own personal situations.

"Casualty" • In "Casualty" matters of life and death are clearly distinguished, as Lessing relates the tale of a group of hospital emergency room patients and their reactions not only to their own plights but also to the hysterics of an elderly woman who feels her condition warrants immediate attention, despite being deemed minor by the head nurse. Only when a critically injured young workman is rushed into the room do the others give pause to their situations, and then only temporarily in the case of the older woman, who appears to the reader to be a casualty of another kind.

"Storms" • Lessing's love of London comes through clearly in "Storms," the story of a woman's encounter with a cranky old taxi driver with whom she is paired upon her return from a visit to Frankfurt. Adding to the driver's dim disposition is the debris covering the streets through which he is attempting to maneuver following an overnight storm. With each compliment the woman expresses for her hometown on the drive back, the driver immediately counters with an invective. By journey's end the woman comes to the realization that the litany of complaints she was hearing was born of sorrow, not of age.

"Two Old Women and a Young One" • "Two Old Women and a Young One" explores the seemingly unlimited capacity of people to deal in delusional thoughts, particularly when engaged in social intercourse with the opposite sex. Beginning with the two women of the title who grossly misinterpret the charms of their young male host at a business luncheon, to the host himself, who later mistakes the attentions of an attractive young woman at the same affair, there is little but empty rhetoric. The conversations reflect neither the personal needs nor the identities necessary to building a human connection. It is a rampant self-absorption that inflicts many of Lessing's characters throughout her work, no matter the setting.

Mary Baron
With updates by Mary LeDonne Cassidy, William Hoffman, and the Editors

Other major works

PLAYS: *Each His Own Wilderness*, pr. 1958; *Play with a Tiger*, pr., pb. 1962; *Making of the Representative for Planet 8*, pr. 1988 (libretto); *Play with a Tiger, and Other Plays*, pb. 1996.

NOVELS: *The Grass Is Singing*, 1950; *Martha Quest*, 1952; *A Proper Marriage*, 1954; *Retreat to Innocence*, 1956; *A Ripple from the Storm*, 1958; *The Golden Notebook*, 1962; *Landlocked*, 1965, 1991; *The Four-Gated City*, 1969; *Briefing for a Descent into Hell*, 1971; *The Summer Before the Dark*, 1973; *The Memoirs of a Survivor*, 1974; *Shikasta*, 1979 (also known as *Re: Colonized Planet 5, Shikasta*); *The Marriages Between Zones Three, Four, and Five*, 1980; *The Sirian Experiments*, 1981; *The Making of the Representative for Planet 8*, 1982; *Documents Relating to the Sentimental Agents in the Volyen Empire*, 1983; *The Diary of a Good Neighbour*, 1983 (as Jane Somers); *If the Old Could . . .*, 1984 (as Jane Somers); *The Diaries of Jane Somers*, 1984 (includes *The Diary of a Good Neighbour* and *If the Old Could . . .*); *The Good Terrorist*, 1985; *The Fifth Child*, 1988; *Canopus in Argos: Archives*, 1992 (5 novel cycle includes *Re: Colonized Planet 5, Shikasta, The Marriages Between Zones Three, Four, and Five, The Sirian Experiments, The Making of the Representative for Planet 8*, and *Documents Relating to the Sentimental Agents in the Volyen Empire*); *Playing the Game*, 1995; *Love, Again*, 1996; *Mara and Dann*, 1999; *Ben, in the World*, 2000; *The Sweetest Dream*, 2001; *The Story of General Dan and Mara's Daughter, Griot and the Snow Dog*, 2005; *The Cleft*, 2007.

MISCELLANEOUS: *The Doris Lessing Reader*, 1988 (selections).

NONFICTION: *Going Home*, 1957; *In Pursuit of the English: A Documentary*, 1960; *Particularly Cats*, 1967; *A Small Personal Voice*, 1974; *Prisons We Choose to Live Inside*, 1987; *The Wind Blows Away Our Words*, 1987; *African Laughter: Four Visits to Zimbabwe*, 1992; *A Small Personal Voice: Essays, Reviews, Interviews*, 1994; *Doris Lessing: Conversations*, 1994 (also known as *Putting the Questions Differently: Interviews with Doris Lessing, 1964-1994*, 1996); *Shadows on the Wall of the Cave*, 1994; *Under My Skin*, 1994 (autobiography); *Walking in the Shade*, 1997 (autobiography); *Time Bites: Views and Reviews*, 2005.

POETRY: *Fourteen Poems*, 1959.

Bibliography

Butcher, Margaret. "'Two Forks of a Road': Divergence and Convergence in the Short Stories of Doris Lessing." *Modern Fiction Studies* 26 (1980): 55-61. Asserts that "Homage to Isaac Babel" provides a rebuttal that Lessing's later stories move away from her earlier larger concerns with moral and political issues and retreat into a feminine world of social satire. In her appreciation of Babel's detachment and control, Lessing has at last learned that mannerism and a directness in writing are neither mutually exclusive nor antithetical.

Fishburn, Katherine. *The Unexpected Universe of Doris Lessing: A Study in Narrative Technique*. Westport, Conn.: Greenwood Press, 1985. This study considers Lessing's science fiction from *Briefing for a Descent into Hell* through the Canopus in Argos series. It argues that the science fiction has the purpose of transforming reality and involving the reader in ideas and the intricacies of the texts rather than in characterization. Fishburn also published *Doris Lessing: Life, Work, and Criticism* (Fredericton, New Brunswick, Canada: York Press, 1987), which provides a brief overview of Lessing's life and works, including literary biography, critical response, and an annotated bibliography.

Greene, Gayle. *Doris Lessing: The Poetics of Change*. Ann Arbor: University of Michigan Press, 1997. Greene centers this study on how Lessing's novels are concerned with change. Several different critical approaches to Lessing's works, including Marxist, feminist, and Jungian, are included in the study.

Halisky, Linda H. "Redeeming the Irrational: The Inexplicable Heroines of 'A Sorrowful Woman' and 'To Room Nineteen.'" *Studies in Short Fiction* 27 (Winter, 1990): 45-54. Discusses the inexplicable behavior of the protagonist of Lessing's story by comparing it to Gail Godwin's "A Sorrowful Woman." Argues that the heroine of "To Room Nineteen" is inexplicable only if one is locked into a belief that reason is the only integrating, sense-making force. Discusses the redemptive force of mythic truth in the story.

Klein, Carole. *Doris Lessing: A Biography*. New York: Carroll & Graf, 2000. Unauthorized biography that nonetheless draws on extensive interviews with Lessing's friends and colleagues. Klein draws many connections between events in Lessing's life and episodes in her novels.

May, Charles E., ed. *Masterplots II: Short Story Series, Revised Edition*. 8 vols. Pasadena, Calif.: Salem Press, 2004. Designed for student use, this reference set contains articles providing detailed plot summaries and analyses of six short stories by Lessing: "The Day Stalin Died" (vol. 2), "Homage for Isaac Babel" (vol. 3), "How I Finally Lost My Heart" (vol. 4), "Mrs. Fortescue" (vol. 5), "To Room Nineteen" (vol. 7), and "A Woman on a Roof" (vol. 8).

Perrakis, Phyllis Sternberg. *Spiritual Exploration in the Works of Doris Lessing*. Westport, Conn.: Greenwood Press, 1999. Interesting collection of essays that look at spiritual themes in Lessing's work, touching on both the realistic and the science-fiction novels.

Pickering, Jean. *Understanding Doris Lessing*. Columbia: University of South Carolina Press, 1990. Brief, clear overview of Lessing's work. Begins with a chapter providing a biographical and analytical look at Lessing's career, then continues with a short but sharp analysis of her fiction through *The Fifth Child* (1988). Includes an index and an annotated bibliography of books and articles about Lessing.

Tyler, Lisa. "Our Mothers' Gardens: Doris Lessing's 'Among the Roses.'" *Studies in Short Fiction* 31 (Spring, 1994): 163-173. Examines the mother-daughter relationship in Lessing's short story "Among the Roses"; argues that the breach between mother and daughter suggests a division between two worlds—one of female community and another of heterosexuality.

Yelin, Louise. *From the Margins of Empire: Christina Stead, Doris Lessing, Nadine Gordimer*. Ithaca, N.Y.: Cornell University Press, 1998. The section on Lessing focuses on the process of her "Englishing" after leaving Rhodesia.

Jack London

Born: San Francisco, California; January 12, 1876
Died: Glen Ellen, California; November 22, 1916

Principal short fiction • *The Son of the Wolf*, 1900; *The God of His Fathers, and Other Stories*, 1901; *Children of the Frost*, 1902; *The Faith of Men, and Other Stories*, 1904; *Love of Life, and Other Stories*, 1906; *Moon-Face, and Other Stories*, 1906; *Lost Face*, 1910; *South Sea Tales*, 1911; *When God Laughs, and Other Stories*, 1911; *A Son of the Sun*, 1912; *Smoke Bellew Tales*, 1912; *The House of Pride, and Other Tales of Hawaii*, 1912; *The Night-Born*, 1913; *The Strength of the Strong*, 1914; *The Turtles of Tasman*, 1916; *The Human Drift*, 1917; *The Red One*, 1918; *On the Makaloa Mat*, 1919; *Dutch Courage, and Other Stories*, 1922.

Other literary forms • Jack London's more than fifty published books include plays, children's fiction, novels, sociological studies, essays, and short stories. Although generally known as a writer of short fiction, London is remembered also for two novels, *The Call of the Wild* (1903) and *The Sea-Wolf* (1904), both of which have been made into motion pictures several times. London is also credited with pioneering work in the development of tramp fiction (*The Road*, 1907) and science fiction (*The Star Rover*, 1915).

Achievements • Jack London's numerous stories and his many novels capture with a bold and sometimes brutal reality the confrontation between humans and nature, which by some writers may easily have been portrayed romantically. Instead, London was at the forefront of the move toward naturalistic fiction and realism. He was influenced by social Darwinism, and his stories often reflect the idea that human beings, to survive, must adapt to nature yet are themselves creatures of nature, subject to forces they do not really understand. London was also interested in Marxism, and his work often employs a working-class hero.

London's realistic stories were very popular in the United States when they were first published and continue to be so. He has also achieved wide popularity abroad, with his work being translated into more than fifty languages. His stories in the naturalistic mode continue to influence writers.

Biography • Largely self-educated, Jack London was the product of California ranches and the working-class neighborhoods of Oakland. London's rise to fame came as a result of the Klondike Gold Rush. Unsuccessful in his attempt to break into the magazine market, he joined the flood of men rushing to make instant riches in the Yukon. Although he found little gold, he returned after the winter of 1897 with a wealth of memories and notes of the Northland, the gold rush, and the hardships of the trail. London married Elizabeth May Maddern in 1900, and the couple settled in Oakland, soon adding two daughters to the family. The marriage, however, was not successful, and London divorced his wife in 1905 and married Charmian Kittredge the same year. With Charmian, he sailed across the Pacific aboard a small yacht, intending to continue around the world on a seven-year voyage. The trip ended in Australia, however, when ill health forced London to abandon the voyage after only two years. London's last years were spent in the construction of a scientifically run ranch complex in Glen Ellen, Sonoma County, California. It was there that he died at the age of forty, on November 22, 1916. His death still has not been satisfactorily explained.

Analysis • Jack London's fame as a writer came about largely through his ability to interpret realistically humans' struggle in a hostile environment. Early in his career, London realized that he had no talent for invention and that in his writing he would have to be an interpreter of the things that are rather than a creator of the things that might be. Accordingly, he turned to the Canadian Northland, the locale where he had gained experience, for his settings and characters. Later on he would move his setting to the primitive South Seas, after his travels had also made him familiar with that re-

Library of Congress

gion. By turning to harsh, frontier environment for his setting and themes, London soon came to be a strong voice heard over the genteel tradition of nineteenth century parlor-fiction writers. His stories became like the men and women about whom he wrote—bold, violent, sometimes primitive. London was able to give his stories greater depth by using his extraordinary powers of narrative and language, and by infusing them with a remarkable sense of irony.

"To Build a Fire" • "To Build a Fire" has often been called London's masterpiece. It is a story which contrasts the intelligence of human beings with the intuition of the animal and suggests that humans alone cannot successfully face the harsh realities of nature. The story begins at dawn as a man and his dog walk along a trail which eventually could lead them, thirty-two miles away, to a companion's cabin and safety. The air is colder than the man has experienced before, and although the man does not know about the cold, the dog does. Although the animal instinctively realizes that it is time to curl up in the snow and wait for warmer weather, the man lacks the imagination which would give him a grasp of the laws of nature. Such perception would have enabled him to see the absurdity of attempting to combat the unknown, especially since an old-timer had warned him about the dangers of the cold to inexperienced men. With his warm mittens, thick clothes, and heavy coat, the man feels prepared for the cold and protected while the dog longs for the warmth of a fire. As the man walks along the trail, he looks carefully for hidden traps of nature, springs under the snow beneath which pools of water lie, since to step into one of these pools would mean calamity. Once he forces the dog to act as a trail breaker for him, and, when the dog breaks through and ice immediately forms on its extremities, the man helps the dog remove the ice.

At midday the man stops, builds a fire, and eats his lunch. The dog, without knowing why, feels relieved; he is safe. The man, however, does not stay beside the fire; he continues on the trail and forces the dog onward too. Finally, almost inevitably, the man's feet become wet. Although he builds a fire to dry out, snow puts out the fire, and before he can build another fire, the cold envelops him, and he freezes to death. The dog senses the man's death and continues on the trail toward the cabin, wherein lies food and the warmth of a fire.

The irony of the story is that the man, even with the benefit of all the tools with which civilization has provided him, fails in his attempt to conquer nature and instead falls victim to it, while the dog, equipped only with the instinct which nature has provided, survives. The story, representing London's most mature expression of pessimism, stresses the inability of human beings to shape their environment and conquer the unknown. Unlike the dog, they cannot draw from instinct since civilization has deprived them of it. They are therefore unfit and totally unequipped to face the unknown and conquer the cosmic power.

"Law of Life" • "Law of Life" exhibits another recurring theme in London's work, the inability of humans to assert positive values. It tells the story of the last moments of life for an old Native American. As the tale begins, the old man, son of the chief of the tribe, sits by a small fire with a bundle of wood nearby. The tribesmen are busy breaking camp in preparation for departure since they must go to new hunting grounds in order to survive. The old man, too old to benefit the tribe further, represents only a burden to the rest of his society and must therefore stay behind. As the man sits beside the fire, he remembers the days of his youth and an incident when he tracked an old moose. The animal had become separated from the rest of the herd and was being trailed by wolves. Twice the young Native American had come across the scene of a struggle between the moose and the wolves, and twice the moose had survived. Finally, the Native American witnessed the kill, the old moose dying so that the wolves might live. The moose-wolf analogy to the old Native American's situation is obvious, and as the story closes, the old Native American feels the muzzle of a wolf upon his cheek. At first he picks up a burning ember in preparation for battle, but then resigns himself to the inevitability of fate and extinguishes it.

London uses several vehicles to express his pessimism. Like the protagonist in "To Build a Fire," the old Native American is a man of limited vision. Encircled by an ever-constricting set of circumstances, he waits by a dying fire for his own death. Finally, as the moose-wolf analogy has foretold, the inevitability of nature dominates. As the story ends, the fire goes out, the wolves are no longer kept at bay, and the reader is left repulsed by the knowledge of the Native American's horrible death. London employs a number of symbols in this story as well. The fire gives light which symbolizes life, as does the white snow which falls gently at the beginning of the story. As the fire ebbs, the man remembers the grey wolves, and at the end of the moose-wolf analogy, London writes of the dark point in the midst of the stamped snow, foretelling the end of the fire, and thus of life.

Although London's earlier stories embody a pessimism which reflects humans' helplessness in challenging the unknown, his later ones mark a dramatic change-over. Following an intensive study of Carl Jung and Sigmund Freud, London began writing stories in the last years of his life which reflected his discovery of some unique human quality that enabled humans to challenge successfully the cosmos and withstand the crushing forces of nature. One of London's last stories, also with a Northland setting, reflects this change of philosophy and contrasts markedly with the earlier "To Build a Fire" and "Law of Life."

"Like Argus of Ancient Times" • "Like Argus of Ancient Times" begins as a largely autobiographical account of London's trek to Dawson City with a man known as "Old Man" or "John" Tarwater. Unlike the unnamed protagonist of "To Build a Fire," Tarwater is totally unequipped to face the rigors and challenges of the north. He is old and weak; furthermore, he arrives on the trail without money, camping gear, food, and proper clothing. Somehow he manages to join a group of miners, serve as their cook, and earn his passage to Dawson. Although the winter snows force the group to make camp until spring, Tarwater (who is also called "Old Hero" and "Father Christmas") is driven by gold fever. He strikes out on his own, gets lost in a snowstorm, and falls to the ground, drifting off into a dreamlike world between consciousness and unconsciousness. Unlike London's earlier characters, Tarwater survives this confrontation with nature, awakens from his dream, turns toward the "rebirthing east," and discovers a treasure of gold in the ground. Couched in Jungian terms, the story is directly analogous to the Jungian concepts of the wandering hero who, undertaking a dangerous night journey in search of treasure difficult to attain, faces death, reaches the highest pinnacle of life, and emerges in the East, reborn. "Like Argus of Ancient Times" marks London's return to the many stories he wrote in which the hero feels the call of adventure, encounters difficulties and confronts nature, battles with death, and finally achieves dignity.

Often called the successor to Edgar Allan Poe, an imitator of Rudyard Kipling, or a leader of writers emerging from the nineteenth century, London wrote stories which mark the conflict between the primitive and the modern, between optimism and pessimism. He created fiction which combined actuality and ideals, realism and romance, and rational versus subjective responses to life. More than a new Poe, imitator of Kipling, or new genre writer, however, London is a legitimate folk hero whose greatness stems from his primordial vision and ability to center upon the fundamental human struggles for salvation and fears of damnation.

David Mike Hamilton
With updates by Karen M. Cleveland Marwick

Other major works

CHILDREN'S LITERATURE: *The Cruise of the Dazzler,* 1902; *Tales of the Fish Patrol,* 1905.

PLAYS: *Scorn of Women,* pb. 1906; *Theft,* pb. 1910; *The Acorn-Planter,* pb. 1916; *The Plays of Jack London,* pb. 2001.

NOVELS: *A Daughter of the Snows,* 1902; *The Call of the Wild,* 1903; *The Sea-Wolf,* 1904; *The Game,* 1905; *Before Adam,* 1906; *White Fang,* 1906; *The Iron Heel,* 1907; *Martin Eden,* 1908; *Burning Daylight,* 1910; *Adventure,* 1911; *The Abysmal Brute,* 1913; *The Valley of the Moon,* 1913; *The Mutiny of the Elsinore,* 1914; *The Scarlet Plague,* 1915; *The Star Rover,* 1915; *The Little Lady of the Big House,* 1916; *Jerry of the Islands,* 1917; *Michael, Brother of Jerry,* 1917; *Hearts of Three,* 1920; *The Assassination Bureau, Ltd.,* 1963 (completed by Robert L. Fish).

NONFICTION: *The Kempton-Wace Letters,* 1903 (with Anna Strunsky); *The People of the Abyss,* 1903; *The War of the Classes,* 1905; *The Road,* 1907; *Revolution, and Other Essays,* 1910; *The Cruise of the Snark,* 1911; *John Barleycorn,* 1913; *Letters from Jack London,* 1965 (King Hendricks and Irving Shepard, editors); *No Mentor but Myself: Jack London on*

Writers and Writing, 1979, revised and expanded, 1999 (Dale L. Walker and Jeanne Campbell Reesman, editors).

Bibliography

Auerbach, Jonathan. *Male Call: Becoming Jack London.* Durham, N.C.: Duke University Press, 1996. Auerbach reverses the trend of earlier London studies, emphasizing how London used his writing to reinvent himself. Above all, Auerbach argues, London wanted to become a successful author, and in that respect he shaped his life to suit his art. Includes detailed notes but no bibliography.

Cassuto, Leonard, and Jeanne Campbell Reesman, eds. *Rereading Jack London.* Stanford, Calif.: Stanford University Press, 1996. Essays on London as "representative man," his commitment to authorship, his portrayal of American imperialism, his handling of power, gender, and ideological discourse, his relationship to social Darwinism, and his status as writer/hero. Includes end notes, but no bibliography.

Furer, Andrew J. "Jack London's New Women: A Little Lady with a Big Stick." *Studies in American Fiction* 22 (Autumn, 1994): 185-214. Discusses London's representation of "new womanhood" that emphasizes physical power and capability and an economic and intellectual independence, but is nonetheless feminine and heterosexual.

Howard, Ronald W. "A Piece of Steak." In *Masterplots II: Short Story Series,* edited by Charles E. May. Rev. ed. Vol. 6. Pasadena, Calif.: Salem Press, 2004. Analysis of "A Piece of Steak" with sections on themes and meaning and style and technique. Also includes a detailed synopsis of the story.

Kershaw, Alex. *Jack London: A Life.* New York: St. Martin's Press, 1997. Concentrates on the "powerful drama" of London's life. Includes notes, illustrations, bibliography, and several helpful maps.

Labor, Earle, and Jeanne Campbell Reesman. *Jack London.* Rev. ed. New York: Twayne, 1994. This clear introduction, first published in 1974, takes into account the twenty years of scholarship after the volume first appeared. This volume also takes issue with the widespread belief that the quality of London's work declined in the last decade of his life. Includes chronology, notes, and an annotated bibliography.

McClintock, James I. *White Logic: Jack London's Short Stories.* Grand Rapids, Mich.: Wolf House Books, 1975. McClintock's work is the only one to focus solely on London's short stories. He provides a detailed analysis of the stories in a clear and useful way.

Reesman, Jeanne Campbell. "'Never Travel Alone': Naturalism, Jack London, and the White Silence." *American Literary Realism* 29 (Winter, 1997): 33-49. Argues that even in London's most naturalistic stories, readers find the search for spirit, the desire for community, and the need to address the Other. Provides a detailed analysis of "To Build a Fire" to illustrate these concepts.

Stefoff, Rebecca. *Jack London: An American Original.* New York: Oxford University Press, 2002. Examines the life, beliefs, adventures, and works of London. Three-page bibliography and index.

Welsh, James M. "To Build a Fire." In *Masterplots II: Short Story Series,* edited by Charles E. May. Rev. ed. Vol. 7. Pasadena, Calif.: Salem Press, 2004. Student-friendly analysis of "To Build a Fire" that covers the story's themes and style and includes a detailed synopsis.

Carson McCullers

Born: Columbus, Georgia; February 19, 1917
Died: Nyack, New York; September 29, 1967

Principal short fiction • *The Ballad of the Sad Café: The Novels and Stories of Carson McCullers*, 1951; *The Ballad of the Sad Café and Collected Short Stories*, 1952, 1955; *The Shorter Novels and Stories of Carson McCullers*, 1972.

Other literary forms • Carson McCullers's remarkable first novel, *The Heart Is a Lonely Hunter* (1940), establishes the themes that were to concern her in all her other writing: the spiritual isolation of individuals and their attempt to transcend loneliness through love. Thereafter, she wrote short stories, some poetry (mostly for children), three other novels, and two plays. The most popular of the novels, *The Member of the Wedding* (1946), she adapted for the stage; the play was a great success on Broadway and was also made into an award-winning film. *The Heart Is a Lonely Hunter* and her somber Freudian novel, *Reflections in a Golden Eye* (1941), were also adapted for film. McCullers also wrote a number of significant essays, which are collected in *The Mortgaged Heart* (1971). The essays that are most important to understanding the method and content of her fiction, especially her use of the grotesque, are "The Russian Realists and Southern Literature" and "The Flowering Dream: Notes on Writing." Her unfinished autobiography was published in 1999.

Achievements • Carson McCullers was the winner of a number of literary awards during her lifetime, including membership in the National Institute of Arts and Letters, two John Simon Guggenheim Memorial Foundation Fellowships, and an Arts and Letters Grant. She also won the New York Drama Critics Circle Award, a Gold Medal, and the Donaldson Award (all for the play version of *The Member of the Wedding*). Her fiction and nonfiction works were published in a number of reputable magazines, including *The New Yorker, Harper's Bazaar, Esquire*, and *Mademoiselle*. For her story "A Tree. A Rock. A Cloud," she was nominated for an O. Henry Award.

A praiseworthy writer of short fiction, McCullers succeeds with objective narration, the theme of loneliness, and her lyric compression. Although McCullers is perhaps not as great a writer of short stories as her peers Flannery O'Connor, Eudora Welty, and Katherine Anne Porter, she is nevertheless successful at affecting her readers' emotions. The brevity and compression of stories such as "The Jockey" and "The Sojourner" are remarkable based on any standards. Although her techniques are not as innovative as those of many other postmodern fiction writers, she influenced, among others, Truman Capote, Flannery O'Connor, and Anne Tyler, particularly with the expert use of the grotesque and the freakish, and the portrayal of human alienation. Her knowledge of human psychology also makes her a great spokesperson for the complexity of human experience.

Biography • Carson McCullers, born Lula Carson Smith, was reared in a small southern town, a milieu that she used in much of her fiction. Exhibiting early talent in both writing and music, she intended to become a concert pianist but lost her tui-

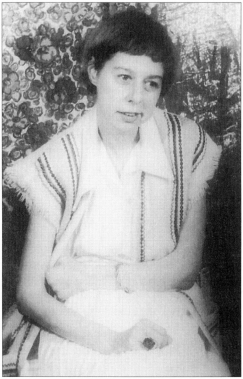

Library of Congress

tion money for the Juilliard School of Music when she went to New York in 1935. This loss led her to get part-time jobs while studying writing at Columbia University. She earned early acclaim for her first novel, *The Heart Is a Lonely Hunter,* written when she was only twenty-two. Her friends included many prominent writers, including Tennessee Williams, W. H. Auden, Louis MacNeice, and Richard Wright. Her health was always delicate; she suffered early paralyzing strokes, breast cancer, and pneumonia. She stayed remarkably active in literature and drama, however, even when confined to bed and wheelchair. She died of a stroke at the age of fifty.

Analysis • Carson McCullers's short stories (ruling out for the moment the novella *The Ballad of the Sad Café,* 1943, serial; 1951, book) often explore the intense emotional content of seemingly undramatic situations. Plot is minimal, although there is often at least one unusual or grotesque element. "Wunderkind," for example, deals with the confused feelings of a gifted fifteen-year-old girl at a piano lesson. Her social development has been sacrificed to her musical talent; now her mastery of the keyboard is faltering, and she is profoundly humiliated. The reader realizes that part of her difficulty is the awakening of sexual feelings for her teacher, Mister Bilderbach. Neither the teacher, who thinks of her as a child prodigy, nor the young girl herself understands her tension and clumsiness.

"The Jockey" • "The Jockey" describes an even more ordinary situation—a brief encounter in a restaurant between a jockey and three other men identified as a trainer, a bookie, and a rich man whose horse the jockey has ridden. The dwarflike jockey, called Bitsy Barlow, is one of those grotesque figures who seem an embarrassing mistake in nature. The point of the story is the ironic contrast between the three "normal" men's callous pretense of sympathy for a rider's crippling accident on the track and the jockey's bitter grief for that rider, who is his closest friend. Although the jockey, because of his physical deformity, seems a caricature of humanity, the intensity of his sorrow makes the other men's callousness seem the more monstrous.

"Madame Zilensky and the King of Finland" • "Madame Zilensky and the King of Finland" is, on the most obvious level, at least, a revelation of the emotional price of artistic excellence. Like "Wunderkind" and "The Jockey," the story concerns the subjective significance of seemingly minor events. Mr. Brook, head of a college music department, hires Madame Zilensky, a famous composer and teacher, for his faculty. He is tolerant of her several eccentricities, her tales of adventures in exotic places, and even her somewhat shocking assertion that her three sons are the offspring of three different lovers. When she claims to have seen the King of Finland, however, Mr. Brook realizes that she is a pathological liar, since Finland has no king. Mr. Brook is sensitive enough to intuit the motive for her prevarications: the terrible constriction of her actual experience. "Through her lies, she lived vicariously. The lies doubled the little of her existence that was left over from work and augmented the little rag end of her personal life."

Point of view is vital in this story. The pathetic emotional dependence of Madame Zilensky on fantasy is the explicit and obvious content, but the story's real focus is on the growing perception of Mr. Brook, who has himself led a somewhat dull, repetitive life in academia. It is his character which receives the more subtle delineation. He represents those countless ordinary people whose individuality has been subdued, but not utterly extinguished, by professional duties. When Mr. Brook, in his official capacity, feels he must reprimand Madame Zilensky for propagating lies about herself, he comes face to face with stark tragedy. The terrible emotional deprivation he is about to expose echoes in his own solitary soul. Compassion for her loneliness and his own makes him realize that truth is not the highest virtue.

This terrified retreat from reality into the most banal of polite conversation ironically combines tragedy and sardonic humor. To use the name of love in this context is surprising, at once accurate and absurd. A final symbolic image captures the grotesque irrationality embedded in the most familiar landscape. As Mr. Brook looks out of his office window later, he sees, perhaps for the hundredth time, a faculty member's old Airedale terrier waddling down the street. This time, however, something is strange: The dog is walking backward. He watches "with a kind of cold surprise" until the dog is out of sight, then returns to the pile of student papers on his desk.

This story is thematically typical of McCullers's fiction. Love, which has little or nothing to do with sexuality, is the only way to bridge the terrible isolation which separates individuals. Too many other factors in the situation, however—habit, social custom, human perversity, the demands of artistic creativity, or simply devotion to duty—conspire against the goal of giving love and comfort to one another. All persons are trapped, incommunicado, in the little cages they have chosen.

"A Domestic Dilemma" • The irrational persistence of love and its inadequacy to solve the everyday problems of existence are also apparent in "A Domestic Dilemma." Here, too, the story is told from the point of view of a patient, kindly man whose attitude toward his alcoholic wife is a curious blend of compassion, love, and angry exasperation. He fears for the welfare of his two children. He comes home to the suburbs from his New York office to find his children unattended, playing with Christmas tree lights, a supper of cinnamon toast on the kitchen table, untouched except for one bite. The little boy complains, "It hurt. The toast was hot." His wife, Emily, had mistaken cayenne pepper for cinnamon.

The bewildered children do not understand the painful scene between mother and father, in which Emily vacillates drunkenly between belligerent defense of her behavior and tearful shame. Martin finally persuades her to go to bed and let him feed the children, bathe them, and put them to bed. He successfully reestablishes an atmosphere of tender solicitude, hoping the children will not remember their mother's puzzling behavior. How long will it be, he wonders, before they understand and despise her? There are moments when Martin hates his wife, imagining "a future of degradation and slow ruin" for himself and his children. When he finally lies down beside Emily and watches her sleeping, however, his anger gradually dissipates. "His hand sought the adjacent flesh and sorrow paralleled desire in the immense complexity of love."

One interpretation offered for "A Domestic Dilemma" points to the stresses of an urban lifestyle on a woman reared in an emotionally supportive small southern town. In suburbia, Emily is isolated from everyone she ever knew, while Martin commutes long distances into the inner city. Thus, it is social isolation that is destroying her. This interpretation has considerable validity, although the cause of her alcoholism is not really central to the story; isolation and loneliness occur in all kinds of social situations in McCullers's fiction, and small southern towns are as deadly as urban suburbs in that regard. Isolation is a metaphysical affliction more than a cultural one. Emily's social isolation is analogous to Bitsy Barlow's physical deformity or even Madame Zilensky's enslaving musical genius—one of the many accidents of nature or situation over which people have little control. As Mr. Brook's empathy for Madame Zilensky cannot alleviate her isolation, Martin's love for his wife will not necessarily save her from her unhappiness. In McCullers's fiction it is usually the act of love, not the comfort of being loved, that has power to transform the lover.

"A Tree. A Rock. A Cloud" • One of the most anthologized of McCullers's stories is "A Tree. A Rock. A Cloud," which was chosen for the 1942 *Prize Stories: The O. Henry Awards*, even though it may be inferior, in some ways, to "A Domestic Dilemma," "Wunderkind," and "Madame Zilensky and the King of Finland." It deals more philosophically and perhaps more ironically with the art of loving. The lover, in this case, is an old, boozy wanderer who waylays a newspaper delivery boy in a café. He is compulsively dedicated to explaining how he learned to love "all things both great and small." The quotation comes not from the story but from *The Rime of the Ancient Mariner* (1798), which is quite possibly its inspiration. The irony of Samuel Taylor Coleridge's Ancient Mariner waylaying an impatient wedding guest with his story of salvation through love is translated here into a somewhat different context.

Three persons, rather than two, are involved. Although the tale is addressed to the naïve newspaper delivery boy, it is overheard by Leo, the proprietor of the café, who is early characterized as bitter and stingy. When the wanderer accosts the boy and says distinctly, "I love you," the initial laughter of the men in the café and their immediate return to their own beer or breakfasts suggest both a widespread cynicism and an utter indifference concerning the welfare of the boy. Although Leo is also cynical and often vulgar, he listens to the conversation carefully. When the old man orders a beer for the boy, Leo brings coffee instead, reminding the other man, "He is a minor."

Although Leo soon understands that the old man's intention is not to proposition the boy, he continues to interject insulting remarks into the wanderer's sad tale of love for a wife who deserted him for another man. The old man struggles to explain the unifying effect of love on the fragmented psyche. Before his marriage, he says, "when I had enjoyed anything there was a peculiar sensation as though it was laying around loose in me. Nothing seemed to finish itself up or fit in with other things." His wife, however, transformed his experience of himself—"this woman was something like an assembly line for my soul. I run these little pieces of myself through her and I come out complete." Yet, after years of frantic search for the lost wife, the man realizes with horror that he cannot even remember distinctly what she looked like. It was then that he began his "science" of love.

At this point, Leo explodes in exasperation:

> Leo's mouth jerked with a pale, quick grin. "Well none of we boys are getting any younger," he said. Then with sudden anger he balled up a dishcloth he was holding and threw it down hard on the floor. "You draggle-tailed old Romeo!"

The wanderer solemnly explains that one must practice the art of loving by starting with small or inanimate things—a tree, a rock, a cloud—and graduate from one thing to another. He learned to love a goldfish next. Now he has so perfected the science of loving that he can love anything and everyone. By this time, Leo is screaming at him to shut up.

As an explanation of Platonic love, this, to be sure, may be feeble. The reactions of Leo and the boy do, however, provide depth to the story. The newsboy is puzzled and confused—presumably because he has yet to pass through adolescence, when the importance and complexity of love will become clearer to him. After the old man leaves, the boy appeals to Leo for answers. Was the man drunk? Was he a dope fiend? Was he crazy? To the first two questions Leo says, shortly, "No." To the last, he is grimly silent. Probably Leo responds so emotionally to the old man's tale because it makes him too keenly aware of his own barren lovelessness. His role is somewhat analogous to that of Mr. Brook in this respect. He recognizes, perhaps, that the old man, unlike himself, has found a way to transcend his wretchedness. Can it be "crazy" to be at peace with oneself, in spite of outwardly miserable circumstances? If so, it is a craziness a sane man might covet. The boy, thinking of nothing else to say, comments that the man "sure has done a lot of traveling." As the story ends, McCullers emphasizes therefore that the story is about adolescent versus adult perceptions of love.

Autobiographical Elements • McCullers's short fiction, like her most popular novel, *The Member of the Wedding*, has many autobiographical elements. Her own absorption in music and early aspirations to be a concert pianist are reflected in "Wunderkind" and "Madame Zilensky and the King of Finland." The particular mode of Madame Zilensky's escape from a narrowly focused existence is even more pertinent to McCullers's short, intense life. She escaped the limitations of her frail body through fantasy, transforming it into fiction and drama.

Even the situation in "A Domestic Dilemma" echoes her own life, curiously altered. She lived both the Emily role, that is, the maimed personality who desperately needs love and companionship, and the Martin role, the hopeless lover of the psychologically disabled person. McCullers's husband, whom she divorced and later remarried, was an alcoholic whose drinking was aggravated by the fact that, although he fancied himself a writer, she was so much more successful than he. She has disguised the personal element in the situation by changing the presumed cause of the alcoholism (although she, too, knew the effect of migrating from a small southern town to New York) and by projecting her role more on the husband than the wife.

Both Martin and Mr. Brook exhibit qualities ordinarily ascribed to women— intuition, gentleness, patience, and unselfish love. McCullers's blurring of gender roles (Miss Amelia in "The Ballad of the Sad Café" is strikingly masculine) was probably not motivated by a feminist revolt against stereotyped sex roles; she was not a polemicist but a lyrical writer, projecting her own personality, feelings, dreams, and fears. If her men act like women or vice versa, it is because she was herself decidedly androgynous. She loved both men and women and somehow contained them both. Some of her most ardent attractions were for women who repudiated her attentions (or at least did not remain in her vicinity), which may account for the wistful need for love in some of her fictional characters.

In spite of her personal sorrows and her emotional isolation and loneliness, McCullers was beloved by many friends and generous in her own affections. Even the odd triangular love affairs that appear in *The Member of the Wedding* and *Reflections in a Golden Eye* have some autobiographical parallels. Both Carson and her husband, according to McCullers's biographer, Virginia Spencer Carr, were intimately involved with Jack Diamond, a concert musician. It is not an accident that McCullers was one of the first American writers to deal openly (in *Reflections in a Golden Eye*) with repressed homosexuality. In the case of her husband, at least, his homosexual orientation was not always repressed; whether she was an active bisexual is more ambiguous.

McCullers's personal life and her fiction both seem marked by a curious combination of sophisticated intuition into human motives and an odd childlike quality that sometimes verges on immaturity. Most writers, for example, would not write of Mr. Brook that he could not speak until "this agitation in his insides quieted down"; nor would many writers try to express the blurred Platonic idealism of "A Tree. A Rock. A Cloud." Although the situational irony of that story saves it from being naïvely expressed philosophy, one has a lingering impression that the writer is mocking a sentiment that she really wants to advocate.

"The Ballad of the Sad Café" • "The Ballad of the Sad Café," sometimes grouped with novellas, sometimes with short stories, is the most successful of McCullers's ventures into the grotesque. The melancholy mood suggested by the title is appropriate; like many a folk ballad, it tells a mournful tale touched with sardonic humor. The story celebrates the love of a cross-eyed, mannish woman for a conceited, hunchbacked dwarf. It also involves a curious love triangle, for the climax is a grotesque battle between the protagonist, Miss Amelia, and her former husband for the affection of the dwarf.

True love, paradoxically, is both a cruel joke and the means of redemption, not only for the lover, Miss Amelia, but also for the whole ingrown, backwoods community, which otherwise dies of emotional starvation. The inhabitants of this stifling southern village, like a somber chorus in a Greek tragedy, observe and reflect the fortunes of Miss Amelia, their leading citizen. Cousin Lymon, the hunchback, appears out of nowhere at the door of Miss Amelia, who runs the town store and the best distillery for miles around. To everyone's amazement, instead of throwing him out, as she has done to others who claimed kinship, Miss Amelia takes in the wretched wanderer and even falls in love with him. Cousin Lymon becomes a pompous little king of the castle, although not, apparently, her bed partner. Love transforms the mean, hard, sexless Miss Amelia into a reasonable facsimile of a warmhearted woman. She opens a café in her store because Cousin Lymon likes company, and her place becomes the social center of the community. Miss Amelia blossoms; the community blooms with goodwill, until the arrival of another person who is to destroy this interlude of happiness and peace.

Miss Amelia had once married the town bad boy, who had unaccountably fallen in love with her. Her motivation had apparently been solely commercial, the hope of acquiring a strong helper in her business; when the bridegroom expected sexual favors, Miss Amelia had indignantly refused. After ten stormy days, she threw him out entirely, earning his undying hatred for causing him such frustration and humiliation; he turned to a life of crime and landed in the penitentiary. Now he is out of jail and returns with malevolent thoughts of revenge. Poor Miss Amelia, now vulnerable in a new and surprising way, accepts his unwelcome presence in her café because Cousin Lymon is fascinated with him, and Miss Amelia and her former spouse become rivals for the affection of the dwarf.

This rivalry culminates in a ludicrous variation of the western showdown, solemnly witnessed by the whole community, when Miss Amelia and her former husband have a battle of fisticuffs in the café. Moreover, Miss Amelia, who has been quietly working out with a punching bag in preparation for the event, is winning. At the last moment, however, the traitorous Cousin Lymon leaps onto her back, and the two men together beat her senseless. Afterward, they vandalize her store and her still in the woods and flee. Miss Amelia thereafter closes her business and becomes a permanent recluse in a town now desolate and deserted.

Katherine Snipes
With updates by D. Dean Shackelford

Other major works

CHILDREN'S LITERATURE: *Sweet as a Pickle and Clean as a Pig*, 1964.

PLAYS: *The Member of the Wedding*, pr. 1950, pb. 1951 (adaptation of her novel); *The Square Root of Wonderful*, pr. 1957, pb. 1958.

NOVELS: *The Heart Is a Lonely Hunter*, 1940; *Reflections in a Golden Eye*, 1941; *The Ballad of the Sad Café*, 1943, serial (1951, book); *The Member of the Wedding*, 1946; *Clock Without Hands*, 1961.

MISCELLANEOUS: *The Mortgaged Heart*, 1971 (short fiction, poetry, and essays; Margarita G. Smith, editor).

NONFICTION: *Illumination and Night Glare: The Unfinished Autobiography of Carson McCullers*, 1999 (Carlos L. Dews, editor).

Bibliography

Bloom, Harold, ed. *Carson McCullers*. New York: Chelsea House, 1986. Essays on McCullers's novels and major short stories. Includes introduction, chronology, and bibliography.

Carr, Virginia Spencer. *Understanding Carson McCullers*. Columbia: University of South Carolina Press, 1990. Thoughtful guide to McCullers's works by the author of *The Lonely Hunter: A Biography of Carson McCullers* (1975). Includes bibliographical references.

Clark, Beverly Lyon, and Melvin J. Friedman, eds. *Critical Essays on Carson McCullers*. New York: G. K. Hall, 1996. Collection of essays ranging from reviews of McCullers's major works to tributes by such writers as Tennessee Williams and Kay Boyle, to critical analyses from a variety of perspectives. Most helpful to a study of the short story is Robert Philips's "Freaking Out: The Short Stories of Carson McCullers."

James, Judith Giblin. *Wunderkind: The Reputation of Carson McCullers, 1940-1990*. Columbia, S.C.: Camden House, 1995. Examines McCullers's place in literature as a southern female author. Bibliographical references and an index are provided.

Jenkins, McKay. *The South in Black and White: Race, Sex, and Literature in the 1940's*.

Chapel Hill: University of North Carolina Press, 1999. Covers McCullers along with several other writers in a consideration of the role of race and sex in southern literature.

McDowell, Margaret B. *Carson McCullers.* Boston: Twayne, 1980. Good general introduction to McCullers's fiction, with a chapter on each of the novels, the short stories, and *The Ballad of the Sad Café.* Also included are a chronology, endnotes, and a select bibliography. Stressing McCullers's versatility, McDowell emphasizes the lyricism, the musicality, and the rich symbolism of McCullers's fiction as well as McCullers's sympathy for lonely individuals.

May, Charles E., ed. *Masterplots II: Short Story Series, Revised Edition.* 8 vols. Pasadena, Calif.: Salem Press, 2004. Designed for student use, this reference set contains articles providing detailed plot summaries and analyses of four short stories by McCullers: "The Ballad of the Sad Café" (vol. 1), "Madame Zilensky and the King of Finland" (vol. 5), "A Tree. A Rock. A Cloud" (vol. 7), and "Wunderkind" (vol. 8).

Savigneau, Josyane. *Carson McCullers: A Life.* Translated by Joan E. Howard. Boston: Houghton Mifflin, 2001. The McCullers estate granted Savigneau access to McCullers's unpublished papers, which enables her to deepen the portrait painted by previous biographers.

Westling, Louise. *Sacred Groves and Ravaged Gardens: The Fiction of Eudora Welty, Carson McCullers, and Flannery O'Connor.* Athens: University of Georgia Press, 1985. In this study, important comparisons are made between these three major southern writers of short fiction and novels. Although Westling is not the first to use a feminist approach with McCullers, the book offers useful insight concerning the portrayal of the female characters and the issue of androgyny in McCullers's fiction. Her analysis of *The Ballad of the Sad Café* is particularly good. Supplemented by useful endnotes and a bibliography of secondary material.

Whitt, Margaret. "From Eros to Agape: Reconsidering the Chain Gang's Song in McCullers's *Ballad of the Sad Café.*" *Studies in Short Fiction* 33 (Winter, 1996): 119-122. Argues that the chain gang was a rare visual example of integration in an otherwise segregated South; notes the irony suggested through the song—that the men must be chained together to find harmony.

Bernard Malamud

Born: Brooklyn, New York; April 26, 1914
Died: New York, New York; March 18, 1986

Principal short fiction • *The Magic Barrel*, 1958; *Idiots First*, 1963; *Pictures of Fidelman: An Exhibition*, 1969; *Rembrandt's Hat*, 1973; *The Stories of Bernard Malamud*, 1983; *The People, and Uncollected Stories*, 1989; *The Complete Stories*, 1997 (Robert Giroux, editor).

Other literary forms • Bernard Malamud devoted his writing career to fiction. In addition to his highly praised short stories, he wrote seven well-received novels: *The Natural* (1952), *The Assistant* (1957), *A New Life* (1961), *The Fixer* (1966), *The Tenants* (1971), *Dubin's Lives* (1979), and *God's Grace* (1982). He is also the author of many literary essays and reviews.

Achievements • Of the last half of the twentieth century, Bernard Malamud is one of the best American writers. In his seven novels and numerous short stories, he transcends the Jewish experience so ably chronicled by the so-called Jewish literary renaissance writers (such as Saul Bellow and Philip Roth) by using Jewish life as a metaphor for universal experience. Critic Robert Alter has proclaimed that short stories such as "The First Seven Years," "The Magic Barrel," "The Last Mohican," "Idiots First," and "Angel Levine" will be read "as long as anyone continues to care about American fiction written in the 20th century."

Both a traditionalist and an experimenter in his fiction, Malamud won rave reviews, literary plaudits, and many awards. *The Magic Barrel* brought a National Book Award in 1959. In 1967, *The Fixer* won for him a second National Book Award as well as a Pulitzer Prize. In addition, he was president of the International Association of Poets, Playwrights, Editors, Essayists, and Novelists (PEN Club) from 1979 to 1981.

Biography • Born on April 26, 1914, Bernard Malamud was the eldest of two sons of Max and Bertha Malamud. His parents, who had emigrated from Russia, ran a grocery store. Both Yiddish and English were spoken in the Malamud household, where much emphasis was placed on the cultural aspects of Judaism.

This milieu as well as his father's tales of life in czarist Russia provided much fodder for Malamud's fiction. He was also influenced by many trips to the Yiddish theater on Manhattan's Second Avenue, and by novels such as his favorite Horatio Alger stories and a multivolume *Book of Knowledge* that his father gave him when he was nine.

Throughout his boyhood in the back room of the family store, where he wrote stories, and his high school days at Erasmus Hall in Brooklyn, where he was an editor of the literary magazine, he was devoted to storytelling. In 1936, he graduated from City College of New York. He had written a few stories in college and continued to write during a series of odd jobs. While working on a master's degree at Columbia University, he taught at Erasmus Hall Evening High School and wrote. In 1945, he married a Gentile, Ann de Chiara.

During the 1940's, Malamud's stories appeared in some noncommercial maga-

© Jerry Bauer

zines. Then, in 1949, he sold the appropriately titled "The Cost of Living" to *Harper's Bazaar*. That same year, he moved with his family to Corvallis, Oregon, where he worked at Oregon State University. Finally adjusting from the urban to the rural lifestyle, Malamud developed a new perspective and a weekly routine that allowed him much quality time for writing: He taught three days a week and wrote four. Without a doctoral degree, he was forced to teach composition, not literature, so his favorite course was a compromise—a night workshop in short-story writing for townspeople. His stories began to appear in such noted magazines as *Partisan Review, Commentary,* and *Harper's Bazaar*.

The *Natural,* his first novel, appeared in 1952 to mixed reviews. Some critics were put off by what they saw as an obscure symbolism, while others applauded the masterful use of fable and its art of ancient storytelling in a modern voice. In 1956, the *Partisan Review* made him a fellow in fiction and recommended him for a Rockefeller grant, which made it possible for Malamud to spend a year in Europe. In 1957, his next novel, *The Assistant,* was published, winning for him many awards and establishing him as a major Jewish American writer. The short-story collection *The Magic Barrel* came out in 1958, followed by his third novel, *A New Life.* In 1961, he moved to Bennington College, where he taught for more than twenty years. *Idiots First* was followed by *The Fixer,* which was researched during a trip to Russia.

From 1969 until his death in 1986, Malamud continued to publish both novels and short stories. His works include *Pictures of Fidelman: An Exhibition,* a collection of stories about one character; *The Tenants,* a novel; *Rembrandt's Hat,* another short-story collection; *Dubin's Lives,* a novel; *God's Grace,* a novel; and *The Stories of Bernard Malamud,* still another collection.

Analysis • All Bernard Malamud's fiction seems based on a single affirmation: Despite its disappointments, horror, pain, and suffering, life is truly worth living. His work may be best understood in the context of mid-twentieth century American literature. When Malamud arrived upon the literary scene, he disagreed with the period's twin pillars of negativism and nihilism, and his work is a reaction to this prevailing trend. "The purpose of the writer," contends Malamud, "is to keep civilization from destroying itself." Therefore, his characters, no matter how bad their lot, push toward a better life, a new life. "My premise," notes the author, "is that we will not destroy each other. My premise is that we will live on. We will seek a better life. We may not become better, but at least we will seek betterment."

In this respect, for Malamud the most important element of fiction is form, a belief that appropriately reinforces his thematic beliefs. Literary form as "ultimate necessity" is the basis of literature. The writer's duty, he argues "is to create the architecture, the form." This element of structure, so prevalent in both his short and long fiction, runs counter to the practice of many of his contemporaries, who preferred the inherent formlessness of the so-called New Novel. The essence of this form, says Malamud, is "story, story, story. Writers who can't invent stories often pursue other strategies, even substituting style for narrative. I feel that story is the basic element of fiction."

This belief, however, raises the question of what for Malamud constitutes a good story. Here Malamud is likewise a traditionalist, returning to such nineteenth century influences as Fyodor Dostoevski, Leo Tolstoy, and Gustave Flaubert. Malamud's stories grow out of character. More often than not, the typical protagonist is the schlemiel (usually Jewish, though sometimes Italian). According to the author himself, "A Malamud character is someone who fears his fate, is caught up in it, yet manages to outrun it. He's the subject and object of laughter and pity." When Malamud began publishing his stories, the emphasis was often on case studies rather than elaborate personality development, a trend that irritated Malamud:

> The sell-out of personality is just tremendous. Our most important natural resource is Man. The times cry out for men of imagination and hope. Instead, our fiction is loaded with sickness, homosexuality, fragmented man, "other-directed" man. It should be filled with love and beauty and hope. We are underselling Man. And American fiction is at its weakest when we go in for journalistic case studies instead of rich personality development.

A typical Malamud story, then, is an initiation story, the classic American pattern. Malamud admits that his American literary roots lie in Stephen Crane, Ernest Hemingway, and Sherwood Anderson. The story usually begins with a youth—or an older man with arrested personality development—who has led an unfulfilled life because of undeveloped emotions, failed relationships, and questionable morality. This protagonist then encounters a father figure—similar to the Hemingway tutor-tyro technique—who guides him through his odyssey by prodding him to ask the right questions, teaching him the meaning of suffering and spirituality, and ultimately coaxing him to accept the responsibility for his own life.

Because Malamud is Jewish, his protagonists are, more often than not, Jewish as well. Given Malamud's background—his father was a Jewish immigrant and passed on his knowledge of the Yiddish tradition of storytelling—this is to be expected. Malamud himself admits, "I write about Jews because I know them. But more important, I write about them because Jews are absolutely the very *stuff* of drama." By itself, this assertion is misleading, for unlike his fellow members of the Jewish literary renaissance, Malamud is not preoccupied with the uniqueness of the Jewish experience. The Jew for Malamud is a metaphor for all human beings. "Jewishness is important to me," Malamud asserts, "but I don't consider myself only a Jewish writer. I have interests beyond that, and I feel I am writing for all men." Malamud's method, then, is synecdochic—by detailing the plight of his Jews, he reveals the human's common humanity.

Throughout his career Malamud alternated writing novels with short stories. Of the two forms, he confesses to "having been longer in love with short fiction." One aspect of the short story that Malamud especially enjoys is "the fast payoff. Whatever happens happens quickly." A related matter is compression. Short fiction, Malamud argues, "packs a self in a few pages predicating a lifetime. . . . In a few pages a good story portrays the complexity of a life while producing the surprise and effect of knowledge—not a bad payoff."

Ironically, this fastness and compression are part of the ultimate illusion of Malamud's art. For him the writing of a short story is a long task that demands constant revision. "I would write a book, or a short story," Malamud admits, "at least three times—once to understand it, the second time to improve the prose, and a third to compel it to say what it still must say."

"The First Seven Years" • "The First Seven Years," which first appeared in the *Partisan Review* in 1950 and later in *The Magic Barrel,* is a straightforward tale set in the favorite Malamudian milieu, the New York Jewish ghetto. Feld, the shoemaker, decides to play matchmaker for his nineteen-year-old daughter, Miriam, whom he desires to attend college. Feld's choice is Max, a college boy, but the shoemaker is disappointed to learn that Max is a materialist (he wants to be an accountant), and for this reason his daughter rejects the chosen suitor. Simultaneously, Sobel, Feld's assistant, quits his job, and Feld has a heart attack.

The story turns on a typical Malamud irony. What Feld has failed to realize is that he, like Max, is a materialist and that his dreams of his daughter's having "a better life" are wrapped up in money, her marrying well. Malamud here also reverses the typical older-man-equals-tutor, younger-man-equals-tyro pattern. Apparently, Feld is teaching Sobel the shoemaker's trade, but in truth, Sobel is the instructor: He admits that he has worked cheaply and lived poorly for the past five years only to be around the woman whom he truly loves, Miriam. As Malamud might have punned, the assistant teaches the master the difference between soles and souls. Finally, Sobel agrees to remain an assistant for two more years before asking Miriam to marry him.

Malamud's symbolism is both simple and mythic. Feld suffers literally from a damaged heart and metaphorically from an organ that is too materialistic. The rebirth pattern is inherent in the story's time frame, which moves from winter toward spring. The seven-year cycle of fertility—Sobel's wait—suggests that he is in tune with larger forces in the universe. Interestingly, the story is also an early version of the tale on which Malamud would elaborate in *The Assistant.*

"The Magic Barrel" • "The Magic Barrel" utilizes another familiar Malamud pattern, the fantasy. Here, he blends elements of the traditional fairy tale with Jewish folklore. The story in fact begins like a fairy tale, with the line "Not long ago there lived. . . ." In the story, Leo Finkle, a rabbinical student searching for a wife, is the prince; Salzman, the marriage broker with the "magic" barrel and his sudden appearances, is the supernatural agent; and Stella, Salzman's prostitute daughter, is the princess of the tale. The plot is likewise reminiscent of a fairy tale as the prince finally meets the princess and through the intervention of the supernatural agent has a chance at a happy ending.

Malamud's fairy tale borrows elements from Jewish folklore. The characters are certainly stereotypical: the marriage broker, the schlemiel, and the poor daughter. The setting is the usual lower-class milieu. With Leo helping Salzman at the end (each man plays both tutor and tyro), the plot has the familiar reversal, and the story is based on the age-old subject of parent as matchmaker. Even the theme is familiar:

Love is a redemptive force earned through suffering and self-knowledge. Malamud also infuses his story with humor. Aside from the stock characters and stock situations, he utilizes puns (for example "Lily wilted"), hyperbole, and comic juxtaposition (prospective brides are described in the jargon of used-car salesmen). Finally, the story contains social criticism directed at the Jews. Leo Finkle, the would-be rabbi, has learned the Jewish law but not his own feelings. He takes refuge in his self-pity (a frequent Malamud criticism), he wants a wife not for love but for social prestige, and he uses his religion to hide from life.

"Angel Levine" • "Angel Levine" is part fable, part fantasy, and an example of the typical Malamud theme, the brotherhood of all people. Manischevitz, a Malamudian Job-victim, seeks relief from his suffering and aid for his sick wife, Fanny. In the Malamudian world, help comes from human rather than divine sources; here, the aide is a Jewish Negro angel, Angel Levine. In his narrow religious pride and prejudice, Manischevitz can only wonder why God has failed to send him help in the form of a white person. The tailor's subsequent refusal of aid, an act saturated with egotistical pride, fails to lead to relief.

Eventually, Manischevitz, in pursuit of aid, roams into Harlem, where, finding Angel Levine in Bella's bar, he overhears the essential Malamudian lesson about the divine spark in all persons: "It de speerit," said the old man. "On de face of de water moved de speerit. An' dat was good. It say so in de Book. From de speerit ariz de man. . . ." God put the spirit in all things.

Socially color-blind at last, Manischevitz can now believe that the same spirit dwells within every human, uniting them all. In a scene reminiscent of Felicity's vision at the end of Flaubert's "Un Cœur simple," Manischevitz is rewarded by the sight of a dark figure flying with dark wings. The final meaning of his experience he conveys to Fanny when he admits, "Believe me, there are Jews everywhere." Here, he is Malamud's rationalizer, mouthing the familiar theme of brotherhood.

"The Last Mohican" • "The Last Mohican" introduces the recurring Everyman character Arthur Fidelman (the stories about him were collected in *Pictures of Fidelman: An Exhibition*) and reveals Malamud's growth and artistry in enlarging the scope of his essentially Jewish materials. Although the setting is not New York City but Rome, the protagonist is familiar. Fidelman, "a self-confessed failure as a painter," is also a failure as a human being, a self-deluded egotist who knows little about his self. His teacher is the familiar aged Jew—this time called Shimon Susskind in typical Malamudian gentle irony, "a Jewish refugee from Israel."

The essential lesson is again brotherhood. As Susskind persists in asking for help on his own terms, Fidelman inquires, "Am I responsible for you, Susskind?" The elderly Jew replies, "Who else . . . you are responsible. Because you are a man. Because you are a Jew, aren't you?" Like Dante descending into the depths of Hell, Fidelman must enter the personal hell of his own ego to learn the powerful lesson. Fearing that Susskind has stolen his manuscript-laden briefcase, Fidelman discovers the refugee in the Jewish ghetto of Rome, "a pitch black freezing cave." Susskind admits to burning the Giotto manuscript inside the case because "the spirit was missing."

This "rebirth of the spirit" story reads less like a Jewish parable than do many of Malamud's stories. Malamud has set the tale in Rome, and he has obviously undergirded it with mythic dimensions by using *Inferno* motifs (using, for example,

"Virgilio" Susskind and a street named Dante). Some critics even contend this is the best of the stories in *The Magic Barrel*. Perhaps this story is more believable than others, for rather than merely learning an abstract lesson, Fidelman actually begins to care about Susskind, even forgiving him.

"Idiots First" • "Idiots First," the title story of his second collection, reveals Malamud's willingness to experiment. The story is a strange combination of fantasy and fable. Although set at night in his familiar territory, this New York is more of a dreamscape, a nightmare, than a realistic environment. No character motivation is provided, key information is omitted, and one Jewish character, Ginzburg, matter-of-factly introduced à la the fairy godmother in "Cinderella," follows an elderly Jew named Mendel, has the ability to freeze people, and seems to represent God/death. Malamud has either invented a new dramatic form or reverted to an old, nineteenth century American mode known as the romance.

Mendel, convinced that he will die that night, desperately seeks thirty-five dollars in order to send his mentally disabled son to Uncle Leo in California. What is not made clear is that Mendel seems to have made a pact with Ginzburg—he will go willingly to his death if he is given time to take care of his son. Mendel is helped not by the rich (a pawnbroker or the supposedly philanthropic Mr. Fishbein), but by the poor, a dying rabbi who gives him a coat, and by death (or Ginzburg) himself, who gives him extra time.

Whereas earlier Malamud stories usually had contrivances such as obvious symbols or preachy *raisonneurs*, "Idiots First" offers no such aid. On one level, the story seems almost metaphysical, a questioning of God/death for being so detached ("What will happen happens. This isn't my responsibility") and wrathful (Ginzburg sees wrath mirrored in Mendel's eyes) that He no longer understands what it means to be human. In any case, this open-endedness and general ambiguity represent a new development.

"Black Is My Favorite Color" • "Black Is My Favorite Color," first appearing in *The Reporter* in 1963, is representative of another of Malamud's frequent concerns, the relationship among the races. Like "Angel Levine" before it and the novel *The Tenants* after it, this story explores the fragile love-hate bonds between Jews and African Americans.

Nat Lime, a white Jew who operates a liquor store in Harlem, professes to be color-blind ("there's only one human color and that's the color of blood"). Throughout his life, Lime has befriended "colored" people, but they all seem to resent his attempts. Buster Wilson, his would-be childhood buddy, Ornita Harris, the black woman to whom he proposes marriage, and Charity Sweetness, his current maid, all reject his overtures of friendship and more.

This story is difficult to understand. Both Lime's words and his actions indicate that he is free of prejudice. He operates a business in black Harlem, and he hires black workers. In return, he is rejected by the three black people he truly likes and helps; twice, he is beaten and robbed by blacks, once obviously for dating a black woman. Yet, through it all, Lime retains his good sense as well as his good humor, and he pursues his cleaning lady everywhere ("Charity Sweetness—you hear me?—come out of that goddamn toilet!"). Malamud appears to be indicating that prejudice and divisiveness can reside in black people as well as white.

"The German Refugee" • "The German Refugee," one of the few first-person stories in the Malamud canon, also illustrates the theme of brotherhood. The narrator, Martin Goldberg, relates his attempts to teach English to a German refugee, Oskar Gassner, who is scheduled to give a lecture in English about Walt Whitman's relationship to certain German poets.

Two distinct stories emerge: Oskar's anguish over his failure to comprehend English and the irony of Goldberg's failure to understand why. Thus, once again, each man is both tutor and tyro. While Martin teaches Oskar English, the German army begins its summer push of 1939. What the narrator fails to grasp is his pupil's deep involvement in his former country's fate and that of his non-Jewish wife, whom he left there.

To emphasize the irony, Malamud uses references to Whitman. Oskar ends up teaching his teacher the important lesson when he declares about the poet that "it wasn't the love of death they [German poets] had got from Whitman . . . but it was most of all his feeling for Brudermensch, his humanity." When Oskar successfully delivers his speech, the narrator feels only a sense of pride at what he taught the refugee, not the bonds of *Brudermensch* that have developed between them. When Oskar commits suicide, the narrator never sees that he is partially responsible.

"The Jewbird" • "The Jewbird" is a modern, urban version of "The Raven." Just as the raven flew through the open window of Edgar Allan Poe's narrator and stayed to haunt his conscience, so Schwartz, this black jewbird, which looks "like a dissipated crow," flaps through the window of Harry Cohen's top-floor apartment and lingers to bedevil him. "Bird or devil," demands Poe's narrator; "How do I know you're a bird and not some kind of a goddman devil?" asks Cohen.

Malamud's beast fable, however, is concerned with more than nebulous guilt over a lost love. On one hand, the tale is lighthearted with a considerable amount of hyperbole, sarcasm, and comic banter; on the other, "The Jewbird" focuses on a heavier theme, prejudice. When Schwartz first enters the Cohen apartment, the bird announces that it is running from "anti-Semeets." At the conclusion of the story, young Maurie Cohen goes in search of the bird, which had been driven from the apartment by his father. Finding the damaged jewbird by the river, the boy asks his mother who so hurt Schwartz, and his mother replies, "Anti-Semeets." In other words, Harry Cohen is anti-Semitic.

Malamud's story, however, is still more than a parable of anti-Semitism. Harry Cohen is a cruel man and an inherently selfish father who has little to do with his son. When Schwartz begins to help Maurie with his reading, math, violin lessons, and even games, the narrator notes that the bird "took on full responsibility for Maurie's performance in school." Harry Cohen is so self-absorbed that he has been unable to function successfully as a parent.

"Rembrandt's Hat" • Nathaniel Hawthorne once admitted that a few of his tales suffered from an inveterate love of allegory. The same diagnosis might apply to some of Malamud's stories. "Rembrandt's Hat," the title story from the collection that was published in 1973, is typical of the essentially two-person psychological dramas that Malamud does so well. Often in such stories, two people who apparently work closely together never grasp what is truly going on in each other. As a result, painful misunderstandings occur, with a major one and its subsequent suffering leading to self-knowledge as well as a greater understanding between the two. Feld and Sobel,

Finkle and Salzman, Manischevitz and Levine, Goldberg and Gassner, Fidelman and Susskind—the names change, but the pattern remains.

In "Rembrandt's Hat," Rubin, a sculptor, and Arkin, an art historian, are colleagues at a New York art school, and they run into each other occasionally and utter polite, meaningless words. One day, Arkin makes a chance remark to Rubin that the latter's white headwear resembles a hat that Rembrandt wears in one of his self-portraits. From this point on, Rubin grows silent and starts shunning his colleague. Then, each wearing a different hat, the two art teachers go to great lengths to avoid each other. Ultimately, Arkin apologizes, Rubin weeps, and the two men resume their tenuous friendship.

The story turns on another prominent Malamud motif; like Henry James before him, Malamud uses art as a touchstone of character. For example, Fidelman's success as a human being is mirrored in his self-appraisal as an artist. Arkin, like some other Malamud characters, uses art to hide from life; it occurs to him that "he found it easier to judge paintings than to judge people." Rubin's self-portrait is sculpted in a single welded piece, a dwarf tree in the midst of an iron jungle. Thus, when Arkin makes the innocent comment, Rubin's inferiority complex interprets it as a comparison of the sculptor to the old master, Rembrandt, with the sculptor much less prominent. Finally, all the hats, from Arkin's white Stetson to Rubin's railroad engineer's cap, become self-Rorschach tests of the story's participants.

"Notes from a Lady at a Dinner Party" • "Notes from a Lady at a Dinner Party," appearing in *Rembrandt's Hat*, is a typical Malamud tale about the relationship between the sexes. In the Malamudian world, men and women desperately seek out each other, reach the verge of true commitment, but find it difficult to communicate, often to commit. Thus, Sobel silently pursues Miriam for seven years without revealing his true feelings, and Fidelman in "Naked Nude" finds it necessary to forge paintings in a whorehouse.

At a dinner party, Max Adler finds himself attracted to Karla Harris, the young wife of his former professor who is more than twice her age. Adler and Harris develop an alluring intimacy by secretly passing notes back and forth. An artist mired in the traditional role of wife-mother, Karla flirts with Adler, who, though previously daring only in his architecture, kisses her. After planning a late-night rendezvous at a nearby motel, they both get cold feet, part, and return to their separate lives of quiet desperation.

Both Karla and Adler are different versions of Malamud's self-limiting human beings. For the most part, Adler can only express his desires in architecture, while Karla's inner self comes out only in the relative safety of watercolors and romantic notes. In Malamud's twentieth century America, then, would-be lovers still cling to the courtly love tradition. Art is a medium not solely to express one's feelings but a place to hide and sublimate. Love rarely blossoms. Adler is divorced. Karla is content to write enticing notes to strange men and keep getting pregnant by her aging husband. Other Malamud men never marry. Oskar Gassner and his wife live in two different countries and are separated by war. Mendel's wife has died. Feld claims his wife does not understand man-woman relationships. Fidelman ultimately becomes bisexual.

"God's Wrath" • "God's Wrath" is another story about parent-child relationships. As with the sexes and the races, Malamud indicates that there is very little communication between parents and children. Glasser, a retired sexton, is a Lear-like figure with three daughters (by two wives) who have all been disappointments. His hope for one's having a better life is pinned on his youngest daughter, Luci, who quits college, leaves her job, and moves out of his apartment. After a long search, Glasser finally locates Luci, learning that she has become a prostitute. "God's Wrath" offers little explanation for the reason things are the way they are, except that God occasionally winks an eye. The story's conclusion is once again open-ended. Unable to dissuade his daughter from a life of prostitution, Glasser stations himself at her haunts and calls down God's wrath on her. Interestingly, at this point, Malamud switches from the past to the present tense, which indicates a sort of never-ending tension between parent and child, a perpetual inability to communicate, and the ultimate ignorance about how a parent affects a child. In the midst of a pessimistic, naturalistic universe, Malamud suggests that certain conflicts are eternal.

Malamud is an acclaimed twentieth century master of the short story. Often writing realistic fantasy, he is able to imbue his initiating Jews with a mythic dimension, while simultaneously depicting social and spiritual squalor in a realistic manner. His tales contain a great depth of feeling that is occasionally marred by obvious moralizing and transparent mythology. He evinces a deep concern for his fellow human beings. His major flaw has been called the narrowness of his subject matter, the plight of the lower-class Jew, but this problem is only a misunderstanding when one realizes that the Jew is a symbol for people everywhere.

Hal Charles

Other major works

NOVELS: *The Natural,* 1952; *The Assistant,* 1957; *A New Life,* 1961; *The Fixer,* 1966; *The Tenants,* 1971; *Dubin's Lives,* 1979; *God's Grace,* 1982; *The People,* 1989.

NONFICTION: *Talking Horse: Bernard Malamud on Life and Work,* 1996 (Alan Cheuse and Nicholas Delbanco, editors).

Bibliography

Abramson, Edward A. *Bernard Malamud Revisited.* New York: Twayne, 1993. Abramson's chapter on the short stories is a brief, general introduction, divided into such categories as fantasies, Italian stories, father-son stories, and sociopolitical stories. Echoes a familiar judgment that in his stories Malamud is a moralist in the tradition of Nathaniel Hawthorne and Henry James, but that he writes with the rhythms of Yiddish and the contours of the folktale.

Avery, Evelyn, ed. *The Magic Worlds of Bernard Malamud.* Albany: State University of New York Press, 2001. Wide-ranging collection of essays on Malamud and his writings, including personal memoirs by members of his family and friends.

Bloom, Harold, ed. *Bernard Malamud.* New York: Chelsea House, 2000. Part of the Modern Critical Views series, this collection of essays assesses the whole spectrum of Malamud's writings. Includes a chronology of his life and a bibliography.

Giroux, Robert. "On Bernard Malamud." *Partisan Review* 64 (Summer, 1997): 409-413. A brief general discussion of the life and work of Malamud, commenting on his major novels and short-story collections, his reception of the Pulitzer Prize, and the National Book Award.

Malamud, Bernard. Introduction to *The Stories of Bernard Malamud.* New York: Farrar, Straus and Giroux, 1983. This untitled introduction by Malamud offers an invaluable insight into the mind and theories of the writer himself. After a short literary autobiography, Malamud details his belief in form, his assessment of creative writing classes, and the reasons he loves the short story.

_____. "Reflections of a Writer: Long Work, Short Life." *The New York Times Book Review* 93, no. 20 (March, 1988): 15-16. This essay, originally a lecture at Bennington College, offers numerous anecdotes and details about Malamud's life as a writer. He elaborates upon his influences, his various professions, his friends, and some of his theories.

May, Charles E., ed. *Masterplots II: Short Story Series, Revised Edition.* 8 vols. Pasadena, Calif.: Salem Press, 2004. Designed for student use, this reference set contains articles providing detailed plot summaries and analyses of ten short stories by Malamud: "Angel Levine" and "Black Is My Favorite Color" (vol. 1); "Idiots First," "The Jewbird," and "The Last Mohican" (vol. 4); "The Magic Barrel" (vol. 5); "The Prison" and "Rembrandt's Hat" (vol. 6); and "A Summer's Reading" and "Take Pity" (vol. 7).

Ochshorn, Kathleen. *The Heart's Essential Landscape: Bernard Malamud's Hero.* New York: Peter Lang, 1990. Chapters on each of Malamud's novels and his short-story collections. Seeks to continue a trend in Malamud criticism that views his heroes as tending toward the *mensch* and away from the *schlemiel.* Includes a bibliography but no notes.

Sío-Castiñeira, Begoña. *The Short Stories of Bernard Malamud: In Search of Jewish Post-immigrant Identity.* New York: Peter Lang, 1998. Excellent study of Malamud's short fiction and its major themes.

Sloan, Gary. "Malamud's Unmagic Barrel." *Studies in Short Fiction* 32 (Winter, 1995): 51-57. Argues that everything that Pinye Salzman does in "The Magic Barrel" can be accounted for in naturalistic terms; claims that the story is more dramatic and ingenious as a naturalistic story than as a supernatural fable.

Smith, Janna Malamud. *My Father Is a Book: A Memoir of Bernard Malamud.* Boston: Houghton Mifflin, 2006. Intimate and extensive biography of Bernard Malamud, depicting his personal life and writing career.

Watts, Eileen H. "Jewish Self-Hatred in Malamud's 'The Jewbird.'" *MELUS* 21 (Summer, 1996): 157-163. Argues that the interaction of assimilated Jew and the Jewbird in the story reveals the political, social, and psychological fallout of assimilated Jew as good tenant, unassimilated Jew as bad, and Gentile as landlord.

Thomas Mann

Born: Lübeck, Germany; June 6, 1875
Died: Zurich, Switzerland; August 12, 1955

Principal short fiction • *Der kleine Herr Friedemann*, 1898; *Tristan*, 1903; *Das Wunderkind*, 1914; *Erzählung*, 1922; *Children and Fools*, 1928; *Stories of Three Decades*, 1936; *Ausgewahlte Erzählungen*, 1945; *Death in Venice, and Seven Other Stories*, 1954; *Stories of a Lifetime*, 1961; *Collected Stories*, 2001.

Other literary forms • In addition to his short fiction, Thomas Mann wrote novels, essays, and some poetry. When he received the Nobel Prize in Literature in 1929, his novel *Buddenbrooks* (1901; English translation, 1924) was cited specifically, though many of his later novels have received wide acclaim. Especially widely read and written about are the novel *Der Zauberberg* (1924; *The Magic Mountain*, 1927), a philosophical exploration of post-World War I dilemmas, and the four volumes of *Joseph und seine Brüder* (1933-1943; *Joseph and His Brothers*, 1934-1944, 1948), a modern mythology based on biblical tales. Mann's essays, collected in *Adel des Geistes* (1945; *Essays of Three Decades*, 1947), cover a broad range of political and literary issues.

Achievements • During more than half a century of writing and publishing both fiction and nonfiction, the German writer Mann received at least a dozen honorary doctoral degrees from universities in Europe and the United States. Though Mann lost both his honorary doctorate from the Rheinische Friedrich Wilhelm Universität in Bonn and his German citizenship in 1936, when he was accused of "subversive attacks on, and the gravest insults to, the Reich," he was reinstated as an honorary doctor at Bonn in 1947. Among his other honorary doctorates, two stand out in particular: One was his honorary doctorate from Harvard University, which he received together with Albert Einstein in 1935; the other was an honorary doctorate of natural sciences from the Eidgenössische Technische Hochschule of Zurich in 1955, a degree that especially pleased Mann because it was so unusual.

Mann received the Nobel Prize in Literature in 1929, and he received numerous other honors throughout his writing career, including the Herder-Prize of Czechoslovakia for exiled writers in 1937. During his international travels, both before and during his exile, Mann received many personal honors. In 1935, he was the guest of American president Franklin D. Roosevelt and his wife at a private dinner at the White House. From 1938 to 1941, he was a visiting professor at Princeton University, and in 1953, two years before his death, Mann saw Pope Pius XII in private audience.

Mann's fiction is diverse, sometimes reflecting conventions of the nineteenth century, as in Mann's early novel *Buddenbrooks*, sometimes exploring philosophical dilemmas, as in his novel *The Magic Mountain*, sometimes experimenting with stream-of-consciousness writing, as in the final chapter of his novel *Lotte in Weimar* (1939; *The Beloved Returns*, 1940), and sometimes rewriting mythology, as in the tetralogy *Joseph and His Brothers*, based on a biblical story, and the novella *The Transposed Heads*, adapted from a Hindu legend. Always, however, Mann infused a new irony into his fiction. He is a key figure in Western literature.

Biography • Thomas Mann was born on June 6, 1875, in Lübeck, Germany. He was the son of Johann Heinrich Mann, a minor politician and grain merchant, and Julia Mann (née da Silva-Bruhn), an accomplished musician, born and reared in Brazil. The dichotomy between the burgher and the artist, embodied in Mann's parents, is one of the themes of Mann's fiction, appearing in such works as the novella *Tonio Kröger*. One of five children, Mann was especially close to his older brother Heinrich, who traveled through Italy with him. The philosophical and political conflicts between the brothers fueled some of the debates in Mann's fiction, particularly in *The Magic Mountain*.

Though Mann worked briefly as an editor and an insurance agent, he was primarily a writer. When he was nineteen years old, the prestigious journal *Die Gesellschaft* published his first short story, "Gefallen"; after this first publication, Mann continued to write and publish until his death.

In 1905, Mann married Katya Pringsheim, whose father was a mathematics professor at the University of Munich. The Manns had six children: three girls and three boys. Their oldest son, Klaus, who was a writer, took his own life in 1949 at the age of forty-three.

In addition to the influence of Mann's family on his writing, there were two other sources of influence: the political climate of Europe and the social environment of the artist. It was the political climate of Europe that brought about Mann's exile. According to André von Gronicka's account of Mann's life, the "immediate cause of Mann's exile" from Germany was Mann's reading of the essay on Richard Wagner ("Leiden und Grösse Richard Wagner," "The Suffering and Greatness of Richard Wagner") at the University of Munich in 1933. Shortly after the reading, the Manns went to Holland, where they received a call from their children, warning them not to return. As a result, the Manns went into self-imposed exile, spending a brief time in Holland, Switzerland, and the south of France. In 1934, Mann made his first visit to the United States at the invitation of the publisher Alfred A. Knopf. In 1936, when Mann lost his German citizenship, he and his wife became citizens of Czechoslovakia. In 1938, they returned to the United States, and in 1944, they became American citizens. Though Mann's writing has an international flavor, as is evident in the wide range of settings in his fiction, Mann was acutely aware of his German roots. Only briefly between 1933 and his death was he able to return to his homeland.

Mann's social environment as an artist was especially diverse. Because he published from the age of nineteen, in 1894, until his death, in 1955, he had lifelong friendships with such artists as Bruno Walter and Hermann Hesse, and he often visited other friends and acquaintances, such as Hugo von Hofmannsthal, André Gide, Sigmund Freud, and Gustav Mahler.

In 1953, the Manns returned to Europe and went to Kilchberg, Switzerland, where they bought their last home. Though Mann had begun to show signs of ill health as early as 1945, his death was fairly sudden. On August 12, 1955, he suffered a sudden collapse. By eight o'clock that evening, he was dead.

Analysis • Thomas Mann's early stories are set in late nineteenth century and early twentieth century Europe, primarily in Germany and Italy. The protagonists are artists, disillusioned romantics with an ironic view of the cost of their art, which is an isolation from others. They are often burghers turned artist, often physically deformed, further isolating them from life around them and traditional courtship. To avoid the pain and disappointment of love, these protagonists retreat to art and nature, but in midlife, usually when they reach thirty years of age, they are suddenly overwhelmed by passion, usually for an unworthy and superficial beloved. Simultaneously, the disillusioned romantic usually comes face to face with his own superfluity, as does Mann's dilettante, in the story "Der Bajazzo" ("The Dilettante"), when he recognizes himself as "a perfectly useless human being." Though the sense of superfluity is quite often triggered by unrequited love, the object of the love, the beloved, is treated only superficially.

Such is the case, for example, with Amra in "Luischen" ("Little Lizzy"), who obliviously orchestrates her husband's destruction and stares vacantly at him while he dies of grief over her mistreatment of him. Mann says of Amra that she is not "sensitive enough to betray herself because of a guilty con-

© The Nobel Foundation

science." The disillusionment, in fact, has little to do with the beloved. Rather, the disillusionment is a device to trigger the protagonist's introspection, his moment of awareness brought on by the experience. The moment of awareness for Amra's husband, Christian Jacoby, kills him. Other protagonists live on, lacking the will even to kill themselves, such as the narrator in Mann's story "Enttäuschung" ("Disillusionment"), who says of his disillusionment that it has left him "alone, unhappy, and a little queer."

Mann's protagonists yearn for experience, for connection with the day-to-day living of those around them, and for a synthesis between body and spirit, discipline and impulse, reason and passion, involvement and withdrawal, action and inaction. They are fascinated by grief, death, and disease. In Mann's story "Der Kleiderschrank" ("The Wardrobe"), for example, the dying man is drawn to the boardinghouse of a woman who has a "repulsive eruption, a sort of fungus growth, on her brow." Again, in Mann's story "Tobias Mindernickel," Tobias is fascinated by a child's bleeding injury and by his dog Esau's injury. He is so fascinated by Esau's injury that, after it has healed, he tries to reinjure the dog and, in the process, kills it.

Two works typical of Mann's early short fiction are "Der kleine Herr Friedemann" ("Little Herr Friedemann") and *Tonio Kröger.* In these works, Mann develops the Symbolist theme of the artist's solitude, the theme of the burgher turned artist, and the themes involved in the battles between body and mind, passion and intellect, action and inaction.

"Little Herr Friedemann" • In "Little Herr Friedemann," the title story from Mann's 1898 collection of stories, Mann explores the themes of obsession with beauty and disillusionment with romanticism. Johannes Friedemann, a hunchback because he was dropped by his drunken nurse when he was an infant, seeks a life of fulfillment through art and nature. This pursuit is encouraged by his ailing mother, who, after fourteen years of a lingering illness, dies, leaving Friedemann with his three unmarried sisters. Like other protagonists in Mann's short fiction, Friedemann "cherishes" his grief over his mother's death and moves further into his solitary existence. To the extent that he thinks of his own death, he envisions it like his mother's death, a "mild twilight radiance gently declining into dark." At the age of thirty, after constructing a rigorously disciplined life, Friedemann becomes obsessed with a beautiful woman, Frau Gerda von Rinnlingen. Battling between passion and reason, between action and inaction, Friedemann finally summons his courage to go to Frau Rinnlingen and confess his love. He hopes that she will feel pity for him. She instead dismisses him with a "short, scornful laugh" as she clutches his arm and flings him sideways to the ground. The rejection leaves Friedemann "stunned and unmanned" and shuddering. In this moment of awareness, he directs his anger against himself. He is filled with "a thirst to destroy himself, to tear himself to pieces, to blot himself utterly out." He drags himself to the river and, with a faint splash, drowns himself. The final image is a "faint sound of laughter" in the distance. Friedemann is among Mann's disillusioned romantics who do not survive their moment of awareness.

Friedemann, often considered a prototype of Gustave von Aschenbach in the novella *Death in Venice*, illuminates the struggle between passion and intellect, a leitmotif linking the various stories in the first volume together. It is the disillusioned romanticism embodied in Friedemann that moves Mann, in his second volume of stories, *Tristan*, toward what critics have called a "new artistic intellectualism."

Tonio Kröger • In the novella *Tonio Kröger*, Mann again develops the burgher-artist theme, evident in the title name itself. The name "Tonio," for Mann, symbolizes the artistic heritage of Italy, and "Kröger" symbolizes the disciplined intellectualism of his German father. The protagonist, Tonio Kröger, is a sort of synthesis of the artist and intellectual. An outsider in his youth, Tonio later considers isolating himself from society, but he rejects the impulse, thus allowing himself to find a sort of consolation.

The novella begins as Tonio waits for his childhood friend Hans Hansen, so that they can go for a walk, something Hans has almost forgotten while Tonio has "looked forward to it with almost incessant joy." Though Tonio does not want to be like Hans, he loves Hans, not only because he is handsome but also because he is "in every respect his [Tonio's] own opposite and foil." Tonio is brooding, sensitive, and introspective, while Hans is lively, insensitive, and superficial.

Hans and Tonio are separated, years pass, and when Tonio is sixteen years old, his passion for Hans turns to Ingeborg Holm, who makes his heart throb with ecstasy. Tonio, like Friedemann in "Little Herr Friedemann," is aware that his beloved is "remote and estranged," but still he prefers her company to that of Magdalena Vermehren, who understands him and laughs or is serious in the right places. Tonio, realizing the implications of his unrequited love for Hans and later for Inge, speaks of being flung to and fro forever "between two crass extremes: between icy intellect and scorching sense."

In contrast to Hans and Inge is Lisabeta Ivanova, Tonio's close and candid artist-friend of approximately his own age. Though she offers Tonio consolation during his turmoil, she also calls him bourgeois, because he is drawn to the superficial Hans and

Inge and because he wants to be ordinary. Lisabeta and Tonio explore in dialogue the implications of the artist's existence. Lisabeta, unlike Tonio, is reconciled to her role as an artist.

After thirteen years, Hans returns, and Tonio comes upon him with Inge; Hans and Inge, two of a type, get along well together. Nevertheless, when Tonio, Hans, Magdalena, and Inge all end up at a dance, Tonio tries to make Inge jealous by dancing with Magdalena. Like many of Mann's disillusioned romantics, Tonio hopes that his beloved will suddenly return the passion that he feels for her. Inge, however, is incapable of feeling passion for Tonio. She is, in fact, oblivious to his anguish and remains at the dance with Hans. Dejectedly, Tonio returns to his room.

The novella ends with a letter that Tonio writes to Lisabeta from his room at Aalsgard. In the letter, Tonio concludes that he can be happy with the unrequited love of his ideal beauty. He says to Lisabeta of his unrequited love that it is "good and fruitful." He relishes the "longing" in it and the "gentle envy." He concludes that, through the love, he experiences a "touch of contempt and no little innocent bliss." Unlike the unrequited love of Johannes Friedemann that leads to Friedemann's self-loathing and death, the unrequited love of Tonio Kröger somehow consoles and sustains him.

A significant change in Mann's later short fiction appears in his treatment of aging. In the earlier works, the protagonists tend to be thirty-year-old disillusioned romantics, characters drawn to youth as much as beauty. The culminating point of this fascination with youth is in the story "Das Wunderkind" ("The Infant Prodigy"), in which the protagonist is eight, looks nine, and is given out for seven. The child, dressed in white silk, has dark circles around his eyes and is already bored, isolated, and somewhat cynical. Nevertheless, the audience is spellbound by the prodigy's youth.

In Mann's later works, the protagonists develop a fear of aging. For example, Gustave von Aschenbach in the novella *Death in Venice* and Frau Rosalie von Tümmler in the novella *The Black Swan*, upon reaching their early fifties, fall passionately in love as they are dying, Aschenbach of cholera and Tümmler of cancer. As in Mann's early works, the beloved ones are young. In the later works, however, the protagonists dread their own aging, eventually creating young-old death masks for themselves, masks that, ironically, turn out to be their death masks. In addition to exploring the fear of aging, Mann begins to explore new ideas, such as the effects of evil on passive people, as in *Mario and the Magician*, and the implications of mythologies, as in *The Transposed Heads*.

Death in Venice • *Death in Venice* has received high critical acclaim; it is often called Mann's finest novella and one of the finest novellas of Western literature. Mann explores several themes in the novella: the conflict between discipline and impulse, the fear of aging, the draw to beauty that destroys, the death wish, the draw to homoerotic love, and the battle between passion and reason.

Death in Venice is set in the early twentieth century in Munich, Germany, and Venice. The central character, Gustave von Aschenbach, is a well-known German author in his early fifties. At the beginning of the novella, Aschenbach, suffering from insomnia, takes a walk near his home in Munich. On the walk, he encounters a man near the burying ground. The man, who later appears in Venice, awakes in Aschenbach an irresistible longing to travel. This longing eventually puts him on board a ship bound for Venice, where he encounters a repulsive "young-old man," masquerading as one of the youths and trying to keep pace with them. The man, "pitiably drunk," approaches Aschenbach, and as the young-old man drools and stutters nonsense, the upper plate of his false teeth falls loose. Clearly disgusted by the young-old man, Aschenbach escapes. This encounter foreshadows Aschenbach's later battle against his own aging.

In Venice, Aschenbach becomes obsessed with the beautiful Tadzio, a Polish youth about fourteen years old. Mixed with Aschenbach's passion for Tadzio's beauty is a conscious fascination with Tadzio's mortality. For example, as Aschenbach watches Tadzio play, he realizes that it is not Tadzio he sees, "but Hyacinthus, doomed to die because two gods were rivals for his love." When Aschenbach recognizes Tadzio's ill health, he thinks that Tadzio will "most likely not live to grow old." This idea gives Aschenbach pleasure, but Aschenbach refuses to analyze his response. Later, upon the same realization, "compassion" struggles with "reckless exultation" in Aschenbach's heart. Though Aschenbach chooses not to explore this exultation, clearly one part of his joy lies in what critics have called "the seduction of the individual by disease and death" and the other part in Tadzio's avoidance of the aging that disgusts and frightens Aschenbach. Aschenbach feels exultation not because Tadzio will die but because Tadzio will not live to grow old.

As Venice becomes plague-ridden with Asiatic cholera, Aschenbach himself begins to look haggard. He is plagued by the odor of carbolic acid from the man from the burying ground, an odor that Aschenbach suspects others may not detect. He is repulsed by the pervasive stench of germicide and by the "odour of the sickened city." At this point, in his own battle against the physical effects of his declining health and his aging, Aschenbach dyes his hair black and "freshens up" his skin, making himself into a ghoulish "young-old man."

Aschenbach, nearing his end, has a terrifying dream about the "bestial degradation of his fall." In the dream, he realizes that he has lost the battle between passion and reason. Tadzio has smiled at Aschenbach and has, in that small gesture, left Aschenbach feeling "quite unmanned." Aschenbach, still made up into a young-old man, dies in Venice of the cholera. Aschenbach's death reinforces Mann's theme that in the battle between spirit and body, there are no winners. In death, Aschenbach satisfies his need to be free of the yearning that is opposed to his art, the "lure, for the unorganized, the immeasurable, the eternal—in short, for nothingness."

Finally, in *Death in Venice*, Mann explores again, as he does in "Little Herr Friedemann," the theme of the artist being drawn to "beauty that breaks the heart." Even while Aschenbach recognizes the superficiality of the physical attraction, even of his beloved, as he comes to the subtle realization that the lover is "nearer the divine than the beloved," he finds that beauty compelling. He concludes, as does Tonio Kröger, that "in almost every artist is inborn a wanton and treacherous proneness to side with the beauty that breaks the heart, to single out aristocratic pretensions and pay them homage." It is this homage to beauty that makes Aschenbach incapable of action and holds him in Venice to meet his death.

Mario and the Magician • A novella in a different vein is *Mario and the Magician*, published between World War I and World War II. It is generally considered an attack on fascism. The story begins with a German family visiting Italy and experiencing a series of minor humiliations. The family later becomes part of the audience of an evil hypnotist, Cipolla, who humiliates the members of his passive audience, one at a time, until one of them, Mario, shoots him, an act that leaves the audience liberated.

Early in the novella, Mann introduces the theme of peace. He says, "We all know how the world at once seeks peace and puts her to flight—rushing upon her in the fond idea that they two will wed, and where she is, there it can be at home." Peace, however, is treated ironically, in that the desire for peace keeps the passive audience from acting, even as they become the humpbacked magician's victims. Mann's narrator soon begins to realize that in "yielding to another person's will—there may lie too small a space for the idea of freedom to squeeze into." In contrast to Johannes Friedemann, who is destroyed when he acts, the audience in *Mario and the Magician* is saved only through action.

Among Mann's last short fiction, first published between 1940 and 1955, are *The Transposed Heads* and *The Black Swan*. Significant in these last major works of short fiction are two characteristics of Mann's work. The first is one of adapting mythology in new contexts, as he does in the novella *The Transposed Heads*, an adaptation of a Hindu legend about seeking harmony between the inner and outer self. The second characteristic is one represented in the novella *The Black Swan*, in which Mann's earlier theme of the conflict between youth and age, life and death, occurs.

The Transposed Heads • In *The Transposed Heads*, Mann creates his most abstract and mythic characters. Shridaman, a merchant and the son of a merchant, represents spirit and intellect, while Nanda, a smith and a cowherd, represents body and intuition. The girl represents beauty. Though Mann called this work "a metaphysical farce," it offers an integral vision of a new humanity. It is in this tale that Mann includes his clearest synthesis of the unity between "Shridaman" and "Nanda":

> This world is not so made that spirit is fated to love only spirit, and beauty only beauty. Indeed the very contrast between the two points out, with a clarity at once intellectual and beautiful, that the world's goal is union between spirit and beauty, a bliss no longer divided, but whole and consummate.

Following this vision, Mann returns to the farce, concluding, "This tale . . . is but an illustration of the failures and false starts attending the effort to reach the goal."

The Black Swan • In *The Black Swan*, Mann retells the story of Gustave von Aschenbach of *Death in Venice* but with a new twist. The novella, set in Düsseldorf in the 1920's, tells the story of Frau Rosalie von Tümmler, a fifty-year-old widow, who is caught up in passion for her son Eduard's youthful tutor, Ken Keaton, an American expatriate. Once again, the lover is closer to the divine than the beloved. Ken Keaton is variously described by critics as insipid, mediocre, and commonplace, an amiable nonentity. Like Aschenbach, Rosalie, as she becomes increasingly obsessed with her beloved, dyes her hair and applies cosmetics to conceal her age. Like Aschenbach, she does active battle against physical aging.

Rosalie von Tümmler's daughter Anna, born with a clubfoot, paints abstract art and tries to purge all feeling from her work. It is she, recognizing her mother's unhealthy passion, who urges her mother to establish a more socially acceptable relationship with Keaton. Still, Rosalie ignores her daughter's advice.

In an ironic twist, Mann has Rosalie develop cancer of the womb before she can go to Keaton's room to consummate their relationship. The cause of the cancer is, again ironically, the agitation that she experiences during menopause, her passion for Keaton thus leading to her own death in a matter of weeks. A further irony is evident in that the rejuvenation that Rosalie feels in her passion for Keaton is, in fact, a symptom of her physical decay.

Unlike Aschenbach, however, Rosalie regains her dignity during the final weeks of her life. She yearns for the aristocratic black swans, a death symbol. The German title, *Die Betrogene*, means "the deceived," and Rosalie von Tümmler is indeed deceived, by both her passion and her body, which has sent her messages of a new vitality even while she was mortally ill. Still, unlike Aschenbach, whose passion remains unresolved, Rosalie dies a "gentle death, regretted by all who knew her."

Throughout Mann's lengthy writing career, from 1894 to 1955, the bulk of critical opinion of his work was consistently favorable. It has remained so after his death. Nevertheless, significant changes occur between his early and late short fiction. To some extent, Mann's protagonists do achieve, if not a synthesis of polarities, at least a complex worldview in which they find consolation. The shift in worldview is particularly evident in Mann's treatment of the conflicts between self-destruction and survival, between passion and discipline, and between action and inaction.

First, in the conflict between self-destruction and survival, Mann's early protagonists cannot survive their disillusionment. Johannes Friedemann in "Little Herr Friedemann" is filled with self-loathing and drowns himself. Christian Jacoby in "Little Lizzy" becomes suddenly aware of his wife's infidelity and dies instantly from shock and grief. With Mann's development of Tonio Kröger in *Tonio Kröger*, however, the disillusioned romantic finds a new, though not fully gratifying, illusion that can permit him to survive. Some critics have referred to this new worldview as Mann's artistic intellectualism. This artistic intellectualism is based on a sort of ironic realization that perhaps the wanting is superior to the having, an idea that acknowledges both the passion and the intellect. Mann explores another sort of synthesis of the conflict between self-destruction and survival in Frau Rosalie von Tümmler in *The Black Swan*. Though Frau Tümmler's passion triggers the cancer that kills her, she clearly comes to terms with her self-destructive passion. Her death is not a suicide but rather a "gentle" death, the sort envisioned by Johannes Friedemann before his disillusionment.

Second, in the conflict between passion and discipline, Mann's early protagonists are undone by their passion. Johannes Friedemann and Christian Jacoby illustrate Mann's early theme that in conflicts between passion and discipline, body and intellect, there are no winners. Though Tonio Kröger provides a respite from the conflict, as he learns to live with unrequited love, Mann explores this conflict in a new light with Gustave von Aschenbach in *Death in Venice*. Aschenbach does not act on his passion, except insofar as he does not leave the plague-ridden Venice, an inaction that, in fact, becomes a self-destructive action. Unlike Johannes Friedemann and Christian Jacoby, however, Aschenbach does not confess his love to his beloved; to that extent, he displays discipline. Nevertheless, the inaction caused by his passion leads as clearly to his destruction as if he had taken his own life, and though he dies with his self-loathing at what he calls his "bestial degradation," he has not destroyed his reputation as a novelist. Mann does a final exploration of the battle between passion and discipline in the character of Rosalie von Tümmler. Frau Tümmler, fully prepared to act on her passion despite her daughter's advice, collapses on her way to meet her beloved and consummate their passion. To that point, Frau Tümmler has lost her battle between passion and discipline, but through the remainder of her mortal illness, she has a second chance to retrieve her dignity, and she does so with grace.

Finally, in the conflict between action and inaction, Mann's protagonists become increasingly complex. In the early stories, characters who act, especially on their passion, destroy themselves. For example, when Johannes Friedemann in "Little Herr Friedemann" acts on his passion for Frau Rinnlingen, the action leads to his death. When Christian Jacoby in "Little Lizzy" acts on his wife's wishes and against his better judgment, he faces a moment of awareness that destroys him. Later, Mann's Tonio Kröger in *Tonio Kröger* opts for inaction with his beloved Inge. That inaction saves him. Mann's treatment of Gustave von Aschenbach in *Death in Venice* is among Mann's most complex explorations of the conflict between action and inaction. Had Aschenbach not acted on the yearning to travel, triggered by the stranger at the burying ground in Munich, he might not have been in Venice during the cholera epidemic. Aschenbach's failure to act by leaving Venice when he had the opportunity, however, results in his death of cholera. Mann introduces another new complexity into the conflict between action and inaction in Mario in *Mario and the Magician*. The audience sits by passively while the magician victimizes them, one after another. When Mario acts, killing the magician, his action liberates the audience. In Mann's final exploration of the conflict between action and inaction, Rosalie von Tümmler, in her decision to act on her passion, loses her option for further action on her passion, but in her final weeks of illness, she acts again, this time to reclaim her dignity. Her final action leads to her self-respect and to a gentle death.

Part of the resolution of conflicts in Mann's later short fiction undoubtedly comes from his use of his own experience in the creation of his protagonists. In fact, in 1936, when *Stories of Three Decades* was published, Mann, then officially in exile, referred to the collection as "an autobiography in the guise of a fable." In Mann's work during his years of exile, he moved increasingly toward exploring syntheses of the conflicts in his earlier protagonists. As a result, his later protagonists, as they expand their worldviews, begin to synthesize humanism, culture, and philosophy, and through these protagonists, one sees, always, Mann's ironic observations of the world.

Carol Franks

Other major works

PLAY: *Fiorenza*, pb. 1906.

NOVELS: *Buddenbrooks: Verfall einer Familie*, 1901 (English translation, 1924); *Tonio Kröger*, 1903 (novella; English translation, 1914); *Tristan*, 1903 (novella; English translation, 1925); *Königliche Hoheit*, 1909 (*Royal Highness*, 1916); *Der Tod in Venedig*, 1912 (novella; *Death in Venice*, 1925); *Herr und Hund*, 1919 (novella; *Bashan and I*, 1923; also known as *A Man and His Dog*, 1930); *Der Zauberberg*, 1924 (*The Magic Mountain*, 1927); *Unordnung und frühes Leid*, 1926 (novella; *Disorder and Early Sorrow*, 1929); *Mario und der Zauberer*, 1930 (novella; *Mario and the Magician*, 1930); *Die Geschichten Jaakobs*, 1933 (*Joseph and His Brothers*, 1934; also as *The Tales of Jacob*, 1934); *Joseph und seine Brüder*, 1933-1943 (collective title for previous 4 novels; *Joseph and His Brothers*, 1948); *Der junge Joseph*, 1934 (*The Young Joseph*, 1935); *Joseph in Ägypten*, 1936 (*Joseph in Egypt*, 1938); *Lotte in Weimar*, 1939 (*The Beloved Returns*, 1940); *Die vertauschten Köpfe: Eine indische Legend*, 1940 (novella; *The Transposed Heads: A Legend of India*, 1941); *Joseph, der Ernährer*, 1943 (*Joseph the Provider*, 1944); *Doktor Faustus: Das Leben des deutschen Tonsetzers Adrian Leverkühn, erzählt von einem Freunde*, 1947 (*Doctor Faustus: The Life of the German Composer Adrian Leverkühn as Told by a Friend*, 1948); *Der Erwählte*, 1951 (*The Holy Sinner*, 1951); *Die Betrogene*, 1953 (novella; *The Black Swan*, 1954);

Bekenntnisse des Hochstaplers Felix Krull: Der Memoiren erster Teil, 1954 (*Confessions of Felix Krull, Confidence Man: The Early Years,* 1955).

MISCELLANEOUS: *Gesammelte Werke,* 1956 (12 volumes; includes critical writings in volumes 10-11); *Gesammelte Werke,* 1960-1974 (13 volumes; includes critical writings in volumes 9-11); *Werkausgabe,* 1980-1986 (20 volumes; includes 3 volumes of critical writings).

NONFICTION: "Friedrich und die grosse Koalition," 1915 ("Frederick and the Great Coalition," 1929); *Betrachtungen eines Unpolitischen,* 1918 (*Reflections of a Nonpolitical Man,* 1983); *Rede und Antwort,* 1922; *Bemühungen,* 1925; *Die Forderung des Tages,* 1930; *Lebensabriss,* 1930 (*A Sketch of My Life,* 1960); *Three Essays,* 1932; *Past Masters and Other Papers,* 1933; *Leiden und Grösse der Meister,* 1935; *Freud, Goethe, Wagner,* 1937; *Achtung, Europa!,* 1938; *Dieser Friede,* 1938 (*This Peace,* 1938); *Vom künftigen Sieg der Demokratie,* 1938 (*The Coming of Victory of Democracy,* 1938); *Deutsche Hörer!,* 1942 (*Listen, Germany!,* 1943); *Order of the Day: Political Essays and Speeches of Two Decades,* 1942; *Adel des Geistes: Sechzehn Versuche zum Problem der Humanität,* 1945 (*Essays of Three Decades,* 1947); *Neue Studien,* 1948; *Die Entstehung des "Doktor Faustus": Roman eines Romans,* 1949 (*The Story of a Novel: The Genesis of "Doctor Faustus,"* 1961); *Altes und Neues: Kleine Prosa aus fünf Jahrzehnten,* 1953; *Versuch über Schiller,* 1955; *Nachlese: Prosa, 1951-1955,* 1956; *Last Essays,* 1958; *Briefe,* 1961-1965 (3 volumes; partial translation *Letters of Thomas Mann, 1889-1955,* 1970); *Addresses Delivered at the Library of Congress,* 1963; *Wagner und unsere Zeit,* 1963 (*Pro and Contra Wagner,* 1985); *Reden und Aufsätze,* 1965 (2 volumes); *Essays,* 1977-1978 (3 volumes); *Tagebücher,* 1977-1986 (6 volumes; partial translation *Diaries 1918-1939,* 1982); *Goethes Laufbahn als Schriftsteller: Zwölf Essays und Reden zu Goethe,* 1982; *Frage und Antwort: Interviews mit Thomas Mann 1909-1955,* 1983; *Thomas Mann's "Goethe and Tolstoy": Notes and Sources,* 1984.

POETRY: "Gesang vom Kindchen," 1919.

Bibliography
Berlin, Jeffrey B., ed. *Approaches to Teaching Mann's "Death in Venice" and Other Short Fiction.* New York: Modern Language Association, 1992. Part 1 (materials) focuses on general introductions, reference works, and critical studies. Part 2 (approaches) contains perceptive essays on Mann's handling of many themes and his approach to comedy, tradition, modernism, Sigmund Freud, and other thinkers and writers. Includes an extensive bibliography.

Cullander, Cecil C. H. "Why Thomas Mann Wrote." *The Virginia Quarterly Review* 75 (Winter, 1999): 31-48. Examines Mann's statements about his creativity, his fiction, and his journals and diaries; argues that his diaries helped him come to terms with his homosexuality and to know himself.

Kurzke, Hermann. *Thomas Mann: Life as a Work of Art, a Biography.* Translated by Leslie Willson. Princeton, N.J.: Princeton University Press, 2002. Work celebrated in Germany that provides a balanced approach to Mann's life and work. Addresses his homosexuality and relationship to Judaism. The translation, however, is not good. Index.

Lesér, Esther H. *Thomas Mann's Short Fiction: An Intellectual Biography.* Madison, N.J.: Fairleigh Dickinson University Press, 1989. Lesér states the purposes of her biography as twofold: "as a reference work in which each story may be read individually with its comprehensive study materials, and as an organic study of Thomas Mann's intellectual development." The chapters are arranged thematically, each integrating analyses of representative works.

Mann, Thomas. *Death in Venice.* Edited by Naomi Ritter. Boston: Bedford Books, 1998. Reprinting of a widely acclaimed translation of Mann's novella, along with the presentation of five critical essays that serve to familiarize students to the novella.

May, Charles E., ed. *Masterplots II: Short Story Series, Revised Edition.* 8 vols. Pasadena, Calif.: Salem Press, 2004. Designed for student use, this reference set contains articles providing detailed plot summaries and analyses of eight short stories by Mann: "Death in Venice" and "Disorder and Early Sorrow" (vol. 2), "Gladius Dei" (vol. 3), "The Infant Prodigy" and "Little Herr Friedemann" (vol. 4), "Mario and the Magician" (vol. 5), and "Tonio Kröger" and "Tristan" (vol. 7).

Reed, T. J. *Thomas Mann: The Uses of Tradition.* New York: Oxford University Press, 1996. Meticulously researched and well-documented study on Mann's thought and fiction. Includes bibliographical references and index.

Robertson, Ritchie, ed. *The Cambridge Companion to Thomas Mann.* New York: Cambridge University Press, 2002. Thorough reference source on Mann. Bibliography and index.

Votteler, Thomas, ed. "Thomas Mann: 1875-1955." In *Short Story Criticism, Excerpts from Criticism of the Works of Short Fiction Writers.* Vol. 5. Detroit: Gale Research, 1990. The entry begins with a brief introduction to Mann, but it is primarily a series of excerpts of the criticism of Mann's short fiction.

Winston, Richard. *Thomas Mann: The Making of an Artist, 1875-1911.* New York: Alfred A. Knopf, 1981. Winston arranges the biographical information chronologically, but he intersperses chapters of thematic analysis and explication. The book, aimed at readers of literary biography, covers Mann's early years.

Katherine Mansfield

Born: Wellington, New Zealand; October 14, 1888
Died: Fontainebleau, France; January 9, 1923

Principal short fiction • *In a German Pension,* 1911; *Bliss, and Other Stories,* 1920; *The Garden Party, and Other Stories,* 1922; *The Doves' Nest, and Other Stories,* 1923; *Something Childish, and Other Stories,* 1924 (also known as *The Little Girl, and Other Stories,* 1924).

Other literary forms • Although Katherine Mansfield is best known as a writer of short stories, she also wrote poems and book reviews, which were collected and edited posthumously by her second husband, John Middleton Murry. She once began a novel, and several fragments of plays have survived. She left a considerable amount of personal documents; their bulk greatly exceeds that of her published work. Murry edited the *Journal of Katherine Mansfield* (1927; "Definitive Edition," 1954), *The Letters of Katherine Mansfield* (1928), *The Scrapbook of Katherine Mansfield* (1939), and *Katherine Mansfield's Letters to John Middleton Murry,* 1913-1922 (1951).

Achievements • Although extravagant claims have been made for her, many critics insist that Mansfield's achievements were modest. She completed no novel, and, although she wrote about a hundred stories, her fame rests on no more than a dozen. Yet, in any age, her stories would be remarkable for their precise and evocative descriptions, their convincing dialogue, their economy and wit, and their dazzling insights into the shifting emotions of their characters.

In her own age, she was a pioneer. She and James Joyce are often credited with creating the modern short story. Though this claim may be an exaggeration, her stories did without the old-fashioned overbearing author-narrators, the elaborate settings of scenes, and the obvious explanations of motives and themes of earlier fiction. Instead, she provided images and metaphors, dialogues and monologues with little in between. Like T. S. Eliot's *The Waste Land* (1922), her stories seem to have had their nonpoetic dross deleted.

Mansfield's stories have influenced such writers as Elizabeth Bowen, Katherine Anne Porter, and Christopher Isherwood; the standard "*New Yorker* story" owes much to her. Most important, many decades after her death, her stories are read with pleasure.

Biography • Almost everything Katherine Mansfield wrote was autobiographical in some way. It helps a reader to know about Mansfield's life because she often does not identify her stories' locations. For example, readers may be puzzled by her combining English manners and exotic flora in her New Zealand stories.

Mansfield was born Kathleen Mansfield Beauchamp in Wellington, New Zealand, on October 14, 1888. (In her lifetime, she used many names. Her family called her "Kass." She took "Katherine Mansfield" as her name in 1910.) Her father, Harold Beauchamp, was an importer who became chairman of the Bank of New Zealand and was knighted in 1923. In 1903, the Beauchamps sailed for London, where Kass was enrolled at Queen's College, an institution for young women much like a university.

She remained at Queen's until 1906, reading advanced authors such as Oscar Wilde and publishing stories in the college magazine. Her parents brought her back to Wellington in 1906, where she published her first stories in a newspaper. She left New Zealand for London in 1908, never to return.

Mansfield's next decade was one of personal complexities and artistic growth. She was sexually attracted to both women and men. At Queen's College, she met Ida Baker, her friend and companion for much of her life. Back in London, she fell in love with a violinist whom she had known in New Zealand. After she learned that she was pregnant by him, she abruptly married George C. Bowden on March 2, 1909, and as abruptly left him. At her mother's insistence, she traveled to Germany, where she had a miscarriage. The Bowdens were not divorced until April, 1918.

In Germany Mansfield met the Polish translator Floryan Sobieniowski, who, in the opinion of biographer Claire Tomalin, infected her with gonorrhea. Most of her medical problems may have come from this infection: the removal of a Fallopian tube, rheumatic symptoms, pleurisy, and eventually tuberculosis. Back in London, Mansfield met the future editor and critic John Middleton Murry. Their on-again, off-again relationship endured until her death. They were married on May 3, 1918; after she died, Murry edited her stories, letters, and journals. Meanwhile, she was strongly affected when her brother was killed in France in 1915. His death and her own worsening health were probably strong influences on her stories.

During these years, Mansfield and Murry knew many famous writers and artists, particularly those who frequented Lady Ottoline Morrell's famous salon at Garsington: Lytton Strachey, Dora Carrington, David Garnett, Aldous Huxley, Dorothy Brett, J. M. Keynes, T. S. Eliot. She and Virginia Woolf had an off-and-on friendship and professional association; she seriously flirted with Bertrand Russell. The Murrys' most notable friendship was with D. H. and Frieda Lawrence; "Gudrun" in D. H. Lawrence's *Women in Love* (1920) is said to be based on Mansfield. Both Woolf and Lawrence were influenced by Mansfield; both made nasty remarks about her in her last years.

Another result of Mansfield's meeting Sobieniowski in Germany may have been her reading the works of Anton Chekhov. Her story "The Child-Who-Was-Tired" is a free adaptation—perhaps a plagiarism—of a Chekhov story. During 1910 and 1911, she published a number of bitter stories with German settings, collected in *In a German Pension*. For the next seven years, Mansfield experimented with many styles and published stories in journals such as *New Age, Rhythm,* and *Blue Review* before she discovered a mature voice. Her first great story, "Prelude," was published as a booklet in July, 1918, by Virginia and Leonard Woolf's Hogarth Press.

Mansfield's health had not been good for several years; her gonorrhea remained undiagnosed until 1918. From the time she learned that she had tuberculosis in December, 1917, she spent most of each year out of England. Accompanied by Murry or Ida Baker, she traveled to France, Switzerland, and Italy, trying to fight off her disease. In 1922, her search led her to Georges Ivanovitch Gurdjieff's Institute of the Harmonious Development of Man near Paris, where she seems to have been moderately happy until she died.

During Mansfield's last five years, she wrote most of the stories for which she is best known. They were often published in journals such as *Athenaeum, Arts and Letters, London Mercury,* and *Sphere.* Many were then collected in *Bliss, and Other Stories* and *The Garden-Party, and Other Stories.*

Analysis • Katherine Mansfield's themes are not hard to discover. In 1918, she set herself the tasks of communicating the exhilarating delicacy and peacefulness of the world's beauty and also of crying out against "corruption." A reader will soon make his or her own list of themes: the yearnings, complexities, and misunderstandings of love; loneliness, particularly of independent women; the superficiality of much of modern life; the erosions of time and forgetfulness; the beauty and indifferent power of the natural world, especially plant life and the sea. Her exact meanings are not so easily pinned down, for her tone is complex: She mixes witty satire and shattering emotional reversals. Moreover, she uses dialogue and indirect speech extensively, and she does not often seem to speak directly in her own voice; the reader is not sure exactly who is speaking. It is vital for readers to understand that Mansfield (like Chekhov, to whom she is often compared) does not conceal a hidden "message" in her stories. If a story appears to point in many directions, not all of which are logically consistent, that is the way Mansfield feels the whole truth is most honestly communicated. This essay suggests some of the ways these stories may be read.

The action of Mansfield's stories (again, like Chekhov's) does not surge powerfully forward. Often her stories are designed, by means of quick changes in time and by surprise turns, to lead the reader to unexpected moments of illumination or epiphanies. Her stories are economical, edited so that there is usually not one unnecessary or insignificant word. She can be witty if she chooses, but more often her stories provide arresting descriptions and startling metaphors, which evoke shifting states of happiness, yearning, or despair.

"In a Café" • Mansfield's stories often evoke the complexities of the conversational give-and-take between women and men and the unexpected courses that passion can take. An early story, "In a Café," portrays a youthful "new woman" and her male acquaintance, a musician. They flirt as they discuss life, art, and the future. Before he leaves, he asks the girl for her violets, but once outside he drops them because he must keep his hands warm for performing. The young woman is totally happy until she sees the violets on the sidewalk. The reader knows that her love has been crushed, but, new woman that she is, she kicks the flowers and goes her way laughing.

"Epilogue II" • "Epilogue II" (also known as "Violet") is more complex. At a pension in France, where the acidly worldly narrator is recovering from an attack of nerves, she reports a long conversation with an exasperating woman named Violet, who in turns tells of a conversation she has had with a man named Arthur. Violet says that, after a few dances, Arthur asked her if she believed in Pan and kissed her. It was her first adult kiss, and they immediately became engaged. The narrator can hardly believe what Violet tells her and is repelled by how easily the naïve Violet and Arthur have found each other. The story (a conversation within a conversation) ends with the narrator thinking that she herself might be too sophisticated. (In this story, Mansfield has imported a piece of conversation from real life. Sometime before she wrote "Epilogue II," she startled a man by asking him if he believed in Pan.)

"Psychology" • In "Psychology," Mansfield dissects the ebb and flow of attraction between two older artists, culminating in a moment of potential, a moment which, because of their agonizing self-consciousness, they miss. This story shows both minds, but readers are left with the woman and with another characteristically unexpected psychological twist. An older female acquaintance brings her flowers—violets again. This spontaneous gift revitalizes the woman, and with renewed hope she begins an intense letter to the man who has left her. Readers may guess that their next meeting will be no more satisfying than their last.

"Je Ne Parle Pas Français" • Mansfield often portrays more complex and ambiguous sexual and psychological relationships and, as usual, constructs her story to lead her reader in roundabout ways into unexpected territory. Though she often takes readers briefly into male minds, the story "Je Ne Parle Pas Français" has one of her rare male narrators. Raoul Duqette, a grubby Parisian writer, pimp, and gigolo, tells of an Englishman, Dick Harmon, and the woman nicknamed "Mouse," whom he brings to Paris. Not all critics agree on whom the story concerns. Although the reader learns much about the English couple's tortured relationship (Dick leaves Mouse because he cannot betray his mother, and Mouse knows she cannot return to England), many readers think that the story centers on the Frenchman. Incapable of deep emotion, Raoul spies on those with fuller lives than his own; he despises women, is sexually attracted to Dick, and is able to recognize only dimly the suffering that he has witnessed. At the end, he revels in Mouse's sorrow and imagines selling a girl like her to an old lecher.

"Bliss" • The triangle in "Bliss" is different, and again, Mansfield mixes her tones. Bertha seems childishly happy in her marriage, her home, her child, and her arty friends. She gives a marvelous party in which sophisticated guests make inane, decadent conversation. Meanwhile, Bertha finds herself physically attracted to one of her guests, the cool Miss Fulton, and thinks that she detects Miss Fulton giving her a signal. Together in the garden, they contemplate a lovely, flowering pear tree, and Bertha senses that they understand each other intuitively. Again Mansfield surprises the reader. Bertha transfers her feelings for Miss Fulton to her husband; for the first time, she really desires him. When she overhears him making an assignation with Miss Fulton, however, her life is shattered. In "Bliss," as elsewhere, Mansfield's brilliant and precise descriptions of the nonhuman world are always evocative. Although sometimes nature simply reveals an unsympathetic force, allied to human passions but beyond human control, some natural features demand to be interpreted as symbols, such as the phallic pear tree in this story. Phallic it is, but it may be feminine as well, for Bertha identifies with it. The story is read, however, and the pear tree cannot be explained simply. Neither can the reader's final reaction: Is Bertha trapped in an evil world? Is she a free adult at last?

"The Lost Battle" • Mansfield also explores the problems of lonely women, often by showing the reader their inmost trains of thought. In "The Lost Battle," a woman traveling alone is escorted to her room in a French hotel by an overbearing man who makes demeaning and insinuating remarks: A bed in a small room will be enough for her, he implies. She asserts herself and demands a better room, one with a table on which to write. She wins her struggle and is happy with her new room—its size, the view from its windows, and its sturdy table. When she overtips the boy who delivers her bags, however, her joy somehow leaves her. In a convincing but mysterious moment typical of Mansfield's stories, the woman's bravery collapses in self-consciousness, memory, tears, and desire.

"Miss Brill" • Perhaps Mansfield's best-known version of the lonely woman is the central character of "Miss Brill." The reader follows Miss Brill's thoughts as she arrives at the public gardens. The first faint chill of fall and the noise of the band signal that a new season has begun. Miss Brill's sympathetic interest extends to the various sorts of people in the park; the reader senses an older, precise woman who yearns that happiness and gentleness will come for herself and others. Even some unpleasantries fail to shake Miss Brill's enjoyment, as she rejoices that everyone there is performing in some wonderful, happy play. Her illusions, however, are shattered by two insensitive young lovers who simply wish that the fussy old woman would move. Again the reader is taken into a lonely woman's mind as she undergoes a psychic shock.

"The Daughters of the Late Colonel" • In "The Daughters of the Late Colonel," the shock is muffled, and the reader does not enter the two sisters' minds so deeply so soon. The story at first appears to center on the familiar Mansfield theme of male domination. The sisters seem to react alike to the death of their domineering father. They are still under his spell. Mansfield shows her dry wit as their hesitant and ineffectual efforts to assert themselves with the nurse and their maid are pathetic and hilarious at the same time. Even sisters, however, may be alone. Not only have they lost their father and are without prospects of marriage, but also they differ so much in temperament that they will never understand each other—the older sister is prosaic, the younger one dreamy. It is only at the end of the story that each sister shows small signs of vitality. The prosaic sister hears a cry from within, muses on lost chances, and feels a hint of hope. When Mansfield takes readers into the thoughts of the younger sister, they discover that all along she has been living in a secret and extravagant imaginary world of repressed desire: her real life. For a moment, each sister thinks that some action could be taken, but the moment passes without communication. Their lives will never bear fruit.

Mansfield's wit is sometimes closer to the center of a story. In "Bliss," many early pages show a devastating view of the world of artists that Mansfield knew so well at Garsington and elsewhere. "Marriage à la Mode" is more purely a social satire. A nice, plodding husband, William, supports his wife Isabel's ambitions. They move from a cozy little house to the suburbs and entertain her artistic friends. Mansfield's acute ear for conversation enables her to give the reader the wonderful remarks that pass for wit among the arty set. The reader cheers when William, in a dignified letter, asks for a divorce. Isabel's friends mock the letter. Isabel herself realizes how shallow they are, but she runs to them laughing. The story has a moral, but its chief impact is satirical. This is also true of "The Young Girl." The title character is the disgustingly spoiled and overdressed teenage daughter of a selfish mother who is mainly interested in gambling at a casino. By the end of the story, the girl has revealed her youth and vulnerability, but a reader probably remembers the story's vapid world most vividly.

"The Fly" • Mansfield's modernist method seldom gives the reader straightforward statements of her themes; the reader needs to interpret them carefully. Her most deliberately ambiguous and hotly debated story is "The Fly." A businessman ("the boss") is reminded of his beloved son's death in World War I and how he has grieved. Now, however, the boss is troubled because he can no longer feel or cry. At this point, he rescues a fly caught in his inkwell; the fly carefully cleans itself. Then the Mansfield surprise: The boss drops another gob of ink on the fly, admires its courage as it cleans itself again, but then drops more ink. The fly is dead. The boss feels wretched and bullies an employee. The story may remind some readers of William Shakespeare's "As flies to wanton boys are we to the gods;/ They kill us for their sport."

Murry said that "The Fly" represents Mansfield's revulsion from the cruelty of war; other critics discover her antipathy to her own father. Whatever its biographical source, the reader must try to decide his or her reaction to the boss. Where are the readers' sympathies? At first they are with the aged employee who jogs the boss's memory and perhaps with the boss himself. When readers hear of the son's death, they do sympathize with the father. What do they make of his torturing—yet admiring—the fly? Do readers despise him as a sadistic bully? Do they sympathize with him? Is the fly simply another victim of society's brutality, the boss's brutality? Are readers to see Mansfield as the fly, unfairly stricken with tuberculosis? Does the boss refuse to admit his own mortality until he sees himself as a victim, like the fly? At the very end, is he repressing such thoughts again? Critics are divided about this story, but what is clear is that its ambiguities raise a host of issues for consideration.

"The Man Without a Temperament" • Another story that poses problems is "The Man Without a Temperament." The reader has trouble establishing where the story is taking place and who are its characters. Gradually it can be determined that the story takes place at a continental hotel and that the central characters are, not the grotesque guests like The Two Topknots, but The Man (Robert Salesby) and his invalid wife (Jinnie—Mrs. Salesby). The Mansfield woman here is not only lonely but also sick—sick with something that resembles the author's own tuberculosis. The reader's difficulties are slightly compounded when Mansfield manipulates time; readers soon decide that the dislocations in the story are Robert's memories of happier days in England. This story's greatest problem, however, is what the reader is to think of Robert. At first glance, he seems without temperament; all his care is for his wife, her comfort, her health, and her whims. Soon, the tension that he is under becomes obvious. He is tortured by his memories. When his wife encourages him to take a walk by himself, he quickly agrees and almost forgets to return. The exquisite tact and humor that his wife loves so much ring hollow: Readers know that he suspects that she will not live much longer. Is he an icy, resentful, and disgusting hypocrite? Some readers may think so. Is he admirably patient and forbearing? Murry, who acknowledged that Robert was a portrait of himself, thought it was drawn with admiration.

New Zealand Stories • Soon after her return to London, Mansfield wrote some stories based on her experiences among the common people of New Zealand. "The Woman at the Store" is a chilling and dramatic tale in which three travelers stop far from civilization at a dilapidated store run by a slatternly woman and her child. Although the travelers feel sympathy for the woman's hard life, they also laugh at the woman and child—laugh until the child's drawing makes clear that the woman has murdered her husband. The travelers leave quickly. "Ole Underwood," a character sketch based on a real Wellington character, lets readers see into the mind of a deranged former convict as he makes his way around town, driven by memories of his wife's infidelity. In both cases, Mansfield tries to get into the minds of lower-class people, people much different from those she usually depicts. Another story that deals sympathetically with the doomed struggles of a lower-class character is "The Life of Ma Parker."

When Mansfield returned in earnest to telling stories of the New Zealand life that she knew best, she produced her finest work. (The critic Rhoda B. Nathan thinks that the New Zealand stories, taken as a group, can be considered as a Bildungsroman, or story of an artist's growth.) The family drama of her childhood provided material for many of these stories. Her mother was attractive but delicate. Her father was forceful and successful. They lived in a substantial house in Wellington just on the edge of a poor district, then in a nearby village, and later at the edge of the sea in Wellington harbor. She was the third of five surviving children living among a number of aunts and cousins, an uncle and a grandmother.

"Prelude" • Mansfield's two longest works of fiction, "Prelude" and "At the Bay," are strikingly different from conventional short stories. Both take a slight narrative line and string on it a number of short episodes and intense renderings of the inner lives of members—mainly female—of an extended family. In both, readers are set down among these people without preparation; they must work out their relations for themselves. In both, readers must take time to discover the rich vision that Mansfield is giving them.

In "Prelude," the reader enters the consciousness of several members of the family as they adjust to a new house in the country. (The Beauchamps moved from Wellington to Karori in 1893.) The reader is led into the minds of the child Kezia (the character who resembles the author as a girl), her hearty father (Stanley), her pregnant mother (Linda), and her unfulfilled aunt (Beryl). Their relations are strained, and they reveal their hopes, loves, and anxieties. Gradually, Mansfield's emphasis becomes clear. She gives most weight to Linda and Beryl, whose inner worlds invite a range of analysis. Analysis begins with the aloe tree. Mansfield had earlier prepared readers for this huge, ugly, ominous growth, which flowers only once every hundred years. Readers sense that the tree is somehow symbolic. Linda is fascinated by it. When she sees the tree by moonlight, its cruel thorns seem to embody the hate that she often feels, or do they embody the masculine force that she hates? Either way, the aloe tree brings out for the reader the secret that Linda keeps from everyone else: Alongside her other emotions (dislike for her children, love and concern for her husband) is pure hatred. She wonders what Stanley would think of that. Beryl, too, has her secret self. The story ends with her taking an inventory of her attractive qualities and wondering if she can ever get beyond her poses, her false life, to the warm authentic life that she thinks is still within her. Mansfield's apparently haphazard plot has in fact been drawing the reader to two striking female visions.

"At the Bay" • "At the Bay" tells about the same household perhaps a year later. Some characters, such as Kezia, appear to have changed. Mansfield's methods, however, are much the same, though the sea that frames this story does not insist on its symbolic force so obviously as did the aloe tree. Stanley forges off to work. The women he leaves are happy that he is gone, especially Linda, his strangely passive wife, who still loves him but dislikes their children, including a new baby boy. The children and their cousins play games. Kezia almost faces death when she pleads with her grandmother not to leave them. Linda's weak brother does face his failure. Beryl has a new friend, a vivid witchlike woman with an attractive younger husband. Though Linda briefly finds love with Stanley, this story, like "Prelude," ends with two dissimilar kinds of unfulfilled love. Linda loves her baby only for a moment. Beryl yearns for sexual contact but is terrified and revolted when she finds the real thing.

Perhaps at the end, the sea (as a possible symbol of female fecundity, time, and destruction) sympathizes with human desires, perhaps not. Mansfield's way of presenting her incidents and structuring her story creates intense sympathy for her characters, yet simultaneously lets readers see them, without obviously judging them, from a distance.

"The Doll's House" • Two shorter New Zealand stories probably show Mansfield at her finest, and they show most clearly how her narrative surprises and moments of brilliant revelation of character and motive can be concentrated in a single phrase, in what might be called a domestic epiphany: a small moment of great importance not easily summarized. In "The Doll's House," Kezia and her sisters are given a vulgar plaything. The house is despised by Aunt Beryl but loved by the girls (Kezia is particularly enthralled by a tiny lamp in the diminutive dining room) and much admired by their schoolmates. The story seems to be about adult cruelty and juvenile snobbery. All along, however, there appear to be two social outcasts, Lil Kelvey and her silent little sister, Else, both daughters of a washerwoman and (perhaps) a criminal. When Kezia impulsively invites them to look at the house, Aunt Beryl orders them away. Lil says nothing, but her silent, wretched little sister had got one glimpse of the beautiful doll's house and remembers, not her humiliation, but that she saw the house's tiny lamp. A small human spirit asserts itself.

"The Garden-Party" • "The Garden-Party" is based on what happened at a real party that the Beauchamps gave in Wellington in 1907. Part of its meaning concerns the relations between two social classes. The central character is Laura, clearly a Mansfield-like character, an adolescent Kezia. Laura is thrilled by the promise of festivity, but in the middle of the expensive preparations—canna lilies, dainty sandwiches, a small band to play under the marquee—she learns of the death of a poor man who lived close by in a wretched house. Readers see the clash of generations when Laura demands that the party be canceled, but her worldly mother says no. The party is a grand success. As usual in Mansfield, important matters slip the mind; Laura enjoys herself immensely, especially because her large new hat is widely admired. After the guests have left, her mother sends Laura with a basket of party food to the house of the dead man. Her journey at dusk is phantasmagoric. Her sympathies, forgotten at the party, return. She is shocked by the somber house of death and by the grieving wife, and overwhelmed by the stillness, even the beauty, of the corpse. Laura feels that she must say something: "Forgive my hat." What she says is certainly inadequate, but it seems to signal a moment of understanding and growth—or does it? Laura has found a moment of beauty in death. Is that evasive or profound? She accepts the sympathy of her brother at the very end. He understands—or does he?

George Soule

Other major works

NONFICTION: *Novels and Novelists*, 1930 (J. M. Murry, editor); *The Collected Letters of Katherine Mansfield*, 1984-1996 (4 volumes); *The Katherine Mansfield Notebooks*, 1997 (2 volumes).

POETRY: *Poems*, 1923 (J. M. Murry, editor).

Bibliography

Alpers, Antony. *The Life of Katherine Mansfield.* Rev. ed. New York: Viking Press, 1980. Standard biography, sensible, balanced, and detailed. Alpers draws on years of research and includes interviews with people who knew Mansfield, such as Murry and Ida Baker, and their comments on his earlier book, *Katherine Mansfield: A Biography* (1953). He offers some analyses, including passages on "At the Bay," "Prelude," and "Je Ne Parle Pas Français." Includes notes, illustrations, index, a detailed chronology, and a full bibliography.

Daly, Saralyn R. *Katherine Mansfield.* Rev. ed. New York: Twayne, 1994. Revision of Daly's earlier Twayne study of Mansfield, based on the availability of Mansfield manuscripts and letters. Interweaves biographical information with discussions of individual stories, focusing on method of composition and typical themes.

Darrohn, Christine. "'Blown to Bits': Katherine Mansfield's 'The Garden-Party' and the Great War." *Modern Fiction Studies* 44 (Fall, 1998): 514-539. Argues that in the story Mansfield tries to imagine a moment when class and gender do not matter; claims the story explores the conflicting demands of the postwar period, specifically, the painful task of mourning and recovery and the ways in which this task complicates the project of critiquing a society that is founded on the structures of exclusion, hierarchy, and dominance that foster wars.

Hankin, C. A. *Katherine Mansfield and Her Confessional Stories.* New York: St. Martin's Press, 1983. Hankin's thesis is that Mansfield's stories are confessional, with the result that this book connects each story as precisely as possible to its sources in Mansfield's life. The detailed analyses of each of the major stories are more valuable than the thesis suggests. Hankin's readings are subtle and detailed, especially when they discuss the complexities of characters and symbols.

Mansfield, Katherine. *The Complete Stories of Katherine Mansfield,* edited by Antony Alpers. Auckland: Golden Press/Whitcombe and Tombs, 1974. Not the complete short stories but a full and comprehensive collection of almost all of them, scrupulously edited and arranged chronologically in natural and instructive groups. Alpers's notes provide basic facts about each story and much essential information about many of them. The notes also list all the stories not included in this collection, thus forming a complete catalog of Mansfield's short fiction.

May, Charles E., ed. *Masterplots II: Short Story Series, Revised Edition.* 8 vols. Pasadena, Calif.: Salem Press, 2004. Designed for student use, this reference set contains articles providing detailed plot summaries and analyses of eleven short stories by Mansfield: "At the Bay" and "Bliss" (vol. 1); "The Daughters of the Late Colonel" and "The Doll's House" (vol. 2); "Her First Ball," "The Fly," and "The Garden-Party" (vol. 3); "Marriage à la Mode" and "Miss Brill" (vol. 5); "Prelude" (vol. 6); and "The Woman at the Store" (vol. 8).

Nathan, Rhoda B. *Katherine Mansfield.* New York: Continuum, 1988. Detailed and useful chapter on the New Zealand stories considered as a group. Includes comments on the "painterly" qualities of "Je Ne Parle Pas Français." The final two chapters discuss Mansfield's achievement with regard to other writers.

_____, ed. *Critical Essays on Katherine Mansfield.* New York: G. K. Hall, 1993. Organizes previously published and new essays on Mansfield into three categories: "The New Zealand Experience," "The Craft of the Story," and "The Artist in Context." Essays represent a variety of approaches: feminist, postcolonial, and historicist.

New, W. H. "Mansfield in the Act of Writing." *Journal of Modern Literature* 20 (Summer, 1996): 51-63. Argues that Mansfield's notebooks are an active guide to the process of reading her stories; discusses three categories of manuscript commentary and revision: those that emphasize figure and performance, those that change lexicon and syntax, and those that deal with agency and other larger strategies of arrangement.

Robinson, Roger, ed. *Katherine Mansfield: In from the Margin.* Baton Rouge: Louisiana State University Press, 1994. Reprints papers from two Mansfield centenary conferences. Features essays on Mansfield's feminine discourse, her interest in the cult of childhood, the narrative technique of her stories, and her position in the modernist tradition.

Tomalin, Claire. *Katherine Mansfield: A Secret Life.* New York: Alfred A. Knopf, 1987. Very readable biography, though without many critical comments, emphasizing the medical consequences of Mansfield's sexual freedom and treating the question of her plagiarizing "The Child Who-Was-Tired." An appendix gives *The Times Literary Supplement* correspondence on this topic.

Bobbie Ann Mason

Born: Mayfield, Kentucky; May 1, 1940

Principal short fiction • *Shiloh, and Other Stories*, 1982; *Love Life*, 1989; *Midnight Magic: Selected Stories of Bobbie Ann Mason*, 1998; *Zigzagging Down a Wild Trail*, 2001; *Nancy Culpepper*, 2006.

Other literary forms • Between 1985 and 2005, Bobbie Ann Mason published four novels: *In Country* (1985), *Spence Lila* (1988), *Feather Crowns* (1993), and *An Atomic Romance* (2005). Her nonfiction writings include *Nabokov's Garden: A Guide to "Ada"* (1974), *The Girl Sleuth: A Feminist Guide to the Bobbsey Twins, Nancy Drew, and Their Sisters* (1975 & 1995), *Clear Springs: A Memoir* (1999), and *Elvis Presley* (2002).

Achievements • Bobbie Ann Mason has earned a place in American literature with her short stories. She won the Ernest Hemingway Foundation Award for first fiction in 1983 for her first collection of short stories, *Shiloh, and Other Stories*. That collection also earned for Mason nomination for the National Book Critics Circle Award (1982), the American Book Award (1982), the PEN/Faulkner Award for Fiction, a National Endowment for the Arts Fellowship, and a Pennsylvania Arts Council grant (1983), a John Simon Guggenheim Memorial Foundation Fellowship, and an American Academy of Arts and Letters award (1984). Mason received the Appalachian Medallion Award (1991), and her novel *Feather Crowns* was cowinner of the Southern Book Award for fiction and a finalist for the National Book Critics Circle Award (1994). Mason's writing for newspapers and magazines includes work as a society columnist for the *Mayfield Messenger* in Kentucky and as a writer of fan magazine stories for the Ideal Publishing Company in New York City. She has also written "Talk of the Town" columns and feature articles for *The New Yorker*.

Mason's novels have reinforced her reputation. The first of her novels, *In Country* (1985), was particularly well received, and a film (also titled *In Country*) based on the book was released by Warner Brothers in the fall of 1989. That year the Vietnam Veterans of America gave Mason its first President's Citation, which honors a nonveteran who promotes public understanding of the war and its residual effects.

Biography • Bobbie Ann Mason was born in rural Kentucky, and her southern background appears to have been a major force in shaping her fiction. She attended a country school through the eighth grade and then attended Mayfield High School. Her descriptions of country schools in "State Champions" certainly ring true, and apparently her novel *Spence Lila* (1988) fictionalizes a part of her parents' experience. Another aspect of her high school life echoes in her fiction: her love of rock and roll.

Mason majored in English at the University of Kentucky in Lexington, where she wrote for the university paper, *The Kernel*. While in college, she also wrote the summer society column for the *Mayfield Messenger*. After graduating with a bachelor's degree in 1962, she spent fifteen months in New York City working for the Ideal Publishing Company writing for fan magazines such as *Movie Life* and *TV Star Parade*. In addition to her undergraduate degree, Mason earned a master's degree in literature from the State University of New York at Binghamton in 1966, as well as a doctoral degree in literature from the University of Connecticut in 1972. In her doctoral dissertation, she analyzed the garden symbolism in *Ada or Ardor: A Family Chronicle* (1969), by Vladimir Nabokov. Nabokov's artistry in presenting the details of his characters' lives apparently touched a chord in Mason. While pursuing her Ph.D., she met Roger B. Rawlings at the University of Connecticut; they were married in 1969.

From 1972 to 1979, Mason was an assistant professor of English at Mansfield State College (which later became Mansfield University) in Pennsylvania, where she taught journalism as well as other English courses. She had been writing short stories during this period and had received encouraging responses from editors who, nevertheless, rejected her stories for publication. In 1979, Mason stopped teaching to write fiction. She settled in rural Pennsylvania, sometimes giving readings and sometimes writing for *The New Yorker.* In 1990, she and her husband moved back to Kentucky. Her life, with its movement from rural to urban and back to rural living, mirrors a typical concern of her fiction: the tension between rural and urban life. Apparently her own feelings match those of many of her protagonists.

Analysis • Often compared with Ann Beattie, Raymond Carver, and Frederick Barthelme, Bobbie Ann Mason writes fiction that reads like life. Her characters struggle with jobs, family, and self-awareness, continually exuding a lively sense of being. Those who people her stories often transcend circumstance without losing their rootedness in place. Most often her characters struggle to live within a relationship, but are frequently alone. In fiction that resonates with rock-and-roll music and family conflicts, her descriptions leave a reader sometimes feeling uncomfortably aware of a truth about families: Caring does not guarantee understanding or communication.

The short stories are for the most part set in small towns in Kentucky and explore the lives of lower-middle-class people from small towns or farms. Kentucky, a North/South border state, is emblematic of Mason's concerns with borders, separations, and irrevocable decisions. Mason's stories typically explore a conflict between the character's past and future, a conflict that is often exemplified in a split between rural and urban leanings and a modern as opposed to a traditional life. Most often, the point of view in Mason's short fiction is limited omniscient. She is, however, adept with first-person narration as well. Readers are most often left with a sense of her characters' need to transcend their life scripts through action, frequently a quest. Her stories typically lack resolution, making them uncomfortably true to life.

Shiloh, and Other Stories • "Shiloh," the title story in Mason's first collection, is a story about love, loss, and history. A couple, Leroy and Norma Jean, have been married for sixteen years. They married when Norma Jean was pregnant with their son Randy, a child who died as an infant. Leroy is home recuperating from an accident he had in his truck. His leg is healing, but he is afraid to go back to driving a truck long distances. He takes on traditionally feminine activities in the story: He starts doing crafts, watches birds at the feeder, and remains the passenger in the car even after his leg has healed enough for him to drive.

The accident that forced Leroy to remain at home for months recuperating is the second crisis in the couple's marriage. The earlier crisis had been their baby's death. After the baby died, Leroy and Norma Jean remained married but emotionally isolated from each other:

They never speak about their memories of Randy, which have almost faded, but now that Leroy is home all the time, they sometimes feel awkward around each other, and Leroy wonders if one of them should mention the child. He has the feeling that they are waking up out of a dream together.

Now that Leroy is at home, he "sees things about Norma Jean that he never realized before." Leroy's staying at home so much leads to several important changes for Norma Jean: She begins to lift weights, takes a writing course, and curses in front of her mother. In response to the repeated suggestion of Norma Jean's mother, the couple drives to the Shiloh battleground for a second honeymoon trip. At Shiloh, Norma Jean tells Leroy that she wants to leave him. The history of Shiloh is significant to the story of this marriage. Shiloh, an early battle in the Civil War (1861-1865), proved that the Civil War would be a long and bloody one. The story concludes with Leroy merging family history with battleground history and Norma Jean literally flexing her muscles. Their civil war will be Leroy fighting for union and Norma Jean seeking her independent self.

A contemporary history lesson on the fear of polio and communists, "Detroit Skyline, 1949" narrates in first person the summer spent by a nine-year-old girl, Peggy Jo, and her mother as they visit the mother's sister and her family in Detroit. The story reveals the conflict between rural and city life through the perceptions and desires of Peggy Jo. Seeing her aunt's neighborhood for the first time, Peggy Jo immediately knows that she wants to live "in a place like this, with neighbors." When she plays with the neighbor child, however, Peggy Jo is made to feel incompetent because she does not know how to roller-skate, so she instead spends her time watching television and examining newspaper articles and pictures in her aunt's scrapbook.

Peggy Jo feels isolated that summer. She observes the smoothness with which her mother and aunt converse, how natural their communication is. When she attends a birthday party for the neighbor child, Peggy Jo notes:

> I did not know what to say to the children. They all knew each other, and their screams and giggles had a natural continuity, something like the way my mother talked with her sister, and like the splendid houses of the neighborhood, all set so close together.

For Peggy Jo there is little "natural continuity" of speech or gesture within her aunt's household that summer. Her own comments are most often cut short, silenced, or discredited by the others. By the end of the summer, Peggy Jo realizes that her "own life [is] a curiosity, an item for a scrapbook."

Another of Mason's stories concerning rural isolation is "Offerings," in which the isolation is redemptive for Sandra, who stays in the couple's country home instead of traveling with her husband, Jerry, to Louisville, "reluctant to spend her weekends with him watching go-go dancers in smoky bars." She instead spends her time growing vegetables and tending her cats, ducks, and dogs. Her cobweb-strewn house is not her focus; the outdoors is. The offerings that Sandra makes are many: to her mother, tacit agreement to avoid discussing the separation from Jerry; to her grandmother, the fiction of Jerry's presence; and to the forces of nature around her, her tamed and dependent ducks. Sandra finds grace through the natural world, exemplified within the final image of the story: dewy spiderwebs that, in the morning, are trampolines enabling her to "spring from web to web, all the way up the hill to the woods." She cannot be honest with her grandmother and avoids truth in conversation with her mother, but she feels at peace and at home with her yard, the woods, and the wildlife there.

In "Residents and Transients," Mason's narrator is also married to a man who has gone away to work in Louisville. Mary, the narrator, is finding her place within a relationship as well as a location. Several images in this story reinforce the theme of stability as opposed to movement. The cats Mary cares for on the farm represent her dilemma of moving to Louisville. To Stephen, her lover, she explains that she has read about two basic types of cats, residents and transients. She cites difference of opinion by researchers over which type is truly superior: those who establish territories and stay there or those who show the greatest curiosity by going from one place to another. Mary is drawn to the stability of her parents' old farmhouse, feeling the pull of traditional value of place. The single image that most succinctly and horrifically mirrors her dilemma is a rabbit, seen in the headlights as she is driving home. The rabbit at first appears to be running in place, but she realizes that its forelegs are still moving despite the fact that its haunches have been run over. Throughout the story, Mary has been literally running in place, running from her relationship with her husband by taking a lover and running from her life with her husband by remaining in her parents' old home.

Mary's position at the end of the story is mirrored by the image of the odd-eyed cat, whose eyes shine red and green. The narrator has been waiting for some signal to move. Her husband's words do not convince; Mary thinks of them as words that are processed, computerized renderings. She needs more than words; she needs an integrated part of her world to spur her to act. Because her husband is no longer an integral part of her world, she listens and looks for other cues. Apparently, the dying rabbit has spurred her to action. The story ends with Mary "waiting for the light to change."

Love Life • Within Mason's second collection of short fiction, *Love Life*, the reader sees continued the skillful treatment of people's decisions and perceptions. "State Champions" is a reminiscence of twenty years past, so it offers a perspective different from that of other works. "State Champions" further explores Mason's theme of rural versus urban experience by recounting the success of the Cuba Cubs, Kentucky state champions in basketball in 1952. The narrator, Peggy (who appeared earlier in "Detroit Skyline, 1949" but is three years older when this story begins), had seen the team as glamorous, certainly larger than life. As an adult in upstate New York, Peggy is surprised to hear the team referred to as "just a handful of country boys who could barely afford basketball shoes." Although Peggy had shared in the excitement of the championship season, "State Champions" presents her perceptions of being different from the rest even at that time. She rebelled against authority at school by talking back to the history teacher. She surprised her friend Willowdean with the assertion that she did not want to get pregnant and get married, a normal pattern for the girls at the high school. From her adult perspective, Peggy ascribes her own struggle for words with Glenn, the boy she cared about in 1952, to her status as a "country kid":

> I couldn't say anything, for we weren't raised to say things that were heartfelt and gracious. Country kids didn't learn manners. Manners were too embarrassing. Learning not to run in the house was about the extent of what we knew about how to act. We didn't learn to congratulate people; we didn't wish people happy birthday. We didn't even address each other by name.

Ironically enough, what triggers Peggy's recollection of the state championship year is the comment by *The New Yorker* about the poor country boys' basketball team, certainly a comment not springing from a mannered upbringing.

In "Coyotes," Mason provides a third-person account from the perspective of a young man, Cobb, who embodies the ambivalence and sensitivity often seen in Mason's characters. He has asked Lynnette Johnson to marry him, and he continues to look for signs and indications that marriage is the right thing to do. Cobb sees a young clerk in a drugstore showing her wedding ring to a young couple. Their conversation is flat: no congratulations, no excitement. The matter-of-fact nature of the exchange haunts Cobb. He wants his marriage to be the subject of excitement, hugs, celebration. Marriage in general presents itself as a risk, leading him to look further for signs that his own marriage will work. He wonders if Lynnette will find more and more things about him that will offend her. For example, he fails to tell her about having hunted after she tells him that his sweatshirt, on which is written "Paducah, the Flat Squirrel Capital of the World," is in bad taste. He is reassured by their similarities—for example, the fact that they both pronounce "coyote" with an *e* sound at the end. Lynnette's past, with a mother who had attempted suicide, is something he recognizes to be significant to them, but he nevertheless speaks confidently with Lynnette about their future. Lynnette fears that her past will somehow intrude on their future, and so, in fact, does Cobb. Their relationship is, as is typical of Mason's fiction, freighted with all those tangled possibilities.

Past and future as conflicting forces also form a theme of "Private Lies," in which the male protagonist, Mickey, reestablishes his relationship with his former wife and decides to search for the child they gave up for adoption eighteen years earlier. Mickey's wife, Tina, has compartmentalized their lives with a regular television schedule and planned activities for their children. Tina has forbidden him to tell their children about his daughter. Mickey, however, cannot ignore the eighteenth birthday of his daughter given up to adoption. The story concludes with Mickey and his former wife, Donna, on the beach in Florida, the state in which they gave up their daughter for adoption. Donna insists that she does not want to find their daughter and that searching is a mistake. She nevertheless accompanies him to Florida, where Mickey seeks to stop telling lies (by silence) and where Donna still seeks to avoid the search, exemplified by her refusal to look inside shells for fear of what she may find in them. Mickey seeks the daughter who will be his bridge between past and future. He seeks to make a new present for himself, a present free of Tina's control.

Midnight Magic • All of the stories in *Midnight Magic* appeared earlier in either *Shiloh, and Other Stories* or *Love Life*, but this collection provides a new arrangement and a new introduction by the author. The protagonist of the title story, Steve, is a young man whose personal power is no match for that of his showy "muscle" car. Like other Mason characters, he takes to the road in search of elusive secrets of life, but most of the time Steve merely drives in circles around his small hometown. When he finally heads for a specific destination (the Nashville airport to pick up his recently married friend), he is several hours late. His lateness for this appointment parallels his tardiness in maturing. After seeing a body lying beside the road, Steve tries to report it to a 911 emergency operator. Unfortunately, he cannot discover his specific geographic location just as he cannot define his place on the road of life. Steve's girlfriend, Karen, finds guidance in the spiritual teachings of Sardo, an ancient Native American now reincarnated in the body of a teenager. Steve also "wants something miraculous" but simply "can't believe in it." Thus, his persistent hope outstrips his fleeting faith.

Mason recalls that as a college student she associated late-night hours with a "mood of expectation"—"the sense that anything might happen." Thus, the title "Midnight Magic" suggests sympathy for a feckless but engaging misfit. In her introduction Mason describes Steve as a "guy who keeps imagining he'll get it together one day soon, who seeks transcendence and wants to believe in magic."

Another story with a confused male protagonist is "Big Bertha Stories." Written while Mason was working on *In Country*, this story also dramatizes the lingering effects of the war in Vietnam. Donald has come back from war physically, but he cannot make it all the way home emotionally. He operates a huge machine in a strip mine, and his destruction of the land recalls the horrors of war. Attempting to create some order in his life, Donald makes up stories about powerful superheroes. These stories begin with humor and high hopes but break off in chaos. Just as Donald cannot complete his journey home, he can never bring his fictions to a suitable conclusion. Having lost his youth in Vietnam, he becomes old prematurely and can no longer function as husband and father.

Still another story from *Midnight Magic* that tries to reconcile past with present is "Nancy Culpepper." Here the title character is apparently based on Mason herself, and she reappears in the story "Lying Doggo" and the novel *Spence Lila*. The key symbols in "Nancy Culpepper" are photographs. Nancy recalls that the photographs from her wedding were fuzzy double exposures, just as the wedding itself was a superimposition of a strange new identity upon her southern rural past. Several years after the wedding she returns home to Kentucky to rescue old family pictures. She searches in particular for a likeness of her namesake, but this particular photograph is not found, just as her own sense of identity remains elusive.

Janet Taylor Palmer
With updates by Albert Wilhelm and the Editors

Other major works

NOVELS: *In Country*, 1985; *Spence Lila*, 1988; *Feather Crowns*, 1993; *An Atomic Romance*, 2005.

NONFICTION: *Nabokov's Garden: A Guide to "Ada,"* 1974; *The Girl Sleuth: A Feminist Guide to the Bobbsey Twins, Nancy Drew, and Their Sisters*, 1975, 1995; *Clear Springs: A Memoir*, 1999; *Elvis Presley*, 2002.

Bibliography

Blythe, Hal, and Charlie Sweet. "The Ambiguous Grail Quest in 'Shiloh.'" *Studies in Short Fiction* 32 (Spring, 1995): 223-226. Examines the use of the Grail myth in "Shiloh"; claims the story is a contemporary version of Jessie Weston's "Waste Land." Argues that the myth lends universal significance to the minutiae-laden lives of a twentieth century western Kentucky couple in a troubled marriage.

Eckard, Paula Gallant. *Maternal Body and Voice in Toni Morrison, Bobbie Ann Mason, and Lee Smith*. Columbia: University of Missouri Press, 2002. Focusing on southern and African American women writers, Eckard explores the way female authorship subjectivizes the experience of motherhood, as opposed to the objectification of motherhood by male writers.

Giannone, Richard. "Bobbie Ann Mason and the Recovery of Mystery." *Studies in Short Fiction* 27 (Fall, 1990): 553-566. Claims that Mason's rural characters are caught between an incomprehensible otherworldly force and the loss of their this-world anguish; they are mystified by contemporary life while robbed of the mysteries of their lives. Discusses "Shiloh," "Retreat," and "Third Monday."

May, Charles E., ed. *Masterplots II: Short Story Series, Revised Edition.* 8 vols. Pasadena, Calif.: Salem Press, 2004. Designed for student use, this reference set contains articles providing detailed plot summaries and analyses of four short stories by Mason: "Big Bertha Story" (vol. 1), "Graveyard Day" (vol. 3), and "Residents and Transients" and "Shiloh" (vol. 6).

Pollack, Harriet. "From *Shiloh* to *In Country* to *Feather Crowns:* Bobbie Ann Mason, Women's History, and Southern Fiction." *The Southern Literary Journal* 28 (Spring, 1996): 95-116. Argues that Mason's fiction is representative of southern women authors who, without general recognition, have been transforming southern literature's characteristic attention to official history.

Price, Joanna. *Understanding Bobbie Ann Mason.* Columbia: University of South Carolina Press, 2000. Part of the Understanding Contemporary American Literature series, this study provides fairly comprehensive coverage of all Mason's works.

Rothstein, Mervyn. "Homegrown Fiction: Bobbie Ann Mason Blends Springsteen and Nabokov." *The New York Times Biographical Service* 19 (May, 1988): 563-565. This essay reports Mason's love of rhythm and blues in high school and notes the semiautobiographical details of *Spence Lila.*

Ryan, Maureen. "Stopping Places: Bobbie Ann Mason's Short Stories." In *Women Writers of the Contemporary South,* edited by Peggy W. Prenshaw. Jackson: University Press of Mississippi, 1984. An overview of Mason's themes and character portraits, this sampling provides a brief treatment of many different works.

Thompson, Terry. "Mason's 'Shiloh.'" *The Explicator* 54 (Fall, 1995): 54-58. Claims that subdivisions play an important role in the story for gaining a full appreciation of the two main characters; argues that the subdivision is a metaphor for the marriage of the couple.

Wilhelm, Albert E. *Bobbie Ann Mason: A Study of the Short Fiction.* New York: Twayne, 1998. This critical study of Mason's short fiction examines the influence of her femininity and her identity as a southerner on her writing. Includes such topics as the place that Kentucky plays in her work as well as a bibliography and index.

_____. "Bobbie Ann Mason: Searching for Home." In *Southern Writers at Century's End,* edited by Jeffrey J. Folks and James A. Perkins. Lexington: University Press of Kentucky, 1997. Discusses the effect of American involvement in Vietnam in "Big Bertha Stories" and *In Country.* Argues that these two stories of soldiers' attempts to return home expand the theme of social dislocation to mythic proportions.

W. Somerset Maugham

Born: Paris, France; January 25, 1874
Died: Nice, France; December 16, 1965

Principal short fiction • *Orientations*, 1899; *The Trembling of a Leaf: Little Stories of the South Sea Islands*, 1921; *The Casuarina Tree: Six Stories*, 1926; *Ashenden: Or, The British Agent*, 1928; *Six Stories Written in the First Person Singular*, 1931; *Ah King: Six Stories*, 1933; *East and West: The Collected Short Stories*, 1934; *Cosmopolitans*, 1936; *The Favorite Short Stories of W. Somerset Maugham*, 1937; *The Round Dozen*, 1939; *The Mixture as Before: Short Stories*, 1940; *Creatures of Circumstances: Short Stories*, 1947; *East of Suez: Great Stories of the Tropics*, 1948; *Here and There: Selected Short Stories*, 1948; *The Complete Short Stories*, 1951; *The World Over*, 1952; *Seventeen Lost Stories*, 1969.

Other literary forms • A dedicated professional, W. Somerset Maugham earned more than three million dollars from his writing, a phenomenal amount for his day. Between 1897 and 1962, a career spanning eight decades, Maugham published twenty novels, four travel books, more than twenty stage plays, an autobiography of ideas, and innumerable essays, belles lettres, and introductions, in addition to more than one hundred short stories, of which about ninety are readily accessible in different editions. Much of his work has been adapted for use by television and cinema.

Achievements • W. Somerset Maugham is best known for his urbanity, his wit, his controlled sense of writing, and his ability to describe not only objectively but also so realistically that he has been accused of lifting stories directly from life. Many of his stories do spring from real incidents or actual people, but the perceptions and surprise plot twists are always Maugham-inspired. In fact, Maugham is expressly known as a master of the surprise or twist ending to an inextricably woven plot in his short stories, many of which have been converted to film. His early work, under the influence of Oscar Wilde and his cult of aesthetes, shows a refined and civilized attitude toward life. Several of his novels illustrate the demanding sacrifices that art necessitates of life, or that life itself can become, in turn, an art form, thereby demonstrating the "art of living" (*The Razor's Edge*, 1944).

Maugham was curiously denied many conspicuous honors (such as knighthood) usually conferred on a man of letters of his distinction, but he was awarded by the Royal Society of Literature the title of Companion of Literature, an honor given to "authors who have brought exceptional distinction to English letters." Furthermore, the occasion of his eightieth birthday was celebrated with a dinner at the Garrick Club, a distinction given to only three writers before him: Charles Dickens, William Makepeace Thackeray, and Anthony Trollope.

Biography • When William Somerset Maugham was eight, his mother died, and his father, a solicitor for the British Embassy in Paris, died two years later. Shy and speaking little English, Maugham was sent to Whitstable in Kent to live with an uncle, the Reverend Henry MacDonald Maugham, and his German-born wife, and thence almost immediately to King's School, Canterbury. These wretched and unhappy years

Library of Congress

were later detailed in Maugham's first masterpiece, the novel *Of Human Bondage* (1915). A stammer, which stayed with him for life, seems to have originated about this time. At the age of seventeen, Maugham went to Heidelberg and attended lectures at the university. His first play, *Schiffbrüchig* (*Marriages Are Made in Heaven*), was written during this year abroad and first performed in Berlin in 1902.

Returning to London, he began the study of medicine at St. Thomas' Hospital, where the misery of the nearby Lambeth slums profoundly impressed him. He took his medical degree in 1897, the same year *Liza of Lambeth*, his first novel, was published, then abandoned medicine. By 1908, Maugham had an unprecedented four plays running simultaneously in London, and by 1911, he had become successful enough to buy a fashionable house in Mayfair.

In 1915, he married Syrie Barnardo Wellcome. Divorced in 1927, they had one daughter, Liza, who became Lady Glendevon. During World War I, Maugham served as a medical officer in France and as an agent for the British Secret Service in Switzerland and Russia, where he was to prevent, if possible, the Bolshevik Revolution. During and after the war, he traveled extensively in Hawaii, Samoa, Tahiti, China, Malaysia, Indochina, Australia, the West Indies, various Central and South American countries, and the United States. In 1928, Maugham settled on the French Riviera, buying Villa Mauresque. Maugham died in Nice, France, on December 16, 1965.

Analysis • W. Somerset Maugham first claimed fame as a playwright and novelist, but he became best known in the 1920's and 1930's the world over as an international traveler and short-story writer. Appearing in popular magazines such as *Nash's*, *Collier's*, *Hearst's International*, *The Smart Set*, and *Cosmopolitan*, his stories reached hundreds of thousands of readers who had never attended a play and had seldom read a novel. This new public demanded simple, lucid, fast-moving prose, and Maugham's realistic, well-defined narratives, often set amid the exotic flora of Oceania or Indochina, were among the most popular of the day.

The Trembling of a Leaf • *The Trembling of a Leaf: Little Stories of the South Sea Islands* collected six of these first "exotic stories" and assured Maugham fame as a short-story writer on equal footing with his established renown as novelist and dramatist. It was actually his second collection, coming twenty years after *Orientations*, whose title clearly bespeaks its purposes. Apparently, Maugham had found no suitable possibilities for short fiction in the meantime until, recuperating from a lung infection between World War I assignments for the British Secret Service, he took a vacation to Samoa and Hawaii:

> I had always had a romantic notion of the South Seas. I had read of those magic islands in the books of Herman Melville, Pierre Loti, and Robert Louis Stevenson, but what I saw was very different from what I had read.

Although Maugham clearly differentiates life as he saw it in the South Seas from life as he had read about it in the writings of his "romantic" predecessors, his stories of British Colonials, of natives and half-castes in exotic environments, are reminiscent of these authors and also of Rudyard Kipling. Maugham's assessment of Kipling, the only British short-story writer he thought comparable to such greats as Guy de Maupassant and Anton Chekhov, neatly clarifies their similar subject, as well as their ultimate stylistic differences. Kipling, Maugham writes,

> opened a new and fruitful field to writers. This is the story, the scene of which is set in some country little known to the majority of readers, and which deals with the reactions upon the white man of his sojourn in an alien land and the effect which contact with peoples of another race has upon him. Subsequent writers have treated this subject in their different ways, but . . . no one has invested it with more romantic glamour, no one has made it more exciting and no one has presented it so vividly and with such a wealth of colour.

Maugham's first South Seas stories are essentially criticisms of the "romantic glamour" of Kipling and his predecessors, especially Stevenson, his most immediate literary forefather in terms of location. Rather than repeat their illusions, Maugham tries to see the "alien land" as it really is, without poetic frills. "Red," which Maugham once chose as his best story, is a clear example of this process.

"Red" • A worldly, gruff, and overweight skipper of a bedraggled seventy-ton schooner anchors off one of the Samoan Islands in order to trade with the local storekeeper. After rowing ashore to a small cove, the captain follows a tortuous path, eventually arriving at "a white man's house" where he meets Neilson. Neilson seems a typical character out of Robert Louis Stevenson, a life deserter unable either to return to his homeland or to accommodate himself completely to his present situation. Twenty-five years ago he came to the island with tuberculosis, expecting to live only a year, but the mild climate has arrested his disease. He has married a native woman called Sally and built a European bungalow on the beautiful spot where a grass hut once stood. His walls are lined with books, which makes the skipper nervous but to which Neilson constantly and condescendingly alludes. Offering him whiskey and a cigar, Neilson decides to tell the skipper the story of Red.

Red was Neilson's romantic predecessor, Sally's previous lover, an ingenuous Apollo whom Neilson likes to imagine "had no more soul than the creatures of the woods and forests who made pipes from reeds and bathed in the mountain streams when the world was young." It was Red who had lived with Sally in the native hut, "with its beehive roof and its pillars, overshadowed by a great tree with red flowers." Glamorizing the young couple and the lush habitat, Neilson imagines them living on "delicious messes from coconuts," by a sea "deep blue, wine-coloured at sundown, like the sea of Homeric Greece," where "the hurrying fish were like butterflies," and the "dawn crept in among the wooden pillars of the hut" so that the lovers woke each morning and "smiled to welcome another day."

After a year of bliss, Red was shanghaied by a British whaler while trying to trade green oranges for tobacco. Sally was crestfallen and mourned him for three years, but finally, somewhat reluctantly, she acceded to the amorous overtures of the newcomer Neilson:

> And so the little wooden house was built in which he had now lived for many years, and Sally became his wife. But after the first few weeks of rapture, during which he was satisfied with what she gave him, he had known little happiness. She had yielded to him, through weariness, but she had only yielded what she set no store on. The soul which he had dimly glimpsed escaped him. He knew that she cared nothing for him. She still loved Red. . . .

Neilson, admittedly "a sentimentalist," is imprisoned by history. His books, a source of anxiety to the skipper, are a symbol of what Maugham believes he must himself avoid: useless repetition of and bondage to his forebears. As creation, Neilson does repeat Stevenson, but as character, he shows the absolute futility of this repetition. The dead romance assumes priority from the living one, and priority is everything. For the sentimentalist Neilson, tropical paradise has become living hell and the greatest obstacle preventing his own present happiness, the fulfillment of his own history, is his creation of an insurmountable predecessor, one whose "romantic glamour" is purer and simpler than his own reality.

The final irony, that the skipper, now bloated and bleary-eyed, is in fact the magnificent Red of Neilson's imagination and that when Sally and he meet they do not even recognize each other, snaps something in Neilson. The moment he had dreaded for twenty-five years has come and gone. His illusions disintegrate like gossamer; the "father" is not insurmountable:

> He had been cheated. They had seen each other at last and had not known it. He began to laugh, mirthlessly, and his laughter grew till it become hysterical. The Gods had played him a cruel trick. And he was old now.

In "Red," Neilson's realization of failure and waste do prompt some action, possibly an escape from the cell of his past. Over dinner, he lies to Sally that his eldest brother is very ill and he must go home. "Will you be gone long?" she asks. His only answer is to shrug his shoulders.

In its natural manner, Maugham's prose in these stories never strains for effect; each could easily be retold over coffee or a drink. Like Maupassant, Maugham is a realist and a merciless ironist, but while his narrator observes and his readers chuckle, characters such as Neilson grapple in desperate roles against the onrushing determination of their lives. In the style of the best "magazine" stories, incidents in Maugham almost inevitably build one on top of the other, slowly constraining his protagonists until, like grillwork, these incidents all but completely bar the protagonists from realizing their individual potential and freedom. Maugham's predilection for the surprise ending helps some find a final success, but not all; most end as we have believed they would—like the cuckolded Scotsman Lawson in "The Pool" who, after losing job, friends' respect, wife, and self, is "set on making a good job of it" and commits suicide "with a great stone tied up in his coat and bound to his feet."

Lawson, another "great coward" in the Stevenson mold, has married a beautiful half-caste and, naïvely assuming human nature the same the world over, has treated her as he would a white woman. By providing primarily in terms of his own culture's expectations, Lawson unwittingly shoulders "the white man's burden," that bequest of Kipling's, until he becomes himself a burden. Maugham implies, with great irony, that if Lawson had been less "a gentleman" and had taken the girl as a mistress, his tragedy might have been averted. As the reader must see the "alien land" for what it really is, so must they see its peoples.

"Rain" • "Rain," Maugham's best-known short story, develops many of these same themes. Pago Pago is unforgettably described, but no one could confuse it with the romanticized "loveliness" of Neilson's island. When the rain is not falling in torrents, the sun is oppressive. Davidson, the missionary, and Sadie, the prostitute, act out their parts with the same furious intensity. Neither is banalized; Maugham neither approves nor condemns. Only the "mountains of Nebraska" dream foreshadows Davidson's lust. (With its overtones of sexual repression, this dream makes "Rain" a notable pioneer in Freudian fiction.) Other than that, however, Davidson's sincere religious fervor seems convincingly real, inspired though it is by his "mission," yet another example of "the white man's burden." In the ensuing struggle between spiritual and "heathen" sensuality, the ironic stroke is that the prostitute wins; up to the last few pages, the story's outcome looks otherwise. Finally, Davidson must admit that he cannot proscribe human nature, not even his own. Neither saint nor sinner, he is simply human. On a more universal level than either "The Pool" or "Red," "Rain" shows that in human nature, only its unaccountability is predictable.

Maugham's detachment and moral tolerance, as well as assuring Davidson's and Sadie's vitality as characters, benefits his handling of the tale. The restraint exercised in *not* portraying for the reader either of the two "big scenes," Sadie's rape or Davidson's suicide, gives Maugham's story "Rain" an astounding dramatic power. The "real life" genesis of "Rain" is well known. Maugham jotted down his impressions of a few passengers aboard ship traveling with him in the winter of 1916 from Honolulu to Pago Pago; four years later he created a story from these notes. Of his prototype for Sadie Thompson he wrote:

> Plump, pretty in a coarse fashion perhaps not more than twenty-seven. She wore a white dress and a large white hat, long white boots from which the calves bulged in cotton stockings.

Six Stories Written in the First Person Singular • This practice of taking characters and situations directly from life is nowhere better elaborated in Maugham than in the volume entitled *Six Stories Written in the First Person Singular.* The personal touch—clear in the book's title—leaves a strong impression of reality. Whereas "Rain" seems a small classic in its theme, conflict, effective setting, and dramatic ending, it has one difficulty: The reader is unable to sympathize clearly with any one character, and this detracts from a greater, warmer effectiveness it might otherwise have. When the narrator-as-detached-observer is introduced as a character, however, there is no such problem with sympathy. This creation, the consistent and subsequently well-known cosmopolite, the story*teller* for his stories, is one of Maugham's finest achievements.

In "Virtue" the narrator—here differentiated as "Maugham"—browses at Sotheby's auction rooms, goes to the Haymarket, and dines at Ciro's when he has a free morning; he was once a medical student and is now a novelist. In "The Round Dozen," he is a well-known author whose portrait appears in the illustrated papers. He is at Elson, a tattered seaside resort "not very far from Brighton," recovering from influenza. There, "Maugham" coincidentally observes a well-known bigamist—whose portrait at one time had also graced the pages of the press—capture his twelfth victim. In "Jane," the versatile man-of-the-world is introduced as a writer of comedies, while in "The Alien Corn" he is a promising young novelist who has grown middle-aged, written books and plays, traveled and had experiences, fallen in and out of love. Throughout *Six Stories Written in the First Person Singular,* "Maugham" is intermittently away from London, "once more in the Far East." Such frank appeals to verisimilitude (in other words, that "Maugham" is in fact Maugham) succeed extremely well.

"The Human Element" • In "The Human Element," the narrator is a popular author who likes "a story to have a beginning, a middle, and an end." He meets Carruthers, whom he does not much like, one night at the Hotel Plaza in Rome during the late summer "dead season." Carruthers is inhumanly depressed and tells Maugham why: He has found his life's love, the woman he would make his wife, Betty Weldon-Burns, living in Rhodes "in domestic familiarity" with her chauffeur.

Carruthers, also a short-story writer, has been praised by critics for "his style, his sense of beauty and his atmosphere," but when "Maugham" suggests he make use of his experience for a story, Carruthers grows angry: "It would be monstrous. Betty was everything in the world to me. I couldn't do anything so caddish." Ironically, the story ends with Carruthers's excuse that "there's no story there." That "Maugham" has in fact just made a story of it suggests that life can and does provide limitless possibilities for art if we are only ready to accept them.

Maugham specifically delineates these dual creative principles, life and art, in his introduction to the six stories in the collection. Defending the practice of drawing fictional characters from personal experience, Maugham cites Marie-Henri Beyle (Stendhal), Gustave Flaubert, and Jules Renard. "I think indeed," he writes, "that most novelists and surely the best, have worked from life." The concern of Maugham's South Seas stories, to convey what he "saw" rather than what he "had read," is continued here on a higher plane. Maugham qualifies that there must also be art:

> A real person, however eminent, is for the most part too insignificant for the purposes of fiction. The complete character, the result of elaboration rather than of invention, is art, and life in the raw, as we know, is only its material.

Illustrating the unaccountability of human behavior (for how could he endeavor to account for it?), "Maugham" remains a detached observer of life. Critics have wished for more poetry, loftier flights of imagination, more sympathy for his characters, and even occasional indirection; the lack of these things constitutes the limitation of Maugham's style. Rejecting both the atmospheric romanticism of his predecessors and the exhaustive modernism of his contemporaries, Maugham's short stories do not seek to penetrate either landscape or life. His reader, like his narrator, may experience admiration, annoyance, disgust, or pity for the characters, but he does not share or become immersed in their emotions. This point of view of a calm, ordinary man, so unusual for the twentieth century, is instructive, teaching careful and clear consideration of life's possibilities, its casualties and successes, banalities, and gifts. In this way, objective understanding is increased by reading Maugham much as intersubjective facilities are by reading James Joyce, D. H. Lawrence, or the other moderns.

Kenneth Funsten
With updates by Sherry Morton-Mollo

Other major works

PLAYS: *A Man of Honor*, wr. 1898-1899, pr., pb. 1903; *Loaves and Fishes*, wr. 1903, pr. 1911, pb. 1924; *Lady Frederick*, pr. 1907, pb. 1912; *Jack Straw*, pr. 1908, pb. 1911; *Mrs. Dot*, pr. 1908, pb. 1912; *The Explorer*, pr. 1908, pb. 1912; *Penelope*, pr. 1909, pb. 1912; *Smith*, pr. 1909, pb. 1913; *The Noble Spaniard*, pr. 1909, pb. 1953; *Landed Gentry*, pr. 1910 (as *Grace*; pb. 1913); *The Tenth Man*, pr. 1910, pb. 1913; *The Land of Promise*, pr. 1913, pb. 1913, 1922; *Caroline*, pr. 1916, pb. 1923 (as *The Unattainable*); *Our Betters*, pr. 1917, pb. 1923; *Caesar's Wife*, pr. 1919, pb. 1922; *Home and Beauty*, pr. 1919, pb. 1923 (also known as *Too Many Husbands*); *The Unknown*, pr., pb. 1920; *The Circle*, pr., pb. 1921; *East of Suez*, pr., pb. 1922; *The Constant Wife*, pr., pb. 1926; *The Letter*, pr., pb. 1927; *The Sacred Flame*, pr., pb. 1928; *The Breadwinner*, pr., pb. 1930; *The Collected Plays of W. Somerset Maugham*, pb. 1931-1934 (6 volumes; revised 1952, 3 volumes); *For Services Rendered*, pr., pb. 1932; *Sheppey*, pr., pb. 1933.

NOVELS: *Liza of Lambeth*, 1897; *The Making of a Saint*, 1898; *The Hero*, 1901; *Mrs. Craddock*, 1902; *The Merry-Go-Round*, 1904; *The Bishop's Apron*, 1906; *The Explorer*, 1907; *The Magician*, 1908; *Of Human Bondage*, 1915; *The Moon and Sixpence*, 1919; *The Painted Veil*, 1925; *Cakes and Ale*, 1930; *The Narrow Corner*, 1932; *Theatre*, 1937; *Christmas Holiday*, 1939; *Up at the Villa*, 1941; *The Hour Before Dawn*, 1942; *The Razor's Edge*, 1944; *Then and Now*, 1946; *Catalina*, 1948; *Selected Novels*, 1953.

MISCELLANEOUS: *The Great Exotic Novels and Short Stories of Somerset Maugham*, 2001; *The W. Somerset Maugham Reader: Novels, Stories, Travel Writing*, 2004 (Jeffrey Meyers, editor).

NONFICTION: *The Land of the Blessed Virgin: Sketches and Impressions in Andalusia*, 1905 (also known as *Andalusia*, 1920); *On a Chinese Screen*, 1922; *The Gentleman in the Parlour: A Record of a Journey from Rangoon to Haiphong*, 1930; *Don Fernando*, 1935; *The Summing Up*, 1938; *Books and You*, 1940; *France at War*, 1940; *Strictly Personal*, 1941; *Great Novelists and Their Novels*, 1948; *A Writer's Notebook*, 1949; *The Writer's Point of View*, 1951; *The Vagrant Mood: Six Essays*, 1952; *Ten Novels and Their Authors*, 1954 (revision of *Great Novelists and Their Novels*); *The Partial View*, 1954 (includes *The Summing Up* and *A Writer's Notebook*); *The Travel Books*, 1955; *Points of View*, 1958; *Looking Back*, 1962; *Purely for My Pleasure*, 1962; *Selected Prefaces and Introductions*, 1963.

SCREENPLAY: *Trio*, 1950 (with R. C. Sherriff and Noel Langley).

Bibliography

Archer, Stanley. *W. Somerset Maugham: A Study of the Short Fiction*. New York: Twayne, 1993. Introductory survey of Maugham's short fiction, focusing on style and technique of the stories and the frequent themes of how virtue ironically can cause unhappiness, how colonial officials come in conflict with their social and physical environment, and how people are often unable to escape their own cultural background. Reprints some of Maugham's own comments on short fiction and three previously published critical excerpts.

Connon, Bryan. *Somerset Maugham and the Maugham Dynasty*. London: Sinclair-Stevenson, 1997. Connon examines the influence that the Maugham family had on the life and works of W. Somerset Maugham. Includes bibliography and index.

Holden, Philip. *Orienting Masculinity, Orienting Nation: W. Somerset Maugham's Exotic Fiction*. Westport, Conn.: Greenwood Press, 1996. Examines the themes of homosexuality, gender identity, and race relations in Maugham's works.

_____. "W. Somerset Maugham's Yellow Streak." *Studies in Short Fiction* 29 (Fall, 1992): 575-582. Discusses Maugham's story "The Yellow Streak" as a dialectical tale made up of the opposites of civilized/savage, male/female, and racial purity/miscegenation. Considers the treatment of the relationship between the two men in the story.

Loss, Archie K. *"Of Human Bondage": Coming of Age in the Novel.* Boston: Twayne, 1990. One of Twayne's masterwork studies, this is an excellent analysis.

_____. *W. Somerset Maugham.* New York: Frederick Ungar, 1987. The chapter on short fiction in this general introduction to Maugham's life and art focuses largely on his most familiar story, "Rain," as the best example of his short-story technique and subject matter. Discusses Maugham as a tale-teller and argues that the voice of the narrator is the most important single element in a Maugham short story.

May, Charles E., ed. *Masterplots II: Short Story Series, Revised Edition.* 8 vols. Pasadena, Calif.: Salem Press, 2004. Designed for student use, this reference set contains articles providing detailed plot summaries and analyses of four short stories by Maugham: "The Alien Corn" (vol. 1), "An Official Position" (vol. 5), "The Outstation," and "Rain" (vol. 6).

Meyers, Jeffrey. *Somerset Maugham.* New York: Alfred A. Knopf, 2004. This well-reviewed examination of Maugham's life and work provides comprehensive detail and new insights.

Rogal, Samuel J. *A Companion to the Characters in the Fiction and Drama of W. Somerset Maugham.* Westport, Conn.: Greenwood Press, 1996. Alphabetical listing of the characters—animal, human, unnamed, named—in Maugham's drama and fiction. Each entry identifies the work in which a character appears and the character's role in the overall work.

_____. *A William Somerset Maugham Encyclopedia.* Westport, Conn.: Greenwood Press, 1997. Contains information on Maugham's life as well as his works. Includes bibliographical references and an index.

Guy de Maupassant

Born: Château de Miromesnil, near Dieppe, France; August 5, 1850
Died: Passy, Paris, France; July 6, 1893

Principal short fiction • *La Maison Tellier*, 1881 (*Madame Tellier's Establishment, and Short Stories*, 1910); *Mademoiselle Fifi*, 1882 (*Mademoiselle Fifi, and Other Stories*, 1922); *Clair de lune*, 1883; *Contes de la bécasse*, 1883; *Les Sœurs Rondoli*, 1884 (*The Sisters Rondoli, and Other Stories*, 1923); *Miss Harriet*, 1884 (*Miss Harriet, and Other Stories*, 1923); *Contes du jour et de la nuit*, 1885 (*Day and Night Stories*, 1924); *Toine*, 1885 (*Toine, and Other Stories*, 1922); *Yvette*, 1885 (*Yvette, and Other Stories*, 1905); *La Petite Rogue*, 1886 (*Little Rogue, and Other Stories*, 1924); *Monsieur Parent*, 1886 (*Monsieur Parent, and Other Stories*, 1909); *Le Horla*, 1887 (*The Horla, and Other Stories*, 1903); *Le Rosier de Madame Husson*, 1888; *L'Inutile Beauté*, 1890 (*Useless Beauty, and Other Stories*, 1911); *Eighty-eight Short Stories*, 1930; *Eighty-eight More Stories*, 1932; *Complete Short Stories*, 1955.

Other literary forms • Although he became famous above all for his well-crafted short stories, Guy de Maupassant also wrote poems, plays, and three successful novels: *Une Vie* (1883; *A Woman's Life*, 1888), *Bel-Ami* (1885; English translation, 1889), and *Pierre et Jean* (1888; *Pierre and Jean*, 1890). His preface to *Pierre and Jean* has attracted a considerable amount of attention over the years because it reveals the profound influence that Gustave Flaubert exerted on Maupassant's development as a writer. Maupassant was not, however, a major literary theoretician, and many critics have agreed with Henry James's perceptive comment that Maupassant as a "philosopher in his composition is perceptibly inferior to the story-teller." Maupassant also wrote several volumes of fascinating letters to such eminent writers as Flaubert, Ivan Turgenev, and Émile Zola.

Achievements • Guy de Maupassant is generally considered to be the most significant French short-story writer. Unlike other important nineteenth century French prose writers such as Honoré de Balzac and Flaubert, who are better known for their novels than for their short stories, Maupassant created an extensive corpus of short stories that reveals an aesthetically pleasing combination of wit, irony, social criticism, idealism, and psychological depth. Although his short stories deal with readily identifiable situations and character types in France during the 1870's and 1880's, they explore universal themes such as the horrors of war and the fear of death, hypocrisy, the search for happiness, the exploitation of women, and contrasts between appearance and reality. His characters illustrate the extraordinary diversity in modern society, from prostitutes to adulterous husbands and wives and from peasants to aristocrats. Even during his lifetime, his short stories were appreciated both within and beyond the borders of France. He had the special ability of conveying to readers the universal elements in everyday situations. He used wit and an understated style in order to create aesthetically pleasing dialogues. His work exerted a profound influence on many major short-story writers, including Thomas Mann, Katherine Mansfield, and Luigi Pirandello.

Biography • Henri-René-Albert Guy de Maupassant was born on August 5, 1850, in the Château de Miromesnil in the French province of Normandy. He was the first child of Gustave and Laure de Maupassant. Guy de Maupassant spent his childhood and adolescence in Normandy. His parents grew to dislike each other intensely, and they eventually separated. Laure did not want Gustave to play any role in rearing either Guy or their second son, Hervé. She was an overly protective mother, and she did not allow Guy to attend school until he was thirteen years old. Until he became a student in 1863 at a Roman Catholic seminary school, Guy's only teacher was the local parish priest. Guy became indifferent to religion, and at the age of seventeen he was expelled from the seminary school because of behavior judged to be unacceptable by his teachers. He completed his secondary studies in 1869 at a boarding school in Rouen.

In 1867, Maupassant met the celebrated novelist Flaubert, whom Laure had known for almost twenty years. Some fanciful critics have suggested that Flaubert was not only Maupassant's literary mentor but also his biological father. Although there is no evidence to support this hypothesis, Maupassant did react with extreme displeasure and perhaps with excessive sensitivity to the frequently repeated remark that Flaubert was his father.

Maupassant began his law studies at the University of Paris in 1869, but with the outbreak of hostilities in the Franco-Prussian War in 1870, he enlisted in the French army. He served in Normandy, where he experienced firsthand the humiliation of the French defeat and the severity of the Prussian occupation. After his return to civilian life, he became a clerk in the Naval Ministry. He remained in government service until 1880, when he resigned his position in the Ministry of Public Instruction so that he could dedicate all of his efforts to writing.

Starting in 1875, Flaubert became Maupassant's literary mentor. At first, Maupassant slavishly imitated his master's style, but gradually he began to explore themes and situations such as the tragic effect of war and occupation on French society, which Flaubert had chosen not to treat. Maupassant received further intellectual stimulation by frequenting Flaubert's weekly literary salon, which was attended at various times by such eminent writers as Turgenev, Zola, Alphonse Daudet, and Edmond de Goncourt and Jules de Goncourt. In late 1879, Maupassant and five other French authors agreed that each would write a short story on the Prussian occupation of France for a volume to be entitled *Les Soirées de Médan* (1880; the evenings in Médan). Maupassant's contribution was "Boule de Suif." The other contributors to this volume were Zola, Joris-Karl Huysmans, Paul Alexis, Henry Céard, and Léon Hennique. Almost all critics agreed with Flaubert's assessment that "Boule de Suif" was "a masterpiece of composition and wit." This extremely favorable reaction encouraged Maupassant to become a very prolific writer of short stories and novels. During the 1880's, he earned a good living as a writer, but gradually his health began to deteriorate as a result of syphilis, which he had contracted in the 1870's and which his doctors had failed to diagnose until it was too late for him to be cured. On January 2, 1892, Maupassant tried to kill himself. After this unsuccessful suicide attempt, he was committed to a psychiatric asylum at Passy, in Paris, France, where he died on July 6, 1893.

Analysis • Although his active literary career began in 1880 and lasted only ten years, Guy de Maupassant was nevertheless an extraordinarily productive writer whose short stories dealt with such diverse themes as war, prostitution, marital infidelity, religion, madness, cultural misunderstanding between the French and the English, and life in the French provinces, especially his native Normandy. His short stories varied greatly in length from only a few pages to more than forty pages. His stories are extremely well organized, and there is much psychological depth in his insights into the complex motivations for his characters' behavior. His work explores the full spectrum of French society. He describes characters from various professions and social classes with sensitivity and humor. Although Maupassant was himself very pessimistic, rather chauvinistic, and also distrustful of organized religions, his characters do not simply mirror his own philosophy. He wrote about topics of interest to his French readers in the 1880's, but he also enriched his short stories with psychological and moral insights, which continue to fascinate readers born generations after his death. Maupassant examined how ordinary Frenchmen and Frenchwomen, with whom readers can

Library of Congress

readily identify, reacted to unexpected social, historical, moral, and business situations. His short stories mirror life because in fiction, as in life, things never turn out exactly as one thinks they will.

Although Maupassant wrote on a wide variety of topics, the major recurring themes in his short stories are war, prostitution, and madness. Why Maupassant explored these themes instead of others is problematic. In their excellent biographies of Maupassant, Paul Ignotus and Francis Steegmuller showed that the Prussian occupation of France had been a traumatic experience for him. Even his mentor Flaubert realized that Maupassant was promiscuous, and he warned his disciple of the physical consequences of sleeping with prostitutes. By the middle of the 1880's, Maupassant began to write very frequently about characters who fear losing their minds. This would, in fact, happen to Maupassant himself, but not until late 1891. Although it is tempting to interpret Maupassant's short stories in the light of his personal experiences, such an approach is not very useful for literary criticism. Other Frenchmen of his day were scarred by the Prussian occupation of France or frequented houses of prostitution, but they did not possess his literary talents. His biography may well explain his preference for certain themes, but it does not enable readers to appreciate the true value of his short stories.

Maupassant wrote more than two hundred short stories. Even in a relatively long essay, it would be impossible to do justice to all of his major works. This article will examine four representative short stories in order to give readers a sense of Maupassant's refined artistry. These works are "La Folle" ("The Madwoman"), "Boule de Suif," "La Maison Tellier" ("Madame Tellier's Establishment"), and "Le Horla" ("The Horla").

"The Madwoman" • "The Madwoman" and "Boule de Suif" both describe personal tragedies that can result from war and military occupation. These two short stories are significantly different in length. In Albert-Marie Schmidt's 1973 edition of Maupassant's short stories, "The Madwoman" is four pages long, whereas "Boule de Suif" fills forty pages. Both, however, describe women who are victimized by the arbitrary abuse of power during the Prussian occupation of France. The structure of "The Madwoman" consists of a story within a story. The narrator is an unnamed man from Normandy. He tells his listener, Mathieu d'Endolin, that hearing woodcocks reminds him of a terrible injustice that took place during the Prussian occupation of Normandy. This odd reference to woodcocks is explained only at the end of this short story. The narrator speaks of a woman who went mad from grief after her father, husband, and baby had all died within a month of one another in 1855. She went to bed, became delirious, and screamed whenever anyone tried to take her out of her bed. The narrator is a sensitive man who feels pity for this woman. He wonders if she still thinks about the dead or if her mind is now "motionless." Her isolation from the world is absolute. She knows nothing about the world outside her room. During the Prussian occupation of the town in which the narrator and this madwoman live, German soldiers were assigned to the various houses. The madwoman and her maid had to receive twelve soldiers.

For reasons that are totally incomprehensible to the narrator, the German officer in charge of the soldiers in this house convinces himself that the madwoman will not talk to him because she holds Germans in contempt. He orders her to come downstairs, but the madwoman cannot understand his demand. He interprets her silence as a personal insult, and he orders his soldiers to carry the woman in her bed toward a nearby forest. For nine months, the narrator learns nothing about the fate of this woman. During the fall hunting season, he goes to the forest and shoots a few woodcocks. When he goes to retrieve these woodcocks, he finds a human skeleton on a bed. The awful truth is revealed to him. The madwoman had died from exposure to the cold, and "the wolves had devoured her." The narrator does not end this tale by denouncing the Germans but rather by praying that "our sons will never again see war" lest other innocent victims suffer similar tragedies. Readers from any country or generation can identify with the hopes of this narrator. Readers and the narrator know all too well that many innocent victims have been killed in war. "The Madwoman" is a powerful short story that expresses one's revulsion over the death of any innocent victim of war.

"Boule de Suif" • Although his most famous short story, "Boule de Suif," also deals with the horrors of war, "Boule de Suif" is a much more complicated tale, and it has eleven major characters. At the beginning of "Boule de Suif," Maupassant evokes the terror felt by many French citizens who came to fear the abuse of power by the occupying soldiers. This short story begins in the Norman city of Rouen. The Prussian general in Rouen grants ten inhabitants of this city special permission to travel by coach from Rouen to Dieppe. Their intention is to reach the port of Le Havre, from which they can leave France for safety in England. Their motivaton is clear. They hope to lead better lives in a free country.

The ten travelers are from different social classes. There are three married couples. Mr. and Mrs. Loiseau are wine merchants whose integrity has been questioned by many of their customers. Mr. and Mrs. Carré-Lamodon are well-to-do owners of cotton mills, but Maupassant describes Mr. Carré-Lamodon as a hypocritical politician. The Count and Countess of Bréville are very rich, but their noble title is of questionable value. Rumor has it that King Henry IV of France had impregnated an ancestor of the Brévilles. In order to avoid an unpleasant situation, he made the lady's husband a count and appointed him as the governor of Normandy. This placated the husband. In the coach, there are also two nuns, an inoffensive leftist named Cornudet who is more interested in drinking beer than in reforming society, and finally a prostitute named Boule de Suif. Her name, which means "ball of tallow," evokes her rotund figure. Although the three respectable couples feel superior to Boule de Suif, they do not hesitate to accept food from her once they realize that she alone has brought food for this trip.

When their coach stops in the village of Tôtes, a German officer orders the ten passengers to stay in the local inn until Boule de Suif agrees to sleep with him. As a patriotic Frenchwoman, she refuses to yield to this blackmail. The next day she goes to church and asks God to grant her the strength to remain faithful to her moral principles and to France. She assumes that the other passengers will support her, but she is wrong. The married couples and the two nuns conspire to put pressure on Boule de Suif. The elder of the two nuns is especially reprehensible because she distorts the clear meaning of several biblical passages in order to convince Boule de Suif that it would be praiseworthy for her to sleep with the Prussian officer. Boule de Suif feels abandoned by her fellow citizens and by two representatives of her church. In despair, she yields to the Prussian's ultimatum. The three married couples and the two nuns celebrate this action by drinking champagne. Their insensitivity and general boorishness are obvious to the reader, who feels much sympathy for the victim. As they are traveling from Tôtes to Dieppe, Boule de Suif begins to weep, and the others take out their newly purchased picnic baskets filled with cheese, sausage, and bread, but they do not offer to share their food with Boule de Suif, who had been so generous during the earlier trip. A silent rage builds within her, but the proud Boule de Suif says nothing. She realizes that they are unworthy of her.

Ever since its publication in 1880, "Boule de Suif" has been considered Maupassant's masterpiece. Its structure is admirable, and the parallel scenes of eating in the coach serve to reinforce in the reader's mind Boule de Suif's alienation from the other passengers. Her patriotism causes her to sacrifice herself for them, but now they want nothing to do with her. Both "Boule de Suif" and "The Madwoman" reveal Maupassant's artistry in describing the unpredictable and destructive effect of war and occupation on innocent victims.

"Madame Tellier's Establishment" • Although the title character in "Boule de Suif" is a prostitute, the story's main theme is war and not prostitution. In Maupassant's equally celebrated short story "Madame Tellier's Establishment," the principal theme is prostitution, but Maupassant develops this theme with much sensitivity and wit. Madame Tellier runs a bordello, but she is a shrewd businesswoman who does a fine job in marketing. She hires prostitutes representing the different types of feminine beauty "so that each customer could find there the satisfaction" of his sexual fantasies. The men in her town feel very much at ease in her bordello, and she treats her prostitutes and clients as members of her extended family. One Friday evening, however, the routine is disrupted when her customers see a sign with the words "Closed Because of First Communion" at the entrance of her business. Madame Tellier has decided to close her bordello for a day so that she and her five employees can attend the First Communion of her niece, who lives in the rural community of Virville.

The train ride to Virville contains a marvelously comic scene. Seated with Madame Tellier and her five prostitutes are a traveling salesman and an elderly peasant couple, who are transporting three ducks not in cages. The husband and wife watch with disbelief as the five prostitutes take turns sitting on the salesman's lap while playing with the ducks. The salesman then takes out brightly colored garters, and he cajoles the prostitutes and even Madame Tellier into allowing him to place the garters on their legs. All of this is accompanied by much laughter. The peasants cannot believe their eyes. As they get off the train with their ducks, the wife tells her husband: "They are sluts on their way to the wicked city of Paris." She is partially correct, but their actual destination is the nearby village of Virville.

After they have breakfast on her brother's farm, Madame Tellier leads her prostitutes into the local church for the First Communion services. The parishioners have never before seen such gaudily dressed women. The worshipers find it difficult to concentrate on the Mass. The prostitute named Rosa thinks of her First Communion; she begins to cry, and her tears become contagious. First the other prostitutes, then Madame Tellier, and finally all the adults in the church begin to weep uncontrollably, and the tears do not end until the elderly priest has distributed Communion to the last child. He is so moved by their tears, which he interprets as the expression of profound religious emotion, that he decides to give a sermon. For him, this is "a sublime miracle" that has made him the "happiest priest in the diocese." He speaks of the "visible faith" and "profound piety" of the out-of-town visitors. Although this priest would most probably have expressed himself differently had he known of their profession, readers cannot question his sincerity or the reality of the religious emotions experienced by the worshipers in this small church.

After the Mass, life returns quickly to normal for the ever-practical Madame Tellier. She tells her brother that they must take the midafternoon train so that she can reopen her business within a few hours. That evening, there is a festive atmosphere in her bordello. Much champagne is drunk, and Madame Tellier is unusually generous. She charges her customers only six francs for a bottle of champagne instead of the normal rate of ten francs. This is a well-structured short story in which scenes in the bordello precede and follow the First Communion sequence. Maupassant describes characters from widely different professions and social classes in a nonjudgmental manner. The refined artistry and style of "Madame Tellier's Establishment" may explain why Thomas Mann, who was himself renowned for his short prose works, concluded that Maupassant "would be regarded for centuries as one of the greatest masters of the short story."

"The Horla" • "The Madwoman," "Boule de Suif," and "Madame Tellier's Establishment" are all effective third-person narratives, but Maupassant also experimented with other narrative techniques. In 1886, he wrote two versions of a short story that he entitled "The Horla." Both versions describe the mental illness of a Frenchman who believes that an invisible being called "the Horla" has taken possession of his mind. In the first version, a psychiatrist named Dr. Marrande asks seven colleagues to listen to a patient who is sure that the Horla entered his locked bedroom, drank milk and water, and then took over his personality. The psychiatric patient assures his listeners that he "saw" the Horla: He looked in a mirror but did not see his own image. After the patient stops talking, Dr. Marrande makes a very strange remark for a psychiatrist: "I do not know if this man is mad or if we are both mad or if our successor has actually arrived." The first version of "The Horla" is ineffective for several reasons. First, it lacks a clear focus because both Dr. Marrande and his patient speak of their reactions to the Horla. Second, Dr. Marrande's comment that he may have gone mad does not inspire much confidence in him. Third, the very nature of this narration does not enable readers to experience the gradual development of the patient's psychiatric problems.

Maupassant wisely decided to revise this short story into a first-person narrative presented in the forms of diary entries written by the patient himself. In his first entry, dated May 8, the diarist seems to be a calm individual who mentions in passing that a Brazilian boat has just passed by his house, which overlooks the Seine. He soon develops a fever, has trouble sleeping, and writes of a recurring nightmare. He dreams that a being is on his bed and is trying to strangle him. This nightmare returns several nights in a row. For the month of June, he is on an extended vacation, and he considers himself cured. When he returns home, however, he has new nightmares. This time, a being is trying to stab him. Although he keeps his bedroom locked at night, a spirit always drinks the water and the milk left in carafes by his bed. Gradually, he comes to accept the presence of this thirsty spirit. By mid-August, however, he concludes that a spirit has taken over his mind. The spirit orders him to read a book and an article on invisible spirits from Brazil that like to drink water and milk. In a desperate effort to free himself from the Horla, he traps the Horla in his bedroom and then burns down his house. It does not occur to him to think of his servants, who are asleep in his house. They die in the fire, and the diary does not indicate what happened to the diarist. Has he been arrested for murder or has he been committed to an insane asylum? In his very last entry, the diarist assures the reader that if the Horla is still alive, he will have to commit suicide. The second version of "The Horla" is very effective because it enables the reader to experience the gradual transformation of the diarist from a sensible person into a terrified and self-destructive individual who no longer appreciates the value of human life.

Although some critics have hypothesized that the second version of "The Horla" somehow prefigures the serious psychological problems that Maupassant himself would develop five years later, this is a fanciful interpretation. Maupassant did not try to kill himself until January, 1892, and he was still perfectly lucid when he wrote "The Horla" in 1886. This first-person narrative is a powerful short story that enables readers to experience the process by which a person can develop a serious mental illness. "The Horla" had a profound effect on generations of readers. In 1938, Arnold Zweig wrote of his recollection of this short story, which he had read years earlier:

> I still remember my emotion and admiration. I do not even need to close my eyes to see the white ship passing his country-house from which the strange guest, the split ego, invaded the life of the sick person.

Maupassant is still admired for his well-structured and beautifully written short stories. He is generally considered to be the best French short-story writer, although since the early years of the twentieth century, his works have been held in much higher esteem outside France (especially in England, the United States, and Germany) than in his homeland. It is not clear why so many French critics have been less than enthusiastic in their assessment of his short stories. Perhaps the critical standing of Maupassant would be higher than it is among modern French critics if he had explored a wider variety of themes. Readers should not forget that Maupassant died at the relatively young age of forty-two. His short literary career of only ten years did not give him sufficient time to develop the extraordinary breadth and diversity of a writer such as Victor Hugo, whose literary career spanned more than six decades. Despite the relatively limited number of themes that he explored in his short stories, Maupassant wrote short stories of such stylistic beauty and psychological depth that they still continue to please readers and to inspire creativity in short-story writers from many different countries.

Edmund J. Campion

Other major works
NOVELS: *Une Vie*, 1883 (*A Woman's Life*, 1888); *Bel-Ami*, 1885 (English translation, 1889); *Pierre et Jean*, 1888 (*Pierre and Jean*, 1890); *Forte comme la mort*, 1889 (*Strong as Death*, 1899); *Notre cœur*, 1890 (*The Human Heart*, 1890).

MISCELLANEOUS: *The Life Work of Henri René Guy de Maupassant*, 1903 (17 volumes); *The Works of Guy de Maupassant*, 1923-1929 (10 volumes).

NONFICTION: *Au Soleil*, 1884 (*In the Sunlight*, 1903); *Sur l'eau*, 1888 (*Afloat*, 1889); *Le Vie errante*, 1890 (*In Vagabondia*, 1903); *Lettres de Guy de Maupassant à Gustave Flaubert*, 1951.

POETRY: *Des Vers*, 1880 (*Romance in Rhyme*, 1903).

Bibliography
Artinian, Artine. *Maupassant Criticism in France, 1880-1940*. New York: Russell and Russell, 1969. First published in 1941, this important book explores critical reactions to Maupassant's works both in France and outside France. Artinian also includes thoughtful comments on Maupassant by some of the most important American and European writers of the 1930's. An essential work for all critics interested in Maupassant. Contains a thorough bibliography.

Fusco, Richard. *Maupassant and the American Short Story: The Influence of Form at the Turn of the Century*. University Park: Pennsylvania State University Press, 1994. Argues that Maupassant was the most important influence on American short-story writers in the late nineteenth and early twentieth centuries. Focuses on his effect on Kate Chopin, Ambrose Bierce, Henry James, and O. Henry. Arranges Maupassant's stories into seven categories based on narrative structure.

Harris, Trevor A. Le V. *Maupassant in the Hall of Mirrors: Ironies and Repetition in the Work of Guy de Maupassant*. Houndmills, England: Macmillan, 1990. Critical evaluation of Maupassant's use of irony and repetition.

Ignotus, Paul. *The Paradox of Maupassant*. London: University of London Press, 1966. In this fascinating but subjective interpretation of Maupassant's genius, Ignotus believes that Maupassant was a paradoxical writer because he was obsessed with sex and was nevertheless a creative genius. At times, Ignotus's arguments are not terribly convincing, but this book does discuss very well Maupassant's ambivalent attitudes toward his literary mentor, Gustave Flaubert.

Jobst, Jack W., and W. J. Williamson. "Hemingway and Maupassant: More Light on 'The Light of the World.'" *The Hemingway Review* 13 (Spring, 1994): 52-61. A comparison between Hemingway's "The Light of the World" and Maupassant's "La Maison Tellier." Discusses how both stories focus on a single prostitute rising above stereotypes.

Lloyd, Christopher, and Robert Lethbridge, eds. *Maupassant: Conteur et romancer.* Durham, England: University of Durham, 1994. Collection of papers, in both French and English, commemorating the centenary of Maupassant's death in 1993. Papers in English on Maupassant's short stories include an essay on "Mademoiselle Fifi," David Bryant's paper "Maupassant and the Writing Hand," and Angela Moger's essay "Kissing and Telling: Narrative Crimes in Maupassant."

May, Charles E., ed. *Masterplots II: Short Story Series, Revised Edition.* 8 vols. Pasadena, Calif.: Salem Press, 2004. Designed for student use, this reference set contains articles providing detailed plot summaries and analyses of nine short stories by Maupassant: "Boule de Suif" (vol. 1); "A Family Affair" and "The Horla" (vol. 3); "Love: Three Pages from a Sportsman's Notebook," "Madame Tellier's Establishment," "Mademoiselle Fifi," and "The Necklace" (vol. 5); "The Piece of String" (vol. 6); and "Two Little Soldiers" (vol. 8).

Steegmuller, Francis. *Maupassant: A Lion in the Path.* New York: Random House, 1949. Well-documented biography that describes both the nature of Flaubert's influence on Maupassant and the contacts of Maupassant with such major writers as Émile Zola, Ivan Turgenev, and Henry James.

Sullivan, Edward. *Maupassant the Novelist.* Princeton, N.J.: Princeton University Press, 1945. Thoughtful analysis of Maupassant's novels. Sullivan argues persuasively that Maupassant's novels do deserve as much critical attention as his more famous short stories have received over the years. Contains a solid bibliography.

_____. *Maupassant: The Short Stories.* Great Neck, N.Y.: Barron's, 1962. Pamphlet-length introduction to some of Maupassant's basic themes and story types. Particularly helpful are its attempts to place Maupassant's short stories within their proper generic tradition.

Wallace, Albert H. *Guy de Maupassant.* New York: Twayne, 1973. Excellent analysis of recurring themes in Maupassant's major works that discusses with much subtlety Maupassant's representations of war and madness. An essential introduction to the thematic study of Maupassant's major works.

Herman Melville

Born: New York, New York; August 1, 1819
Died: New York, New York; September 28, 1891

Principal short fiction • *The Piazza Tales,* 1856; *The Apple-Tree Table, and Other Sketches,* 1922.

Other literary forms • Herman Melville's sixteen published books include novels, short stories, poetry, and sketches. He is best known for his novels, particularly *Moby Dick* (1851), *The Confidence Man* (1857), and *Billy Budd, Foretopman* (1924).

Achievements • By the middle of the twentieth century, names such as *Moby Dick* and captain Ahab were well known in the popular culture of the United States. Yet one must look to the 1920's and the revival of interest in Melville's work (notably *Moby Dick*) to see the beginning of what came to be Melville's immense stature in American literature. His most significant works received little popular or critical acclaim in his lifetime. One reason for this may have been friction with nineteenth century American tastes. Problems also stemmed, however, from Melville's fascination with forces that seemed (to him) to lie below the placid optimism of his contemporary American culture. Readers were disturbed by the author's tendency to view outward appearances as pasteboard masks that concealed a truer, darker reality. It should come as no surprise that modern students sense an invitation to allegorize Melville's works. Many believe that Melville himself perceived life in a symbolic way.

Many of the short pieces that Melville wrote for various magazines represent conscious attempts, through symbol and irony, to express disturbing layers of meaning beneath a calm surface. In 1855-1856, Melville finished a novel, *The Confidence Man,* rendering a bleak view of the possibility of faith in the world as he knew it. Although Melville openly wrote verse throughout his life, the manuscript that would become his novella, *Billy Budd, Foretopman,* was packed away by his widow and not discovered until the 1920's.

Melville completed *Moby Dick* some forty years before Sigmund Freud began to penetrate the veneer of conventional surfaces in his quest for the causes of hysteria—the salient behavioral aberration of repressive nineteenth century Europe. Yet, Melville (like his contemporary Nathaniel Hawthorne) had already begun to probe beyond the level of mundane appearances in his fiction. Even though some of Melville's stories are lengthy by modern standards, the finest of them exhibit exceptional merit in the short-story genre. "Benito Cereno" and "Bartleby the Scrivener," for example, reveal a rich complexity and density which rival those of modern masterpieces of the form.

Biography • Herman Melville withdrew from school at the age of twelve after the death of his father. He worked in various jobs—in a fur and cap store (with his brother), in a bank, on a farm, and as a teacher in country schools. He made two early sea voyages, one on a merchant ship to Liverpool in 1839, and one to the South Seas aboard the whaler *Acushnet,* in 1841. After about eighteen months, Melville and a friend deserted the whaler, and Melville spent a month in the Taipi Valley on the island of Nuku Hiva. Melville escaped the island aboard an Australian whaler but was imprisoned when he and ten other crewmen refused service. Again he escaped, spent some time on the island of Mooréa, then several months in Hawaii. Eventually, he joined the U.S. Navy and returned home in 1844.

Library of Congress

Out of these early sea adventures came Melville's two successful early novels, *Typee: A Peep at Polynesian Life* (1846) and *Omoo: A Narrative of Adventures in the South Seas* (1847). His experiences aboard the whaling ships led to a novel that was not to be successful in his lifetime, *Moby Dick*. The failure of *Moby Dick* and *Pierre: Or, The Ambiguities* (1852) left Melville financially and morally drained, but he would continue to produce fiction for a while, including the short stories that were guardedly constructed to seem unruffling to the sensibilities of the time but which carried submerged patterns and disturbing undertones.

While still in the limelight of his early success, Melville married Elizabeth Shaw, daughter of a Massachusetts chief justice. They were to have four children; three died in young adulthood and the eldest son committed suicide in his eighteenth year (1867).

Melville was continually plagued by doubt, unrest, and marital problems. His later years were spent trying to adjust to his decline in status and seeking a comfortable living. In 1856, his father-in-law subsidized Melville's travels to the Mediterranean, the Holy Land, and England, where he visited Nathaniel Hawthorne. Unable to secure a naval commission during the Civil War (1861-1865), Melville sold his estate in Massachusetts and settled in New York. Finally, in 1866, he became an inspector in the New York Customs House until, some twenty years later, an inheritance enabled him to retire. He died September 28, 1891, at the age of seventy-two.

Analysis • After the critical and commercial failure of *Moby Dick* and *Pierre*, Herman Melville, who was then supporting his wife and children, his mother, and his four sisters, was desperate for money. So when he received an invitation from *Putnam's Monthly Magazine* to contribute short stories at the rate of five dollars a page, he accepted. He also sold short stories to *Harper's New Monthly Magazine*. Both magazines, however, had very strict editorial policies banning any material which might conceivably offend even the most sensitive reader on moral, social, ethical, political, or religious grounds. This was a shattering limitation to Melville, whose deepest personal

and artistic convictions were bound up in the defiant heroes and themes of highly un-
conventional metaphysical speculation of *Mardi and a Voyage Thither, Moby Dick*, and
Pierre. He genuinely questioned many of the ideas which, although they came to be
freely debated, were sacrosanct in the nineteenth century. These included the existence of a personal God outside the human spirit, the importance of material goods,
the existence of absolute good and absolute evil, and the right of established civil and
religious authorities to impose sanctions against those who expressed ideas that dif-
fered from the ideas of the majority. Obviously, neither *Putnam's Monthly Magazine*
nor *Harper's New Monthly Magazine* would publish stories which dealt openly with opinions that would be objectionable to many of their readers. This left Melville in an apparently unresolvable dilemma: ignore his own strongest beliefs, or allow those
dependent on him to live in poverty.

Not only did Melville find a solution, but he also found one which, while not ideal
from an artistic standpoint, gave him a great deal of rather diabolical satisfaction.
Melville's short stories—all of which were written during this period and under these
conditions—present bland and apparently harmless surfaces under which boil the
same rebellion and the same questioning of established ideas that characterize his
most controversial novels. Furthermore, these stories reflect, in allegorical terms,
the same dilemma that produced them. Beneath apparently innocuous surface plots,
Melville's short stories center on the image of an anguished human being who is
cursed with the ability to see more than the world sees; faced with the hostility that results from his challenge to the established beliefs of a complacent majority, his protagonist either fights against, withdraws from, or surrenders to the world.

"Bartleby the Scrivener" • One of the most effective devices that allowed Melville to
achieve his artistic purpose was his use of reassuringly respectable elderly gentlemen
as narrators. In the very act of allowing them to tell their own stories, Melville in-
jected a subtle but savage mockery which both expressed and concealed his own attitudes. For example, the narrator of Melville's best-known short story, "Bartleby the
Scrivener" (1856), which was collected in *The Piazza Tales*, is an elderly lawyer remi-
niscing about an incident which had occurred some time earlier. The lawyer's own
blindness to the deeper meanings of life is suggested in the first paragraph of the
story, when Melville describes Bartleby as "one of those beings of whom nothing is as-
certainable." As the reader discovers, it is primarily the physical, external facts of
Bartleby's life that are unknown; but to the materialistic lawyer, these are everything.
He sees only surface reality, never inner truth, a point which is underlined in the narrator's next sentence: "What my own astonished eyes saw of Bartleby, *that* is all I know
of him."

The lawyer begins his story by describing the office on Wall Street which he occupied at the time of Bartleby's appearance. The significance of "Wall Street" becomes
apparent immediately; the lawyer has surrounded himself with walls, and his windows command no other view. When the lawyer hires Bartleby as a scrivener, or
copier of law documents, he assigns Bartleby a desk near a window which faces a wall
only three feet away. On one side of Bartleby's desk is a ground glass door separating
him from the other two copyists, and on the other side, the lawyer places a folding
screen. Having imposed upon Bartleby his own claustrophobic setting, the lawyer
gives him law documents to copy. For a while all goes well; Bartleby copies documents
neatly and efficiently. On the third day, however, the lawyer asks Bartleby to examine
his writing.

In ordering him to examine his writing, the lawyer means that Bartleby should read through the copy he has made while someone else reads aloud from the original. This is an extremely boring task, but an accepted part of every scrivener's work. Bartleby replies, "I would prefer not to." The lawyer reacts with characteristic indecision: He feels impelled to expel Bartleby from his office, but does nothing because he is unnerved by Bartleby's total lack of expression, by the absence of "anything ordinarily human about him."

Several days later, when Bartleby again refuses to examine his copy, the lawyer appeals to him in the name of two ideals which are of great importance to the lawyer himself: common usage and common sense. Bartleby is unmoved. Instead of asserting his own authority, the lawyer appeals not only to his other two scriveners but also to his office boy. All these uphold the lawyer's view. He then calls upon Bartleby in the name of "duty"; again, Bartleby fails to respond to the verbal cue.

The lawyer's inability to cope with Bartleby is anticipated in the story by his tolerance of the Dickensian eccentricities of his other two scriveners. The older one, Turkey, works well in the morning, but after a lunch which is implied to be mostly liquid, he becomes reckless, irascible, and messy. The younger copyist, Nippers, is dyspeptic. His irritability takes place in the morning, while the afternoons find him comparatively calm. Thus, the lawyer gets only one good day's work between them. Nevertheless, he always finds some rationalization for his lack of decisiveness.

The first rationalization he applies to his indecision regarding Bartleby is the difficulty of coping effectively with passive resistance. The lawyer feels that Bartleby's unaccountable displays of perversity must be the result of some involuntary aberration, and he reflects that tolerating Bartleby "will cost me little or nothing, while I lay up in my soul what will eventually prove a sweet morsel for my conscience." Even on the comparatively rare occasions when he is sufficiently irritated to confront Bartleby with a direct order to do something which Bartleby "would prefer not to," the lawyer always retires with dire resolutions, but no action.

One Sunday morning, as the lawyer walks toward Trinity Church "to hear a celebrated preacher," he decides to stop at his office. There he finds Bartleby in his shirt sleeves, together with evidence that he has been using the office as his home. The lawyer feels at first a sense of melancholy and pity at Bartleby's loneliness; but as the full realization of Bartleby's isolation dawns on the lawyer, his feelings turn to fear and revulsion. He reflects that Bartleby never reads, never converses, but only works and stands for long periods staring out at the dead walls. Bartleby's presence in the office at night and on Sunday, when the usually bustling Wall Street is silent and uninhabited, reminds the lawyer of Bartleby's essential difference from his own concept of humanity, which revolves around surface society. The lawyer rationalizes his unsympathetic response to these circumstances by reflecting that such depths of soul-sickness as Bartleby's repel the human heart because common sense rejects the idea of pity where there is no realistic hope of offering aid.

The lawyer makes an attempt, on Monday morning, to bring Bartleby inside the narrow circle of external reality which is all the lawyer is capable of comprehending. He asks Bartleby for details of his life: place of birth, family, and the like. Bartleby refuses with his usual "I prefer not." The lawyer notices that he and his other copyists have begun to use that expression, and he fears that the influence of Bartleby will spread throughout the office. Bartleby further irritates the lawyer the next day by refusing to do even the one task he had, until then, been willing to do: copying law documents. When the lawyer asks the reason, Bartleby replies, "Do you not see the reason for yourself?" The lawyer does not see; and ironically, he attributes Bartleby's refusal to copy to trouble with his eyes. When Bartleby finally makes it clear, some days later, that his refusal is final, the lawyer decides to order him to leave. Yet h e feels a sense of pity for the scrivener because "he seemed alone, absolutely alone in the universe."

The lawyer gives Bartleby six days in which to get ready to leave; at the end of that time, Bartleby is still there. The lawyer gives him money, and, ordering Bartleby to be gone by the next day, leaves the office assuming that he will obey. The lawyer's self-congratulations on his masterly application of the doctrine of assumption end abruptly the next day when the lawyer discovers the scrivener still in the office. Then the lawyer rationalizes that it is his predestined fate to harbor Bartleby, and that his charity will be amply repaid in the next world. The gibes of his friends and professional associates, however, undermine his resolve, and again he orders Bartleby to depart. When he does not, the lawyer finally takes decisive action. He packs up his own belongings and moves to a new office, leaving Bartleby alone in an empty room.

The lawyer soon finds, however, that he is not yet free of Bartleby. The landlord of the lawyer's former office, unable to move Bartleby from the building even after the new tenant has expelled him from the office itself, applies to the lawyer for help. The lawyer offers Bartleby several different jobs, and even suggests that he make his home with the lawyer for a time. Bartleby, however, replies that he "would prefer not to make any change at all." The lawyer flees the building and stays incommunicado for several days. When he cautiously returns to his office, he finds that Bartleby has been removed to the Tombs, a prison in New York City. The lawyer visits the Tombs to offer comfort, but Bartleby will not speak to him. He adjures Bartleby to look at the blue sky and the green grass, but Bartleby replies, "I know where I am," and refuses to speak again. The lawyer leaves Bartleby in the prison yard, and on his way out arranges for him to be well fed, but Bartleby refuses to eat. When the lawyer visits Bartleby again, several days later, he finds the scrivener curled up in a ball with his head against the prison wall, dead.

The narrator concludes the story by relating a rumor he has heard to the effect that Bartleby was once employed in a Dead Letter Office. He reflects on the melancholy nature of such work, handling letters containing messages of charity and hope which arrived too late to relieve those to whom they had been sent. "On errands of life," reflects the lawyer, "these letters speed to death." The story ends with the line, "Ah Bartleby! Ah, humanity!"

Although the lawyer seems to be an honest and humane man, he is actually guilty of what Melville considers society's most prevailing sin: self-deception. He labels his pusillanimity prudence, his indecisiveness tolerance, his curiosity concern, as if by doing so he can create a reality which corresponds to his own illusions. He goes to a fashionable church not to worship the God in whom he professes to believe, but "to hear a famous preacher." When he is upset by Bartleby's presence in his office on a Sunday, he does not turn to God for help. Rather, he stays away from church because his perturbation makes him unfit for the only function of church-going that he is aware of: the social function. He constantly thinks in terms of material entities, particularly money and food. Yet the lawyer is not an evil man. By the standards of the world, he is exceptionally charitable and forbearing. He feels for Bartleby's suffering, even if he never understands it; and if the help he offers his scrivener is not what Bartleby needs, still it is all the lawyer has to give. That is Melville's point: Even the best of those who think conventional thoughts, order their lives by conventional rules, and never question conventional commonplaces like "common sense" and "common usage," are incapable of understanding a man like Bartleby.

Bartleby is the only character in the story who makes a point of looking at the walls, who is actually aware of the limitations with which society, represented by the lawyer, has boxed him in. Bartleby's refusal to value meaningless tasks simply because they are important to a shallow and materialistic society reflects Melville's own rage at being ordered to produce literary pabulum by a society which will not even try to understand his ideas. Bartleby is placed in the same economic dilemma which produced the story in which he appears: Produce what society values, regardless of individual needs and beliefs, or die. The solitary Bartleby died; and Melville, equally oppressed by being tied down to a family of dependent women and children, wrote "Bartleby the Scrivener."

"The Fiddler" • Not all the protagonists of Melville's short stories withdraw from the world. The narrator-protagonist of "The Fiddler," for example, responds to the world's contempt for his poetry by abandoning his art and attempting to become a happy failure. The story opens as the young poet, Helmstone, storms out of doors after reading an unfavorable review of his recently published work. He meets a friend, Standard, who introduces him to Hautboy. The three attend a circus, where Helmstone rages at seeing the applause which the world has denied to his poetry being awarded to the antics of a clown. He marvels at the evident enjoyment of Hautboy, whom Helmstone identifies as a man of taste and judgment. Helmstone and Standard later visit Hautboy's home, where he entertains them by playing common tunes on a fiddle. Despite the simplicity of the tunes, Helmstone is struck by Hautboy's style; and Standard finally explains that Hautboy is actually a musical genius who has given up the fame he once had and retired to happy obscurity. The poet, resolved to imitate him, tears up his manuscripts, buys a fiddle, and goes to take lessons from Hautboy.

In "The Fiddler," Hautboy serves as a lesson in the worthlessness of fame because, having had it and rejected it, he is so outstandingly happy. This allows the poet to rationalize his own failure into a deliberate choice to turn his back on the world's opinion of his poetry. In this story, however, as in "Bartleby the Scrivener," the narrator's conformity to the standards of the world (in this case, by ceasing to produce poetry which the world does not appreciate) is an act of self-deception. Either Helmstone's poetry is meritorious but misunderstood by a world whose applause is reserved for clowns, in which case he has betrayed his art by abandoning it, or his poetry is genuinely inferior, in which case he has renounced nothing because he has had nothing, and his attitude of choice is a sham. This reflects another aspect of the situation that produced "The Fiddler." If the kind of literature Melville would have preferred to write was in fact the truth, then in ceasing to write it he was betraying himself; if it was not the truth, he was deceiving himself.

These two examples illustrate the complexity and depth which underlie the surface smoothness of Melville's short tales. His stories are allegorical in nature, expressing his ideas as parables rather than as expositions. Melville often makes his points by means of emblematic symbols, such as the walls in "Bartleby the Scrivener" and the clown in "The Fiddler." In his short stories, as in his novels, Melville emphasizes subjectivity, relativity, and ambiguity. Different characters see the same situation from different perspectives, and there is no omniscient force within the story which can resolve the resulting conflict. Reality is not static and absolute, but shifting and relative; ultimate truth, if it exists at all, is unattainable.

Joan DelFattore
With updates by Mary Rohrberger

Other major works

NOVELS: *Typee: A Peep at Polynesian Life,* 1846; *Omoo: A Narrative of Adventures in the South Seas,* 1847; *Mardi, and a Voyage Thither,* 1849; *Redburn: His First Voyage,* 1849; *White-Jacket: Or, The World in a Man-of-War,* 1850; *Moby Dick: Or, The Whale,* 1851; *Pierre: Or, The Ambiguities,* 1852; *Israel Potter: His Fifty Years of Exile,* 1855; *The Confidence Man: His Masquerade,* 1857; *Billy Budd, Foretopman,* 1924.

MISCELLANEOUS: *Tales, Poems, and Other Writings,* 2001 (John Bryant, editor).

NONFICTION: *Journal up the Straits,* 1935; *Journal of a Visit to London and the Continent,* 1948; *The Letters of Herman Melville,* 1960 (Merrill R. Davis and William H. Gilman, editors).

POETRY: *Battle-Pieces and Aspects of the War,* 1866; *Clarel: A Poem and Pilgrimage in the Holy Land,* 1876; *John Marr, and Other Sailors,* 1888; *Timoleon,* 1891; *The Works of Herman Melville,* 1922-1924 (volumes 15 and 16); *The Poems of Herman Melville,* 1976 (revised, 2000).

Bibliography

Adams, Michael. "Bartleby the Scrivener." In *Masterplots II: Short Story Series,* edited by Charles E. May. Rev. ed. Vol. 1. Pasadena, Calif.: Salem Press, 2004. Analysis of "Bartleby the Scrivener" with sections on themes and meaning and style and technique. Also includes a detailed synopsis of the story.

Bryant, John, ed. *A Companion to Melville Studies.* New York: Greenwood Press, 1986. Articles contributed by various scholars compose this thorough volume, which includes a biography and discussions of the short stories and other works. Some articles give insight into Melville's thought on religion and philosophy and discuss his impact on modern culture.

Delbanco, Andrew. *Melville: His World and Work.* New York: Alfred A. Knopf, 2005. This biography places Melville in his time and discusses the significance of his works, then and now.

Fisher, Marvin. *Going Under: Melville's Short Fiction and the American 1850's.* Baton Rouge: Louisiana State University Press, 1977. Explores the short fiction works with Melville's cultural milieu of the 1850's as a backdrop. Fisher discusses "The Fiddler," "The Lightning Rod Man," and "Bartleby the Scrivener," among other short works.

Hardwick, Elizabeth. *Herman Melville.* New York: Viking Press, 2000. Short biographical study that hits all the high points and some low ones in Melville's life, from his early seagoing expeditions to his settling down in middle age and finally his languishing in his job as a New York customs inspector.

Levine, Robert S., ed. *The Cambridge Companion to Herman Melville.* Cambridge, England: Cambridge University Press, 1998. Indispensable tool for the student of Melville. With bibliographical references and an index.

Newman, Lea Bertani Vozar. *A Reader's Guide to the Short Stories of Herman Melville.* Boston: G. K. Hall, 1986. Newman includes "The Encantadas." Each chapter is divided into sections: publication history, circumstances of composition, relationship to other works, profile of interpretive criticism, and bibliography.

Robertson-Lorant, Laurie. *Melville: A Biography.* New York: Clarkson N. Potter, 1996. This biography includes personal, psychological, social, and intellectual aspects of Herman Melville's life, as well as his travels and adventures in the South Seas and Europe.

Rollyson, Carl E., and Lisa Paddock. *Herman Melville A to Z: The Essential Reference to His Life and Work.* New York: Checkmark Books, 2001. Comprehensive and ency-clopedic coverage of Melville's life, works, and times in 675 detailed entries.

Rosenblum, Joseph. "Benito Cereno." In *Masterplots II: Short Story Series,* edited by Charles E. May. Rev. ed. Vol. 1. Pasadena, Calif.: Salem Press, 2004. Student-friendly analysis of "Benito Cereno" that covers the story's themes and style and in-cludes a detailed synopsis.

Updike, John. "The Appetite for Truth: On Melville's Shorter Fiction." *The Yale Review* 85 (October, 1997): 24-47. Discusses Melville's magazine short fictions of the mid-1850's, which Updike finds to be stiffer than Melville's earlier novels; claims that as a novelist he was exalted by Shakespearean possibilities, but as a short-story writer he saw failure everywhere.

Prosper Mérimée

Born: Paris, France; September 28, 1803
Died: Cannes, France; September 23, 1870

Principal short fiction • *La Double Méprise,* 1833 (*A Slight Misunderstanding,* 1905); *Mosaïque,* 1833 (*The Mosaic,* 1905); *La Vénus d'Ille,* 1837 (*The Venus of Ille,* 1903); *Colomba,* 1840 (English translation, 1853); *Carmen,* 1845 (English translation, 1878); *Nouvelles,* 1852 (*Stories,* 1905); "Lokis," 1869; *Dernières nouvelles,* 1873 (*Last Stories,* 1905); *Carmen, and Other Stories,* 1998.

Other literary forms • Although Prosper Mérimée is best remembered as an important innovator of the short-story form in France, he was, as befits a member of the French intelligentsia of the mid-nineteenth century, a contributor to all of the literary genres. He dabbled in poetry; wrote astonishing plays, romances, and a major novel; contributed as a journalist to the art and literary criticism of his time; distinguished himself as a translator of Russian literature into French; and is largely responsible for introducing Russian literature to the French reading public.

Achievements • Prosper Mérimée may not have been the greatest French writer of his time, but he was certainly one of the most versatile. Ironically, it was his lack of dedication to his craft that gave him his importance. At a time when most French writers took themselves very seriously, and when Germanic Romanticism threatened to inundate the level plain of Gallic thought, Mérimée stood indifferently on his own personal promontory, observant, uncommitted, and completely dry. He began his literary career with two of the most thorough hoaxes ever perpetrated on a reading public and ended it with a tale designed to shock the ladies of Empress Eugénie's court.

Mérimée could afford to be indifferent. Despite his claim that he wrote *Carmen* because he needed new pants, he never had to rely on his pen for either financial support or prestige. His success in his fiction writing was but one of his many accomplishments. He was also a lawyer and a public official important enough in his position as inspector general of public monuments to be retained through the great changes in national political power in 1830 and 1848 and to be made a senator under Louis-Napoleon. Moreover, he was a painter of some talent, a lover of some notoriety, an authority on Russian literature, a member of the French Academy, and a mentor and friend of the empress of the French.

Renowned as a writer of short fiction, Mérinée has also been praised for his painstakingly researched reconstruction of the past in his historical works and his innovations in dramatic theory and practice. Named to the French Academy in 1844, Mérimée was a cosmopolitan figure in the cultural life of Europe. His work was favorably reviewed by contemporary English periodicals.

Biography • Prosper Mérimée was the son of a wealthy art professor and painter; his mother was well known for her own work in the arts as a child-portraitist. Therefore, early in his life, Mérimée was surrounded not only by the arts but also by the atmosphere in which art thrives: There were constant discussions and arguments among friends, an intermingling of art forms, and, above all, an acknowledgment of the art of living. Like his close friend Stendhal, he lived through the Romantic period in France without ever becoming too deeply involved himself, although some of his plays show discernible tendencies to cater to the public's taste of the moment. For many Romantics, art was a game, and in this sense Mérimée excelled: His first publications were elaborate put-ons. *Le Théâtre de Clara Gazul* (1825; the theater of Clara Gazul) purported to be a collection of plays by a Spanish actor and enjoyed great success in Paris. Two years later, Mérimée published *La Guzla* (an anagram of Gazul), a collection purporting to be translations into French of Balkan ballads and folk songs; his techniques were so

Library of Congress

sophisticated that Alexander Pushkin translated the collection into Russian and published it in his own country before the hoax became known. The success of these anonymous works as well as of others confirmed to Mérimée that his true artistic talent lay in the development of shorter fiction since the genre permitted him to exploit his quick wit, cleverness, and extraordinary powers of observation.

In 1829, at the age of twenty-six, Mérimée signed his real name to several short stories that took the reading public by storm: "Mateo Falcone," "Tamango," and "Le Vase étrusque." Several plays were equally successful, bringing Mérimée more and more into the public eye, where his family, friends, and connections paid off with a series of political posts. In 1833, he was appointed chief inspector of historical monuments; the position provided his aesthetic preoccupations an outlet. Thanks to his energetic dedication to his task, which required him to sacrifice his own personal artistic ambitions, Mérimée was instrumental in helping to preserve and upgrade French treasures of Roman and gothic art.

Mérimée's life was filled with successes, including being elected a French senator, remaining close to the emperor Napoleon III and his wife Eugénie, and being elected early (1844) to the Académie Française. Although he was able to indulge himself in every way, his upbringing in the world of art helped guide him instinctively toward ventures that were both noble and aesthetic; he was a learned critic, linguist, and historian with many diverse interests. Although his detractors criticized his calm dispassion, contemporary critics, armed with Mérimée's vast correspondence, perceive that this dispassion was also a pose, concealing an artfully nurtured sensitivity.

Analysis • In Prosper Mérimée, readers encounter an amazingly versatile writer, scholar, and public official. Best known for his short stories, which, as Henry James once commented, are full of "pregnant brevity" and a "magical after-resonance," Mérimée also belonged to the French Romantic generation. With the Romantics, he shared a taste for exoticism, folk culture, and local color, and he practiced unsparingly that uniquely Romantic form of irony, whereby writers distance themselves from their work, mocking themselves and their own creations. In his desire, however, to shock the bourgeoisie, indulge in complex wordplays, and mock Romantic conventions, he resembles the writers of the later Young France movement. Simultaneously, his objectivity and the concision of his narratives link him with realism.

"Mateo Falcone" • Typical of Prosper Mérimée's art is "Mateo Falcone," first published in 1829, and included in the volume *Mosaïque*. Set in Corsica, it is a story of rigorous family pride and personal honor. While Mateo Falcone and his wife are away caring for their flocks, their ten-year-old son Fortunato remains at home alone. A bandit, however, pursued by soldiers, arrives and gives the young boy some coins in exchange for the latter's promise to hide him. Moments later, the soldiers arrive and question Fortunato, who disavows any knowledge of the bandit. The captain, nevertheless, is a clever person; he shows the boy a lovely silver watch that will be his if he reveals the presence of the fugitive. Unable to resist, Fortunato grasps the watch and reveals the hiding place. Mateo and his wife return at this point and hear the bandit cursing the greedy child and his family. Profoundly shocked, Mateo asks his wife if Fortunato is truly his son, for if so, Fortunato is the first member of his race to have betrayed another. Consanguinity confirmed by the mother, father and son walk into the underbrush where Fortunato is ordered to pray and is shot. One of Mérimée's first published works in prose, this short story is powerful precisely because of the author's meticulous control of the material. There are no digressions, no self-serving descriptions, no gratuitous details. Mérimée's sober and rigorous discipline is in marked contrast to the exuberant mood of Honoré de Balzac, his contemporary. The tone of detachment heightens the intensity of primitive passion, giving a mythical quality to the story.

Colomba • Another tale of Corsican passion is *Colomba*, which deals with the notion of vengeance that overpowers all other considerations. After Napoleon's defeat at Waterloo, Lieutenant Orso returns to his native Corsica to learn that his father has been killed. Rumors suggest that the Barricini family is responsible, although the official accounts exonerate them. Because of his European experience and culture, and because his long absence from the island may have dulled his native instincts, Orso's first response is to accept things as they are. His sister Colomba, however, has been eagerly awaiting his return to avenge her father, and she will not allow Orso's complacency. Similar to Electra in Jean-Paul Sartre's *Les Mouches* (1943; *The Flies*, 1946), Colomba drives her brother to action, and thus the cycle begins again. With all the classical intensity of such a work as Pierre Corneille's *Horace* (1640), Mérimée's story builds as the characters fall victim to a terrifying and overpowering thirst for blood.

Carmen • Perhaps the best known of Mérimée's short stories is *Carmen*, the story of the love of a soldier, Don José, for Carmen, the bohemian he is supposed to escort to prison. Infatuated, he allows her to escape and then suffers the humiliation of being demoted for his ineptitude. His love for Carmen prompts him to abandon his career and seek her out, join her, and earn his livelihood as a smuggler. Since he exults in his love for her, he can accept his new life, and he savors his exclusive possession of such a fascinating woman. She, on the other hand, is a bohemian, both capricious and willful, dominated by fate and tradition. When Carmen's husband reappears unannounced, Don José kills him from jealousy since he cannot endure the sight of Carmen with another man. Later, when Carmen throws down her wedding ring in a temper, Don José kills her in a fit of jealous rage. Mérimée adopted for this story the point of view of a young archaeologist, whose scientific detachment makes these extraordinary characters more believable and the overpowering presence of fate in the story more compelling. *Carmen* had many imitators and served as the basis for Georges Bizet's opera of the same name, presented in Paris in 1875.

The Venus of Ille • *The Venus of Ille* develops Mérimée's notions of the supernatural and marks an important step in the evolution of the genre toward its climax in the works of Guy de Maupassant. On the Spanish border in the foothills of the Pyrenees, a collector discovers a lovely statue of Venus, which he cherishes all the more strongly when the local townspeople express their fear of it as an omen of evil. The collector's son is a devotee of the game of *pelote*; on his wedding day he joins some friends in a game, and in order not to be encumbered by the wedding ring which he will soon be placing on his bride's hand, he places the ring on the hand of the statue, where it is forgotten. Later, at the wedding ceremony, another ring must be used. That same afternoon, he returns to the garden to attempt to recover the ring, but it will not come off the statue's finger. In panic because he feels bewitched, the son joins his bride in their room, where he hopes to be comforted and distracted. Once in bed, however, he is kissed by the statue, whose embrace kills him in full view of his bride, who then goes mad. The dispassion of the author in leading the reader from the festive atmosphere of the opening pages to the horror of the conclusion, and his subtle foreshadowing of the hand of fate are excellent examples of Mérimée's art.

Contrary to Gustave Flaubert and his preoccupation with subject matter that could be considered normal, ordinary, or plausible, Mérimée was fascinated by the élan vital of the Mediterranean world. Strong, colorful people from Italy, Corsica, and Spain inhabit his universe; they have violent, primitive passions and are imbued with tradition and a keenly developed sense of honor. In contrast to his contemporaries, Mérimée applied to his prose that dispassionate artistic perspective that neither praises, condemns, nor judges.

Robert W. Artinian
With updates by Anna M. Wittman

Other major works

PLAYS: *Le Théâtre de Clara Gazul*, pb. 1825 (*The Plays of Clara Gazul*, 1825); *La Jaquerie*, pb. 1828; *L'Occasion*, pb. 1829; *La Carrosse du Saint-Sacrement*, pb. 1829; *Les Deux Héritages*, pb. 1850.

NOVELS: *La Famille de Carçajal*, 1828; *Chronique du règne de Charles IX*, 1829 (*A Chronicle of the Times of Charles the Ninth*, 1830).

MISCELLANEOUS: *The Writings of Prosper Mérimée*, 1905 (8 volumes).

NONFICTION: *Histoire de don Pedre Ier, roi de Castille*, 1848 (*The History of Peter the Cruel*, 1849; 2 volumes); *Les Faux Démétrius*, 1852 (*Demetrius, the Impostor*, 1853); *Lettres*

à une inconnue, 1874 (*Letters to an Unknown*, 1874); *Correspondance générale*, 1941-1964 (17 volumes).
POETRY: *La Guzla*, 1827.

Bibliography

Buller, Jeffrey L. "Mateo Falcone." In *Masterplots II: Short Story Series*, edited by Charles E. May. Rev. ed. Vol. 5. Pasadena, Calif.: Salem Press, 2004. Analysis of "Mateo Falcone" with sections on themes and meaning and style and technique. Also includes a detailed synopsis of the story.

Cogman, P. W. M. "Cheating at Narrating: Back to Mérimée's 'La Partie de trictrac.'" *Nineteenth-Century French Studies* 26 (Fall/Winter, 1997/1998): 80-90. Argues that the tale embodies a tension between psychological content and the narrative technique, which seems to mock storytelling and both exploit and subvert narrative expectations; claims the story has two centers.

_____. *Merimée, Colomba, and Carmen*. London: Grant and Cutler, 1992. Examination of the two stories.

Gould, Evelyn. *The Fate of Carmen*. Baltimore: Johns Hopkins University Press, 1996. Thoughtful study of *Carmen*.

Mickelsen, David. "Travel, Transgression, and Possession in Mérimée's *Carmen*." *Romantic Review* 87 (May, 1996): 329-344. Argues that the story should be viewed as an unequal meeting of cultures in which the central figure is not the Gypsy Carmen but the French narrator visiting Spain; claims that examining the role of the narrator helps reveal the cultural imperatives operating within the story, especially its hidden colonialist stance.

Rigolot, François. "Ekphrasis and the Fantastic: Genesis of an Aberration." *Comparative Literature* 49 (Spring, 1997): 97-112. Discusses "The Venus of Ille" as an illumination of the fantastic as a displaced mode of ekphrastic representation.

Seidler-Golding, Marianne. "Destabilized Security in Mérimée's Short Stories." *Paroles-Gelées* 13 (1995): 63-73. Discusses the relationship between explicit violence in Mérimée's stories and implicit violence in the ways the violent actions are depicted, with reference to "Mateo Falcone" and "The Venus of Ille."

Smith, Maxwell A. *Prosper Mérimée*. New York: Twayne, 1972. Readable introductory study of the author's life and works. Especially relevant to the study of the short prose fiction are chapters 6 through 11. Biographical and critical material are supplemented by a chronology of Mérimée's life, a select bibliography, and an index.

Stowe, Richard. "Prosper Mérimée." In *European Writers*. Vol. 6 in *The Romantic Century*, edited by Jacques Barzun and George Stade. New York: Charles Scribner's Sons, 1985. This brief study combines a biographical overview with a discussion of the style and content of Mérimée's major works, including the short fiction. The select bibliography includes editions, collected works, bibliographies, translations, correspondence, and biographical critical studies.

Tilby, Michael. "Languages and Sexuality in Mérimée's *Carmen*." *Forum for Modern Language Studies* 15, no. 3 (1979): 255-263. An analysis of the fictional world of *Carmen*, focusing on its tight and natural organization.

Yukio Mishima

Born: Tokyo, Japan; January 14, 1925
Died: Tokyo, Japan; November 25, 1970

Principal short fiction • *Kaibutsu*, 1950; *Tōnorikai*, 1951; *Manatsu no shi*, 1953 (*Death in Midsummer, and Other Stories*, 1966).

Other literary forms • Yukio Mishima wrote more than eighty short stories; twenty novels; more than twenty plays, several in the manner of the classical Nō dramas, as well as plays for the Kabuki theater; several essay collections; two travel books; a bit of poetry; and a handful of works that defy clear-cut classification.

Achievements • The collected works of Yukio Mishima form thirty-six volumes, more than the literary production of any other writer of his time. The Japanese writer best known outside Japan, from the viewpoint of Western critics he is the most gifted of the post-World War II writers. Mishima also combined his knowledge of classic Japanese literature and language with his wide knowledge of Western literature to produce plays for the Kabuki theater and the first truly successful modern Nō plays.

Although uneven in some volumes, style is the most distinctive feature of Mishima's work. His writing is characterized by beautiful but rarely lyric passages. Figures of speech, notable in his later works, are also present in his juvenilia. He consistently used ornate language, though he could also write realistic dialogue.

A Nobel Prize hopeful at least two times, Mishima is among those Japanese writers closest to attaining the rank of master of twentieth century fiction.

Biography • Kimitake Hiraoka, who began using the pseudonym Yukio Mishima in 1941, was the son of a middle-class government official who worked in Tokyo. When Mishima was less than two months old, his paternal grandmother, Natsu, took the boy to her living quarters; his mother, Shizue, felt helpless to protest, and his father, Azusa, appeared to be totally subjected to his mother's will.

In 1931, Mishima was enrolled in the Gakushūin (the Peer's School), a school attended largely by young aristocrats. In due time, he graduated at the head of his class and received a silver watch from the emperor personally at the imperial palace. By this time, his literary gifts had already become evident, and "Hanazakari no mori" ("The Forest in Full Bloom") was published in 1941.

In 1946, Mishima entered the Tokyo Imperial University to study law. After being employed for a time at the Ministry of Finance, he resigned in 1948 to devote full time to writing. The publication of *Kamen no kokuhaku* (1949; *Confessions of a Mask*, 1958) established him as a literary figure.

The 1950's were eventful years in Mishima's life. During this decade, he produced several novels, two of them major successes. He also traveled to the United States, Brazil, and Europe, and his visit to Greece in particular was a highlight because of its classical associations. During these years, *Shiosai* (1954; *The Sound of Waves*, 1956), a best-seller, was published and film rights were sold, and *Shiroari no su* (1956; the nest of the white ants) established his reputation as a playwright. He also began a body-building program (having been a spare, sickly child) and married Yoko Sugiyama in 1958.

During the first half of the 1960's, writing plays occupied Mishima's time. He trained at the Jieitai (Self-Defense Forces) bases and traveled periodically. He was a strong contender for the Nobel Prize in 1968, the year that his mentor Yasunari Kawabata won. The short story "Yōkoku" ("Patriotism"), in which the hara-kiri (ritual suicide by disembowelment) of a young patriot is described, was published in 1961. He also acted in his first film, a gangster story.

By this time, Mishima's obsession with death was manifested both in word and in deed. He developed a plan for organizing a private army to be used somehow in his death, a step labeled foolish by his friends and ignored by others. During the final five months of his life, he completed the third and fourth books of his tetralogy *Hōjō no umi* (1969-1971; *The Sea of Fertility*, 1972-1974), and on November 25, 1970, he delivered the final volume to the magazine that was publishing it in installments. Later that day, following his plan and schedule implicitly, Mishima went to the Ichigaya Self-Defense headquarters with a group of his Shield Society (a private legion) and, following a nationalistic speech, committed ritual seppuku.

Analysis • The world will never know what course the literary career of Yukio Mishima might have taken had he not died at the age of forty-five. Nevertheless, he was the best known of post-World War II writers among critics and readers outside Japan, and he received a fair share of attention within his own country. Not all of his work was of equal literary merit, but a certain unevenness is almost certain for a prolific writer.

Apart from his style, usually ornate and meticulously wrought, Mishima's success stemmed in part from his effectiveness in capturing the sense of void and despair that typified many Japanese during the postwar period. Another key to his success lay in his unusual interest in Japanese cultural tradition. His abilities, unique among his peers, enabled him to write in the genre of classical Kabuki and Nō plays.

"The Forest in Full Bloom" • Mishima's early works represent a period that both clarified the directions in which his talents would go and developed features that would become trademarks of his later works. He came to realize that poetry was not to be his major effort. In 1941, the year he graduated from the Peer's School, he published his first long work, "The Forest in Full Bloom" in October, at the age of sixteen. The maturity of style in this juvenile work amazed his mentors and peers. The sophisticated word choice is noteworthy, but its maturity goes much further; it establishes the major theme of his life's work, for he was well on his way to evolving the aesthetic formula that would distinguish his work: Longing leads to beauty; beauty generates ecstasy; ecstasy leads to death. Likewise, the sea, an important motif throughout his writing, is associated with death. Indeed, as Donald Keene has noted, Mishima seemed to be "intoxicated with the beauty of early death."

Death in Midsummer, and Other Stories • Preoccupation with death is obvious even in the title of the short-story collection that constitutes Mishima's major short fiction, *Death in Midsummer, and Other Stories*. The title story, "Death in Midsummer," takes an epigraph from one of Charles Baudelaire's poems that translates as "Death affects us more deeply under the stately reign of summer." The psychological realism of Mishima's presentation of the family's reactions to three deaths in the family is the focus of the story. Masaru and Tomoko Ikuta have two sons, Kiyoo and Katsuo, and a daughter, Keiko. Yasue, Tomoko's sister-in-law, is baby-sitting the children while Tomoko takes an afternoon nap. Despite warnings to the children against wandering away, during a brief moment when Yasue is preoccupied with other thoughts, two of the children disappear, leaving the three-year-old Katsuo alone, crying. When Yasue realizes what has happened, she is stricken with a heart attack and dies. Informed of Yasue's accident, Tomoko "felt a sort of sweet emptiness come over her. She was not sad." (This is only one of several passages in which a dearth of feeling is expressed.) Only then does she inquire about the children; she finds Katsuo, who informs her that "Kiyoo . . . Keiko . . . all bubbles." Tomoko is afraid; she sends her husband a telegram telling him that Yasue is dead and that the two children are missing, although by now it is clear that the children have drowned.

Masaru prepares to go down to the resort where the family was vacationing. Devoid of any emotion, he feels more like a detective speculating on the circumstances of death than a distraught father. Intuitively, he senses that the children are dead, not simply missing. When he arrives at the resort, he hears that three people have died, and his thoughts turn to how to approach his wife. Funeral preparations are made. Tomoko is conscious of the incongruity of her almost insane grief alongside her businesslike attention to detail and her large appetite at such a time. She vacillates between a feeling of guilt and her knowledge that she did not cause the deaths. Dissatisfied, she believes that Yasue is lucky to be dead because she does not have to feel that she has been "demoted and condemned" by relatives. Mishima here intrudes to comment that although Tomoko does not know it, it is her "poverty of human emotions" that is most troubling her.

On the surface, life returns to normal, but Tomoko associates almost everything with the tragic accident, while Masaru takes refuge in his work. Tomoko questions the fact that "she was living, the others were dead. That was the great evil. How cruel it was to have to be alive." Autumn comes and goes; and life becomes more peaceful, but Tomoko comes to feel as if she is waiting for something. To try to assuage her empty feelings, Tomoko seeks outside activities. She asks herself why she had not "tried this mechanical cutting off of the emotions earlier." Winter comes. Tomoko, who is to have another child, admits for the first time that the pain of the lost children was gone, but she cultivates forgetfulness in order not to have to deal with her feelings further. After two years, one summer day, Tomoko asks Masaru to return with her to the beach. Grudgingly, he consents. Tomoko is silent and spends much of her time gazing at the sea, as if she were waiting for something. Masaru wants to ask but then realizes that "he thought he knew without asking."

As with much Japanese literature, the cycle of the seasons is prominent. Deaths come in midsummer, when things should be flourishing and in full bloom. When winter comes, the final ritual of burying the ashes of the dead is completed. Tomoko becomes pregnant, and Momoko is born the following summer. Again, it is summer when she returns to the beach. The cryptic ending is typical of some, not all, of Mishima's work. One may speculate that the return to the beach in the summer is a sign of acceptance or an effort by Tomoko to come to terms with her own identity. Possibly, her waiting represents some sense of communication with the spirits of the dead or even indicates a longing for her own death. A less gloomy interpretation of the return to the beach, however, may recall Baudelaire's line suggesting that death in summer is out of place; death is for the winter, when nature, too, is desolate.

"The Priest of Shiga Temple and His Love" • More often anthologized, the story "Shigadera Shōnin no Koi" ("The Priest of Shiga Temple and His Love") manifests Mishima's familiarity with classical Japanese literature. At the same time, the central theme of the story is one that is common in the West but relatively rare in Japanese literature: the inner conflict between worldly love and religious faith. A brief account in a fourteenth century war chronicle of an elderly priest falling in love with the imperial concubine provides the subject matter of the story.

It is the motivation of the concubine and the priest—rather than the events—that is the focus of the story. The priest is an exemplar of virtue; he is old and doddering, physically a "bag of bones"; it is unlikely that he would become infatuated with a beautiful young woman. When the concubine comes to the area to view the springtime foliage, the priest "unwittingly" glances in her direction, not expecting to be overwhelmed by her beauty. He is, however, and he realizes that "what he had imagined to be completely safe had collapsed in ruins." Never had he broken his vow of chastity, but he realizes that this new love has taken hold of him. The concubine, having forgotten their meeting, is reminded of it when she hears a rumor that an old priest has behaved as if he were crazed after having seen her. She, too, is without blemish in that, while she performed her duties to the emperor, she has never given her love to any suitor.

The priest is now tormented by the implications of this love in relation to his attaining enlightenment. He longs to see the lady once more, confident in his delusion that this will provide escape from his present feelings. He goes to her garden, but when the concubine sees him, she orders that his presence be ignored; she is frightened when he continues to stand outside all night. The lady tells herself that this is a one-sided affair, that he can do nothing to her to threaten her security in the Pure Land. Finally, she admits him, and her white hand emerges from beneath the dividing blind that separates them, as custom decrees. She waits, but the priest says nothing. Finally, he releases her hand and departs. Rumor has it that a few days later, the priest "achieved his final liberation" and the concubine begins copying rolls of religious sutras. Thus, the love story between these two who both are faithful to the tenets of *Jōdo* Buddhism focuses on the point at which the ideal world structure that each one envisioned was in this incident "balanced between collapse and survival." If nothing more, the story reflects the aesthetic formed early in Mishima's life, which holds that beauty causes ecstasy which, in turn, causes death.

"Patriotism" • The story "Yōkoku" ("Patriotism"), which was made into a film, is the first of several that focus on ideals of young military officers of the 1930's. To understand this work, it is important to grasp the meaning of the translation of the word "patriotism." The word *yōkoku* means grieving over a country rather than loving a country (*aikoku*), which is a positive emotion. Thus, it is autobiographical in that it expresses Mishima's own grief over the country that he perceived to be in disorder. "Patriotism," according to Mishima's own evaluation, contains "both the best and the worst features" of his writing. The story concerns a young lieutenant, Shinji Takeyama, who commits seppuku because he feels that he cannot do what he has been ordered to do: lead an attack on the young rebels in the Ni Ni Roku Incident, an unsuccessful coup d'état that occurred on February 26, 1936, in Tokyo. Although Mishima was only eleven years old at the time of the incident, its influence on him provided the germ for two other works, a play *Tōka no Kiku* (1961; tenth-day chrysanthemums) and *Eirei no Koe* (voices of the heroic dead). These works confirm Mishima's growing dedication to imperialism. The story contains what is possibly the most detailed account of the samurai rite of seppuku in all of Japanese literature.

Almost everything spoken or written by Mishima fits into a personal cosmology that evolved and was refined throughout his life; the living out of this system led to his death: Beauty leads to ecstasy, ecstasy to death. Literature was central to Mishima's cosmos and was virtually inseparable from it. To understand one is to comprehend the other. Mishima was obsessed with death, and to create beauty in his works, in his system, led almost inevitably to his death.

Victoria Price

Other major works

PLAYS: *Kantan*, wr. 1950, pb. 1956 (English translation, 1957); *Dōjōji*, pb. 1953 (English translation, 1966); *Yoro no himawari*, pr., pb. 1953 (*Twilight Sunflower*, 1958); *Aya no tsuzumu*, pr. 1955, pb. 1956 (*The Damask Drum*, 1957); *Shiroari no su*, pr., pb. 1955; *Aoi no ue*, pr., pb. 1956 (*The Lady Aoi*, 1957); *Hanjo*, pb. 1956 (English translation, 1957); *Kindai nōgakushū*, pb. 1956 (includes *Kantan, The Damask Drum, The Lady Aoi, Hanjo*, and *Sotoba Komachi; Five Modern Nō Plays*, 1957); *Sotoba Komachi*, pb. 1956 (English translation, 1957); *Tōka no kiku*, pr., pb. 1961; *Sado kōshaku fujin*, pr., pb. 1965 (*Madame de Sade*, 1967); *Suzakuke no metsubō*, pr., pb. 1967; *Waga tomo Hittorā*, pb. 1968, pr. 1969 (*My Friend Hitler*, 1977); *Chinsetsu yumiharizuki*, pr., pb. 1969.

ANTHOLOGY: *New Writing in Japan*, 1972 (with Geoffrey Bownas).

NOVELS: *Kamen no kokuhaku*, 1949 (*Confessions of a Mask*, 1958); *Ai no kawaki*, 1950 (*Thirst for Love*, 1969); *Shiosai*, 1954 (*The Sound of Waves*, 1956); *Kinkakuji*, 1956 (*The Temple of the Golden Pavilion*, 1959); *Kyōko no ie*, 1959; *Utage no ato*, 1960 (*After the Banquet*, 1963); *Gogo no eikō*, 1963 (*The Sailor Who Fell from Grace with the Sea*, 1965); *Kinu to meisatsu*, 1964 (*Silk and Insight*, 1998); *Forbidden Colors*, 1968 (includes *Kinjiki*); *Hōjō no umi*, 1969-1971 (collective title for the following 4 novels; *The Sea of Fertility: A Cycle of Four Novels*, 1972-1974); *Haru no yuki*, 1969 (*Spring Snow*, 1972); *Homba*, 1969 (*Runaway Horses*, 1973); *Akatsuki no tera*, 1970 (*The Temple of Dawn*, 1973); *Tennin gosui*, 1971 (*The Decay of the Angel*, 1974).

MISCELLANEOUS: *Hanazakari no mori*, 1944 (short fiction and plays); *Eirei no Koe*, 1966 (short fiction and essays).

NONFICTION: *Hagakure nyumōn*, 1967 (*The Way of the Samurai*, 1977); *Taiyō to tetsu*, 1968 (*Sun and Steel*, 1970); *Yukio Mishima on "Hagakure": The Samurai Ethic and Modern Japan*, 1978.

Bibliography

Keene, Donald. "Mishima in 1958." *The Paris Review* 37 (Spring, 1995): 140-160. Keene recalls his 1958 interview with Mishima, in which Mishima discussed influences, his delight in "cruel stories," the importance of traditional Japanese theater for him, and his novels and his other writing.

May, Charles E., ed. *Masterplots II: Short Story Series, Revised Edition.* 8 vols. Pasadena, Calif.: Salem Press, 2004. Designed for student use, this reference set contains articles providing detailed plot summaries and analyses of three short stories by Mishima: "Death in Midsummer" (vol. 2), "Patriotism" (vol. 6), and "Swaddling Clothes" (vol. 7).

Miyoshi, Masao. *Accomplices of Silence: The Modern Japanese Novel.* Berkeley: University of California Press, 1974. Chapter 6 in part 2, "Mute's Rage," provides studies of two of Mishima's major novels, *Confessions of a Mask* and *The Temple of the Golden Pavilion*, as well as comments on works that Miyoshi considers to be important. Includes notes and an index.

Napier, Susan J. *Escape from the Wasteland: Romanticism and Realism in the Fiction of Mishima Yukio and Ōe Kenzaburō*. Cambridge, Mass.: Harvard University Press, 1991. Napier uncovers shocking similarities as well as insightful dissimilarities in the work of Mishima and Ōe and ponders each writer's place in the tradition of Japanese literature.

Nathan, John. *Mishima: A Biography*. 1974. Reprint. Cambridge, Mass.: Da Capo Press, 2000. The classic biography of Mishima, with a new preface by Nathan. Index.

Scott-Stokes, Henry. *The Life and Death of Yukio Mishima*. Rev. ed. New York: Noonday Press, 1995. Following a personal impression of Mishima, Scott-Stokes presents a five-part account of Mishima's life, beginning with the last day of his life. The author then returns to Mishima's early life and the making of the young man as a writer. Part 4, "The Four Rivers," identifies the rivers of writing, theater, body, and action, discussing in each subsection relevant events and works. Part 5 is a "Postmortem." Supplemented by a glossary, chronology, bibliography, and index.

Starrs, Roy. *Deadly Dialectics: Sex, Violence, and Nihilism in the World of Yukio Mishima*. Honolulu: University of Hawaii Press, 1994. Critical and interpretive look at sex and violence in Mishima's work. Includes bibliographical references and an index.

Ueda, Makoto. *Modern Japanese Writers and the Nature of Literature*. Stanford, Calif.: Stanford University Press, 1976. Mishima is one of eight Japanese writers treated in this volume. Although Ueda discusses certain novels in some detail, for the most part his discussion centers on philosophical and stylistic matters and suggests that Mishima's pessimism derived more from his appraisal of the state of human civilization than from his views on the nature of literature. Includes a brief bibliography and an index.

Wolfe, Peter. *Yukio Mishima*. New York: Continuum, 1989. Wolfe asserts that common sense explains very little about motives in Mishima. "What makes him unusual is his belief that anything of value exists in close proximity to death."

Yourcenar, Marguerite. *Mishima: A Vision of the Void*. Chicago: University of Chicago Press, 2001. This edition of a biography of Mishima published in 1986 contains a foreword by Donald Richie, a well-known critic and Japan expert.

Bharati Mukherjee

Born: Calcutta, West Bengal, India; July 27, 1940

Principal short fiction • *Darkness*, 1985; *The Middleman, and Other Stories*, 1988; "The Management of Grief," 1988.

Other literary forms • In addition to several volumes of short fiction, Bharati Mukherjee has written seven novels, including *The Tiger's Daughter* (1972), *Wife* (1975), *Jasmine* (1989), *The Holder of the World* (1993), *Leave It to Me* (1997); *Desirable Daughters* (2002), and *The Tree Bride* (2004). Her nonfiction writings include a travel memoir, *Days and Nights in Calcutta* (1977; with her husband Clark Blaise); a nonfiction critique of Canadian racism, *The Sorrow and the Terror: The Haunting Legacy of the Air India Tragedy* (1987; in collaboration with Blaise); a political treatise, *Kautilya's Concept of Diplomacy* (1976); the nonfiction studies *Political Culture and Leadership in India: A Study of West Bengal* (1991) and *Regionalism in Indian Perspective* (1992); and several essays and articles.

Achievements • Bharati Mukherjee occupies a distinctive place among first-generation North American writers of Indian origin. She has received a number of grants from the Canada Arts Council (1973-1974, 1977), the Shastri Indo-Canadian Institute (1976-1977), the John Simon Guggenheim Memorial Foundation (1978-1979), and the Canadian government (1982). In 1980, she won first prize from the Periodical Distribution Association for her short story "Isolated Incidents." In 1981, she won the National Magazine Award's second prize for her essay "An Invisible Woman." Her story "Angela" was selected for inclusion in *The Best American Short Stories 1985*, and "The Tenant" was included in *The Best American Short Stories 1987*. Her second collection of short stories *The Middleman, and Other Stories* won the National Book Critics Circle Award in 1988.

Biography • Bharati Mukherjee was born into a well-to-do, traditional Bengali Brahman family in the Calcutta suburb of Ballygunge on July 27, 1940. Her Hindu family's affluence buffered them from the political crises of independence and partition that engulfed the Indian subcontinent in the 1940's, and by the end of that troubled decade her father, Sudhir Lal Mukherjee, a chemist and the proprietor of a successful pharmaceutical company, had moved the family first to London (1948-1950) and then to Switzerland (1951) before returning them to India. Accordingly, Mukherjee explains, she and her two sisters (one older, one younger) "were born both too late and not late enough to be real Indians." Her educational experiences abroad had made her fluent in English at an early age, so that once back in India she began attending Calcutta's Loreto Convent School, an elite institution for girls run by Irish Catholic nuns, where she occasionally glimpsed Mother Teresa early in her ministry to the city's poor. At the time, Mukherjee herself followed the habits of her caste and preferred to turn away from the misery on the streets around her rather than question or reflect upon it.

Neither did she consciously plan to deviate very far from the traditional path of

Tom Victor

Indian womanhood expected of her; even her early interest in becoming a writer, fed by an ever-expanding fascination with the European novels to which her travels and education had exposed her, was tolerated because she was female—such impractical aspirations would have been quickly discouraged in a son, she believes. She has praised her mother for her courageous insistence that she receive a top-flight English education so that she "would not end up, she said, as chattel to a traditional Bengali husband." Although her father intended to have his middle daughter marry a bridegroom of the family's choosing from within their own strictly defined social class, he encouraged her intellectual aspirations in the meantime, and so Mukherjee earned an honors bachelor's degree in English from Calcutta University in 1959 and a master's degree in English and ancient Indian culture in 1961 from the University of Baroda. She then joined "the first generation of Indians who even thought of going to the United States rather than automatically to England" when she accepted a Philanthropic Educational Organization International Peace Scholarship to the University of Iowa Writers' Workshop, receiving a master of fine arts degree in 1963. During that time she also met Clark Blaise, an American writer of Canadian descent, whom she married on September 13, 1963, in an action that, she explains, "cut me off forever from the rules and ways of upper-middle-class life in Bengal, and hurled me into a New World life of scary improvisations and heady explorations." The couple would have two sons, Bart and Bernard, and would, over the course of their long marriage, collaborate on a number of book projects, most strikingly *Days and Nights in Calcutta* (1977), a travel journal of their respective observations during a trip together to India.

Having already taught at Marquette University and the University of Wisconsin at Madison, in 1966 Mukherjee moved with Blaise to Montreal, Canada, where she assumed a teaching position at McGill University, which she held until 1978. She completed a doctoral degree in English at the University of Iowa in 1969 and published her first novel, *The Tiger's Daughter* (1972), soon thereafter. In 1972 Mukherjee became a Canadian citizen but quickly grew disenchanted with her new country as she experienced the persistent racial discrimination and harassment suffered by Indians and other immigrants of color; she registered her protest in a celebrated article entitled "An Invisible Woman" and in several short stories.

After fourteen years in Canada, a period during which she published a second novel, *Wife*, along with *Days and Nights in Calcutta*, Mukherjee and Blaise brought their family to the United States and became permanent residents in 1980. In 1976-1977 she served as director of the Shastri Institute in New Delhi, India. She became writer-in-residence and distinguished professor of English at the University of California, Berkeley. In later years she and Blaise jointly published *The Sorrow and the Terror: The Haunting Legacy of the Air India Tragedy* (1987), which pointedly documents what she regards as Canada's refusal "to renovate its national self-image to include its changing complexion." In 1987 Mukherjee became a naturalized U.S. citizen. Over the course of her career she has taught in numerous American universities, including Emory University, Skidmore College, Columbia University, Queens College, and the University of Iowa Writers' Workshop. Since the 1980's Mukherjee has regarded herself squarely as an "American" writer (categorically eschewing hyphenated Asian- or Indian-American labels) and describes her geographic relocation as the seminal moment in her artistic maturation. In Canada she had come to view herself, for the first time in her life, as

> a late-blooming colonial who writes in a borrowed language (English), lives permanently in an alien country, and is read, when read at all, in another alien country, the United States.

That multilayered dispossession ended in the United States as she found herself moving "away from the aloofness of expatriation to the exuberance of immigration." The ideological legitimacy of the immigrant story in American culture has in fact become one of her central literary themes, one in which she explores "America" as "an idea" and "a stage for transformation." Her impressive literary production since arriving in the United States has included a number of critically acclaimed novels centered on strong-willed American or Americanized heroines (*Jasmine, The Holder of the World,* and *Leave It to Me*) and several expansive short-story collections (*Darkness* in 1985 and *The Middleman, and Other Stories* in 1988, the latter the recipient of the National Book Critics Circle Award). Her enthusiasm has not blinded her to political backlash against America's most recent newcomers; in 1997 she warned in *Mother Jones* magazine against a spreading "cultural crisis" wherein "questions such as who is an American and what is American culture are being posed with belligerence, and being answered with violence." Because she sees such polarization as having "tragic" consequences not only for its victims but also for the unique "founding idea of 'America'" itself, which rejected "easy homogeneity" for a "new version of utopia," she urges instead, "We must think of American culture and nationhood as a constantly reforming, transmogrifying 'we' that works in the direction of both the newcomer and the culture receiving her."

Analysis • Bharati Mukherjee has herself become one of the literary voices whose skillful depictions of the contemporary non-European immigrant experience in the United States she credits with "subverting the very notion of what the American novel is and of what American culture is." In Canada she kept her "Indianness" smugly intact despite—or because of—a painful awareness of her displacement in the West. She consciously regarded other immigrants, as she notes in the introduction to *Darkness,* as "lost souls, put upon and pathetic," in contrast to the more ironically sophisticated postcolonials with whom she identified: people "who knew all too well who and what they were, and what foul fate had befallen them," and who therefore escaped the emotional turmoil of divided loyalties or assimilationist incongruities.

After arriving in the United States, Mukherjee found herself drawn toward those same immigrant "outcasts" she once pitied—and not just the ones from the subcontinent. In Mukherjee's two critically acclaimed short-story collections she sets out to "present a full picture, a complicated picture of America," one in which evil as well as good operates and where "we, the new pioneers, who are still thinking of America as a frontier country . . . are improvising morality as we go along." Although she unblinkingly paints the bigotries that bedevil her protagonists, she resists casting them as victims

> because they don't think of themselves as victims. On the contrary, they think of themselves as conquerors. We have come not to passively accommodate ourselves to someone else's dream of what we should be. We've come to America, in a way, to take over. To help build a new culture . . . with the same guts and energy and feistiness that the original American Pilgrims had.

Darkness • Mukherjee's first collection of short fiction is something of a transitional work in documenting the shift in sensibility that occurred when she left Canada for the United States. Three of its twelve stories reveal a lingering bitterness about Canadian prejudice toward its Indian citizens and concern themselves with the problems that such prejudice generates in the lives of individuals still wrestling with the question of whether they believe themselves to be in voluntary exile or hopeful self-transformation. The stories set in the United States, by way of contrast, regard the immigrant experience more dynamically and offer "a set of fluid identities to be celebrated" as a result of Mukherjee's having personally "joined imaginative forces with an anonymous, driven underclass of semi-assimilated Indians with sentimental attachments to a distant homeland but no real desire for permanent return." In this new context her own "Indianness" functions less "as a fragile identity to be preserved against obliteration" than as "a metaphor, a particular way of partially comprehending the world." The U.S.-based Indian protagonists of *Darkness* generate stories "of broken identities and discarded languages, and the will to bond oneself to a new community, against the ever-present fear of failure or betrayal."

In an interview published in *The Canadian Fiction Magazine*, Mukherjee stated, "My stories center on a new breed and generation of North American pioneers." The "new pioneers" inhabiting her fictional world include a wide variety of immigrant characters—most of them India-born and others, increasingly, from Third World countries—who pull up their traditional roots and arrive in the New World with dreams of wealth, success, and freedom. Her first collection of short stories, *Darkness*, focuses on immigrant Indians in North America and deals primarily with the problems of expatriation, immigration, and cross-cultural assimilation. Of the twelve stories in this collection, three reflect on the Canadian situation and the rest are set in the United States. Mukherjee calls the Canadian stories "uneasy stories about expatriation," as they stem from the author's personal encounters with racial prejudice in Canada.

"The World According to Hsü" • Among the Canadian pieces in *Darkness*, a notably painful and uneasy story about expatriation and racial prejudice, "The World According to Hsü," explores the diasporic consciousness of Ratna Clayton, an Indian woman married to a Canadian professor of psychology at McGill University, Montreal. Her husband, Graeme Clayton, has been offered the chair at the University of Toronto. Ratna dreads the thought of moving to Toronto: "In Toronto, she was not Canadian, not even Indian. She was something called, after the imported idiom of London, a Paki. And for Pakis, Toronto was hell." Hoping that a vacation would be the ideal setting to persuade his wife to move, Graeme arranges a trip to a beautiful African island. Upon their arrival, they find themselves caught in the midst of a revolution and constrained by a night curfew. The threat of violence unleashes memories of Toronto in Ratna's mind:

> A week before their flight, a Bengali woman was beaten and nearly blinded on the street. And the week before that an eight-year-old Punjabi boy was struck by a car announcing on its bumper: KEEP CANADA GREEN. PAINT A PAKI.

At the dinner table, when her husband reads her an article by Kenneth J. Hsü about the geological collision of the continents, Ratna wonders why she had to move to Toronto to experience a different kind of collision—racial and cultural. Finally, she brings herself to accept her situation when she realizes that "no matter where she lived, she would never feel at home again."

"Tamurlane" • Another story in *Darkness*, "Tamurlane," depicts the lives of Indian émigrés at the opposite end of the class hierarchy from the one Ratna occupies. It dramatizes the precarious situation of illegal aliens who, lured by the dream of a better life, are smuggled into Canada, where they are forced to lead an anonymous, subhuman, underground existence, sleeping in shifts and living in constant fear of being raided by immigration authorities. "Was this what I fled Ludhiana for?" poignantly asks the narrator, an illegal Indian working as a waiter at a dingy Indian restaurant in Toronto. The title of the story (alluding to Tamerlane, a lame Mongol warrior) refers to the restaurant's chef Gupta, who had been maimed six years earlier when he was thrown on the subway tracks. During a raid on illegals at the restaurant, Gupta orders the Mounties to leave. When they refuse and threaten to use force against him, he picks up a cleaver and brings it down on the outstretched hand of one of the policemen. He then defiantly holds his Canadian passport in front of his face. "That way," the story ends, "he never saw the drawn gun, nor did he try to dodge the single bullet."

"Nostalgia" • The immigrant experience dramatized in the American stories is less about the humiliations inflicted on the newcomer by New World intolerance than about the inner struggles of that newcomer in mediating between the pull of old cultural loyalties and the pressures to assimilate to the new context. Dr. Manny Patel, in "Nostalgia," is an Indian psychiatrist working at a state hospital in Queens, New York. His American Dream has come true; he lives in an expensive home, drives a red Porsche sports car, is married to an American nurse, and sends his son to school at Andover. Counting his manifold acquisitions and blessings, he regards himself as "not an expatriate but a patriot." Yet he knows that, despite becoming a U.S. citizen, he will forever continue to hover between the Old World and the New. Being the only child of his parents, he feels it is his duty to return to India and look after them in their old age. Caught in a mood of remorse and longing, he drives one day into Manhattan, is smitten by the beauty of an Indian saleswoman, Padma, and invites her on a date, which she readily accepts. They go to an Indian restaurant for dinner and then to bed at an expensive hotel. The whole experience makes him so nostalgic that he wishes "he had married an Indian woman" and "had any life but the one he had chosen." At the end of their tryst, Padma's uncle enters the hotel room with a passkey and accuses Dr. Manny of the rape of his minor niece. Shocked and humiliated, Dr. Manny discovers that "the goddess of his dreams" was nothing more than a common prostitute in collusion with her uncle-pimp to deceive him for profit. The uncle extorts not only seven hundred dollars but also a physician's note on hospital stationery to secure immigration for a nephew.

Afterward Dr. Manny defecates into the bathroom sink, squatting as he had done in his father's home, and writes "WHORE" on the bathroom mirror and floor with his excrement, now become "an artist's medium." Just before dawn he drives home, doubly chastened by having succumbed so foolishly to the siren's song of a culture to which he no longer truly belongs and whose gilded memories he now sees for what they are. As he approaches his home he finds the porch light still on, "glow[ing] pale in the brightening light of morning," and he decides to take his wife on a second honeymoon to the Caribbean, in effect repledging his troth to the tangible reality of America itself.

"A Father" • The conflict between Old World and New World takes a different form in "A Father." Mr. Bhowmick, a traditional Bengali, works as a metallurgist with General Motors and lives in Detroit with his Americanized wife and a twenty-six-year-old engineer daughter. He worships the goddess Kali in his home shrine, believes in the sanctity of Hindu superstitions, and lives in constant awe of the unseen powers he believes govern his destiny. Every day he finds himself making frequent compromises between his beliefs and the American pragmatism that surrounds him. When he discovers, to his horror, that his unmarried daughter is pregnant, his first reaction is that she should get an abortion to save the family honor. He blames his wife for this unhappy situation because coming to the United States was her idea. Then he tries to be reasonable. He pities the double life between conflicting values that his daughter must live; he hopes that maybe she has already married secretly; he prays that his hypothetical son-in-law turns out to be a white American. He even secretly enjoys the thought of having a grandson (for he is sure, in this rosier scenario, that the child must be a male).

Thus he reconciles himself to this new situation without resorting to the draconian measures a father in India would be expected to take, only to be confronted with an even more contemporary twist: His daughter reveals that she was impregnated by artificial insemination and with all the fury of Kali herself bluntly counters her parents' revulsion at the "animality" of such calculated procreative behavior with assurances that she has secured a sperm donor who meets all the standard bourgeois criteria for a good mate, just as they would have done in arranging a "good" marriage for her were they still in India: "You should be happy—that's what marriage is all about, isn't it? Matching bloodlines, matching horoscopes, matching castes, matching, matching, matching." Her caustic deflation of the traditions he still venerates defeats his effort to rise to the challenges of modernity, and he strikes out at her, hitting her swelling belly with the rolling pin he has just taken away from his wife. The story ends with Mrs. Bhowmick forced into an unthinkable violation of family honor: She calls the police, thus relying on outsiders to intervene publicly in the self-destruction of her family. In the ways it pulls the reader's sympathies back and forth inconclusively among its characters, "A Father" simulates the actual see-sawing of loyalties characteristic of the multigenerational acculturation process itself.

The Middleman, and Other Stories • Although *Darkness* focuses primarily on the experience of immigrants from the Indian subcontinent, Mukherjee's second collection, *The Middleman, and Other Stories*, is broader in range and scope, as it explores the

American experience of immigrants from across the developing world, including India, Afghanistan, Iraq, the Philippines, Sri Lanka, Trinidad, Uganda, and Vietnam. Moreover, four of the eleven stories in this volume have white American protagonists who offer another perspective on the contemporary immigrant situation. (It is worth noting, however, that the concluding piece, "The Management of Grief," once more returns to Mukherjee's deep animus toward the special form of bigotry suffered by Asians in Canada; it renders fictively the same subject with which she and Blaise have dealt in *The Sorrow and the Terror*.)

Virtually all of the stories examine the compromises, losses, and adjustments involved in the process of acculturating newcomers to American life and remaking American culture to reflect their presence: In fact, the volume virtually hums with the hustle of modern American cultural diversity played out across an equally various set of U.S. locations ranging from Atlanta to Detroit to Miami to Iowa. Most of the "new pioneers" in this collection are, in a metaphoric sense, middlemen and women caught between two worlds and cultures (and sometimes more), as even a brief sampling of the cast of characters suggests: an Amerasian child reunited with her veteran father; a Trinidadian "mother's helper"; a fully assimilated third-generation Italian American and her Afghan lover; an Iraqi Jew being chased by police in Central America; a Filipino makeup girl. Such international pedigrees bespeak the widespread political breakdowns that on a shrinking planet increasingly link people who once inhabited completely different worlds. She consistently uses the cross-cultural romance as locus for the societal frictions and emotional barriers that exemplify and exacerbate the problems of communication across culturally constructed differences. The faith of the newest aspirants to the American Dream is frequently contrasted with the decadent malaise of "ugly Americans," who no longer have to travel abroad to betray or defile peoples of other lands. The vigorous immediacy of the American vernacular (to which Mukherjee confesses a delighted addiction) penetrates the speech of these characters, many of whom speak directly to the reader in the first person, and conveys the volatile excitement of the dreams ignited in them by what Mukherjee calls "the idea of America."

The volume's title story is narrated by Alfred Judah from Baghdad, an individual regularly mistakenly for an Arab or an Indian. When not on the job, he lives in Flushing, Queens, and he was once married to an American, but he nonetheless feels like an eternal outsider, for "there are aspects of American life I came too late for and will never understand." As such he remains on the margins by working for an illicit border-jumper, gun smuggler Clovis T. Ransome. In this story Judah's job is as middleman delivering contraband weapons, when the armed uprising in the Central American country where they had been operating in callous indifference to the politics of their customers violently ends their exploitative enterprise and leaves Judah (through the casual intervention of Ransome's bloodthirsty mistress and his own recent lover Maria) to negotiate his way back to "civilization" by drawing yet again upon his basic repertoire of survival in the New World: "There must be something worth trading in the troubles I've seen."

The Middleman, and Other Stories, like *Darkness* before it, contains many melodramatic situations and a pronounced streak of violence. Mukherjee does not always provide sufficient context for the behaviors and attitudes of her characters. Nevertheless, she imparts a potent voice to these "new pioneers" and reveals the dynamic world of America's newest wave of self-inventors—people often invisible to those in the mainstream. Many of them suffer from racism and prejudice; others seem welcome only in the shady underworlds of sex, crime, and drugs; and some merely scramble for a living in their struggle for survival. To adapt to their new milieu, even professional men and women have to make compromises and trade-offs between their old belief systems and the New World ethos. In the process, many suffer cultural disorientation and alienation and undergo traumatic changes—psychological, cultural, linguistic. Yet Mukherjee appears to have no doubt that such a break is desirable. As she has told journalist Bill Moyers,

> America is a total and wondrous invention. Letting go of the old culture, allowing the roots to wither is natural; change is natural. But the unnatural thing is to hang on, to retain the old world . . . I think if you've made the decision to come to America, to be an American, you must be prepared to really, emotionally, become American and put down roots. . . . In doing that, we very painfully, sometimes violently, murder our old selves. . . . I want to think that it's a freeing process. In spite of the pain, in spite of the violence, in spite of the bruising of the old self, to have that freedom to make mistakes, to choose a whole new history for oneself, is exciting.

Admittedly, the new selves that emerge from her stories are not always models of virtue, but "pioneering does not necessarily equate with virtue. . . . I like to think my characters have that vigor for possessing the land," with all the mother wit, ruthlessness, and tenacity of their predecessors. Yes, she admits,

> the immigrant's soul is always at risk. . . . I have to make up the rules as I go along. No one has really experienced what the nonwhite, non-European immigrants are going through in the States. We can't count on the wisdom and experience of the past of the old country; and we can't quite fit into the traditional Eurocentric experiences of Americans.

In telling their stories, then, she regards herself as "writing a fable for the times. I'm trying to create a mythology that we can live by as we negotiate our daily lives."

"Danny's Girls" • In "Danny's Girls," a young Ugandan boy living in Flushing works as a middleman for a hustler, Danny Sahib (originally "Dinesh," a Hindu from northern India), whom the boy calls "a merchant of opportunity." Danny started out selling tickets for Indian concerts at Madison Square Garden, then for fixed beauty contests, and eventually went into the business of arranging green cards through proxy marriages for Indians aspiring to become permanent U.S. residents. The latter launched a business of mail-order brides, with Danny in partnership with the African boy's aunt, Lini, in selling Indian and other Asian girls to American men eager for reputedly "compliant" wives. The young narrator has always looked up to Danny and has wanted, like his hero, to attain financial independence in the big world of the United States. When he falls in love with a Nepali girl for whom Danny had arranged a green card, however, he determines to liberate both of them from Danny's clutches, accepting the challenge of becoming his own man by resisting Danny's commodifying ethic—surely American opportunity should mean more.

"Jasmine" • "Jasmine" is the story of an ambitious Trinidadian girl of that name, who, through a middleman, illegally enters Detroit over the Canadian border at Windsor. She finds a job cleaning and keeping the books at the Plantations Motel, a business run by the Daboo family, Trinidadian Indians also trying to remake their destinies in Michigan. In picaresque fashion Jasmine later goes to Ann Arbor and works as a live-in domestic with an easygoing American family: Bill Moffitt, a biology instructor, Lara Hatch-Moffitt, a performance artist, and their little girl, Muffin. When Lara goes on the road with her performing group, Jasmine is happily seduced by her boss, and as they make love on the Turkish carpet, she thinks of herself as literally reborn, "a bright, pretty girl with no visa, no papers, and no birth certificate. No nothing other than what she wanted to invent and tell. She was a girl rushing wildly into the future." The story in many ways presages the improvisational Indian heroine of Mukherjee's full-length novel *Jasmine*, published in 1989.

"A Wife's Story" • Not all of *The Middleman, and Other Stories* deals with characters struggling to move from the margins into the mainstream of American opportunity: "A Wife's Story" and "The Tenant" focus on well-educated Indian women. In the first, Mrs. Panna Bhatt, married to the vice president of a textile mill in India, has come to New York on a two-year scholarship to get a doctoral degree in special education. Haunted by memories of the oppressive gender roles imposed on her mother and grandmother, she believes that she is making something new of her life; her choice of special education as a field of study provocatively mirrors the kind of intervention in her own constricted development that she is undertaking with her radical experiment abroad. She even develops a friendship with a married Hungarian man with whom she attends the theater. When an actor makes obscene jokes about Patel women, however, she feels insulted:

> It's the tyranny of the American dream that scares me. First, you don't exist. Then you are invisible. Then you are funny. Then you are disgusting. Insult, my American friends will tell me, is a kind of acceptance. No instant dignity here.

Yet when her husband comes for a short visit, as a reminder of the more decorous world she misses, she must feign enthusiasm for him. She tries to make up to him for her years away, pretending that nothing has changed, but finally she refuses to return to India with him. When forced to choose between the vulgar freedoms of the United States and the repressive if "safe" institutions of her homeland, she realizes she has already crossed over to another country psychologically.

"The Tenant" • "The Tenant" goes to the other extreme by showing how an attractive, middle-class, young Bengali woman becomes vulnerable when she breaks with her traditional ways and tries to become part of mainstream America. Maya Sanyal from Calcutta came to the United States ten years earlier, at the age of nineteen. In smooth succession she received a doctoral degree, married an American, became a naturalized citizen, got divorced, and now teaches comparative literature in Cedar Falls, Iowa. During that time she has indiscriminately slept with all kinds of men, except Indians, in a seemingly ambivalent repudiation of the constrictive gender mores of her homeland. Now, afraid that her bachelor landlord might make sexual advances toward her, she calls the other Bengali professor on campus, Dr. Chatterji, and secures an invitation to tea. The traditional atmosphere of his life prompts a newly awakened longing for her homeland, even as his pathetic attempt at seduction leaves her embarrassed. Tired of the fact that her unattached status makes her vulnerable to the lust of every passing male and newly nostalgic for her homeland traditions, she responds to an *India Abroad* matrimonial advertisement from a countryman seeking "the new emancipated Indo-American woman" with "a zest for life," "at ease in USA [sic]," but still holding on to values "rooted in Indian tradition." To her surprise, as she meets Ashoke Mehta at the Chicago airport, she suddenly feels as if a "Hindu god" is descending to woo her—a handsome Indian man who has indeed merged his two cultures in ways that seem to make them destined for each other. Yet witnessing his seamless acculturation also erodes her own self-confidence:

> She feels ugly and unworthy. Her adult life no longer seems miraculously rebellious; it is grim, it is perverse. She has accomplished nothing. She has changed her citizenship but she hasn't broken through into the light, the vigor, the hustle of the New World. She is stuck in dead space.

More to the point is their mutual recognition that each carries a complicated romantic history to this moment—a history that makes each wary of the other and precludes Ashoke's contacting her again for several months. During that time she resumes her life in Cedar Falls and, when her landlord abruptly marries, moves to a new room rented to her by an armless man named Fred, whose lover she soon becomes, "two wounded people" who "settle into companionship." She also recognizes uncomfortably that this liaison speaks to some sense of her own deficiency as a rootless émigré in flight from her own past: "She knows she is strange, and lonely, but being Indian is not the same, she would have thought, as being a freak." When at last Ashoke calls and obliquely concedes the entanglements that had kept him from committing to her, she knows she will accept his invitation to join him out East—each has made peace with the contradictory emotions about their shared legacy they arouse in each other.

Chaman L. Sahni
With updates by Barbara Kitt Seidman and the Editors

Other major works

NOVELS: *The Tiger's Daughter,* 1972; *Wife,* 1975; *Jasmine,* 1989; *The Holder of the World,* 1993; *Leave It to Me,* 1997; *Desirable Daughters,* 2002; *The Tree Bride,* 2004.

NONFICTION: *Kautilya's Concept of Diplomacy,* 1976; *Days and Nights in Calcutta,* 1977 (with Clark Blaise); *The Sorrow and the Terror: The Haunting Legacy of the Air India Tragedy,* 1987 (with Blaise); *Political Culture and Leadership in India: A Study of West Bengal,* 1991; *Regionalism in Indian Perspective,* 1992.

Bibliography
Alam, Fakrul. *Bharati Mukherjee.* New York: Twayne, 1996. Looks at India, women, and East Indian Americans in literature. Includes a bibliography and index.

Bowen, Deborah. "Spaces of Translation: Bharati Mukherjee's 'The Management of Grief.'" *Ariel* 28 (July, 1997): 47-60. Argues that in the story, the assumption of moral universalism is a crucial precursor to the problems of negotiating social knowledge. Mukherjee addresses questions of cultural particularization by showing how inadequately translatable are institutionalized expressions of concern.

Drake, Jennifer. "Looting American Culture: Bharati Mukherjee's Immigrant Narratives." *Contemporary Literature* 40 (Spring, 1999): 60-84. Argues that assimilation is portrayed as cultural looting, cultural exchange, or a willful and sometimes costly negotiation in her stories; notes that Mukherjee rejects the nostalgia of hyphenated "Americans" and their acceptable stories and portrays instead settlers, Americans who want to be American—not sojourners, tourists, guest workers, or foreigners.

Ispahani, Mahnaz. "A Passage from India." Review of *Darkness*, by Bharati Mukherjee. *The New Republic* 14 (April, 1986): 36-39. Ispahani believes that the short stories in this collection "treat the classical theme of diaspora—of exile and emigration." She singles out five stories for analysis to demonstrate her point. The review includes a brief comment on Mukherjee's style.

May, Charles E., ed. *Masterplots II: Short Story Series, Revised Edition.* 8 vols. Pasadena, Calif.: Salem Press, 2004. Designed for student use, this reference set contains articles providing detailed plot summaries and analyses of these four short stories by Mukherjee: "Jasmine" (vol. 4), "The Management of Grief" (vol. 5), and "A Wife's Story" and "The World According to Hsü" (vol. 8).

Mukherjee, Bharati. "American Dreamer." *Mother Jones,* January/February, 1997. Depicted literally as wrapped in an American flag while standing in a cornfield, Mukherjee speaks to her passionate sense of herself as an American writer and citizen.

_____. "Interview." In *Speaking of the Short Story: Interviews with Contemporary Writers,* edited by Farhat Iftekharuddin, Mary Rohrberger, and Maurice Lee. Jackson: University Press of Mississippi, 1997. Mukherjee discusses the origins of her stories and the process by which they are composed. She criticizes Marxist and other social critics who reduce stories to sociology and anthropology.

_____. "An Interview with Bharati Mukherjee." Interview by Geoff Hancock. *The Canadian Fiction Magazine* 59 (1987): 30-44. In this important interview, Mukherjee discusses her family background, formative influences, and work. She provides illuminating comments on her fictional characters, themes, and voice.

Nazareth, Peter. "Total Vision." *Canadian Literature: A Quarterly of Criticism and Review* 110 (1986): 184-191. Nazareth analyzes Mukherjee's first collection of short stories, *Darkness,* to show how she has distinguished herself by becoming "a writer of *the other America,* the America ignored by the so-called mainstream: the America that embraces all the peoples of the world both because America is involved with the whole world and because the whole world is in America."

Sant-Wade, Arvindra, and Karen Marguerite Radell. "Refashioning the Self: Immigrant Women in Bharati Mukherjee's New World." *Studies in Short Fiction* 29 (Winter, 1992): 11-17. An analysis of "The Tenant," "Jasmine," and "A Wife's Story" as stories in which immigrant women refashion themselves and are reborn. In each story the women's sense of possibility clashes with a sense of loss, yet their exuberant determination attracts the reader to them and denies them the power of pity.

Vignisson, Runar. "Bharati Mukherjee: An Interview." *Span* 3-4 (1993). An expansive discussion covering Mukherjee's childhood, her experiences in Canada and the United States, her evolution as a writer, her views on feminism, and some of the ideas informing her novel *Jasmine.*

Alice Munro

Born: Wingham, Ontario, Canada; July 10, 1931

Principal short fiction • *Dance of the Happy Shades*, 1968; *Something I've Been Meaning to Tell You: Thirteen Stories*, 1974; *Who Do You Think You Are?*, 1978 (pb. in U.S. as *The Beggar Maid: Stories of Flo and Rose*, 1979); *The Moons of Jupiter: Stories*, 1982; *The Progress of Love*, 1986; *Friend of My Youth: Stories*, 1990; *Open Secrets: Stories*, 1994; *Selected Stories*, 1996; *The Love of a Good Woman: Stories*, 1998; *Hateship, Friendship, Courtship, Loveship, Marriage*, 2001; *No Love Lost*, 2003; *Runaway: Stories*, 2004; *Vintage Munro*, 2004; *The View from Castle Rock*, 2006.

Other literary forms • Alice Munro is first and foremost a writer of short fiction. However, the line between long and short fiction is sometimes blurred in her writings. She has published one book that is generally classified as a novel, *Lives of Girls and Women* (1971), but she herself prefers to view it as a group of linked stories. On the other hand, some reviewers, including author John Gardner, have suggested that the stories in her collection published in the United States as *The Beggar Maid* are so intricately related that *that* book might be viewed as a novel. Most critics, however, treat it as short fiction.

Achievements • Alice Munro has gained recognition as a consummate writer, principally of short, psychological fiction. She received the Governor General's Award (Canada's highest literary award) for *Dance of the Happy Shades*, *The Beggar Maid*, and *The Progress of Love*. Her novel *Lives of Girls and Women* won the Canadian Booksellers Association Award in 1972, as did *Open Secrets* in 1995. In 1990 the Canada Council awarded her the Molson Prize for her contribution to Canada's cultural and intellectual life. In 1977 and 1994 she received the Canada-Australia Literary Prize, and in 1995 *Open Secrets* won the W. H. Smith and Son Literary Award for the best book published in the United Kingdom. Munro received the National Book Critics Circle Award from the United States in 1999 for *The Love of a Good Woman*.

Biography • Alice Munro was born July 10, 1931, in Wingham, Ontario, Canada, where her father raised silver foxes. A scholarship covering the years 1949-1951 to the University of Western Ontario led to her bachelor's degree in 1952. Her marriage to bookstore owner James Munro produced three daughters. After a 1976 divorce, Munro married geographer Gerald Fremlin; they established homes in Clinton, Ontario, and Comox, British Columbia.

Analysis • Alice Munro has been compared to Ernest Hemingway in the realism, economy, and lucidity of her style, to John Updike in her insights into the intricacies of social and sexual relationships, to Flannery O'Connor and Eudora Welty in her ability to create characters of eccentric individualism, and to Marcel Proust in the completeness and verisimilitude with which she evokes the past. She is an intuitive writer, who is less likely to be concerned with problems of form than with clarity and veracity. Some critics have faulted her for a tendency toward disorganization or diffusion—too many shifts in time and place within a single story, for example. On her strengths as a writer, however, critics generally agree: She has an unfailing particularity and naturalness of style, an ability to write vividly about ordinary life and its boredom without boring her readers, an ability to write about the past without being sentimental, a profound grasp of human emotion and psychology. Chief among her virtues is her great honesty: her refusal to oversimplify or falsify human beings, emotions, or experience. One of her characters states, "How to keep oneself from lying I see as the main problem everywhere." Her awareness of this problem is everywhere evident in her writing, certainly in

Courtesy, Vancouver International Writers Festival

the distinctive voices of her narrator-protagonists, who are scrupulously concerned with truth. Finally, her themes—memory, love, transience, death—are significant. To explore such themes within the limitations of the short-story form with subtlety and depth is Munro's achievement.

"Dance of the Happy Shades" • One of Alice Munro's recurring themes is "the pain of human contact . . . the fascinating pain; the humiliating necessity." The phrase occurs in "The Stone in the Field" and refers to the narrator's maiden aunts, who cringe from all human contact, but the emotional pain that human contact almost inevitably brings is a subject in all of her stories. It is evident in the title story of her first collection, "Dance of the Happy Shades," in which an elderly, impoverished piano teacher, Miss Marsalles, has a "party" (her word for recital) for a dwindling number of her students and their mothers, an entertainment she can ill afford. The elaborate but nearly inedible refreshments, the ludicrous gifts, and the tedium of the recital pieces emphasize the incongruity between Miss Marsalles's serene pleasure in the festivities and the grim suffering of her unwilling but outwardly polite guests. Their anxieties are intensified by the mid-party arrival of Miss Marsalles's newest pupils, a group of mentally disabled children from a nearby institution. The other pupils and their mothers struggle to maintain well-bred composure, but inwardly they are repelled, particularly when one of the mentally disabled girls gives the only accomplished performance of a sprightly piece called "The Dance of the Happy Shades." The snobbish mothers believe that the idea of a mentally disabled girl learning to play the piano is not in good taste; it is "useless, out-of-place," in fact very much like Miss Marsalles herself. Clearly, this dismal affair will be Miss Marsalles's last party, yet the narrator is unable at the end to pity her, to say, "Poor Miss Marsalles." "It is the Dance of the Happy Shades that prevents us, it is the one communiqué from the other country where she lives." The unfortunate Miss Marsalles is happy; she has escaped the pain she would feel if she could know how others regard her, or care. She is living in another country, out of touch with reality; she has escaped into "the freedom of a great unemotional happiness."

"The Peace of Utrecht" • Few of Munro's characters are so fortunate. In "The Peace of Utrecht," for example, the inescapable emotional pain of human contact is the central problem. Helen, the narrator, makes a trip with her two children to Jubilee, the small town where she grew up, ostensibly to visit her sister Maddy, now living alone in their childhood home. The recent death of their mother is on their minds, but they cannot speak of it. Maddy, who stayed at home to look after their "Gothic Mother," has forbidden all such talk: "No exorcising here," she says. Yet exorcism is what Helen desperately needs as she struggles with the torment that she feels about her sister's "sacrifice," her mother's life, and her own previous self, which this return home so vividly and strangely evokes. Mother was a town "character," a misfit or oddity, even before the onset of her debilitating and disfiguring illness (she seems to have died of Parkinson's disease). For Helen, she was a constant source of anxiety and shame, a threat to Helen's own precarious adolescent identity. (Readers who know Munro's novel *Lives of Girls and Women* will find a strong resemblance of Helen's mother to Del Jordan's bizarre mother. She also appears as recognizably the same character in the stories "The Ottawa Valley," "Connection," "The Stone in the Field," and perhaps "The Progress of Love.") Recalling the love and pity denied this ill but incorrigible woman, Helen experiences raging guilt, shame, and anger that she and her sister were forced into "parodies of love." Egocentric, petulant, this mother

> demanded our love in every way she knew, without shame or sense, as a child will. And how could we have loved her, I say desperately to myself, the resources of love we had were not enough, the demand on us was too great.

Finally, Helen and her sister withdrew even the pretense of love, withdrew all emotion:

> We took away from her our anger and impatience and disgust, took all emotion away from our dealings with her, as you might take away meat from a prisoner to weaken him, till he died.

Still, the stubborn old woman survived and might have lived longer except that Maddy, left alone with her mother and wanting her own life, put her in the hospital. After she tried to run away, restraint became necessary; she did not survive long after that.

Some critics believe that Munro's strongest works are those which draw on her own small-town origins in western Ontario, stories of Jubilee, Tuppertown, Hanratty, Dalgleish. Munro has confessed in an interview that "The Peace of Utrecht" is her most autobiographical story and thus was difficult to write. Perhaps its emotional power derives in part from its closeness to her own experience, but it exhibits those qualities for which her writing has been praised: the effortless clarity of style, the psychological penetration of character, the evocation of time and place, the unfailing eye and ear which convey an impression of absolute authenticity—these are the hallmarks of Munro's finest fiction, and they are evident even in her earliest stories. For example, in "The Peace of Utrecht," Helen's visit to two memorable residents of Jubilee, her mother's sisters, Aunt Annie and Auntie Lou, demonstrates a deftness of characterization and a sureness of touch which are remarkable but typical of this writer at her best. Helen finds them spending the afternoon making rugs out of dyed rags. They are very old now. They sit in a hot little porch that is shaded by bamboo blinds; the rags and the half-finished rugs make an encouraging, domestic sort of disorder around them. They do not go out any more, but they get up early in the morning, wash and powder themselves, and put on their shapeless print dresses trimmed with rickrack and white braid.

Later, after tea, Aunt Annie tries to press on Helen a box of her mother's clothing (painstakingly cleaned and mended), seemingly oblivious to Helen's alarm and pain at the sight of these all-too-tangible reminders of her mother. To Aunt Annie, things are to be used up; clothes are to be worn. Yet she is not insensitive, nor is she a fool. Revealing to Helen (who did not know) the shameful facts about her mother's hospitalization against her will, her pitiful, frantic attempt to escape one snowy January night, the board that was subsequently nailed across the bed to immobilize her, and Maddy's indifference to it all, Aunt Annie begins "crying distractedly as old people do, with miserable scanty tears." Despite the tears, however, Aunt Annie is (as Helen is not), emotionally tough, "an old hand at grief and self-control." Just how tough she is is conveyed by Aunt Annie's final, quietly understated words: "'We thought it was hard,' she said finally. 'Lou and I thought it was hard.'"

Helen and Maddy, with less emotional resilience, try to come to terms with their own complex anguish through evasion, rationalization, and finally, admonishment—"don't be guilty"—but Munro is too honest to imply that they can be successful. In the final lines of the story, Helen urges her sister to forget the past, to take hold of her own life at last. Maddy's affirmation, "Yes I will," soon slips into an agonized question: "But why can't I, Helen? *Why can't I?*" In the "dim world of continuing disaster, of home," there is no peace of Utrecht, not for Munro's characters, perhaps not for Munro.

The preoccupation in Munro's fiction with family, usually as a "continuing disaster," is striking. Assorted eccentric aunts, uncles, and cousins appear and reappear; a somewhat miscreant brother appears in "Forgiveness in Families" and "Boys and Girls." Sometimes the family portraits are warmly sympathetic, as in the case of the grandmother in "Winter Wind" or especially the gentle father who calmly prepared for his death in "The Moons of Jupiter." Even the neurotic mother and father in "The Progress of Love" are treated sympathetically. There, the mother's fanatical hatred of her own father leads her to burn the desperately needed money she inherits from him at his death. Clearly, for Munro, family origins matter, sometimes as the source of humor and delightful revelation but more dependably as the source of endless mystery and pain. This is particularly true of "the problem, the only problem," as stated in "The Ottawa Valley": mother. At the story's conclusion, the narrator confesses that

she is the one of course that I am trying to get; it is to reach her that this whole journey has been undertaken. With what purpose? To mark her off, to describe, to illumine, to celebrate, to *get rid*, of her; and it did not work, for she looms too close, just as she always did. . . . She has stuck to me as close as ever and refused to fall away, and I could go on, and on, applying what skills I have, using what tricks I know, and it would always be the same.

Some relationships, some kinds of "fascinating pain," can be recorded or analyzed but not exorcized. Clearly, these may become the inspiration for significant literature. In Munro's fiction, the view of the emotional entanglements called "family" is unflinchingly honest, unsentimental, but always humane, at times even humorous.

"Bardon Bus" • Another important dimension of Munro's short stories is sexual relationships, particularly in the "feelings that women have about men," as she stated in an interview. In "Bardon Bus," the narrator, a woman writer spending time in Australia, meets an anthropologist (known as "X") and begins a deliberately limited affair, asking only that it last out their short time in Australia. Later, when both have returned to Canada, she is miserable, tortured by memory and need: "I can't continue to move my body along the streets unless I exist in his mind and in his eyes." Finally, she realizes her obsession is a threat to her sanity and that she has a choice of whether to be crazy or not. She decides she does not have the stamina or the will for "prolonged craziness," and further that

> there is a limit to the amount of misery and disarray you will put up with, for love, just as there is a limit to the amount of mess you can stand around a house. You can't know the limit beforehand, but you will know when you've reached it. I believe this.

She begins to let go of the relationship and finds "a queer kind of pleasure" in doing this, not a "self-wounding or malicious pleasure," but

> pleasure in taking into account, all over again, everything that is contradictory and persistent and unaccommodating about life. . . . I think there's something in us wanting to be reassured about all that, right alongside—and at war with—whatever there is that wants permanent vistas and a lot of fine talk.

This seeming resolution, however, this salvation by knowing and understanding all, is subtly undercut by the conclusion of the story. The narrator's much younger friend, Kay, happens to mention her involvement with a fascinating new "friend," who turns out to be X. The story ends there but the pain (presumably) does not.

"Tell Me Yes or No" • The female protagonist of "Tell Me Yes or No" is also sifting through the emotional rubble of an adulterous affair, which has ended, perhaps because of the death of her lover, or perhaps it has merely ended. In this story, it is difficult to distinguish reality from fantasy, and that may be the point. The other lives and other loves of her lover may be real, or they may be a fantasy (as defense mechanism) of the protagonist, but the central insight is the realization of how

> women build their castles on foundations hardly strong enough to support a night's shelter; how women deceive themselves and uselessly suffer, being exploitable because of the emptiness of their lives and some deep—but indefinable, and not final!—flaw in themselves.

For this woman, none of the remedies of her contemporaries works, not deep breathing, not macramé, and certainly not the esoteric advice of another desperate case: to live "every moment by itself," a concept she finds impossible to comprehend, let alone practice. The irony of her difficulty is evident, considering Munro's passionate concern throughout her fiction for "Connection" (the title of one of her stories). Here, it seems that there is some connection between past choice and present desolation:

Love is not in the least unavoidable, there is a choice made. It is just that it is hard to know when the choice was made, or when, in spite of seeming frivolous, it became irreversible. There is no clear warning about that.

"Labor Day Dinner" • Munro's clear-eyed, self-aware narrators are never easy on themselves. They are constantly requiring themselves to face reality, to be aware of and responsible for the consequences of their own choices. In "Labor Day Dinner," the narrator, forty-three-year-old Roberta, has for the past year been living on a run-down farm with George, a younger man and former art teacher. His ambitious plan is to restore the farm and create a studio in which do to his sculpture. Roberta's daughters Angela, seventeen, and Eva, twelve, are spending the summer with her. The atmosphere is emotionally charged, prickly, and tense. George does not approve of the way Roberta indulges her daughters, allowing them to practice ballet instead of doing any work. George does not approve of Roberta, who seems to be indulging herself with tears and moody idleness. On the other hand, Roberta (weeping silently behind her sunglasses) does not approve of George's cooling ardor, his ungallant awareness of her age as evidenced by his request that she not wear a halter top to his cousin's Labor Day dinner because she has flabby armpits. So far, this sounds like the unpromising stuff of the afternoon soaps. (In fact, some of Munro's short stories first were published in popular magazines.) The difference is in what Munro is able to do with her material, the way in which she prevents her characters from deteriorating into stereotypes or her theme into cliché.

Roberta (who has reduced her waist only to discover that her face now looks haggard) reflects mournfully:

How can you exercise the armpits? What is to be done? Now the payment is due, and what for? For vanity. . . . Just for having those pleasing surfaces once, and letting them speak for you; just for allowing an arrangement of hair and shoulders and breasts to have its effect. You don't stop in time, don't know what to do instead; you lay yourself open to humiliation. So thinks Roberta, with self-pity—what she knows to be self-pity—rising and sloshing around in her like bitter bile. She must get away, live alone, wear sleeves.

The self-awareness, the complex mingling of humor and pathos, the comic inadequacy of the solution, to wear sleeves (rivaling Prufrock's momentous decision to wear his trousers rolled), these lend to the character and to the story a dimension which is generally missing in popular fiction.

Roberta's daughters are close observers of as well as participants in this somewhat lugubrious drama. Angela, watching the change in her mother from self-reliant woman to near wreck and viewing George as a despot who hopes to enslave them all, records in her journal, "If this is love I want no part of it." On the other hand, sensitive Eva, watching her older sister develop the unpleasant traits of a typical adolescent, wants no part of that—"I don't want it to happen to me."

The characters all nearly get what they want, a way out of the emotional trauma in which they find themselves. On the way home from the Labor Day dinner, the pickup truck in which they are riding (the girls asleep in the back) comes within inches of being hit broadside by a car that came out of nowhere traveling between eighty and ninety miles an hour, no lights, its driver drunk. George did not touch the brake, nor did Roberta scream; they continue in stunned silence, pull into their yard and sit, unable to move.

What they feel is not terror or thanksgiving—not yet. What they feel is strangeness. They feel as strange, as flattened out and borne aloft, as unconnected with previous and future events as the ghost car was.

The story ends with Eva, waking and calling to them, "Are you guys dead?" and "Aren't we home?"

The ending shocks everything in the story into a new perspective, making what went before seem irrelevant, especially Roberta's and George's halfhearted playing at love. For Munro, it seems that the thought of the nearness, the omnipresence, and the inevitability of death is the only thing which can put lives and relationships into true perspective, but this (as Munro states at the conclusion of "The Spanish Lady") is a message which cannot be delivered, however true it may be.

The Love of a Good Woman • Munro continues at the top of her form in *The Love of a Good Woman*, where the pain of human contact, in its various guises, remains her central theme. In the title novella, Enid, a middle-aged, practical nurse finds herself attending the dying Mrs. Quinn. Lonely, kind Enid strives to do good, resisting her dislike of the sick woman. As an intruder in a household that cannot function without her, she is unaware of her attraction to the husband, a former classmate, until his wife implicates him in the death of a local optometrist. If the dying woman's story is true, Enid must decide whether to confront the husband or to believe in his innocence as she begins to lose hers. This complex, loosely structured work ends ambiguously, as do most of the stories, with Enid hesitating between motion and stillness.

"Cortes Island" is the most troubling story of this group, perhaps because of its ambiguity, perhaps because human lives have gone terribly wrong. A newlywed couple rents a basement apartment from the elderly Gorries. When the young woman needs a job, Mrs. Gorrie asks her to sit with her wheelchair-bound husband. A stroke has rendered Mr. Gorrie virtually speechless, but by grunts he can make himself understood. He wants her to read scrapbook articles from Cortes Island, where long ago a house burned to the ground, a child escaped, and a man died. What happened on Cortes Island, where Mr. Gorrie operated a boat? Was the death an accident, suicide, murder?

This story is so subtly written that events are not immediately clear. Typically, Munro offers only hints, although the young woman realizes that the Gorries once had an intense relationship. With harsh noises, the disabled Mr. Gorrie demands, "Did you ever think that people's lives could be like that and end up like this? Well, they can." This marriage is a wreck of love, a ruin.

As always, Munro exhibits masterful use of irony. In "Jakarta," two young wives argue over D. H. Lawrence's assertion that a woman's happiness lies in a man and that her consciousness must be submerged in his. Kath is a proper Canadian wife and mother, but Sonje, her pot-smoking, commune-dwelling friend, is an American. Over the years, conservative Kath breaks away from her stuffy marriage to become strong and self-reliant. Sonje, who has routinely accepted her husband's wish to switch sexual partners, remains faithful to him even after he disappears in Jakarta.

In other stories, a daughter seeks to ease a strained relationship with her abortionist father by revealing the birth of her child, but she is talking to a dead man. A young girl realizes that she is completely, utterly alone. In the best kind of horror story, one that will chill any parent's blood, a woman tries to entertain her grandchildren with a game that turns sinister as she glimpses the danger, as well as the pain, implicit in any human contact.

Munro has stated in an interview that her need and desire to write

has something to do with the fight against death, the feeling that we lose everything every day, and writing is a way of convincing yourself perhaps that you're doing something about this.

Despite her characteristic concern for honesty and her determination to tell only the truth, it seems in this passage that she may be wrong about one thing: It seems clear that Alice Munro's writing is destined to last for a very long time.

Karen A. Kildahl
With updates by Kenneth W. Meadwell and Joanne McCarthy

Other major works
NOVELS: *Lives of Girls and Women*, 1971.

Bibliography

Canitz, A. E. Christa, and Roger Seamon. "The Rhetoric of Fictional Realism in the Stories of Alice Munro." *Canadian Literature*, no. 150 (Autumn, 1996): 67-80. Examines how Munro's stories portray and enact the dialectic between legend-making and demythologizing; discusses techniques that Munro uses to adapt the opposition between fiction and reality to the expectations and ethical beliefs of her audience.

Carrington, Ildikó de Papp. *Controlling the Uncontrollable: The Fiction of Alice Munro*. De Kalb: Northern Illinois University Press, 1989. Good critical study of Munro's fiction. Includes a bibliography.

Clark, Miriam Marty. "Allegories of Reading in Alice Munro's 'Carried Away.'" *Contemporary Literature* 37 (Spring, 1996): 49-61. Shows how the stories in Munro's *Friend of My Youth* and *Open Secrets* dismantle the foundations of realist narrative, figuring or disclosing the many texts in the one and so refiguring the linked practices of writing and reading; claims that "Carried Away" addresses allegorically the politics of the library and the ethics of reading.

Crouse, David. "Resisting Reduction: Closure in Richard Ford's 'Rock Springs' and Alice Munro's 'Friend of My Youth.'" *Canadian Literature*, no. 146 (Autumn, 1995): 51-64. Discusses how Ford and Munro deal with the problem of realistic closure and character growth in their short stories by manipulating time. Shows how they use various narrative devices to give more interpretive responsibility to the reader.

Hiscock, Andrew. "'Longing for a Human Climate': Alice Munro's *Friend of My Youth* and the Culture of Loss." *The Journal of Commonwealth Literature* 32 (1997): 17-34. Claims that in this collection of stories, Munro creates complex fictional worlds in which character, narrator, and reader are involved in the business of interpreting versions of loss, tentatively attempting to understand their function and status in a mysteriously arranged reality.

May, Charles E., ed. *Masterplots II: Short Story Series, Revised Edition*. 8 vols. Pasadena, Calif.: Salem Press, 2004. Designed for student use, this reference set contains articles providing detailed plot summaries and analyses of eleven short stories by Munro: "The Beggar Maid" and "Boys and Girls" (vol. 1); "Floating Bridge" (vol. 3); "How I Met My Husband" (vol. 4); "The Love of a Good Woman," "Meneseteung," and "The Moons of Jupiter" (vol. 5); "Royal Beatings" and "Save the Reaper" (vol. 6); and "Walker Brothers Cowboy" and "Wild Swans" (vol. 8).

Mayberry, Katherine J. "'Every Last Thing . . . Everlasting': Alice Munro and the Limits of Narrative." *Studies in Short Fiction* 29 (Fall, 1992): 531-541. Discusses how Munro's characters use narrative as a means of coming to terms with the past, how they manage their pain by telling. Argues that most of Munro's narrators come to realize the imperfections of narrative because of the incongruence between experience and the story's effort to render it.

Rasporich, Beverly. *Dance of the Sexes: Art and Gender in the Fiction of Alice Munro.* Edmonton: University of Alberta Press, 1990. Very interesting analysis focusing on male/female contrasts and relationships in Munro's fiction. Augmented by a critical bibliography.

Ross, Catherine Sheldrick. *Alice Munro: A Double Life.* Toronto: ECW Press, 1992. Literary biography by a scholar who has written extensively on Munro's fiction.

Smythe, Karen E. *Figuring Grief: Gallant, Munro, and the Poetics of Elegy.* Montreal: McGill-Queen's University Press, 1992. Generic study of Munro's stories based on the premise that her fiction, with its emphasis on loss and the importance of story telling as a way of regaining knowledge of the past, enacts a poetics of elegy.

Vladimir Nabokov

Born: St. Petersburg, Russia; April 23, 1899
Died: Montreux, Switzerland; July 2, 1977

Principal short fiction • *Vozrashchenie Chorba*, 1930; *Soglyadatay*, 1938; *Nine Stories*, 1947; *Vesna v Fialte i drugie rasskazy*, 1956; *Nabokov's Dozen: A Collection of Thirteen Stories*, 1958; *Nabokov's Quartet*, 1966; *A Russian Beauty, and Other Stories*, 1973; *Tyrants Destroyed, and Other Stories*, 1975; *Details of a Sunset, and Other Stories*, 1976.

Other literary forms • Vladimir Nabokov's fifty-year career as a writer includes—besides his short stories—novels, poetry, drama, memoirs, translations, reviews, letters, critical essays, literary criticism, and the screenplay of his most famous novel, *Lolita* (1955). After his death, three volumes of lectures on literature that he had delivered to students at Wellesley, Stanford, and Cornell were scrupulously edited by Fredson Bowers and published as *Lectures on Literature: British, French, and German* (1980), *Lectures on Russian Literature* (1981), and *Lectures on Don Quixote* (1983).

Achievements • Vladimir Nabokov occupies a unique niche in the annals of literature by having become a major author in both Russian and English. He wrote nine novels, about forty stories, and considerable poetry in Russian before migrating to the United States in 1940. Thereafter, he not only produced eight more novels and ten short stories in English but also translated into English the fiction that he had composed in his native language, sometimes with the collaboration of his son, Dmitri. Reversing his linguistic field, he translated his *Lolita* into Russian.

Nabokov's work has received considerable critical acclaim; a modern master, he has influenced such diverse literary figures as Anthony Burgess, John Barth, William H. Gass, Tom Stoppard, Philip Roth, John Updike, and Milan Kundera. Nabokov's fiction is never intentionally didactic or sociological; he detested moralistic, message-ridden writing. Instead, he delighted in playing self-consciously with the reader's credulity, regarding himself as a fantasist, a Prospero of artifice. He manipulates his characters as so many pieces on a chessboard, devising problems for absorbing, intricate games of which he and Jorge Luis Borges are the acknowledged modern masters. His precision of language, lexical command of multilingual allusions, and startling imagery have awed, delighted, but also sometimes irritated critics and readers. Few writers have practiced art for the sake of art with such talent and discipline. Nabokov's advice to students suggests the best approach to his own fiction:

> In reading, one should notice and fondle details. . . . We must see things and hear things, we must visualize the rooms, the clothes, the manners of an author's people . . . above all, a great writer is always a great enchanter, and it is here that we come to the really exciting part when we try to grasp the individual magic of his genius and to study the style, the imagery, the pattern of his novels or poems.

Biography • Vladimir Vladimirovich Nabokov's life divides neatly into four phases, each lasting approximately twenty years. He was born on Shakespeare's birthday in

Library of Congress

1899 to an aristocratic and wealthy family residing in St. Petersburg. His grandfather was State Minister of Justice for two czars; his father, Vladimir Dmitrievich, a prominent liberal politician, married a woman from an extremely wealthy family. Vladimir Vladimirovich, the first of two sons, was reared with much parental love and care, eloquently evoked in his lyrical memoir, *Conclusive Evidence: A Memoir* (1951), later expanded and retitled *Speak, Memory: An Autobiography Revisited* (1966).

In 1919, the October Revolution forced the Nabokovs to flee Russia. Vladimir, who had learned both French and English from governesses during his childhood, enrolled in the University of Cambridge, took a degree in foreign languages in 1923, and published two volumes of poetry the same year. Meanwhile, his father and the other family members settled in Berlin. There, Vladimir Dmitrievich was assassinated in 1922 by two right-wing extremist Russian expatriates who had intended their bullets for another victim. Vladimir took up residence in Berlin in 1923, and in 1925 he married a Jewish émigrée, Véra Slonim, with whom he maintained a harmonious union. Between 1924 and 1929, he published, in Russian-language exile newspapers and periodicals, twenty-two short stories. Many were collected in a 1930 book *Vozvrashchenie Chorba* (the return of Chorb), whose contents were later translated into English and distributed among several collections of Nabokov's short stories.

To avoid confusion with his well-known father, the younger Nabokov assumed the pen name "V. Sirin," after a mythological, multicolored bird featured in ancient Russian literature; he used this name until leaving Europe in 1940. The Nabokovs stayed in Berlin until 1937, even though Vladimir never learned German and usually drew his German fictive personages unfavorably. In his writings during these years, he dramatized the autobiographical themes of political exile from Russia, nostalgia, grief, anguish, and other variations of vagrant rootlessness. His most important novels during the 1920's and 1930's are commonly judged to be *Zashchita Luzhina* (1929; *The Defense*, 1964) and *Dar* (1937-1938, 1952; *The Gift*, 1963).

Nabokov's third life-stage began in 1940, when, after a three-year stay in Paris, he was glad to escape the Nazi menace by emigrating to the United States. After a one-term lectureship at Stanford University, he distributed his time for the next seven years between teaching at Wellesley College and working as a research fellow in entomology at Harvard's Museum of Comparative Zoology, pursuing his passion for lepidoptera. During these years, he began to establish himself as an American writer of note and, in 1945, became a naturalized citizen. He published two novels, *The Real Life of Sebastian Knight* (1941) and *Bend Sinister* (1947); a brilliant but eccentric study of the Russian writer who had most deeply influenced him, *Nikolai Gogol* (1944); a number of stories and poems; and sections of his first autobiography. In 1948, Cornell University lured him away from Wellesley by offering him a tenured professorship. He became a celebrated ornament of the Ithaca, New York, campus for ten years, specializing in a course called Masters of European Fiction, alternately charming and provoking his students with witty lectures and difficult examinations.

Nabokov wrote *Lolita* during his summer vacations in the early 1950's, but the book was refused publication by several American firms and was first issued in 1955 by Olympia Press, a Parisian English-language publisher that usually featured pornography. By 1958, the work had become celebrated as well as notorious, and Putnam's issued it in New York. It became the year's sensational best-seller, and Nabokov, taking an abrupt midyear leave from Cornell, thereupon moved to an elegant hotel on the banks of Switzerland's Lake Geneva for what were to prove nineteen more fecund years.

During this last arc of his career, Nabokov basked in the aura of worldwide recognition as an eminent writer yet continued to labor diligently: He revised his autobiography; resurrected his Russian long and short fiction in English translations; produced a four-volume translation of and commentary on Alexander Pushkin's novel in verse, *Yevgeny Onegin* (1833; Nabokov's English translation, *Eugene Onegin*, appeared in 1964); and wrote several new novels, including two–*Pale Fire* (1962) and *Ada or Ardor: A Family Chronicle* (1969)—worthy of consideration among the twentieth century's leading literary texts. Despite many losses and difficulties in his arduous life, Nabokov never yielded to self-pity, let alone despair. His career demonstrated not only artistic resourcefulness but also the personal virtues of resolution, resilience, and capacity for renewal.

Analysis • Vladimir Nabokov's early stories are set in the post-czarist, post-World War I era, with Germany the usual location, and sensitive, exiled Russian men the usual protagonists. Many are nascent artists: wistful, sorrowful, solitary, sometimes despairingly disheartened. Many evoke a Proustian recollection of their Russian pasts as they try, and often as not fail, to understand an existence filled with irony, absurdity, and fortuity. These tales display Nabokov's abiding fascination with the interplay between reality and fantasy, between an outer world of tangs, scents, rain showers, sunsets, dawns, butterflies, flowers, forests, and urban asphalt, and an inner landscape of recondite, impenetrable, mysterious feelings. He loved to mix the disheveled externals of precisely described furnishings, trappings, and drab minutiae with memories, myths, fantasy, parody, grandeur, hilarity, masks, nostalgia, and, above all, the magic of artistic illusion. He celebrates the unpredictable permutations of the individual imagination over the massive constraints of the twentieth century's sad history. He is the supreme stylist, dedicated to forging his vision in the most dazzling verbal smithy since James Joyce's.

"The Razor" • One of his first stories, "Britva" ("The Razor"), is a clever adaptation of motifs used in Nikolai Gogol's "Nos" ("The Nose") and Pushkin's "Vystrel" ("The Shot"). A White Russian émigré, Colonel Ivanov, now a barber in Berlin, recognizes a customer as the Red officer who had condemned him to death six years before. He toys with his victim, terrorizing him with caustic, cruel remarks, comparing his open razor to the sharp end of a sword, inverting the menace of their previous confrontation in Russia. Yet he shaves his former captor gently and carefully and finally releases him unharmed. By doing so, Ivanov also releases himself from his burning desire for vengeance. Nabokov uses the multivalent symbol of the razor compactly and densely: The acerbic Ivanov both sharpens and encases his razorlike temperament.

"The Doorbell" • In "Zvonok" ("The Doorbell"), Nabokov delineates a tragic encounter between past and present in a complex tale fusing realism and symbolism. A son, Galatov, has been separated from his mother for seven years, during which time he has fought in the post-1917 Russian Civil War and wandered over Africa, Europe, and the Canary Islands. He learns that his mother's second husband has died and left her some real estate in Berlin. He searches for his mother there, meets her dentist, and through him obtains her address. Structurally, Galatov's visits to the dentist, a Dr. Weiner, anticipate his reunion with his mother: This Weiner is not Galatov's childhood dentist, yet he does happen to be his mother's. When Galatov finally meets his mother, he learns that she, too, is not the mother of his childhood: He meets, in the Berlin apartment, not the faded, dark-haired woman he left seven years earlier but an aged courtesan awaiting the arrival of a lover who is three years younger than her son. Galatov realizes that her fervent greeting of him had been intended for her paramour. When the doorbell announces the latter's arrival, Galatov learns, observing his mother's distraction and nervousness, that her new déclassé circumstances leave no room for him. He hurriedly departs, vaguely promising to see her again in a year or thereabouts. He knows now that not only has the mistress supplanted the mother but also his mother may never have cherished him as dearly as his previous need for her had deluded him into believing. The story's structural symmetry between memory and new reality is impressively achieved.

"A Matter of Chance" • "Sluchainost" ("A Matter of Chance") is one of Nabokov's most poignant tales. Its protagonist, Aleksey Luzhin—whose surname reappears five years later as that of the hero of *The Defense*—is a Russian exile who, like Galatov, has traveled to many places and worked many jobs. Currently, he is a waiter on a German train; having had no news of his wife, Elena, for five years, he is deeply depressed and has become addicted to cocaine. He plans his suicide for the night of August 1, the ninth anniversary of his wedding and the day of this story. On this particular trip, an old Russian princess, Maria Ukhtomski, is joined in her compartment by a young woman who arrived in Berlin from St. Petersburg the previous day, Elena Luzhina, who is seeking her lost husband. The story's rising action is full of suspense: Will the unsuspecting spouses find each other on the train? Luzhin sniffs cocaine in the toilet, on the day he has resolved to make his last. The princess has known the Luzhin family and recalls its former aristocratic opulence. Ironically, when the now plebeian Luzhin announces the first seating for dinner, his cocaine-rotted mind can only dimly note the princess; he cannot connect her to his elegant past.

The links between the two plots never interlock. Elena, disturbed by a rudely aggressive fellow passenger, decides to forgo the dinner in the dining car where she would probably have met her husband. She loses her prized golden wedding ring in the vestibule of the train's wagon; it is discovered by another waiter as Luzhin leaves the wagon and jumps to his death before another train: "The locomotive came at him in one hungry bound." Missed chances abound—perhaps too many: Nabokov's uses of coincidence and his insistence of the malignity of haphazard events strain credulity.

"The Scoundrel" • Perhaps Nabokov's most accomplished story of the 1920's is "Podlets" ("The Scoundrel," retitled by the author "An Affair of Honor" for its English publication). In his foreword to the English translation, Nabokov explains that "'An Affair of Honor' renders, in a drab expatriate setting, the degradation of a romantic theme whose decline had started with Anton Chekhov's magnificent story 'The Duel' (1891)." Nabokov situates the duel within the traditional love triangle. The husband, an affluent banker named Anton Petrovich, returns home early from a business trip to find an arrogant acquaintance, Berg, nonchalantly getting dressed in his bedroom while his wife, Tanya, whom the reader never sees, is taking an interminable bath. Anton Petrovich challenges Berg to a duel. He pulls off his new glove and tries to throw it at Berg. Instead, it "slapped against the wall and dropped into the washstand pitcher." The ludicrous failure of Anton Petrovich's challenge sets the farcical, burlesque tone for the tale.

Anton Petrovich is a loving, tender, hardworking, amiable fellow whose major fault—abject cowardice—becomes his undoing. Anton Chekhov would have treated him gently and compassionately; Nabokov handles him disdainfully and absurdly, emphasizing his fondness for his shiny fountain pen, expensive shoes and socks, and monocle which "would gleam like a foolish eye on his belly." A duel is arranged but does not actually take place. Anton Petrovich, who has never fired a weapon, shakes with increasing fear at the prospect of confronting a former White Army officer who boasts of having killed hundreds. Before entering the woods where the combat is to occur, he and his caricatured seconds stop at a tavern for a round of beers. Anton Petrovich thereupon runs into the bar's backyard, slides and slips ridiculously down a slope, stumbles his way back to a train, and thence rides back to Berlin. He fantasizes that his craven flight will have been overshadowed by Berg's even earlier change of mind about dueling and that his wife will leave Berg and return to him, filled with love, delighted to satisfy him with an enormous ham sandwich.

Abruptly, Anton Petrovich awakens from his fiction. "Such things don't happen in real life," he reflects. He realizes that his reputation, his career, and his marriage are now ruined. He orders a ham sandwich and, animalistically, "grabbed the sandwich with both hands, immediately soiled his fingers and chin with the hanging margin of fat, and grunting greedily, began to munch." Nabokov has here begun to command the art of grotesquerie, precisely observed, relentlessly rendered, contemptuously concluded. Anton Petrovich would serve as a model for Albinus Kretschmar, cuckolded lover and failed artist in the novel *Kamera obskura* (1932; *Camera Obscura*, 1936; revised as *Laughter in the Dark*, 1938). Kretschmar in turn is a prototype for *Lolita*'s Humbert Humbert.

"The Admiralty Spire" • An amusing as well as saddening early exercise in playing mirror games, which were to become more and more convoluted in Nabokov's fiction, is his 1933 story "Admiralteyskaya Igla" ("The Admiralty Spire"). Its narrator addresses a trashy Soviet female writer who uses the pseudonymous male name Sergey Solntsev. He asserts that her cheap romantic novel, *The Admiralty Spire*, is a vulgar version of his first love affair, sixteen years earlier, with a young woman named Katya, whom the writer has renamed Olga. He accuses her of "pretentious fabrication" and of having "encroached with astonishing insolence on another person's past!" The letter proceeds to lecture the writer on the correct, nostalgic use of the sentimental past, but in the process of recall, the writer admits his distaste for Katya's "mendacity, her presumption, her vacuity" and deplores her "myopic soul" and the "triviality of

[her] opinions." He did, however, once love her. The narrator ends with the speculation that the mediocre novelist he is addressing is probably Katya herself, "who, out of silly coquetry, has concocted a worthless book." He hopes against the odds that his presumption is erroneous. The atmosphere of overlapping dimensions of reality established here was to be splendidly employed in such later novels as *Pale Fire* and *Ada or Ardor.*

"Cloud, Castle, Lake" • In "Oblako, ozero, bashnya" ("Cloud, Castle, Lake"), the protagonist, a timid, intellectual bachelor, Vasili Ivanovich, wins a pleasure trip at a charity ball for Russian expatriates in Berlin. He is the kind, meek, saintly soul familiar in Russian literature since Gogol's stories. He does not really want to take the journey but is intimidated by bureaucratic mazes into doing so. Obstacles thwart him persistently: Trying to settle down with a volume of Russian poetry, Vasili is instead bullied by a squadron of husky German fellow travelers, with monstrous knapsacks and hobnailed boots, into forced communal games that prove witless and humiliating. When the group pairs off, no one wants to romance him: He is designated "the loser and was forced to eat a cigarette butt." Unexpectedly, they come upon "a pure, blue lake," reflecting a large cloud and adjoining "an ancient, black castle." Overjoyed, Vasili wishes to surrender to the beautiful prospect and remain the rest of his life in the inn from which he can delight in this tableau. Unfortunately for Vasili, the group insists on dragging him back and beats him furiously during the return journey.

The tale is manifestly an allegory mourning the defeat of individuality and privacy in an ugly world determined to enforce total conformity. "Oh, but this is nothing less than an invitation to a beheading," protests Vasili as the group grimly denies him his room with a view. By no accident, Nabokov would soon write his novel, *Priglashenie na kazn'* (1938, 1935-1936; *Invitation to a Beheading*, 1959), whose main character, Cincinnatus C., is condemned to death for not fitting into a totalitarian culture. Nabokov may have occasionally presented himself as an arrogant, coldhearted puppeteer lacking any world-mending concerns, but he does clearly condemn all cultures of regimentation and authoritarianism.

"Spring in Fialta" • "Vesna v Fialte" ("Spring in Fialta") was to become the title work of a collection of Nabokov's short stories; some critics regard it as the masterpiece among his stories, although others prefer "Signs and Symbols." The narrator of "Spring in Fialta," Victor, is a Russian émigré businessman who, over the course of fifteen years, has had sporadic meetings with a charmingly casual, pretty, vital woman named Nina. These encounters are sometimes sexual but never last more than a few hours and occur outside their continuing lives and separate marriages. "Again and again," Victor notes, "she hurriedly appeared in the margin of my life, without influencing in the least its basic text." So, at least, he believes. He has his respectably bourgeois world "in which I sat for my portrait, with my wife, my young daughters, the Doberman pinscher." Yet he finds himself also drawn to Nina's world of carefree sexuality mixed with "lies . . . futility . . . gibberish." This tension that Victor experiences is common in both life and literature, and Nabokov's characters are not immune. Although Nabokov appears to admire uxoriousness, as in the marriages of the Shades in *Pale Fire* or the Krugs in *Bend Sinister,* his protagonists are also mesmerized by *belles dames sans merci*—Margot (renamed Magda) in *Laughter in the Dark,* Lolita, Ada, and many more.

Nina is married to a gifted but repulsive Franco-Hungarian writer, Ferdinand; she also travels with the equally offensive but far less talented writer, Segur. Both men are artist figures: selfish, artificial, buoyant, heartless. Nina, while adaptable and "loyally sharing [Ferdinand's] tastes," is not really his muse: rather, she represents life's vulnerability, and her attempt to imitate Ferdinand's world proves fatal. When the car in which the three of them ride crashes into a truck, Ferdinand and Segur, "those invulnerable rogues, those salamanders of fate . . . had escaped with local and temporary injury . . . while Nina, in spite of her long-standing, faithful imitation of them, had turned out after all to be mortal." Life can only copy art, not replace it.

"Signs and Symbols" • In "Signs and Symbols," Nabokov wrote his most sorrowful story. An elderly, poor Russian émigré couple intend to pay a birthday visit to their son, institutionalized in a sanatorium, afflicted with "referential mania," in which "the patient imagines that everything happening around him is a veiled reference to his personality and existence." On their way to the sanatorium, the machinery of existence seems to malfunction: The subway loses its electric current between stations; the bus is late and crammed with noisy schoolchildren; they are pelted by pouring rain as they walk the last stretch of the way. Finally, instead of being able to see their son, they are informed that he has again attempted suicide and should not be disturbed. The couple return home with the present that they cannot give him, wordless with worry and defeat, the woman close to tears. On their way they see "a tiny, half-dead unfledged bird . . . helplessly twitching in a puddle."

After a somber supper, the husband goes to bed, and the wife reviews a family photo album filled with the faces of mostly suffering or dead relatives. One cousin is a "famous chess player"—Nabokov's oblique reference to Luzhin of *The Defense*, who commits suicide. In his previous suicide attempt, the son had wanted "to tear a hole in his world and escape." In the story's last section, the time is past midnight, the husband is sleepless and in pain, and the couple decide to bring their boy home from the institution; each parent will need to spend part of each night with him. Then the phone rings: a wrong number. When it rings a second time, the wife carefully explains to the same caller how she must have misdialed. After a while the phone rings for the third time; the story ends. The signs and symbols in all likelihood suggest that the last call is from the sanatorium, to announce that the son has succeeded in escaping this world.

Artistically, this story is virtually flawless: intricately patterned, densely textured, remarkably intense in tone and feeling. For once, Nabokov the literary jeweler has cut more deeply than his usual surfaces; for once, he has entered the frightening woods of tragic, unmitigated grief; for once, he has forsaken gamesmanship and mirror-play, punning and parody and other gambits of verbal artifice to face the grimmest horrors of a sometimes hopeless world.

Gerhard Brand

Other major works

PLAYS: *Dedushka*, pb. 1923; *Smert'*, pb. 1923; *Polius*, pb. 1924; *Tragediya gospodina Morna*, pb. 1924; *Chelovek iz SSSR*, pb. 1927; *Izobretenie Val'sa*, pb. 1938 (*The Waltz Invention*, 1966); *Sobytiye*, pr., pb. 1938.

novels: *Mashenka*, 1926 (*Mary*, 1970); *Korol', dama, valet*, 1928 (*King, Queen, Knave*, 1968); *Zashchita Luzhina*, 1929 (serial), 1930 (book; *The Defense*, 1964);

Kamera obskura, 1932 (*Camera Obscura*, 1936; revised as *Laughter in the Dark*, 1938); *Podvig*, 1932 (*Glory*, 1971); *Otchayanie*, 1934 (serial), 1936 (book; *Despair*, 1937; revised 1966); *Priglashenie na kazn'*, 1935-1936 (serial), 1938 (book; *Invitation to a Beheading*, 1959); *Dar*, 1937-1938 (serial), 1952 (book; *The Gift*, 1963); *The Real Life of Sebastian Knight*, 1941; *Bend Sinister*, 1947; *Lolita*, 1955; *Pnin*, 1957; *Pale Fire*, 1962; *Ada or Ardor: A Family Chronicle*, 1969; *Transparent Things*, 1972; *Look at the Harlequins!*, 1974.

NONFICTION: *Nikolai Gogol*, 1944; *Conclusive Evidence: A Memoir*, 1951; *Drugie berega*, 1954; *Speak, Memory: An Autobiography Revisited*, 1966 (revision of *Conclusive Evidence* and *Drugie berega*); *Strong Opinions*, 1973; *The Nabokov-Wilson Letters, 1940-1971*, 1979; *Lectures on Literature: British, French, and German*, 1980; *Lectures on Russian Literature*, 1981; *Lectures on Don Quixote*, 1983; *Vladimir Nabokov: Selected Letters, 1940-1977*, 1989.

POETRY: *Stikhi*, 1916; *Dva puti*, 1918; *Gorny put*, 1923; *Grozd'*, 1923; *Stikhotvorenia, 1929-1951*, 1952; *Poems*, 1959; *Poems and Problems*, 1970.

SCREENPLAY: *Lolita*, 1962.

TRANSLATIONS: *Anya v strane chudes*, 1923 (of Lewis Carroll's novel *Alice's Adventures in Wonderland*); *Three Russian Poets: Translations of Pushkin, Lermontov, and Tiutchev*, 1944 (with Dmitri Nabokov); *A Hero of Our Time*, 1958 (of Mikhail Lermontov's novel; with Dmitri Nabokov); *The Song of Igor's Campaign*, 1960 (of the twelfth century epic *Slovo o polki Igoreve*); *Eugene Onegin*, 1964 (of Alexander Pushkin's novel).

Bibliography

Boyd, Brian. *Vladimir Nabokov: The Russian Years*. Princeton, N.J.: Princeton University Press, 1990.

_____. *Vladimir Nabokov: The American Years*. Princeton, N.J.: Princeton University Press, 1991. In the course of the two volumes of this critical biography, Boyd discusses virtually all Nabokov's stories. Boyd generally provides a brief summary of each story, relating it to Nabokov's development as an artist and noting recurring themes. Each volume includes illustrations, extensive notes, and an exceptionally thorough index.

Connolly, Julian W. *The Cambridge Companion to Nabokov*. New York: Cambridge University Press, 2005. Concise introduction to Nabokov's life and his writing.

Grayson, Jane, Arnold B. McMillin, and Priscilla Meyer, eds. *Nabokov's World: Reading Nabokov*. New York: Palgrave Macmillan, 2002. Collection of fifteen essays focusing on intertextuality in Nabokov's works and their literary reception.

May, Charles E., ed. *Masterplots II: Short Story Series, Revised Edition*. 8 vols. Pasadena, Calif.: Salem Press, 2004. Designed for student use, this reference set contains articles providing detailed plot summaries and analyses of five short stories by Nabokov: "Cloud, Castle, Lake" (vol. 2); "The Return of Chorb" (vol. 6); "Signs and Symbols" and "That in Aleppo Once" (vol. 7); and "The Vane Sisters" (vol. 8).

Nicol, Charles. "'Ghastly Rich Glass': A Double Essay on 'Spring in Fialta.'" *Russian Literature Triquarterly*, no. 24 (1991): 173-184. One of two pieces devoted to Nabokov's short fiction in this special Nabokov issue, Nicol's article on "Spring in Fialta" has two concerns: "First, a consideration of the plot structure . . . and second, a further perspective on the vexed question of whether this story has any autobiographical relevance or personal reference to its author."

Nicol, Charles, and Gennady Barabtarlo, eds. *A Small Alpine Form: Studies in Nabokov's Short Fiction.* New York: Garland, 1993. Contains sixteen essays on Nabokov's stories from a variety of critical points of view. The essays discuss themes, sources, parallels, and symbols in such stories as "Spring in Fialta," "Signs and Symbols," and several others.

Parker, Stephen Jan. "Vladimir Nabokov and the Short Story." *Russian Literature Triquarterly,* no. 24 (1991): 63-72. Parker worked with Nabokov and Véra Nabokov in the early 1970's to establish a precise chronology of Nabokov's short stories in Russian and to discuss possible titles for the English translations. Listed here are the results of their conversation and correspondence. Also included is a previously unpublished interview (conducted by mail) centering on the short story as a genre, with some characteristically provocative responses from Nabokov.

Shrayer, Maxim D. "Mapping Narrative Space in Nabokov's Short Fiction." *The Slavonic and East European Review* 75 (October, 1997): 624-641. Discusses the figurations of space in Nabokov's stories; emphasizes rendering three-dimensional space on an atomistic scale and the way in which a whole narrative serves as a travel guide to its own space; compares Nabokov's method of rendering the narrative space with that of his Russian predecessors.

_____. *The World of Nabokov's Stories.* Austin: University of Texas Press, 1999. Detailed analysis of Nabokov's mastery of the short-story form and his worldview. Traces Nabokov's literary practice from the early 1920's to the 1930's; focuses on Russian stories, such as "The Return of Chorb" and "Cloud, Castle, Lake." Also discusses Nabokov's relationship to Anton Chekhov and Ivan Bunin.

R. K. Narayan

Born: Madras, India; October 10, 1906
Died: Madras, India; May 13, 2001

Principal short fiction • *Malgudi Days,* 1941 (expanded, 1982); *Dodu, and Other Stories,* 1943; *Cyclone, and Other Stories,* 1944; *An Astrologer's Day, and Other Stories,* 1947; *Lawley Road: Thirty-two Short Stories,* 1956; *Gods, Demons, and Others,* 1964; *A Horse and Two Goats, and Other Stories,* 1970; *Old and New,* 1981; *Under the Banyan Tree, and Other Stories,* 1985; *The Grandmother's Tale and Selected Stories,* 1994.

Other literary forms • A prolific writer, R. K. Narayan published—besides the collections of short stories cited above—more than a dozen novels, a shortened prose version of each of the two famous Indian epics, *The Ramayana* and *The Mahabharata,* several travel books, volumes of essays and sketches, a volume of memoirs, and numerous critical essays. His novel *The Guide* (1958) was made into a successful motion picture, both in English and in Hindi.

Achievements • R. K. Narayan, an internationally recognized novelist and the grand patriarch of Indo-Anglian writers (writers of India writing in English), received a number of awards and distinctions. In 1961, he received the National Prize of the Indian Literary Academy (Sahitya Akademi), India's highest literary honor, for his very popular novel *The Guide.* His other honors include India's Padma Bhushan Award for distinguished service of a high order, 1964; the United States' National Association of Independent Schools Award, 1965; the English-speaking Union Award, 1975; the Royal Society of Literature Benson Medal, 1980; and several honorary degrees. In 1982, Narayan was made an honorary member of the American Academy and Institute of Arts and Letters. He was named a member of India's nonelective House of Parliament, the Rajya Sabha, in 1989.

Narayan invented for his writings the town of Malgudi, considered by critics a literary amalgam of Mysore, where he lived for several decades, and Madras, the city of his birth. He gently asserted that "Malgudi has been only a concept but has proved good enough for my purposes." In its imaginative scope, Narayan's Malgudi is similar to William Faulkner's Yoknapatawpha County, but whereas Faulkner's vision is complex and dark-hued, Narayan's vision is simpler, ironic, sad at times, yet ultimately comic.

Biography • Rasipuram Krishnaswami Narayan was born in Madras, South India, on October 10, 1906. Until the family moved to Mysore, he remained in Madras with his grandmother, who supervised his school and college education. In his autobiography, *My Days* (1974), Narayan admits his dislike of education: he "instinctively rejected both education and examinations with their unwarranted seriousness and esoteric suggestions." Nevertheless, in 1930, he graduated from Maharaja's College (now the University of Mysore).

In 1933, he met a woman by the name of Rajam and immediately fell in love with her. In 1935, after overcoming almost insurmountable difficulties (to begin with, their horoscopes did not match), Narayan and Rajam were married. She was a great help in his creative work, but she lived to see publication of only three novels. She died of typhoid in 1939. Narayan's fourth novel, *Grateful to Life and Death* (1953), dedicated to his dead wife, centers on the trauma of this loss and on a hard-won sense of reconciliation. Rajam is portrayed in some detail as Sushila in that novel and, later, as Srinivas's wife in *The Printer of Malgudi* (1957).

Narayan had not begun his career as a writer without some false starts. Indeed, only after having worked at a number of jobs without satisfaction and success—he worked for a time in the civil service in Mysore, taught for a while, and served as a correspondent for *Madras Justice*—did Narayan finally embark upon writing as a full-time career. In the beginning, many of his writings were rejected—a traumatic experience which he bore with fortitude. He was firm in his resolve to make his living as a writer. Experiencing bitter dejection when several British publishers rejected his first novel, *Swami and Friends* (1935), Narayan instructed a friend not to mail the manuscript back to him in India but to throw it into the Thames. Instead, his friend took the manuscript to Graham Greene, who was successful in finding a publisher for the novel. Thus, from a frustrating experience began the literary career of an eminent Commonwealth writer whose books are known throughout the world. Narayan settled in Mysore, India, and his involvement with Indian Thought Publications led to the publication of several of his works.

Narayan continued to write and publish well into his nineties, concentrating on short fiction and essays. He experimented with "table talk," a new form of his own devising, which he described as a loosely structured reflection on any subject. Narayan died in Madras, India on May 13, 2001.

Analysis • R. K. Narayan said that he found English the most rewarding medium to employ for his writing because it came to him very easily: "English is a very adaptable language. And it's so transparent it can take on the tint of any country." Critics frequently praise the unaffected standard English with which Narayan captures the Indian sensibility, particularly the South Indian ambience. His unpretentious style, his deliberate avoidance of convoluted expressions and complicated grammatical constructions, his gentle and subtle humor—all this gives his writing an elegant, unforced simplicity that is perfectly suited to the portrayal of ordinary life, of all classes and segments of Indian society—household servants, herdsmen, saints, crooks, merchants, beggars, thieves, hapless students.

Narayan was essentially an old-fashioned storyteller. With Addisonian wit, Twainian humor, and Chekhovian irony, he depicted everyday occurrences, moments of insight; while some of his stories are essentially sketches, quite undramatic, others feature the ironic reversals associated with O. Henry. Although Narayan's characters are imbued with distinctively Indian values, their dilemmas are universal.

Malgudi Days • Among the nineteen stories in Narayan's first collection, *Malgudi Days*, there are two stories, "Old Bones" and "Neighbours' Help," that are laced with supernatural elements. This volume includes such memorable stories as "The Gold Belt," "The White Flower," "An End of Trouble," and "Under the Banyan Tree." Some of the stories may be viewed as social criticism; Narayan looks with a satiric eye on various aspects of traditional South Indian society, particularly the dowry system and the powerful role of astrology and other forms of superstition.

One of the finest stories in the collection, "The Mute Companions," centers

Library of Congress

on the ubiquitous Indian monkey, asource of meager income for poor people and a source of delight for children. Adopting the omniscient point of view yet without moralizing or judging, Narayan portrays the life of Sami the dumb beggar, whose "very existence depended on the behavior of the monkey." Having taught the monkey several tricks, Sami is able for a time to subsist on the earnings of the clever creature, who is his "only companion." This brief story is an excellent specimen of Narayan's art, revealing his ability to portray a segment of society that typically goes unnoticed. The story emphasizes the passiveness characteristic of the poor Indian, his acceptance of his Karma, or fate. Narayan's gentle social criticism, too, emerges: "Usually [Sami] avoided those big places where people were haughty, aloof, and inaccessible, and kept formidable dogs and servants." As in many of his stories, Narayan in "The Mute Companions" blends humor and sadness.

Malgudi Days, it should be noted, is also the title of a later collection, published in the United States in 1982. Eight of the thirty-two stories in this collection—"Naga," "Selvi," "Second Opinion," "Cat Within," "The Edge," "God and the Cobbler," "Hungry Child," and "Emden"— were previously uncollected; the remaining stories were selected from Narayan's two earlier volumes, *An Astrologer's Day* and *Lawley Road*.

Dodu, and Other Stories • In his second collection, *Dodu, and Other Stories*, Narayan focused on themes related to motherly love, South Indian marriages, the financial and economic frustrations of the middle class, and childhood. Among the outstanding pieces in this volume of seventeen stories are "Dodu," "Gandhi's Appeal," "Ranga," "A Change," "Forty-five a Month," and "The One-Armed Giant." (Originally published in *The Hindu*, a Madras newspaper, as most of his stories have been, "The One-Armed Giant" was the first story that Narayan wrote.) The title story, "Dodu," satirically focuses on adult attitudes toward children. "Dodu was eight years old and wanted money badly. Since he was only eight, nobody took his financial worries seriously. . . . Dodu had no illusions about the generosity of his elders. They were notoriously deaf to requests." One of the significant contributions of Narayan is his uncanny ability to portray children—their dreams, their mischief, their psychology. "Ranga," an early tale, is a moving story of a motherless child developing into a disillusioned youth. "Forty-five a Month" is a simple and tender story of the relationship of a father and his family—his wife and their young daughter. The conflict between economic security and the little pleasures of life is evocatively and movingly delineated; indeed, this depiction of a white-collar worker eking out his dreary existence reflects the experience of an entire generation in modern India.

Lawley Road • In *Lawley Road*, as in most of his fiction, Narayan is concerned more with character than with plot. He notes that he discovers "a story when a personality passes through a crisis of spirit or circumstances," but some stories present flashes of significant moments in characters' lives without any dramatic circumstances; others simply show "a pattern of existence brought to view." Many of the pieces in this collection have a reportorial quality—there are sketches and vignettes, character studies and anecdotes. Of the twenty-eight stories gathered here, fourteen are reprinted from previous collections. The title story is delightful. Named after a typical thoroughfare in the fictitious city of Malgudi, the story recounts how Kabir Lane is renamed as Lawley Road. The narrator is one of Narayan's most engaging recurring characters, whom the people of Malgudi have nicknamed the "Talkative Man," or TM for short, who lends distance and historicity to the story. In another strong story, "The Martyr's Corner," the focus is on a humble seller of *bondas, dosais* (South Indian snacks), and *chappatis* (wheat-flour pancakes) rather than on the violent action. It is the character of the vendor—his dreary and drab life and his attitude toward existence—that holds the interest of the reader.

A Horse and Two Goats, and Other Stories • *A Horse and Two Goats, and Other Stories* comprises five stories with illustrations by Narayan's brother R. K. Laxman. The title story deals with Muni, a village peasant, and his meeting with a "red man" from the United States. The language barrier is responsible for confusion about a statue and a pair of goats, with hilarious results. The second story, "Uncle," is a masterpiece; it slowly unfolds the mystery that teases a growing boy about his benevolent but inexplicably sinister "uncle." "Annamalai" and "A Breath of Lucifer" deal with two simple, hardworking, faithful servants. Annamalai is an eccentric gardener who attaches himself to a reluctant master. Sam in "A Breath of Lucifer," with an autobiographical preface, is a Christian male nurse. In the end, both Annamalai and Sam, governed by their own impulses, unceremoniously leave their masters. "Seventh House," perhaps a continuation of "The White Flower" in *Lawley Road*, dealing in astrology and superstitions, touchingly explores a husband's tender devotion to his sick wife. Each of the five stories is a character study; all the stories are embellished with picturesque native customs. The dominant tone throughout the collection is casual, understated.

Under the Banyan Tree, and Other Stories • *Under the Banyan Tree, and Other Stories* is a superb retrospective collection of twenty-eight tales, published specifically for American readers; almost all the stories are drawn from earlier volumes. When the collection appeared on the American scene, several glowing reviews were published in the leading weeklies and periodicals. This collection further confirms Malgudi's place as a great imaginary landscape. The title story, fittingly taken from Narayan's first collection, reaffirms storytelling as a central human activity. The villagers of Somal "lived in a kind of perpetual enchantment. The enchanter was Nambi the storyteller." Yet, having regaled his audience for several years with his tales, Nambi spends the rest of his life in "great consummate silence."

The Grandmother's Tale and Selected Stories • *The Grandmother's Tale and Selected Stories* (titled *The Grandmother's Tale, and Other Stories* in the paperback edition) was the first collection of Narayan's fiction that attempted to give a comprehensive overview of his more than fifty years of productivity. Many of the stories, including "A Horse and Two Goats" and "Lawley Road," have been widely anthologized for many years. Others, including "Salt and Sawdust" and the title story, make their first North American appearance in this collection. Many of the stories are based on humble but complex characters engaged in daily life in India. As a collection, they demonstrate the richness of Indian life, which blends ancient tradition with Western technological modernity, but Narayan's stories do not call attention to the setting. Rather, they focus on the characters, showing with gentle humor the wonderful absurdity that makes one human and the ironic twists that shape one's life.

In "Salt and Sawdust," for example, Narayan presents a childless housewife who cannot cook—her sense of taste is so bad that she cannot tell the difference between salt and sawdust. Her poor husband is forced to take over the cooking, while his wife occupies herself with writing a novel. However, when the novel is finally completed, the publisher advises the wife to turn it into a cookbook. Narayan was a master of the small details that make domestic scenes seem true and important. Although the wife is made fun of in "Salt and Sawdust," she is a fully rounded character. The humor is good-natured, and Narayan's respect for humans with all their flaws never wavers.

"The Grandmother's Tale" is adapted from a tale Narayan's mother told him about his own great-grandmother. The story is narrated in a winding fashion by a young boy who is sent to live with his strict grandmother. Although he resents his new situation at first, he gradually comes under the spell of the story she tells him, in bits and pieces, about her own grandmother's life. The grandmother's story is set firmly in India. The heroine is married in a traditional ceremony at the age of seven, but her husband abandons her to take a new wife. The landscape she crosses to reclaim her husband is clearly the Indian subcontinent. Ironically, regaining her husband costs her her independence. "The Grandmother's Tale" is unlike many of Narayan's stories in having a strong and admirable central female character. The framing device of the boy narrator reinforces the timelessness and universality of the grandmother's story, which is equally powerful to a young Indian boy in a small village and to adult readers around the world.

As an old-fashioned storyteller, Narayan sought to convey the vitality of his native India, a land that is full of humanity, oddity, poverty, tradition, "inherited culture," picturesqueness. Narayan realized

> that the short story is the best medium for utilizing the wealth of subjects available. A novel is a different proposition altogether, centralized as it is on a major theme, leaving out, necessarily, a great deal of the available material on the periphery. Short stories, on the other hand, can cover a wider field by presenting concentrated miniatures of human experience in all its opulence.

Narayan's concern was the heroic in the ordinary Indian. John Updike affirms that "all people are complex, surprising, and deserving of a break: this seems to me Narayan's moral, and one hard to improve upon. His social range and his successful attempt to convey, in sum, an entire population shame most American authors, who also, it might be charged, 'ignore too much of what could be seen.'" With dignified simplicity, honesty, and sincerity, Narayan infused his stories with charm and spontaneous humor; his narrative voice guides the reader through his comic and ironic world with an unobtrusive wit.

S. S. Moorty
With updates by Chaman L. Sahni and Cynthia A. Bily

Other major works

NOVELS: *Swami and Friends*, 1935; *The Bachelor of Arts*, 1937; *The Dark Room*, 1938; *The English Teacher*, 1945 (also known as *Grateful to Life and Death*, 1953); *Mr. Sampath*, 1949 (also known as *The Printer of Malgudi*, 1957); *The Financial Expert*, 1952; *Waiting for the Mahatma*, 1955; *The Guide*, 1958; *The Man-Eater of Malgudi*, 1961; *The Sweet-Vendor*, 1967 (also known as *The Vendor of Sweets*); *The Painter of Signs*, 1976; *A Tiger for Malgudi*, 1983; *Talkative Man: A Novel of Malgudi*, 1987; *The World of Nagaraj*, 1990.

MISCELLANEOUS: *A Story-Teller's World*, 1989 (stories, essays, and sketches); *Salt and Sawdust: Stories and Table Talk*, 1993.

NONFICTION: *Mysore*, 1944; *My Dateless Diary*, 1960; *Next Sunday: Sketches and Essays*, 1960; *My Days*, 1974; *Reluctant Guru*, 1974; *The Emerald Route*, 1977; *A Writer's Nightmare: Selected Essays, 1958-1988*, 1988; *The Writerly Life: Selected Nonfiction*, 2001 (includes essays from *My Dateless Diary*, *A Writer's Nightmare*, *A Story-Teller's World*, and *Salt and Sawdust*; S. Krishnan, editor).

TRANSLATIONS: *The Ramayana: A Shortened Modern Prose Version of the Indian Epic*, 1972 (of Vālmīki); *The Mahabharata: A Shortened Prose Version of the Indian Epic*, 1978.

Bibliography

Bery, Ashok. "'Changing the Script': R. K. Narayan and Hinduism." *Ariel* 28 (April, 1997): 7-20. Argues that Narayan often probes limitations and contradictions in Hindu worldviews and identities; analyzes the ways Narayan challenges Hindu doctrines, particularly those that teach that the individual self and the phenomenal world are unimportant; although Hinduism is indispensable to Narayan, it is not unchallengeable.

Jussawalla, Feroza, and Geralyn Strecker. "R. K. Narayan." In *Critical Survey of Long Fiction, Revised Edition*, edited by Carl Rollyson. Vol. 5. Pasadena, Calif.: Salem Press, 2000. Analysis of Narayan's longer fictional works that may offer insights into his short fiction.

Kain, Geoffrey, ed. *R. K. Narayan: Contemporary Critical Perspectives*. East Lansing: Michigan State University Press, 1993. Collection of essays, mostly on the novels, including feminist, cultural, postcolonial, and other contemporary approaches. Other essays focus on irony, satire, transcendence, self-reflexivity, and mythmaking in Narayan's fiction.

Knippling, Alpana Sharma. "R. K. Narayan, Raja Rao, and Modern English Discourse in Colonial India." *Modern Fiction Studies* 39 (Spring, 1993): 169-186. Using Michel Foucault's notion that discourse does not necessarily implicate human intention, Knippling contends that Narayan is not heavily influenced by English discourse and therefore not culpable in the whole Westernizing process.

May, Charles E., ed. *Masterplots II: Short Story Series, Revised Edition*. 8 vols. Pasadena, Calif.: Salem Press, 2004. Designed for student use, this reference set contains articles providing detailed plot summaries and analyses of five short stories by Narayan: "An Astrologer's Day" (vol. 1), "A Horse and Two Goats" and "House Opposite" (vol. 4), and "Uncle" and "Under the Banyan Tree" (vol. 8).

Naik, M. K. *The Ironic Vision: A Study of the Fiction of R. K. Narayan.* New Delhi, India: Sterling, 1983. Perceptive study of Narayan's fiction demonstrating his use of irony, in its various forms, to portray human character and situations and to project his total vision of life. Devotes a chapter to the short stories and contains references, a layout of Malgudi and its surroundings, a select bibliography, and an index.

Ram, Susan, and N. Ram. *R. K. Narayan: The Early Years, 1906-1945.* New Delhi, India: Viking Press, 1996. Prepared with the cooperation of Narayan's family and friends, the Rams' biography of Narayan's early years is excellent.

Sundaram, P. S. *R. K. Narayan.* New Delhi, India: Arnold-Heinemann, 1973. This volume's only aim, according to the author, "is to acquaint the Common Reader with the works of an outstanding writer and to suggest what makes the writing outstanding." Contains a brief thematic study of Narayan's short stories and notes the thematic connections between many of the stories and the novels. Supplemented by notes and references, a select bibliography, and an index.

Urstad, Tone Sundt. "Symbolism in R. K. Narayan's 'Naga.'" *Studies in Short Fiction* 31 (Summer, 1994): 425-432. Discusses Narayan's basic technique of juxtaposing scenes from modern life with the exploits of gods, demons, and heroes in the short story "Naga." Argues that in this story Narayan creates a mythic framework in which humans act out age-old patterns and conflicts.

Venugopal, C. V. *The Indian Short Story in English: A Survey.* Bareilly, India: Prakash Book Depot, 1975. The chapter on R. K. Narayan provides a useful overview of his short fiction. Complemented by references, a select bibliography, and an index.

Walsh, William. *R. K. Narayan.* London: Longman, 1971. Booklet in the British Council Writers and Their Work series, it gives a general critical appraisal of Narayan as a novelist. Walsh discusses Narayan's novels as "comedies of sadness" and argues that "his work is an original blend of Western method and Eastern material." Includes a select bibliography.

DATE DUE

HIGHSMITH 45230